No Future

'No Feelings', 'No Fun', 'No Future'. The years 1976–84 saw punk emerge and evolve as a fashion, a musical form, an attitude and an aesthetic. Against a backdrop of social fragmentation, violence, high unemployment and socioeconomic change, punk rejuvenated and re-energised British youth culture, inserting marginal voices and political ideas into pop. Fanzines and independent labels flourished; an emphasis on doing it yourself enabled provincial scenes to form beyond London's media glare. This was the period of Rock Against Racism and benefit gigs for the Campaign for Nuclear Disarmament and the striking miners. Matthew Worley charts the full spectrum of punk's cultural development from the Sex Pistols, Buzzcocks and Slits through the post-punk of Joy Division, the industrial culture of Throbbing Gristle and onto the 1980s diaspora of anarcho-punk, Oi! and goth. He recaptures punk's anarchic force as a medium through which the frustrated and the disaffected could reject, revolt and reinvent.

Matthew Worley is Professor of Modern History at the University of Reading. He has written extensively on British politics in the interwar period, and more recently on the relationship between youth culture and politics in the 1970s and 1980s. His articles on punk-related themes have been published in *History Workshop Journal*, *Twentieth Century British History* and *Contemporary British History*. His books include *Oswald Mosley and the New Party* (2010), *Labour Inside the Gate: A History of the British Labour Party between the Wars* (2005) and *Class against Class: The Communist Party in Britain between the Wars* (2002). As a co-founder of the Subcultures Network, he has contributed to books such as *Fight Back: Punk, Politics and Resistance* (2015) and *Youth Culture, Popular Music and the End of 'Consensus'* (2015).

No Future

Punk, Politics and British Youth Culture, 1976–1984

Matthew Worley
University of Reading

CAMBRIDGE
UNIVERSITY PRESS

CAMBRIDGE
UNIVERSITY PRESS

University Printing House, Cambridge CB2 8BS, United Kingdom

One Liberty Plaza, 20th Floor, New York, NY 10006, USA

477 Williamstown Road, Port Melbourne, VIC 3207, Australia

4843/24, 2nd Floor, Ansari Road, Daryaganj, Delhi – 110002, India

79 Anson Road, #06-04/06, Singapore 079906

Cambridge University Press is part of the University of Cambridge.

It furthers the University's mission by disseminating knowledge in the pursuit of education, learning, and research at the highest international levels of excellence.

www.cambridge.org
Information on this title: www.cambridge.org/9781107176898
DOI: 10.1017/9781316779569

First published 2017

Printed in the United Kingdom by TJ International Ltd. Padstow Cornwall

A catalogue record for this publication is available from the British Library.

ISBN 978-1-107-17689-8 Hardback
ISBN 978-1-316-62560-6 Paperback

Cambridge University Press has no responsibility for the persistence or accuracy of URLs for external or third-party internet websites referred to in this publication and does not guarantee that any content on such websites is, or will remain, accurate or appropriate.

What are the politics of boredom?*

WHAT ARE THE POLITICS OF BOREDOM?   BETTER RED THAN DEAD.

Contrary to the vicious lies from the offices of Leber, Krebs and Thau, our former "paper tiger" management, the New York Dolls have not disbanded, and after having completed the first Red, 3-D Rock N' Roll movie entitled "Trash" have, in fact, assumed the role of the "Peoples' Information Collective" in direct association with the Red Guard.

This incarnation entitled "Red Patent Leather" will commence on Friday, February 28th at 10 P.M. continuing on Saturday at 9 and 11 P.M. followed by a Sunday matinee at 5 P.M. for our high school friends at The Little Hippodrome--227 E. 56th St. between 2nd and 3rd.

This show is in coordination with The Dolls' very special "entente cordiale" with the Peoples Republic of China.

NEW YORK DOLLS
produced by Sex originals of London
c/o Malcolm McLaren
New York--212-675-0855
all rights reserved

---

* This New York Dolls press release for a gig at the Little Hippodrome in Manhattan, February 1975, was brought back from America by Malcolm McLaren following his brief stint as the band's manager/mentor/haberdasher. It hung on the wall of SEX, the shop McLaren ran with Vivienne Westwood and from where Sex Pistols were launched. The flyer is kept in the England's Dreaming Archive (Liverpool John Moores University) and is reproduced by kind permission of the McLaren Estate.

Contents

Figures

Acknowledgements

This project led me to people I had previously only read about in fanzines and the music papers I devoured as a teenager or heard on the records I continue to value. Almost without exception, everyone I approached has been helpful and instructive. Chris Low and Tim Wells deserve a special mention, both of whom were generous with their time and provided me with links to obscure sources beyond the limited archival deposits available: great people doing great things. Steve Ignorant has become a friend as well as an inspiration. Afternoons in 'the office' lubricated key aspects of this book. Thanks Steve, and the wonderful Jona too. Jon Savage put up with my 'punk pest' picking of his brains and archive; thanks Jon, it is all very much appreciated. Garry Bushell, too, offered me insights and information way beyond the call of duty; again, many thanks Garry. Numerous other people answered my queries and gave up their time in a variety of ways, meaning due mention and gratitude must go to Ian Aitch, Viv Albertine, Alan Apperley, Nic Austin, Simon Beesley, Karl Blake, Richard Boon, Janine Booth, Dunstan Bruce, Julie Burchill, Graham Burnett, Richard Cabut, Nick Cash, Rob Challice, Alan Christie, Kev Clark, Caroline Coon, Rhoda Dakar, Mike Diboll, Tony Drayton, Steve Drewett, Russell Dunbar, Bev Elliott, Jamie Fry, Malcolm Garrett, Gillian Gilbert, Paul Gorman, Chip Hamer, Ian Hayes-Fry, Pete Haynes, Paul and Stuart Henderson, Sadie Hennessy, Kev Hunter, Nick Hydra, Garry Johnson, Jordan, Young Kim, Con Larkin, Colin Latter, Alistair Livingston, John Marchant, Jonny Melton, Mensi, Tom McCourt, Ali McMordie, June Miles-Kingston, Ray Molrham, Tony Moon, Stephen Morris, Kev Nixon, Gary O'Shea, Mark Perry, Lol Pryor, Simon Reynolds, Alan Rider, Penny Rimbaud, John Robb, Tezz Roberts, Peter Ross, Richard Rouska, Martin Ryan,

Hannah Sawtell, Seb Shelton, Steve Smith, TV Smith, Linder Sterling, Fraser Sutherland, Richard Swales, Toast Trojanskin, Jeff 'Stinky' Turner, Cathi Unsworth, Tom Vague, Suzy Varty, Gee Vaucher, Fred Vermorel, Paul Weller, Angus Whyte, Lee Wilson and Mark Wilson. Thanks to Russ Bestley for helping with images and reading the manuscript – a curry banquet awaits. Thanks also to Amy Britton, Nic Bullen, Rich Cross, Pete Keeley, Chris Low (again), Mickey Penguin, Steve Shepherd and Fraser Sutherland for their helpful and insightful comments on drafts – I promise a copy will come your way.

Academically, this project has been bound up with the Subcultures Network founded in 2011. Among the hundreds now part of this, I thank my fellow conspirators in particular: Jon Garland, Keith Gildart, Anna Gough-Yates, Paul Hodkinson, Sian Lincoln, Bill Osgerby, Lucy Robinson, John Street and Pete Webb. It would be impossible to mention everyone who has contributed to the Network's events, books and Facebook site. Nevertheless, Lucy has been especially brilliant and I value the input from everyone involved. Punk Scholars – Russ Bestley, Rebecca Binns, Pete Dale, Mike Dines, Jim Donaghey, Alastair Gordon, Kirsty Lohman, Roger Sabin – I salute you, as I do the KISMIF (Keep It Simple, Make It Fast!) organisers leading the way in the study of DIY (Do It Yourself) cultures in Europe and beyond. Paula Guerra, Tânia, Pedro, Gabriela and everyone else who makes it what it is: long may it run … Thanks, also, to those I have met and enjoyed time with along the way: Angela Bartie, Tim Brown, Laura Cofield, Nigel Copsey, Sam du Bois, Sian Edwards, Felix Fuhg, Mark Hayes, Lez Henry, Nicola Ingram, John Marsland, George McKay, Donna McKean, Lisa McKenzie, Claire Nally, Andy Perchard, Hilary Pilkington (I owe you a Czech beer or two), Herbert Pimlott, Ana Raposo, Bart van der Steen, Simone Tosoni and Chris Warne.

My thanks go to the Leverhulme Trust for funding the research that underpins this book. John Street and David Wilkinson were part of the project and contributed to it in so many ways. Thanks especially for your comments on the drafts. Both John and David have been inspiring and great company – a joy to work with and people I hope to know forever more.

From Reading, or once thereabouts, Jon Bell, Andrew Nash and Emily West remain true friends and colleagues, as do Allison Donnell, Dan Healy, Max Hodgson, Richard Hoyle, Ester Mijers, Jason Parry,

Dan Renshaw, Melani Schroeter, Natalie Thomlinson, Jacqui Turner, Andy Willimott and Coleen Weedon. Further afield, thanks to Gavin Bailey, June Hannam, Ben Harker, David Howell, Karen Hunt, Nev Kirk, Norry, LaPorte, Kevin Morgan, Helen Parr, Daisy Payling, Emily Robinson, Gavin Schaffer, Evan Smith, Paul Stott, Tim Strangleman, Andrew Thorpe and Chris Wrigley for intellectual stimulation. Ben Jones, Camilla Schofield and Alan Finlayson: you are fine thinkers in a fine city; it's always great to meet up.

Closer to home, my thanks to the Norwich punks who got involved and made for a great series of events over 2016. Pete Keeley and Paul Mills, you were an inspiration to me way back when; you continue to be so today. Jonty: thanks for the help and the stories and the organisation – it's been exhausting but worth it. Thanks also to Rachel Ann, Jyl Bailey, Dieter and Karen Coulson, Melanie Easter, Davey Guttridge, Kirsten Francis, Jon Fry, Steve Hansell, Kate Phillips, Jack Pitt, Prem Nick, Mick Smith, Clare Staples, Tom Stocker, Pete Strike, Tox, Russell Turner, Gaz Watts, Andrew Wells and everyone else (too many to mention). RIP Jon Vince and Johnny Appel.

Home, too, is for family. Amelia's love and support have been immense; I am always happiest when I am with you. My two children, Rosa and Sid, make me proud, even though they don't seem to like the 'noise' I've been writing about. I love you all very much; you make the world a better place. Thanks to my parents; to my sister Jo and her fine chap Chris; to Bill and Vin. Also, for drinks and welcome distractions in Norwich's Kings Head, Plasterers, Alexandra and sometimes further afield, due mention must be given to Andrea and Dom, Alex and Rachel, Amy and Asa, Andrew and Jane, Andy A, Andy M, Andrew Smith, Batesy, Bob Smith, Cally and Jon, Dan, Dom W, Dunc and Doreen, Ed and Eileen, Emma, Isabel and Jamie, Jo and Daniel, John Bunker and Kathy, John Currie, John J, Johnny Blanco and Zoe, Lisa, Mark and Anne, Marty and Nic, Mick, Mike Braithwaite, Neil, Paul, Pete and Katie, Pete B, Roger, Sadie, Simon Gitter, Simon and Tizz, Stu and Mel, Terry, Trev, Vicky and Warren. Peter Newland, Chris Smith and Simon Wolstenholme: In Thorpe Hamlet We Trust.

Finally, Scott King – too-rye-aye comrade. Remember how we always said that 'Anarchy in the UK' was the pivot around which our world turned?

On the Ball, City …

TEENAGE WARNING: PUNK, POLITICS AND YOUTH CULTURE

> Obviously, the music is the thing that brings all the people
> together in the first place and a lot of the music, I think, has fairly
> important political comments to make. And those comments
> may be naïve, but I think we've tended to believe over the years
> that because political expression was naïve there was somehow
> something wrong with it ... I think the naivety in the music really
> has very little to do with the sincerity or the accuracy of the
> statements its making politically.[1]
>
> John Peel (1977)

The mood was tense even before the violence erupted. As a benefit concert organised on behalf of six political activists arrested in the summer of 1978 for conspiring to 'cause explosions with persons unknown', the vagaries of the charge and the drawn-out prelude to the trial – which ran from September to December 1979 – served only to affirm the seditious and conspiratorial mind-set of Britain's anarchist milieu.[2] Among the 500-strong crowd of punks, skinheads, students and veteran politicos gathered inside London's Conway Hall, any semblance of a good night out had already been tempered by the politics underpinning the event. This was less a gig than a point of reckoning. The state had conformed to type, it seemed; 'the system' was closing in: 'Beware, the thought police are coming'.[3]

Three punk bands were scheduled to play: Crass, an anarchist collective encamped in a communal house located near Epping on the edge of London; Poison Girls, a staunchly feminist and libertarian band originally from Brighton; Rondos, a Dutch group of ultra-leftists with revolutionary aspirations. Among the audience, meanwhile, a contingent of skinheads aligned to the far-right British Movement (BM) took up position, provoking skirmishes and feeding off the repressive atmosphere enveloping the hall. The police came and went, with the gig's organisers assuring them that the situation was under control, before a call was made to members of the anti-fascist 'squads' formed within the ranks of the Socialist Workers Party (SWP) to mobilise a response. Come ten o'clock and it arrived: a tooled-up mob of battle-hardened anti-fascists forced their way into the venue to beat the Nazi skins into submission. Bottles smashed, fists flew, and the once bullish *sieg heils* that had punctuated the evening were stifled amidst the chaos. In the aftermath, with Crass unable to play their set, the police returned with ambulances in tow to tend the wounded and pick over the debris strewn across a blood-stained floor crackling beneath the crunch of broken glass.[4]

Now, the events of 8 September 1979 may not have constituted a *typical* Saturday night out in the late 1970s, but they were resonant of a time in which youth culture, popular music and politics intertwined in complex, exciting and often ugly ways. Taken altogether, the identifiable subcultural styles (punks and skinheads), the visibility of political 'extremes' (anarchists, revolutionary socialists, fascists), the backdrop of perceived crisis and impending authoritarianism, the violence and the meshing of politics and culture all combined to form a recognisable snapshot of Britain on the eve of the 1980s.[5] Indeed, the purpose of this book is to explore the extent to which the cultural spaces opened up and inhabited by British punk from 1976 informed and were informed by the wider socioeconomic and political environment of which they were part. In other words, it seeks to determine the politics of punk as a musical form and youth culture. If punk was an expression of youthful revolt, as it first appeared and was initially understood to be, then what was it revolting against, in what ways, why, and to what end?

More broadly, the book urges historians to take youth and youth culture seriously.[6] If we return to the Conway Hall in 1979 then we find not just a political benefit, a pop gig and a punch-up, but also a portal into the construction of personal identities; a forum for expression and dissent; an alternate site of information, communication and exchange. Integral to the current study, therefore, is the positioning of youth culture as a space for social and political development. That is, youth culture should not be understood simply as a model of consumption, or a product of media invention, but as a formative and contested experience through which young people discover, comprehend, affirm and express their desires, opinions and disaffections. This, arguably, was made explicit with the emergence of punk, whose early protagonists raised the standard of 'Anarchy in the UK' and set themselves but one criterion: 'Does it threaten the status quo?'[7]

We Are Not in the Least Afraid of Ruins: British Punk, 1976–1984

British punk is synonymous with the Sex Pistols. Though it may be more accurate to see the band as providing a point of convergence for the various influences that informed what eventually became known as punk, there is no doubting that the Pistols served as the fulcrum of a musical and stylistic form that redefined popular culture both in Britain and beyond. If not quite signalling a mythical *year zero*, then the emergence of the Sex Pistols in 1975–76 offered a critical moment of departure that has since come to shape our understanding of the 1970s. The Pistols tore open the cultural fabric, trashing the past and confronting the present to better refine the future. 'As soon as I saw them [Sex Pistols] I knew that rhythm and blues was dead, that the future was here somehow', Joe Strummer (John Mellor) of The Clash claimed in late 1976. 'I just knew … It's the music of now'.[8]

The origins of the Sex Pistols were rooted in London's Shepherd's Bush circa 1973. Steve Jones, Paul Cook and their friend Wally Nightingale, three working-class truants obsessed with The Faces, Roxy Music and the harder-edged r'n'b bands of the mid-1960s, procured by a variety of nefarious means the equipment necessary to form a band.[9] Members came and went, before a connection to the clothes shop owned by Malcolm McLaren and Vivienne Westwood on the King's Road in Chelsea, known as SEX between 1974 and 1976, helped provide the personnel and impetus to move out of the rehearsal room and onto the stage. SEX, too, framed the band in an assortment of cultural and political signifiers that reasserted youth culture as a site of subversion: the clothes and ephemera that emerged from the shop juxtaposed overt sexuality and fetishism (bondage, rubber) with extreme politics (swastikas, anarchism), irreligion and rock 'n' roll.[10] By the time of the Sex Pistols' first gig, on 6 November 1975 at St Martin's School of Art in central London, the band was managed by McLaren and comprised Jones (guitar), Cook (drums) and Glen Matlock (bass), with John Lydon, better known as Johnny Rotten, providing the voice.

The impact made by the Sex Pistols has been well documented.[11] Throughout 1976–77, the band helped forge a distinctive youth culture that challenged the preconceptions of the music industry and provoked a media-driven moral panic that fed into broader concerns as to the nation's well-being. Essentially, the Sex Pistols offered a negation of everything: 'No Feelings', 'No Fun', 'No Future'. In so doing, they initiated what Jon Savage described as an 'intense process of questioning' that infused popular culture with an oppositional sensibility that transcended its immediate cultural context.[12] Live appearances were confrontational, during which Rotten often abused audiences already polarised in their response to the Pistols' aggressively stripped-down rock 'n' roll. An air of violence and unpredictability enveloped the band, fuelled by music press stories of gigs descending into chaos and brawls breaking out among the crowd.[13] Early interviews, too, focused on tales of vandalism, petty crime and remand centres that gave the band's members and affiliates a dangerous air of delinquency.[14] Rotten, in particular, projected an attitude that cut through the pretentions and complacency of what he described as 1970s 'non-reality culture', demanding a music that engaged with and appeared relevant to life in a period of social conflict and recession.[15] Just twenty years old and dressed in ripped-up clothing with short spiky hair alien to the time, his first words to the music press were: 'I hate shit. I hate hippies and what they stand for. I hate long hair. I hate pub bands. I want to change it so there are rock bands like us ... I'm against people who just complain about *Top of the Pops* and don't do anything. I want people to go out and start something, to see us and start something, or else I'm just wasting my time.'[16] 'Everyone is sick of the old way', he told Caroline Coon in November 1976, 'we're just one alternative. There should be several.'[17]

Rotten's rallying cry was soon met by those inspired as a result of seeing or reading about Sex Pistols. Simon Barker, having caught the band at Ravensbourne College in December 1975, alerted his friends and thereby paved the way for the so-called 'Bromley contingent' to form the Pistols' first core audience. Dressed in outfits inspired by the Weimar chic of *Cabaret* (1972) and *The Night Porter* (1974), not to mention the fetish wear pedalled by McLaren, Westwood and exhibited by their shop assistant Jordan (Pamela Rooke), the

Bromleys – who included Susan Ballion (Siouxsie Sioux) and Steven Bailey (Steve Severin) among their ranks – reconciled their loathing of suburbia through a style deliberately designed to shock.[18] In so doing, they helped extend the template for what became punk's defining look while simultaneously taking the aesthetics of SEX into the streets, bars and clubs.[19]

As this suggests, aspirant musicians and artists with similar influences to the Sex Pistols soon gravitated towards the band, providing the personnel for The Clash, The Damned, Siouxsie and the Banshees, The Slits, Chelsea and Generation X.[20] Not dissimilarly, pre-existing bands that favoured a rougher live sound (Cock Sparrer, The Jam, The Stranglers) were absorbed into what by the summer of 1976 was defined by the music press as 'punk rock'. Others, such as Adam Ant (Stuart Goddard), Vic Godard (Victor Napper), Pauline Murray, TV Smith (Tim Smith) and Poly Styrene (Marianne Elliott-Said), immediately resolved to form bands or commit to the Sex Pistols in the wake of seeing them perform. In Manchester, Howard Trafford (Howard Devoto) and Peter McNeish (Pete Shelley) helped pioneer punk's do-it-yourself (DIY) ethos by self-releasing and distributing their own record – Buzzcocks' *Spiral Scratch* EP. Even before this, they had organised two Sex Pistols gigs at Manchester's Lesser Free Trade Hall in June and July 1976 to provide a stimulus to punk's spread beyond the capital.[21] Back in London, Mark Perry – a young bank clerk from Deptford – initially eschewed playing in a group to write about punk in his *Sniffin' Glue* fanzine. Thereafter, a flurry of samizdat magazines emerged from bedsits and bedrooms across the UK to provide personalised commentaries on the gigs, bands and implications of punk's cultural challenge.[22]

Not surprisingly, such a burst of creativity brought music industry and media attention. By November 1976, the Sex Pistols had signed to EMI and appeared on a series of television programmes to preview their debut single, 'Anarchy in the UK'.[23] The record was incendiary. Over Steve Jones' multilayered barrage of guitars, Rotten prophesised in a language of chaos and disorder, raising taboos with antichrists and anarchists before exposing the staid mundanity of a Britain defined by shopping schemes, traffic lines and council tenancies. The final verse, during which Rotten fired off a series of terrorist acronyms (IRA, UDA, MPLA), was later described by Jon Savage as a 'scrambled news-cast from a world beset by terrorist forces'.[24] For Perry – as for many others – 'Anarchy in the UK' was 'the most important record that's ever been released', a polarising moment guaranteed either to incite or repulse.[25] Things intensified, however, following the Sex Pistols' appearance on Thames Television's *Today* programme on 1 December 1976. Bill Grundy, the presenter, had been expecting to showcase Queen's latest single, 'Somebody to Love', before a last-minute hitch necessitated EMI find a replacement.[26] Instead, Grundy's ill-prepared interview provoked Johnny Rotten and Steve Jones to swear live on air and thereby spark a protracted media panic that led to the band being dropped by its record label and prevented from playing the majority of dates on its subsequent tour.[27] Amidst front-page headlines and articles bemoaning the Pistols as 'boorish, ill-mannered, foul-mouthed, dirty, obnoxious and arrogant', punk was first subjected to municipal bans and earnest moral outrage as to its supposed degeneracy before then being codified and commodified by a record industry keen to appropriate, package and market the 'new wave' as saleable product.[28] Punk's *meaning*, Jon Savage argues, was refracted through a media glare, reduced to caricature in the mainstream press and probed for deeper significance in the music papers, broadsheets and periodicals.[29]

Despite such co-option, punk retained its potential to challenge and offend. The Greater London Council (GLC) made it difficult for punk bands to play in the capital throughout 1977 amidst rumours of a 'new wave dossier' that blacklisted certain groups. Local authorities, venue owners and student committees across the country likewise prevented punk gigs or ensured a police presence at those that did go ahead.[30] Most famously, perhaps, the furore that surrounded the Sex Pistols' second single – 'God Save the Queen' – all but eclipsed the controversies of the *Today* programme.[31] Released in late May to coincide with 1977's Silver Jubilee celebrations, the record was seditious and provocative, stripping away the façade of British tradition to reveal a repressively outmoded social structure trapped beneath. Predicting 'no future in England's dreaming', the 7-inch came wrapped in a sleeve that defaced the Queen. In response, the single was prevented from reaching the top of the chart only by the machinations of the music industry, with several retailers refusing to stock the record.[32] A boat trip along the Thames organised to promote the single was then curtailed by river police who arrested members of the band's entourage, while a cross-party group of MPs sought advice towards banning the single. On the ground, Rotten and Jamie Reid, who designed the artwork for 'God

Save the Queen', were attacked by royalists goaded by the tabloids' faux outrage.[33]

Two more singles followed: 'Pretty Vacant', a snarling hymn to irreverence, and 'Holidays in the Sun', a chaotic descent into Cold War paranoia via reflections on commodified leisure and a Jamie Reid design that détourned a Belgian Travel Service brochure to present cartoon families taking a 'cheap holiday in other people's misery'.[34] Inspired by a short trip to Germany, the record bristled with Rotten's anger and frustration, the suffocating dead end of the twentieth century embodied in the concrete block of Berlin's wall. October 1977 saw the release of *Never Mind the Bollocks, Here's the Sex Pistols*, the title enough to provoke another round of headlines and a failed prosecution under the Indecent Advertisements Act (1889).[35] But even after the Sex Pistols imploded on their first American tour in January 1978, punk continued to provide a provocative cultural form that existed beyond the realms of the pop charts and high-street fashion.[36] Intermittently, it would re-emerge into the media consciousness, be it as one of the triggers for the wide-scale urban disturbances of 1981 or as a site of political opposition to the Falklands War in 1982.[37]

Punk's transition from subculture to pop culture ensured that its complexities and contradictions quickly unravelled. The Sex Pistols had fused rhetorical populism with cultural innovation; the proletarian credentials of the band and Rotten's emphasis on engagement were filtered through the art school pretensions of McLaren, Westwood, Reid and erstwhile associates such as Bernie Rhodes (who managed The Clash). Punk appealed on one level because it was visually and aurally exciting; it injected a sense of youthful energy and urgency into pop music. Those drawn to London's Roxy club in early 1977 revelled in punk's creative expression, seizing the opportunity to shock, pose and perform.[38] But it resonated too because it captured a mood. Punk gave vent to frustrations of both socioeconomic and existential origin at the precise moment when Britain itself was passing through a period of uncertainty and change. In other words, punk's language, style and iconography (cut-up Union Jacks, 'blackmail' lettering, ripped clothing) appeared to embody the rhetoric of decline and social dislocation that pervaded the media and political discourse of the time.[39] As a result, punk could be read both as a medium for cultural and musical experimentation that challenged conventional sociocultural structures and values, and as a means of providing a voice for the disaffected, including those Mark Perry described as the 'kids ... waiting out there in the discos, on the football terraces and living in boring council estates'.[40]

Such a tension, between punk-as-art and punk-as-social-commentary, would inform the culture's development into the 1980s.[41] First, and most obviously, punk began to subdivide into a mesh of mutating and overlapping subscenes. In the wake of The Clash, whose early set-list drew on Rhodes' advice to write songs relevant to their everyday lives, a number of bands committed to punk as a form of street-level protest. The music was raw and aggressive, the lyrics either depicting the frustrations and excitement of inner-city living or railing against those social, economic and political forces that restricted opportunity. From this, bands such as the Angelic Upstarts, The Ruts and Sham 69 emerged, presaging the Cockney Rejects' ruck 'n' roll to provide a template for the working-class social realism of Oi![42] Concurrently, punk's distillation of rock was soon honed to a hardened thrash perfected by early-1980s bands like Discharge and The Exploited. The social commentary remained, but now cast in the shadow of the Cold War or bound to the entrenched unemployment of Margaret Thatcher's monetarist policies.[43] Crass and Poison Girls, meanwhile, produced a series of records and publications that critiqued the various systems, ideologies and institutions that maintained power both in Britain and globally. Seeing anarchy not simply as a provocative slogan of self-determination but as the basis for an alternative society capable of sustaining itself beyond existing state and socioeconomic structures, the bands each lived collectively and lent support to a range of radical causes. Inspired by their example, numerous groups – not to mention fanzines, record labels, anarchy centres, squats and campaigns – committed to what has since been labelled 'anarcho-punk', with Conflict, Flux of Pink Indians, The Mob and Subhumans among those to the fore.[44]

The 'art' side of British punk likewise fractured into a number of distinctive subscenes. From the Warhol-via-Bowie influences that informed the Bromley contingent came a more elitist reading of punk's 'otherness', one that took the 'clothes for heroes' slogan raised by Seditionaries (the name adopted for McLaren and Westwood's shop from late 1976) as a means to social, cultural or sexual transgression. The tribes who gathered around Siouxsie and the Banshees and the early Adam and the Ants thereby fed into new romanticism and the proto-gothic 'posi-punks' who emerged into the early 1980s.[45] Others picked up on punk's challenge to the music industry, seeking to confront the expectations and influence of the established sector by forming independent record labels and asserting control over the sound, look and promotion of pop music's production. This often contained an overtly political or subversive motive. Bands such as The Desperate Bicycles and Scritti Politti saw musical experimentation and independent organisation as a means of resisting cultural and economic hegemony. They, alongside groups such as Gang of Four and Ludus, used pop as a medium through which to critique and expose the mechanisms behind gender relations, consumerism and power. Simultaneously, Throbbing Gristle's sensory overload of noise and horror augured an industrial culture intended to reveal and break down the processes of social conditioning.[46]

Such approaches were frequently informed by critical theory, be it Marxist, feminist or via literary avant-gardists such as William Burroughs. For those with less overtly political agendas, however, punk more simply provided an opportunity to reinvent popular music, scrambling the codes of rock and pop to create new forms free from the tenets of rock 'n' roll or the whims of the record industry. In other words, punk served to open up a cultural space in which to fuse musical styles; to inject new sounds and lyrical content into popular music; to explore new ways of expressing emotions both light and, given punk's negative impulse, dark. As this suggests, what has since become known as post-punk placed an emphasis on originality and innovation: a 'new musick' or a 'new pop' that evaded preconceived ideas and genres to perpetuate punk's tendency to confront, demystify and reassemble.[47]

Second, punk's dissemination beyond London ensured that it evolved in divergent ways. This has been mapped extensively by Simon Reynolds, whose survey of post-punk explores how the Sex Pistols' cultural intervention was interpreted and reimagined through the urban, socioeconomic and cultural landscapes of places such as Manchester, Leeds, Liverpool, Sheffield, Bristol and Coventry. But it was also a product of punk's DIY message inspiring local scenes to develop around venues, shops, fanzines, squats, labels and bands.[48] Many of these came and went, in the process providing loose networks of contacts that proved able to sustain and inform punk as a fractured-but-distinctive subculture long after it had fallen off the conveyor belt of London's media taste-setters.

Third, punk's adoption of political signifiers and tendency to social commentary invited divergent interpretation and expression. Early on, McLaren, Westwood and the Sex Pistols' use of the swastika and reference to anarchy formed part of a more general assault on mainstream culture. These were confrontational symbols, often utilised to provoke a reaction and juxtaposed deliberately to avoid easy assimilation. In so doing, however, punk could not prevent political meanings being projected back onto the emergent culture. Just as members of the far right saw punk's swastikas and iron crosses as evidence of white youth becoming aware of their racial identity, so some on the left saw in punk a formative expression of socialist protest.[49] From the outset, therefore, punk became a politically contested cultural form. Accusations of fascism soon led bands such as The Clash to better define their stance, presenting themselves as 'anti-fascist, anti-violence, anti-racist and pro-creative'.[50] They and others aligned themselves with initiatives such as Rock Against Racism (RAR), played gigs in support of political causes and opened the way for bands with relatively distinct political agendas to adopt or utilise punk as a medium for progressive cultural politics. Simultaneously, sections of the far right sought to colonise punk gigs to recruit and mobilise members. Though very few punk bands associated with parties on the right, several had to grapple with the problems thrown up by an audience that included either British Movement or National Front (NF) supporters.

Finally, punk's meshing of subcultural styles combined with its rejection of hippiedom, progressive rock and saccharine pop to initiate – or provide a context for – youth cultural revivals to flourish. Thus, the skinhead, mod, rude boy and rockabilly revivals of the period were often infused with a punk aesthetic or attitude that gave rise to sometimes innovative (and sometimes derivative) cultural (re)inventions. Around all this, a debate ensued as to whether punk represented a return to rock 'n' roll basics or its decimation; whether it was part of a youth cultural continuum or evidence of its fragmentation. On the street, such concerns were played out in subcultural rivalries that added further division to the fallout from punk's detonation.[51]

Punk, then, is here defined in its British context and in relation to people and cultural practices inspired or informed by the Sex Pistols. Such a definition recognises that punk was quick to splinter into multiple subsects that often conflicted with each other, but suggests continuity existed in at least four ways: a stated opposition to a perceived status quo (cultural, social or political); a disregard for symbols of authority and established hierarchies; claims to provide a voice for the marginalised or disaffected; an emphasis on self-sufficiency and overcoming obstacles that prevent access, expression or autonomy. As a term, punk is used to encompass those associated with its initial 'moment' in 1976–77 and those who retained an open affinity to it through to the 1980s. It is also used to comprise elements within the subcultural revivals that formed in punk's wake and the post-1977 diaspora that understood punk to have provided opportunity for both musical and intellectual innovation. Punk, therefore, may best be understood as a cultural process of critical engagement rather than a specific musical or sartorial style. It provided a space to revolt, reject and reinvent. 'You have to destroy in order to create', McLaren told the BBC's *Nationwide* in late 1976, 'you know that'.[52]

Waiting for the Clampdown: Politics, 1976–1984

On the b-side of their debut single, 'White Riot' b/w '1977', The Clash began a countdown to 1984. The bulk of the lyric, written in 1976, depicted London on the verge of collapse. Unemployment had bred antipathy and ennui. Pop culture, so resplendent in the 1960s, had become redundant. The media, detached from everyday life, offered little more than a palliative, while violence stalked London boroughs both rich and poor. On the cover of the single (Figures I.1 and I.2), with a nod to Joe Gibbs and The Professionals' *State of Emergency* reggae album from 1976, Joe Strummer, Mick Jones and Paul Simonon stood with their hands to the wall, as if under arrest.[53] On the back, images of tower blocks, rubble and the police were broken up by texts taken from Charles Hamblett and Jane Deverson's *Generation X* (1965) and Stanley Cohen's *Folk Devils and Moral Panics* (1972) describing youth cultural violence transforming into class warfare. As the song itself built to a climax, the years were ticked off: 'in 1977, sod the Jubilee, in 1978 …, in 1979, stayed in bed, in 1980 …, in 1981, the toilets don't work, in 1982 …, in 1983, here come the police, in 1984!'. The song ends with a jolt, as if the power has been cut and the Orwellian dystopia finally descends.[54]

  Such a scenario chimed with the times. Contemporary analyses of Britain in the mid-to-late 1970s came with titles such as *The Death of*

Figures I.1 and I.2 Sleeve to The Clash, 'White Riot' b/w '1977' (CBS, 1977), designed by The Clash. (Photograph by Caroline Coon, Camera Press London.)

British Democracy (1976) and *Britain in Agony* (1978), their attention focused on a stagnating economy and mounting social tensions.[55] On the picket lines, militant trade unionists were accused of wresting power away from Westminster in preparation for a class war. On the streets, football hooligans and 'muggers' became emblematic of a breakdown in law and order, while racial antagonisms spilt over into violent confrontation with the police. From the margins, a resurgent NF emerged to threaten electoral breakthroughs and take its message of race-hate into the inner cities. The far right, in turn, was complemented by a vibrant – if fractured – revolutionary left infused by the sociocultural transformations of the 1960s. As the old Communist Party fell into decline, new social movements and political groupings arose to contest both the inequities of capital and the repressive forces of imperialism and patriarchy. With the empire receding into the background, so the very point and purpose of the UK appeared open to question: Scottish and Welsh nationalism revived; relations with Europe cut across the political battlelines; the Irish Republican Army (IRA) brought its war to the mainland in bloody and spectacular style.[56] And as successive governments searched to find a way out of the snares set by what was a global recession, so plots and coups were rumoured to be hatching among disgruntled military men and 'apprehensive patriots' fearful of a descent into anarchy and chaos.[57] 'Declinism', Andy Beckett suggests, had become part of the 'British state of mind' by the mid-1970s, with encroaching authoritarianism and social collapse foreseen as alternate futures for a country that had lost its way.[58]

The background to all this is well known, even as historians begin to reassess the nature and extent of the 'crisis' that continues to inform popular memory of the 1970s.[59] Inflationary pressures inherited from the 1960s had led to a steady rise in unemployment and industrial conflict that combined to inaugurate a prolonged period of socioeconomic and political strife. The 1973 oil crisis served only to exacerbate Britain's problems, tipping the economy into recession and providing the backdrop to a miners' dispute that precipitated the fall of Edward Heath's Conservative government in early 1974. Though growth returned in 1975, Britain appeared trapped in a permanent state of disarray. By 1976, unemployment had moved way beyond the symbolic one million mark to reach 1,635,800 (6.8 per cent) in August 1977. Inflation, meanwhile, had rocketed in the early 1970s to almost 25 per cent in 1975 and remained high thereafter.[60]

The Labour government's response to the problems it (re) inherited in 1974 was initially based on a 'social contract' with the trade unions. This sought to curb inflation by limiting pay rises in return for social and legal measures of benefit to the working population. Once a further bout of industrial unrest broke out in mid-1976, however, and the pound fell to an all-time low against the dollar, so the chancellor, Denis Healey, was moved to ask the International Monetary Fund (IMF) for a loan. Healey had already cut public expenditure in an attempt to curtail the wage-price spiral in 1975, but the IMF loan was contingent on far deeper reductions amounting to some £2.5 billion. In effect, Healey set in motion the redirection of the British economy away from the broadly Keynesian principles that had underpinned it from the end of the Second World War towards a monetarist policy that was taken up and extended by the Conservative governments led by Margaret Thatcher following her election in 1979.

The full implications of such a shift would become clear in due course. The structural changes ongoing within the British economy – away from industrial production towards the service sector – were accelerated. The power of the trade unions was curtailed via a mixture of legislation and set-piece industrial disputes epitomised by the bitter miners' strike of 1984–85. Large-scale unemployment, which peaked at 3,407,729 (12.2 per cent) in 1986, became a permanent feature of Britain's economic landscape, while old industrial regions fell into decline from which many have yet to recover.[61] More broadly, the collectivist principles of the welfare state were challenged by those of individualism as the nationalised industries were sold off and the private sector blossomed on the back of cheap credit and government incentive. In the long term, Britain was to emerge rebranded as a financial and service centre geared towards the interests of the customer and entrepreneur. In the short term, the country was racked by inflation, inner-city riots and intense social conflict as the 'popular authoritarianism' that Stuart Hall recognised as the kernel of Thatcherism buried itself in the national psyche.[62]

The late 1970s and early 1980s was therefore a period of significant socioeconomic change, during which a heightened political climate was imbued with a sense of engagement *and* disaffection that facilitated both new ideas and associated reactions. Tensions that had simmered during the immediate postwar years of reconstruction and full employment began to bubble to the surface; the basic assumptions – political, cultural and economic – that gave shape to the so-called 'consensus' in British politics from 1945 began to fragment. As a result, Britain's three mainstream parties each passed through different degrees of readjustment over the last quarter of the twentieth century, while organisations and movements to either side of the political centre became more visible as they jostled for position amidst the flux. Of course, such realignments within the political order were also a product of broader cultural and societal forces: changing demographics; the demands of consumerism and technological advance; shifting attitudes to gender relations, class, race and sexuality. They were, moreover, contained within the geo-political context of a Cold War rekindled at the end of the 1970s to raise the spectre of global nuclear confrontation. But the point here is that these developments fed into cultural currents that, in turn, responded to and informed the socioeconomic and political changes going on around them.[63] As The Clash sang about civil conflict and stencilled their boiler suits with slogans alluding to a government crackdown, so they provided a cultural reflection of the media-filtered political discourse that pervaded throughout a country struggling to reimagine itself.

I'm a Youth, I'm the Truth: Postwar Youth Culture

Youth cultures have long smouldered with a sense of deviance. The teddy boys and girls, born out of postwar reconstruction and armed with a sartorial style that stood resplendent against the bombsite, soon gained a reputation for trouble. They appeared, to the media at least, as dark harbingers of a new age, a perception reaffirmed by their adoption of rock 'n' roll as it crossed the Atlantic to re-wire the aspirations of British youth.[64] Teds liked to dance and were up for a fight; they existed in a space somewhere between the home and the workplace. They were working class, territorial and young, a spectacular affirmation of cultural creativity rooted on the street corner but emblematic of a changing world.

If the teds can lay claim to being the first recognisable youth culture to emerge into the postwar age, then others soon followed.[65] Some of these gathered around music scenes (folk, skiffle, jazz, soul, ska, rock, reggae, glam); others evolved out of street-level fashions to be labelled mods, rockers, skinheads and suedeheads. All, however, were to some extent informed by the socioeconomic shifts that took place after the Second World War. Full employment, growing affluence and technological breakthroughs in mass media and production each served to facilitate an age of consumption. In particular, the postwar baby boom gave rise to perhaps *the* archetypal consumer, the teenager, for whom the availability of popular music, make-up, clothes, radios and record players opened the way to innovative, constructed styles of living. Simultaneously, new cultural forms found synergies with emergent political ideas in a fusion that culminated in the 1960s counterculture.[66] The tendency for popular musicians to take up political causes, or to openly transgress the social mores of mainstream society, complemented a 'cultural turn' in leftist politics that embraced youth as a revolutionary force cutting across the old battlelines of class towards a politics of identity. Demographic changes, too, as a result of greater access to higher education, immigration, national service (to 1960) and patterns of employment, served to modify the ways in which young people interacted with each other and wider society. Be it the student radical marching against the Vietnam War, or the pilled-up mod fighting rockers on the bank holiday beaches, youth culture brokered the dynamics of social change.[67]

As a concept, youth culture is relatively new. It was first introduced by sociologists in the United States and used primarily in relation to juvenile gangs and delinquency.[68] Come the 1950s, and attention turned towards the evermore distinctive and visible cultural forms adopted by young people in the years following the war. Charles Radcliffe, a British journalist ensconced in the political and cultural currents of the time, recognised youth culture as a disaffected product of consumer society. In mods and rockers he saw the 'seeds of social destruction'; he welcomed their 'rage' as a sign of simmering anti-social intent.[69] More prominently, the Birmingham University Centre for Contemporary Cultural Studies (CCCS) was founded by Richard Hoggart in 1964, giving rise to a series of pioneering papers, books and articles that interpreted aspects of youth culture as sites of 'symbolic resistance' to prevailing socioeconomic and cultural relations. In such accounts, youth culture was broadly defined as constituting the ways by which young people developed distinct patterns of life and gave expression to their social and material experience. It was, moreover, interpreted through a Marxist lens that placed youth culture in the context of evolving class struggles. Thus, youth 'subcultures' – incorporating popular music, sartorial style, language and social space – were understood to provide a means for young people to try and resolve the tensions that existed between their class position, their parents' generation and the hegemonic values of capitalism. By existing beyond home-life and those social structures (school, work, church, politics) that conspired to shape the adult future, subcultures founded a site wherein young people symbolically reimagined or reaffirmed their (class) identities by adapting and transforming the raw material of consumerism to their own ends.[70]

Such interpretation has been widely criticised.[71] Most importantly, perhaps, a lack of empirical evidence has led to suggestions that the scholars associated with or informed by the CCCS sought to fit youth culture to their own politically motivated theories rather than any recognisable – more complex – reality. This was compounded by a tendency to focus on 'spectacular' subcultures, an emphasis that, first, excluded those who did not fit to a subcultural type and, second, ignored the amorphous boundaries of subcultural identity that allowed people to flit in and between them.[72] Subsequently, the fluidity of subcultural identity has now become integral to the ideas of sociologists examining contemporary youth cultures, for whom cultural 'choice' and the act of consumption is less politically charged and more embedded into the multiple ways by which culture is utilised and understood by those involved.[73] Amidst all this, CCCS scholars were also criticised for their spatial and gender bias, ignoring female participation in the youth cultures examined and failing to scrutinise those social – and private – spaces deemed more likely to be inhabited by young women.[74]

Each of the charges has substance; and studies of youth culture now encompass an array of competing methodologies and approaches.[75] For a historian examining the 1970s and 1980s, however, the theories developed within the CCCS remain intriguing. Not only do they form part of the political and cultural history of the period, but their basic assertions – that youth cultures provide potential modes of resistance and contain distinct (if differentiated and contested) meanings – also helped shape contemporary readings of punk. Even before it was named, punk's gestation related to subcultural tradition via its drawing on youth cultural signifiers to reflect its separation from the sociocultural mainstream. Elements of teddy boy, mod, rocker and skinhead style formed part of a visual assault that rested initially on rock 'n' roll's primal base. As Dick Hebdige explored in his classic *Subcultures* (1979), punk engaged in a conscious form of 'semiotic guerrilla warfare', using symbols and bricolage to challenge conventional norms and values.[76] Punk, in its music, language and aesthetic, deliberately set out to provoke, disrupt and subvert. By so doing, it provided a means for cultural and political expression through which social commentary and dissent were communicated. Crucially, too, such dissent was often focused on a media and cultural industry that competed to define, appropriate and channel youth's innovations. A fledgling punk rocker did not need to read the situationist texts compiled in Jamie Reid's copy of *Leaving the 20th Century* (1974) to know, as the Cockney Rejects put it, that you had to 'have a laugh before the press get in, ['cos] if you give 'em half a chance, they'll kill the fucking thing'.[77]

The objective of the current study is to examine the processes and products of punk-related cultures. By so doing, it will assess the ways by which punk reflected, critiqued and challenged the broader cultural, socioeconomic and political forces that enveloped it. It will argue, too, that youth cultures may thereby constitute formative sociocultural and political spaces through which young people develop, experiment and acquire understanding. In other words, they provide portals to alternate points of reference and information that help forge individual and collective identities. To paraphrase Savage, the premise throughout is that the music, artworks, fanzines and ephemera produced by punk-related cultures reflected the world of 1976–84; that they connected to events outside the pop cultural bubble and were understood to do so by many of those involved; that there was something more than image and sales at stake.[78] Throughout, reminiscence will be eschewed for contemporary source material, both in order to avoid hindsight and to capture the moods, language and preconceptions of the time. As this suggests, the aim is not to write a narrative history of punk remembered, but to examine the various ways by which punk was constructed, understood and utilised as a cultural medium at a particular historical juncture.

Such an approach has political connotations. Punk's basic message was 'do it yourself', which in the context of the mid-to-late 1970s meant assaulting or circumscribing those cultural, social and political forces that appeared to have suffocated the possibilities promised by the mechanisms of consumption and social democracy. As the first modern youth culture born into recession, the punk generation entered the world and reported back in conflicting and sometimes obnoxious ways. Punk's impact was such, moreover, that it continued to inform aspects of youth (and popular) culture long into the 1980s, during which time ongoing socioeconomic and geo-political changes provided ample material to feed further punk's urge for autonomy.

God Save History: Recovering Punk's Past

Why is such a book necessary? From the outset, those involved with punk have sought to control and protect their own history. The Sex Pistols very quickly recruited a designer (Jamie Reid), photographer (Ray Stevenson, then Dennis Morris) and cameraman (Julien Temple) to collate the band's progress.[79] This, of course, culminated in the quasi-situationist fantasy of *The Great Rock 'n' Roll Swindle* (1980), a filmic attempt by McLaren to claim the Pistols' myth as his own and a classic example of why those who make history are not necessarily best equipped to retell it. The initial point, however, was to secure control of the group's presentation, to set it against and in contrast to the distort-ing lens of the media and the all-too-familiar contrivances of the music industry. In fact, punk actively documented itself from the bottom up. Fanzines such as *Sniffin' Glue* were designed to provide an alterna-tive to a weekly music press (*Melody Maker*, NME, *Record Mirror*, *Sounds*) deemed 'so far away from the kids that they can't possibly say anything of importance'.[80] Film-makers, including Temple, Don Letts and Wolfgang Büld, captured punk's grass-roots development in stark documentary form.[81] The first punk books were almost all photo-graphic collections or compiled press cuttings culled from newspapers and fanzines.[82]

Punk, then, catalogued and reported; it rarely explained.[83] Indeed, attempts to define punk in broader socioeconomic, cultural or political terms tended to receive short shrift. Rotten, for example, com-plained of writers such as Caroline Coon assuming 'social implications that just aren't there' and resented those who sought to interpret or project their own meaning onto his words and actions. The Sex Pistols' recorded version of The Stooges' 'No Fun' even came with its own counter to such analysis, with Rotten presenting a song about boredom as a 'sociology lecture, with a bit of psychology, a bit of neurology, a bit of fuckology'.[84]

As a result, punk's tendency to document but resist explanation has paved the way for three distinct modes of history to formulate
around it. First, the earlier recourse to reportage has continued in the
form of compiled oral testimonies and compendiums of photos, graphics and ephemera.[85] These provide the basis for most popular books
on punk, retaining an emphasis on those involved (re)asserting their
take on its origins, content and passing. They remain, moreover, generally entertaining and informative. Over time, as new angles are sought
and punk's battlelines fade into the past, so they continue to throw up
choice bits of detail to tickle the punk connoisseur and occasionally
shed light on events lost in previous accounts. The curatorial instincts
of Jon Savage have, in particular, provided new insights and recognition of the depth, breadth and scope of punk's influence.[86] At the same
time, the transition from contemporary cultural critique to artefact has
arguably served to blunt the tensions, innovations and contradictions
so resonant of punk. More generally, the relativism and subjectivism of
memoir and most oral testimony have precluded and actively denied
analytical consideration of punk's broader meaning and significance.
Components of punk's diachronic and disparate development continue
to be excluded in favour of personalised histories, apocryphal stories
and the nostalgic hue that surrounds 1976–77.[87]

Second, narrative accounts of punk have begun to multiply as
individual memoirs, group biographies and popular music histories
find publication.[88] Some of these are excellent. Jon Savage's *England's
Dreaming* (1991) will forever remain the definitive study of the Sex
Pistols' rise and fall, locating the band firmly within the cultural, socioeconomic and political context of the mid-1970s. Simon Reynolds, too,
has catalogued punk's experimental diaspora in his *Rip It Up and Start
Again* (2005), which journeys through the various 'post-punk' scenes
that emerged in the Pistols' wake. In so doing, Reynolds argues that
'revolutionary movements in pop culture have their widest impact after
the "moment" has allegedly passed, when ideas spread from the metropolitan bohemian elites and hipster cliques that originally "own"
them, and reach the suburbs and the regions'. That such ideas were
often 'inextricably connected to the political and social turbulence of
the times' is made clear as Reynolds celebrates the musical innovations
and intellectual engagement of artists who 'exposed and dramatised the
mechanisms of power in everyday life' while simultaneously committing to an ethos of 'perpetual change'.[89]

More typically, however, narrative accounts of punk serve only to absorb it into an increasingly uniform continuum of popular music history that is close to saturation point. With a multitude of monthly music magazines dedicated to rock's past and countless documentaries regurgitating well-worn legends *ad infinitum*, so bands such as the Sex Pistols, The Clash, The Jam, Joy Division and the Specials (not to mention US groups such as the Ramones et al.) have become dislocated from – or only superficially related to – their historical context. Consequently, punk has been reduced to but another touchstone in pop's rich tapestry; a distinct *musical* segue between the 1970s and 1980s. True, writers such as Savage, Greil Marcus, Stewart Home, Tom Vague, Fred Vermorel and Paul Gorman have – to different extents – argued for punk's place in a 'secret history' of cultural dissent that passes back through situationist interventions, lettrisme and dada to even the 'King Mob' outrages of the 1780 Gordon Riots and the ranters of the English civil war.[90] Polemical essays, too, have sought to contest or undermine perceived wisdom as to punk's motives, meaning and import.[91] But even these tend to rely on a choice reading of punk that selects what is deemed relevant to the argument and discards what is not. And if the anarcho-punk movement inspired by Crass and the DIY ethos embodied in the independent labels and fanzines that flowered around punk have recently begun to accord greater interest, then other areas of punk's dissemination have yet to be judged worthy of serious comment.[92] Punk's early 1980s resurgence, for example, not to mention the scenes around Oi! and goth's punky prototypes, remain beyond the pervasive narrative of popular music's 'progression'.[93] Too often, it seems, punk's broader culture – its audience, context, language and politics – is lost beneath the minutiae of who played bass for whoever and inventories of gig dates or record releases.

Of course, debate as to punk's wider significance once formed the crux of many a contemporary account, not only in the music press but also in political periodicals and sections of the academy. Though it remains a misnomer to suggest that academic studies of punk are legion, the fact that the Sex Pistols emerged in tandem with both the CCCS' evolving analysis of youth culture and the 'cultural turn' going on across the political left means that we can assert a third strand of punk 'history': the theoretical. In truth, most of these are to be found in areas of social science, particularly in the disciplines of cultural studies, politics and sociology.[94] Their objective, meanwhile, tends towards identifying punk's sociocultural implications, be it as a semiotic attack on conventional codes of meaning (Hebdige), a paradoxical challenge to the music industry (Laing), or the apotheosis of an art school tradition that sought to marry 'bohemian ideals of authenticity' with 'pop art ideals of artifice' at the interface between modernism and postmodernism.[95] In their wake, many of the assumptions first made about punk – its working-class origin, political affinity and subversive intent – have been held up to scrutiny and found wanting.

More recently, or at least from late 1990s, it is punk's *legacies* that have drawn attention. Beyond Roger Sabin's useful compilation of essays on punk's broader cultural impact, so a number of exhibitions and heavy-duty compendiums have been collated to trace the aesthetic ramifications of punk's culture shock.[96] Politically, both RAR and the 'white noise' movement aligned to the far right have provided means to assess punk's racial connotations in a period of acute social tension.[97] David Wilkinson, meanwhile, has drawn from Raymond Williams to apply a cultural materialist approach that locates punk's politics in the progressive struggles of the late 1970s and early 1980s.[98]

As this suggests, academic work on punk and punk-related cultures appears to be broadening in scope.[99] Not surprisingly, the primary role played by women in punk scenes locally and nationally continues to warrant attention, both historically and in relation to contemporary culture.[100] Class, by contrast, has all but fallen off the agenda, though a recent academic study – by Pete Dale – examines the faultlines between a Marxist and an anarchist reading of punk in order to assess the music's ongoing reinvention and claims to empowerment.[101] Likewise, although Nick Crossley's 2015 depiction of the social networks that facilitated punk's cultural impact has little to say on class, his use of network analysis does allow insight into how punk scenes coalesced across England's towns and cities.[102] Indeed, the formation of a Punk Scholars Network looks set to enable evermore insightful work into punk's transmission, bringing together the expertise of Russ Bestley, Mike Dines, Alastair Gordon, Roger Sabin and others to generate conferences, research and the publication of a *Punk and Post-Punk* journal.[103]

Despite such activity, there is much to be done – especially from a historical point of view. As things stand, the existing literature remains bookended by highly theorised accounts that seek to squeeze punk into pre-designated paradigms and numerous popular music histories focused on a particular artist or band. In between, collections of punk ephemera and oral testimonies combine to provide both over-whelming detail and, paradoxically, evermore ahistorical remember-ings of punk circa 1976–78. By way of contrast, the intention here is to re-historicise British punk beyond its media *moment* through to one of its own prescribed end-games of 1984.[104] This means locating punk as an evolving youth culture within a shifting socioeconomic and polit-ical context, focusing on the substance of punk's cultural critique and exploring the varied ways by which it served as a medium to comment on and, occasionally, challenge the last vestiges of postwar consensus and emergent neoliberalism.[105] Punk meant something to a lot peo-ple. To some it was just fun, a focal point for a night out and a cele-bration of youth. To others it was a means of expression, a space for experimentation and a source of inspiration/information. Whatever, it is hoped here to capture something of the cultural and political fission that helped define aspects of British youth culture in the late 1970s and 1980s, giving voice to those who in word, if not always in deed, attempted to destroy the passer-by.

1 WHAT'S THIS FOR? PUNK'S CONTESTED MEANINGS

> It depends doesn't it? Everyone's got their own idea of punk …
> punk is to any person what they think.[1]
>
> 'Hoxton Tom' McCourt (1982)

In December 1982, the music weekly *Sounds* convened a 'punk debate' to discuss an article published just a few days before by its features editor Garry Bushell (see Figure 1.1). The subject was a recurrent one, one that flickered in and out of media discourse from 1977 onwards: Was punk alive or, as Bushell now suggested in deliberately provocative fashion, dead?[2]

Ostensibly, British punk appeared to be in relatively rude health as 1982 drew to a close. December's independent charts were dominated by punk or punk-informed bands, with Crass, the Anti-Nowhere League, GBH, Violators, Theatre of Hate, Sex Gang Children and Southern Death Cult all in the top twenty. Among the albums, Factory and Rough Trade LPs jostled for position with the likes of the Abrasive Wheels, Blitz, Poison Girls, Dead Kennedys and The Damned.[3] Once again, John Peel's 'all-time festive 50' for 1982 was topped by 'Anarchy in the UK' and featured nothing released prior to late 1976. His listeners' chart for songs issued only in 1982 covered the gamut of punk and post-punk styles, topped by New Order but including Action Pact, The Clash, The Cure, The Jam, Josef K, Killing Joke and Siouxsie and the Banshees.[4] Street fashion and even national chart acts retained elements of punk style or attitude across their varied forms. Earlier in the year, too, Crass had proven punk's ability to retain a subversive intent, spearheading a vocal protest against the

DECEMBER 25, 1982 35p

PHIL COLLINS · STEVO · TONY BENN · OZZY
TEST TUBES · PRESSBUTTON · XMAS QUIZ

sounds
THE
PUNK
DEBATE

WITH: BEKI BONDAGE
JELLO BIAFRA
VI SUBVERSA
MENSI
ATTILA THE
STOCKBROKER
AND OTHERS   DEAD OR ALIVE?

Figure 1.1 'The Punk Debate', *Sounds*, 25 December 1982.

Falklands War that provoked questions in parliament and threats of prosecution.[5] Bushell, however, sensed punk's impact was on the wane, going so far as to ask: 'Does anyone know what punk means anymore?'[6]

His argument was relatively straightforward: where punk once offered a challenge, 'at most to the way society is, at least to the jaded musical establishment', it had now descended into ritual, imitation and narrow-mindedness. 'A movement which once stood proudly and profoundly against uniformity is … just another uniform', he insisted. Stylistically, the punk 'look' had become formulaic (studs, spikes and leather jackets). In musical terms, thrash or wilful experimentation had replaced songs with a point and purpose. Ideologically, punk had sub-divided into what Bushell described as the hippie-inflected libertari-anism of Crass-style bands; the art-for-art's sake impasse of 'musical radicalism' (post-punk); and the blunted 'street socialism' of an Oi! scene deformed by a mixture of middle-class prejudice, media misrep-resentation and far-right encroachment. Punk's spirit remained, Bushell contended, but punk itself – as a music and a culture – had become conservative and introspective. 'If you're going to change anything you've got to look beyond what you're doing, beyond music. Because music ain't never going to change anything.'[7]

Bushell's polemic proved contentious. Readers wrote in to reassert punk's continued relevance, pointing to the prescience of vari-ous punk bands and punk lyrics; to the local scenes and squats that incubated creativity; to the excitement generated by what Alistair Livingston of the influential *Kill Your Pet Puppy* fanzine felt was punk's basic rationale: 'to create our own lives out of the chaos'.[8] The debate itself brought together writers and members of various bands to discuss the problems facing punk in 1982, meaning factionalism, media fad-dism, commercialisation and a fatalism embodied in the nuclear mush-room cloud that decorated many a record sleeve and the discarded glue-bag that littered too many a gig. Not surprisingly, all thought punk remained an important cultural force (even as they recognised punk's distance from the cultural mainstream). As interesting, however, were the attempts to answer Bushell's secondary question: What did punk actually mean?[9]

For Tom McCourt, bassist with archetypal Oi! band the 4-Skins, punk meant people thinking for themselves; it was neither fash-ion nor anything the media said it was. John Baine, otherwise known as the punk-poet Attila the Stockbroker, agreed. He understood punk as a medium through which people could communicate their own ideas. For Vice Squad's Beki Bondage (Rebecca Bond), punk was about being individual and thinking for yourself. And although the Angelic

Upstarts' Mensi (Thomas Mensforth) felt punk should be working class, it was more generally recognised to cut across such social barriers. Poison Girls' Vi Subversa (Frances Sokolov) described punk as 'a reaction to power ... it's a reaction of the powerless ... We're expressing something and we're using music as a medium. But if it stays within there, then we're going to become either ignored or just so much fodder and so much product ... Punk is about life; punk [is] about taking my life for myself.'[10]

Such broad definition recognised punk's potential diversity while also reasserting an underlying commitment to engage with, comment on and critique issues relevant to everyday life. The problem, it seemed, was that punk's initial shock had been absorbed by the music industry and its challenge formalised via a combination of media caricature and the emergence of various subscenes competing to claim ownership of punk's original intent. To define punk was to emasculate it. But if punk was about 'changing things', as Conflict's Colin Jerwood maintained, then the question still remained as to the extent and focus of its protest.[11]

Of course, punk had always been open to interpretation. Having emerged to disrupt the cultural equilibrium of the mid 1970s, it did not thereby provide the basis for a coherent or unified *movement*, be it political or otherwise.[12] From the outset, punk's symbolism, negation and iconoclasm ensured that competing attempts were made to explain or direct its apparent disaffection. First in the music press and then in the tabloids and political periodicals, punk was framed by a politicised discourse that sought to make sense of its emergence and subsequent trajectory.[13] Simultaneously, those drawn to – or inspired by – punk picked through the debris left in the Sex Pistols' wake to find their own means of expression. That these sometimes clashed or appeared contradictory should not be surprising. It was, after all, the tension between punk's urge to destroy and eagerness to create that allowed its influence to reverberate so far and so wide.

Press Darlings

Punk, to some extent, was a construct of the music press. Certainly, punk's British variant was first recognised and then interpreted by journalists writing for the three principal music weeklies: *Melody Maker*, *NME* and *Sounds*. By 1974–75, the *NME* had already focused its attention on a clutch of bands congregated in New York's Bowery district whose aesthetic drew from the sleazy urbanity of the New York Dolls and Velvet Underground to distil rock's template and, more importantly, reclaim rock 'n' roll for the street-level clubs that once nurtured it.[14] Bands such as the Patti Smith Group, Blondie, The Heartbreakers, Television, Suicide and the Ramones all played stripped-back versions of rock 'n' roll that found a home under the label 'punk' codified by Legs McNeil and John Holmstrom in their magazine of the same name from January 1976. Having existed as an adjective for some time in the music press lexicon of the 1970s, punk finally became a noun.[15]

Back in Britain, the impulses that informed New York punk (denoted by Savage as urbanism, romantic nihilism, musical simplicity and a kind of teenage sensibility) were sought and eventually applied to the nascent scene forming around the Sex Pistols.[16] A dry run of sorts had previously been attempted in 1974, with the *NME* noting how UK A&R (artists and repertoire) departments were searching for 'punk rock' bands. The feature centred on the likes of Heavy Metal Kids and The Sensational Alex Harvey Band, groups that aestheticised and dramatised the delinquent kicks of back-street 'aggro'.[17] None wholly convinced, and the article recognised the 'nebulousness of the genre and lack of any truly understandable working definition', thereby paving the way for the Sex Pistols to pose a genuine threat that warranted comparison to the attitude and atmosphere emanating from the US. The Pistols' first live review, by the *NME*'s Neil Spencer, referred to their playing '60s-styled white punk rock', while McLaren's brief sojourn as the New York Dolls' mentor in early 1975 appeared to make the link explicit.[18] The influence of the Dolls, alongside the primal rock 'n' roll noise of The Stooges, proved integral to punk's early sound and attitude. Simultaneously, however, interpretations of British punk soon tended to be viewed through a socioeconomic and cultural lens that distinguished the Sex Pistols from their US counterparts. Punk in the UK, ostensibly at least, contained political connotations absent in America.

The influence of Britain's music press in the 1970s and early 1980s is difficult to overstate. Between them, *Melody Maker*, *NME* and *Sounds* helped shape the contours of British popular culture, constructing narratives and interpretations of popular music history that maintain today. From the later 1960s, the music press became a vehicle for writers keen not just to report on the comings and goings of chart-toppers and the hit parade, but to inject a cultural and political significance into popular music that took it beyond the realms of commerce and entertainment.[19] The *NME*, in particular, gained a reputation as a taste-setter in the early-to-mid 1970s, becoming a gauge for emergent cultural shifts and a gateway to the subterranean worlds of the post-hippie counterculture and rock 'n' roll. Journalists such as Nick Kent and Charles Shaar Murray had honed their craft in the underground press before moving to the *NME*, from where they seemed to live out – as well as report back on and mythologise – the seedy-glamour of rock bohemianism.[20]

In terms of readership, the three principal music papers boasted sales of 209,782 (*Melody Maker*), 198,615 (*NME*) and 164,299 (*Sounds*) in 1974.[21] Between 1976 and 1980, the *NME's* readership rose to a peak of 230,939, while its combined sales with *Sounds, Melody Maker* and *Record Mirror* were more than 600,000.[22] Neither the mainstream press nor television provided much space for popular music at this time; the music featured on Radio 1 and programmes such as *Top of the Pops* was circumscribed to say the least. Likewise, the musical content of popular pre-and-early teen magazines such as *Jackie* or *Look-in* – along with the flurry of short-lived pop-poster mags that thrived in the early 1970s – concentrated primarily on the relatively narrow remit of a designated 'teenybop' audience: glam's fading glitter dissolving into photo-shoots of The Osmonds and Bay City Rollers. As a result, each copy of *Melody Maker, NME* and *Sounds* tended to be shared between those seeking edgier or more critical fare, meaning the readership of the music papers far outstripped the number who bought them.[23] By 1979, the *National Readership Survey* estimated that more than three million people read the weekly music press.[24] The impact of punk, moreover, meant both a resurgence in readership (following a mid-1970s slump) and a notable change in style and tone. New writers – many of whom began with their own punk-inspired fanzines – emerged to reflect on and charter punk's cultural offensive. Most famously, the *NME* advertised in July 1976 for 'hip young gunslingers' to revitalise its staff list, thereby enabling Julie Burchill, Tony Parsons and, ultimately, Paul Morley, Paul Du Noyer, Ian Cranna and Ian Penman to usher in a new generation of music writers. Not dissimilarly, *Sounds* enlisted Jon Savage (Jon Sage), Jane Suck (Jane Jackman) and Sandy Robertson as its principal punk reporters in 1977, before Garry

Bushell joined in 1978 to focus the paper's attention on the street cultures that flowered around punk. Consequently, *Sounds'* readership rose steadily through to 1982, briefly overtaking the *NME* and, in punk terms, becoming the primary record of its development among the high-street weeklies. *Melody Maker*, meanwhile, provided space for Caroline Coon to track punk's emergence before recruiting Savage, Vivien Goldman, Mary Harron and Simon Frith in the later 1970s. Although the 1980s brought cultural, technological and political challenges that effectively neutered the weeklies' influence, the music press continued to provide a medium through which culture and politics were fused and disseminated. It was, for many, the place where meaning and interpretation of popular music were sought and discovered.

The first writers to engage seriously with the Sex Pistols were Caroline Coon and Jonh Ingham. Though they wrote for rival papers (*Melody Maker* and *Sounds* respectively), both were quick to recognise the band's significance and produce a series of articles that did much to shape the parameters of how British punk was initially understood. Where Ingham emphasised the Sex Pistols' *difference*, Coon applied a sociologically honed eye to assert the band's relevance both to popular music and British society in the context of the mid-1970s. Thus, Ingham's April 1976 piece on the Pistols focused on style and antagonisms. 'Flared jeans were out. Leather helped. All black was better. Folks in their late twenties, chopped and channelled teenagers ... People sick of nostalgia. People wanting forward motion. People wanting rock and roll that is relevant to 1976'. The music's energy and power was celebrated; its lack of virtuosity transformed into a virtue; the aura of violence noted. Most importantly, Ingham gave space to Rotten's decimation of pop's recent history: hippies, pub rock and even the contemporary New York scene were dismissed as a 'waste of time'.[25] Later, Ingham wrote of 'boundaries being drawn by the Pistols', boundaries he defined in more detail in an October issue of *Sounds* billed as a 'punk rock special': youth, an irreverence for rock's pantheon, a predominantly working-class background, a commitment to *doing* rather than consuming, a rejection of '70s style (flares, long hair, platform shoes). Punk was pitted *against* the music industry and the 'old farts' who dominated it.[26] 'The great ignorant public don't know why we're in a band', Rotten is quoted as saying: 'It's because we're bored with all the old crap. Like every decent human being should be'.[27]

Coon's interpretation of punk pushed towards more explicit associations. In particular, she made much of the Sex Pistols' working-class background, using it, first, to explain their evident disaffection and, second, to distinguish punk from a rock 'aristocracy' made up of ageing millionaires no longer connected to their audience. 'It was natural', she suggested, 'that if a group of deprived London street kids got together and formed a band, it would be political'.[28] In cultural terms, this placed the young punks in opposition to the likes of Mick Jagger – who Coon dismissed as 'elitist, the aristocracy's court jester, royalty's toy' [a reference to his friendship with Princess Margaret] – and the 'multi-national corporations' of Led Zeppelin, Elton John and The Who. In contrast to bands such as Pink Floyd, Soft Machine, Yes, Genesis, Jethro Tull and Queen, who comprised 'middle-class, affluent or university academics' playing 'progressive rock' dependent on musical dexterity, Coon presented punk as a return to street-level music that the 'average teenager' could relate to and make themselves.[29]

Class formed the basis of punk's ire, Coon suggested. Her early interviews with the Pistols, The Clash and The Damned centred on broken homes, criminal convictions and failed education.[30] She probed for political comment and opinion, relating punk's antipathy towards contemporary rock 'n' roll to the 'increasing economic severity' of the mid-1970s. Punks 'reflected and expressed the essence of the society they experienced every day', Coon argued. Theirs was the 'violence of frustration'; a rejection of 'romantic escapism'. 'In 1967 the maxim was peace and love. In 1976 it is War and Hate'.[31]

As this suggests, Coon and Ingham did much to define punk as a distinctive cultural form. They helped denote its musical characteristics and drew various bands under its label to provide a sense of coherence.[32] Not only did they highlight punk's irreverence to rock's established canon, but they also linked such iconoclasm to a sartorial rejection of all things hippie that exposed a generational rupture and placed attention on punk's audience as much as on the bands.[33] Most significantly, perhaps, they invested punk with political connotations that tied cultural disaffection to the socioeconomic context from which it emerged. In other words, punk was presented as a creative outlet for a generation coming of age in a period of crisis.

As we shall see, such analysis did indeed reflect attitudes expressed by many of those caught in the Sex Pistols' wake. More to the point, the various elements brought together to give form to British punk remained in flux and open to interpretation. Almost from the outset, a debate ensued as to punk's significance and intent. For the *NME*'s 'young gunslingers', punk's relevance was all too clear. Punk was 'reality rock 'n' roll', Julie Burchill insisted, akin to 'being on the terraces' with an audience comprising 'working-class kids with the guts to say "No" to being office, factory and dole fodder'.[34] For Parsons, punk meant 'amphetamine-stimulated high energy seventies street music, gut-level dole queue rock 'n' roll, fast flash, vicious music played by kids for kids'.[35]

Crucially, Burchill and Parsons appeared to capture punk's spirit in written form. Where Coon's punk sympathies revealed roots that stretched back to the sixties counterculture, Burchill and Parsons were seventeen and twenty-two respectively when they joined the *NME*.[36] Both, along with *Sounds*' Jane Suck and Jon Savage's early writings, offered breathless prose that read as punk felt; they lashed out at non-believers and revelled in punk's impudence. Burchill, in particular, embraced punk for its clearing a space for new voices (young working-class voices) to enter pop and the media; the music was all but immaterial. Parsons was more earnest, seizing on punk's social commentary and urbanity to politicise its relevance in the face of the media storm and municipal bans that followed the Grundy incident. Famously, too, Burchill and Parsons embodied punk's cultural shift by barricading their own space in the *NME* offices, building a 'bunker' from which to do (sometimes physical) battle with the hippies and boring old farts who maintained the rest of the paper.[37]

Over time, as punk proliferated, so Burchill and Parsons' demands hardened. Those who seemed intent to ride punk's bandwagon were summarily dismissed.[38] Political rhetoric and signifiers were assessed and judged against a self-defined street-savvy socialism built on class awareness and anti-racism. In particular, those flirting with swastikas or fascism were taken to task.[39] The 'battle of Lewisham', in which anti-fascists clashed with far-right National Front (NF) marchers on 13 August 1977, became bound to Burchill and Parsons' vision of punk activism.[40] 'The honeymoon's over', Parsons wrote in October, the 'naïve euphoria of 1976 has subsided enough for everyone to turn on the light, straighten the hem of their plastic bin-liner and work up the bottle for imperative re-evaluation judgements'.[41] Inevitably, such high expectations led to disappointment. By the end of 1977, both Burchill and Parsons despaired of what they saw as the dilution of the Sex Pistols' genuine rage and the co-option of punk's early challenge by the media, music and clothing industries. Rock 'n' roll was dead, they concluded, with punk but another illusion of rebellion transformed into commodity.[42]

For others, punk's politics and form should never have been so rigidly defined. Before joining *Sounds* in the spring of 1977, Jon Savage used his *London's Outrage* fanzine to celebrate punk's ability to reflect Britain's social and psychological faultlines, going so far as to predict the development of a 'peculiarly English kind of fascism' – 'mean and pinched' – with Margaret Thatcher as the 'Mother Sadist'.[43] Punk, Savage suggested, was a mode of critique rather than a definite answer or solution. It confronted, challenged and gave vent to a disaffection that was resonant but politically ambiguous. Once punk's shock and provocation had gained space and attention, moreover, so Savage moved to chart its continued evolution. Not only did he predict that the mainstream would fill with punk clones and *nouveau pop* flirtations with the 'new wave', but he also held fast to punk's potential to engage. 'Fresh energy' would be provided by the 'regional centres', he contended, while new sounds and influences would be sourced to map Britain's 'mass nervous breakdown' as 'crisis' gave way to post-industrial (and post-imperial) stasis.[44]

In effect, Savage pointed towards what he called 'post-punk projections': a 'New Musick' built on textures ('harsh urban scrapings/controlled white noise/massively accented drumming') that challenged preconceived notions of punk but reflected the sense of anxiety that would usher in the 1980s. On relocating to Manchester in 1979, he pursued punk's aesthetic through scrutiny of bands such as Joy Division, Wire, Throbbing Gristle and Cabaret Voltaire, focusing on those he felt best chronicled their time and complemented punk's urge to question and experiment.[45]

Savage was not alone in exploring punk's impetus beyond the confines of London and rock 'n' roll. Integral to the culture's vitality was the emergence of local scenes that either reinforced or reimagined punk's template. In particular, punk's do-it-yourself (DIY) ethos and the expansion of independent record labels ensured the music press enlisted regional correspondents to report back on places where, throughout the late 1970s and early 1980s, punk continued to inspire. The most notable of these was Paul Morley, who kept the *NME* informed about Manchester before moving to London and cultivating his own theories of pop's cultural significance.[46]

Morley's early communiqués from the North West made much of punk's serving as a pivotal moment. Before the Sex Pistols played the city's Lesser Free Trade Hall in the summer of 1976, he reported, Manchester had not existed as a 'rock 'n' roll town': 'it had no identity, no common spirit or motive'. Thereafter, bands began to form, venues opened, fanzines developed and a recognisable community emerged to 'attack' the 'insipidity' of 1970s rock. From such a premise, Morley located punk's importance in its opening up 'all the freedoms that can be imagined'.[47] In other words, punk facilitated new ideas, vocabularies and sounds to reinvigorate popular music at both a regional and national level.

Initially at least, Morley embraced a range of punk styles. Though he favoured its more cerebral exponents (Buzzcocks, Magazine, The Prefects, Subway Sect, Joy Division), he recognised punk's urge to protest, writing favourable reviews of proto-Oi! bands such as Sham 69 and Angelic Upstarts.[48] Far from bemoaning the death of rock 'n' roll, Morley celebrated its rebirth. There must be *choice*, he argued in early 1979, as he surveyed a burgeoning underground of punk-inspired bands ready to maintain the challenge to radio playlists and the music industry.[49]

Simultaneously, Morley began to warn against those who subscribed to a definitive punk sound or aesthetic. He disavowed any attempt to politically align punk. Punk's politics lay in its practice, he argued, in its ability to pleasure, surprise, transgress, inspire, question and imagine. The sloganeering of the Tom Robinson Band or blunt social realism of The Jam served only to stifle its potential.[50] Nor did he have time for those he felt offered style over substance. A band such as Bauhaus, for example, who dramatised punk's foreboding in gothic imagery, were described as performing 'rehearsed melodrama' that revealed them to be little more than 'bullshitters in a fine art shop'.[51] Most importantly, he recognised punk as a catalyst for pop's perennial renewal. Just as his prose became evermore baroque and infused with hints of postmodern theory, so he eventually renounced rock in favour of music that sought to redraw the boundaries of pop by avoiding cliché and embracing technology. By the 1980s, he dismissed those clinging to punk as being trapped in a kind of 'folky traditionalism', preferring instead to champion groups that at once celebrated and critiqued pop's pretensions and possibilities.[52]

If Savage and Morley saw punk's challenging the conventions of cultural form as crucial to its impact, then others found greater purpose in its reclaiming rock 'n' roll as a vehicle for rebellion. On joining *Sounds* in 1978, Garry Bushell reasserted the notion of punk as working-class protest, focusing on bands such as Sham 69, The Ruts, Angelic Upstarts and Cockney Rejects to define an authenticated version of punk mythology. That is, a working-class culture made by and for the kids from the council estates and football terraces that Burchill, Parsons and *Sniffin' Glue*'s Mark Perry envisioned back in 1976–77.[53]

Bushell's take on punk was inherently political. As a young member of the International Socialists (Socialist Workers Party [SWP] from 1977) he had been quick to recognise punk as a cultural response to the socioeconomic travails of the mid-1970s.[54] Not only did he urge his comrades to take punk seriously in the pages of *Socialist Worker*, but he actively supported Rock Against Racism (RAR) and contributed to its fanzine, *Temporary Hoarding*. Punk reflected the anger of a generation that had graduated from school only to serve its time on street corners and the dole, he argued. It was the SWP's job to channel such revolt 'into a real revolutionary movement'.[55] Though he had left the party by the turn of the decade, Bushell retained what he termed a 'street socialist' outlook that prioritised collective action rooted in the working class itself. This, in turn, would shape his conception of Oi! as 'a loose alliance of volatile young talents, skins, punks, tearaways, hooligans, rebels with or without causes united by their class, their spirit, their honesty and their love of furious rock 'n' roll'.[56]

From 1980 to 1983, Bushell was punk's most visible champion in the music press. While record industry and media attention turned to the styles and sounds that supposedly superseded punk, Bushell continued to cover those who proudly bore the label into the 1980s. 'The anarchy beat stayed on the streets', he argued in a survey of punk circa 1981, 'growing, changing, transmutating, diversifying, the bands staying true to their roots or getting forgotten, and finally resurging now stronger than ever'. Punk meant thinking for yourself, freedom of speech and finding room to move. It was not about art school pretension but 'energy and teen rebellion – even when it's only rebellion against the boredom'.[57] Bushell retained a critical perspective. He chastised those who appeared absorbed into the music establishment (including The Clash by 1979) or prioritised musical experimentation (Magazine, Public Image Ltd). He condemned bands that chose to circumnavigate rather than engage with either the music industry or society more generally.[58] By conceiving Oi! as a distinct cultural form, he sought to tie punk into a broader stylistic and class-based lineage that ran through teds, mods and skinheads onto punk and 2-Tone.[59]

Punk, then, was both constructed and deconstructed within the music press. Indeed, those who most convincingly defined punk and provided it with a sense of purpose were often moved to mourn its failings once expectations ceased to be met. By as early as mid-1977, 'punk rock' had been reduced to a basic sound, what the *NME* labelled 'ramalamadolequeue', ensuring that many bands and journalists looked to move beyond the parameters of speedy three-chord rock 'n' roll. Those who retained a recognisably punk style were increasingly criticised for succumbing to cliché or negating its original spirit of challenge and change.

Nevertheless, the shadow of 1976–77 remained cast over much of what followed into the 1980s. The cultural spaces cleared by punk were understood by most in the music press to have enabled the innovations of 'post-punk' and 'new pop'. Punk informed the aesthetic and the socialist discourse that underpinned RAR and continued to inspire bands such as the Redskins, bIG fLAME and Test Dept – none of whom played archetypal 'punk rock'. Punk was also recognised as the stimulus for the independent labels that flowered from 1977 and the social-realist edge that fused punk with ska to create 2-Tone.[60] Even those who charted journeys into post-punk's more esoteric corners noted a connection to the breakthroughs of 1976–77. So, for example, writers such as Richard Cabut, Steve Keaton and Mick Mercer plotted punk's transgressive undercurrent towards a 'positive punk' that foresaw and fed into goth.[61] Not dissimilarly, Chris Bohn and Dave Henderson followed Throbbing Gristle's industrial lead through the new musick into a brutalised hinterland that connected transglobal artists revelling in the abject and extreme.[62] For those reading the music papers, such narratives and debate helped make sense of the sounds and cultures that unfolded from 1976, informing their understanding of popular music and providing them with templates and opinions to actively embrace or react against.

The Sun Says (So It Must Be True)

If the music press provided multiple interpretations of punk's emergence and development, then the wider media tended towards a more reductionist reading.[63] Punk became the latest in a long line of youthful 'folk devils' that were defined culturally but simultaneously presented as indicative of some deeper malaise.[64] Much of the reporting that followed the Sex Pistols' appearance on *Today* was fanciful: the epitome of a fabricated 'moral panic' designed to sell copy rather than provide insight on a distinct youth culture.[65] Even so, the version of punk captured in the media glare contributed towards both the evolution of the culture and the ways in which it was more broadly understood. First, the mainstream media's recoil from punk became part of its appeal, a sign of punk's impact and proof of the media fallacies that helped fuel its critique. Second, media exposure gave greater form and substance to punk's cultural identity. Though press and television reports often caricatured and distorted punk's early stirrings, they also fed back into the culture to fashion its myths and codify its signifiers.[66] Third, media coverage enabled access to those beyond the remit of the music papers or early punk milieu. In so doing, it served to raise punk above the level of a subculture. Finally, as Bill Osgerby has noted, the media discourse that enveloped punk contributed to the dramatisation of a wider sense of crisis that characterised Britain in the mid-to-late 1970s.[67] Beneath the mock outrage of the tabloids lay insecurities and socioeconomic tensions for which punk provided a ready outlet.

Initially at least, the mainstream media's take on punk swung between intrigue and incredulity. Early exposés in the tabloids concentrated on punk style; a 'crazy ... shock-cult' defined by chains, rips and colour. So, for example, *The Sun* featured 'Suzie' (later Siouxsie Sioux) and Steve Havoc (later Severin) in torn and see-through clothes to explain the 'craziest pop cult of them all', while the *Sunday People* pictured a young punk – Mark Taylor from Newport, who along with his friends Steve Harrington (Steve Strange) and Chris Sullivan had been quick to pick up and adopt new styles glimpsed on trips to London and Ilford's Lacy Lady – replete with nose chain. The report read: 'If you thought you'd seen it all, dig this latest line in crazy gear. As you can see, one end of that chain is actually through his nose, the other through his ear ... It's the face of a Punk Rocker, Britain's latest pop trend. And there's more to the whole bizarre look than this. Like vividly dyed hair, oozes of make-up, ballet tights and ripped plastic or leather T-shirts. And that's for fellas. The girls are even more way out. They wear razor blades for earrings as well'.[68] Though passing reference was made to punk's being born of economic recession and reaction against rock's excesses, the emphasis was on punk as fashion.

Not surprisingly, perhaps, more in-depth enquiry came from the broadsheets and features such as those on the BBC's *Nationwide* and LWT's *Weekend Show* (both 1976). These took their cue from Coon, Ingham and Parsons' early writings, picking up on the Sex Pistols' cultural offensive against the pop 'establishment' and what McLaren defined as their attempt to 'transform what is basically a very boring life'. Punk, McLaren insisted on *Nationwide*, was about 'kids' reclaiming rock music, 'making music from the streets ... born out of a frustration to get something across that is of their own'.[69] From such analysis, the trope of 'dole queue rock' briefly embedded itself in the media lexicon.[70]

Ultimately, it was the Sex Pistols' appearance on *Today* that fixed the press' conception of punk. Attention thereafter focused on punk's anti-social mannerisms – the swearing, the spitting and the violence. Already, punk's association with the COUM Transmissions exhibition *Prostitution*, held at the Institute of Contemporary Arts (ICA) in October 1976, had presaged the furore that engulfed the Sex Pistols. The exhibition, which effectively launched Throbbing Gristle's mission to subvert popular music, also featured the punk band Chelsea (playing as LSD) and art works that comprised Cosey Fanni Tutti's (Christine Newby) explorations in pornography and sculptures adorned with used tampons.[71] The media took the draw, reigniting debate on the use of public money to fund the arts and feeding concern as to the extent to which such a 'celebration of evil' could undermine Britain's supposed moral values.[72] Notably, however, the much-repeated quote of the Tory MP Nicholas Fairbairn, that 'these people are the wreckers of civilization', was juxtaposed in the *Daily Mail* next to pictures of Siouxsie Sioux, Steve Severin and Debbie Wilson, all of whom had attended the event's opening 'party'.[73]

The media response to the Grundy incident would eclipse all this of course. As expletives and bodily functions became headline staples, so punk's challenge was distilled into crude caricature: the 'foul mouthed yob' with coloured hair and safety pins who, by the 1980s, had become a light entertainment cliché.[74] More immediately, punk appeared to tap into a perennial fear of disaffected youth that found renewed expression in a period of recession and growing unemployment.[75] If the *Sunday People*'s verdict on punk was that 'it is sick. It is dangerous. It is sinister', then the *Daily Mirror* felt punk was 'tailor-made for youngsters who feel they have only a punk future ... a brave new generation of talent and purpose is turning sour before our very eyes'.[76] In effect, any substance contained within punk's critique was buried beneath media narratives designed to stoke age-old concerns or confirm predetermined opinion. Punk was caught in a media freeze-frame, primed and ready to decorate tabloid tales of street-fighting, glue-sniffing or obscenity for years to come. In media terms, punk was but a signpost for delinquency and decay.[77]

Bloody Revolutions

Politics formed but a subtext of the media's understanding of punk. Intermittently, concern that punk harboured a fascist germ found its way into a tabloid exposé. The *Evening News*' John Blake seemed keen on this angle for a while in 1977, belatedly picking up on punk's use of the swastika to hint at links to the NF.[78] The controversies surrounding Oi! in the early 1980s also related to broader media interest in the far-right's attempts to recruit young skinheads. Having been conceived as an amalgam of punk, skinhead and terrace culture, Oi! became headline fodder once a gig featuring 4-Skins, The Business and The Last Resort at the Hambrough Tavern in Southall on 3 July 1981 was attacked by local Asian youths objecting to the arrival of a large skinhead contingent in an area with a history of racial conflict. Thereafter, the tabloids (and the *NME*) conflated Oi! with skinheads and racism, a reductionist reading that was nevertheless fuelled by the fact Nicky Crane, a member of the British Movement (BM), was featured on the cover of 1981's *Strength Thru Oi!* compilation.[79] Even so, Simon Barker made it onto Grundy's *Today* programme wearing a Nazi armband without undue fuss in 1976, and the uproar that greeted the Sex Pistols' commentary on 1977's jubilee celebrations, 'God Save the Queen', focused less on its perceptive critique of Britain's 'mad parade' and more on its reinforcing the Pistols' yobbish credentials. 'Punish the punks', the straplines admonished, as the lyrics were misquoted and attention shifted to the beatings meted out on Rotten, Cook and Jamie Reid in the aftermath.[80]

For those of an overtly political bent, however, punk's arrival had definite implications. Its oppositional stance – not to mention its display of political signifiers – contained an obvious appeal to both the left and the right.[81] In many ways, punk rekindled the debates of the 1960s and early 1970s as to the meaning of specific (youth) cultural forms and their use as a medium for social and political change.

The Communist Party of Great Britain (CPGB) had, between 1973 and 1975, engaged in a protracted discussion on just such a subject, exploring the extent to which youth cultures were simply the commercialised products of capital or, as the party's Martin Jacques argued, a formative site of class struggle relevant to prevailing material conditions.[82] Paul Bradshaw, the editor of the party youth section's newspaper (*Challenge*), actually predicted in mid-1976 that 'new forms of culture, especially through music, [will] develop and give expression to the problems facing youth' in a period of rising unemployment and social tension.[83] For at least some young communists, songs such as 'Anarchy in the UK' and The Clash's 'Career Opportunities' delivered just that. The Young Communist League (YCL) even sent the Sex Pistols an 'open letter' in 1977, suggesting a consolidation of punk and communist forces.[84]

Others on the left were equally alert to punk's political potential. In the SWP, Roger Huddle joined with Bushell to argue that punk was an expression of youthful (working-class) discontent that needed to be directed into the socialist movement.[85] Letters to *Militant*, *Challenge* and *Socialist Worker* debated punk's progressive and reactionary tendencies; articles wrestled with the relationship between punk, politics and culture.[86] Even the Workers' Revolutionary Party (WRP) overcame its early reading of punk as inherently fascist to include favourable coverage in *Young Socialist* from mid-1978.[87] Though dissenting voices remained, some leftist publications adopted punk graphics in the late 1970s and provided space to interview the more politically committed bands, poets and artists.[88] To attend a political festival or benefit at this time was to catch sight of X-Ray Spex, The Ruts, Crisis, Gang of Four, The Pop Group, The Fall and others all too ready to lend support to a cause or, it must be said, take advantage of the opportunity to play live.[89] Without doubt, Red Saunders and those who formed RAR saw punk's inclusion as integral to its success, ensuring that punk bands performed at the carnivals arranged in conjunction with the Anti-Nazi League (ANL) between 1978 and 1981 and at countless gigs organised by local RAR clubs throughout the late 1970s.[90] These, as well as high-profile rallies such as that held by the Campaign for Nuclear Disarmament (CND) in Trafalgar Square in October 1980, helped align punk's protest to distinct political positions.[91]

Not surprisingly, perhaps, punk's champions on the left were relatively young. Some, including Jacques, Huddle and David Widgery, had cut their political teeth in the 1960s and viewed punk within a broader tradition of youthful protest. Others, such as Bushell or *Temporary Hoarding*'s Lucy Whitman (also known as Lucy Toothpaste), were politicised over the 1970s and recognised in punk a spirit and an approach that complemented (and soundtracked) their own sense of revolt. More searching analysis was occasionally offered. Dave Laing, who in 1976 addressed the CPGB's Art and Leisure Committee on 'trends in rock music', drew from Walter Benjamin to explain how punk's 'shock effect' opened up contested cultural spaces of ideological struggle.[92] But the left's relevance to constructing punk's meaning or purpose really came with its providing connections between youthful discontent and prevailing sociopolitical issues – be it anti-racism, feminism, unemployment or nuclear disarmament. If, by the 1980s, the theories of Theodor Adorno were more readily applied to explain punk's failure to overturn the music industry or instigate socialist revolution, then the early enthusiasms that fed into RAR, CND and unemployed demonstrations continued to lend political gravitas to bands, scenes and the records released in the wake of 1976.[93]

On the right, meanwhile, there were also activists keen to forge links between politics and youth. Though the aged leaderships of the NF and BM were repulsed by popular music in all its forms, seeing it as a 'manifestation of the jungle', younger members began to combine their interest in fashion and fascism.[94] Not only did an anonymous contributor to the BM's *British Patriot* claim to recognise in punk signs of a general rightward shift in rock music, but a cabal of young BM and NF members formed an increasingly visible and assertive contingent among London's punk audience from 1977.[95] This, initially, led to tensions on the far right. According to Gary Hitchcock, 'a few of us' were expelled from the BM for being 'degenerate for going to gigs'.[96] But the left's success in student recruitment and initiatives such as RAR helped prompt the establishment of a Young National Front (YNF) in 1977 and encourage the BM's cultivation of a skinhead vanguard thereafter.[97]

The far right's claims for punk varied. At an organisational level, its engagement formed part of a wider drive for youthful members. In London, Joe Pearce headed the YNF and edited its *Bulldog* magazine. As a teenager in the mid-to-late 1970s, Pearce appreciated the importance of youth culture to his potential recruits and tailored *Bulldog* accordingly, focusing on football, music and promoting YNF discos.[98]

Not dissimilarly, Eddy Morrison used his position as an NF regional organiser to provide the foundations for Rock Against Communism (RAC).[99] In the BM, the drive to recruit working-class youth offered a violent political outlet for a mainly skinhead milieu that included Hitchcock, Glen Bennett, the Morgan brothers and Nicky Crane.[100]

As this suggests, the far right's adoption of youth cultural motifs reflected its younger members' coming of age in a period when pop music and subcultural style were established parts of everyday life. Like their rivals on the left, they also accepted popular music and youth culture as a politically charged means of expression. Morrison was a David Bowie fan who endeavoured to find Aryan – or at least European – roots for pop music.[101] Pearce, whose brother Stevo ran a 'futurist disco' and a punk-informed label (Some Bizarre), focused on street-level youth cultural styles: 'Punks, Mods, Skins and Teds – All Unite to Fight the Reds!'[102] To this end, affinities were sought between nationalist politics and everything from the mod and skinhead revivals of the 1970s to new romantics and football hooligans. Even 2-Tone bands were coveted, though this more than anything revealed the contradictions inherent in a racial interpretation of either popular music or youth culture more generally.[103] In relation to punk, the emergence of Oi! was belatedly seized upon as 'music of the ghetto. Its energy expresses the frustrations of white youths. Its lyrics describe the reality of life on the dole … It is the music of white rebellion'.[104]

It was, however, through active intervention – stage invasions, *sieg heils* and co-ordinated violence – that the far right sought to colonise the cultural and physical spaces opened up by punk. Bands were claimed for the nationalist cause irrespective of whether they wanted such attention or not. Gig venues became sites of political confrontation to be fought for and won. Once a band rejected the far right's overtures, they became a target for reprisal. Most notoriously, Sham 69's 'farewell to London' gig at the Rainbow Theatre in July 1979 was violently broken up by the BM, though less renowned instances were commonplace before and after. Three years on and the YNF attacked a Bad Manners gig at the same venue, warning that 'our attitude is that bands who are not our friends are our enemies, and will be treated as such … remember what happened to Sham 69'.[105]

Ultimately, the tenuous relationship between racist politics and existing youth cultures necessitated that the far right form its own variant. This was concentrated around RAC and Skrewdriver, a

Lancastrian punk band whose singer, Ian Stuart, first moved to London in 1977 and became involved with the NF. With most punk, Oi! and 2-Tone bands refusing to endorse a fascist following, so Skrewdriver claimed to speak the language of the white working class and set in train what became a transglobal network of 'white power' bands that later gathered under the auspices of Blood & Honour.[106] The music, initially at least, was crude punk rock, with lyrics that were overtly racist and ultra-nationalist targeted at an audience drawn primarily from a section of the skinhead subculture that fused class and racial identity into a distinctive style.[107]

The ways by which organised politics informed punk's cultural development will be explored in due course. The key point here is that both the left and right sought to assign political meaning to punk and provide opportunity for music, youth culture and politics to coalesce. This was never wholly successful; punk and its associated cultural forms remained too amorphous and diverse to forge a coherent politics. But by projecting onto punk ideological intent or potential, activists from the left and right helped delineate the music and youth cultures that emerged from 1976 as sites of political engagement. This, in turn, was further facilitated by a music press that was receptive to ideas of a politicised youth culture wherein music – in terms of both its form and content – mattered beyond the realm of personal taste.[108] In the heightened political climate of the late 1970s and early 1980s, punk was utilised to revive the notion of popular music as a vehicle for protest and youth culture as a signal of revolt.

All the Young Punks ...

When Johnny Rotten was asked in 1976 if he was happy being known as a 'punk', his reply was curt: 'No, the press give us it. It's their problem, not ours. We never called ourselves punk'.[109] As this implies, there was initially some resistance to a label that had already been used to describe American garage bands from the 1960s and their more recent descendants in New York. 'New wave' was preferred by some, even amongst the Sex Pistols' inner circle, but it lacked the perfunctory offensiveness of a word that contained criminal and sexually subversive etymological roots.[110] For Tony Parsons, the term punk was 'too old, too American, too inaccurate'; it failed to do justice to what he regarded as a genuine upsurge of young British bands who reflected their time and place. 'Kids rock [sic]', he suggested, was a more accurate descriptor – if one be needed at all.[111] Not dissimilarly, Paul Morley had touted 'S' rock, as in 'surge', to define the Sex Pistols' 'controlled chaotic punk muzak', while Jonh Ingham made a belated pitch for '(?) rock'.[112] Nevertheless, the fact that Caroline Coon's early pieces defined the Sex Pistols as 'punk', and the fact that it allowed older journalists to locate the emergent new wave in a recognisable rock 'n' roll lineage, meant the term prevailed.[113] Although antipathy remained, primarily in recognition of the way such media-devised labels served to 'dehumanise/ isolate/ humiliate/ segregate/ divide up [and] create bull-shit and dull acceptance' (*Toxic Grafity*), 'punk' was adopted by the mainstream press and, crucially, by Mark Perry, Jon Savage, Tony D (Drayton), Steve Burke, Paul Bowers and others who helped catalogue the embryonic culture at a grass-roots level.[114] The impact made by the Ramones, too, should not be underestimated with regard to defining a punk sound and forging affinities with the already branded US scene.[115]

Beyond the name, of course, the ways and means by which punk was interpreted continued to vary. Punk's impact was often visceral: it was fun, fast and exciting. Though *who* and *what was* (or *was not*) punk may have formed the basis of perennial schoolyard/college/pub debates, precise definition or prescribed meaning counted little to many of those prompted to form a band, dress up, buy a record or go to a gig in the wake of discovering the Sex Pistols.[116] To flick through fanzines or to read the letters published in the music press is to reveal the nebulous ways by which punk was understood and acted upon. For the enthused, punk revitalised popular music – lending credence to the idea that its primary effect was to reassert rock 'n' roll's initial impetus and recover youth culture's snottily subversive gene.[117] Likewise, the oft-cited incentive born of punk's disregard for musical proficiency (anyone can do it) was not always recognised to contain the implicit political or sociological connotations that it undoubtedly did. Despite certain tropes being easily mouthed – anarchy, boredom, bondage, city, hate, fascism, liar, nowhere, sick, suburbia – The Damned's insistence that 'I don't need politics to make me dance' rang true for many a self-defined punk rocker.[118]

Certainly, there was always a degree of disjuncture between the music press' desire to define musical genres and a youthful embrace of the numerous bands and styles that evolved from 1976. Punk-inspired fanzines, for example, regularly covered anything and everything deemed to exist as an alternative to a perceived mainstream.[119] If punk informed the soundtrack of someone's youth, then its meaning – or resonance – transcended the intellectual conceits of the music press.

For others, punk's importance ran deeper. At a local level, the fanzines produced from 1976 soon progressed from celebrating fledgling punk bands (and their precedents) to personalised critiques of the music industry and society in general. 'Zines such as Lucy Toothpaste's *Jolt* proffered feminist assessments of punk's early stirrings, while ruminations on the wearing of Nazi symbols found their way into *Ripped & Torn* before it transformed into the more overtly anarchistic *Kill Your Pet Puppy*.[120] *Vague*, which began as a fairly conventional fanzine from Wiltshire, eventually developed through in-depth analyses of punk's sociocultural relevance to expanded essays on situationist practice and the Red Army Faction.[121] *Rapid Eye Movement*, too, morphed from a punk 'zine into a book-length compendium exploring what its founder, Simon Dwyer, called 'occulture'.[122] In so doing, punk served to establish links to currents of political and cultural dissent someway beyond the typical preserve of pop music.

This was undoubtedly the case with regard to the samizdat publications that fused anarchism and punk in the early 1980s. The contents of *Anathema, Enigma, Fack, New Crimes, Pigs for Slaughter, Scum, Toxic Graffitti* [sic][123] and countless others mixed limited music coverage with political tracts directed against the various organisational and intellectual props of 'the system'. Collages, poems and essays became essential weapons in the punk arsenal, complementing the words and imagery of bands whose politics were unpicked and assessed in critical fashion. As a result, fanzines formed an integral part of the subterranean networks that connected punk collectives, labels and venues across the UK (and beyond) into the 1980s.

Nor did those who formed bands necessarily limit their understanding of punk to music. From Rotten and The Clash's insistence that pop should be relevant to its time and place, so punk may in part be measured by its ability to reflect and critique. Quite what this entailed was again open to interpretation. At one end of the spectrum, humour lent itself to irreverence and a wilful puerility designed to offend and titillate in equal measure.[124] At the other, a sense of engagement could be defined in terms of social reportage or political activism. For those with a keen eye on the motivations of McLaren and Westwood, punk emerged as an exercise in creative destruction; an aesthetic provocation that translated into lives lived 'heroically' amidst the ruins of the twentieth century.[125] In between, punk cultivated a DIY ethos committed to opening up channels of independent production that strove either to reimagine the boundaries of popular music or reset them against all that was deemed to have become clichéd and impotent. Rotten, when pushed, retained a more open-ended definition : 'You can't put it [punk] into words. It's a feeling. It's basically a lot of hooligans doing it the way they want and getting what they want'.[126]

In many ways, therefore, people could find what they needed in punk. For Sham 69's Jimmy Pursey, punk was 'a kid in Glasgow, Liverpool, London, Southampton, who lives in a little grimy industrial estate, wears an old anorak, dirty jeans, pumps, goes out at night, has a game of football on the green, throws a couple of bricks through a window for a bit of cheek, a kick. He likes the things he likes; no fucking about ... they're the kids that THIS was supposed to get over to'.[127] Others picked up on punk's challenge to musical convention, both in terms of sound and lyrical content. Bands such as Scritti Politti and The Pop Group appreciated punk's innovation and '*bona fide* political fervour', but sought to extend its relatively limited palette via continued experimentation.[128] In other words, they understood punk as a temporal moment that provided the impetus and the processes by which to enable access to new cultural forms and production. Penny Rimbaud (Jeremy Ratter), meanwhile, seized on punk's anarchic symbolism to conceive a more overtly activist strand of protest linked back to the 1960s counterculture. Rimbaud, who co-founded Crass with Steve Ignorant (Steve Williams) in 1977, recognised punk as 'an all-out attack on the whole system'.[129]

As should be clear, punk could infer many things. The debate that rumbled across the letter-pages throughout the short life-span of *Punk Lives* magazine (1982–83) flitted between those bemoaning the inclusion of certain bands not deemed to be punk and discussion as to the culture's meaning. But despite sometimes serious division, such as between the anarchist punks inspired by Crass and the more class-orientated punks and skinheads who related to Oi!, what tended to bind the various interpretations together was a sense of difference or opposition to perceived sociocultural norms.[130] Most of those involved in or inspired by punk saw it as having either opened up or provided an alternative cultural space through which to operate, escape to or exist in. Punk served as a medium for agency; it stirred people to act.

It could, moreover, be *used* in different ways. Punk could be enjoyed purely for the music, the style and the excuse to play in a band or go to a gig. Simultaneously, British punk's template – as sketched by the Sex Pistols, The Clash and developed by others thereafter – meant it harboured more serious intent. It provoked, questioned and lent empowerment to those who aligned to it.[131] This could mean voicing an opinion or registering a protest; it could also be read in purely cultural terms, as a reaction to prevailing music or stylistic trends. At its most committed, punk pertained to a politicised youth culture that, in the words of Conflict, 'meant and still means an alternative to all the shit tradition that gets thrown at us. A way of saying No to all the false morals that oppress us. It was and still is the only serious threat to the status quo of the music business. Punk is about making your own rules and doing your own thing.'[132]

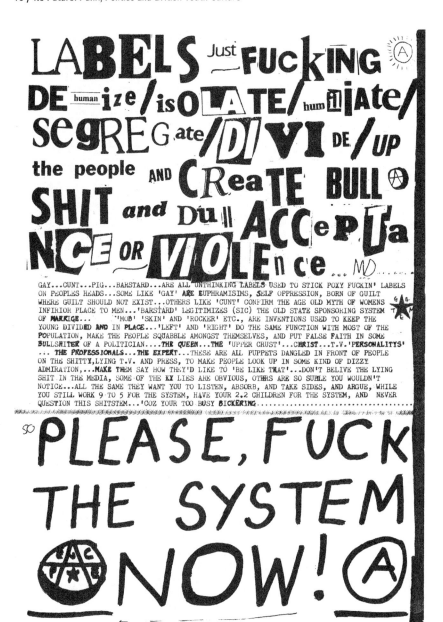

Figure 1.2 *Toxic Grafity*, 5, 1980.

2 ROCK AND ROLL (EVEN): PUNK AS CULTURAL CRITIQUE

> We wanted to change the reasons for playing rock music. We
> didn't want it to be rock for rock's sake; we wanted it to be a
> medium for ideas rather than a release from boredom ... It's not
> as if we're saying 'wipe out the whole of rock 'n' roll' ... We're
> just saying 'go about things in a different way'. Don't just use it
> as a way of releasing peoples' tension so that they can go back to
> work the following morning [...] rock could be made into a really
> good secondary education system.[1]
>
> Vic Godard (1978)

One of the prevailing media tropes applied to punk is that 1976–77
marked a 'year zero', a levelling of pop music's cultural terrain that disavowed the past in order to clear a path for the future. Early interviews
with the Sex Pistols made much of Johnny Rotten's claim to have no
musical heroes. His customised 'I Hate Pink Floyd' T-shirt combined
with his dismissal of rock's prevailing icons as 'redundant' appeared to
signal a cultural shift. Hippies, so emblematic of the previous generation, were cast as the enemy: the antithesis of punk's assertive urbanity.[2] The year 1977, The Clash forewarned, meant 'No Elvis, Beatles
or the Rolling Stones' – a prophecy that seemed to gain credence with
Presley's death and Keith Richards' arrest on drug charges in Canada at
the start of the year.[3] Lest we forget, Paul McCartney's Wings released
'Mull of Kintyre'.

Such portents of 'cultural patricide' – as mediated through the
music press and oft-reaffirmed in early punk interviews – have since
hardened into the narrative that prefaces most books, overviews or

documentaries on the period, to wit: rock 'n' roll in the 1970s had travelled so far from its primal beginnings as to appear lost in a world of
fantasy and self-indulgence, a process seemingly embodied in the musical excesses of 'prog rock' and the wealthy lifestyles of an ageing rock
elite. Not only had the foremost rock acts of the time become prone
to signing on for expensive and irregular stadium gigs, but mainstream
pop had fallen fallow after glam and succumbed to an endless stream
of novelty acts and diluted disco. At a local level, the student union circuit provided scant relief from the multitude of jobbing bands playing
cover versions of assorted 'classics' to disinterested audiences in local
pubs and workingmen's clubs. Punk, so the story goes, arrived to provide the necessary antidote to all this, serving both to challenge and
reinvigorate a record industry suffering from falling album sales and
the effects of an ongoing recession.

Things were not quite so simple. Reggae, northern soul and
disco each provided signs of youth cultural life beyond the parameters of the rock press. The influence of progressive rock was not as all
pervasive (or besmirched) as subsequent accounts suggest. Scratch the
surface and glam's glitter continued to scatter across pop's evolving
sounds and styles, while punk's do-it-yourself (DIY) practice was often
facilitated through infrastructures connecting back to people, politics
and places informed by a still-active counterculture, be it via creative
spaces, retail outlets or community printing presses. Hawkwind and
Pink Fairies certainly registered as a formative influence on at least some
of those who later cut and spiked their hair.[4] Nevertheless, Rotten's
claim that rock 'n' roll 'had nothing to do with anything relevant …
it's just background music while they buy their jeans – FLARED jeans',
had traction.[5] It tallied with the mood at *Sounds* and the *NME*, whose
end of year reviews for 1975 bemoaned the state of popular music and
paved the way for Mick Farren's 'The Titanic Sails at Dawn' article
of June 1976 to lament rock 'n' roll's co-option into cultural respectability.[6] It echoed David Bowie's disavowal of a form he described
as a 'toothless old woman'.[7] It was implicit, too, in the emergence of
pub rock bands committed to playing r'n'b tunes that predated the
advent of psychedelia and the 60s' rock boom. It also reflected the
effect of a vertically integrated music industry dominated by six major
companies that prioritised established artists and records aimed at a
cross-generational (and transnational) market.[8] Most importantly, perhaps, it corresponded with contemporary accounts that recognised the

impetus engendered by punk at the provincial level for those whose tastes resided away from the dance floor or campus.[9]

Even before the Sex Pistols had found their way into the tabloids, numerous articles and letters to the music press revealed a growing dissatisfaction with rock's apparent separation from its audience. Just as Clem Gorman, the deputy administrator of London's Roundhouse, wrote to *Melody Maker* forewarning that government subsidies would be needed to prevent inflation making rock concerts prohibitive, so Robert Plant's complaint about his tax bill in February 1976 provoked a series of letters from readers bemoaning 'middle-aged millionaires' and 'big business bands' that left them feeling 'cheated'. Others began to deride the unoriginality of groups such as Queen and 10cc, or railed against a music industry that one correspondent described as 'the last outpost of classical capitalism'. For Ms J Rose of Shrewsbury, the reasoning was clear: 'Rock music has become so sophisticated nowadays, especially in its recording, but even in its performance (dressed up with the now obligatory lasers), that many fans, while appreciating the new complexity, are bound to feel alienated ... I think it's important that at least some forms of rock remain accessible so that would-be musicians don't get the feeling they've got to be geniuses before they start.'[10]

Within such a context, the Sex Pistols emerged to provide what Pete Dale has called a 'new-sense'. That is, the Pistols *felt* like the start of something new and distinct.[11] By actively positioning themselves in opposition to the prevailing motifs of 1970s rock, they provoked a re-evaluation of rock 'n' roll as a cultural form. In other words, punk served as a mode of cultural critique. It questioned the point and purpose of popular music while simultaneously endeavouring to reassemble, reassert and reinvent its basic concepts.

This, as already noted, could be expressed in a variety of ways. But even at its most basic, punk provided an opportunity to question just who and what rock 'n' roll was for and about. As significantly, punk's critique extended not only to the business that produced, packaged and presented popular music, but also to the media that framed and sought to define (youth) culture in the late twentieth century. Among the list of 'hates' on McLaren, Rhodes and Westwood's 'You're gonna wake up one morning and *know* what side of the bed you've been lying on' T-shirt, produced in 1974 as a manifesto-like precursor to punk, were 'television ... magazines that treat their readers as idiots ... Good Fun Entertainment when it's really not good or not funny ...

the narrow monopoly of media causing harmless creativity to appear subversive.'[12] From the outset, therefore, punk engaged with and parodied the media, utilising tabloid text as graphics, exposing its banalities and cursing its pacifying influence. By railing against the alienating effects of a culture reduced to commodity and spectacle, punk urged people to take the initiative – to *do it* rather than consume it.

Chuck Berry Is Dead?

Punk's relationship to rock 'n' roll was complicated. To be sure, it is easy to find irreverent statements about rock's elder statesmen – be it Rotten's dismissal of Mick Jagger as a 'pathetic old bastard' or the cheers that greeted the announcement of Elvis Presley's death at the Vortex on 16 August 1977.[13] To make an impact, punk had to differentiate itself from the rock and youth cultural mores of the mid-1970s, meaning 'short hair versus long hair; straight legs versus flares; uptight versus mellow; amphetamines versus marijuana; short songs versus extended guitar solos; pointed lyrics about real-life teenage problems and the state of the world versus identikit pop banalities'.[14] But a closer look at the substance of punk's critique reveals it to have provoked multiple – sometimes contradictory – responses to rock's condition in the mid-1970s. Though punk appeared to oppose what rock 'n' roll had *become*, it did not thereby reject its past. Quite the opposite in fact: many in the early punk period proved keen to recover some kind of lost rock 'n' roll essence. In so doing, alternative musical trajectories were referenced and later juxtaposed to forge the more innovative permutations of the 1970s and early 1980s. Attention to where popular music had supposedly *gone wrong* ensured that the mechanics of rock 'n' roll were held up to scrutiny and often found wanting.

For those attracted to or enthused by the Sex Pistols, punk signalled a new beginning, a dividing line beyond which pop music and its associated culture could be reclaimed for those who made and listened to it. What this entailed varied in both form and practice, but three sometimes overlapping approaches may be discerned. First, punk was read as a return to 'basics': rock 'n' roll played 'in its lowest form', as Mark Perry's first issue of *Sniffin' Glue* (1976) described it, 'on the level of the streets. Kids jamming together in the dad's garage, poor equipment, tight clothes [and] empty heads (nothing to do now you've left school).[15] This, originally, was understood in purely musical terms before broader sociocultural connotations were drawn from and projected onto the bands that fostered punk's emergence. Or, to quote *Ripped & Torn*'s Tony D:

> It makes you fucking puke when you think of those boring cunts (like the whole of Led Zeppelin, The Who, Paul McCartney, Stevie Wonder etc.) lazing away in some hot tropical paradise, whilst us poor punters have to make do with any shit they care to pour on us. But it's all over now (Rolling Stones are another, so's Elton John), with the emergence of such saviours as the Sex Pistols, Clash, Damned. Already you can hear the shrieks of the old rich as they finally realise they're being made redundant by the energy ridden bands who work out of necessity in cheapo clubs with lousy P.A's. THAT'S ROCK & ROLL.[16]

As this suggests, a premium was placed on age, energy and accessibility, a new wave of bands that comprised 'kids' playing 'good fast rock 'n' roll'.[17] The notion of 'rock star' was degraded to insult and any sign of punk producing its own elite was subject to vigilance.[18] If rock had seemingly mellowed – or matured – with age, then punk signalled its rejuvenation. 'Who wants to see and hear 45 year old rock stars?', The Damned's Rat Scabies (Chris Millar) asked, 'what about the sixteen-year-old kids on the street who ain't had no life?'[19]

Over time, the primacy of youth and speed conflated with claims to cultural or political relevance. 'If punk means anything', Dublin's *Heat* fanzine mused as it tried to determine just what separated punk from 'good energy rock', then 'it's putting yourself against establishment systems. Stickin' your neck on the block. Makin' a stand and clearing the way for other bands to follow.'[20] The British punk 'voice' was anglicised, its language made coarse and direct. Lyrically and visually, punk's preoccupation with social reportage or subjects of negation, demystification and taboo established new precedents. Love songs, dismissed by Rotten as 'a myth brought on by Mickie Most and co. to sell records', tended to be forsworn in favour of words and imagery that confronted, attacked or critiqued.[21] Cover versions also became less common over time, either in a bid to highlight a band's contemporaneity or, in the case of those with a political imperative, not to distract from any overriding message. Doing covers was 'just like playing records on a Juke Box', Buzzcocks' Pete Shelley insisted. '[Unless] you play all your own stuff you are just recycling other people's ideas.'[22]

The very speed by which punk bands formed, wrote songs and took to the stage ensured that their rough-hewed sound contrasted with the increasingly slick production of most rock and pop in the mid-1970s and defied the more tutored formulas of rock 'n' roll.

Punk, therefore, marked a generational shift that reasserted rock 'n' roll's grass-roots credentials whilst simultaneously seeking to affirm its own distinctiveness. It purged the past to repopulate the present. As a consequence, most self-defined punks tended only to cite other punk bands as influences from about 1978, with a flick through the pen-pals section of *Punk Lives* magazine (1982–83) revealing few if any correspondents referring to music made prior to 1976. Nevertheless, bands from The Clash through to the UK Subs, Discharge, The Exploited and even onto the anarchist groups that accepted no compromise with rock's pre-existing structures continued to recognise rock 'n' roll as a vehicle for youthful (and political) expression – albeit one stripped back to the raw and recast to reflect a perceived *here and now*.[23]

Secondly, if more contentiously, punk harboured tendencies to rewind popular music history, as if seeking to reroute its future by returning to a *moment* circa 1966 or 1956 when r'n'b, rock 'n' roll and pop were deemed more club based, youthful and immediate. The recovery of 'lost' 7-inch '60s nuggets from thrift stores or the racks of London stalls such as Rock On revealed an archivist culture underpinning punk's exasperation at rock's evolution. This, arguably, formed part of Malcolm McLaren's early intent, complementing his well-documented affection for original rock 'n' roll.[24] Punk embodied 'the same attitude … that Eddie Cochran probably had, that any *real* rock and roller had', he told the *NME*.[25] It also explains how Generation X could celebrate *Ready Steady Go*, Britain's first televised pop show broadcast between 1963 and 1966, whilst trying to 'forget' the 1960s generation that had subsequently outgrown the programme's original pop thrill.[26]

Initially, therefore, proto-punk figures on rock's margins were recovered as influences (Velvet Underground, Stooges, MC5, New York Dolls, 1960s garage bands) and the formative work of groups since perceived to have lost their way (The Who, Mott the Hoople, Roxy Music) was acknowledged. Most early punk sets included sped-up – re-energised –cover versions ('Louie Louie', 'Whatcha' Gonna' Do About It', 'Substitute', 'Circles', 'So Sad About Us', 'Slow Down', 'Help', 'Steppin' Stone', 'I Can't Control Myself', 'No Fun', 'I'm Waiting for the Man'), while countless punk 45s accelerated and applied suitably acerbic lyrics to standard rock 'n' roll or r'n'b riffs.[27] Punk style also co-opted recognisable elements of (non-hippie) youth cultures – brothel creepers, mohair sweaters, leather jackets, boots, Sta-Prest.[28] Though early fanzines and bands celebrated punk's shock-of-the-new, they continued to locate punk in an identifiable tradition.[29] The point, again, was not to dismiss rock 'n' roll out of hand, but to revitalise its original spirit – its 'primal scream', as The Fall's Mark E. Smith put it.[30]

The Jam provide a suitably neat example of a band looking forwards and backwards at the same time. Led by Paul Weller, aged eighteen as 1976 became 1977, The Jam committed to the 'new wave' but proved suspicious of punk's supposedly political import and claims to innovation. Weller openly acknowledged his debt to The Who and the mod culture of the 1960s; the band wore mohair suits and produced records such as *All Mod Cons* (1978) that made clear their affinities. Nevertheless, Weller was scathing about rock's apparent self-indulgence – 'you can't play rock 'n' roll with a beer gut' – and insisted that the time was right for Pete Townsend and others to 'give way to some of the younger bands'. Punk's new wave, he contended, meant 'today's pop music for kids, it's as simple as that'.[31] Given all this, The Jam's relationship to punk was contentious; they were often dismissed as old-fashioned and resisted the 'punk' tag. Yet they played with anger and energy, shared a significant part of the fledgling punk audience, and adopted a social realist approach that became characteristic of the time. In the midst of the mod 'renewal' that came in The Jam's wake, Weller was even quoted as saying: 'We're a punk band ... We started as a punk band and that's where we're staying'.[32]

It was this urge to reconvene the past that enabled various subcultural revivals to flourish over the late 1970s, many of which revolved around club-nights and bands motivated by punk's agency but repulsed by aspects of its style or aesthetic.[33] Just prior to the 'new mods' inspired by The Jam and galvanised by the 1979 film version of The Who's *Quadrophenia* (for which Johnny Rotten was considered to play the lead role), skinheads re-emerged to provide part of the audience for bands such as Sham 69, Cock Sparrer, Menace and Skrewdriver. Skinheads had their roots in the later 1960s, developing out of mod to forge a starkly proletarian youth culture that claimed early reggae as its music of choice. The culture evolved over the 1970s but never wholly disappeared. Come 1977 and its revival gave rise to a new generation of skins who could relate to punk's aggression and the class implications of its street-level rhetoric. The culture's origins, moreover, fed into a 2-Tone movement that blended punk and ska to forge a cross-cultural amalgam that also drew from mod and rude boy/girl.[34]

Few of the youth cultural styles revived in tandem with punk were simple pastiche; they sought to update rather than mimic. Unlike the teddy boys who reappeared to complement the rock 'n' roll revival of the early 1970s, the new breed of skinhead formed, joined and followed punk bands. New mods may also have chosen to reject punk's aesthetic, but the flurry of Jam-like bands that appeared in 1978–79 tended to write material that reflected the 1970s rather than the 1960s.[35] 2-Tone, meanwhile, brokered a genuinely original musical hybrid that proffered stark social-realist lyrics. Even the rockabilly revival, which boasted an underground presence from at least 1977, was distorted into an overtly punk form by 1980.[36] Known as psychobilly, the UK scene centred on bands such as The Meteors and clubs such as London's Klub Foot.

Perhaps the most systematic attempt to determine where 'it all went wrong' developed amidst the groundswell of independent labels evident from 1977. Punk's DIY assertions, combined with its more general dismissal of rock's excesses, allowed for sixties obsessions to inform an almost puritan sense of what pop music *should be*: amateurish, provincial, 7-inch based, uncorrupted by 'the industry', guitar-bass-drums, forever adolescent. Beat groups, girl bands, Phil Spector and Warhol's Factory formed an imagined pop lineage to rival rock 'n' roll's transformation into 'prog' virtuosity or heavy rock machismo.[37] 'We know our pop history', Kevin Pearce wrote in his *Hungry Beat* fanzine, 'the inspired/inspirational parts have all been absorbed and past mistakes will be avoided at all costs … pop music/punk rock – it's the same thing, right?'[38] Accordingly, groups such as the Television Personalities, Orange Juice, The Pastels and June Brides began to filter a mix of 1960s pop and stylistic influences through a select punk canon (Ramones, Buzzcocks, Subway Sect, The Undertones), the result of which was a swathe of bands whose sound had distilled by the mid-1980s into a jangly 'indie-pop' as recognisable as the 'punk rock' of 1977.[39]

Both the impulses to reclaim rock 'n' roll and reconvene earlier youth cultural styles shared a presumption that popular music and the culture surrounding it had become detached from its core (predominantly teenage) constituency. If the rhetoric of the time complained of rock's self-indulgence, complacency and inaccessibility, then punk was understood as a response that invoked youth cultural and musical forms devised by or performed by those who lived through and listened to it. An emphasis on agency complemented claims to relevance and innovation; a disregard for technique and the recognised signifiers of 'success' redirected attention towards the neoteric or provincial. Simultaneously, punk triggered a period of cultural interrogation that allowed new subject matter and influences to feed into popular music. Third, therefore, punk provided space for both the disavowal and reinvention of rock 'n' roll.

Such inclinations were evident early on, and not just in the mocking of Rod Stewart's tax status or the denim-clad image of the George Hatcher Band singled out by The Clash for embodying rock 'n roll's debasement (see Figure 2.1).[40] Subway Sect, who formed in the wake of a Sex Pistols performance at the Marquee in early 1976, set out to challenge and undermine the banalities of rock's sound and performance. Not only did the band's singer, Vic Godard, delight in giving wilfully absurd interviews in which he claimed 'East European programmes for children' as an influence, but the band's live appearances – monochrome, stationary, lyrics read from paper, instruments held at odd angles – were designed to communicate a stated aim: 'We oppose all rock and roll'. The objective, Godard suggested, was to push at the limits of rock; to inject new influences into it and embrace imperfection. Ordinary (or familiar) chord structures were shunned in favour of treble and discord; the joys of bird watching, reading and geography were extolled over rock's more traditional pursuits. Northern Soul, Françoise Hardy and Jane Birkin were cited as inspirations, while The Beatles, Godard provoked, made him 'physically sick sometimes'.[41]

> Old conceptions justified/ Tradition stays in tune/ You make guitars talk information/ That tells you what to do!
>
> We use no belief in the pre-existing school/ And since we've got this test/ We've just been waiting for it to fall/ We oppose all rock and roll/ It's held you for so long/ You can't refuse/ It's too much to lose
>
> The lines that hit me again and again/ Afraid to take the stroll/ Off the course of twenty years/ And out of Rock and Roll![42]

Page 24   NEW MUSICAL EXPRESS   September 25th, 1976

Figure 2.1 The George Hatcher Band, targeted by The Clash as an example of 1970s rock 'n' roll debasement.

Less sardonically, Wire sought to deconstruct rock's form in order to build songs around a particular sound, image or lyrical focus. Their guitarist, Bruce Gilbert, compared the band's approach to painting: 'A number of processes are very similar: the stepping back ... And wanting to get it finished before you get bored with an idea ... And the economy thing – the economy of effort, to write a statement that is the essence of what you're trying to do'. As this suggests, each song (and the band's artwork) was designed to be distinct and devoid of obvious precedent. Initially, at least, such an approach meant short songs – most of which lasted only as long as there were lyrics to be sung – before later developing into lengthier pieces that continued to explore subjects beyond rock's typical remit ('Map Ref, 41°N 93°W'). Like Subway Sect, Wire's stage presence deliberately reacted against what was expected of a rock or pop performance: detached with stark lighting and, later, comprising absurdist theatre. Their aim, Graham Lewis insisted, was to innovate and avoid the 'childishness' of rock 'n' roll posturing.[43]

Wire's relationship to punk revealed an art school pedigree. Others, however, interpreted 'back to basics' in a more literal sense, with some bands taking to the stage even before their members had learnt to play instruments. Siouxsie and the Banshees' impromptu debut performance at the 100 Club in September 1976 was perhaps the most celebrated example, twenty minutes of grinding noise that took in 'Twist and Shout' and 'The Lord's Prayer' via 'Deutschland Uber Alles' and 'Knocking on Heaven's Door'. But groups such as The Worst, The Slits and The Prefects also adopted similar approaches. The Worst, from Manchester via Preston, built their set on primitive guitar riffs and lyrics culled from newspaper articles or improvised by the singer, Allan Deaves. The effect, as described by Paul Morley, was 'by liberal intellectual standards, destructive and anti-social', but it also served to invert all sense of musical convention, be it rock 'n' roll or otherwise.[44] Not dissimilarly, The Slits – whose singer, Ari Up (Ariane Forster), was fifteen in 1977 – were born from a musical chaos that centred on pummelling drums and, eventually, dub-inflected basslines. The fact that the band was all female served only to expose further the gendered prejudices of the rock press, audience and industry.[45] The Prefects, meanwhile, played in a simple and repetitive style that effec- tively parodied rock 'n' roll. One song, 'VD', lasted seven seconds – a riposte to the tendency of 1970s rock bands to 'jam' and extend their live sets over time. Another, 'Going Through the Motions', offered a slow dirge that critiqued the performer-audience divide and was played as its title suggested. 'Faults' was a hymn to the imperfections engen- dered by the band's being wilfully under-rehearsed.

The important point to note, of course, is that such approaches were deliberate.[46] Bands began to develop strategies and manifestos designed not to revive or reclaim rock 'n' roll but to move beyond it. The Mekons initially set out to democratise the rock process, refusing either to be photographed or reveal their surnames. The objective was to disarm the notion of 'pop star' and demonstrate 'that anybody could do it … that there was no set group as such, anybody could get up and join in and instruments would be swapped around; that there'd be no distance between the audience and the band'.[47] The Gang of Four, too, deconstructed rock's form and function through their lyrics and performance, while the gender conventions of rock 'n' roll were dissected in the work of Ludus, Poison Girls, The Raincoats and others.[48] Rock's clichés – lyrical ('baby', 'man' etc.) and presentational (guitar hero, sex symbol) – were subject to scorn: 'cock rock' and 'rockism' became terms of abuse. Production values and standard compositions were rejected in order to radicalise the form as well as the content of popular music. Some groups even talked of 'un-learning' their instruments. '[Too] much theory in your head … restricts your imagination', The Raincoats' Vicky Aspinall explained to *After Hours* fanzine.[49]

The results of such approaches varied. Bands began to look first to reggae and then to funk, jazz, electronics, 'krautrock' and even improvisatory composition to expand pop's palette and dilute rock's traditional formulae. The Pop Group, from Bristol, meshed all of these influences into one cacophonous whole; in Manchester, Martin Hannett's production resculptured the blunt punk of Warsaw into the bleak panoramas of Joy Division. Public Image Ltd (PiL), the band formed by John Lydon in 1978 after the Sex Pistols' dissolution, intentionally set out to avoid all traces of a musical form they felt 'obsolete'.[50] Lydon had already revealed experimental tastes predisposed to reggae and rock's margins during a 1977 radio interview with Tommy Vance.[51] PiL, therefore, was presented as an attempt to forge something wholly distinct and original. 'I've said it before', he told Danny Baker in 1979, 'rock 'n' roll is stone dead. It's had it. How much more 12-bar din-dun-der-dun can you jumble up?'[52]

Such experimentation has since been termed 'post-punk'. In truth, it formed part of the same cultural critique that instigated the more straight-forward punk rock of the period. Both 'punk rock' and the multifarious strands of 'post-punk' were defined in opposition to rock and pop as perceived *at the time*; they provided musical alternatives and modes of expression initiated 'from below'. Just as Graham Lewis understood punk to have facilitated the opportunity for Wire's experimentation, so Scritti Politti's Green Gartside (Paul Strohmeyer) could insist that his group's 'roots' were 'very firmly with punk rock … I don't think you need to go back any further than that', even as they began to musically and lyrically unravel rock's form.[53] Cabaret Voltaire, whose name revealed their dadaist influence, recognised rock 'n' roll to mean more than simply 'regurgitating Chuck Berry riffs', preferring instead to use dissonance, tape cut-ups and the infrastructures that grew out of punk to challenge and communicate.[54] 'One thing [that] differentiated Edinburgh amongst other punk movements in the country', Paul Mackie of Scars suggested, was that people 'wanted to move on from punk really quickly and make their own original music: punk was a starting point, but it wasn't supposed to be perfecting formula'. His compatriot, Malcolm Ross of Josef K, concurred: 'the board has been wiped clean … it was a question of starting again.[55]

Within such a context, punk was seen to have broken down rock's edifice and enabled new musical fusions and processes to collapse the distinction between 'popular' and 'experimental'.[56] This, as noted earlier, often contained political intent. The experiments engendered through punk were regularly couched in terms of provocation and consciousness-raising. But whether punk was seen to comprise 'certain individuals' fighting the 'rock 'n' roll gig syndrome' (Charles Hayward, This Heat) or simply those 'having a laugh … doing what you want to do and refusing to adjust to the system' (Wattie Buchan, The Exploited), the impetus was to some extent driven by an urge to confront, offset or reject the conservative forces that mediated youth culture.[57]

It Was Easy, It Was Cheap, Go and Do It

Punk's critical relationship to the music industry may best be understood as a challenge on two fronts. First, as an effort to open-up – or break into – a cultural medium dominated by a relatively small number of 'major' record companies and seemingly closed to all but a select canon of established or suitably temperate artists. Second, as an attempt to forge an alternative to the industry establishment, either by working in spaces not wholly taken over by the larger labels or by existing outside and in parallel to pop's commercial structures.

As Dave Laing has shown, the principal record companies of the mid-1970s exerted extensive control over the production, manufacture and distribution of popular music, with EMI even staking claim to retail via HMV. There were, of course, relatively smaller labels such as Island and Virgin that competed with the likes of EMI, CBS and Polygram. But these had corporate aspirations that ensured they operated along similar business lines to the majors in the mid-to-late 1970s. A scattering of independents existed, most of which functioned through negotiated deals with the more established labels and thereby contributed to – or made little impact on – the larger companies' two-thirds market share.[58] Mickie Most's RAK Records, for example, along with Dick Leahy's Bell UK, issued their run of early 1970s bubble-gum pop and disco-glam hits through EMI. In response, punk appeared to contest the industry's claims to rock 'n' roll culture by reasserting ownership ('we created it, let's take it over') and rejecting its prevailing values, tropes and motifs ('don't accept the old order, get rid of it').[59] From such a perspective, the industry feeding frenzy that took place in and around the Sex Pistols' wake may be taken as a sign of success. It allowed new voices to be heard, be it Johnny Rotten, Howard Devoto, Siouxsie Sioux or Poly Styrene; new writers to enter the music press, many from the provinces or 'trained' on fanzines; new 'stars' to be cultivated (Adam Ant, Boy George, Toyah, U2).[60] At the very least, punk helped repopulate and rejuvenate pop music as a cultural form into the 1980s, even as its oppositional edge was thereby smoothed along the way.[61]

Simultaneously, the speed with which punk was appropriated exposed the limits of its difference. As The Clash complained of their contemporaries 'turning rebellion into money', and as fanzines bemoaned the emasculation of their once favoured bands, so questions emerged as to the point and purpose of punk's initial revolt. Was it simply to replace one set of pop stars with another while injecting some youthful energy back into rock 'n' roll? Or did punk represent a more fundamental challenge to a co-opted culture in thrall to the profit margin? 'Here we are in the summer of '78', David George wrote in his *Dirt* fanzine, 'and after the promise of last summer what's going on now? Fuck all'. For George, as for others, punk had 'failed' because the record companies were still thriving via a 'cleverly disguised rip off of you and me by capitalistic orientated bands, managers and companies'.[62] New strategies were therefore needed if punk was to signal more than just coloured vinyl and cartoon attitudes – attempts had to be made to exert control over what Mark Perry summed up as 'everything, including posters, record covers, stage presentation, the lot!'[63] To this effect, independent labels were soon seen to represent a 'new underground' in 'opposition' to the record industry.[64] For Lucy Toothpaste, writing in her *Jolt* fanzine, those 'contained' by the music business had to be eclipsed by 'dozens of other bands and other fanzines' emerging as a result of the Sex Pistols' and *Sniffin' Glue*'s example.[65]

Each of these responses built on the premise of punk representing some kind of challenge to the music industry. The problem, or so it seemed, was how best to effect any kind of change. From within, as a 'poison in the machine' designed to destabilise the industry while using its commercial reach to influence ideas, tastes and attitudes? Or as an independent alternative that spurred creativity and enabled culture to flourish beyond the rigged confines of the marketplace? Such debate underpinned much of the discourse surrounding punk, especially as interpretations of the Sex Pistols' broken relationship with EMI (and A&M) filtered into broader analysis of the band's significance. It also echoed ongoing political discussion as to the benefits of 'entryism' in pursuit of radical ideals and the role played by culture in the struggle for hegemony. Add in Buzzcocks' self-release of *Spiral Scratch* in early 1977, and arguments over the democratisation of music that allowed artists to control the process of production gained tangible expression.[66]

For those keen to follow the Sex Pistols' and The Clash's lead, the objective was to utilise the established channels of the music industry as a platform for expression or a vehicle to reconstitute popular music. If, as Gang of Four argued, record companies were all part of the same (capitalist) system, then it made sense to sign to one that paid a weekly wage and allowed artists to channel radical messages through extensive promotional and distribution networks. The power structures of the status quo would not be affected, the band's Andy Gill recognised, but music and lyrics could still disrupt conventional attitudes and change how people thought.[67] Others talked of *using* major labels to agitate, innovate and communicate, suggesting that by so doing they could avoid 'preaching to the converted' or becoming culturally ghettoised.[68] 'That independent bullshit!', Davy Henderson said of his band Fire Engines' attempt to revitalise British pop, 'we want to get across to as many people as possible so we will use all the aspects of the business around us to our own advantage'.[69]

Come the 1980s, and perhaps the most resolute argument in favour of working 'inside' the music industry came from the Redskins.

Although the band comprised members of the Socialist Workers Party (SWP), which rejected political entryism and was scathing of the Red Wedge initiative launched in 1985 to mobilise young voters for Labour, they signed to Decca Records and evolved through punk to adopt a soul-infused sound to back their explicitly socialist lyrics. 'If The Supremes had been three steelworkers from Petrograd', Chris Dean suggested, then they would have sounded like the Redskins.[70]

Originally formed as No Swastikas in York in 1981, before changing their name in 1982 as they endeavoured to marry punk's intensity with a pop sensibility targeted at the charts, the Redskins rejected any suggestion that signing to a major label diluted their political message. In a letter to the SWP's *Socialist Review*, the band's bass player, Martin Hewes, defined his position as a worker earning money off the ruling class. But, he maintained, the Redskins had influence because of the nature of popular music as a medium; they had access to a potentially mass audience.[71] Not dissimilarly, Lynden Barber's concern that the distribution of Marxist agit-prop by a transnational capitalist company simply confirmed an inherent contradiction was met with disdain. Dean recognised the juxtaposition and the limitations of music serving as a force for political change, but he also insisted that pop's ability to communicate made it a useful *part* of a broader revolutionary appeal.[72] Consequently, he combined his singing duties with journalism (as X Moore in the *NME*) and conducted interviews that typically comprised extended political debates espousing the SWP line on everything from Thatcherism and the miners' strike to the 'treacherous' nature of the Trades Union Congress (TUC) and Labour Party. Appropriately, the band's gigs saw songs introduced with reference to ongoing industrial disputes and global struggles, many of which served as benefits for the anti-apartheid, anti-fascist and unemployed causes of the time.[73]

But if the Redskins' agit-prop as agit-pop was the most explicit attempt to utilise existing record industry structures for political purposes, then others sought to subvert by more nefarious means. Most obviously, McLaren's version of the Sex Pistols' story was dependent on their having an impact at the heart of the commodity, from where the tensions between art and commerce could be revealed and exploited. *The Great Rock 'n' Roll Swindle* was nothing if not a fictionalised exposé of the music business, something McLaren sought to take further with Bow Wow Wow from 1980. Where the *Swindle* focused on ways to exploit the cultural vacuity of the record industry, so Bow

Wow Wow were designed to expose its duplicity and immorality, particularly the paedophilic tendencies that lurked within. Alongside the advocacy of home taping onto cassette – then feared by the record industry as a death-knell for music[74] – Bow Wow Wow were fronted by a fourteen-year-old singer, Annabella Lwin, whose sexuality formed the basis of the band's lyrics and marketing campaign. A magazine, *Chicken*, was even formatted as a way of promoting the band, before its content of children in sexually provocative poses made too obvious McLaren's ruse.[75]

More typically, perhaps, bands informed by punk tended to present themselves in a struggle with their corporate pay-masters.[76] They recognised the exploitative nature of the relationship but sought to counter or reveal it through their lyrics, approach and imagery. The results were sometimes messy. The Clash, for example, made public their battles with CBS and used them to assert a sense of integrity in the face of accusations of 'selling out'. When, in mid-1977, the label released 'Remote Control' as a single without the band's consent, Strummer responded by writing a follow-up entitled 'Complete Control' that bemoaned the 'c-o-n' of his contract. According to a Clash-endorsed statement, the song told the 'story of conflict between two opposing camps. One side sees change as an opportunity to channel the enthusiasm of a raw and dangerous culture in a direction where energy is made safe and predictable. The other is dealing with change as a freedom to be experienced so as to understand one's true capabilities, allowing a creative social situation to emerge'.[77] Thereafter, The Clash prided themselves on retaining an affinity with and providing value-for-money for their fans (non-album singles, cut price LPs, etc.), even if the label was no doubt aware that such gestures emboldened their 'product'.[78]

That said, the spaces opened up by punk did allow for innovation. Record sleeves provided one site of communication that major label distribution ensured found its way into the marketplace. Seen in this way, Buzzcocks' 'Orgasm Addict' (1977) was more than just an attempt to extend and subvert pop's language; it was also a conduit for Linder's photomontage and Malcolm Garrett's design critiques of commodification (see Figure 2.2).[79] Jamie Reid's artworks, too, proved integral to the Sex Pistols' attack, be it the cut-up Union Jack that promoted 'Anarchy in the UK', the defaced symbolism of 'God Save the Queen', the buses to 'boredom' and 'nowhere' on the back of 'Pretty

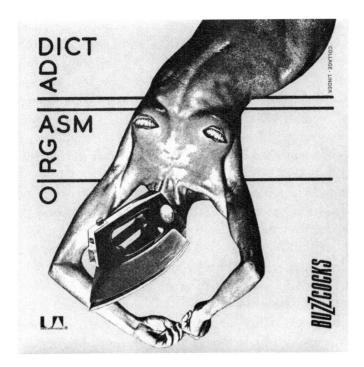

Figure 2.2 Buzzcocks, 'Orgasm Addict' (United Artists, 1977), sleeve design by Malcolm Garrett (Arbi-trary Im-ages) featuring montage by Linder. (Photographs by Richard Rayner-Canham.)

Vacant', the détourned tourist brochure of 'Holidays in the Sun', the profanity of *Never Mind the Bollocks* or the self-aware deconstruction of punk's co-option that marketed the *Great Rock 'n' Roll Swindle*.[80]

Others used the opportunities afforded by punk to assert their cultural capital in the form of experimental releases or presentation. Bands – including Siouxsie and the Banshees, who signed to Polydor – talked of assuming full control of their releases and artwork, resisting co-option and refusing to compromise with the dictates of the industry.[81] A few bands set up label imprints that functioned through the distribution, promotional and manufacturing networks of larger companies. The Specials, for instance, signed 2-Tone to Chrysalis in a move that helped both them and the larger label promote the 2-Tone movement of 1979–81.[82] PiL even defined themselves as a limited company rather than a group, adopting a corporate identity to run their own affairs without 'middle men' – managers, producers, artistic directors, secretaries – interfering in the creative process.[83]

Not all such ventures were successful. The willingness of a conventional record company to tolerate or lend its marketing clout to projects soon paled once sales fell or attentions turned elsewhere.[84] Nor did the reality of signing to a major label always match the expectations or stated intent of those seeking to subvert pop's form from the inside. Compromises *were* made, be it in terms of promotional schedules, marketing schemes or self-censorship.[85] One listen to the Angelic Upstarts' *Still from the Heart* (1982) reveals the damage that signing to a major label could do, with ill-fitting synths and polished production blunting the band's necessarily hard edge. Indeed, the fickle nature of the pop industry and the capacity of labels to exploit their artists became a recurrent theme in songs such as the Sex Pistols' 'EMI', The Boys' 'Do the Contract', Stiff Little Fingers' 'Rough Trade', Cock Sparrer's 'Take 'em All', and The Jam's 'All Mod Cons' and 'To Be Someone (Didn't We Have a Nice Time)'. Nevertheless, the idea of working through the mainstream remained an objective for those who saw pop music as both a reflection and a way out of the preset patterns of 'ordinary' life. It also provided subsequent justification – albeit decorated in postmodern language – for much of the so-called 'new pop' of the early 1980s.[86]

Alternative strategies did exist. Few of the majors ventured far beyond London's borders before the end of 1977, preferring instead to 'cherry pick' from the conveyor belt of bands playing at The Roxy club opened in London's Covent Garden from December 1976 or at other venues on the capital's gig circuit.[87] In response, a network of smaller labels, retailers, studios and manufacturers emerged to cater for punk-informed scenes evolving beyond the metropolitan monopoly, culminating in the compilation of an 'independent chart' by the British Market Research Bureau from 1980.[88] As 'the industry' concerned itself with an unprecedented drop in production, from 250 million to 190 million units between 1978 and 1981, so the number of independent labels rose from 231 to 322 in the same period, with more than 800 listed in 1980.[89]

Early on, punk-related independents formed simply to produce and market records by bands passed over or ignored by the larger companies.[90] In other words, they filled a gap in the market and were typically run by industry 'veterans' with some understanding of how the business worked. Stiff Records, for example, was formed in 1976 by Jake Riviera (Andrew Jakeman) and Dave Robinson in reaction to the majors' failure to pick up on pub rock and the early stirrings of London punk, while Step-Forward Records was owned by Miles Copeland, an erstwhile manager of progressive rock bands.[91] As punk's influence spread and diversified, so a combination of entrepreneurs, enthusiasts and mavericks founded labels to cover locales or scenes in and beyond London.

Simultaneously, labels began to materialise organically from punk's dissemination, primarily out of independent record shops that stocked, distributed and eventually produced records inspired by a DIY ethos. An early template was Chiswick, formed in 1975 through Ted Carroll's Rock On retail stalls. Thereafter, Beggars Banquet, Rough Trade and Small Wonder began as London record shops before widening their remit in the wake of punk. Outside the capital, Remember Those Oldies in Cambridge begat Raw Records and Bruce's from Scotland helped launch a series of small labels before the likes of Attrix (Brighton), Backs (Norwich), Good Vibrations (Belfast), Probe (Liverpool), Red Rhino (York) and Revolver (Bristol) did likewise to serve as regional fulcrums and, in some cases, components of the Cartel cultivated by Rough Trade's Richard Scott to co-ordinate a nationwide distribution network.[92]

Finally, and most significantly perhaps, those inspired by a combination of the Sex Pistols' attitude and Buzzcocks' initiative resolved to self-release their own records. This was sometimes conceived as a means-to-an-end, a way of generating interest by securing press coverage and airplay via John Peel's late-night radio show. Several well-known bands – 999, Angelic Upstarts, The Exploited, Joy Division, The Skids, Stiff Little Fingers – first recorded on their own imprints before moving to larger or more firmly established labels. Equally, the process of starting a label, self-releasing a record or cultivating a cassette network became a raison d'être in itself, spawning a DIY aesthetic rooted in punk's back-to-basics attitude but willing to experiment within its own limitations.[93] 'Nothing's fucking easy is it', Charlie Deane of Six Minute War complained, a band whose three EPs offered an archetypal example of punk's 'DIY not EMI' approach. 'But it's no excuse for signing to any fucking label … you don't go round making money out of your art. As soon as you say I'm gonna do this as a job you're gonna start writing songs that will sell and not what you believe in'.[94] To be independent was to stand in opposition to the existent music industry and provide space for cultural (and political) alternatives.

Such a perspective was clearly stated by The Desperate Bicycles, one of the first groups to follow Buzzcocks' example. *Spiral Scratch* had emerged at the beginning of 1977, cheaply made in a local studio and self-released on the New Hormones label set up with Richard Boon. Its sleeve, fronted by a Polaroid picture of the band, listed the number of 'takes' (mainly one) and overdubs used for the recording. The Desperate Bicycles soon followed suit, coining punk's DIY mantra and, on the cover of their second single ('The Medium Is Tedium' b/w 'Don't Back the Front'), demystifying the means of production with the following statement:

> The Desperate Bicycles were formed in March 1977 specifically
> for the purpose of recording and releasing a single on their own
> label. They booked a studio in Dalston for three hours and with
> a lot of courage and a little rehearsal they recorded 'Smokescreen'
> and 'Handlebars'. It subsequently leapt at the throat. Three
> months later and The Desperate Bicycles were back in a studio
> to record their second single and this is the result. 'No more time
> for spectating' they sing and who knows? they may be right.
> They'd really like to know why you haven't made your single
> yet. 'It was easy, it was cheap, go and do it' (the complete cost of
> 'Smokescreen' was £153). The medium may very well have been
> tedium but it's changing fast. So if you can understand, go and
> join a band. Now it's your turn ...[95]

The objective, as the band's Roger Stephens explained, was to enable access to the manufacturing and production of records. 'You see, the record industry will keep on churning out so-called anti-establishment lyrics quite happily until you start attacking the pricing structure of records or attacking their profits. And that's really where to start. We need a continued attack'. Agency took priority over ability; the studio was envisaged as being 'like a passport photo booth' and a maximum retail price (70p) was printed on the front of the subsequent *New Cross, New Cross* EP (1978).[96] Though songs could carry a message (anti-fascism in 'Don't Back the Front'), the politics of punk were more readily discerned in its processes than its content.

Others took up the baton, booking into cheap studios (Arrow, Cargo, Spaceward, Street Level); mastering and pressing limited runs of vinyl at small plants; printing labels and sleeves to fold in kitchens and bedrooms; dropping off copies at local record shops or Rough Trade to distribute.[97] Among the most outspoken were Scritti Politti, whose early singles on Rough Trade and their own St Pancras label again featured a breakdown of costs and included songs that dissected the structures of the music industry.[98] 'Scritlock's Door', for instance, explored the relationship between groups and market forces, bemoaning the ways by which creativity was dictated by profit margins as the 'interest is kept and money is made by changing the scenery/ Fashion is fab when the product is made without necessity'.[99] Indeed, Scritti served briefly as the ideologues of punk's DIY diaspora, providing interviews with the music press and fanzines that explained their adoption of independent production as representing far more than a simple response to punk's impetus.[100] 'We are interested in ... keeping out of the sweaty palms of the record companies', Gartside argued, '[we're] interested in DIY records, co-operation with other groups, seeing how ... large an alternative can be built, a positional alternative rather than a run-away-and-hide alternative'.[101] As this suggests, Scritti's rationale was informed by Gramscian theory (Gartside was a young communist in 1978–79), with independents posited as part of a counter-hegemonic 'war of position'.

Though Gartside later swapped Marx and improvisation for Derrida and the luxuriousness of pop, his band's connection to Rough Trade was telling. Established as a shop by Geoff Travis in 1976, Rough Trade evolved to become the principal hub of punk's claim to provide an independent alternative by the end of the 1970s. As well as stocking, distributing and helping to finance record releases (and fanzines), it combined punk's growing sense of autonomy with libertarian-leftist politics traceable to the 1960s counterculture.[102] The shop, label and distribution were run collectively, with staff paid equal wages regardless of position and contributing to debates on the content of fanzines, record sleeves and lyrics. Profits were shared evenly between the bands and the label (sometimes in the band's favour), with artists retaining the rights to their master tapes and long-term contracts eschewed for short-term deals. In effect, Rough Trade presented itself more as a workspace than a business, an ethos articulated by bands such as Essential Logic and The Raincoats who held fast to the label's progressive intent.[103] 'Changing things from the inside is nonsense', Travis argued in 1980. 'It doesn't matter how much "creative control" a band is given ... you're still indentured'.[104]

Quite clearly, Rough Trade's approach stood in deliberate contrast to that of a conventional record label. Its practices were based on a political reading of the power relations that existed inside the wider music industry and were assumed, to varying extents, by other independents. Just as Factory's Tony Wilson first signed Joy Division by agreeing – reputedly in his own blood – that the band owned everything and the label nothing, so Terri Hooley envisaged his Good Vibrations imprint to be more than a profit-orientated cash cow. 'We could have done a distribution deal with somebody like WEA', he told *Melody Maker* in 1979, '[but] we won't because we don't want to sell out. We offer our groups 50 per cent of the profits now and we couldn't do that if we went with a major. The idea of the label anyway is as a co-operative. Everybody helps everybody else out. I haven't liked much of what I've seen of the music business, to be honest, so I'm not anxious to be a part of it … We'd rather be failures than be owned'.[105] Rough Trade's early ethos, too, fed into labels such as Ron Johnson and Vinyl Drip, whose bands – including A Witness, Bogshed, The Membranes and Vee VV – ploughed determinedly independent furrows throughout the 1980s. bIG fLAME, formed out of Manchester in 1982 to release a series of rigorously abrasive EPs on Ron Johnson, issued the following statement of intent:

PROLOGUE – We are … born out of a common dismay/disgust/distrust at the way creativity and individuality in pop music has once again been stifled by the music industry in their efforts to regain control over the highly profitable and easily exploitable business since losing it in 1977 …

OBJECTIVES – To provide a positive and constructive alternative to the bland and corrupt world of pop through the application of honesty, integrity and dynamic enthusiasm. To show to others that it can be done without selling your soul!

EXECUTION OF OBJECTIVES – Everything we do is pre-meditated and deliberate. Anything we produce is based on 100% effort – nothing less will do …

a) recordings – we will only release 7" 3-track e.p.'s … the best and most innovative bands were single bands – Buzzcocks, Orange Juice, Josef K and numerous early punk bands – … we'll never get a major record deal because we'll have to compromise so much that we'd become everything we hated in the 'music-biz, man' …

b) Live performances – we play a 9 song, 25 minute set … We feel that people tend to get bored after that …

c) Musical content (!) – we made a deliberate decision to follow a certain musical path, derived from our influences [who] produced an attitude of independence …

d) <u>Lyrical content</u> – … Based on the personal (as to write about things you don't know anything about would be disgraceful), the lyrics employ wit, satire and play on words to convey any ideas/inspiration/observations that we feel need relating, be it on society or otherwise. We HATE clichés … 'Hey, girl, I wanna dance with ya all night long' is definitely OUT

e) <u>Political content</u> – if, by highlighting what we see as wrongs in 'today's society' and allowing others to appreciate that and hopefully motivating <u>them</u>, we are labelled political, then that is fine by us … Also, because of the way we approach our music, we feel that the sound we produce is political in music circles because it is so radical and anti-complacency when compared to the crap that we are being fed now from all angles, be it large companies or the so-called 'independents'. So, we feel we are striving for change in music and a betterment of our way of life […]

EPILOGUE – things that disturb us in modern pop music: i) the return to rockism; ii) the apathy of young people ALL YOU YOUNG PUNKS who are locked in their time warp circa 77; iii) the return of the POP STAR and all the hype/corruption/dupery rip offs that accompany him/her; iv) the stifling REAL talent and the promotion of smug complacency by £££££'s in the interest of generating more ££££££'s; … If we can influence people to get up and do something, to provide that spark of inspiration and enthusiasm, to promote change, then, despite how many records we've sold, we will have succeeded in our aims …[106]

The only question, in terms of point and purpose, was whether the 'indies' wished to compete with the mainstream or forge a distinct alternative to it – a tension that became acute once bands gained commercial success or expectations began to exceed the limits of a label's capabilities.[107]

There was no such ambiguity with the avowedly anarchist bands whose own self-formed labels were underpinned by a critical analysis of the music business' place in the system. Record companies and their associated media were deemed to function only in the interests of capital and control; the likes of EMI's links to the arms industry or animal experiments were unveiled and condemned.[108] To engage with them on any level was to be 'bought up, cleaned up, souped up' and transformed into 'just another cheap product for the middle-class consumer'.[109] Effectively, and whether consciously or unconsciously, what Crass, Conflict, Subhumans and others offered was a hardened interpretation of Adorno and Horkheimer's argument determining the role and meaning of popular culture against its mode of production. From such a perspective, punk's entry – or absorption – into the music industry not only disarmed it of any radical or oppositional potential, but in fact made it part of the problem rather than part of the solution.[110] Or, to quote Poison Girls, 'state control and rock 'n' roll ... it's all good for business'.[111]

Crass' response was to pursue a determinedly independent path. Their first record, *The Feeding of the Five Thousand* (1978), had been issued in early 1979 on Pete and Marian Stennett's Small Wonder label, running into trouble when a foreman at an Irish pressing plant objected to the blasphemous content of the opening track ('Asylum').[112] Thereafter, Crass took full control of their releases, forming a close relationship with John Loder's Southern Studios to keep retail costs down to a minimum ('pay no more than ...') and opening up the label to like-minded artists committed to working outside the structures of the music industry.[113] By so doing, the anarchist tenets of the band became realisable and the potential use of the medium more encompassing. Crass releases came in fold-out sleeves that visually and literarily complemented the political sentiments explored on the records. To take just one example, 'Persons Unknown' b/w 'Bloody Revolutions', a joint single with Poison Girls from 1980, came wrapped in a Gee Vaucher illustration critiquing punk's appropriation via the Sex Pistols depicted as Queen, Pope, Lady Justice and Margaret Thatcher. Inside, a series of essays outlined the bands' critique of leftist power politics and the possibilities of anarchy. Details of the 1978–9 'persons unknown' trial were offered alongside a short statement promising funds from the record would support the establishment of a London anarchist centre. Around the sleeve's edge ran a list of contact addresses for collectives, fanzines, campaigns and book shops. As intended, the record appeared closer to a political communiqué than a pop product – an example followed by the numerous anarchist bands and labels (Bluurg, Mortarhate, Spider Leg) founded in Crass' wake.

Of course, not all independents committed to the same modus operandi. Fast Product, set up in Edinburgh by Bob Last and Hilary Morrison, presented itself as an 'operation' intervening in the media by using design techniques to package ostensibly non-commercial records in sleeves that communicated the mechanisms of production and consumption. Inspired, Tony Wilson and Alan Erasmus' Factory Records followed suit, forging a regional identity centred on Manchester with a roster that included A Certain Ratio, Durutti Column, Joy Division/New Order and, from 1982, the Hacienda nightclub. Industrial Records, founded by Throbbing Gristle, conspired to parody the music industry, issuing annual reports, newsletters and promotional material for product that defied the conventions of popular music.[114] More typically, labels developed in ad hoc fashion. Some lasted but briefly; a few – such as 4AD, Creation and Mute – transformed from small-scale ventures into global companies over the 1980s. Others, including Beggars Banquet, followed the traditional route of pre-punk independents by establishing manufacturing, promotional or distribution deals with major labels, while a combination of business pressures, technological changes and cultural shifts forced even the likes of Rough Trade to adopt more conventional commercial practices over time.[115]

Nor were independents immune to criticism. The very notion of working 'outside' the music industry was often challenged as naïve given the pop cultural medium in which records existed and the economic forces that determined their production.[116] As noted earlier, bands and labels disagreed as to whether they were seeking to compete with or bypass the established industry. This, in turn, prompted accusations of elitism or ghettoisation to be directed at those keen to retain their autonomy.[117] Not only was the DIY aesthetic soon cast as 'dour' or 'grey' against the glitz of much early 1980s pop, but the 'thinness' and ramshackle nature of indie production was also set negatively against the technological possibilities available to bands willing to work through the majors.

Politically, Rough Trade and Crass were both scorned for their 'hippie' derivations, especially by those the labels deemed to have produced 'ideologically unsound' work or felt their collective approach prevented them functioning as effective record companies.[118] More damningly, perhaps, the impetus that founded small independents was compared to the entrepreneurial spirit championed by Thatcherism. The indies were akin to 'grocers … they're just Margaret Thatchers', Malcolm McLaren taunted with a nod to the then prime minister's family background; '[they're] poverty stricken in terms of imagination, street suss and feeling'.[119] Rough Trade, Gang of Four's Jon King mocked, was

PRODUCTION NOTES.

Towards the end of 1979,Stortbeat,a small independent local label,run by a group of friends,offered to do a single with us,we agreed,naively thinking that,although they were a commercial venture,their independent status would at least ensure a degree of honesty,it wasn't long before we learnt better.

By coincidence,on the day that we were going into the studio to record the single,Crass rang us up to ask if we'd like to do a single on their label,by then we were committed to Stortbeat,but we did make it a condition of the contract that we would be free to record with Crass whenever we wanted.We went ahead and recorded 1970's knowing that we could do the single with Crass at a later date.

After the record was released we realised that Stortbeat were not living up to their agreement,they hadn't paid the recording fees and weren't making the right kind of efforts to move the single.We were getting pissed off with them so we contacted Crass to arrange starting work on a new single with them.When Crass looked through the contract we had signed with Stortbeat we found that the clause freeing us to record with Crass was invalid.We contacted Stortbeat but they were unwilling to help,in fact they started placing all sorts of stupid conditions on Crass so,for the while,we dropped the project.

As time went by Stortbeat lost interest in us and we were at last able to record Neu Smell on the Crass label. Around this time we decided to nick the materials for pressing 1970's from the pressing plant that did Stortbeats work,we were fed up with them doing nothing with it and we wanted to get it out,if only to pay back the cost of recording it.The result of this fiasco was that we pressed 1000 before Stortbeat found out and generously offered legal action for our troubles,we gave it back to them before the sheriff came round.

By now Neu Smell was topping the alternative charts and Stortbeat decided to capitalise on our success by re-releasing 1970's.We contacted them,telling them that we had now started our own label,Spider Leg Records,and that we were prepared to buy the pressing rights from them.They said they wanted £300 plus 2% production fees etc,the production fees were probably to pay off the dope bill run up by the 'production team' at the original recording session,which probably accounts for many of the 'special effects'.We told them to piss off and they went ahead and pressed the record with no proper label and a shitty cover,to retail at £1,which by any standard is a rip-off.What they were doing is a complete contradiction of what we stand for,so we decided to rerecord the single,with the old band,with decent labels and cover and sell it for 75p.

When we tried to get the old band together,Richard,the drummer,didn't want to do it,so we asked our new drummer if he'd mind doing it,he agreed,so we booked the same studio,Spaceward,and at last seemed to be getting somewhere.On the morning of the recording the drummer failed to turn up,we'd noticed that his old band was playing at the Rainbow that day,so we added things together,paid off the studio,£120,and headed for London.We arrived at the Rainbow in time to find our new drummer and guitarist coming off stage-as we disagree with a great deal of what many of the bands playing that day represent,(high entrance prices,dressing-rooms,roadies,rip-offs and so called 'real punk chaos'),we were left with no alternative but to tell them that we couldn't work together any more.So, we'd lost half our band,£120 and the chance to stop Stortbeats little game.

Later that day we spoke to Crass about it as we were supposed to be gigging with them over Xmas and Penny offered to drum with us if we wanted to have another go-we booked in at Southern Studios and recorded and mixed the new 1970's in five hours,(by then we couldn't afford any more).We think the result is worthwhile-at least it was honestly produced by people who care,which is fucking rare in the shitty world of the music business.

CONCLUSIONS.

Punk is a way of life,a working together of people who want to reject the system.We've found that a lot of people who claim to be punks are no better than the business men who exploit us all.We've heard of 'punk' bands buying themselves into the charts,'punks' who let other people do the shitty work while they star it up in the dressing-rooms,'punks' who think money is more important than frienship.We stood in for one so called punk band who cancelled a gig so they could be on Top of the Pops and then read about them slagging us off in the music-press, NOW WHO'S EXPLOITING WHO?

Figure 2.3 Extract from The Epileptics' *1970s* EP (Spider Leg Records, 1981).

'the Virgin of tomorrow'.[120] At the very least, manipulative contracts and nefarious business practice were by no means the preserve of major labels – as the cover and 'production notes' for The Epileptics' reissue of their *1970s* EP (1981) made clear (see Figure 2.3).[121]

To sum up, punk's cultural politics harboured an innate distrust of the music business. The exploitative nature of the industry and its processes of cultural commodification were regularly dissected and bemoaned in fanzines, interviews, songs and artworks, while details of a band's contract and the implications of signing to a major label became perennial topics of discussion. Part of punk's motivation, therefore, was to engage with the tensions that existed between culture, commerce, identity and consumption.[122] This, on occasion, had an ideological foundation – resulting in strategies to subvert or counter the prevailing structures of the music industry. Simultaneously, it was born of experience and observation, for which punk at least appeared to offer a means of agency and access denied to fledgling bands by larger (London-based) labels. In either case, the objective was to assert some kind of control over the form and content of popular music. Whether punk provided a platform for protest, creative expression or just a channel for youthful exuberance, it was recognised as a means to contest the industry standard.

Television's Over

The media of 1970s Britain was extensive in reach but limited in scope, a paradox that shaped many a punk-informed response to it. Though 97 per cent of homes owned a television by the turn of the decade (almost 75 per cent colour), just three channels broadcast intermittently throughout the day before closing down towards midnight.[123] The earthy populism of *The Sun* had somewhat ruffled the style and political balance of a national press read by 14.3 million people in 1978, but the launch of the *Daily Star* in the same year marked the first wholly new daily paper to appear since the war.[124] On the newsstands more generally, the countercultural undertow of the music press and titles such as *Cosmopolitan* offered slight respite from the staid functionality of a newsagent's 'general interest' racks (including the increasingly risqué top shelf). The radio, meanwhile, remained the preserve of the BBC, though pirate stations and, from 1972–3, commercial broadcasters had begun to broaden the style of news, music and entertainment available.

Viewed in wider perspective, however, the 'media-scape' was evidently mutating. Alongside the steady commercialisation of broadcasting and the mainstream press, so technological advances and cultural shifts pointed towards the continued expansion of form and content. If the 1960s brought moon landings, World Cup finals and war into the nation's front rooms, then the media's remit of information and communication transformed as TV and tabloids became bastions of popular culture. Indeed, the 1970s marked perhaps the highpoint of a genuinely *mass* media in Britain, with its relative lack of diversity allowing for a far more communally shared culture to be forged than any time previously or since. Thereafter, new channels, mediums, newspapers and magazines became totems of the 1980–90s, encouraged by

the market-orientated politics of Thatcherism and destined to fragment
the mass even as the all-pervasive twenty-four-hour media of science
fiction became contemporary fact. In the midst of all this, pop music
and youth culture existed at an ever more blurred interface between
media, leisure and commerce, provoking the question as to whether
pop was the teenage news or just another cog in a globalised industry
machine.

Of course, the growth and expanse of the media had long provoked debate as to its moral, social and political implications. Fears
of Americanisation and 'levelling down' rumbled throughout much of
the century; the media's conversion from a source of information to a
site of entertainment provoked much consternation. If media studies
was still in its infancy by 1976–77, then the influence and effect of the
media was very much to the forefront of public and intellectual debate.
Most obviously, Mary Whitehouse's conservative National Viewers and
Listeners' Association (NVLA) ensured that media content – both print
and celluloid – was continually subject to scrutiny by self-appointed
moral guardians. Simultaneously, theoretical analyses had begun to filter through to the public domain, primarily as a result of work developed by Marshall McLuhan and academics gathered in the Glasgow
University Media Group and the Centre for Contemporary Cultural
Studies (CCCS).[125]

Punk engaged with and critiqued such developments, both in
terms of substance and aesthetic. Tabloids were derided for their cheap
sensationalism and partial truths; the press generally was portrayed as a
mouthpiece for vested interests and a means of shaping public opinion
on behalf of government, commerce or elites. Both television and radio
were depicted as a substitute for agency and a distraction from the
realities of everyday life. Advertising, in particular, was recognised as
more than just a motor for consumption, but rather a simulacrum – an
ideal for living that reinforced social constructs and channelled desires.

In reply, punk détourned symbols of the press and challenged
the camera's distorting lens. Tabloid typography became an essential
punk signifier, not only in the use of ransom-note lettering to spell out
group names and fanzine text, but also on sleeve designs culled from
newsprint to frame records in headlines of '6 Minute War Madness',
'Fun, Kill, Love, Horror, Money, Dream, Terror' or 'Fires Rage in
London Riot'.[126] PiL's first single, 'Public Image' (1978), came in a
replica newspaper replete with mock-tabloid stories about the group's

members, while Linder and Jon Savage's *The Secret Public* (1978) comprised photomontages that spliced together pornographic images with household appliances to expose the gendered false promise of the advertising hoarding.[127] Band names, too, were taken from headlines (Buzzcocks, The Clash, Crisis, Six Minute War) or chosen in recognition of the mediated context through which pop music existed (The Adverts, Alternative TV, Magazine, The Media, Television Personalities). Audio extracts from news reports were even incorporated into songs (Chelsea's 'Government', Crass' 'Angels', Scritti Politti's '28/8/78') and, in one famous incident featuring The Clash at London's 100 Club (1976), fed live through the PA to become part of a gig's soundtrack. In other words, punk inserted itself into the media by reproducing its language, fears and predilections.

Examples of bands critiquing the media in song are legion. The first Sex Pistols' b-side, 'I Wanna Be Me', set its sights on the 'typewriter gods' that constructed and demolished personal identities through the press.[128] The Clash's 'London's Burning' depicted television as a 'new religion', a cause of the ennui settling over the nation's capital.[129] Not dissimilarly, 'FM' by The Slits accused the media of cultivating fears and false solutions, while Subway Sect encapsulated punk's default position in the lyric to 'Nobody's Scared': 'Media teach me what to speak, take my decisions/ It's how to find your inner-self time, on the television'.[130]

Thereafter, punk and post-punk bands continued to attack and deconstruct the media's nefarious influence. Both Wire and Gang of Four produced debut albums that obsessed with the media, including songs – 'Reuters' and '5.45' respectively – that explored how war reports were refracted through print and screen to become sanitised or merely another form of entertainment: 'the corpse as a new personality'.[131] Simultaneously, Crisis and The Radiators from Space portrayed television as a mental prison, with the latter promising to stick their telecasters through the television screen. The gap between mediated reality and lives actually lived became a particular concern. The Cortinas, for instance, used their 'Television Families' to mock the idealised domesticity portrayed on TV. The Members, meanwhile, satirised the phone-in shows peddled by commercial radio as 'cheap entertainment … five minutes of glib advice when you've nowhere left to go'.[132]

Much of this was intuitive. The tabloid reaction to punk in late 1976 through 1977 demonstrated clearly how far media interpretations could diverge from personal experience, a fact bemoaned in many a fanzine from the time.[133] Early on, moreover, punk's criticism of the media focused on its failure – or unwillingness – to reflect the interests of young people. Just as the pop industry was deemed not to provide music made by or relevant to teenagers in the mid-1970s, so the dearth of popular music coverage in the newspapers or on television was cited as a key instigator of punk's emergence. For The Clash's Paul Simonon, at least, punk was partly a product of 'kids who watch *Top of the Pops* and they see all these shitty groups and there's nothing to do ... It is ... kids getting up and doing something on their own'.[134]

In effect, punk positioned itself as an alternative media – an Alternative TV, to use Mark Perry's band as exemplar. Beyond the social reportage that informed many a group's lyrics, punk reconceived rock 'n' roll as a medium to posit opinions, actions and perspectives excluded from the mainstream. Fanzines, similarly, justified their existence as an antidote to a music press in thrall to the fickle interests of the industry and thereby detached from pop's grass-roots gestation.[135]

As this suggests, instinctive distrust of the media was complemented by more sophisticated analysis. Much has been made of the situationist influence that informed the ideas of McLaren and Jamie Reid, both of whom were aware of Guy Debord's conception of 'the spectacle' as an 'inversion of life'.[136] According to Debord, building on Marx's critique of alienation under capitalism, the media served as an agent of reification: 'Everything that was directly lived has moved into a representation'.[137] The result was a society of passive consumption and vicarious living, wherein culture was commodified, fact and fiction coalesced, and celebrities (including the 'pop star') *seemingly* lived out lives to compensate for the fractured and banal existence of lives *actually* lived.[138] To negate the spectacle, its processes had to be disrupted, revealed and subverted, thereby providing a neat conceptual framework to locate the Sex Pistols and a palette of ideas to complement the band's ire.[139]

Similar thinking was manifest elsewhere. Richard Boon, who managed Buzzcocks and ran the New Hormones record label, was using situationist ideas to write a dissertation on the function of art when he first saw the Sex Pistols. Tony Wilson, too, admitted in 1978 to being an 'armchair situationist' who recognised in punk certain approaches that he later applied to Factory Records.[140] The first Durutti Column album thus came wrapped in a sandpaper sleeve, an anti-consumerist gesture borrowed from Debord's collaboration with Asger Jorn, *Mémoires* (1959), while the group's name was itself a reference to a situationist-informed pamphlet designed by André Bertrand from Strasbourg University in 1966. With an albeit misspelt nod to the Spanish anarchist Buenaventura Durruti, the text, which came in the form of a détourned comic strip featuring – among much else – two cowboys discussing reification, further provided the album's title: *The Return of the Durutti Column* (1979).[141] More famously, the Hacienda nightclub opened by Factory in 1982 was named after an Ivan Chtcheglov essay that conceived new visions of time and space through architecture and urban planning.[142]

Nor was Manchester the only northern city to harbour situationist influences. Over in Leeds, the ideas of Gang of Four, The Mekons and Delta 5 were partly informed by the presence of Tim (TJ) Clarke in the university's fine arts department, where members of all three bands were studying in the mid-to-late 1970s. Clarke had briefly been a member of the Situationist International. Back in London, beyond the likes of McLaren and Reid, situationist ideas circulated among London's anarchist milieu into the 1980s, finding their way onto records such as The Apostles' *Smash the Spectacle* EP (1985) and into a number of fanzines.[143]

That said, it is important not to overstate the impact of situationist practice on punk more generally. Though apparent, the influence of Debord, Raoul Vaneigem and others formed but part of a far wider cultural critique that ranged across the varied contours of the New Left and counterculture. This, certainly, was the case with Crass, a band that included members whose politics and worldview had been shaped by the cultural upheavals of the 1950s and 1960s. Given such a context, Crass recognised the media as integral to the maintenance of existing social structures and modes of control. 'Every day the TV, the radio and the newspapers manipulate and direct the thoughts of the general public, tell them what to think and how to think, but it's not because they want to improve the "quality" of thought, it's more that they are required, by the establishment interests that run them, to reinforce "standard" social values; serve that which serves you, or else. When media is controlled almost exclusively by the wealthy, ruling elite, censorship becomes unnecessary; money speaks louder than words.'[144] Subsequently, Crass' approach was designed to provide alternative lines of communication to challenge the dominant media. Beyond the communiqués that formed the record sleeves described previously, the band issued statements through the punk fanzine network that developed from 1976, collaborated with the film-maker Mick Duffield, and published a series of papers, pamphlets and artworks.[145]

Not surprisingly, Crass' lyrical focus often concentrated on media-related themes. 'Nineteen Eighty Bore', for example, defined television as an Orwellian form of social control, while 'Mother Earth' recast the media's fascination with the Moors murderess Myra Hindley as a fetish that revealed the moral duplicity of generating profit via images of death and destruction. Television was 'today's Nuremberg', Crass insisted on *Yes Sir, I Will* (1983), a means of dampening anger, constructing social stereotypes and distracting from 'real problems'. 'We look for alternatives, but the enormous power of the media makes it so difficult to establish foundations. Their lies and distortions are so extreme that everything becomes poisoned and corrupted. We can become media personalities but it is always on their terms'.[146]

Similar sentiments were oft-repeated by the bands formed in Crass' wake, with titles such as 'Bullshit Broadcast', 'TV Scream', 'Media Friend', 'TV Dinners' and 'Channel Zero' giving a sense to their content.[147] But perhaps the most coherent media critique beyond Crass came from the industrial culture that likewise saw music as a medium to disseminate ideas and the media more generally as an insidious form of social control. To this end, groups such as Cabaret Voltaire and Throbbing Gristle aligned musical performance with other forms of media to expose the disparity between mediated reality and life itself. Noise, cut-up visuals, found sounds and extreme imagery were presented as an assault on the senses, a means to disrupt perceived notions of order and normality. For Genesis P-Orridge (Neil Megson), the objective was to 'decondition people's responses, demystify creative, musical activity and life too, and most of all … make people think for themselves, decide for themselves and direct their own lives by their own values and experiences, by experiences learned BY THEM from life and not second hand, unproven experiences handed down by education and religion and dogma politics'.[148]

Throbbing Gristle formed out of COUM Transmissions, an art collective from Hull that included P-Orridge, Cosey Fanni Tutti and, following their relocation to London, Peter Christopherson. From 1969–70, COUM experimented with music, performance and mail art to challenge prevailing social values and negate the conventions of the cultural establishment. As this suggests, the troupe obsessed with sex, violence and the body, their 'actions' pushing at the boundaries of taste through use of nudity, bodily fluids, pornography, vandalism, infantilism and waste. With Throbbing Gristle, the focus shifted from the gallery space to popular culture, providing for an anti-music group to explore the disturbing atmospheres 'gristleized' through Chris Carter's customised effects unit. According to P-Orridge, both Throbbing Gristle and his follow-up group Psychic TV were 'interested in infiltrating the media because it's the main channel of control. At the moment the media is promoting pessimism and vacuous fun. And the reasons are quite obvious to us. If people are pessimistic and distracted they don't pose much of a threat'.[149] In response, Throbbing Gristle engaged in an 'information war', deliberately locating themselves – in terms of their presentation, sound, content, production and record label – at odds with the prevailing mores of the music business.[150]

In practical terms, such an approach entailed parodying and subverting the commercialism that sustained popular music. Titles, imagery and photos were infused with multiple or conflicting meanings designed to interrogate how the media and consumers interpreted the information relayed through and to them. So, for example, the cover image of four group members smiling on a seaside cliff-top beneath the title *20 Jazz Funk Greats* (1979) was read differently once the location was revealed as the renowned suicide spot Beachy Head and the record's contents proved some way removed from the album title. Their label name, Industrial Records, and slogan, 'music from the death factory', both forged a brand identity and commented on the commodification of culture. More practically, Throbbing Gristle's experiments opened up new channels of enquiry to provide gateways to cultural extremes. The group's 'newsletter', *Industrial News*, featured contact addresses and pieces on such key influences as William Burroughs.[151] Through reading interviews and picking up on references, the inquisitive could amass extensive film and book lists to later pursue.

Similar methods were applied by Cabaret Voltaire. They, too, experimented with forms of multimedia; like Throbbing Gristle, they proved quick to employ video as a complementary means of communication. Both bands were fascinated by technology, utilizing synthesizers and tapes while simultaneously exploring the dystopian ramifications of mechanisation. Both presented themselves as closer to journalists than to musicians, documenting and reporting back from behind the media curtain.[152] Stephen Mallinder, who formed Cabaret Voltaire with Richard Kirk and Chris Watson in 1973, described his band's methods as a 'course of exploration' designed to facilitate self-knowledge and 'change people's conceptions'.[153] Neither band took a political or moral position, preferring instead to relay information and media snippets alongside reportage on the extremities of a 'real life' desensitised by media overload. 'The point is', Mallinder insisted on being questioned with regard to the violent images projected at the band's live show, 'people see them but aren't aware of them … when people see it on the news they're totally punch-drunk. It's news, and the news has become a fantasy as much as *Hart to Hart* [a US television drama]. You see it in a totally different context and it has far more impact on you'.[154]

Punk and industrial cultures portrayed the media as both a source of disinformation and a palliative – a medium that conditioned, distracted and deadened the senses. In response, punk and industrial groups sought to cut through the artifice to engage with and reflect life-as-lived. This could mean circumnavigating the media and music industry by prioritising activities and producing alternative lines of communication (gigs, fanzines, self-produced records). Alternately, it could mean intervening to subvert the processes of popular music's commodification by reconstituting its form and substance. The importance of the Grundy incident, beyond the moral panic it instigated, was its momentary rupture of the media sheen. The Sex Pistols were 'off script'; their appearance would have been edited if pre-recorded, but *Today*'s live transmission allowed for a fleeting glimpse of something 'other' to seep through the pretence. Be it the swear words, indifference or irreverence shown by the band to their surroundings, the Grundy interview allowed what Rotten called 'real eyes' to penetrate – and so realise – the media artifice.[155]

3 TELL US THE TRUTH: REPORTAGE, REALISM AND ABJECTION

> Words are the most important thing about punk. If I just wanted to pogo, there's hundreds of bands I could go and see – that's just as bad as Disco. What I'm interested in is people who tell the truth. That's what I believe in.[1]
>
> Jimmy Pursey (1977)

> All our songs are about being honest, right? The situation as we see it … otherwise we'd be writing bullshit!![2]
>
> Mick Jones (1976)

The story behind The Clash's 'White Riot' has become part of punk folklore. As told on LWT's *London Weekend Show* in November 1976, Joe Strummer and Paul Simonon used it to explain The Clash's commitment to writing about 'what's going on at the moment'.[3] The song itself related to the Notting Hill carnival of just a few weeks earlier, during which ongoing tensions between police and the area's black population gave way to violence. According to newspaper reports, some 300 police and 131 members of the public were injured during the disturbance, bringing to the fore questions of race relations, inner-city policing and political stability.[4] In fact, the trouble was such that the Home Office subsequently authorised the introduction of riot shields (first used the following year during clashes between the National Front [NF] and anti-racists in Lewisham), with images from the time showing policemen wielding truncheons and cowering behind dustbin lids, smashed-up shop fronts and rubble-strewn streets, black youths fleeing from police or throwing bricks. 'We was down there, me and him', Strummer recounted with a nod to Simonon, 'and we got searched by policemen, looking for bricks, like. And then, later on, we got searched by Rasta, looking for pound notes in our pockets'. 'And all we had were bricks and bottles,' the bass-player finishes.[5]

Such a tale would feed into The Clash's own mythology, helping to align their punk protest with the roots reggae that provided a suitably dread soundtrack to the unrest in Notting Hill and affirming the band's conception of themselves as street-level rebels reporting back from the urban frontline.[6] The song's lyrics celebrated the riot and urged white youth to have the guts to do the same. Photos from the day provided copy for the band's record sleeves and stage backdrops; the fact that Strummer and Simonon had *been there* helped authenticate their aural snapshot of mid-1970s London.

This lived experience was important. The Clash aspired to a significance they felt had been lost in most popular music. Their early songs were peppered with local references to the 'Westway', 'Bakerloo', 'Knightsbridge', 'Hammersmith', 'the 100 Club' and 'London Town'; they spoke of 'escalators', 'Ford Cortinas', 'skin-flicks', the dole 'office' and 'fighting in the road'; they described social tensions, ennui, unemployment, petty crime and political impotency. Or, as Tony Parsons put it, The Clash offered a 'mirror reflection of the kind of ... white, working-class experiences that only seem like a cliché to those people who haven't lived through them'.[7] In so doing, they helped forge a template that informed much British punk and punk-related styles into the 1980s: that is, an aggressive sound, image and rhetoric that proffered social reportage rooted in practice.[8] As is well known, Strummer's middle-class background and the art school enrolment of all three core members soon provided critics with the necessary information to challenge the group's street-savvy stance. But the *idea* of the early Clash – not to mention their evident sincerity – meant the band remained integral to punk's cultural evolution. In effect, both Oi! and the more socially conscious punk of the period strove to maintain or better fulfil a bona fide version of The Clash's original intent.

Simultaneously, 'White Riot' – alongside many other Clash songs – hinted at a morality beyond mere reportage. Early interviews revealed the band to accept the political connotations of an approach that tended more towards a form of consciousness-raising than any specific doctrine – '[We're] making people aware of a situation they'd otherwise tend to ignore', Simonon insisted.[9] Nevertheless, lyrics such as 'all the power in the hands, of the people rich enough to buy it' lent

The Clash a missionary zeal that inspired many a fledgling socialist to embrace punk.[10] In Strummer's words, 'the only thing I'm interested in is my personal freedom … [But] it ain't no use me having the right to choose unless everybody else has too'.[11]

More typically, perhaps, punk represented a medium of social realism that was often political by default.[12] In producing records that sought to reflect, report and comment on their time and place, bands such as Sham 69, The Ruts, Angelic Upstarts and Cockney Rejects infused popular music with voices, subject matter and perspectives that had rarely been so explicitly stated in a pop cultural context.[13] This, in turn, was further evident in the work of The Jam and much early 2-Tone, which redirected punk's social realism through different musical and stylistic routes. Though most such bands rejected any overtly political label, punk signified a means to register a protest, highlight a social problem or celebrate a localised – often class-based – culture. Similarly, while squabbles about authenticity became a feature of punk and post-punk discourse, the principal effect of its tendency to social realism was to dramatise British youth culture at a significant historical juncture. Just as the novels of Alan Sillitoe or the films of Tony Richardson depicted the tensions and transformations of postwar Britain into the 1950s and 1960s, so the starkly urban insights of The Jam, The Ruts and Specials captured the anxieties occasioned by the socioeconomic insecurities and sociocultural changes manifest by the 1970s and 1980s.[14]

In practice, punk-derived social realism oscillated between the thrills and frustrations of urban living. It fretted over adolescent insecurities and celebrated the empowerment of subcultural style. It documented the spectacular, as with 'White Riot', but simultaneously sought to tap into and engage with the provincial concerns of those 'Saturday's Kids' from 'council houses' who wore 'V-neck shirts and baggy trousers'/'cheap perfume 'cos it's all they can afford'.[15] It veered, uneasily at times, between reportage and political commentary. In the main, however, bands tended to reject accusations of preaching, preferring to see their music as a means to 'observe' or 'tell the truth' about the world around them.[16]

Not all were convinced. For their critics, bands such as The Jam confirmed rather than challenged their audience's expectations and thereby neutered punk's radical spirit via a combination of fatalism and reaction.[17] Sham 69 and their successors were soon dismissed – as

Parsons forewarned – as projecting working-class caricatures that revelled in street-level violence and failed to demonstrate a positive response to the problems they highlighted. By 1981 and the emergence of Oi!, such brusque rock 'n' roll and a lyrical focus on (male) working-class culture was even dismissed as inherently 'racist-sexist-fascist'.[18] But these bands were not writing or performing for aspiring cultural commentators, academics or self-proclaimed socialist revolutionaries. Rather, they formed part of a wider youth culture that encompassed clothes, clubs, friends and locales. The bands' lyrical concerns were designed to resonate with their audience – to trigger points of recognition via the language used, the places referenced and the experiences shared. As this suggests, gigs – especially those in smaller venues – were as important as the records made. Gigs served as a place of commonality that was reaffirmed by the terrace-style sing-a-long nature of songs that dissolved the band–audience divide and reclaimed pop music for the proverbial 'kids on the street'. In other words, the 'way out' offered by rock 'n' roll and pop music from the 1950s was again made tangible by bands that celebrated the moment and warned against the dismal future of adult life.

Tears of a Nation

When, in 1976, James Callaghan warned the Labour conference that the 'cosy world is gone', he made something of an understatement.[19] The immediate problem was serious enough: the pound's value against the dollar had plunged to a record low of $1.68 in September 1976, thereby prompting Britain to apply for an International Monetary Fund (IMF) loan to offset the market's lack of confidence and allay fears of a currency collapse.[20] More broadly, the Labour government's appeal to the IMF proved but an especially humiliating episode among a series of political and economic crises that rumbled throughout the 1970s into the 1980s. As the Sex Pistols set out on their ill-fated 'Anarchy in the UK' tour of December 1976, so a year that had begun with inflation rates of over 20 per cent (not to mention an IRA bomb attack on London's West End) culminated in public spending cuts that effectively signalled a fundamental realignment of the British polity.

Of course, Callaghan's once 'cosy' Britain was itself something of a chimera. His comments alluded to the sustained period of economic growth and full employment that followed the war; to the

technological optimism of the 1960s, the implementation of the welfare state, increased access to education and social mobility. In Labour
terms, it denoted a steady improvement in working-class living standards and trade union influence from 1945. Yet such developments had
always been undercut by tensions and anxieties. British growth and
material progress occurred relative to other developed (and developing) economies expanding at a greater rate than the UK.[21] Inflationary
pressures and the recession of 1973–75 exacerbated deeper concerns
about the validity of the postwar settlement, especially among a middle
class vexed by taxation, falling property prices and shrinking share
dividends. Cultural changes raised questions of morality. Social mobility and immigration tendered fears of personal status aggravated by a
fragile economy and loss of empire. Industrial strife triggered alarm
about governance and stability. As a result, talk of 'decline' – a recurring feature of the British political lexicon since the late nineteenth
century – moved to the centre of public debate in the mid-1970s.[22]

Alwyn Turner and others have done much to reveal the extent
to which such political and economic portents found cultural expression.[23] Be it through newspaper editorials, political journals, novels,
artworks, film or television series, Britain's decay was anticipated
and dramatised to multiple effect. Vistas of urban dereliction and
social conflict became commonplace as testimonies to a dying country informed serious drama, comedies, documentaries and even end-
of-year soliloquies by popular light entertainers. Anyone tuning into
BBC Two during September–October 1977, for example, would have
found themselves presented with a vision of 1990, a Wilfred Greatorex
series starring Edward Woodward that foresaw national bankruptcy,
a state of emergency transformed into civil service dictatorship, and
a closed-border Britain falling into disrepair as it struggled to prevent
its citizens from leaving. The premise, common among those who saw
public ownership and the welfare state as a precursor to East European
style socialism, was a morally duplicitous Labour government resort-
ing to evermore statist solutions to allay its economic mismanagement.
A few months previously, *The Money Programme* had cast a similar
eye to the near future. Broadcast in July 1976, two scenarios of Britain
in 1980 were presented: one a country bedevilled by crumbling infra-
structure and devoid of public services but economically buoyant in
terms of exports and the city; the other – understood to be more of a
continuum – a decimated wasteland of abandoned factories, inner-city

decay, mass unemployment and runaway inflation. Come the end of the year, on 27 December 1976, it was left to Hughie Green, the presenter of *Opportunity Knocks*, to provide a suitably ascetic sermon of despair. Bidding farewell to a year that had seen Britain 'old and worn, on the brink of ruin, bankrupt in all but heritage and hope', he asked for 1977 to be 'our year'. For otherwise, he feared, the British people would 'lose our freedom forever'.[24]

On both the political left and right, the socioeconomic difficulties of the period were certainly recognised as a crisis of … something. Whether this meant the collapse of capitalism or the end-days of social democracy depended on authorial bias. But as the Labour government tried to balance prices, wages and inflation against a global economic downturn, so its Keynesian panacea appeared battle worn and broken. 'Fear is more potent than hope', an internal Tory paper instructed in 1978, finding ready outlet in a 'winter of discontent' that seemingly confirmed the prevailing mood of a nation sliding into chaos.[25]

A correlation between punk's emergence and Britain's 'decline' was easily made.[26] As well as the lyrical focus of 'Anarchy in the UK', 'White Riot' and other early songs, punk's aesthetic drew from and reflected the media and political discourse that defined its time. The Sex Pistols' 'no future' tallied with the cataclysmic language that permeated the 1970s; punk's aggression, rips, zips and images of decay complemented tabloid fears of social disintegration. Punk's discord signalled social discord – a tattered Union Jack held together by safety pins and bull clips. 'Take a depression', Jon Savage wrote in late 1976, 'spice with a castrating bureaucracy (all the power to the men in grey) and a sexually & socially frustrated people living off past (WW 2) glories & violence recycled *ad nauseam* – add an accepted intolerance-as-a-way-of-life at all levels (ask any West Indian) and you get the vacuum tedium of a country OD'd on its own greed'.[27]

In response, punk appeared to filter youthful obsessions and disaffection through the prevailing sense of catastrophe that provided its socioeconomic, political and cultural context. This could be instinctive, expressed via blunt statements of antipathy and disillusionment. But interviews from the time also reveal how the language of crisis and decline informed the perspectives of those drawn into punk's orbit. In late 1976, for example, The Stranglers' Jean-Jacques Burnel contextualised punk's implicit political meaning thus: 'There's decay everywhere. We've always lived with the assumption that things were getting better and better materially, progress all the time, and suddenly ... you hear every day there's a crisis ... Things being laid off, people are not working. Everything's coming to a grinding halt'.[28] More generally, premonitions of social collapse or authoritarian clampdown repeated through punk's formative years, having gained substance with every slim election victory and minority administration that struggled to govern over the 1970s.

In terms of reportage, therefore, punk tended towards the general: state-of-the-nation addresses that offered snapshots of society in conflict or decline. Neither 'Anarchy in the UK' nor 'God Save the Queen' worked as systematic appraisals of British polity, but as verbal collages that evoked the tenor of their time: shopping schemes and council tenancies, fascism and terrorism, H-bombs and the 'mad parade' of a Jubilee celebrating a nation on the wane. No Future. Anarchy. Destroy.

The Clash took a more narrative approach, detailing their environment and reporting back on events that defined their understanding of the world in which they lived. The Clash album 'reflects all the shit', Mark Perry enthused, 'it tells us the truth ... It's as if I'm looking at my life in a film'.[29] Thereafter, punk provided space for bands and writers to document their time and place, typically relaying moods and experiences in three-minute bursts of variable quality and sophistication. Recurring themes emerged. Portrayals of national decay were played out in songs such as The Adverts' 'Great British Mistake', depicting a country weighed down by complacency and unable to adapt as it sunk into media-saturation and, ultimately, authoritarianism. Not dissimilarly, the Tom Robinson Band's 'Up Against the Wall' and 'Winter of '79' imagined state-sanctioned clampdowns to stave off social change, while the first Jam LP, *In The City* (1977), flitted between pathos at Britain's fading prowess and invective against a discredited establishment: 'Whatever happened to the great empire? You bastards turned it into manure'.[30]

Come 1978–79 and bands such as Stiff Little Fingers and The Ruts built on The Clash's model. The former reported back from Northern Ireland, imagining an 'Alternative Ulster' as they transmitted the very real pressures experienced by those growing up at the heart of the Troubles. 'We've said all along we're not giving solutions', the band's Jake Burns told the *NME*. 'We're just telling people all around us what's going on.'[31] The Ruts, meanwhile, proffered mini-dramas of contemporary society infused with unease. Their songs were often mired in violent imagery, depicting a society rife with social tensions exacerbated by limited opportunities and the repressive forces of the state. 'Jah War', for instance, documented the violence meted out by police on anti-fascist protesters in Southall in 1979, during which Blair Peach was murdered and Clarence Baker beaten into a coma.[32] As effectively, their single 'Babylon's Burning' captured a *sense* of Britain at the end of the 1970s, conveying a nation smouldering with anxiety, ignorance and hate, ready to combust. 'What you see has to come out in your lyrics', the band's Malcolm Owen insisted, 'everyone's anxious. Everyone's worried'.[33]

If dystopian visions helped inform punk's worldview, then the frailties of social cohesion were charted in its sound, image and attitude. Street-level animosities were documented in songs such as The Jam's '"A" Bomb in Wardour Street', The Ruts' 'Staring at the Rude Boys' and Chron Gen's 'Mindless Few', each of which offered redolent accounts of gig-related clashes between the youth cultural tribes given fresh impetus by punk. As this suggests, perennial hostilities found ever more spectacular expression as culture commodified and the cameras rolled. Turf wars became style wars: mods versus rockers became punks versus teds; the skinheads hated everybody. More to the point, *The Sun*'s 'Violent Britain' series of 1978 found ready complement in punk's depictions of urban brutality. Across the Fatal Microbes' 'Violence Grows', Vivien Goldman's 'Private Armies', the Newtown Neurotics' 'Mindless Violence' and Blitz's 'Someone's Gonna Die Tonight', the bloody consequences of random beatings were captured in depressing detail.

In effect, punk instigated commentary on Britain's sense of malaise. The deficiencies of the postwar consensus were detailed across the late 1970s; the effects of Thatcherism and the reignited Cold War were recorded over the early 1980s. Fanzines offered their own youthful reflections on the time, interspersing record reviews and band interviews with collages of newspaper headlines and tabloid images of police, the NF, militarism and war. Short articles on the threat of fascism, police harassment and unemployment became common; youth cultural and racial tensions were dissected and bemoaned.[34] In particular, the process of deindustrialisation began to inform countless record sleeves and posters, represented by graffitied walls and urban dereliction that later doubled as post-apocalyptic visions of a bombed-out

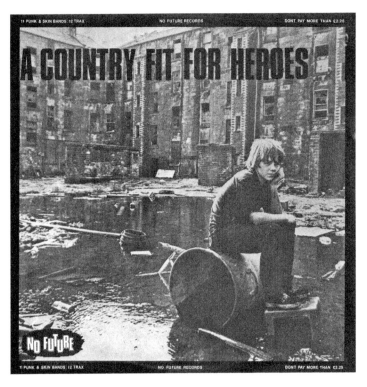

Figure 3.1 Desolate punk sleeve from the No Future label: Various Artists, *A Country Fit for Heroes* (1982).

UK (see Figures 3.1 and 3.2). Singles, not to mention EPs, albums and posters, portrayed Britain as a country no longer caught in the midst of decline but plunged into desolation; their titles – 'Dead Cities', *Burning Britain* (1982), 'Give Us a Future', *No Hope for Anyone* (1982) – harbouring the fatalistic fury of doomed youth. 'Look through this broken window', the Subhumans ruminated on 'Black and White', 'from normality into the ghetto/ broken – through madness, hate and boredom/ UK – a disunited kingdom'.[35]

The first term of Margaret Thatcher's Conservative government (1979–83) was certainly bellicose. A large pay increase granted to the police sent one signal; realignments in macroeconomic policy – cuts in income tax, increases in VAT and interest rates, loosening control over the exchange of foreign currency, market determination of prices and incomes – sent another. Thereafter, manufacturing contracted by some 25 per cent as unemployment soared to more than 3 million by

Figure 3.2 Desolate punk sleeve from the No Future label: Blitz, *All Out Attack* EP (1981).

1982. Simultaneously, trade union influence was curbed, cautiously at first but more robustly over time, while state power was both central-ised and 'rolled back' via promises to cut borrowing and public expen-diture, sell off council housing, limit the influence of local government and, more extensively from 1984, privatise state-owned industries and services.[36] The language of opposition became the language of govern-ment: 'freedom' was measured in economic rather than social terms; enemies within – trade unionists, leftists, squatters and onto Peter Lilley's 'little list' of 1992 – were distinguished from 'hard working families', the 'quiet majority' and 'our people'.[37]

In reply, bands such as Blitz, The Exploited and Vice Squad (whose album title, *No Cause for Concern* [1981], reportedly came from a Thatcher quote relating to growing youth unemployment) depicted a country broken and violent. Punk's aesthetic traits became more raggedy; the once stylised apparel became faded and worn; battered leather jackets and boots served as austerity-wear. Appropriately, too, the 'Apocalypse Now' tour showcasing four of the leading 'new punk' bands of the early 1980s – Anti Pasti, Chron Gen, Discharge and The Exploited – set off in the summer of 1981 as riots erupted across Britain's inner cities, prompting even sceptical journalists to register a connection.[38] 'Last week's Commons reports [on the riots] read like paraphrased Pistol songs', the *NME*'s Chris Bohn reported, noting how punk's continued references to anarchy resonated once more as 'chaos asserted its new reign elsewhere'.[39] Or, to quote Wattie Buchan of The Exploited's reading of the riots: 'Kids are fed up. If they've got nowt to do they'll do something stupid. Like vandalise or something ... If kids go straight from school to the dole, it's not their fault is it? They cannae go out and get a job. The government creates boredom and there's no way you can protest about it ... They never bother until something actually happens ... Punk today is the backlash of reality.'[40]

Famously, of course, the Specials' 'Ghost Town' was at number one in July 1981, providing a bleak panorama of Britain's decaying inner cities that all but prefaced the findings of the Scarman Report commissioned by the government in the wake of the 'Brixton disorders' of April 1981. The song's fusion of reggae-dread, punk-ire and pointed social commentary embodied the cross-cultural fusion forged by 2-Tone amidst the racial tensions of the period. As disorder continued to unfold through Liverpool, Leeds, Bristol, Birmingham, Nottingham, Manchester and elsewhere, so deprivation, poor housing and a lack of employment provided a common link. A racial element existed in many areas; but this was less the 'black versus white' scenario envisaged by Enoch Powell then stoked by the far right, and more the result of long-running animosities between local communities and a police force committed to heavy-handed strategies suffused with racial prejudice.[41] As for punk, the riots inspired a series of songs – such as Blitz's 'Nation on Fire' and Violators' 'Summer of '81' – that duly reported events as an upsurge of youthful anger against the government, unemployment and police.[42]

Not surprisingly, such analyses lent themselves to political interpretation. As we shall see, socialist, anarchist and fascist adaptations of punk's (and 2-Tone's) reportage were not uncommon. Though many continued, like Jake Burns, to insist that commentary did not thereby pertain to a proposed solution, it did raise questions of cause and effect. Tirades against 'the system' bore the stamp of a critical consciousness. More broadly, reportage confirmed punk's conception of a youth culture that engaged with the world of which it was part – that 'confronted' the situation, as Killing Joke's Jaz Coleman put it.[43] By so doing, punk tapped into real and media-refracted stresses within the social fabric: industrial conflict and police brutality, youth cultural rivalries and political extremes, unemployment and substance abuse. For every government report on violence at rock concerts, glue sniffing or inner-city policing, punk offered cultural supplements that aspired to Joe Strummer's conviction that 'the truth is only known by guttersnipes'.[44]

Living with Unemployment

There was a moment in late 1976 when punk flirted with the moniker of 'dole queue rock'. References to the dole or 'signing on' featured in most early interviews with the Sex Pistols, The Clash and The Damned, particularly once Tony Parsons ascribed punk's 'reality stance' to its being 'a product of the United Kingdom in the 1970s'.[45] If Labour wasn't working, as the famous Tory campaign poster later insisted against a decade increase of almost a million registered unemployed (from 601,333 in 1968 to 1,475,042 in 1978), then punk was seen to represent what *New Society*'s Peter Marsh described as the 'empty life' of a jobless teenager.[46]

Such interpretation had its limits. A closer look at punk's initial demographic and the substance of its early texts reveal it to have been born of more than just the 'right to work'. Most notably, as Simon Frith was quick to observe, punk's expression of teenage frustration was complemented by art school and countercultural influences that inclined as much towards the bohemian as the innate street-level protest Parsons and Marsh attributed to it. Pop music had long provided succour from the tedium of work, school and home life, be it temporal (dancing, listening, dressing up, hanging around) or actual (becoming a musician/singer). In a sense, therefore, punk followed this tradition, albeit filtered through what Frith recognised as the 'intractable economic situation' of the mid-1970s.[47]

Whatever their motivation, punk bands utilised the dole queue as a symbol of Britain's wider condition. Just as one Peterborough band called themselves The Dole in 1977, so references to unemployment peppered early songs by Alternative TV, Chelsea, The Clash, Menace,

Sham 69 and others in the same way as record sleeves and gig flyers featured urban topographies of tower blocks and 'the street'.[48] Signing-on or working in a series of low-paid jobs served to demarcate punk's pioneers from the rock 'n' roll superstars they sought to contest. The infamous pseudonyms adopted by punks were often done so to deflect social security officials ('SS snoopers') from discovering the minor earnings received from gigs, singles or fanzines.[49]

By the 1980s, moreover, as unemployment became entrenched and increased to average more than 3 million between 1982 and 1986, so youth culture's relationship to the dole became more explicit. Beyond the dole-queue skank of UB40, whose name and debut album referenced the signing-on documentation of the time, the early days of Thatcherism were recorded across overtly punk tracks such as the Abrasive Wheels' 'Vicious Circle': 'Forgotten youth just waste away/ Sniffing glue to face the day/ Walking streets, signing on/ Government schemes go on and on'.[50] Indeed, a steady stream of dole-queue songs emerged from punk's hinterlands over the early 1980s, ranging from the defiant (Emergency's 'Points of View') to the fatalistic (Infa Riot's 'Each Dawn I Die'). In between, government initiatives were dismissed, as on The Exploited's 'YOP', and conspiratorial scenarios of unemployed youths being conscripted into the army became rife under the darkening cloud of the Cold War.[51]

Much of this was born from experience. Whereas, in the 1970s, the dole could be seen as a means to facilitate creative activity and effectively help support an alternative lifestyle, so the 1980s limited any sense by which unemployment retained a practical – even optional – quality. Running parallel to the rising number of young unemployed (averaging 25 per cent of sixteen- to nineteen-year-olds by 1985), a series of government schemes were introduced to push those out of work into training and employment.[52] Incremental benefit restrictions were also enforced, culminating in the removal of sixteen- to eighteen-year-olds from the unemployed register in 1988. As a result, the permanency of mass unemployment – especially in those areas north of London devastated by deindustrialisation and the logic of monetarist economics – fed into the popular culture of the period.[53]

In punk terms, the bands and fans who sustained an avowedly punk identity into the 1980s related far closer to the 'dole queue kids' of 1977 folklore than their forebears, adopting self-applied labels such as 'reject' and 'victim' to signal their sense of disenfranchisement. No doubt, Discharge's perception of themselves as social outcasts was reinforced by three members' being fined for receiving earnings while claiming supplementary benefits in 1980–81, proving also that pseud-onyms did not always do the trick.[54] Equally, such a perspective could feed into a glue-, drug- or alcohol-fuelled nihilism that became subject to graphic depiction, both as warning and a glimpse of where des-peration ends. While Action Pact urged young punks to throw away their 'Suicide Bag' and fight back, the A-Heads' 'Dying Man' had gone past the point of no return: hiding in doorways, riddled with self-pity, addicted to the glue.[55] More typically, punk bands simply registered their protest, documenting and dramatising the frustrations of a gen-eration struggling to adapt to a shifting socioeconomic environment over which they felt no control. 'We're just part of an experiment', Anti Pasti's nineteen-year-old Will Hoon stated in 1981 with some insight. 'Monetarism is being tried out on us. And I don't wanna be a guinea pig'.[56]

There was a parallel narrative. From the outset, punk-informed protest set itself as much against the tedium and futility of work as it did against unemployment per se. One consequence of the postwar consensus was to broaden further education opportunities and provide sufficient welfare provision for the young working class and disaffected middle class to step outside the '9-to-5' grind and gain perspective on it. Forming a band offered a means to defer – maybe even escape from – the regimented toil of an 'ordinary life', with punk's import stemming in part from its recovering access to pop's medium. The Jam, Paul Weller explained, originated from the fact that 'you wake up one morning and you don't wanna go and work in a poxy factory'.[57] Steve Diggle, too, joined Buzzcocks after experiencing the working alterna-tive. '[I] decided I'd never work again in my life', he told the *NME*. 'What I was going to do was read and play guitar, do all the things I wanted to do. Do artistic things …'[58] In tune with Simon Frith's notion of punk bohemia, Mick Jones ruminated on signing-on to supplement his art school grant by insisting that being on the dole was only 'hard if you've been conditioned to think you've gotta have a job'.[59]

As this suggests, the stultifying effect of employment provided a constant of punk-informed social realism. The Fall's 'Industrial Estate' captured its subject's bleak surroundings via stark observation ('and the crap in the air will fuck up your face'), culminating in a Valium prescription for depression. Sham 69's 'I Don't Wanna' was equally curt, refuting both a life of work and the dole on route to a gold-watch pension sign-off and a council flat coffin 'up in the sky'.[60] More eloquently, perhaps, The Jam, whose songs included several character portraits of the aspiring petty-bourgeoisie ('Mr Clean', 'Man in the Corner Shop'), released 'Just Who Is the Five O'clock Hero' as a single in 1982, a record that offered a snapshot of an ageing factory worker, always tired and forever poor, locked into a living death. The Subhumans, too, followed the day-cycle of a beleaguered worker on their 'Get to Work on Time', as did The Fakes, whose 'Production' comprised a plodding, clock-watching dirge to the factory and back. From Manchester, The Mothmen issued 'Factory/Teapoint/Factory' in 1980, a song with a recorded canteen break sandwiched between its metronomic portrait of life on a production line. The Wall, meanwhile, debuted with 'New Way', a single that portrayed technological change as a conduit for mechanised slave labour, a subject implicit in Steve Ignorant's Crass-rant about his home town of Dagenham's Ford factory ('End Result'). Or, to get really blunt about it, The Maniacs wrote an unreleased song called 'I Don't Wanna Go To Work' that combined class insight ('I've had enough of this, working for the capitalist') with trademark punk insolence ('I just want to get pissed').[61]

Workplace politics were occasionally tackled. Poet-ranters such as Oi! The Comrade delivered by turn angry and humorous diatribes against the 'Guvnor's Man' and exploitative employment.[62] Not dissimilarly, The Business' 'National Insurance Blacklist' exposed the persecution of militant workers in the building trade, while the Redskins espoused the importance of trade unionism and played with other punk-inspired bands at numerous gigs in support of striking workers up to and throughout the 1984–5 miners' dispute. By then, however, any focus on work tended to fuse with the deepening problem of unemployment. Thus, in 1980–81, as unemployed rates passed 2 million, so the Angelic Upstarts' north-east roots were explored in paeans to the mining and dockyard communities from where the band came and an album, 2,000,000 Voices (1981), that referenced back to the Depression of the 1930s. Mensi even presented a 1984 Play at Home (Channel 4) documentary that looked into the effect of unemployment on Tyneside.[63]

Such accounts of work and unemployment were generally experiential. But while punk's protest and sense of frustration moved beyond simply 'living for the weekend', its political significance remained diffuse and contested. Simultaneously, therefore, competing theoretical perspectives attempted to concentrate punk's disaffection. From a Marxist point of view, attention focused on the mechanics of labour and capital, as in The Mekons' '32 Weeks', which chartered the relationship between work and consumption via a breakdown of the hours needed to buy a car, a bed, some food and a drink. The extension of market forces into social relations also formed the basis of many a Gang of Four song, while Six Minute War's 'Strike' detailed the class dynamics of industrial struggle ('maximize on profit that's all they want to do/ exploit the working class and that means you').[64] Again, however, the 1980s saw attention shift to unemployment, a problem typically registered as a by-product of Thatcherite economics. So, for example, the Newtown Neurotics indicated the changing mood of the 1970s and 1980s on their 'Living with Unemployment', an update of a Members' song – 'Solitary Confinement' – written in 1978 that told the story of someone moving to London only to get stuck in a bed-sit on low-paid work and a long commute. In the Neurotics' version, released in 1983, the job had been lost, 'working all day long' had become 'sleeping all day long', and the subsequent alienation was no longer a consequence of exploitative labour but part of a Tory plan to subjugate the working class.[65]

Alternately, anarchist and countercultural approaches paved the way to more radical responses. On the one hand, McLaren's situationist roots revealed themselves through Bow Wow Wow, whose 'W.O.R.K.' disavowed the work ethic in favour of 'primitive' pleasures and 'piracy'. Unemployment, McLaren argued, should be embraced as liberation; kids should dress up, fuck, steal and have fun.[66] More seriously, Debord's advice to 'Ne travaillez jamais' [never work] – first daubed across a wall on Paris' Rue de Seine in 1953 – inspired a *Vague* essay by Pete Scott that posited unemployment and a creative 'life on society's outer fringe' as preferable to the drudgery of labour.[67] Indeed, such ideas proved integral to the ideological foundations of punk's anarchist milieus and found regular expression in fanzines such as *Toxic Grafity*: 'As far as I can see work in its present form is nothing but slavery. There must be more to life than this. The myth that work brings purpose and meaning to your life is crap ... who wants to spend fifty-or-so years of your life doing this ... And to think people actually march for the right to do this ... STAY FREE.'[68]

Punk's relationship to unemployment was therefore contained within a broader range of pressures and concerns affecting young people in the late 1970s and early 1980s. The dole queue was a component of punk's dystopian vision and punk-informed bands played unemployed benefit gigs from 1977 onwards.[69] But responses to the problem varied. Famously, to the chagrin of those who interpreted Chelsea's 'Right to Work' as a bold statement in support of the Socialist Workers Party's campaign for jobs, the song was aimed (in part) at restrictive trade union practice.[70] More to the point, working for the 'rat race' and committing to a factory or office job brought into sharp relief the sentiment captured by the situationist-inspired King Mob's graffiti that greeted London commuters each day between Ladbroke Grove and Westbourne Park. Reproduced in Savage's *London's Outrage*, it read: 'same thing day after day – tube-work-diner-work-tube-armchair-tv-sleep-tube-work – how much more can you take: one in ten go mad – one in five cracks up'.[71] 'Kids don't want to just get a job in the system', Poly Styrene of X-Ray Spex said in 1978, being 'pushed around in a factory for 20 years and get a gold watch – they've got more suss now … Nothing much has changed since the days of serfdom except that you get paid a wage, but just enough to make you go back next week'.[72] Nevertheless, the deepening impact of unemployment into the 1980s helped reassert initial readings of punk's motivation. Unemployment was taken up in the music press, including pieces by Garry Bushell, Chris Dean and Ray Lowry, and calls for the government to provide jobs or a future became recurrent slogans.[73] If 'dole queue rock' proved too narrow a description to encompass punk's original impetus, then (the spectre of) unemployment formed at least part of the backdrop to its social realist drama.

What a Wonderful World This Is

Released in late 1978, Sham 69's *That's Life* followed a day in the life of a working-class teenager. The story was irregular: the lead character changes and its fragments do not quite hold together in a coherent whole. Nevertheless, the album provided a compelling piece of punk social realism, what Paul Morley described as a dramatised depiction of youth's social and domestic claustrophobia. 'The sense is that of a person who doesn't control their own life, a feeling we all know'.[74]

The narrative to *That's Life* – later made into a short film for the BBC's *Arena* series – is deliberately simple.[75] The day starts with a missed alarm clock, a moaning mum and an occupied bathroom. There follows a daily commute to a hated job fuelled only by thoughts of the weekend and stoic indignation: 'who gives a damn ... we're all dogsbodies'. But lateness leads to the sack and the rest of the day is spent in the café, bookies and pub trying to salvage *something* from an uncertain future – 'I don't know where I'm going, but I gotta get there soon'. Money is won, drinks are drunk, a girl is met and a fight is squared, before the Sunday morning nightmare starts all over again. 'Where am I?', our hero asks. 'You're at home, where do you think you bleedin' are?', his dad replies.[76]

Formed in 1976, Sham 69 were fronted by Jimmy Pursey, a sinewy motor-mouth who 'thinks as he speaks and speaks as he thinks'.[77] They hailed from Hersham, a small Surrey town that lent the band its name, and were briefly touted as a necessary reaction to punk's descent into stylised pose. Sham 69 'feel like you and me', Danny Baker wrote in *Sniffin' Glue*, 'genuine' street kids sussed to punk's commodification and 'part of what I always thought this lark was about'.[78] Sham were the sound of someone 'screaming at the bastards', Tony Parsons concurred, caught in a state of constant conflict with the 'lifeless, soulless, joyless Establishment Order'.[79] As a result, the band attracted a loyal following cut from their own cloth: 'working-class kids, out of school who [no-one] gives a fuck about', as Gary Hitchcock, a member of the 'Sham Army', put it.[80] Many of these, like Pursey, were ex- or revived skinheads; a few, too, including Hitchcock, found an outlet for their disaffection in fascism and violence. But Sham's politics were never explicit and never aligned. Though Pursey lent support to Rock Against Racism, his focus was on articulating the frustrations of what he understood to be 'ordinary kids', replete with their faults, contradictions and imperfections.[81] The band's early signature tune, 'Song of the Streets', centred on a call-and-response refrain, 'What have we got? Fuck all', with lyrics that rejected the solutions of detested politicians.[82] Instead, Sham 69 rallied round a naïve but heartfelt call for youth cultural unity – 'If the Kids Are United' – that clung to an identity based on spirit and class affinity.

Sham's approach embodied the idea of punk connecting to the lives of those who made, played and listened to rock 'n' roll. This, typically, meant lyrics focused on contemporary everyday concerns

expressed in contemporary everyday language. Relationships, antagonisms, frustrations and anxieties shorn of pop's sheen to be stated
bluntly and unashamedly; the 'kids on the street' recast as an emblem
of pop's provenance. Analogous to Sham 69, therefore, were bands
such as Slaughter and the Dogs and Menace who respectively celebrated 'boot boys' from Wythenshawe and asked 'If we're the working
class why ain't we got jobs?'[83] From Custom House in London's East
End came the Cockney Rejects, eschewing songs about love and politics in favour of tales from the backstreets and the terraces. 'We stand
for punk as bootboy music', a teenage 'Stinky' Turner told *Sounds* in
1980, 'Harringtons, boots, straights, that's what we're all about'.[84]
Cock Sparrer, too, whose early gigs appealed to 'football hooligans,
skinheads and clockwork orange lookalikes', evoked the thrill of a
Saturday afternoon, combining celebrations of youthful exuberance
with an existential fear of the future.[85] On both 'Runnin' Riot' and
'Chip on my Shoulder', they extolled disrupting the 'peace and quiet'
to offset the dreaded tomorrow of mortgages and a life spent 'digging
holes in the road'. 'Getting old sure bothers me', they admitted, 'it bothers me to death'.[86]

    By the 1980s, Sham's prototype had helped pave the way for
Oi!, under whose banner bands such as 4-Skins, The Business and
Infa Riot transmitted both the empowerment and the tensions inherent in the adoption of youth cultural style. If Oi! meant 'punk without the posers' and 'facing up to reality', as The Business' Micky Fitz
insisted, then its lyrical focus combined protest ('Work or Riot', 'Bread
or Blood') with snapshots of working-class life and culture.[87] Local
characters – Jack-the-lads, plastic gangsters, clockwork skinheads –
were immortalised in song; pub conversations about bank holiday
beanos, street fights, petty crime and personal misfortune were set
to a punk backbeat. This was sometimes humorous. From Brighton,
Peter and the Test Tube Babies specialised in tall tales of being banned
from local pubs or getting into scrapes with teds, moped lads and
convincing transvestites. Back in London, The Gymslips provided a
female counterpart to Oi!'s primarily male persona, 'rockin' with the
renees' via odes to the pub's optics and the joys of pie 'n' mash. But
Oi!'s social realism more generally concentrated on the frustrations of
being young, male and working-class. Beneath the bravado lay a sense
of anger and frustration, an existential disaffection with *the state of
things*.

Among the best at expressing this were the Angelic Upstarts, whose songs – 'Teenage Warning', 'I'm an Upstart', 'Leave Me Alone', 'Out of Control' – railed against the teachers, social workers, politicians, police and social structures that seemingly shaped and bound possibilities. Infa Riot, too, sung of cages and catch-22s, portraying lives trapped by circumstance and caught in a game to which the rules were rigged. 'Feel the rage', Lee Wilson sung, 'building up ... breaking out'.[88] Like teenage Arthur Seatons transported from Sillitoe's 1950s Nottingham to the inner-city 1970s and '80s, punk's social realists came of age embittered by the material, political and economic confines that determined their lives.

Not surprisingly, given their shared milieu, the 2-Tone bands that emerged to prominence in 1979 covered similar lyrical concerns. Both Oi! and 2-Tone tapped into youth cultural styles that predated punk (skinheads, rude boys, mod); both claimed street-level credentials; both suffered from the attentions of the far right recruiting among their audience; both celebrated their cultural origins as they registered a protest. Where Oi! aspired to 'having a laugh and having a say', 2-Tone's energy and ska-based sound emphasised its commitment to pleasure in the face of 'too much pressure'.[89]

Coming from the midlands, The Beat, The Selecter and Specials used social realist lyrics to affirm their cross-cultural origins and environment. Anti-Thatcherite diatribes rubbed against tales of subcultural conflict. Tales of grotty nightclubs and unwanted teenage pregnancies gave way to youthful defiance and paeans to fashion. As importantly, the bands' anti-racism was transmitted through words and practice. The 1970s, after all, had seen racial tensions exacerbated by a resurgent NF and the socioeconomic effects of recession. In response, Specials' 'Concrete Jungle' and The Beat's 'Two Swords' captured the merger of territorial, political and racial identities over the decade, while 'Doesn't Make It Alright' and 'Why?' questioned the attitudes of racist elements in the 2-Tone audience. The result was to marry both critique and resolution, forging a cultural politics rooted in the everyday experience of Coventry and Birmingham that found expression in the bands' musical fusion and multiracial composition.[90]

The provincial, or localised, nature of much punk-informed social realism was important. As Russ Bestley has argued, it confirmed a sense of grass-roots authenticity that connected bands to their environment and audience.[91] Local signifiers were used on sleeves; songs engaged with specifically resident concerns; independent labels were formed to document regional scenes. The *Wessex '82* EP may serve as a good example, comprising four bands from the south-west on a local label (Bluurg) wrapped in a sleeve featuring the famous white horse of Westbury Hill. Notably, too, such provincialism marked a disregard for the London-centric media and music industry. By engaging with a 'Nottingham Problem' or documenting a falling out with a local pub landlord ('Black Horse'), Resistance '77 and Cult Maniax displayed their indifference to the potential of pop as a career or business.

Of course, provincialism did not have to be overtly confrontational. The Undertones relayed pop's youthful obsessions – love, lust, fun and dancing – in parochial terms that suggested provenance rather than idealisation: teenage kicks, perfect cousins, chocolate and girls. Coming from Derry, such concerns had political connotations when set against a backdrop of the Troubles. But they also resituated the clichés of pop's lexicon in a way that transformed the ordinary into points of connection. In time, songs about the minutiae of everyday life – about boys and girls, bus stops and rainy Sundays – became standard for an indie pop focused on personal relationships caught at the moment of adolescence.[92]

Punk's tendency to social realism injected new voices and subject matter into popular music. By so doing, feelings and experiences were expressed in ways designed to reassert pop music's relevance to the youth cultures that formed around it. This was often infused with a class sensibility – a street-level riposte to pop's commercial whimsy. In Centre for Contemporary Cultural Studies terms, it may be seen as a 'magical' solution to broader socioeconomic oppressions, a means of dealing with the boredom and frustration that punk described.[93] Certainly, some of those involved in punk and 2-Tone recognised it as such. 'Our music is a solution', Joe Strummer said, 'because I don't have to get drunk every night and go around kicking people and smashing up phone boxes … [like] Paul [Simonon] used to do'.[94] The Selecter's Pauline Black sung of teaching 'myself a new philosophy' as 2-Tone lived out the racial and cultural unity it espoused in the face of political and socioeconomic stresses.[95] For Paul Weller, it meant taking 'everyday experience' and turning 'it into art', something The Jam did in ways that combined evocative depictions of British life with an underlying sense of critique. From the late-night terrors of the London Underground to class conflict and the ideological pyres of Thatcherism,

The Jam's run of 7-inch singles through 1977–82 embodied the feelings and effects of Britain's changing socioeconomic landscape. On 'Town Called Malice' especially, Weller balanced pop's joy de vivre with a sad vision of social dislocation. 'It's enough to make you stop believing', he sang over a furious Motown beat, as the tears came 'fast and furious' and the choice between beer and the kids' new gear became the soundtrack for *Top of the Pops*' number one spot in the early weeks of 1982.[96]

Dirt Behind the Daydream

There were darker and stranger components to punk-informed realism. From the outset, punk gave rise to tendencies keen to recover the marginal and the suppressed, to scrape away the veneer of British propriety to reveal what lay beneath. Among McLaren and Westwood's early designs were images of sexual transgression, blasphemy, criminality and political extremity. Naked cowboys, bare breasts, fetish wear and pornographic images were displayed to break down the boundaries of fascination and repulsion, drawing from Wilhelm Reich's ideas of sexual liberation to expose the tensions between private and public desire.[97] Not dissimilarly, inverted crucifixes, swastikas and anarchist slogans coexisted to provoke and subvert towards some kind of reaction. According to McLaren, the ideal customer of SEX and Seditionaries was a sixteen-year-old girl from the suburbs who bought a rubber mini-skirt at the weekend to wear to work on the Monday.[98]

Again, such an approach overlapped with the industrial culture of Throbbing Gristle, Cabaret Voltaire and others, for whom the 'reality' constructed by forces of social and political control (politics, media, religion, family, work, etc.) could be challenged through the presentation of behaviours that rubbed against the grain of supposed normality.[99] To this end, punk and industrial culture shared an interest in the abject and the taboo, in violence and the profane, subjects that could shock and disrupt the fragile equilibriums of modern society. Crucially, too, both tended – or claimed – to draw their alternative realities from life itself.

There are numerous examples. Where the Sex Pistols' 'Bodies' described the gurgling bloody mess of an abortion via the life-story of a fan suffering from severe mental illness, Lydon's early PiL lyrics recounted media reports of exorcism and rape.[100] Siouxsie and the

Banshees claimed to find inspiration for their macabre songs of mental breakdown ('Suburban Relapse'), alienation ('Jigsaw Feeling') and necrophilia ('Carcass') in the tabloids and obscure corners of popular culture. '[The] bloke who put his leg on the railway line because he wanted to claim more money as a war hero', Siouxsie reflected, and 'the woman who wheeled a chopped-up body around in a pram. It's all there in *The Sun* every day.'[101] Like the Velvet Underground, whose influence on the band was manifest, the Banshees subverted the mores of popular music, producing 'chilling vignettes of minor atrocities and gruesome indulgences, of frustration or unrequited love. From the dark side of life, grinning, perverted', they specialised in revealing 'ugly truths … set against the pointlessness of life.'[102]

Throbbing Gristle's approach was more conceptual, drawing from ideas honed in the performance work of COUM Transmissions. Back in 1975, COUM had committed to revealing the 'secret fears and neuroses' of society, exposing repressed emotions and desires as a means to confront prevailing social values.[103] Throbbing Gristle took this on, initially producing a harsh, grinding noise through which a fascination with the body and mechanisms of social control served as a commentary on both the 'savage realities' of modernity and the sanitised projections of 'real life' disseminated by the media.[104] Over a series of records, videos, newsletters and live performance, detailed depictions of murder, violence, pain, the Holocaust and sexual taboo coalesced in a gruesome tableau that dared the listener/viewer to confront or retreat. A subsequent group, Coil, formed by John Balance (Geoff Burton) with Peter Christopherson in 1983, even issued an album, *Scatology* (1984), that journeyed deep into the recesses of humanity's base instincts, culminating in a story of sexual caprophagy. 'Gold and excrement are akin in the subconscious', the sleevenotes quoted from Salvador Dali, pointing the way to the group's own dark obsessions and 'private mythology'.[105]

Wars past and envisaged provided subject matter and imagery for countless record sleeves, fanzines and posters. Just as the Second World War and the horrors of Nazism nurtured a morbid interest in those wishing to explore the extremes of humankind, so the Cold War and its nuclear endgame informed the anti-militarist politics of punk over the 1980s.[106] Discharge, in particular, engaged with the 'realities of war', producing a series of records that gruesomely depicted the effects of nuclear destruction or military intervention: 'men, women and children cry and scream in pain, wounded by bomb splinters/

Streets littered with maimed and slaughtered in rigid pathetic heaps'.[107] Murderers, maniacs and madness likewise weaved their way through the punk-informed canon. The Cambridge Rapist (Peter Cook), Yorkshire Ripper (Peter Sutcliffe) and Moors Murderers (Ian Brady and Myra Hindley) provided pertinent signifiers of society's disturbing underbelly, creeping their way into SEX, Seditionaries, band names and the music of Throbbing Gristle, Siouxsie and the Banshees, The Exploited and Sutcliffe Jugend.[108] Less gratuitously, perhaps, juxtapositions of real life horror and media-drawn promises of a better tomorrow became a staple of songs and fanzine collage. The dirt behind the daydream, Gang of Four called it, as they undercut advertising lingo with references to Britain's war in Ireland and the onset of North Sea oil.[109]

Things got messy if the propensity to shock fell out of context. A fascination with the macabre could also drift into fantasy, relinquishing any claim to realism in favour of schlock horror or, later, the romantic darklands of what became goth. Equally, where band names such as The Moors Murderers or Raped began to push at the boundaries of taste with barely a hint of dissident intent beyond the desire to offend, then records such as Stench's 'Raspberry Cripple' or Chaotic Dischord's 'And There Wuz Cows' plunged deep into the mire. To be sure, the giddy thrill of saying-the-unsayable – or wearing-the-unwearable – struck a chord with teenagers looking to provoke a reaction.[110] But swastikas, in particular, retained a potency for reasons that could not be so easily disarmed when projected away from Seditionaries' clashing symbols or the archly camp Weimar references of the Bromley contingent.[111] Several bands were accused of harbouring Nazi sympathies as a result of using imagery drawn from the Third Reich. Most famously, perhaps, Joy Division's name (taken from a book, *House of Dolls*, which depicted sex slavery in a concentration camp) and debut EP (its sleeve featuring a Hitler Youth drummer boy) prompted rumours of fascist leanings.[112]

Certainly, the line between fascination and fetishisation could all too easily be crossed. If the ambiguous symbolism presented by Joy Division, The Skids, Theatre of Hate and others was noted on the far right and prone to misinterpretation, then Death in June's obsession with National Socialist history led to at least one member (Tony Wakeford) engaging with active fascist politics.[113] Groups like Whitehouse – formed by erstwhile Essential Logic guitarist William

Bennett with the aim of being 'violently uncompromising, both musically and lyrically' – repudiated the critical detachment retained by Throbbing Gristle, dedicating their records of harsh 'power electronics' to serial killers and filling their fanzines with texts of rape and murder.[114] Predictably, Whitehouse's Come Organisation adopted a swastika-like symbol and built records around fascist language and iconography (*Buchenweld*, *New Britain*, *Für Ilse Koch*), tracing a line from the Marquis de Sade to the death camps and the extremes of human cruelty.[115] The results were mixed: disturbing, repulsive, fascinating and juvenile in about equal measure.[116]

As this suggests, an interest in the abject could lead to dubious ends. Simultaneously, however, punk stimulated transformative impulses that sought out the absurdities of everyday life, facilitating a social *surrealism* rooted in the contemporary but attuned to the incongruities that lurked beneath any semblance of 'normality'. Best of all were The Fall, emerging from Prestwich as 1976 turned to 1977. Musically, The Fall recognised the potential to break down and reconstitute popular music in the wake of punk's emergence. The band's sound combined rock 'n' roll primitivism with disciplined repetition, 'mistreating instruments' to a get a 'feeling over', as Mark E. Smith put it.[117] All affectation was removed. Their songs contained no solos or musical frills; records were produced to emphasise the emergent rawness of their content, rejecting the sheen of studio production in favour of a discordant, deliberately distorted sound. Fall songs appeared caught in what Michael Goddard and Benjamin Halligan have described as 'a state of becoming', unruly, chaotic, perpetually mutating.[118] Stylistically, too, the band projected an anti-image, adopting none of punk's sartorial props and distancing themselves from the expectations of pop or rock presentation. Live, the band was uncommunicative and functional; the music press, music industry and most contemporary bands were held in disdain. Record sleeves were cut 'n' pasted, covered in Smith's scrawl as if to trash any reverence afforded to rock's product status. Indeed, The Fall's uncompromising approach and commitment to perpetual creativity was interpreted by Smith to mean his band were among the 'only ones who represented what the whole thing [punk] was supposed to be'.[119]

Smith remains one of rock's most innovative lyricists. From the outset, his words, accent and delivery located The Fall within their regional and socioeconomic context while simultaneously reimagining the environments they described. Just as photos and videos of the band were typically taken in situ (Prestwich streets and pubs), so Smith's lyrics referred to local and contemporary signifiers that connected to a particular time and place: fags, pubs, industrial estates, Hovis adverts, Kwik Save, CB radio, Manchester parks, Prestwich halls, and so forth. In their articulation, however, Smith's words complemented the band's sound, fragmenting narratives and cultural critiques into unique patterns of language and imagery. The songs' characters were often grotesques, such as 'Fiery Jack', an amphetamine-ravaged pub intellect, forty five years old and living off pies as he drinks, thinks and burns.[120] Humdrum locales were transformed into strange worlds that filtered literary influences such as M. R. James, H. P. Lovecraft, Malcolm Lowry and Arthur Machen through Smith's own speed-and-alcohol fuelled imagination.[121] The effect was to transform the ordinary into the extraordinary, contesting and disrupting preconceptions by undermining their apparent rationale. In other words, Smith claimed and defended his proudly working-class heritage against the commercial, cosmopolitan and intellectual forces that conspired to dilute it: 'Northern white crap that talks back'.[122]

Other bands did similar. The Prefects morphed into The Nightingales, allowing Robert Lloyd to perfect his tales of urban ospreys and crafty fags. The Membranes, from Blackpool, sung of tatty seaside towns and Spike Milligan's tape recorder. A Witness, Bogshed and The Three Johns followed suit, mangling rock 'n' roll's form while combining a pub-honed wit with lyrics that found the surreal amidst the mundane. Most comparable to Smith, perhaps, was John Cooper-Clarke, the Salford poet who came to prominence in tandem with The Fall. Cooper-Clarke was twenty-eight in 1977, having honed his craft in northern clubs (frequented by young pre-Fall members) and thereby connecting to aspects of the pre-punk counterculture. Nevertheless, he recognised in punk an interest in words and ideas, appreciating its attempts to expand rock's lexicon and deconstruct its formulas. 'It's the nearest thing that there's ever been ... to the working classes going into areas like surrealism and Dada ... It only widens your perspective ... The Pistols put you in a context where it's possible to understand more. I mean, it's probably a cliché now, but words like fascist and fascism jumped out. Things like that just weren't in pop songs'.[123]

Like Smith, Cooper-Clarke surveyed and transformed his environment. His poems could be humorous and fantastical, such as '(I

Married a) Monster from Outer Space', but always rooted – linguisti-
cally and verbally – in recognisably urban locales full of buses, dirt,
concrete and disease.[124] His flights of imagination were underpinned
by a social critique informed by the structural changes affecting his
native Salford. Thus, among his most well-known poems, 'Evidently
Chickentown' and 'Beasley Street' travel deep into the distresses of
everyday life, depicting poverty and decay via evocative descriptions of
sights, sounds, people and smells.[125]

     The reportage and realism that signalled punk's engagement
with the world it was born into developed in distinct ways. The path
from The Clash's 'White Riot' to Bogshed's 'Fat Lad Exam Failure' was
hardly a straight line. Many of those informed by punk's emergence
quickly shed any commitment to a predetermined musical form or
sense of style even as they retained comparable attitudes and lyrical
concerns. In other words, the diverse sounds and cultures that evolved
from 1976 shared an aversion to the banal platitudes of much rock
'n' roll and a conviction that popular music should reflect and inform
the lives of those who made and listened to it. Motivations varied of
course. Where Throbbing Gristle sought to confront their audience,
Tom Robinson endeavoured to raise political consciousness. Where
Sham 69 rallied in celebratory protest, The Fall scrambled preconceptions and stimulated imaginations. Even then, there remained a sense
by which the cultural spaces opened up by punk should hold a relevance to recognisable places, events and life-as-lived. More to the
point, beneath the anger, abjection and absurdity lay hint of an even
darker stimulus: a boredom born of alienation and despair.

4 SUBURBAN RELAPSE: THE POLITICS OF BOREDOM

You're left to expect nothing. You get nothing. You start off in school and they take your soul away. They take your brains away; you're not allowed to have an opinion that differs from theirs. You've got to think what they tell you to think. So when you leave school, your only future is getting married. And by the time you're about 29, and you've got two kids, you just want to commit suicide.[1]

Johnny Rotten (1977)

And from ground zero there are only two ways out, two kinds of nihilism: active and passive.[2]

Raoul Vaneigem (1967)

Released in early 1977, Buzzcocks' *Spiral Scratch* EP proved significant for a number of reasons. It signalled punk's evolution beyond London and confirmed Manchester's position as a vibrant hub of the emergent new wave. It provided an archetype for punk's do-it-yourself (DIY) culture, comprising four tracks captured 'live' over a single day and then self-released in a cheaply pressed sleeve that detailed the recording process. Musically, too, the EP embodied punk's opposition to the conventions of most mainstream rock and pop. Its production, by Martin 'Zero' Hannett, was trebly and energetic; its songs were short and fast, stripped down to their essence without recourse to musical flourish. The one discernible guitar solo on the record was in fact an anti-solo: two discordant notes repeated over and over in a deliberate parody of virtuosity.[3]

As important as the EP's form, however, was its lyrical content. That is, *Spiral Scratch* documented what Howard Devoto described in

1977 as the 'trials and tribulations of boredom, waiting and nascent enlightenment'.[4] Not only did the record exude a sense of urgency in its sound and presentation, as if Buzzcocks were impatient with the processes of becoming a 'proper' band recording a 'proper' 7-inch single, but its lyrics explored the ennui of everyday life. 'Breakdown' depicted a personality fragmenting into bits, a collapse born not of 'austerity' but 'all these livid things you never get to touch'. 'Time's Up' began in a supermarket queue before charting moments of time passing in the post office, smoking, in a waiting room, hanging around for a friend. 'Boredom' expressed the alienating effects of a life transformed into representation: 'Now I'm living in this movie, but it doesn't move me'. In less than ten minutes, the EP offered a playful (its catalogue number – ORG-1 – was inspired by Wilhelm Reich) but simultaneously existential rumination on contemporary life.[5]

The themes that ran through *Spiral Scratch* – alienation, boredom, frustration, mental breakdown – were integral to punk's aesthetic. They dove-tailed neatly with the 'politics of boredom' that McLaren discerned as the root of the Sex Pistols' delinquent discontent.[6] They also helped connect the frustrations of teenage angst with the more cerebral analyses that framed punk's development. In boredom, the alienation of consumerism and a world projected through media-image collided with the adolescent urge to break free and live. Thus, the Sex Pistols' cover of The Stooges' 'No Fun' was released on the b-side of a record ('Pretty Vacant') housed in a sleeve featuring the image of two buses heading to 'nowhere' and 'boredom'.[7] Where the situationist Raoul Vaneigem spoke of 'stifling mediocrity and this absence of passion' in a world defined through product and simulation, so Johnny Rotten could look out over London and bemoan there being 'nowhere to go'.[8]

As this suggests, boredom appeared to be both stimulus and explanation for punk's dissatisfaction. It soon became a punk trope, cropping up in song titles, interviews and fanzines.[9] So, for example, The Clash insisted London burned with boredom and that they were bored of the USA; The Adverts depicted 'Bored Teenagers' looking for 'emotional rages' to 'fill the vacuum'; The Damned were bored with school; Slaughter and the Dogs were bored of druggy hippies; The Slits feared 'A Boring Life'; Crass lamented the boring media; Honey Bane dreaded 'Boring Conversations' and The Prats just had nothing to do.[10] Amidst punk's complex semiotics, boredom became a default setting.

'Johnny Rotten looks bored', Caroline Coon noted in August 1976, with an 'emphasis on the word "looks"', his demeanour reflecting a cultural malaise that the Sex Pistols resolved to overturn.[11]

The cause and effect of punk's boredom varied. On the one hand it suggested a recognisably teenage riposte to a world not of one's own making. It also carried generational overtones in its rejection of parental society and, given punk's cultural context, the rock 'n' roll legacy of the 1960s. More deeply, it challenged the presumptions of modern consumer capitalism, disavowing the delights and distractions of things bought, sold and idealised via media simulacrum. In the midst of the 1970s and 1980s, moreover, it complemented the sense of Britain falling into disrepair. With socioeconomic (and imperial) dislocation came dereliction and despondency.

On the other hand, boredom gave hint towards a prognosis of punk's condition – an explanation for the anxieties, breakdowns and alienation explored on *Spiral Scratch* and in countless punk songs and images thereafter. For punk was not only bored, it was 'messed up', 'screwed up', 'fucked up' and 'sick'.[12] And once the symptoms had been described and displayed, so they were also diagnosed. First, of course, the answer was sought in the immediate socioeconomic and cultural environment from which punk emerged: 'dole queue rock' and the state of rock 'n' roll. A closer look, however, revealed punk's ailments to stem from deeper trauma. It was, after all, nurtured as much behind the hedge-lined streets of suburbia as beneath the urban underpass, in the bedroom as well as the art school and backstreet. Punk's import and influence communicated not just in British cities, but in the small towns, new towns and provincial back waters. Consequently, beyond pop's ongoing concern with love-sick lusting and other teenage urges, punk's angsty and antsy expression began to ruminate on life itself.

Punk's boredom enveloped a gamut of concerns and emotions: social alienation, the stifling ordinariness of everyday life, the ramifications of 'No Future'. Simultaneously, dialectically even, boredom served as motivation. Returning to Devoto, he later admitted to Nick Kent that 'I get bored very easily and that boredom can act as a catalyst for me to suddenly conceive and execute a new vocation ... In fact, negative drive was always what I believe the punk ethic was about'.[13] Beyond the repercussions of rock 'n' roll's entering middle-age and the deleterious effects of broader socioeconomic change, punk's cultural critique encompassed deeper reflections on the pain of existence. In response, to quote Jamie Reid's disjointed notes for a Sex Pistols book that never materialised, punk marked an attempt to '[turn] and utilise violence from frustration and boredom, make it positive and directional to destroy the environment, packaged culture, make it more interesting. Take on that medium which exists and its machine and give it a new life – revitalising – kids become rock 'n' roll ... the Intention has grabbed their imagination. Fired to make their own culture – music used as a launching pad for attitudes [sic]'.[14]

New Towns, Small Towns and Sweet Suburbia

For all its inner-city rhetoric and urban imagery, punk was also the sound of the suburbs. In fact, The Members' well-known song of the same name took its inspiration from Camberley, a commuter town located to the west of London from wherein the stereotypes of sub-urban life were easily drawn upon: the gendered family unit, with mother in the kitchen cooking Sunday dinner, father washing his car, teenage son in his bedroom; the quiet stillness of home-lined streets broken only by the roar of Heathrow jets and the nearby Broadmoor hospital siren being tested every Monday in suitably punctual fash-ion. Next door, an old woman lives out her days alone in a house she has not left since her husband died. Nearby, people trudge through a shopping precinct as kids loiter in mild intimidation. 'Johnny', mean-while, stares from his window into nothingness, breaking the bore-dom by practising his 'punk rock electric guitar' and joining – or maybe just dreaming of joining – a group to play at the local youth club.[15]

Caustic reflections on suburbia have long found expression in British culture.[16] From the poetry of Stevie Smith through the comedy of Tony Hancock and the novels of J. G. Ballard, the suburbs appear to embody a very particular sensibility. As if caught between somewhere and nowhere, they represent a site of deluded aspiration; a place to move to or escape from, where the upwardly mobile (or relocated) working class meet the middle class to often ill effect. Behind the archi-tectural uniformity and surface calm lurk psychological dramas and shackled ambitions. Or, put another way, the suburbs appear to offer a superficial meshing of town and country signified by trimmed hedges and twitching net curtains hung to conceal inner turmoils born of lone-liness, repressed sexualities, prejudice and addiction.[17]

Simultaneously, as Michael Bracewell and others have recognised, British pop music has oft been fuelled by such 'suburban sensibilities'.[18] '[The] violence of English talent incubates in the frustrations of suburbia or the bland estates on the edges of indifferent conurbations. What turns a spotty Mod into a glorious pop hero is not the glamour of London but the confines of his dismal bedroom in the suburbs'.[19] And punk proved no different. 'I hated suburbia', Siouxsie Sioux told Jon Savage. 'I thought it was small and narrow-minded'.[20] In response, Siouxsie – alongside friends such as Steve Severin, Simon Barker, Sharon Hayman, Bertie Marshall [Berlin] and Simone Thomas – wilfully provoked the veneer of suburban respectability. As the so-called Bromley contingent, they sought to escape the cloying ordinariness of the Kent suburbs through stylistic, sexual and artistic transgression. Like Jordan, commuting to London from Seaford dressed in the fetish-wear she helped sell in SEX, their swastikas, sexualities and decadence were weapons in a struggle.[21]

But what are we really thinking about here? As inferred earlier, the notion of suburbia comes with presumptions conceived and defined as much in the cultural mindscape as on the ground.[22] To imagine 'the suburbs' is to imagine tidy gardens, white-collar/middle class, neat rows of semidetached houses in close proximity to London. During the 1970s, the suburbs were personified in such recognisable television characters as Reggie Perrin, Beverly Moss, Jeffrey Fourmile and Margo Leadbetter, their comedic value mocking but nevertheless affirming the prevailing sense by which home, family and social status served as the drivers to life's ambition.[23] And yet, the impulses attributed to pop's suburban sensibility – essentially a pining for authentic experience signified by 'the city' (where *things happen*) or the means to transcend the mundanity of everyday life – merge very easily into those of provincial Britain more generally: the small towns, new towns, villages and cities bound by their own drab peripheries.[24] As importantly, any correlation between suburbia and middle-class aspiration/disaffection risks reducing the desire to challenge, circumnavigate or escape the hegemonic values of a standardised life to a particular social group.[25] This may work well with regard to Siouxsie and the Banshees or the young Robert Smith plotting The Cure from his parents' 'comfortable' house in Crawley.[26] But it sits less easily with Paul Weller's eulogies to London as viewed from his working-class home in Woking, or Morrissey's slow emergence from his council house bedroom in Stretford.[27] In other words, the suburbia of the cultural imagination does not necessarily reflect Britain's shifting demographic, even as it does provide space to explore the social tensions contained within it.[28]

There is, after all, a broader context to consider. Britain's topography changed notably from 1945. The slum clearances of the prewar period continued thereafter, giving way to housing estates and suburban enclaves of variable quality. The expansion of service industries relative to a decline in industrial labour assisted the transformation of landscape as well as identity. A steady drift in population took place, from the urban centre to the boundary, as new towns flowered and the suburbs extended to provide homes for both working- and middle-class families.[29] London alone saw its population decrease by more than a million between 1961 and 1981, presaging a period of inner-city decay signified by crumbling Victorian terraces, sink estates and desolate docklands. Across Britain's seven conurbations, the urban population fell by some 1.8 million over the same period.[30] Elsewhere, town planners reimagined urban spaces as retail precincts and commuter corridors, while population growth led to overspill and the strictures of government spending ensured Britain's postwar Jerusalem did not always match the 'metro-land' or 'garden city' image that helped provide the suburban template.[31] True, improved living standards and advances in transport helped ease the transition. For many, the promise of home ownership and escape from the grime of city living remained a measure of progress. But while suburbanisation, technology and consumerism transformed the home lives and leisure patterns of many, so residual cultural practices and associated tensions endured.[32] The entrapment of a (young) life lived on the edge of *somewhere* or deep in a housing estate could lead easily to frustration. Steve Williams, recalling his pre-Steve Ignorant days living on the Heath Park estate in Dagenham, later wrote of the 'dead time' spent pacing his mother's flat as a teenager.

> [As] with most things in the suburbs it was sterile. Mind-numbingly sterile … Boredom and monotony. Monotony and boredom. Day after day after sodding drawn-out day … I couldn't go out because I didn't have a front door key, so I'd wander through the flat. Lost and aimless. Kitchen, living room, bedroom. Kitchen, living room, bedroom. Kitchen, living-room, bedroom. Hour after hour. Or I'd stand and stare out of the window … watching the streetlights come on and the streets empty … I'd stand there in an empty flat looking at empty streets in an empty estate.[33]

Equally, of course, the modernist vision that drove much post-war town planning had provoked fierce reaction by the 1970s.[34] Just as conservatives and conservationists found offence in the functional nature of housing 'units' and the demolition that accompanied urban renewal, so others began to recognise processes of social atomisation and alienation beneath the façade.[35] It was not by accident that Jamie Reid nurtured his disaffection in Croydon, from where copies of *Suburban Press* rehearsed punk's politics of boredom in samizdat-style early in the 1970s. Across six issues, Reid interspersed images of suburban landscapes, living spaces and consumer goods with text that conflated the drab ordinariness of suburbia with consumption and alienation:

> We feel isolated. Our isolation is reflected in both the physical and mental environments in which we live. The destruction of the city is almost complete. The exploitation and redevelopment of the city to make way for more offices, expensive flats and yachting marinas, has brought a gradual erosion of urban/communal life. This in turn has created a major shift of population to outer suburbs, thus alienating people from their traditional city relationship. The oral traditions of language and communication have been substituted by new media languages.[36]

Indeed, many of the fanzines that flourished from late 1976 originated in suburban bedrooms, cut 'n' pasted by young teenagers living on the outer limits of an urban sprawl. Some even displayed their 'suburban sensibilities' in their titles: *Apathy in Ilford*, *Suburban Revolt*, *Surrey's Burning*, *Surrey Vomet*.

True to form, punk's cultural critique tended to explore the bleaker recesses of the suburban and small-town experience. Most obviously, the bland conformity of the suburbs' proposed utopia was exposed. 'This could be heaven', John Lydon sang on PiL's 'No Birds' (having already shown his disdain for suburbia with the Sex Pistols' 'Satellite'), equating the 'planned idle luxury' of ordered lawns with 'well-intentioned rules' that 'dignify a daily code' of 'standard views'.[37] From Dunfermline, The Skids offered a rather different take on 'Sweet Suburbia' via a lyrical jigsaw that alluded to a modern high-rise located on an 'open plain' beneath the Forth Road Bridge. Inside, cocooned in concrete boxes, the nameless occupants lived, mated and died. Back in Surrey, meanwhile, Action Pact recorded an ode to their hometown Stanwell in 1982, a non-descript place like many others across the country ('sweet suburbia is all the same'). Underlying class distinctions and generational tensions were noted, as 'precious lawns' were mown and youthful boredom expressed itself in graffiti scrawl.[38]

Not dissimilarly, a number of punk bands presented Britain's 'new towns' as the epicentre of suburban alienation. Facilitated by the New Towns Act of 1946, places such as Harlow, Hatfield, Livingston, Stevenage and Telford were built around existing locales to rehouse communities bombed during the war or transferred following slum clearance. In time they further accommodated those who aspired to leave the city behind and embrace the planned contours of modern housing, roadways and leisure facilities. By the mid-1970s, Milton Keynes – with its grid system designed to ensure maximum consumer and commuter comfort – signalled the latest new town ideal.[39]

Again, Jamie Reid had rehearsed a punk critique of new-town life through his Suburban Press in the early 1970s, producing a mock-advert to promote 'A New Town Like the Old Town – but New!' With its promise of safe living ('troublemakers need not apply') and shopping zones to 'spend the fruits of your increased productivity in total secu-rity', the poster mimicked the sterile vision proffered by the publicity that announced Milton Keynes' development.[40] Thereafter, The Slits' 'New Town' honed in on the low-level violence and drug-taking that too often passed as a youthful response to boredom. The Now, from Peterborough (designated a new town in 1967), sung of 'Development Corporations' producing facile schemes for social improvement, while Skroteez immortalised the Scottish new town of Livingston on their 1982 *Overspill* EP (Figure 4.1). Its lead track, 'Newtown', contrasted the promise of a 'new life' with the reality of unemployment and noth-ing to do. 'They should blow it all up, or else burn it all down', the band suggested in faint echo of John Betjeman's 'solution' for Slough.[41]

One of the most sustained critiques came from the Newtown Neurotics, whose name referred to their hometown of Harlow and inspired a song, 'Newtown People', which depicted a soulless popula-tion lost in a maze of identikit housing and grey concrete. Vandalism and glue offered one respite; submission to ennui another. 'You have to walk for half an hour … to get from one pub to another', Steve Drewett complained in one of a series of interviews that described the frustra-tions of the new town experience. 'Everything is so spaced out. Even the main railway station's a good few miles away from the town centre. It's so inhospitable for anyone coming to visit'. Like other new towns, Harlow comprised 'very shiny glass, lots of concrete and millions of

Figure 4.1 Skroteez, *Overspill* EP (Square Anarchy Music, 1982).

roundabouts', Colin Dredd [Colin Masters] continued. 'It's the town to come to if you want to buy shoes or jewellery or sports clothes, or go to discos'.[42]

More generally, perhaps, the cosy home life idealised through suburbia provided a perennial source of punk disaffection, with pictures of living rooms and household appliances decorating many a record cover, poster or fanzine spread.[43] This reached its apotheosis in the early 1980s among punk's anarchist cadre, for whom the family home represented a cosseted incubator of gendered power politics. The second issue of Crass' *International Anthem* (1979) was themed around 'domestic violence', comprising Gee Vaucher's stark juxtapositions of male and female stereotypes culled from advertisements and détourned to distort their faux-suburban setting.[44] Likewise, the Poison Girls' *Hex* (1979) was largely dedicated to exploring the pressures contained within the constructs of the nuclear family. In a vein similar to Siouxsie and the Banshees' 'Suburban Relapse' ('I was washing up the dishes … when my string snapped'), Vi Subversa drew from her own experience as a mother in her forties to chart how the pressures of a 'normal day' could lead to breakdown: 'Peel the onions, ask no questions, hit the baby, stop it screaming …, normal normal, crisis crisis'. By the album's end, the deceit of domestic bliss had led to Valium, with the weekly shop viewed through a blur broken only by the odd 'reality attack'. 'Be strong', Subversa urged, 'nothing takes the pain away for long'.[45]

Of course, the male suburbanite was also targeted across punk's varied cultures. Where The Jam's 'Smithers-Jones' revolved around the fragile existence of a suburban drone on the 8 a.m. train, wife, kids and car at home, never late, always diligent, but easily laid-off by his sun-tanned boss, so Adam and the Ants' 'Cartrouble' mocked the suburban male's preference for 'polishing the chrome' (while all the 'mothers and the sisters and the babies, sit and rot at home').[46] The Anti-Nowhere League even named themselves in opposition to those the band defined as 'somebody who gives up on life at a very early age and becomes totally non-existent. Nowheres get married early and finish their lives. They've got no future'.[47] Soft Cell, meanwhile, debuted with an EP, *Mutant Moments* (1980), that included a bleak industrial dirge dissecting the 'Frustration' of a balding 'ordinary bloke' stuck in a domestic straightjacket ('I want to die').[48] In short, domesticity and the suburban represented a punk dystopia: a panorama of tedium and banality wherein 'your future dream is a shopping scheme'.[49]

Finally, a number of bands reapplied the motifs of punk's suburban sensibility to document the frustrations of life in the provinces.[50] Some revelled in tales of small-town violence and conformity, with The Mob's 'Witch Hunt' standing out as a particularly astute dissection of provincial conservatism 'stubbing out progress where seeds are sewn, killing off anything that's not quite known'.[51] Others simply restated the boredom punk served as a response to. Among the hundreds of DIY singles produced from 1977 came roughly hewn elegies to small towns defined by their languor. The Head, perhaps, put it most succinctly on their 'Nothing to Do in a Town Like Leatherhead' single from 1980. But similar sentiments may be found on the Nuclear Socketts' 'Shadow on the Map' (an oblique reference to their hometown of King's Lynn) or the 'O' Level's depiction of East Sheen as a 'dirty shit hole'.[52]

Such expressions of provincial disaffection were sometimes more snotty belligerence than deep-set angst, their gleeful negation all part of punk's provocative fun. But complex reflections also emerged. New Model Army, formed in Bradford in 1980, wrote a series of songs exploring the claustrophobia of life beyond London's glittering allure. 'Smalltown England', in particular, picked its way through a provincial night out, capturing the routines, petty squabbles and simmering animosities that fuelled the violence of a weekend. 'Is it a crime to want something else?' Justin Sullivan asked, as he surveyed those holding fast to what they had, refusing to 'rock the boat' in order to 'protect the cage they're in'.[53]

Simultaneously, New Model Army – alongside the poet Joolz [Julianne Denby], with whom they continue to work closely – retained an affinity to the people and spaces that inspired them. Their songs and poems regularly evoked the dramatic landscape of Yorkshire's old mill towns and moors. 'Bradford … it's a very beautiful town and a very hard town', Sullivan explained to *Rigor Mortis* fanzine, 'it's something about the hardness of the place like wherever you are you can see the sky and the moors … It's sort of died. The unemployment rate is about 16/17% … it's a beautiful town. I love it and yet there is something I hate about it as well'.[54] Sullivan, in fact, was the only member of the band not from Bradford, though his sentiments were shared and filtered through virtues of passion and commitment to forge a tribal ethos embodied in a dedicated following that adopted the group's ragtaggle image.[55] And while Sullivan's wanderlust remained (satiated, in part, by extensive touring), the delusions behind London's bright lights were regularly exposed. On 'Green and Grey', Sullivan joined with the band's drummer Rob Heaton to ruminate on those who left Bradford for the capital, recognising the drive of ambition but bemoaning the conceit of thinking life was something that happened only somewhere else.[56]

New Model Army's ambivalent relationship with Bradford was telling. As Keith Gildart has suggested, popular music and youth culture did not just offer people a vicarious means to escape the trials of everyday life. They also provided a medium through which to reassert or redefine local, class and personal identities. 'From the 1950s, working-class youth performed and consumed popular music as a source of escape from the mine, mill and factory, but also as an affirmation of a particular connection to community and locality.'[57] In punk terms, we may think here of the Cockney Rejects; Oi! was very much a reassertion of class and local identity through boisterous punk rock. But such observation could also relate to the Newtown Neurotics, who remained in Harlow to help set up The Square as a gig venue, or to the many punk-inspired bands for whom 'making it' in the sense of achieving pop stardom was not the prevailing motive.[58] The numerous bands, labels, fanzines and venues that emerged across the UK from 1976 were often responding to the boredom of life in the provinces. But many of those involved stayed put to initiate and cultivate distinct local cultures.

As should be clear, both the suburbs and 'small town England' provided suitable backdrops to punk's 'negative drive'. The suburban sensibilities denoted by Bracewell, Simon Frith and others were certainly evident among those who responded to punk's impetus, though not just contained within the peaceful mews of Chislehurst or Camberley. Debbie Wilson, for example, found her way to the same places as the Bromley contingent from an Edgware council estate; Adam Ant's route through art school to punk-pop piracy came via a St John's Wood tenement.[59] Equally, the adoption of youth cultural identity and popular music as a means to renegotiate class and local identities was integral to punk, both in the northern industrial towns highlighted by Gildart and the shifting contours of London and its surround. As Vicky Lebeau has argued, punk's suburban disaffection was not just that of the young middle-class malcontent. It also tapped into the frustrations of a displaced working class reimagining an urbanity lost through family relocation. An obvious example would be Sham 69's fetishisation of all things cockney from the leafy commuter town of Hersham, Surrey. But Joy Division's Bernard Sumner also recalled the loss he felt on being moved from a Victorian two-up two-down in Salford's Lower Broughton to a high-rise flat in nearby Greengate. '[The] tower blocks just isolated people', he remembered. '[All] the history, people, families, homes, pride, dignity – everything – had gone … you can hear the death of a community … in my contribution to the music of Joy Division'.[60]

In effect, punk helped make explicit what had always been implicit in pop and rock 'n' roll: the desire to transcend the travails of everyday life through experience, feeling and dreaming. By so doing, punk and its post-punk descendants filtered an existential urge through landscapes real and imagined, both urban and suburban. This, in itself, was not new. The Kinks and The Who had both explored similar terrain. In the context of the mid-to-late 1970s and early 1980s, however, punk's response was set against a backdrop of socioeconomic change defined, in part, by conflicting media-driven images of (suburban) domesticity and a discourse of crisis and decline. As the planners' dream faded and the economic basis of the postwar consensus began to crumble, so the smiles on the advertising hoardings no longer beamed so bright for those who stopped to contemplate them.

I Am a Product

Postwar youth cultures comprised a range of styles, musical forms, aesthetics and accoutrements. These, in turn, were bound closely to the mechanisms of commercial production; they communicated, in large part, through acts of consumption and display.[61] Indeed, youth culture – and pop music in particular – served in the vanguard of postwar consumerism, with the 'teenager' deployed to signal the emergence of an affluent, classless society in which social mobility and aspiration were but a (hire) purchase away.[62]

Things were never so simple of course. The transition from industrialism to consumerism triggered anxieties across the political spectrum and at all levels of society, be it in response to the supposed 'Americanisation' of British culture or the 'delinquent' connotations of youth cultural style.[63] Nor was the relative prosperity of the postwar decades based on a secure economic foundation: inflationary pressures, sluggish growth and residual inequalities continued to simmer even as London swung and the white heat of technology pushed towards the future age. By the end of the 1960s, even some of the young beneficiaries of the postwar 'boom' were in revolt. Certainly, the student protests and the counterculture of the period were often interpreted as a 'reaction against the excessive materialism of consumer society'.[64] In the background, the spectre of Herbert Marcuse's 'one-dimensional man', for whom affluence bred passivity and new forms of repression, lurked in ominous presence.[65]

Amidst such concerns, the signs and signifiers of youth culture and popular music remained a site of contention. As capital extended its reach into the world of leisure and culture became evermore commodified, so the ways by which products were *used* continued to mark 'the subculture off from more orthodox cultural formations' (Hebdige).[66] In other words, youth (sub)cultures distinguished themselves by repositioning and recontextualising commodities in ways that made it difficult 'to maintain any absolute distinction between commercial exploitation on the one hand and creativity/originality on the other'.[67] As a result, the tension between the social and the commercial uses of culture – between the creative process and the process of manufacture, between the 'authentic' and the replicated, between the fun of *doing* and the power relations that enabled dissemination – continued to inform the development of just about every popular music or style-based youth culture into the twenty-first century.[68]

Punk, again, was no different. Debate as to who constituted the 'real' or the 'part-time' punks recurred through many a fanzine; the form and content of punk's trajectory soon constituted a hard-fought terrain. At the same time, punk stimulated exploration of the contradictions thrown up by the construction of identity through consumption, bricolage and homology.[69] In fact, punk wilfully embraced those contradictions, decoding and critiquing the processes of youth cultural production while revelling in the pleasures discovered therein. Fashion, records, record sleeves, gigs, posters and media became both a platform for protest and a source of expression. Even the most hardened punk anarchist had, at some point, been enthused by the possibilities of pop music and rock 'n' roll.[70]

Among punk's early exponents, few examined the faultlines of pop-cultural consumerism better than X-Ray Spex. The band was fronted by Poly Styrene, a rebellious teen from Stockwell in London who found herself disaffected with the hippie trail and the world of low-paid employment looming by the mid-1970s. Having flirted with a pop career in 1976, releasing a solo single (as Mari Elliott), she embraced punk after seeing the Sex Pistols at Hastings Pier Pavilion in July of the same year. Around the same time, Styrene opened a stall on Beaufort Market on the King's Road, selling clothes and bright plastic bric-a-brac that informed both her own distinct sense of style and the lyrical focus of her band. 'I was … interested in consumerism, plastic, artificial living', she told Jon Savage, with a nom-de-plume that reasserted her point: 'this is what you have done to me, turned me into a zombie. I am your product'.[71]

Related themes informed much of the band's set and many an interview. X-Ray Spex's signature tune was 'Oh Bondage, Up Yours', a joyous negation of restriction in general but material restrictions and the binds of consumerism in particular. The lyrics linked the chainstore to the chain gang, with the act of consumption becoming but another form of enslavement. Essentially, Styrene offered a pop version of György Lukács' theory of reification. 'It's completely unreal. People don't become people', Styrene observed in *Melody Maker* as she contemplated the alienating effect of shops full of products bought only to satiate some vague sense of desire/need.[72]

The band's only album, *Germfree Adolescents*, was released in 1978 to expand on Styrene's preoccupations. It made reference to Day-Glo plastics, household consumables and genetic engineering, as if documenting the ways by which material reality had succumbed to synthetic reproduction. On the title track and songs such as 'Art-I-ficial', 'Obsessed with You' and 'Plastic Bag', Styrene sung of being 'reared on appliances', corresponding 'to all those ads' and becoming just another figure for the 'sales machine'.[73] At the album's centre was 'Identity', a frightening depiction of a psyche fragmenting amidst a barrage of media images and expectations that would later prove predictive. Styrene herself buckled under the pressures of fame while on tour in 1978 – a process captured on an *Arena* documentary broadcast in early 1979.[74]

X-Ray Spex were not alone in recognising both the danger and the appeal of consumerism (the important thing, Styrene told *Temporary Hoarding*, was that people use products rather than let the products use them).[75] Buzzcocks, too, combined a celebration of pop's form – the 7-inch single as a means of communication and a source of pleasure – with appreciation of its function in the market place. So, for example, Malcolm Garrett's sleeve designs emphasised the enclosed record's catalogue number and label logo.[76] Adverts for the single 'I Don't Mind' (1978) were published under the slogan 'Marketing Ploy: The Single from the Album', while initial copies of the LP itself (*Another Music in a Different Kitchen*) came packaged in a plastic bag stamped 'product'. As this suggests, the deleterious effect of commodification was a theme that ran through many a Buzzcocks song, from the self-explanatory 'Fiction Romance' and 'I Need' ('I used to only want but now I need') to later songs that complained 'everything's fake nothing's real' and obsessed with thwarted desire. For Richard Boon, writing a typically arch press release for the band in late 1977, Buzzcocks proved able to describe 'both the love object of a supermarket society and the process that transforms nostalgia and romance into yet more consumer goods'.[77]

The use of pop's packaging to détourn and demystify the process of cultural commodification became a common strategy. XTC's second album, *Go 2* (1978), came in a Hipgnosis-designed cover that comprised just text on black background: 'This is a RECORD COVER.

This writing is the DESIGN upon the record cover. The DESIGN is to help SELL the record … We're letting you know that you ought to buy this record because in essence it's a PRODUCT and PRODUCTS are to be consumed and you are a consumer …'[78] In the same year, the launch of Bob Last and Hilary Morrison's Fast Product label drew attention to the commodity fetish that helped stimulate record sales. According to Last:

> It's a product world. The old ideas of product as impersonal "stuff" tend to be illusions. I'm positively coming to grips with the real situation, as it actually is. You live in a world of product. I may not like the present situation but if you want to do any- thing positive, you've got to accept certain things about it and work on its terms … Even the most independent of 45s, however obscure or politically committed, is the end of a product system, a cog – no matter how small – in the entertainment industry machine.[79]

In response, Last and Morrison's own product sought to reveal and exploit this process. So, for example, the first Mekons' single – 'Never Been in a Riot' (1978) – was released in a sleeve that drew attention to the relationship between the band, the product and its consumption. An image of a microphone provided the cover, signifying the recording process. The label's motif – and the word 'product' – was repeated across the record's packaging to denote and affirm its com- modity status. The objective was to make the consumer/listener aware of the recording process and commercial context, a strategy drawn from Berthold Brecht, whose theatre deliberately applied alienating effects (*verfremdungseffekt*) designed to instil the viewer with a critical distance that prevented emotional attachment and revealed the deeper mechanisms shaping the 'realities' of everyday life.[80] The Mekons' sec- ond single – 'Where Were You?' (1978) – came in a sleeve that featured gold discs piled on a record company floor.

Last also worked with Gang of Four, another group alive to the contradictions inherent in culture's commodification. For their Fast Product release, the band issued an EP led by a title track – 'Damaged Goods' – that transferred the language of commerce to the realm of romance. Not only did the song's lyric bind the affairs of the heart to the rules of consumption, but the record also came replete with a complimentary sticker that featured a negative photo of unidentifiable people socialising in a supermarket. On the back, Last presented a newspaper-cutting of a matador sent to him by the band. The intention was for captions to be attached: the matador explaining to the bull that they were part of the entertainment business and that she did the job for money rather than pleasure. The bull was to reply: 'I think that at some time we have to take responsibility for our actions'. Last, however, presented the cutting without the captions, instead locating it next to the Gang of Four's original letter outlining how the sleeve should look. The result, of course, was a further deconstruction of the production process.[81]

Clearly, the blurred boundaries between art, commerce and life itself preoccupied Last and the groups he worked with. Alongside records, Last also issued conceptual works ('The Quality of Life') that masqueraded as product: a plastic bag filled with bits of consumer debris and photocopied collages culled from magazines, an ad campaign for non-existent products ('instead of sex: SeXes – devote a minute a day to your most valuable asset: Fiction Romance').[82] Fire Engines, who signed to Last's Pop:Aural label, were ostensibly the antithesis of a commercial pop band: discordant, indecipherable and renowned for fifteen-minute sets that antagonised their audience. Members of the group – along with their manager, Angus Whyte, and art-school friends such as Paul Steen, who helped bring out the band's first single on Codex Communications in 1980 – had previously spent much time in Last's Edinburgh flat and the nearby Tap O'Lauriston pub.[83] Therein, ideas were swapped among the various fledgling musicians, artists and designers to provide the impetus for a series of records issued in sleeves decorated with household products and built around titles – 'Get Up and Use Me' (Figure 4.2), 'New Thing in Cartons', *Lubricate Your Living Room* (1980) – that parodied the language of advertising.

As for The Mekons and Gang of Four, both continued to release records that explored the processes of commodification. For the former, this meant songs measuring life in terms of goods bought and money earned-then-spent. The chorus to 'Trevira Trousers' deconstructed and critiqued masculinity via a list of products and leisure pursuits: 'drinks, fags, fun at night, dirty books and a Ford Cortina, randy girls in plastic shoes'.[84] Even blunter, 'Work All Week' condensed the function of work down to saving money in order to buy 'that certain kind of something, for that certain kind of life'. Gang of Four, meanwhile, issued *Entertainment!* in 1979, an album preoccupied with reification and

Figure 4.2 Fire Engines, 'Get Up and Use Me'. (Design by Angus Whyte, Codex Communications, 1980.)

the distorting influence of the media. From its title through to songs focusing on the profits made on the 'disco floor' and the 'purchase' of leisure, it served to problematise the correlation between commerce and human relations.[85] Even its recording process was done so as to accentuate the distance between the band and the listener/consumer, its dry production deliberately eschewing any attempt to capture the band playing live or in real time. This was, as Simon Reynolds notes, 'a studio artefact, a cold-blooded reconstruction'.[86]

If Gang of Four's engagement with consumer-based alienation appeared relatively sophisticated, then it nevertheless encompassed themes that repeated across punk's diverse canon. Most explicitly, The Pop Group's 'We Are All Prostitutes' revolved around the notion of 'consumer fascism', with department stores presented as new cathedrals. And while The Clash got 'Lost in the Supermarket' searching for identity amidst the special offers, so The Jam wrote similarly of the alienation engendered by 'Shopping' and the somnambulant effect of the supermarket aisles.[87] More obscurely, perhaps, The Cravats took aim at the 'Precinct', depicting people shuffling round looking at their shoes as they pondered buying rubbish that would never be used, while Annie Anxiety wrote 'Buy Now, Pay As You Go' for Crass, risking her dignity as she gazed down the aisles at 'brushed chrome shit' and 'plastic crap' before refusing to become a possession junkie.[88]

A whole host of punk-informed songs captured or bemoaned the transformation of the individual into *a thing*, sometimes in relation to the music industry or media, sometimes as a result of consumerism.[89] A particularly good example was Adam and the Ants' 'Boil in the Bag Man', whose subject became the embodiment of the cheap convenience products he consumed. But the Vital Disorders' 'Prams' also chartered how consumer goods helped define a socially constructed identity, in this case a housewife surrounded by appliances that marked the death of her childhood dreams.[90] Indeed, the idealisation and reification of the female-self through marketing, media and consumption recurred. Essential Logic ('Aerosol Burns'), The Raincoats ('Fairytale in the Supermarket', 'Odyshape') and The Slits ('Spend, Spend, Spend') all wrote songs exposing how the language of advertising and the chimera of consumption conspired to shape and confine female identities.[91]

To an extent, the relatively sustained critique of consumerism that became manifest through punk was an extension of the disaffection that underpinned its emergence. It was but a short step from bemoaning the state of pop, fashion and rock 'n' roll to bemoaning the mechanisms that facilitated and disseminated youth culture.[92] Looked at this way, drawing attention to cultural commodification was an end in itself, part of the consciousness-raising or critical thinking that many bands claimed to encourage. 'If we're responsible for anything', Johnny Rotten told the BBC's *Rock On*, 'it'll be to make people think about things like that, like the media, what fools they are'.[93] To understand the processes of cultural production allowed more astute choices to be made, both within and without the market place.

Not surprisingly, therefore, navigating the cultural-commercial tensions exposed through punk brought varied ends. For exponents of DIY autonomy and anarcho-punk, the perceived threat of commodification meant redefining the parameters of cultural production. 'New ways of relating to people' were necessary, the Poison Girls reasoned, ways that did not conform to industry models of style, image, music and the 'simple pop message of "be my baby"'.[94] Similarly, 'independence' opened up alternative spaces parallel to and distinct from the perceived mainstream: against the 'official' singles and album charts stood the alternative ('indie') chart; against the music press, the fanzine; against the high-street disco, the subterranean night club or self-organised gig.[95]

Alternately, punk's initial challenge may be understood as an attempt to gain access to the opportunities afforded by the music industry. Once done, so a section of punk's milieu proved quick to embrace – rather than shun – the possibilities therein. By 1980–81, the emergence of new romanticism and what Paul Morley christened 'new pop' saw the likes of Adam Ant, Boy George, Martin Fry (ABC) and Green Gartside dismiss the darker, realist or confrontational aspects of punk in favour of style, glamour and technology.[96] Protest gave way to pleasure, reimagining pop as a site of 'play … one glorious, un-erasable mistake [with] no claim to authenticity [and a] love of kitsch, [a] love of "the future" [and a] sense of fun'.[97]

Subversion remained. New romanticism was cultivated in London's club-land by Steve Strange and Rusty Egan, combining flamboyant dress with Bowie-worship and connections to the more fashionably *outré* corners of the capital's gay underground.[98] First in Billy's (1979), then at Blitz (1979–80) and Hell (1980), gender boundaries were flouted; the scene's coiffured artifice extending punk's Weimar fixation to encompass a broader European sense of fin-de-siècle that enlivened the bleak landscape of late 1970s Soho and Covent Garden.[99] Musically, choice pieces of punk, disco, glam, Kraftwerk, industrial and early synth-pop provided 'futurist' sheen to complement a detached, alienated pose.[100] As for new pop, most of those associated with the term boasted punk pedigrees and critical sensibilities expressed either through adroit dissections of pop's form (ABC, Scritti Politti) or 'transgressive' sexualities (Boy George, Dead or Alive, Frankie Goes To Hollywood, Marilyn, Soft Cell). Beneath Orange Juice's fey aesthetic lay a deep critique of rock machismo. The state-of-the-art pop of Heaven 17 presented an album – *Penthouse and Pavement* (1981) – that revealed the corporate basis of the music industry on its sleeve. Among the band's hit singles were '(We Don't Need This) Fascist Groove Thang' (1981), about Ronald Reagan, and 'Crushed by the Wheels of Industry' (1983), a deposition on the alienating effects of capitalism.

Arguably, however, the politics of both new pop and new romanticism were bound to what Robert Hewison (following Lyotard) described as the 'post-modern condition': a miasma of mediated signs and images that dove-tailed neatly with neoliberal economics and postmodern theory.[101] Very quickly, new romanticism's transformation of self-into-art-object revealed a narcissism defined primarily by portentousness and, later, faux-sophistication.[102] For Strange, the scene revolved around people living out 'their fantasies', dressing up, escaping from work and 'all the greyness and depression'.[103] Looked at another way, it appeared to foreshadow what Savage called the 'toytown nihilism' of the 1980s, where style eclipsed content in an age of 'endless consumption'.[104] Even the scene's most detailed chronicler has suggested it tended to comprise individuals 'looking for a leg up into the limelight' rather than 'trying to make a romantic gesture of refusal'.[105]

Nor would Scritti Politti continue to reference Gramsci and seek a 'war of position'. Instead, Gartside wrote paeans to Jacques Derrida, issued records in sleeves based on luxurious consumer products, signed to Virgin and sought meaning only in 'what sells'.[106] 'The politics have moved', Gartside explained to the *NME* in 1981 following a year-long sojourn during which he recovered from a nervous collapse by reconsidering his attitude to making music with high doses of post-structuralism. Rather than 'an essentialist and reductionist position in which we believed in a history of science which could make sense of the future [Marxism]', Scritti now adhered to a politics that 'realised that what you've got is needs, demands and desires, and you go out and you fight for them'.[107] Fittingly, perhaps, Bob Last helped manage Gartside's transformation.

How to explain such a shift? Postwar youth cultures emerged in tandem with the defining motifs of postmodernism: mass consumption, the media, the scrambling of linearity, the debasing of perceived 'truths' or 'grand narratives', the collapse of representation into reality. In punk and its related cultures, the tensions born of such developments were engaged with and played out in various ways. What proved interesting about punk's turn to new romanticism and new pop was how it coincided with the realigned political landscape presided over by Margaret Thatcher from 1979. As social democracy succumbed to 'crisis' and leftist ideas fragmented through deconstruction, so the politics of neoliberalism gained leverage. Notions of 'freedom', 'individuality' and 'innovation' were framed in the language of the market; human activities – lifestyles – were recognised in terms of commodification.[108] In the world of pop, moreover, including the youth cultural spaces it soundtracked (clubs, discos, bedrooms and, via the Sony Walkman launched in 1979, the street and inner space), the will to pleasure was all too easily harnessed by the 'heroic entrepreneurs' beckoned by Joseph Schumpeter and trumpeted by Friedrich Hayek and Thatcher thereafter.[109] Not by accident did a flowering of young fashion designers emerge from the new romantic milieu who clubbed at Billy's and Blitz, attuning their business antennae as they tested their creativity amidst London's self-defined elite.[110] Nor, too, was it by chance that the *stars* of new pop defined their aesthetic as much through lavish video and studio production as music and performance. The new mood, Morley suggested during a 1980 interview with ABC, was 'towards a brightness'; clever pop bands with a sense of style who offered 'choice and value' as they sought a 'big display in the supermarkets' rather than getting 'stuck on a high shelf in the corner shop'.[111] In 1981, *Smash Hits'* Mark Ellen celebrated the new pop artists' 'business-wise' control of their 'careers'.[112] Within such a context, the commodity was no longer a signal of reification but a means of liberation. Dress for success; play to win. If youth was an age when 'you are starting to mature and become sexually aware', Spandau Ballet's Gary Kemp told the *NME*, then it was also time to 'realise you've got a body to sell'.[113]

In a Rut (Gotta Get Out of It)

The Ruts' signature tune, released as a single in January 1979, proved a bleakly prophetic record. Built around a circular bassline and produced with dub-like space between the instrumentation, 'In a Rut' travelled deep into a troubled psyche. The lyrics hinted at a sense of purposelessness. The song's subject, drawn from singer Malcolm Owen's own experience, was unable to concentrate, to feel 'straight' or feel anything at all. In verse two, the allusion to drug addiction repeated, this time pointing to suicide. The chorus – 'You're in a rut, you gotta get out of it' – was ambiguous. Did getting 'out of it' mean taking more drugs? Did it mean death? Was it positing some practical solution? Seemingly, the 'rut' of the song's title was ground somewhere between narcotic dependency and the brutal realities of life itself.[114]

Owen died of a heroin overdose in 1980, a tragedy that lent gravitas to the drug references peppering his lyrics.[115] Arguably, however, Owen's heroin addiction was bound to the broader struggles that underpinned his songs: the social tensions, politics and relationships that made his late 1970s such a 'Savage Circle'.[116] Looked at this way, the pathos of 'In a Rut' appeared less a product of hapless delinquency and more a youthful glimpse into the void. In other words, Owen's 'rut' was born of existential crisis, yet another strand of the politics of boredom that unravelled from 1976–77.[117]

Of course, such insights were never the sole preserve of punk. Just as anomie and boredom informed the best of modern literature, so they also provided a kernel of pop: the Rolling Stones' '(I Can't Get No) Satisfaction' alluded to far more than Mick Jagger's festering sexual urge.[118] That said, there appeared to be a notable overlap between punk and an existentialist mind-set. Both emphasised the individual and recognised subjective experience as determining meaning. Both shared a tendency to reject prescribed labels as a bind on individuality; both overturned binary distinctions between 'good' and 'bad'. Both represented perseverance in the face of life's absurdity; both tended to dismiss prevailing social mores and structures as meaningless constructs (and so shared a propensity towards nihilism). Both, too, identified as outsiders, either alienated from or rejected by mainstream society.[119] The Sex Pistols' early interviews stood out partly on account of Rotten's scathing critiques of just about anything and everything, from the music industry to the education system. 'They try to ruin you from the start', he told *Record Mirror* in 1976. 'They take away your soul. They destroy you. "Be a bank clerk" or "join the army" is what they give you at school … You have no future, nothing. You are made to feel unequal'. *Ordinary* patterns of life – refined over time through school, work, marriage and mortgage – were anathema. 'I don't believe in marriage, mortgage or houses in the country', Rotten insisted. 'All these bores who have crawled out of their little Surbiton huts. The only constructive thing left for them to do is kill themselves. You've met one – you've met them all. Their personality is governed by what they do … and they do nothing worth talking about. They don't like people to have notions because they accept how they live'.[120]

Religion offered no respite. Rotten's Catholic education left scars that later found expression in 'Religion', a contemptuous attack on the church rehearsed briefly as the Sex Pistols imploded before gaining release on the first PiL album in 1978.[121] Thereafter, religion (and Christianity in particular) became a standard punk target. Crass' 'Asylum' berated Christ on the cross for the repression enacted in his name, a trope oft-repeated by anarchist bands and many an 'anarcho' fanzine.[122] New Model Army's 'Christian Militia' and the Subhumans' 'Religious Wars' chartered religion's historical legacy of bloodshed and division. The sanctity of death and the temptations of sin offered sites of transgression for fledgling goths and those attracted to the darker corners of the human psyche. Indeed, the likes of Coil, Current 93 and Psychic TV peeled back the mystique of religious ritual to uncover dark pathways to chaos, magick, paganism and the occult.[123] Even The Damned berated the Catholic Church on 'Anti-Pope', while The Blood's 'Megalomania' offered a manic dissection of the 'gap' between Catholicism's claim to care for the needy and the pope's 'robes of silk and gold'.[124] In short, religion was another symptom of the 'hypocrisy, monotony, consistency' that Rotten defined punk in opposition to. '[Punk] is against the unacceptable face of capitalism, against religion, against any organised establishment movement', he told Caroline Coon in 1978.[125]

For Rotten, joining a band and educating himself provided his own (existential) solution. More generally, such thinking helped inject British youth culture with a dose of critical introspection: a questioning of life's purpose and the mechanisms that maintained the prevailing social and political order. On the one hand this meant verbal attacks against 'the system', epitomised by 'God Save the Queen' but replicated in countless songs by countless bands thereafter. On the other, it allowed existential moods and questions to ferment in a period of economic depression, political change and, from 1979–80, a reignited Cold War.

Expressions of punk existentialism flickered intermittently from the outset. 'Life' by Alternative TV was perhaps the most explicit example, with Mark Perry taking a journey through work, the dole queue and the high street before determining that life was 'about as wonderful as a tramp lying dead in the road'. 'Life', he re-emphasised as the song built to a Beckettian close, was as wonderful 'as nothing'.[126] But existential disaffection also helped fuel the anger of much punk-informed social realism, with Sham 69's 'What About the Lonely?' and 'I'm a Man, I'm a Boy' providing two reflective examples. It ran through The Lurkers' affinity with 'God's Lonely Men' and provided inspiration for Sandy Robertson's imaginary band: The Young Existentialists.[127] Equally, life's absurdities loomed large in the lyrics of, say, Robert Lloyd or Phil Hartley (Bogshed), not to mention The

Fall's Mark E. Smith, whose band was named after an Albert Camus novel. Even the anarchism associated with Crass bore an existential stamp. Not for nothing did Penny Rimbaud disseminate his publications through the in-house Exitstencil Press [sic].[128]

By 1979–80, such tendencies had begun to inform a recognisable aesthetic, with Joy Division – whose singer, Ian Curtis, succumbed to suicide in 1980 – serving as an archetype. Curtis' own personal demons related to a failing marriage and the debilitating effects of being diagnosed with epilepsy. But he also bore cultural influences (Ballard, Bowie, Burroughs, Dostoyevsky, Gogol, Herzog, Hesse, Kafka, Nietzsche, Iggy Pop, Sartre, Velvet Underground) that helped map a darkening perspective. In his notebooks, published posthumously, Curtis' lyrics and prose evolved from fascinated depictions of human atrocities ('Ice Age', 'No Love Lost', 'Walked in Line') to alienated ruminations on the pains of existence ('Digital', 'Exercise One', 'Glass') to personal dissections of a crumbling relationship ('Atmosphere', 'Love Will Tear Us Apart', 'Passover'). Scenarios were often set in lonely rooms or desolate cityscapes, they evoked – as Jon Savage noted – 'the heightened emotions of a particular post-teenage state: the desire to be different and the searching for oddity and extremity, the dreadful sense that you're not quite good enough, that you're letting everyone down, and the immersion in books as an inspiration and a method ... of staving off isolation'.[129] 'Dark ages' were coming, Curtis predicted in a scribbled note, the prevailing 'social or intellectual position holds no bright prospects for future. Trapped in corners – solitary'.[130]

Joy Division's influence was telling. Their relatively slower, bass-led sound – rough and abrasive live; spaciously produced by Martin Hannett on record – was much imitated. Their image, all heavy coats, dark shirts and thrift-store slacks, likewise inspired a recognisable 'type'; a 'long mac brigade' of young men with weights on their shoulders and Penguin classics in their pockets. Their music – combined with the substance of Curtis' lyrics and the stark-but-stylish sleeve designs of Peter Saville – conflated with what Paul Morley described as 'the horror of the times' and Jon Savage recognised as the 'decay and malaise' of post-industrial Manchester.[131] By remaining on Factory and aloof from the media, the band retained a punk ethos while extending their sound and language into new, innovative areas.

As this suggests, Joy Division captured *something*; the band appeared to be what Martin Hannett described as 'one of those channels for the gestalt'.[132] But similar moods permeated the (post-)punk diaspora over the late 1970s and early 1980s. Cast in the shadow of Rotten's predicted No Future, an existential dread infused the paranoid media-scapes of Cabaret Voltaire and much industrial culture; the 'death disco' of PiL and Killing Joke; the self-proclaimed 'grey' tenor of fanzines such as *Dangerous Logic* ('run on turmoil'); the doom-laden early releases of 4AD and Factory; the nuclear war fixation of much early 1980s punk.[133] The temper was bleak and introspective, the aesthetic monochrome. Occasionally, it drew from distinct literary influences. Or, to quote David Stubbs: a 'new Europhilia revealed itself in a host of artists' names, song titles and lyrics: Magazine's Dostoyevsky-inspired "Song From Under the Floorboards", Warsaw, Josef K, Spandau Ballet, Bauhaus, Cabaret Voltaire, Wire's "Midnight Bahnhof Café", the Associates' "White Car in Germany", Simple Minds' "Kant-Kino" and "I Travel"'.[134]

The origins of this punk-informed Europhilia were varied: the cold ambience of Bowie's 'Berlin phase', especially *Low* (1977); a rejection of rock 'n' roll clichés and associated American influences; the Weimar-chic adopted by those around Siouxsie and the Banshees; a persistent fascination with the horrors of Nazism; the *otherness* of Eastern Europe at a time of Western economic depression and hardening Cold War. More to the point, the existential reflections of modernist literature, theatre and film complemented the mood of the times. Like Joy Division, Josef K drew from literary sources to explore the human condition in pop form, their Kafka-referencing name a clue to songs also inspired by writers such as Camus and Dostoyevsky.[135] Famously, too, The Cure's debut single, 'Killing an Arab' (1978), paid homage to Camus' *The Outsider*, after which the band released a series of records imbued with an existentialist influence. *Pornography*, from 1982, was especially desolate, a suffocating drum-heavy descent into self-disgust amidst lyrics of imagined deaths and inner abjection.[136]

Of course, well-stocked bookcases might help explain life's anxieties, but they neither solved nor cured them. According to The Pop Group, life's 'traps' were actually reinforced by language and reason.[137] For others, the struggle against a 'mortgage mentality' (The Business), a 'stupid marriage' (Specials) or a 'wasted life' in the army/paramilitary (Stiff Little Fingers) took on more immediate form. Accordingly, dramatised accounts of nervous breakdowns and existential crises had become a punk staple by the 1980s. These, in turn, were occasionally aligned to the deleterious effects of early Thatcherism, but often hinted at a deeper malaise. While GBH's 'Self Destruct' proffered a suicide solution to a desperation born of 'their' recession, The Exploited's 1982 single 'Attack' depicted an inner turmoil caught somewhere between a nasty speed comedown and the psychological effects of loneliness, paranoia and pent-up frustration.[138] The Partisans, too, provided a prescient snapshot of life on the cusp of adulthood. Their 'Blind Ambition' began by describing a sense of social detachment before ruminating on the need to find a 'way out' from a life lived on the 'never-never'. By its end, the song had turned from angst to defiance, railing against 'plastic people' whose latent violence was a product of conforming to a ritualised lifestyle of car-house-kids and a yearly-holiday in Spain.[139]

As with Owen and Curtis, a fixation on the futility or struggles of existence could sometimes lead to a sorry end. Nick Blinko from Rudimentary Peni expressed his own personal torments through the intricate drawings of foetal skeletons and plagued souls that decorated his band's records. Lyrically, his fascination with the macabre preceded his eventual stay on a psychiatric ward.[140] Equally, refusing or dismantling life's structures could lead to destructive – as well as existential – conclusions. Punk's most famous casualty, Sid Vicious, was very much an idiot savant; his descent into rock 'n' roll cliché underpinned by a despair that occasionally seeped through in amusing – if simultaneously dispiriting – interviews. 'Ordinary life is so dull', he told *Melody Maker*'s Allan Jones, 'I get out of it as much as possible'.[141]

Punk's existential instincts reflected multiple concerns. They bore trace of the adolescence that most of those involved in developing the culture were passing through. They touched on personal worries or experiences that informed wider perspectives and sensibilities; 'soul mining', as The The's Matt Johnson called it.[142] They also tapped into anxieties relevant to the time. 'The world's only going to get worse', Rotten opined in mid-1977, echoing the mood of declinism then permeating so much media and political discourse.[143]

Conversely, such insights stimulated the 'negative drive' denoted by Devoto. And while some fell by the wayside, ravaged by drugs, mental illness or suicide, the impetus to agency remains one of punk's abiding legacies. Rather than succumb to the boredom of everyday life, punk and its associated cultures represented a conscious attempt to alleviate it: to form a band, write a fanzine, dress up, go out and do-it-yourself. For Jah Wobble, the bass player in PiL and once-close associate of Rotten, the punk generation harboured 'absolutely no illusions, we knew it was a rigged game'.[144] That is, punk stemmed from recognition that the future looked bleak, that the music industry was exploitative, that politicians lied, that the media distorted, that capital corrupted and life was a treadmill from cradle to grave. In his 1953 novel *The Unnameable*, Samuel Beckett concluded with a famous refrain: 'I can't go on. I'll go on'. In 1976, Johnny Rotten introduced the Sex Pistols' first televised performance of 'Anarchy in the UK' with a command: 'Get off your arse'.[145]

5 WHO NEEDS A PARLIAMENT? PUNK AND POLITICS

> Every law, every act of government, is carried through with the
> aim of maintaining the position of the rulers over the ruled. It
> makes no difference if the government is 'right', like Thatchers,
> or 'left', like Castros. It is a gigantic barrier to peoples liberation.
> All governments are by their very nature conservative, static,
> intolerant of change and opposed to it.[1]
>
> Ronan Bennett (1980)

Punk's political orientation was contested from the outset. That it registered disaffection was immediately apparent in the attitude, look, language and sound of the Sex Pistols. Less clear, however, was the extent
to which such discontent contained any discernible political tendency.
Commentators from the left and right both claimed and disowned
punk in about equal measure, prompting lively debate as to its significance and potential.[2] In the music press, the writings of Coon, Burchill
and Parsons quickly sought to draw and direct political meaning from
punk's aggression. As for the bands themselves, often comprised of
teenagers yet to vote in a general election, they initially offered mixed
signals when pushed as to political allegiance or sympathies. Many
rejected politics altogether, revealing a sense of disengagement that suggested the machinations of parties and government were either irrelevant or detrimental to their everyday lives. The Sex Pistols' Steve Jones
claimed not even to know who the prime minister was in 1977, while
Rotten described politically aligned rock 'n' roll as a 'loser stance'.[3]
Others volunteered vague sensibilities. Where The Clash talked of
attending left-wing workshops and committed to anti-fascism, Siouxsie

Sioux's 'low tolerance of people who can't help themselves' and Paul Weller's bemoaning the power of trade unions spoke in a language that presaged the Conservative victory of 1979.[4]

To be fair, both bands soon modified their position. The Banshees went on to play benefit gigs – such as for handicapped children in 1979 – and made explicit their objections to Thatcherism.[5] Weller's 1977 quote that he intended to vote Conservative was almost immediately qualified by the fact he thought both 'Jim Callaghan AND Margaret Thatcher are cunts. I don't trust any of them. All I said at the time was that I thought the Tories would do a less bad job'.[6] He then moved sharply to the left to become a stalwart supporter of the Campaign for Nuclear Disarmament (CND) and co-instigator of Red Wedge in 1985.[7] Nevertheless, his comments in 1977 – affirmed in The Jam's Labour-baiting 'Time for Truth' ('the truth is you lie Uncle Jimmy') – were indicative of how punk's protest could not simply be claimed as innately progressive. Punk, after all, was born into a period of Labour government, for which much antipathy and disillusionment was clear. Not for nothing did Rotten sometimes dedicate the Sex Pistols' 'Liar' to Harold Wilson, while Joe Strummer's description of Jim Callaghan as 'a robot' reading from scripted speeches related to a sense by which Labour had lost its way amidst the financial and political turmoil of the 1970s.[8] Consequently, talk of 'individuality' and songs bemoaning the repressive apparatus of the state found ready echo in the language of the New Right.[9] Likewise, anger at powerlessness or limited life chances was not always targeted towards those in authority: misogyny and racism cast ugly shadows across punk-informed cultures.

The fact that punk emerged into a period of political flux served only to further confuse matters. While the Conservative and Labour parties dominated the political mainstream, neither proved able to govern with significant majorities over the 1970s. By 1976–77, as punk entered the public consciousness, economic problems and social tensions combined to ensure disaffection with the status quo was apparent inside and out of the establishment. Beyond broader debate as to the UK's post-imperial relationship to Europe, the US and a potentially devolved self, the roots of what became known as 'Thatcherism' were being tendered in think tanks and discussion groups designed to break the Conservatives free from the yoke of postwar 'consensus'. Labour, in power, struggled to balance its promises of a better tomorrow against economic conditions that fanned industrial unrest and undermined its credibility. Post-1979 it split, spawning the Social Democratic Party (SDP) as it sought to refocus a socialist vision blurred further by militant tendencies and the combative politics of Thatcherite Conservatism.

From the margins, meanwhile, the 1970s saw the far right and far left proffer political alternatives that fuelled the increasingly apocalyptic tone of the media. Growing support for the National Front (NF) offered an ugly glimpse of incipient fascism; student revolutionaries, militant trade unionists and an intellectually vigorous New Left pushed at the fissures of labourism and capitalism. Even then, internecine divisions served to fracture the revolutionary subsects and movements that strove to break into or smash the prevailing political mainstream. The boundaries that demarcated across the left and right continually dissolved and readjusted beneath competing priorities, tendencies and identities.[10]

Any political impulses bound up in punk's emergence were therefore diffuse and open to interpretation. The initial vagaries of punk's disaffection allowed for exploration and connections to be made as teenage frustrations tangled with the shortfalls of Labour social democracy and nascent Thatcherism. From the left, unemployment, anti-racism and the connotations of independent record labels began to shape the ways by which punk's political implications were understood and communicated. Personal politics, with regard to sexuality and gender, found expression through revaluation of rock 'n' roll mores. On the right, punk's urbanity and fascination with fascism coincided with NF recruitment drives geared to exploit the territorial proclivities of youth. More generally, perhaps, a rejection of traditional and hierarchal political organisation found expression through punk-associated claims to autonomy: anarchy transferred from rhetorical device to practice.[11]

Of course, a closer look reveals political residues filtering into and informing punk's development. The countercultural and art school grounding of McLaren, Reid, Rhodes and others are well known, through which ideas cultivated in radical leftist milieus were absorbed and redirected into punk. Both Crass and Throbbing Gristle emerged on the other side of Penny Rimbaud, Gee Vaucher and Genesis P-Orridge's experience of the late 1960s and early 1970s counterculture. Many of punk's facilitators – from Caroline Coon to Geoff Travis – shared comparable pedigrees, complementing tertiary education with radical politics. Across the UK, nascent punk scenes were nurtured in leftist or bohemian networks that sometimes included the politically aligned, but more generally centred on groups of friends drawing from political, artistic and literary sources that fed into the sound, image and content of punk's dissemination.[12]

To an extent, therefore, punk provided a further – critically attuned – medium to explore agendas and processes already evolving as a result of the cultural turn initiated from within leftist politics from the 1950s.[13] Recognition that culture served as a site of political struggle was complemented by an emphasis on the personal politics that flowed from social movements centred on race, gender and sexuality. Not only did young political activists seize on and intervene in punk's development, but organisations on the left and right recognised music and youth cultures as forces of change. In other words, punk appeared to represent a signal of youthful discontent resonant with political possibilities.

Such a reading was not always welcomed. For those who understood punk in purely musical terms, or as an expression of youthful exuberance, political agendas served only to drain pop's energy and spoil its fun. To this end, Mick Jones told *Sniffin' Glue* of an argument he had with Brian James of The Damned, whose insistence on 'enjoying himself' rubbed against Jones' belief that punk channelled rock 'n' roll rebellion into a conduit for 'change and creativity'.[14] In response, The Damned wrote 'Politics', a song that took aim at The Clash, McLaren and Rock Against Racism (RAR), dismissing political 'rules and regulations' in favour of 'fun, not anarchy'.[15]

But despite such objections (and they were oft-repeated), punk's negation and adoption of political signifiers invited political interpretation. For young activists and the instinctively disaffected coming of age in a world of popular culture and heightened political tensions, punk reasserted rock 'n' roll as a means of protest and transgression. The question was to what end such rebellion could best be channelled; were the Sex Pistols harbingers of change or reaction?

Militant Entertainment

In May 1977, a two-day 'socialist festival of music' was organised by Music for Socialism at the Battersea Arts Centre in London.[16] The event involved performances, workshops and discussion designed to explore the links between revolutionary politics and musical practice. Some 550 people attended, drawn from across the left and representing 'progressive' musicians of both an avant-garde and folk persuasion. All committed to 'attack a system under which music is made for a passive market rather than a dynamic relationship with a real audience or community'. Women's participation in music-making was celebrated and demonstrated via the Women's Theatre Group Band; the need to break down barriers between audience and performer was regularly asserted. Disagreement occurred, however, once attention turned to questions of political action and cultural tradition, rekindling long-rumbling debates about musical form and content. Should radical culture take a radical form in order to break down 'working-class cultural conservatism' forged from capitalist mass consumption; or should music serve the people by expressing working-class struggles in a direct and accessible way? Could radical musicians work within the confines of the music industry; or should they remain independent of it? Abuse flew, 'anarchist wankers' against 'militaristic robots', before someone mentioned punk.

Day two of the festival had already been scheduled to conclude with a film of the Sex Pistols.[17] In the event, both days ended in acrimonious debate as to whether punk was progressive or reactionary. According to Cornelius Cardew, a former avant-garde musician transformed into a Maoist member of People's Liberation Music, punk was 'fascist'. 'The monopoly capitalist class consciously selects for promotion the most reactionary elements of culture', he argued. This meant punk in 1977, to which end Cardew produced the first Clash LP as evidence. No song had to be played: the Union Jack on the cover, worn by Paul Simonon, proved it imperialist; the CBS logo revealed it to be capitalist; the back sleeve photograph of police charging rioters in Notting Hill served as propaganda for the state's forces of oppression. As for the Pistols' film, Cardew dismissed it as an advert for the NF.[18] Others objected, suggesting punk's use of political symbolism was intended to offend 'the bourgeoisie', its aesthetics designed to reflect contemporary society. Henry Cow's Geoff Leigh pointed to punk's working-class pedigree ('these cats live in the street'); Simon Frith, later to write up the event for *Village Voice*, countered that punk revealed far more about the music industry than it did about unemployment.

The debate bore no firm conclusion. Indeed, Cardew's criticisms continued to echo elsewhere, and not only under Maoist cover.

Trotskyists in the Workers' Revolutionary Party (WRP) were just as likely to regard punk as a capitalist ruse to distract the working class in 1977, while at least one young communist accused punk of being 'nihilistic, anti-social and degenerate in the extreme'.[19] Simultaneously, activists politicised in the 1960s or coming of age as punk emerged into the mid-1970s began to dissect Clash lyrics and relate punk's protest to the social realities of capitalist deficiency. At the very least, punk bands were applauded for introducing 'politics to thousands of young people, through their performances, songs and through interviews with fanzines'.[20] During the course of 1977–78, moreover, punk bands received regular invites to play benefit gigs for a range of causes organised by parties across the left. Following its 'open letter' to the Sex Pistols, the Young Communist League (YCL) held a 'new wave forum' at its 1977 Red Festival to which Sham 69 provided the live soundtrack.[21] There were, too, a smattering of young revolutionaries motivated to form bands: Tony Friel (The Fall), Green Gartside and Niall Jinks (both Scritti Politti) were in the YCL; Pauline Black came to The Selecter through the WRP; Crisis included Tony Wakeford and Douglas Pearce from the Socialist Workers Party (SWP) and the International Marxist Group respectively; the Redskins wore their SWP membership with pride; a few of punk's ranter-poets, including Attila the Stockbroker and Seething Wells, also came through the SWP.

But such card-holding affiliations were rare. The left of the 1970s comprised a range of campaigns, tendencies and movements. Disillusionment with the Soviet Union and the Labour Party had given rise to ideological and strategic realignments that transformed the style and substance of leftist politics over the 1960s–70s.[22] Older commitments to class and party began to give way to new ideas shaped by a mixture of New Left discourse and countercultural experimentation. Social movements centred on racial, sexual and gender identities demarcated 'new' sites of struggle. With regard to punk, this meant leftist influences more typically reflected sensibilities than party-political loyalties. That is, the spaces opened up by punk allowed for critical engagement with questions of cultural practice and social interaction rather than organisational strategies. Nevertheless, attempts to formally align cultural politics and popular music were made. Most obviously, RAR reignited debate as to music and youth culture's ability to serve as mediums for social change.

RAR formed in the wake of a co-authored letter sent to the music press by Red Saunders and published on 11 September 1976. The impetus came from Eric Clapton's drunken pledge of support for Enoch Powell during a Birmingham Odeon concert the previous August, a sorry spectacle made sadder by Clapton's reputation for being Britain's foremost blues guitarist. Powell, of course, had courted controversy since 1968 when he predicted bloody racial conflict as a consequence of continued immigration into the UK. 'Own up', Saunders demanded of Clapton, 'half your music is black. You're rock music's biggest colonist ... We urge support for Rock Against Racism'.[23]

Two weeks later, Saunders and Roger Huddle restated their initiative in the *Socialist Worker*, presenting an ad hoc RAR committee that called for rock music – 'black and white' – 'to be part of the struggle to change the system'.[24] Letters of support were already forthcoming, paving the way for an inaugural event to be held at a Forest Gate pub in east London featuring the folk-singer Carol Grimes. Thereafter, RAR expanded dramatically. Following a more formal launch on 10 December 1976 at the Royal College of Art, hundreds of gigs were held in London under the auspices of RAR between 1977 and 1981. In 1979, a 'Militant Entertainment' tour criss-crossed the UK, bringing together various punk, pop, rock and reggae bands to rally support prior to a general election contested by 303 NF candidates.[25] By this time, too, a series of carnivals had been held in conjunction with the Anti-Nazi League (ANL), the first of which – at Hackney's Victoria Park in April 1978 – featured The Clash and attracted an estimated crowd of 80,000.[26] According to the *NME*, some 90 local RAR clubs had formed by the spring of 1979, organising approximately 800 gigs in the process.[27]

RAR's base was in London, from where access to the SWP's facilities allowed for the production of *Temporary Hoarding*, a fanzine-styled paper with a readership of 12,000 by 1979. A steady flow of circulars, badges, posters, stickers and publicity material was distributed to local clubs and interested correspondents.[28] Intermittently, conferences and workshops were held to discuss political and organisational concerns, before internal tensions and the election of a Conservative government in 1979 meant RAR was effectively wound down in 1980–81.[29] With anti-racism embedded into British pop culture, the left's attention turned to the threat posed by Thatcherism.[30]

The wider context to RAR's development is important. Both the NF and National Party were making electoral in-roads in 1976–77, polling significant votes in by-elections and local elections. More pertinently, perhaps, Britain's socioeconomic problems fanned racial tensions that the NF exploited to recruit amongst disaffected white youths. According to one estimate, thirty-one suspected racial murders took place in Britain between 1976 and 1981, as the NF marched and the British Movement (BM) mobilised to claim ownership of the streets.[31] In response, with fire bombs, graffiti, fascist paper sales and day-to-day abuse evermore common, activist groups organised locally or initiated by anti-fascists on the left resolved to meet the far-right offensive, presaging the SWP's launching of the ANL in late 1977 as a broad-based movement comprising Labour, trade union and Communist Party of Great Britain (CPGB) support.[32] In other words, the ANL provided a political force to supplement what Huddle called RAR's 'gut' response 'by socialists and music fans to the unbelievable hypocrisy of musicians who made their money out of black music and then turn against black people'.[33]

As for punk, affinities to reggae were claimed early on. Jamaican rude boys, King Tubby and dreadlocks were included on the 'Loves' side of McLaren, Rhodes and Westwood's 'You're Gonna Wake Up One Morning…' t-shirt. Both Johnny Rotten and Paul Simonon brought knowledge of reggae to their respective bands, with the latter citing The Ethiopians and The Rulers as key influences to *Sniffin' Glue* in 1976.[34] As a result, connections between reggae and punk were made both in terms of their social commentary and 'rebel' stance.[35] 'We'd just like to bridge the gap between the two things [punk and reggae]', Strummer told the *NME*, an approach that gained substance via Don Letts, a Rastafarian who DJ'd at The Roxy and worked in Acme Attractions on the King's Road (where he exposed fledgling punks to dread sounds fresh from Jamaica as they shopped for clothes).[36] Certainly, The Clash's version of Junior Murvin's 'Police and Thieves' on their debut album paved the way for similar covers or dub inflections to decorate many a punk LP thereafter.[37] By 1978, particularly in cities with a notable ethnic mix, such cross-cultural pollination extended to club nights and the experiments of PiL, The Pop Group, Scritti Politti, The Slits and others. Shoop in Birmingham had long mixed heavy dub, glam, rock and soul together before absorbing punk in 1977.[38] Even beyond the initiatives of RAR and 2-Tone, dub poets (Linton Kwesi Johnson, Benjamin Zephaniah), punk-aligned poets (John Cooper-Clarke) and ranters (Attila the Stockbroker, Janine Booth, Seething

Wells, Tim Wells) performed together to cement spoken-word traditions that found expression in dancehall spaces and punk gigs.

Of course, the punky-reggae party celebrated by Bob Marley on his 1977 *Exodus* album was not without its tensions. Punk, looked at in isolation, remained a primarily 'white' culture, even if a number of bands and local milieus were multi-racial.[39] Early talk of punk as a 'white' complement to reggae also tended to essentialise the two cultures along racial lines, albeit with affirmative intent.[40] Nor, indeed, was punk immune from racism, as Roger Sabin has demonstrated.[41] If Adrian Thrills' reference to 'paki fleapits' in his *48 Thrills* fanzine offered one random example, then numerous songs, interviews and letters to the music press revealed similar attitudes permeating punk's evolution.[42] Most notoriously, perhaps, Siouxsie and the Banshees' original 'Love in a Void' – with its reference to 'too many Jews for my liking' – delivered an early point of controversy.[43]

Despite such contestations, punk and RAR developed something of a symbiotic relationship. Just as RAR was quick to pick up on and champion The Clash's commitment to anti-racism, so countless punk-informed bands played RAR gigs alongside British reggae acts such as Aswad, The Cimarons, Matumbi, Misty in Roots and Steel Pulse.[44] By so doing, RAR helped to inject a purpose into punk's rebellion; to play an RAR gig was to take a position and, ostensibly at least, support a cause.[45] It also helped dissolve what Savage described as the 'miasma of fascism' that still hung over punk's use of the swastika, particularly in the wake of the street-level confrontation between anti-fascists and NF marchers at Lewisham in August 1977.[46] The 'battle', which saw more than 200 arrests amidst the violence, was attended by Burchill and Parsons, whose report for the *NME* coincided with their own attempts to better direct punk towards a broadly leftist position. The time had come, they argued, for 'backing up the words with action. This late in the day, too few people are carrying the weight of responsibility for all of us'.[47]

Already, RAR had begun to adopt aspects of punk's aesthetic. In *Temporary Hoarding* and on RAR posters, punk's do-it-yourself (DIY) approach fed into designs redolent of prewar radical cultures. Punk lyrics served as slogans, while montages of NF rallies, police ranks, demos and strikes took their cue from both the anti-fascist artwork of the dadaist John Heartfield and the cut 'n' paste style of punk fanzines and sleeves. The music-related content of *Temporary*

Hoarding certainly lent towards the new wave, with bands quizzed on their political opinions and interviews with Johnny Rotten, Adam Ant, Mark Perry, Jimmy Pursey, Tom Robinson and Poly Styrene featuring alongside polemics on racism, gender and authoritarianism. Even the paper's staff list ensured that 'seasoned' activists – Ruth Gregory, Roger Huddle, Red Saunders, Syd Shelton, David Widgery – were accompanied by politically attuned younger writers enthused by punk: Garry Bushell, Sharon 'Spike' Fox, Lucy Toothpaste and Irate Kate [Webb].

By 1978, therefore, RAR's political roots had begun to feed into and inform punk's development. Beyond the Tom Robinson Band's 'conscious' lyrics reproducing the broader concerns of the libertarian left ('Glad to Be Gay', 'Right on Sister', 'Winter of '79'), anti-fascist songs and fanzine pieces helped formulate punk's politics. RAR badges mingled with those of punk bands on shirts, jumpers, bags and jackets; the ANL–RAR slogan of 'We are black, we are white, together we are dynamite' found its way onto at least two punk singles; an RAR record label released singles by Alien Kulture, The Proles and others in DIY style.[48] For Dave Widgery, punk allowed *Temporary Hoarding* to transform Marxist ideas from 'badly translated Russian' into 'plain English prose', formulating a 'punk Marxism' relevant to the 1970s.[49] Musically, Crisis emerged from the footfall of Right to Work and ANL marches as a band designed to be a 'concept unto itself of all things left – anti-racist, anti-fascist, anti-boss ... anti-sexist and for the liberation of women and gays'.[50] For a while, before a mixture of political doubt and a fascination with fascism led Pearce and Wakeford to obsess about National Socialism, their songs documented leftist fears of impending authoritarianism and engaged with prevailing themes of alienation, police brutality and intra-leftist debate.[51] 'Militant', an early unreleased song, name-checked Lewisham and the Grunwick industrial dispute that ran through 1976–78. On 'White Youth', the band proffered class unity ahead of right-wing appeals to race and nation ('a capitalist creation'). 'Red Brigades', from the band's 1980 mini-album *Hymns of Faith*, referred to events in Italy, beginning with the lines 'Urban terrorism is no substitute for the building of a revolutionary working-class party. Comrades gone wrong, they feed the fuel of a capitalist class'.[52]

Although many of its originators were active in the SWP, RAR was ostensibly open to anyone committed to anti-racism. This, in turn, was encouraged by a generally supportive music press whose own letters' pages fizzed with debate as to the relationship between punk, pop music and politics.[53] RAR also helped connect those drawn to punk's implicit oppositionism by fuelling political impulses and providing conduits to further campaigns and ideas.[54] Gigs allowed space for meetings, paper sales and pamphleteering. The ANL–RAR carnivals, in particular, followed organised protest marches captured in Chris Brazier's description of a 'vast range of badges and banners ... an abundance of radical literature', speeches ranging from the 'embarrassing' to the 'rabble-rousing' and a primarily young crowd composed of varied subcultural styles.[55] More regularly, RAR clubs, workshops and conferences staged debates on questions of gender, sexuality, unemployment and Ireland that subsequently found outlets in songs, record sleeves and fanzines.[56] In Leeds, for example, an RAR club was organised by the SWP's Paul Furness at the city polytechnic. Not only did it arrange gigs, but it also provided recruitment for the ANL and facilitated campaigns relating to feminism and gay rights activism.[57] The most well-known Leeds bands – Delta 5, Gang of Four, The Mekons – were all associated with RAR and leftist politics.[58]

But while RAR's embrace of punk did much to reassert music as a medium of protest, such intervention proved contentious. There grew a sense by which RAR pressured bands into taking definite political positions, a tendency captured on the Tom Robinson Band's 'Better Decide Which Side You're On'. Thus, Sham 69 agreed to play an RAR gig with Misty in Roots in early 1978, primarily to rebut accusations of harbouring right-wing elements in their audience.[59] Others, including the Specials and Madness, were criticised for not doing enough to combat young NF members at their gigs, while *Temporary Hoarding* interviews came close, at times, to political interrogations, with bands pushed to justify their actions, attitudes and aesthetics.[60] According to Mark E. Smith, his enthusiasm waned once RAR organisers failed to recognise The Fall's music and mixed-gender line-up as political *in itself*, instead wanting 'you to make announcements between songs; they see you as an entertainment – you might as well be singing Country & Western'.[61] Not surprisingly, talk of vetting, censoring and blacklisting raised concern that RAR sought to codify and control punk's form and function.[62]

More problematically, such action brokered reaction. Following their endorsement of RAR, Sham 69's performances were regularly disrupted by contingents of the NF and BM, their gigs effectively transformed into a political battleground. Over the course of 1978, RAR venues and the ANL office were fire bombed, while London's second ANL–RAR carnival, in Brockwell Park, was met by far-right reprisals enacted, first, in a mobilisation along the largely Asian-populated Brick Lane.[63] As this suggests, territorial and youth cultural tensions began to take on a political dimension that found an outlet at gigs. This was often piecemeal and localised, though none the less intimidating for being so. Occasionally, however, the violence was spectacular and worked both ways, as at Hatfield on the 1979 2-Tone tour, where anti-fascists stormed the fire exits to attack suspected Nazis in the audience.[64]

RAR's association to the SWP certainly reinforced suspicions. Strummer, Pursey and Malcolm Owen were among those who insisted their anti-racism should not be read as an endorsement of revolutionary socialism or any particular socialist group.[65] Indeed, distrust of the organised left became an oft-repeated motif in punk. Fanzine articles and letters to the music press perceived ulterior motives behind RAR, suggesting it served as a recruiting agent for the SWP.[66] Paul Morley's report on the 1978 Manchester ANL–RAR carnival complained of being weighed down by leaflets and harangued by speeches and slogans orchestrated by 'a horde of political extremists and crackpots [who] have now honed in on a ready-made mass target of youth'.[67] Others connected the far left to 'student' or 'trendy' politics, with one review describing an RAR gig's roll-call of leaflets, speeches and stalls as being akin to an 'Ideal Socialist Exhibition'.[68] For Johnny Rotten, socialists always appeared 'separated from reality'. 'It's fine talking about revolution', he told *Temporary Hoarding* in 1977, 'but that's all they tend to do. They ... don't get into the people they are trying to involve. It comes across as a condescending attitude which isn't appreciated'.[69] RAR remained too much of 'an organisation', Mark Perry argued, revealing a mistrust of ideologies and institutions that he felt stifled individuality and provoked – rather than healed – division.[70] Or, as he more crudely put it, 'I don't need to be told by a commie organisation to love blacks ...'[71]

A similarly scathing critique came from Crass and Poison Girls, for whom RAR amounted to little more than an expression of 'white liberal shit' in thrall to constructed – and, ultimately, patronising – racial identities.[72] Though they played anti-racism benefits, both bands repeated concern that RAR's political agenda was too closely tied to the SWP.[73] In particular, the formation of organised 'squads' to physically confront the far right convinced Crass that the left was but another variant of the power politics they wished to transcend. Having witnessed 'left-on-right' violence first hand at their Conway Hall gig in September 1979, slogans such as 'pogo on a Nazi' were deemed an incitement to violence rather than a defence against reaction. In other words, 'the siding of left and right has given us nothing but bloodshed', Crass stated in an essay for *Kill Your Pet Puppy*, accusing the 'SWP/RAR' of politicising punk, dividing its audience and attempting to assert their own politics on 'our culture' via censorship and coercion.[74] Instead, both Crass and Poison Girls rejected the assumption that the only way to respond to the presence of far-right sympathisers at gigs was to physically fight back. They and other anarchist bands adopted the risky (and somewhat idealistic) strategy of seeking to confront repellent ideas with a countercultural alternative that was both visceral and philosophical. The aim was not to 'beat the fascists' into cowed submission, or to harden their hatred as they nursed the bruises of physical assault, but to encourage them to think afresh about the causes of their alienation and anger. Crass' 'Bloody Revolutions', released as a split-single with Poison Girls in 1980, may therefore be seen as the band's definitive statement on the matter, critiquing the theory and practice of the organised left as but another variant of authoritarianism: 'just another set of bigots, with their rifle-sights on me'.[75]

Conversely, young socialists keen to utilise music as a political medium questioned the politics and remit of RAR. This was sometimes organisational. Delegates to the 1979 RAR conference in Birmingham censured the London-based central committee for its lack of financial acumen and local representation.[76] But it also related to attempts to extend RAR's platform to the Troops Out Movement campaigning against Britain's military presence in Ireland. Gender politics, too, began to challenge the primacy given to anti-racism. Feminist critiques of 'cock rock' were soon applied to punk, with gigs occasionally picketed by feminists objecting to certain bands playing under the RAR banner. In Liverpool, for example, feminists protested against RAR's providing a stage for The Accelerators, whose drummer's 'all women's libbers are cunts' badge not surprisingly caused offence.[77] As problematically, RAR's alignment of punk and reggae generated friction between feminists and Rastafarian members of bands committed to RAR.[78]

Despite such antagonisms, RAR provided an important counter to racist attitudes in popular music and society more generally.
Though many went to gigs and carnivals purely for the music (including young NF supporters), numerous personal accounts tell of those
politicised – or at least affected – by attending RAR-sponsored events.[79]
Alongside the ANL, RAR mobilised a visible opposition to far-right
attempts to recruit among white youths in Britain's inner cities. With
regard to punk, RAR augmented and encouraged a cognisant reading of its political potential, building on The Clash's 'pro-creative' and
anti-racist comments to enable leftist interpretation. As importantly,
it gave substance to punk's stated affinity to reggae, bringing together
two forms of 'crisis music' behind a united cause. According to John
Baine, there were 'two sorts of punks': Sex Pistol punks 'who thought
no future' and Clash punks who were 'highly politically motivated,
anti-fascist, communist'.[80] This oversimplifies matters, but it does give
sense to how young socialists found emotional sustenance in punk's
oppositionism and the collective experience provided by a politicised
cultural environment.[81]

More generally, RAR set something of a precedent that was
imitated but never wholly replicated thereafter. The regrowth of CND
from 1980 was expressed through large-scale rallies complemented
by regular benefit gigs featuring punk-related bands committed to the
anti-war movement. But to flick through the music press of the late
1970s and early 1980s is to see bands playing benefits for causes as
diverse as Amnesty, animal liberation, disabled children, gay rights, the
Greater London Council (GLC), one-parent families, prisoners' rights,
striking workers and the unemployed. If punk enabled a sense of social
and political engagement evident in the upsurge of benefit gigs and
politicised pop from 1976, then it was suitably diffuse: bricolage politics across a bricolage culture.

As for the organised left, interest in punk – as a youth culture
and musical form – gave way to anxiety about the political commitment of musicians and the content of their songs. Against the complexities of building a culture, the CPGB, SWP et al. remained more likely
to associate with bands and performers who suited their own prevailing political concerns. Examples of punk-informed groups adopting
an openly socialist position remained. The Newtown Neurotics played
alongside Billy Bragg and the Redskins over countless benefits into
the mid-1980s, while the burgeoning independent sector gave rise to

networks of left-leaning bands, venues and fanzines informed by punk and socialist politics but not thereby restricted by aesthetic codes.[82] In many ways, Rough Trade embodied these overlapping traits in the late 1970s and early 1980s, with debate as to form and content – independence or entryism – continuing to spark division as punk splintered into a range of styles and subscenes.[83] But common cause did not thereby translate into cohesive movement. Ironically, but not unconnectedly, the fractures and fissures of political allegiance across the late twentieth century found complements within the contested cultures of punk.

Rocking the Reds

If RAR made claims to be the third mass protest movement of the postwar period, following CND and the 1960s Vietnam Solidarity Campaign, then its political 'other', Rock Against Communism (RAC), was an altogether more marginal affair.[84] Small and ill-supported, RAC existed on the fringes of British punk. Nevertheless, it planted a nefarious seed from which a global scattering of Nazi-inspired bands, labels and fanzines continued to flower into the twenty-first century.[85]

RAC originated in Leeds, where the NF's regional organiser for Yorkshire, Eddy Morrison, recognised in punk the 'frustration of white working-class youth'.[86] Morrison was already something of a seasoned political activist by 1977, aged in his late twenties and entrenched in the factional world of the far right. As a David Bowie fan, he was also attuned to the political implications of popular music. Bowie, after all, had regularly alluded to fascism in interviews over the mid-1970s, from which Morrison – in contrast to RAR – found positive inspiration.[87] Thus, in April 1977, Morrison wrote to *Sounds* urging a 'racist backlash' against RAR, envisioning a 'Rock for Racism' concert of 'all-white bands' playing 'all-white music', headlined by Bowie but co-ordinated by punk rockers, Hell's Angels, teds and 'Bowie youth'. These youth cultures, Morrison reasoned, were 'the storm-troop stewards of the racism you'll never take out of the young'.[88]

The reality of Morrison's 'backlash' was nowhere near as grand. In the short term, it centred on exploiting 'town versus gown' hostilities to mobilise opposition to Leeds' RAR-affiliated punk scene. Gigs by The Mekons, Gang of Four and others were attacked; claims were made to the punk nights held at the city's F-Club.[89] A fanzine, *Punk Front*, was also issued in 1978, with 'rock against communism' raised as a slogan to 'let people know that there are bands around who won't be brainwashed'.[90] Just who those bands were remained a moot point. The Dentists and The Ventz from Leeds briefly rallied to RAC, as did White Boss from Coventry. Others were named but quickly shied away or denied affiliation; none released a record.[91] By the time RAC held its inaugural London gig at the Conway Hall on 18 August 1979, only The Dentists and White Boss agreed to play to an estimated crowd of 150.[92]

RAC's transferral to London was not by chance. The Young National Front (YNF) had been established in 1977, from which point its London headquarters set about recruiting from among the capital's young working class. Simultaneously, Michael McLaughlin's tenure as leader of the BM (following Colin Jordan's arrest for stealing women's underwear) was marked by his cultivating a street-fighting image that appealed to territorial loyalties and made in-roads to the east end. As a consequence, punk's audience began to include those for whom aggression, rebelliousness and claims to working-class authenticity coalesced with fascist and ultra-nationalist politics. Or, as 'Chubby' Chris Henderson put it: 'The lads fought on a Saturday afternoon, and new punk bands sang about it later in their raw unrefined lyrics ... now the boys would smash up a pub to the sound of The Clash or Generation X instead of the Four Tops'.[93]

As this suggests, far-right claims to punk were initially vicarious. Bands were adopted and followed irrespective of their political views. Beyond Sham 69, groups such as The Lurkers and Menace were among those chosen to facilitate displays of territorial pissing; punk and RAR gigs became targets for retribution.[94] Very quickly, a skinhead image – understood to be more authentically proletarian once punk's art school origins were revealed – was cultivated by young BM and NF members keen to colonise the cultural spaces opened up by punk. Gary Hitchcock, a young BM skinhead in 1977, claimed not to have related to punk at first. But 'all the clubs were either disco or punk and the discos never let us in, so we used to go to punk clubs to meet and have a beer'.[95] The Vortex, in Wardour Street, became known for its intimidating atmosphere.[96]

Despite the presence of a young fascist milieu at London's punk gigs, it took a while before bands openly aligned to the far right. Skrewdriver, a punk group from Poulton-le-Fylde near Blackpool, relocated to London in 1977 and soon gained an audience that included

BM and NF members in its ranks. For some time, however, the group's singer, Ian Stuart, prevaricated as to his political and subcultural allegiance, disavowing his skinhead following in 1978 and repeatedly splitting and reforming his band in search of a more congenial musical career.[97] In 1979, despite having by then joined the NF, he declined RAC's invitation to play the Conway Hall gig for reasons of 'record company pressure'. It was only in 1982 that Stuart finally broke cover, once more reforming Skrewdriver and issuing the single 'White Power' in 1983 on the White Noise Records label set up by Joe Pearce and financed by the NF. Two years later, Skrewdriver's *Blood & Honour* album provided the name for what would become a global franchise of Nazi-affiliated music, clothes and magazines.[98] Prior to Skrewdriver's emergence as figureheads of an openly Nazi music scene, RAC existed more in name than in substance. *Bulldog*, the YNF magazine edited by Pearce, included an RAC page from 1979, featuring short articles on bands and an 'RAC Chart' made up primarily of punk songs. An RAC fanzine, *Rocking the Reds*, also emerged, comprising a similar mix of items and reviews. In both cases, the political allegiance of a band or the intended meaning of a song was less relevant than the trigger response accorded to words such as 'white', 'England' or images that evoked fascism and ultra-nationalism. The Skids' *Days of Europa* (1979), for example, was featured for its cover artwork's reference to the 1936 Olympics and choice quotes about European pride and nationalism were attributed to the band's singer, Richard Jobson. Alternately, a song such as 'Dresden' by UK Decay could be extolled for its World War II reference.[99] The Clash, Crass, Specials and Stiff Little Fingers were among those listed in the RAC chart, without any hint of irony.

Nor was RAC firmly committed to punk. The revived skinhead youth culture of the mid-1970s coincided with the NF and BM's recruitment drive among the young working class, contentiously fusing skinhead style with far-right politics. This was often just a pose, as Suggs (Graham McPherson), singer in Madness and part of London's skinhead milieu, made clear.

> [You] go round all these kids houses and they've got, like, Union Jack jackets and British Movement shirts, and it's all this game of going down Brick Lane every Sunday marching for the British Movement and it all gets a bit heavy … It gives them something.

"WE ARE SOMETHING" ... There's a lot of horrible perverts backing all these things, but the average punter doesn't know what the fuck's going on. He sees the Union Jack, hears the national anthem, remembers what his old man was saying about the war ...[100]

For others, however, far-right politics became a vocation that found cultural expression in music and style. Both the NF and BM sought to exploit this, providing young skinheads with a political focus to express their disaffection and territorialism. In *Bulldog*, bands associated with 2-Tone received attention on account of their skinhead audience; gigs by the likes of Bad Manners became sites for paper sales and political display.[101] Chants of *seig heil* too often rung out as a signal of violent intent and a ready-made goad to students or 'the left'.

More surprisingly, perhaps, both Morrison and Pearce wrote enthusiastic articles about new romanticism and electronic music. Where Pearce's *Bulldog* featured pieces celebrating the 'white European dance music' of Spandau Ballet, so Morrison traced his interest in Bowie through to the electronic music of Ultravox and the Human League. Writing in the NF's *Spearhead* journal, Morrison described synth pop as combining 'strains of classical and traditional Aryan music' to form a modern folk music.[102] By 1982, the 'haunting' Death in June also featured in *Bulldog*, completing Pearce and Wakeford's transition from left-wing agitators to right-wing avant-gardists producing sullen hymns to the holocaust.[103]

Crude punk rock, however, remained RAC's music of choice. Beyond *Bulldog*'s coverage of punk and Oi! bands unconnected to the far right, a few young fascists began to join or form their own groups. The BM's Glen Bennett and, occasionally, Nicky Crane, played in The Afflicted; Henderson became the singer of Combat 84; Hitchcock helped his erstwhile BM comrade Gary Hodges form the ostensibly non-political 4-Skins. By the early 1980s, moreover, a smattering of bands – Brutal Attack, Diehards, London Branch, The Ovaltinees, Peter and the Wolf – began to write ultra-nationalistic and explicitly racist songs that moved some way from punk/Oi!'s occasionally patriotic dystopianism. Most of these bands had BM roots or tendencies, thereby explaining perhaps their absence from the NF-aligned *Bulldog* prior to RAC's official relaunch in 1983 (intra-right-wing rivalries could be fierce). Nevertheless, it was they who combined with Skrewdriver to form the nucleus of a distinctly nationalist, 'white power' scene in the UK. The clandestine London gig held in April 1983 to relaunch RAC comprised Skrewdriver, The Ovaltinees and Peter and the Wolf.[104]

Gigs featuring nascent 'white power' bands initially took place in small pub venues or at clubs in support of better-known bands. Skrewdriver, for example, made their 1982 'comeback' at the 100 Club in Oxford Street, while Skunx (later Streets) at the Blue Coat Boy in Islington put on punk gigs in the early 1980s that attracted a far-right audience to see the likes of Brutal Attack. The Agricultural pub nearby became a regular for young NF and BM skinheads in the 1980s. Over time, however, as the politics became more overt, so bands found gigs harder to come by. The music press steered clear beyond the odd exposé of a particular band's Nazi sympathies, while anti-fascists organised as Red Action mobilised to drive the far-right underground.[105] 'Sussed' skinheads began to distinguish themselves from the 'boneheads', reasserting the subculture's cross-cultural origins in sixties soul, ska and early reggae.[106] Some even began to suggest punk and Oi! had distorted the culture's style and substance.[107] Ultimately, too, the audience for songs extolling National Socialism and race hatred was a limited one that few bands wanted anything to do with. The Cockney Rejects and Angelic Upstarts chose to physically beat the BM element out of their audience.[108]

As a result, fascist punk retreated underground into a world of internecine struggles. Not only did divisions on the far right break the connection between Skrewdriver and the NF in the mid-1980s, but gigs had to be held secretly in order to avoid censor or anti-fascist reprisals. Directions to meeting points were circulated surreptitiously; venues were often not known until the day of the event or found far from the usual music circuit. The White Noise Club's summer festivals took place on a Suffolk farm belonging to the father of future British National Party (BNP) leader Nick Griffin. In effect, a self-contained micro scene developed, with a collection of bands playing regularly together and associated fanzines providing interviews and coverage.[109] Conversely, as Nazi flags and Nordic imagery came to predominate, so connections were made to far-right milieus on the continent and in the US.[110] Blood & Honour, established by Ian Stuart and others in 1987, morphed into its own music-based political movement, nominally independent from any recognised far-right party but replete with its own internal rivalries, financial disagreements and sexual scandals.[111]

That punk inspired a fascist variant should not really surprise. Sophie Richmond, who worked on Suburban Press with Jamie Reid before managing the Sex Pistols' office in 1976–79, worried that punk's 'rebellious stance at this point of political time could equally lead rightwards as leftwards'. In her diary, she recorded discussions between Reid and McLaren as to the Pistols' political potential: 'It's all double edged but at least it's not the dead-end that I feel the political parties to be ... perhaps the message is not as important as the practice'.[112] Certainly, the utilisation of Nazi symbolism and fascination with all things abject revealed dark impulses that led potentially beyond the provocative or voyeuristic. As Jon Savage noted in *London's Outrage* (1976): '[The] bully-boy sex-power of Nazism/fascism is very attractive & an easy solution to our complex moral and social dilemmas ... The cult of the powerful ... is just too right for the vacuum following failed hippie / acid mysticism & ethos'.[113] For this reason, industrial music similarly accommodated those whose interest in extremes led to Nazism, while in between emerged a neo-folk sound from the likes of Death in June, Above the Ruins and Sol Invictus through which the more esoteric roots of fascism were explored.[114] Read literally, punk's use of the swastika pointed to a reactionary radicalism with transgressive appeal: the ultimate and ugliest anti-social gesture.

Strive to Survive Causing Least Suffering Possible ...

British punk's relationship to anarchy may be traced back to its origins. 'Anarchy in the UK' represented the Sex Pistols' first real statement of intent, a call to arms that suggested a subversive ideological undercurrent lay beneath all the noise and confrontation. In its title and lyrics, the song served both as a cry for personal freedom and a totem of the UK's decline amidst the perceived crises of 1976–77.[115] Initial pressings of the single came wrapped in a sheer-black sleeve that signalled the anarchy flag and a nihilistic urge to destroy.

Then again, of course, use of the term 'anarchy' did not thereby commit the Pistols (or punk) to a political creed. The symbol of a circled 'A' was part of a far broader mix of radical and seditious references drawn by McLaren, Reid and Westwood from the extremes of politics, sex, crime and irreligion. McLaren, as revealed by his brief connection to King Mob, was in thrall to the disruptive pleasure suggested by anarchy rather than its intellectual gravitas.[116] Talking to the

NME in 1976, he stated: 'I just see it [anarchy] as a reaction against the last five years of stagnation ... a statement of self-rule, of ultimate independence, of do-it-yourself'.[117] As for Rotten, he sung of wanting to 'be' anarchy; to embody it rather than pursue it as an aim in itself. 'You should write about what's happening', he told *Melody Maker* in 1977. But '"Anarchy in the UK" was about MUSICAL anarchy', a way to 'overcome the boredom'.[118]

In time, both anarchy-the-word and anarchy-the-symbol became synonymous with punk. Both featured regularly on the clothes produced by Westwood for Seditionaries and fed into the DIY designs that festooned shirts, armbands and leather jackets into the 1980s. The anarchy symbol became a graffiti staple, a recurrent motif to be inserted into band names, logos and punk record covers.[119] As a result, discussion as to just what anarchy *meant* soon began to inform debates triggered by punk.

Early on, the nihilist implications of punk's disruption fanned discussion. Mick Farren, writing in the *NME*, wondered if anarchy signified an 'attack on conventional greyness' or a 'destructive free-form Nazism' that incited violence and hate.[120] The all-consuming nature of the Sex Pistols' fury – 'we hate everything'[121] – imbued their reference to anarchy with a wilful negation that compounded Rotten's prophecy of no future. Arguably, the Sex Pistols' potency came from their apparent amorality; the transgressive, chaotic joy of delinquency played out in public at the heart of the spectacle. To this end, the media's response to punk reflected long-held establishment fears of the unruly mob: 'foul mouthed yobs' let loose to riot and devastate.

More typically, perhaps, the term was used descriptively to capture punk's irreverence and creative fervour. Punk's immediacy – and stated disregard for predetermined social or cultural mores – harboured an anarchistic urge. Thus, Jonh Ingham's first review of the Sex Pistols, written before 'Anarchy in the UK' had made the set list, described the band's creating an atmosphere of 'anarchy, rebellion and exclusiveness'.[122] Not dissimilarly, The Stranglers' Hugh Cornwell spoke of anarchy's 'applied meaning' in a cultural context, denoting rock 'n' roll as a primal force, a 'means of releasing parts of the unconscious repressed or buried in modern society'.[123] Boiled down, 'anarchy' encapsulated punk's allusions to 'be yourself', 'think for yourself' and 'do what you want to do'. In other words, it served to denote a desire for individual freedom simultaneously expressed through songs such as 'Oh Bondage, Up Yours!' (X-Ray Spex), 'I Just Wanna Be Myself' (Drones) or Buzzcocks' 'Autonomy'.[124]

For others, raising the black flag necessitated more serious intent. Crass, in particular, emerged over the late-1970s to give substance to punk's anarchic impulse.[125] This took time. Though formed in 1977, the band remained relatively obscure prior to releasing their first record in early 1979. Initially, too, Crass mirrored the Sex Pistols in presenting the anarchy symbol as part of an evolving linguistic and semiotic arsenal designed to provoke, confuse and disrupt. Where the Pistols used sex and politics to goad a reaction, so Crass used the anarchy sign alongside the peace emblem associated with CND and a distinctive motif that comprised a mesh of cross, swastika and Union Jack. 'The whole appearance is designed to be a barrage of contradictions', Rimbaud explained to *The Leveller*, 'we try and challenge people on every ground we can. The appearance is fascist. We wear black. The symbol which hangs behind us looks a mish-mash of different flags. The contradictions are with what we are and what we're singing about. We look macho and we're not macho'.[126] Unlike the Sex Pistols, however, Crass committed to working wherever possible outside the mechanisms of the culture industry, a decision further motivated by the problems surrounding the 'antichrist/feminist' statement 'Asylum' on their debut Small Wonder release (see Chapter 2).[127]

Such experience, combined with a growing disaffection at the ways by which punk had been co-opted and codified over the course of 1977–78, spurred Crass to hone and disseminate their political perspective. Record sleeves and fanzine interviews became sites of communication and information, revealing an evolving philosophy and approach that sought to give meaning to punk's protest. Anarchism, meanwhile, allowed Crass to retain a link to punk's initial revolt while also steering a pathway between the binaries of 'left' and 'right' that they understood as two opposing manifestations of political power. Thus, as RAR gave cultural expression to the ANL's campaign to nullify the NF, and as the NF and BM mobilised to colonise punk gigs, so Crass adopted anarchy as a workable description of their own modus operandi: living collectively, forging a creative existence that challenged the prevailing structures of society, circumnavigating the music industry and commercial media.[128]

As this suggests, the anarchism associated with Crass and, by extension, the 'anarcho-punk' culture they inspired, was not based on a close reading of any pre-existing doctrine. Though Poison Girls boasted a history that had seen members selling the anarchist paper *Freedom* long before punk, Crass pioneered a kind of DIY-anarchism that drew from a range of countercultural, literary and artistic influences.[129] As a critique, the artwork of Gee Vaucher, Andy Palmer and the writings of Penny Rimbaud, Pete Wright, Eve Libertine (Bronwyn Lloyd Jones) et al. combined to demystify the socioeconomic, political and cultural structures that maintained existing power relations. 'We are born free', Rimbaud wrote, 'but almost immediately we're subjected to conditioning in preparation for a life of slavery within the system.'[130] From such reasoning, religion was recognised as an archaic root of oppression, a moral and institutional construct deployed historically to protect ruling elites by mentally, emotionally and physically enslaving those over whom they governed. The state, meanwhile, was presented as an apparatus of repression that wielded power in defence of vested interests (politicians, the owners of capital); its forces – the police, military and law courts – provided the tools by which all vestige of resistance was controlled, suppressed and destroyed. The media, of course, served as an opiate for the masses and means of indoctrination. At a social level, the family existed as a site of conditioning through which gender roles, patriarchy and hegemonic values were imposed and further reinforced via the education system. The advance of capital was serviced through the exploitation of science and a war machine that projected the threat of nuclear holocaust to both terrorise and subjugate; the Cold War was a power play of two elite systems engaged in a destructive endgame. From a British perspective, Margaret Thatcher emerged to become an icon of state oppression: the instigator of war and the public persona of a system willing to crush those seeking to exist outside or challenge her vision of Britain's 'new beginning'.[131]

Crass were careful not to present their ideas as an ideology or programme. The underlying 'message' was eventually encapsulated in the slogan 'There Is No Authority but Yourself'. Nevertheless, the band did claim to guide by example. As anarchists, they strove 'to break the circle of violence', to 'make their own decisions and choices in life free from imposed restrictions'. By so doing, Crass recognised the need to 'respect those rights in others', a position that allied their anarchy to pacifism. In Rimbaud's words, Crass sought to 'subvert the system that perverts our lives', be it through actions (political and cultural) or developing alternative social structures, meaning squats, communes and housing co-ops; information services; gardening and health groups; free schools; community centres and 'work banks' to exchange individual skills for the skills of others.[132] 'The most powerful of our non-violent methods', the band's film-maker Mick Duffield added, 'are non-co-operation with the establishment and the building up of different ways of life and survival'.[133] To this end, Crass' own Dial House served as a creative hub that inspired countless bands, record labels and political initiatives to unfold over the 1980s.

Clearly, Crass' anarchism extended beyond the pop-cultural form they used as a means of communication. Though the band's ideas evolved over time – and began to take a harsher, more confrontational tone in the wake of the 1982 Falklands crisis and Thatcher's election victory in 1983[134] – their roots stretched back to at least the 1960s counterculture; to the commune movements, experimental art and free festivals that Crass subsequently recast through punk's angry aesthetic.[135] The band applied films – such as Duffield's *Autopsy* – to augment their live performance, confronting the audience with a barrage of images spliced from news reports, documentaries, found and original footage. Leaflets, pamphlets and badges were printed and distributed at gigs and through fanzines, lending support to an array of causes and providing information as to living cheaply or what to do if arrested. By design, Crass kept costs to a minimum, playing non-commercial venues – church halls, community centres, scout huts – scattered across the country and away from the standard gig circuit. In so doing, they helped forge networks that grew to sustain a recognisably anarchist strand within punk's broader culture into the 1980s and beyond.

More concerted political actions were also undertaken. A graffiti campaign was organised across the London underground throughout 1979, applying stencilled slogans – 'Fight War Not Wars: Destroy Power Not People' – to walls and advertising hoardings. In late 1982, the band helped arrange a squat gig to be held eventually at London's Zig Zag club, reclaiming the venue to stage a day-long event replete with 'free food, free shelter, free information, free music, free ideas ...'[136] A year later, having already produced two records condemning the Falklands War that led to questions in parliament and the threat of prosecution, Crass sparked an internal government enquiry by circulating a hoax-tape pertaining to a conversation on military brinkmanship between Margaret Thatcher and Ronald Reagan.[137] Less seriously, the band had previously tricked *Loving* magazine into giving away a free flexi-disc of a song, 'Our Wedding' (1981), that critiqued the institution of marriage beneath a saccharine synthesiser tune replete with church bells and Joy de Vivre's (Joy Haney's) words of passive obedience.

Such activity led Crass to connect with existent political campaigns. The band's anti-war sentiment and adoption of the peace symbol facilitated contact with CND, for whom they played benefits and circulated anti-war material to a growing audience. Fund-raising gigs were also organised for radical publications and fanzines (*Final Straw*, *The Leveller*, *Peace News*, *Toxic Graffitti*); support was given to initiatives such as the Autonomy Centre set up in London's Wapping in 1981. Provisional conversations were even held with anarchist collectives, to the extent that Crass have since been identified as a 'catalyst' towards the revitalisation of British anarchism over the 1980s, replenishing its advocates and reimagining its potential.[138]

As this suggests, it is difficult to overestimate the influence of Crass in terms of transforming punk's anarchist rhetoric into practice. And yet, the band did not exist in a vacuum. Early on, following formative gigs supporting the UK Subs, they played with a smattering of like-minded artists who sought similar substance from punk's revolt. Poison Girls, in particular, presented scathing anarcho-feminist critiques of family, rock 'n' roll and militarism that complemented Crass' approach.[139] Having relocated from Brighton to Burleigh House in Epping (and then to Leytonstone in late 1980), they set up their own Xntrix label to disseminate early releases by Fatal Microbes (with Small Wonder), The Mob (on their All the Madmen label), Conflict and Rubella Ballet.[140] Annie Anxiety (Ann Bandez), who arrived at Dial House from New York in 1978, also worked closely with Crass, splicing sounds together and bemusing audiences with poems of 'cyanide tears'.[141] Zounds, from Oxford, became associated with Crass at the turn of the decade, primarily on account of their possessing a comparable countercultural heritage in their experience of 1970s free festivals.[142]

Over time, however, Crass' influence saw bands form or develop as a direct consequence of their example. So, for instance, Flux of Pink Indians changed their name from The Epileptics to develop a far more politicised approach after performing with Crass and Poison Girls. Their debut EP, *Neu Smell* (1981), was released on Crass Records and featured animal rights lyrics that soon became a staple of punk's anarchist politics.[143] Flux were suitably motivated, moreover, to establish a label (Spider Leg Records) that issued records by bands who in turn formed their own labels – an ongoing process repeated by numerous others thereafter. Certainly, by the early 1980s, the number of groups citing Crass as an influence or coming to prominence through playing or recording with the band was legion. Conflict emerged from working-class Eltham; Subhumans formed fresh from boarding school in Wiltshire; Alternative set up in Dunfermline; Chumbawamba in Burnley; Anthrax, Antisect, Dirt, Icons of Filth, The Sinyx, The System ad infinitum. The *Bullshit Detector* albums (1980–84), compiled from the hundreds of cassettes sent to Dial House, now serve as testament to Crass' commitment to affording access to the means of production. The usually poorly recorded but enthused snapshots of bands half-formed and emergent from provincial practice rooms across the UK embody punk's notion that anybody can (try to) do it.

Like Crass, most of these bands – and the milieus from which they emerged – connected their punk protest to broader political sensibilities. Squats, housing co-ops and communal digs provided creative living spaces to both disengage from and challenge 'the system'. Events were self-organised, often as anti-war or anti-vivisection benefits, for which posters, flyers and pamphlets were hand-made and self-distributed.[144] In London, the Autonomy Centre (1981–82) and Centro Iberico (1982) provided short-lived but vibrant locations to combine music and agitation. The first of these had links to the London Autonomists, whose leaflets and activities served to inform the gigs, fanzines, bands and political groupings (Anarchist Youth Federation) conceived there to varying effect.[145] The Centro Iberico, meanwhile, was located in an old school building on Harrow Road where Spanish anarchists had already established a base. Lasting barely half a year, it nevertheless hosted a series of performances by Conflict, The Mob, Rubella Ballet and others all too willing to perform on a hand-made stage built from old cookers and classroom doors.[146]

Similar locales developed beyond London. In Bradford, the 1in12 Club was set up by the local Claimants' Union in 1981 to hold gigs for the young unemployed. Based initially at The Metropole Hotel and then at the Market Tavern, the club staged performances by Anti-System, New Model Army, Southern Death Cult and a coterie of poets (Joolz, Little Brother, Seething Wells, Nick Toczek), thereby serving as a cultural and political nexus for anarchists and socialists that maintains today on Albion Street.[147] Further north, in Dunfermline, The

Pad was established by members of Alternative, allowing bands to meet, play and rehearse; in Sunderland, The Bunker was organised by punk anarchists keen to provide practice space and benefit gigs for associated causes.[148] Important, too, were the anarchy centres formed in Belfast, initiatives born of youthful punk agency and connections made through Dave Hyndman in the city's anarchist bookshop, Just Books.[149]

Visual and textual evidence of punk's interplay with anarchism can be found in fanzines. By 1980, debates as to the meaning of anarchy were commonplace as 'zine writers grappled with punk's political connotations. For Tony D, in *Kill Your Pet Puppy*, anarchy provided a means of regaining the 'self-respect [and] personal identity' stolen by socially contrived 'myths' and the illusions of power wielded by institutions. '[When] an individual confronts the system with its own irrelevance', he wrote, 'it is an anarchistic act … "Punk" exposes the myth – punks are the frontline, the shock troops that herald the collapse of … a civilisation that ruled by fear'.[150] Also influential was Mike Diboll's *Toxic Graffitti*, a 'zine that evolved away from band interviews towards politically charged collage and acerbic diatribes against state repression. Issue five, produced as 1979 became 1980 and subtitled the 'mental liberation issue', effectively comprised a collection of nihilistic ruminations on the illusion of organised politics and the stifling abjection of everyday life.

> It's time to stop the farce, time to realise the REAL truth, to break thru the smoke-screen that is put in our way … the truth is that from cradle to grave we are fed an illusion of reality, we think we know what's going on … we think our life has a purpose beyond that of a commercial work producing unit, we are divided, dilluded, the sources of our dillusion are manyfold, the illusion of control over our rulers by voting, the illusion that we can be 'rebels' … OUR ANARCHY IS OUR LIBERATION, let no-one bullshit you otherwise … people should live independently of the system, don't vote, resist the call up if there is ever one, run factory's independently of any bosses, rent strikes, squats, make their own alternatives, obviously there are targets of common oppression that should be attacked, prisons, the church, the sausage factory that is school etc etc … THE ILLUSION IS AROUND US, DEATH IS OBLIVION, PRO-REALITY/PRO-CREATIVITY, ANTI-ROMANCE, R.U.O.K.? … EXIT–STANCE ….[151]

Others did similar, discussing anarchy's implications across elongated interviews with Crass and Poison Girls or conceptualising ways to apply anarchist critiques to the world outside. So, for example, Lee Gibson's various 'zines (*Protesting Children Minus the Bondage, Anathema, Spitting Pretty Pikktures*) featured polemics designed to puncture the 'reality' constructed by politicians and media simulacra. Russell Dunbar, in *Acts of Defiance*, framed his anarchy as a 'state of thinking and acting where you treat everybody as your equals but not your betters'. In *FACK*, produced by Juley and David from 'anarcho house' in North Cheam, anarchy's negative connotations of chaos and disorder were rejected in favour of taking constructive action and responsibility for your own situation.[152] Elsewhere, the scribblings of Paul James (*Cobalt Hate*), Andy Martin (*Scum*) and Ian Rawes (*Pigs for Slaughter*) recalled the millenarian spirit of Britain's seventeenth-century ranters, while more esoteric musings began to conceive a punk-inflected anarchy that centred on 'beating reality rather than escaping it'. For Richard Cabut, who produced *Kick* between 1979 and 1982, anarchism was more of a 'mystic affair than a political one', revolving around an 'experiment in life' that comprised squatting, creativity and resisting the 'conventions and expectations of society'.[153]

In practical terms, punk's anarchism tended to disavow formal political organisation in favour of action. This took a variety of forms: from squatting and attending anti-war demonstrations to mobilising as hunt saboteurs or raising funds for activist groups. Some, including Colin Jerwood from Conflict, aligned closely to the Animal Liberation Front (ALF), committing to the direct action advocated on their *To a Nation of Animal Lovers* EP (1983) that came in a sleeve featuring essays on vivisection alongside lists of animal rights groups and the addresses of scientists, food producers and fur manufacturers. 'This is what they are doing', the sleeve's poster read above a picture of a splayed rabbit cut open and bloody on a metal vivisection table: 'What are you doing?'[154] We should not overstate matters. Complaints about punks talking rebellion but doing nothing were commonplace; memoirs recalling life in punk squats reveal drugs, squalor and social disorientation to have been rife.[155] But to flick through the anarchist 'zines that flourished in the early 1980s is to catch glimpse of a grass-roots punk-activism concentrated around local campaign groups, anarchist book shops and political benefits some way from the pop mainstream or the sanitised stylings of commercial youth culture.

Beyond the large punk presence on CND and anti-war demonstrations in the early 1980s, the most public expression of punk's
anarchism was the Stop the City campaign of 1983–84.[156] A series of
mobilisations were organised across the UK, each without any centralised co-ordinating committee and each without recourse to legal
sanction.[157] The objective, as disseminated through radical publications
and punk's own DIY networks, was to deliver 'carnivals' of action to
disrupt the flow of capital and draw attention to issues of arms manufacture, apartheid and exploitation.[158]

The extent of the protest varied from place to place. Many
were small and ramshackle; others, as in Leeds on 9 August 1984,
aligned to broader protests with some effect.[159] Not surprisingly, the
four held in London predominated. The first, on 29 September 1983,
saw the area around London's financial centre occupied by some two
thousand protestors breaking off into subgroups to blockade traffic
and bamboozle the police. Or, in the words of Penny Rimbaud, writing
shortly after the event,

> Royal Exchange messengers had been prevented from operat-
> ing ... restaurants and cafés had been stink-bombed; fur shops
> attacked; people had spent the day jamming telephone lines to
> banks and offices; there had been lie-ins and sit-ins, street theatre
> and music and innumerable acts of individual subversion from
> lock gluing to flying anarchist banners from the various statues
> that decorate the City.[160]

As may be guessed, arrests were soon made (legal advice had been
circulated in advance), but the day was deemed successful enough for
another to be held on 29 March 1984. Indeed, the second Stop the
City proved larger, with Mick Duffield's film of the event capturing
the chaos and excitement generated by a punk-infused protest replete
with black flags and anarchist banners.[161] It was also more combative.
As the police better co-ordinated their response, so carnival gave way
to confrontation. This time some 400 arrests were made and the disruptive elements of the protest brokered concern among many a seasoned peace campaigner allied to the mobilisation.[162] Because of this,
the third and fourth events, on 31 May and 27 September 1984 respectively, were less well attended and met with a heavy police presence that
quickly nullified the action. Power had been tested, Conflict reported
on their 'Stop the City' statement, but the City was not stopped.[163]

If Stop the City demonstrated the potential of punk's anarchist protest, then it also revealed its limitations. Without doubt, the
anarchist politics that evolved through Crass were the closest British
punk came to formulating a coherent ideologically driven movement. Nevertheless, there were tensions and faultlines that cut into
and across the contours of the culture. First and foremost, punk's
relationship to any pre-existing anarchist tradition was always
fraught. In 1978, David and Stuart Wise had taken the Sex Pistols
to task for engaging with the commercialised spectacle of capitalist
culture, concluding that punk was simply 'the admission that music
has got nothing left to say'. Like all art, it was in fact the 'denial of
the revolutionary becoming of the proletariat'.[164] As for Crass, their
playing a benefit gig for those arrested in the 'persons unknown'
trial of 1979 did not mean suspicions were quelled. A feature on
both Crass and Poison Girls in *Anarchy* magazine came with a pre-
amble accusing them of failing to recognise the need for a 'collective
strategy' of 'revolutionary struggle'. Crass remained too 'subjective',
the article insisted, too self-satisfied in a rural ideal that prioritised
'individual change at the exclusion of all else'.[165] More generally, the
Anarchy Collective feared that punk offered the 'humiliating spectacle of anarchism being devalued into a commodity, with even some
well-intentioned but none the less naïve anarchists helping in the
process'.[166]

Nor were Crass' politics simply accepted without question
across punk's wider anarchist milieu. True, there were many who did
read Crass as doctrine, becoming what Joseph Porter – the drummer
for Zounds and The Mob – later described as 'disciples' picking up a
'comic-strip system of political beliefs' to be repeated 'parrot-fashion'
in judgement over their contemporaries.[167] There were others, however,
who baulked at such a relentlessly bleak vision, not to mention the
associated hair-shirt politics.[168] Rubella Ballet's Day-Glo imagery was
one response to Crass' black-and-white aesthetic. Another was the construction of a 'positive punk' that accentuated aspects of 'instinct, ritual and ceremony' to provide an almost mystical alternative to Crass'
'sexless … bleak' approach. Key to this were bands such as Blood and
Roses, Sex Gang Children, Southern Death Cult and UK Decay, many
of whom had passed through or associated with punk's anarchist culture before developing a proto-gothic style that celebrated 'personal
revolution'.[169]

From a more overtly political perspective, Crass' pacifism and rejection of class struggle soon came in for criticism.[170] *Class War*, an anarchist newspaper and, later, movement that emerged in London via Swansea over the early 1980s, was born partly in response to punk and the ideas emanating from Dial House.[171] 'The only band to carry the musical-politics line forward was Crass', *Class War* noted in its second issue, 'but like [Kropotkin] the politics are up shit creek. Putting the stress on pacifism, they refuse the truth that in the cities, opposition means confrontation and violence if it were to go anywhere'.[172] A year earlier, in fact, *Class War*'s co-founder, Ian Bone, had written to *Sounds* to bemoan both the 'spectacle' of CND's recent Hyde Park rally and to chastise those – including Crass – who thought being in a punk band could be anything other than 'a distraction to stop us fighting the class enemy more effectively'.[173]

Bone's observations resonated with a small-but-growing number of anarchists enthused by punk but in search of more decisive means of protest.[174] Conflict, whose militantly assertive approach promised direct confrontation with the system, emerged as the foremost exponents of such a tendency, producing a series of records that offered a running commentary on punk's activist movement. '[We] are not pacifists', the band clarified on the sleevenotes to *Increase the Pressure* (1984), 'we believe and strive for peace and freedom but will not let people destroy what little we have'.[175] To this end, the liberating 'moment' of disruption – be it the riots of 1981, fighting fascists, heckling 'liberal' CND leaders or rescuing animals primed for vivisection – was celebrated both as a transgressive action in itself and a broader statement of resistance.[176] Not dissimilarly, references to anarcho-syndicalism began to find their way into fanzines and record sleeves. Both Andy Martin and Dave Fanning of The Apostles worked for the Little 'A' press that printed *Black Flag*, the paper set up by Albert Meltzer with Stuart Christie in 1970. Indeed, the first Apostles EP – *Blow It Up, Burn It Down, Kick It Till It Breaks* (1982) – evoked such influences by advocating direct action and rebuffing Crass' pacifist position. Thereafter, Andy Martin's politics flickered intermittently towards various extremes as he strained to provoke punk out of what he perceived to be a smug complacency. But tracks such as 'Proletarian Autonomy', 'Mob Violence', 'Class War' and 'Stoke Newington Eight' (about the Angry Brigade) provide some sense of his consistently stark worldview over the 1980s.[177]

Finally, Crass' anarchism attracted criticism from other strands within the broader punk culture. Both Tony Parsons and Garry Bushell dismissed Crass as being closer to a 'middle-class' hippie counterculture than their favoured understanding of punk as working-class protest.[178] Bushell, in particular, developed a sustained critique of Crass' politics and strategies, namely their disavowal of class and refusal to engage with existing commercial or social structures. For Bushell, Dial House smacked of a bucolic commune; it was 'dropping out' so 'copping out'. 'The real challenge to the system', he argued, 'comes not from music but from the organised working class ... We change the system by being the poison inside, not the snipers outside.'[179] Variations on this theme were oft-repeated. Six Minute War sparked a minor fanzine debate with their song 'Camera', which posited Crass' anarchist ideas as a prelude to violent social collapse.[180] The Redskins' Chris Dean, writing as X Moore in the *NME*, offered a class critique of Crass' 'soft' politics.[181] Others, including The Exploited, objected to Crass' 'Punk is Dead' statement in relation to the culture's commodification, preferring instead to retain an explicitly anti-social understanding of 'anarchy'.[182] More opportunistically, the Colchester band Special Duties sought attention by condemning Crass as wealthy hippies and releasing a single, 'Bullshit Crass' (1982), as a weak pastiche.[183]

In reply, Crass tended to give as good as they got. To Bushell, Rimbaud responded both in song ('Hurry Up Garry (the Parson's Farted)', 'The Greatest Working Class Rip Off') and in word, formulating a lengthy appraisal of Oi! that accused the *Sounds* writer of denying the 'classless roots' of rock 'n' roll in favour of proletarian caricature and the fetishisation of violence. Oi! was divisive, Rimbaud reasoned; yet another music press construct designed to 'control the energies of the bands from whom [it] makes [its] parasitic living'.[184] As this suggests, anarchist bands rarely held back from condemning those who 'sold out' to the music industry or succumbed to the allure of 'stardom'. Autonomy and DIY remained at the core of punk's anarchist vision; to sign to a major label or appear on *Top of the Pops* was to be co-opted and neutered. Thus, while Crass mocked the Sex Pistols and The Clash's absorption into 'the system', so Conflict set their sights on contemporaries such as The Exploited and New Model Army: 'the latest in the long line of scum who chose to turn their backs on our struggle and get rich on the state's money with the feeble excuse being "in order to spread the message to a wider spectrum", Yo fucking ho!!!'[185]

The criticisms levelled at punk's anarchist culture had substance. A sense of superiority, even misanthropy, appeared to run through its depictions of a malleable public rendered ignorant by the somnambulant effects of the media and moulded into hollow husks by the structures of work, family, church and state. Talk of 'little people' and tirades against those not deemed sufficiently active or politically conscious could indeed be read as condescension.[186] As many of their critics argued, class structures did matter and – like questions asked toward the practical implications of anarchy – could not simply be wished away.[187] Nevertheless, punk's adoption of anarchism provided for an important site of political engagement and discussion. Not only did it construct a pertinent and all-consuming critique of the late twentieth-century, but it generated an impressive surge of political activism and cultural production. In effect, the anarchism formulated by Crass, Poison Girls, Conflict and others evolved to fill the void left by punk's broader disavowal of existent political representation. An alternative culture was forged; new ways of being were conceived. To Zounds' request for some 'demystification about what's going on', punk's anarchists proffered answers in wrap-around sleeves, lyrics and samizdat publications generated beneath the radar of Britain's commercial youth culture.[188]

6 ANATOMY IS NOT DESTINY: PUNK AS PERSONAL POLITICS I

> [If] you're singing about life, you're singing politically. Politics is
> life and society in its perversity has made it into something else.[1]
>
> Una Baines (1977)

When Tony Parsons interviewed Gang of Four for the *NME* in 1978,
his probing sparked an argument within the band. Asked as to whether
they were political, Andy Gill said 'yes' and Hugo Burnham said 'no'.
The issue, so it turned out, was one of definition. For Burnham, politics related to sloganeering; to parties and organisations. By contrast,
Gill understood the group's creative processes to be working 'against
the dominant political practice'.[2] In other words, Gang of Four were
political because they problematised rather than propagated.[3] What
the band said and did was inherently political; they didn't need banners or membership cards to affirm it.

   Such debate was indicative of the time. More specifically, it
reflected the late twentieth-century's broadening remit of politics beyond
the traditional realm of party, government and elite. As the personal
became political, so power relations brokered struggles in the family,
bedroom and community. Questions of gender, sexuality and race came
to the fore, challenging the prevailing precepts of class, nationality and
religion.[4] Simultaneously, a politics of consumption – stoked by rising
living standards, technology and expanding media – unlocked social
and cultural arenas through which to reconfigure pre-existing notions
of status, sex and identity. Indeed, youth culture proved central to this;
the sociocultural upheavals of the postwar period were often defined in
generational terms.[5]

As always, cultural change was contested. If the 1960s may generally be seen as a period of liberalisation (both socially and legislatively), then they also fostered reaction. By the 1970s, moreover, the politics of liberation – be they in relation to racial equality, feminism, gay rights or the labour movement – had to contend with the impact of recurrent economic crises and the emergence of a New Right that was as radical in its economic prescription as it was conservative in its morality.[6] Framed in a Cold War context, the notion of 'freedom' founded an ideological battleground. More to the point, the ferment of new ideas fostered by the socioeconomic transformations of the postwar period became ever more difficult to contain within existing political structures. As lifestyles and identities took on political connotations, and as 'the state' came to represent a bulwark against cultural or economic change, so cultural practice (or cultural 'choices') began to cut into and across party-political assumptions. Once again, pop and youth culture were to the fore; corroding racial divisions, extolling sexual freedoms, experimenting with lifestyles (and intoxicants), simultaneously embracing and exposing the transience of consumerism.

This politicised reading of (youth) cultural form and expression was not always recognised. Burnham's response was repeated by others who associated politics with ideological or organisational affinities. So, for example, Jimmy Pursey complained that 'when I sing political songs I sing against politics, I detest leaders. I believe that anyone in power is going to be a dictator, and I'm not going to change my mind 'cos someone thinks I should, or doesn't like my politics, 'cos I ain't got no politics'.[7] The Clash's Mick Jones claimed not to understand why his band's songs were deemed political: 'We just consider [them] statements of … life through our eyes'.[8] Others recognised a distinction between what PiL's Keith Levene denoted as party politics ('bullshit') and people politics ('important').[9] 'We say bollocks to all politics, left, right, centre', The Business' Micky Fitz insisted, 'cos in practice it's always the working class who pay for the politicians' power games'. The band dealt instead with the 'politics of living', he explained.[10] Even then, questions of gender, race and sexuality were often liable to be dismissed as 'trendy' or the preserve of 'students'.[11]

Whatever the difficulties of definition, a politics of identity and social relations ran through punk and its associated cultures. Or, to quote Buzzcocks' Pete Shelley, writing in his self-produced *Plaything* fanzine:

The NEW WAVE is not just about music. It is a challenge to consider everything you do, think and feel. For some it has meant
a change in fashion and in lifestyle. But most of the fashion has
become clichéd and most of the groups have even now become
boring old farts future tax exiles and full of crap such as saying "I
don't want to hear about politics, I just want to have a good time.
It's only rock & roll." But it's not only rock & roll! ... Politics is
people & people is YOU. I'm not talking about party politics, not
the NF or The Tories. I'm talking about PERSONAL politics. The
way that you react to the people around you. The ways that you
love them, fuck them, hate them, slate them ... How often do you
do something to someone & not know why you did it?[12]

   Shelley's checklist replicated the concerns of social movements
that had, in turn, fed into the counterculture of the late 1960s. Shelley
himself had been involved in gay and women's liberation groups while
attending the Bolton Institute of Technology in the mid-1970s, the influence of which was evident in the non-gender specific lyrics he wrote
to unpick the dynamics of personal relationships.[13] More generally,
punk reconnected pop and youth cultural style to the counterculture's
attempts to challenge the patterns and preconceptions of 'straight' society. Accordingly, punk's antipathy to hippiedom was often geared more
towards what the counterculture had become than to its existence per
se. Johnny Rotten railed against hippie complacency and hypocrisy; he
and others poured scorn on hippie aesthetics, naivety ('flowah powah'),
self-indulgence and passivity ('too much dope').[14] But at the same time,
Rotten admitted, '[It's] very hard not to run into those hippie phrases,
because some of them were good, some of them actually meant something. It's just a shame they ruined a lot of 'em with silly ideas about
"I wanna be *free*", which meant fuck all.'[15] Beneath the spikey antagonism, punk retained a countercultural sense that foresaw music and
style as a means of self-liberation: 'I wanna be me'.
   Individuality was a recurrent buzzword, a by-product of the
dialectic that defined and simultaneously challenged the 'consensus'
of Britain's postwar settlement.[16] Among punk's early contingent, the
likes of Rotten, Jordan, Soo Catwoman and Siouxsie Sioux cultivated
wholly distinct images that embodied punk claims to originality. In
local scenes, customised fashions and accoutrements provided marks
of individual distinction.[17] For Tim Niblock, a young Scottish punk
in 1977, 'I wanted to be a part of something, to be different ... I just

wanted to look individual, and [punk] encouraged me to look and think like an individual.'[18] Style-wise, this paved the way for self-reinvention. 'I love the way clothes have the power to change the mind that inhabits them', McLaren later wrote. 'People normally wear a uniform to reflect their job or role in life ... Fashion, used as a disguise, allows you to be something you're not'.[19] That is, clothes for heroes; revolt into style; life becomes art.

Such stylistic transgressions were fun and exciting. They offered a temporal sense of empowerment; a *positive* sense of differ-ence. Intellectually, meanwhile, the primacy of the individual informed punk's adoption of anarchy and autonomy as signals of 'self-rule' ('do what you wanna do').[20] Thereafter, both anarcho-punk and the more esoteric strands of industrial culture centred on liberating the indi-vidual self. Where Crass' 'Big A Little A' urged escape from 'external controls' and insisted that 'I am he and she is she but you're the only you', so Genesis P-Orridge argued that to overcome the ubiquitous-but-amorphous forces that constrained modern society, 'the first and most important thing an individual can do is to become an individ-ual again'.[21] To this end, P-Orridge convened a Temple ov Psychick Youth (TOPY) in 1981 for those 'who wish to reach inwards and strike out ... to find out your SELF' through ritual, magick and arcane belief systems.[22] Richard Cabut, too, conceived of a proto-gothic punk tribe bound by an 'ethos of individuality, creativity and rebellion'. 'So here it is', he wrote in relation to a scene revolving around bands such as Brigandage and Sex Gang Children, 'the new positive punk, with no empty promises of revolution, either in the rock 'n' roll sense or the wider political sphere. Here is only a chance of self-awareness, of per-sonal revolution, of colourful perception and galvanisation of the imag-ination that startles the slumbering mind and body from their sloth.'[23]

The sociology and politics of style have long been (and remain) central to both pop and youth culture, locating the body as a site of expression and struggle.[24] From leather jackets to mini-skirts and on through the poised androgyny of Bowie, the New York Dolls and Patti Smith, a lineage was forged to push against social and sexual conven-tion. Punk was informed by all this.[25] Simultaneously, punk's critical sensibility interrogated the faultlines of emergent identity politics and the social relations they helped fashion. The construction of gender, both socially and through the media, was a preoccupation of Linder, Poison Girls and Cosey Fanni Tutti. Masculinity, particularly in its rock 'n' roll guise, was deliberately challenged by Buzzcocks, Orange Juice and fledgling new romantics. But it was also reasserted by The Stranglers and the male-centric class politics of Oi! Feminism informed the work and approach of The Raincoats, Au Pairs and fanzines such as *Brass Lip* and *City Fun*. The boundaries of sexuality were explored – in very different ways – by Adam and the Ants, the Tom Robinson Band and Coil. Beneath it all, meanwhile, class remained a perennial site of tension, even as its confines blurred through processes of education and socioeconomic change. Put bluntly, punk honed in on the problem, and the problem was you.

Some People Say Little Girls Should Be Seen and Not Heard ...

Brass Lip was a one-off fanzine produced from Birmingham in 1979 by Connie Klassen, Syd Freake and Suzy Varty. Comprising a series of interviews with bands for whom feminism informed their politics and cultural practice (Kleenex, Mekons, Poison Girls, The Raincoats), the 'zine also contained an essay on sexism in rock 'n' roll by the Au Pairs' Lesley Woods. The essay itself was written over an advert for the Rolling Stones' 1976 LP *Black and Blue*, a typical period-piece that featured a bruised and bound woman in a negligée sat astride the album's sleeve. Put together, they presented rock 'n' roll's transformation into the male preserve of 'cock rock', an argument bolstered by lyrics from Jimi Hendrix and reference to the macho posturing of Robert Plant. The music industry was male-dominated, Woods reasoned, pointing to label executives, producers, engineers, promoters and artists: 'the images they [women] have as performers are decided by men'.[26]

Woods' analysis was built on a feminist critique developed through the burgeoning women's movement of the late 1960s and early 1970s.[27] As the limits of the 1960s 'social revolution' became clear, and as misogynist tendencies revealed themselves beneath the banner of 'free love', so feminists began to dissect the gender politics of both the counterculture and wider society. In leftist and feminist circles, moreover, music groups – such as The Derelicts, Jam Today, the Northern Women's Liberation Rock Band and The Stepney Sisters – formed to contest the conventions of music making and the structures of the music industry. Workshops, conferences and benefits were held; discussion groups debated questions as to modes of performance and the gender politics of particular music genres.[28] By the mid-1970s, the Women's Liberation

Music Projects Group argued, it had become 'clear that [women] had no music of our own'; that the songs women listened to and danced to belittled them 'by describing them as babies, chicks, dolls'. As an alternative, the group urged women 'to define their own music' in a way 'that accurately describes us and the situations we find ourselves in'.[29]

For Lesley Woods, punk raised the possibility of forging just such an alternative. She and others – including Lucy Whitman, whose 1977 *Jolt* fanzine was the first to cover punk from a feminist perspective – recognised how punk women could challenge the prevailing stereotypes of female performers.[30] Lynn Hutchinson, writing in a special issue of the YCL's *Challenge*, saw punk's do-it-yourself (DIY) ethos and hostility to the music industry as an opportunity for women to form bands and release records.[31] Caroline Coon, in 1976, presented punk as the first youth culture not to be dominated by males. On the contrary, women such as Viv Albertine (then in Flowers of Romance), Vivienne Westwood, Jordan and Siouxsie Sioux were 'trailblazing a lifestyle and breaking down the barriers'.[32]

Without doubt, women were integral to the conception, dissemination and evolution of British punk.[33] The visual representation of punk's early aesthetic was crafted in Westwood's Thurleigh Court flat, where she and Malcolm McLaren designed and made clothes for SEX and Seditionaries. Their ideas became flesh via, first, Jordan, and then a roll-call of shop regulars and assistants, many of whom were female.[34] The stylistic creations of Siouxsie Sioux and Soo Catwoman helped define a recognisably punk image; in Sioux's case, she also helped forge the template for what became goth.[35] In the music press, Caroline Coon moved fastest and furthest to contextualise and explain punk's meaning, with Jane Suck and Julie Burchill emerging among the most belligerent champions of the new wave. Linder and Gee Vaucher produced definitive punk-related artworks, respectively utilising photo and illustrated montage for their own work and that of Buzzcocks and Crass; Joolz's charcoaled sketches for New Model Army inspired tattoos and leather jacket designs the world over. Musically, women fronted and played in an array of bands formed during and after 1976–77, overturning residual prejudices and bringing new perspectives into both punk and wider pop culture. Behind the scenes, women such as Kay Carroll (manager of The Fall), Mari Stennett (Small Wonder) and Hilary Morrison (Fast Product) provided under-acknowledged contributions to the broader punk narrative.

There were, of course, limits to this. First, not all those involved with punk adhered to feminist politics or cared whether or not women contributed to the culture. The Stranglers, one of the biggest selling bands of the new wave, were routinely criticised for a misogynist worldview that took in a beaten 'honey', 'little' ladies, peaches on the beaches, chicks, pieces of meat and 'muscle power'. In response, they goaded and provoked those who found their attitudes 'retrogressive', precipitating a stand-off with the media that defined the band's early history.[36] Their first album, *Rattus Norvegicus* (1977), was picked apart for its portrayals of male violence and voyeurism; their second album, *No More Heroes* (1977), retaliated with 'Bring on the Nubiles', an ugly expression of male lust that hinted at paedophilia: 'I want to love you like your dad … and hold your little hand … I've got to lick your little puss, and nail you to the floor'.[37] By 1978, following controversies involving the kidnapping of a feminist protester and strippers performing on-stage with the band at Battersea Park, almost every interview or review revolved around questions of 'locker room' machismo.[38]

Nor were The Stranglers alone. Songs such as Eater's 'Get Raped', GBH's 'Slut' or Anti-Nowhere League's 'Woman' make for grim listening, revealing how sexual violence and sexism remained part of punk's arsenal of provocation from the outset through the 1980s. As this suggests, punk milieus continued to include 'regular knob-heads who just happened to have spikey hair', to quote *City Fun*'s Liz Naylor.[39] Predictably, too, the music industry showed little inclination to change its attitude towards women in response to punk. Famously, Stiff Records were quick to use Gaye Advert as a promotional tool for her band (The Adverts), despite this being unusual for a bass-player. In the music press, picture editors and gossip-mongers sought out titillation where they could, while female musicians regularly fell foul of a male journalist's fantasies/prejudices.[40]

Second, the term 'feminist' was not necessarily embraced by those whose actions warranted its use. The Slits, for example, claimed simply to ignore chauvinism wherever they found it, preferring instead to associate with those who 'talk to us as people' rather than as women.[41] For Albertine, speaking to the *NME*'s Deanne Pearson in 1980, the term 'feminism' was a restrictive label loaded with stereotypical associations. '[The] one thing people need above all else is confidence in themselves as individuals', she insisted, seeing herself as more part of a 'peoplist movement'.[42] Her former band mate,

Kate Korus (Kate Corris) of the Mo-Dettes, felt similarly, suggesting feminism was 'almost something that's out of date' given how women were 'doing things they wouldn't or couldn't do 20 years ago'.[43] Even Woods, who attended consciousness-raising meetings and was happy to be known as a feminist, expressed unease as to intuitive criticisms of all things 'male' and the solutions that some in the women's movement were moving towards. 'I don't want to conform to some female sexy stereotype but I'm certainly not gonna go on stage in dungarees with no make-up or whatever just to avoid stupid comments [from journalists]'.[44]

Concern as to the way feminists were perceived (middle-class, puritanical, judgemental, 'anti-men') was oft-repeated. So, too, was the notion that feminism predetermined certain ideas or personalities.[45] In many ways, rejection of the term tallied with a broader antipathy to labels and movements regularly given voice in the cultures spawned by punk. More to the point, bands – including The Raincoats, whose Vicky Aspinall had played with Jam Today and been involved in the women's movement – recognised that the very act of a woman performing, writing and recording music was a positive political statement.[46] Though disagreement existed as to whether all-female or mixed-gender groups served best to demonstrate women's cultural legitimacy, the importance of *doing it* was undisputed.[47]

Whatever the contestations of the feminist label, the women who informed and were inspired by punk met many of the objectives put forward by the women's movement. Sioux, Poly Styrene, The Slits and Vi Subversa were among those who challenged the perceived cultural norms expected of female artists. Where Sioux was stern, assertive and intimidating, the antithesis of a demure female chanteuse, Poly Styrene wore braces on her teeth and expressed awareness of the music industry's machinations.[48] Where The Slits presented a deliberately feral femininity, Subversa was a mother in her forties.[49] They and others – such as Pauline Murray (Penetration), Jayne Casey (Big in Japan/ Pink Military), Fay Fife (The Rezillos), Pauline Black (The Selector), Hilary Morrison (Flowers) and Beki Bondage (Vice Squad) – helped define their respective bands rather than simply front them.[50] Not dissimilarly, female musicians – including Gaye Advert, the all-female Slits and Raincoats, Gil Weston (Killjoys), Shanne Bradley (Nipple Erectors), Ros Allen (The Mekons/Delta 5), Danielle Dax (Lemon Kittens), Lora Logic (X-Ray Spex/Essential Logic), Una Baines and Yvonne Pawlett

(The Fall) – demystified masculine codes of musicianship, both in terms of performance and composition.

With regard to female voices, women broadened the remit of punk-informed social realism and cultural critique with lyrics that developed towards a veritable *écriture féminine*.[51] For Janya Brown, the very sound of singers such as Poly Styrene and Bow Wow Wow's Annabella Lwin complemented and challenged the 'masculinised' anger associated with punk. Their 'shrill, shrieking' voices, Brown suggests, were a response to gendered forms of oppression that broke through the conventions expected of female performers.[52] Most explicitly, songs of rape (The Raincoat's 'Off-Duty Trip'; Rhoda Dakar's chart-bound 2-Tone release, 'The Boiler'; Honey Bane's 'Girl on the Run'; Zos Kia's 'Rape') and harassment (pragVEC's 'The Follower'; The Raincoats' 'Life on the Line') became part of the punk-related canon. Ludus' 'My Cherry is in Sherry' also breached an erstwhile cultural taboo with regard to menstruation. But everyday songs of fledgling relationships and nights out could be equally revelatory when written from a female perspective, be they dissecting the rituals of the disco (Flowers' 'After Dark'), the demands of a needy partner (Vivien Goldman's 'Launderette'), the illusory charms of a prospective suitor (Mo-Dettes' 'White Mice', Figure 6.1) or the problems of a mate two-timing her boyfriend (The Gymslips' 'Complications').[53] The pressure/refusal to conform to pre-determined – often media-driven – constructs of femininity was also a recurring theme, from The Slits' 'Typical Girls' to Girls at Our Best's 'It's Fashion' via Delta 5's 'Make Up' and The Bodysnatchers' 'Easy Life'.

Clearly, the creative spaces opened up by fanzines, local scenes and independent labels enabled alternate sites for female artists and writers to experiment and express ideas. As well as *Brass Lip* and Lucy Toothpaste's *Jolt*, a number of punk and post-punk 'zines were produced by young women, including early trailblazers such as *More On* and *Apathy in Ilford*.[54] To delve into the independent releases of the late 1970s and early 1980s is to find an array of records by punk-informed women pushing beyond rock's standard musical form – even towards a new language in the case of Cocteau Twins' Liz Fraser. Many such projects proved short-lived. Too often they remain unheralded. But even the barely registered likes of The Ettes (Edinburgh), Numbers (Belfast), Catholic Gils (Southampton) and Property Of (Manchester) should be recognised for what they were: pioneers challenging and redefining the parameters of rock, pop and youth culture.

Figure 6.1 Back cover image for the Mo-Dettes' 'White Mice' b/w 'Masochistic Opposite' (Mode, 1979). (Artwork and copyright June Miles-Kingston.)

Girls at Our Best

Of course, possibilities were also artistically realised. Linder, a design student at Manchester Polytechnic in 1976, had been among those to witness the second Sex Pistols' gig at the Lesser Free Trade Hall in Manchester, where she met Howard Devoto and Pete Shelley. In 1977 she provided the cover image for Buzzcocks' 'Orgasm Addict' single, a naked woman's torso with the head replaced by an iron and nipples covered by smiles. In fact, the photomontage was one of a number produced by Linder to decode media images that commodified and objectified the female body (see Figure 6.2). Household appliances and scenes of domesticity were spliced with pornography; body parts became consumer objects or obscured by confectionery.[55] These, in turn, formed part of *The Secret Public* fanzine produced with Jon Savage, before 1978 saw the formation of Ludus.

Figure 6.2 Linder, Untitled, 1978. (Courtesy of the artist and Stuart Shave, Modern Art, London. Collection Paul Stolper.)

For Linder, punk opened up a space to present her work and her politics.[56] Just as her collages revealed and détourned the gendered semiotics of advertising and the media, so Ludus challenged rock's masculine conventions and obsessions. The music tended towards the abstract, almost free-form, avoiding linearity. Menstruation and female sexuality featured prominently; the band's lyrics centred on questions of sexual politics and social anxieties, journeying through the blood, flesh, hair and sweat of a female body some way from the sanitised or disconnected media representations Linder had previously sliced and spliced.[57] One album, *Danger Came Smiling* (1982), comprised a series of short experimental tracks interrupted by laughter, yelps, sobs, screams, vocal ticks and diary readings from Reichian therapy. Live, too, Ludus sought to confront rather than appeal. Most notoriously, the band's Hacienda performance of November 1982 featured Linder in a dress made of meat beneath which she wielded a black dildo. Tampons decorated the venue; raw meat wrapped in pornography was handed to the audience, a comment on the softcore pornography being shown – 'casually and interminably' – in the venue.[58] 'Linder had done the ultimate in making the implicit explicit', Lucy O'Brien later commented. 'Through the use of the meat and tampons she was showing the "reality of womanhood", and with the dildo: "Here's manhood, the invisible male of pornography … it can be reduced to this, a thing that sticks out like a toy"'.[59]

Subsequent work saw Linder use her own body as both 'palette and process' to demonstrate that 'anatomy is not destiny', incorporating photography, cling-film, make-up, bodybuilding and video to look beyond the standardised constructs of femininity. Well into the twenty-first century, her art continues to draw on punk, dada/surrealism and the feminist tracts she read with her friend Morrissey.[60]

Similar terrain, if approached from a very different angle, was explored by Cosey Fanni Tutti.[61] Cosey had long worked with Genesis P-Orridge as a member of COUM and, from 1975, co-founded Throbbing Gristle. In the former, the group's performances and artworks tended to revolve around questions of transgression, culminating in 'actions' that saw Cosey and P-Orridge push at the limits of social and sexual convention. Nudity, sex and bodily functions became key to their work, sometimes exploring the fluidity of gender (1974's 'Orange and Blue' saw Cosey and P-Orridge swap clothes and gestures); sometimes the boundaries of sexuality and the body. One 1975 'action' in Southampton ('Studio of Lust') saw Cosey tear open her tights and pour blood over herself before joining a naked Peter Christopherson and P-Orridge (a tampon hanging from his backside) in a series of sex acts. Every two minutes a camera flashed, documenting the performance.[62]

Feeding into COUM, and central to the infamous 'Prostitution' exhibition at the Institute of Contemporary Arts (ICA) in October 1976, was Cosey's work in pornography. On arrival in London from

Hull in 1973, she performed as a model and, later, a stripper, appearing in numerous pornographic films and magazines. For the exhibition, alongside the bloodied tampons that festooned P-Orridge's 'Tampax Romana' sculptures, her magazine images were framed and collated, pushing the 'pornographic' towards 'art' and thereby blurring any differentiation between the two. As it was, the ICA refused to display the 'portraits', compiling them in sealed containers to be viewed on request. Nevertheless, the exhibition triggered enough controversy to provide new insights into such classic twentieth-century conundrums as to 'what is art' and the parameters of sexual morality. More significantly, perhaps, Cosey explained her venturing into the world of pornography as an investigation, a process of self-exploration that transformed her understanding of self, sex and femininity.

> Through working in a wide variety of photographs/films &
> venues & with an equally wide variety of men & women, all
> involving sex in its many guises, I have lost the element within
> me which suggests as a woman I must always appear sexually
> presentable. Sex is beautiful & ugly, tender & brutal both physi-
> cally & mentally. As our sexuality is a key to our "whole being"
> it has always been extremely important to me to explore & find
> myself ... My actions have always been lessons to me, teaching
> me about myself, taking away barriers which had no meaning
> in reality & replacing them with experiences which enriched
> my whole life & enabled me to go forward as a more sensitive
> human being ready to "live" life & not merely survive it.[63]

Like Linder, Cosey's work served to decode the formulas of pornography. 'I had to become that required sexual archetype', she explained. 'There are specific sexual fantasy types and deviation is not tolerated gladly by the consumer'.[64] Both also used collage as a way to demystify the form and functions of the female body. Unlike Linder, Cosey's work eschewed an overtly feminist or moral perspective.[65] Though she recognised the exploitative nature of pornography, Cosey also claimed to uncover more complex power relations between the performers, audience and producer.[66] In particular, she noted differences between live performance and the reproduction of codified media images. Where performing allowed Cosey to retain agency in her actions and ability to fulfil or dispel the viewer's fantasy/illusion, transferal to film or print saw her identity appropriated and objectified. At different times, in different places or spaces, 'Cosey' was transformed into 'Tessa from Sunderland' or 'Gayle the sizzling swinger'.[67] Looking back, she maintained that the experience taught her a lot: 'I was in control of my sexuality and of the power of being a woman. I chose to enter the sex industry with my own agenda and to explore its reality. That entailed submitting, but not necessarily repetitiously, to what went on ... It's made me a stronger and more confident person'.[68] Equally, of course, Cosey's 'agenda' as an artist ensured her relationship to porn's subterranean world differed from most of those she met on the way through.

As part of a group named after phallic slang, Cosey tended to work within a predominantly male milieu. Where COUM saw sex as 'sensual, delirium, escape', a 'key to magick, joy, excitement', the industrial scene that formed around Throbbing Gristle was primarily concerned with questions of power and control.[69] Sadism and sexual murder proved recurring themes of abjection, through which the female body was more often defiled than demystified. Of course, women artists also helped shape industrial culture, often crossing over from performance art.[70] In Britain, Diana Rogerson and Jill Westwood comprised Fistfuck, combining extreme noise with heavy-duty S&M. Rogerson, who made films as well as music, ran a fetish stall in Kensington Market. Nearby, Christine Glover and Mary Dowd contributed to Produktion, described by David Kennan as a 'hairdressing/performance art unit' that sold Whitehouse records alongside a selection of Produktion tapes.[71] Caroline K (Caroline Walters) was co-founder of Nocturnal Emissions and Sterile Records; Min Kent was part of Ake and Zos Kia. Less centrally, Annie Anxiety shared stages with and contributed to records by the likes of Current 93. Danielle Dax (Danielle Gardner) – as a member of Lemon Kittens and as a solo artist – used primitivism (nudity, body-paint) and surgical collage (the cover of 1983's *Pop-Eyes*) to complement her musical experimentation. In most cases, however, the objective was to reverse/dramatise the power dynamics of sexual/gender relations or retain focus on exposing the underlying viscosity of the human body.[72] By contrast, those women who came to punk with a more avowedly feminist perspective endeavoured to claim their own cultural spaces by, first, challenging sexist attitudes in punk and popular music generally and, second, forging new styles, languages and approaches to express female-centric concerns and experiences.

As this suggests, feminist critiques of rock and pop overlapped with punk's wider disaffection as to the state of popular music. The love songs, musical virtuosity and pomposity that feminists read in gendered terms coincided with the sense of disconnection that drove punk's 'back-to-basics' approach. The turn against rock 'n' roll that informed 'post-punk', 'indie-pop' and 'new pop' also borrowed much from feminism in its rejection of machismo and the 'fake impotency' of heavy metal.[73] Simultaneously, punk's own rock 'n' roll roots came under scrutiny, leading eventually to the formation of Rock Against Sexism (RAS) in November 1978.[74]

Moves towards RAS began in 1977, primarily as an adjunct of Rock Against Racism (RAR).[75] Once formed, the organisation committed to a number of objectives, most obviously to fight sexism in rock music, but also to challenge gender stereotypes and present a positive image of women in rock. Gigs and workshops were to be organised in order to provide opportunities for female musicians; the right of 'everyone to determine their own sexuality' was asserted.[76] Among those to the fore was Lucy Whitman, building on her involvement in RAR and *Temporary Hoarding*. To this end, benefit gigs – featuring the Au Pairs, Delta 5, Gang of Four, Mo-Dettes, The Raincoats and others – were held to assist causes such as the National Abortion Campaign, and a 'bulletin' (*Drastic Measures*) was published over five issues between 1979 and 1981.[77]

RAS proved active but controversial. Local groups were registered across the country, a few of which were based in Brighton, Bristol, Edinburgh, Reading and York. Campaigns and discussion were initiated, debating such issues as 'on stage sexuality' and 'sexism in the rock media'.[78] Links to and from the women's movement were facilitated; 'literally billions [sic]' of gigs were held across the UK.[79] Equally, however, RAS could appear more prescriptive than liberating, offering bureaucratic solutions to contested cultural concerns.[80] Instructions were issued as to what music could be played at RAS discos and what bands could perform at RAS-sponsored events. Dress codes and subject-matter were scrutinised. PA companies and venues were vetted, 'anti-sexist contracts' were proffered.[81] A report of a Spoilsports gig from the first issue of *Drastic Measures* gives a flavour:

> During the evening I became painfully aware of the lack of preparation for the event. First I should have made sure that the people

organizing it understood the importance of it being non-sexist – including the disco and bands. Second ... the band hadn't properly discussed the issues connected with RAS – image, stage gear, chat between numbers etc. The disco was a nice boppy one, but I didn't have time to find out if it was non-sexist or not ... Our new singer, who isn't with us anymore, didn't really dress in a non-sexist way. This was partly the band's fault for not taking the time to discuss non-sexist stage presentation, and partly her own fault – she'd seen us plenty of times ...[82]

More effective, perhaps, were the bands that used the spaces opened up by punk as a means of conversation. In Leeds, around which the Yorkshire Ripper's presence hung heavy as a living expression of male violence against women, feminist ideas proved integral to the left-leaning groups that emerged from the university and polytechnic.[83] Both The Mekons and Gang of Four engaged with gender politics, as did their friends in Delta 5, a unisex band comprising three women and two men.[84] Musically, Delta 5 played a clipped punk-funk that was danceable but abrasive. Their songs, sung mainly by Julz Sale, offered a female counterpoint to rock's masculine prowl that simultaneously denied the passive role commonly demanded of women in pop. Across a series of Rough Trade singles (and subsequent album), the band explored the faultlines of personal relationships, offering female dissections of the romantic idyll or problematising the dynamics of gender relations: 'Can I interfere in your crisis? No, mind your own business'.[85] 'Delta 5 songs are about the distance between people', Greil Marcus wrote in 1980, 'they don't so much try to close those distances as make sense of them'.[86]

The Au Pairs made a similar noise and, though based in Birmingham, played regularly with the Leeds bands. Arguably, perhaps, Lesley Woods' lyrics revealed a more assertive feminism, interrogating the personal relationships she believed essential to enabling social change.[87] 'Obviously, women's experiences of situations are going to be different to men's', she told *The Leveller* in 1981, 'because of the space they occupy in relationships. The songs ... try to describe certain situations between men and women, the positions they occupy in those situations, and the repercussions of them'.[88] This could be both serious and humorous. The band's debut album – *Playing With a Different Sex* (1981) – covered the gamut of gender politics, ranging from the clichés peddled by media-projected male fantasies and fiction romance to domestic violence (via Bowie's 'Repetition'), patriarchal hegemony and, on 'Come Again', the self-imposed pressures of progressive politics. As a couple seek – but fail – to ensure mutual sexual satisfaction, so Woods and Paul Foad play out their inner-turmoil: 'is your finger aching/ I can feel you hesitating …'[89]

In London, punk's diaspora proved quick to absorb musicians with feminist credentials. From The Derelicts came members of The Art Attacks (Marion Fudger), The Passions (Barbara Gogan) and pragVEC (Susan Gogan). The Raincoats, too, used feminist ideas to shape their music and performance. 'Being a woman is both feeling female, expressing female and also … reacting against what a woman is told she "should" be like', Ana da Silva wrote in 1982.[90] To this end, The Raincoats shunned rock's traditional (male-associated) structures while also refusing to adopt the visual or performative tropes expected of women singers/musicians. Lyrically, they offered a resolutely female perspective, demystifying gender relations and exploring themes of love, motherhood and identity.[91] 'We don't have "love" songs and "political" songs', da Silva told the *NME* in 1979, 'we have songs about people [and] I think that anything you do in your life is a political move'.[92]

The Raincoats could seem ramshackle if measured in traditional rock terms. Early on, the band appeared caught in the process of formation; their first records were rough-hewed, held together by Palmolive's (Paloma Romero's) clattered percussion and the scratch of Vicky Aspinall's violin. Later, they began to swap instruments and collaborate with other musicians (male and female), keen to deny the prescribed roles attributed to bass, guitar, drums and move beyond any predefined musical form.[93] By 1981's *Odyshape*, The Raincoats' sound had evolved into something wholly original; loose rather than structured, caught somewhere between the improvised and the scored. Notably, however, such experimentation was not understood to capture some kind of inherently *female* music, the possibility of which was a recurring theme in the feminist discourse of the time. Rather, for Vicky Aspinall at least, the 'whole question about whether there's a definable "women's music"… in one way, it's irrelevant, but in another way, it's a very exciting prospect … I don't want there to be two camps, men's music and women's music. I want there to be one camp, but for none of it to be like cock rock! (laughs) I suppose what I'm talking about is a utopian position – after the revolution, when nobody's sexist!'[94]

The feminism that informed bands such as The Raincoats, Au Pairs and Delta 5 (not to mention Gang of Four and the politics of Rough Trade) was typically underpinned by socialist or cultural influences located on what David Wilkinson defines as the libertarian left. That is, a cultural milieu informed by the New Left of the 1950s but also 'encompassing 1960s student protests, the new social movements of the 1970s, developments on the intellectual left, elements of Eurocommunism and libertarian socialism'.[95] This was a politics born of discussion that found expression in bohemian enclaves, political grouplets, art schools and campus bars. Perspectives were unshackled from orthodox Marxism, reconsidered and then reset to a suitably 'progressive' template. The confines of party/ideology were broken down; personal politics were played out in cultural choices and relationships that brokered new linguistic and behavioural criterions. Over time, such approaches could harden into essentialist identity politics or dissolve into the relativist miasma of postmodernism. In the late 1970s, they remained relatively fluid, endeavouring to reconfigure ideas of how life could be lived when the self was set both in and against society's material structures. For others, meanwhile, anarchism offered the best conduit for feminist ideas to find lived experience.

Poison Girls came together in 1977, emerging out of an experimental theatre group with roots in the pre-punk counterculture. Fronted by Vi Subversa, alongside Richard Famous (Richard Swales), Lance D'Boyle (Gary Robins) and Bella Donna (Sue Cooper), the band proved integral to the Brighton punk scene, helping to open and run The Vault at the local Resources Centre before moving to the edge of London close to Crass' Dial House.[96] Crass and Poison Girls worked closely between 1978 and 1981, sharing live performances, co-releasing records and combining to forge the basis of what became anarcho-punk. Into this, Poison Girls brought an avowedly feminist politics, complementing Crass' anti-statist diatribes with gendered critiques of militarism, labour and the family.[97] *Hex* (1979), for example, bore a cover of identikit female faces, eyes closed behind barbed wire – life as a concentration camp (Figure 6.3). Its follow up, *Chappaquiddick Bridge* (1980), ranged from songs of domestic isolation and male violence to brutally exact depictions of the pressures placed on women from cradle to grave: 'anxious to please, genetic disease'.[98]

Later releases, and *The Impossible Dream* fanzine issued intermittently between 1980 and 1986, extended the analysis: the 'bully

Figure 6.3 Poison Girls, *Hex* (Small Wonder, 1979).

boy' machismo of political violence, the phallocentric symbolism of both rock 'n' roll and war ('toys for the boys'), the boorish constructs of masculinity that sought to 'capture, domesticate, exterminate'.[99] Taken furthest, as on 'Offending Article', a text written for Conflict's *A Nation of Animal Lovers* EP (1983) but rejected by Crass for its apparent call for retributive violence (castration) against male tyranny, Poison Girls presented 'man' as a synonym for all forms of repression.[100] 'We've got to make those connections', Subversa insisted, 'between personal politics and why we've got nuclear bombs'.[101] At root, however, punk and feminism combined as a way for Subversa to make sense of the world. 'I was a mother. I was middle-aged. I was frightened by years of conditioning, frightened to leave the dull but very safe environment of my kitchen'.[102] As a result, Poison Girls songs could be as reflective and anxious as they were angry, yearning for tender human relationships to break through those social, ideological and political structures that 'make machines of my children' and 'denies my existence'.[103]

Poison Girls' influence on punk anarchism was extensive. Not only did they help instil recognition of patriarchy as one of the core props maintaining a totalising system designed to subjugate individuals to the interests of a ruling elite, but they focused attention on the way gender was constructed to perpetuate mechanisms of social control. Pick up almost any anarchist punk fanzine from the early 1980s and an essay on gender will be filed next to those on militarism, wage slavery and animal liberation.[104] Collages, such as *Toxic Grafity*'s 'Forming the Stereotype', depicted the process of conditioning, intertwining gendered media images with agit-prop statements or newspaper headlines reinforcing the message (Figure 6.4).[105] Live and on record, most anarchist groups performed songs that critiqued and dissected gender constructs, typically relating masculinity to violence and femininity to domesticity or sexual objectification.[106] Accordingly, several anarchist groups – beyond Poison Girls and Crass – boasted mix-gender line-ups. Subversa's own children – Gem Stone (Gemma Sansom) and Pete Fender (Daniel Sansom) – played in Fatal Microbes and Rubella Ballet, but bands such as Dirt, Hagar the Womb, Lost Cherrees, Metro Youth and Toxic Shock also bore trace of the Poison Girls' example.[107]

As for Crass, their opening statement, 'Reality Asylum', was a feminist critique of religion. 'His vision/ His cross/ His manhood/ His violence/ Guilt /Sin ... The cross is the virgin body of womanhood that you defile ... He is the ultimate pornography/ He/ He/ Hear us/ Jesus/ You sigh alone in your cock fear/ You lie alone in your cunt fear/ You cry alone in your woman fear/ You die alone in your man fear ... Your fear/ Your fear/ Warfare/ Warfare'.[108] The second issue of *International Anthem* (1979), too, was themed around 'domestic violence', comprising a long Penny Rimbaud essay and a series of Gee Vaucher collages that helped set the template for those that later filled anarchist fanzines. Spread female legs from a pornographic magazine are set beneath a car and the strapline 'You really a ladykiller?'; gender stereotypes are placed in domestic settings or amidst consumer debris; televisions project images of horror to nuclear families; a bride and groom are placed on a wedding cake below a poem: 'To describe us as woman/ To describe us as man/ To set out the rules of this ludicrous game ...'[109]

Crass' definitive feminist communiqué was *Penis Envy* (1981). While feminist themes had been introduced to previous Crass releases, *Penis Envy* brought Eve Libertine and Joy de Vivre's voices to the fore.

Forming the stereotype. . . .

Figure 6.4 *Toxic Grafity*, 5 (1980) by Mike Diboll.

The album's cover featured a blow-up doll, cellophaned and boxed. On the back, a butcher cut through a carcass. Inside, Vaucher's images of bound female bodies decorated a lyric sheet that ranged from the constraints of female fashion to the male-derived ideologies that colonised modernity (from Jesus through Marx, Einstein and Jung). Marriage and romance were deconstructed; 'Poison in a Petty Pill' cast its eye over the glossy pages of the media, alluding to both women's magazines and pornography in its revelation of 'dishonesty and fear'.[110] In 1984, the record's 'Bata Motel' – 'I've studied my flaws in your reflection, and put them to rights with savage correction' – was deemed to contravene the Obscene Publications Act.[111] For all Crass' blasphemy, profanity and talk of insurrection, it was a song about high-heels that eventually fell foul of the law.

Clearly, feminist ideas and concerns fed into the punk-related cultures that evolved from 1976–77. They permeated punk critiques of rock 'n' roll and provided impetus for some of the most innovative artworks, records and performances of the period. At the same time, such engagement was contested. On the one hand, punk harboured gender prejudices and preconceptions that continued to bite even as lip-service was paid to notions of equality and emancipation. The 'knobheads with spikey hair' were not scene specific; they came in crops, dreads and back-combed styles too. We should note, moreover, that the Poison Girls' 'Offending Article' was written partly in response to the macho posturing of much political activism, both anarchist and socialist.[112] On the other, punk opened up a space where feminist ideas were culturally played out.[113] This meant engaging with themes integral to feminist discourse: the male gaze, mediated depictions of sexuality, processes of gender conditioning and deconditioning, the personal politics of social relationships. But it also meant exposing tensions between competing sociocultural identities (class, race, sexuality, religion); between understanding gender as essential or socially constructed; between the signifier and the signified. For the leftist bookshops that refused to stock *The Secret Public* and the Bradford university women's group that censored Buzzcocks for their name and 'Orgasm Addict', see also Rough Trade's debate over the cover of the first Slits LP (the band topless, Amazonian, defiant, covered in mud) or refusal to allow Zounds to issue their 'Demystification' single in a sleeve that featured Margaret Thatcher as a multilimbed – but naked – Indian god.[114] Certainly, by 1981 and the publication of the pop-astute *Shocking Pink*, punk's influence may be seen to have fed back into feminism.[115] The emergence of riot grrrl in the early 1990s represented a further flowering of punk-feminist interaction.[116] Back in the 1970s, however, feminist ideas were only just beginning to feed into the mainstream, infusing punk even as they sometimes snagged on the culture's irreverence and desire for individuality.

7 BIG MAN, BIG M.A.N.: PUNK AS PERSONAL POLITICS II

His mind grasps his body
and his body grasps his flesh,
He's an incarnate satyr
in this twentieth-century mess.[1]

Black Dwarf (1979)

There was a vulnerability to Johnny Rotten, early on, before the media attention toughened his resolve and hardened his public persona. A childhood bout of meningitis had left him stooped, wiping his memory and damaging his eyesight.[2] His skin was sallow, with adolescent spots still visible beneath the speed-induced sheen. Rotten teeth earned him a nickname. His clothes were tattered and torn, hiding a skinny physique scarred by cigarette burns and cuts.[3] Beyond the wit and the venom, Rotten could be shy, sullen and introspective. His bandmates teased him about going home for Sunday dinner with his mum.[4] According to Jordan, Rotten cut 'a diminutive figure' in 1975–76. '[He] wasn't what I would call a sexual creature ... When he performed, it was never masculine ... it was postured'.[5]

To be sure, Rotten presented neither the exaggerated sexual thrust of a Robert Plant nor the boyish good looks of a David Cassidy. There were no Elvis hips or Jagger lips; the only comparable figure was Kilburn and the High Roads' lead singer Ian Dury, whose polio-damaged frame would inform and find space amidst punk's upheaval.[6] By contrast, Rotten's body did not so much confirm, bend or blur a sense of masculinity as by-pass it altogether. He – and punks thereafter – exaggerated the grotesque to deform and distort their bodies.[7] In interviews, Rotten and Sid Vicious poured scorn on rock's supposed sexual impulses and the romantic formulas fashioned by Tin Pan Alley. Sex was demythologised – 'by the time you're 20 you just think, yawn, just another squelch session' – or dismissed.[8] 'I don't believe in sexuality at all', Vicious claimed in typically iconoclastic fashion. 'People are very unsexy. I don't enjoy that side of life. Being sexy is just a fat arse and tits that will do anything you want. I personally look upon myself as one of the most sexless monsters ever'.[9] As for love, Rotten pre-empted the likes of Gang of Four's fascination with the commodification of emotion, complaining that 'when you actually listen to a love song and try to relate to it something that happens in real life, it just doesn't work. There's no connection'.[10]

Of course, the very word 'punk' challenged rock's association with male virility. Its etymology related to the worthless and degenerate, to male prostitutes and imprisoned young delinquents ready or forced to be fucked by their fellow inmates – a connection inferred early on by Throbbing Gristle's Peter Christopherson, whose late 1975 promo-photos of the Sex Pistols bore rent-boy overtones.[11] In pop-cultural terms, 'punk' pointed towards teenage ne'er-do-wells (kids hanging about on street corners, making a racket in their parents' garage) or a subterranean world where the weird and the outcast hid away from a 'straight' society committed to work, sleep and TV entertainment. Simultaneously, therefore, 'punk' – and the fetishes fetishised in Westwood and McLaren's shop – signalled the transgression of social and sexual mores. More generally, punk's critical temper opened the way to reimagine or undermine the unstable constructs of male identity.

Such reimaginings had forever been a feature of postwar youth culture, through which the contours of just what it was to be 'male' could be both reaffirmed and redefined. As Britain's socioeconomic base evolved, and as the institutions of empire began to creak beneath the pressure of a new geo-politics, so sociocultural certainties fragmented. Blue-collar fathers bore white-collar sons, with service sector jobs continuing to replace industrial labour as the foundation of the British economy. It was in the later 1960s that Britain for the first time became a society in which the majority of the workforce was employed in service industries.[12] At the very least, this meant the fusion of British male identity with class and occupation had to be renegotiated, particularly among adolescents on the cusp of adulthood. Educational reform also led to new learning patterns and possibilities (art school became a useful means of postponing employment); consumerism allowed for new signifiers of class and status. As importantly, the slow and contested fusing of the supposedly 'separate spheres' that demarcated genders at home, in work and the community began to have effect, with legislative reform underpinning social change and feminist pressure.[13]

One result of all this, as Michael Bracewell described it, was an existential reappraisal of what it was to be a young man living in modernity: 'gender, presumed robust and inviolable, was open to investigation'.[14] Youth culture, moreover, provided space to play out such a reappraisal, be it teddy boys combining a dandy-esque flourish with violent repute or mods cultivating a style and sensibility that, in Pete Townsend's words, suggested 'being macho was no longer the only measure of manhood'.[15] In the club and on the dancefloor, agility and finesse offered new determinants of physical prowess; the resolutely masculine lines of skinhead style retained a mod-ish attention to detail as they morphed into suedehead. By the early 1970s, with David Bowie pushing the performative boundaries of 'conventional' masculinity beyond long hair towards overt ambisexuality, pop's previously concealed ties to gay subculture began to show through.[16] Punk, as ever, bore traces of such developments, distorting and disfiguring masculine identities through a mixture of teenage confusion and critical instinct.[17]

Sex Is Known as a Screw ...

The evolving frontiers of masculine identity provided yet another faultline to assail across the cultures forged through punk. Most obviously, male attitudes to sex and sexuality were either deconstructed or crudely displayed. This was evident in the very name 'Sex Pistols'. But it was also interpreted through songs and artworks that were deliberately explicit. So, for example, Cane's discovery of the clitoris in 1977 ('College Girls') or, later, GBH's ode to 'Big Women' offered smutty instances of punk juvenility presented without recourse to metaphor or allusion. Likewise, The Stranglers' aforementioned 'Bring on the Nubiles' was consciously blunt and aggressive, written with the intent of both shocking and offending.[18] Taken to their extreme, such depictions of male lust led towards the brutal misogyny explored by Whitehouse, whose power electronics found 'feeling, intensity and relevance' in such punishing noise-pieces as 'Rapeday', 'Dominate You', 'Pro-sexist' and

'Tit Pulp'.[19] By contrast, The Passage's *New Love Songs* EP (1978) was an ironic disposition on masculine desire that was nevertheless equally direct. Beginning with 'Love Song', Dick Witts' lyric shattered all pretence of emotional connection ('I love you 'cos I need a cunt') to reveal the insecurities that drive misogyny: 'you're not a human being dear, you're my private convenience to show I'm not queer'. The EP finished with Tony Friel's call for a 'New Kind of Love'.[20]

Of course, lascivious urges could be expressed or dissected in less cynical ways. Much early punk sounded determinedly *teenage*, its lyrical content some way from the 'adult' concerns of 1970s rock. The Damned's 'New Rose' – oft-recognised as the first British punk single – was a souped-up throwback to pre-rock times, referencing the Shangri-Las as it struggled to keep its desire in check: 'Is she really going out with him?'.[21] Buzzcocks' 'Orgasm Addict', too, was a jerky punk-pop spasm of irrepressible adolescent hormones. Not dissimilarly, The Undertones' early songs of unrequited lusting retained a naivety that captured the nervy excitement of a teenage boy's discovery of sex and himself. For John Peel, at least, the masturbatory insinuations of their 'Teenage Kicks' were never bettered.[22] Typically, however, punk's critical impulse tended to unravel or disabuse the conceits of masculine sexual prowess. On 'Love Lies Limp', Alternative TV's paean to male impotency, Mark Perry succeeded in belittling machismo whilst also presenting an ambisexuality – 'male or female, there's never any incentive' – that sometimes repeated across punk-informed cultures into the 1980s.[23]

Attempts to demystify sexual relations could lead to a suspicion of love itself. From the outset, punk revelled in replacing pop's idealisation of romance with songs of rejection or sexual detachment ('No Feelings').[24] Personal relationships were presented as problematic; in the dystopian present, love had become just another mediated emotion: a fiction romance. This was not simply a 'male' response. The Slits' 'Love and Romance' covered similar ground, sniping ironically at the 'kiss, kiss, kiss' of a 'fun, fun life'.[25] Nor was it always just a gesture of being pretty vacant. Gang of Four's 'Love Like Anthrax' came with a spoken-word exposition that situated the song's title in relation to pop's attempts to universalise, conform and commodify human interaction. 'I don't think we're saying there's anything wrong with love', Andy Gill intoned over harsh feedback and a pounding beat that battered down the song's title. '[We] just don't think what goes on between two people should be shrouded in mystery'.[26]

Over time, however, male sexualities were reconfigured to acquire more positive – if sometimes controversial – readings. Sensuality became a keyword; the allure of love and the minutiae of personal relationships began to find their way onto punk-informed vinyl. Scritti Politti, not to mention Paul Morley and Ian Penman at the *NME*, tried to filter pop through a post-structuralist lens in pursuit of pleasures that freed (male) desire. The 1981 formation of Psychic TV in the wake of Throbbing Gristle's termination also saw Genesis P-Orridge return to sex as a source of magick rather than a site of power. Among the various esoteric strands that ran through the group and its associated Temple Ov Psychick Youth, 'sex magic' provided for a channelling of energy towards new states of consciousness and understanding.[27] In practice, this took the form of transgressive rituals involving sigils, bodily fluids, enemas, binding and cutting – the filming of which later led to a media scandal and P-Orridge's fleeing the country accused of Satanic abuse.[28]

Emerging from Psychic TV were Coil, whose work brought homosexual sex into post-punk and post-industrial culture. For Jon Savage, punk harboured a 'conspiracy of silence' with regard to same-sex relations: 'Feminism yes, but not gay rights or gay consciousness'.[29] Though SEX and Seditionaries had built their notoriety on exposing the aesthetics of subversion, amidst which gay imagery jostled for outrage alongside more *outré* sexual practices, McLaren and Westwood treated homosexuality vicariously – that is, as a trigger of provocation rather than a conduit for transformative social change. By so doing, to quote David Wilkinson, their designs 'deliberately inhabited dominant understandings of unsanctioned sexuality as perverse, sordid and violent'.[30] Indeed, Alan Jones' arrest in July 1975 for wearing a SEX t-shirt depicting two cowboys naked at the waist with penises almost touching was a seminal pre-punk moment.[31] But punk-related cultures were not thereby reconciled to homosexuality per se. Jordan, speaking to the *NME* in 1978, felt free to rail against 'prancing, whining queens' and 'weak' *Gay News* readers defined only by their sexuality.[32] To Jordan, all and any perceived cliché was anathema.

At the same time, such forays into the gay underground ensured that the nuclei of punk's emergent subculture gestated in subterranean clubs or marginal spaces that allowed for stylistic, sexual and musical alternatives to the high-street discothèque or chainstore. The polysexual crowd that first coalesced around the Sex Pistols also gathered in Louise's (a lesbian bar), Bangs (where the Sex Pistols played in July 1976) and El Sombreros, often spending time at Linda Ashby's St James' Court flat from where she worked as a *maîtresse*.[33] The Roxy, punk's most renowned club, was previously Chaugeramas, a transvestite bar in Covent Garden known to Chelsea's Gene October (John O'Hara).[34]

Similar patterns may be found elsewhere, as in Manchester (The Ranch) and Liverpool (Bear's Paw, Masquerade), where Pete Burns, Holly Johnson, Paul Rutherford and others joined Jayne Casey in disrupting prevailing gender conventions.[35] 'One week if you wore make-up you were a queer', Rutherford commented in 1983, 'the next you were a punk'.[36] But even provincial cities such as Norwich developed punk milieus that comprised multiple sexualities, eventually finding home at The Jacquard, taking over from a gay night in 1979.[37] As with glam, punk's frisson was caused, in part, by its combining the marginal and the populist to exhilarating effect. In the mid-to-late 1970s, a teenage sense of subversion bound to the emotional possibilities promised by rock 'n' roll still made for a potent mix.

Even so, punk's polysexual origins were soon swamped as the culture moved overground in 1977. Disaffection and snotty delinquency took many forms; punk's cultural critique encompassed questions beyond sex and gender. More contentiously, affected toughness and claims to street credibility often found expression in prejudices that conflated homosexuality with weakness or camp pretension (and vice versa).[38] Although same-sex relations had been decriminalised following the 1967 Sexual Offences Act, hostility remained. To be gay in the 1970s and 1980s was to be subject to potential violence and ridicule in the face of pervasive cultural stereotypes and residual moral conservatism.[39] Punk-related cultures were far from immune to this.[40]

Still, the silence denoted by Savage was occasionally disturbed. Buzzcocks' Pete Shelley spoke openly about his bisexuality from the outset, contributing also to Manchester's *City Fun* fanzine that mixed punk-informed content with guides to the local gay scene and discussion of gay politics.[41] Even more conspicuously, the Tom Robinson Band formed in punk's slipstream to locate gay rights in the mix of 1977's cultural politics. Robinson's relatively conventional image and defiant insistence that he was 'Glad to Be Gay' drew positive coverage in the music press and prompted reconsideration of clichéd assumptions.[42] Where Julie Burchill had attended an early gig expecting to see a 'limp wristed fag plucking half-heartedly at the soft strings of an acoustic guitar and singing songs about wanting to settle down with a mortgage and the boy he loves', she came away in thrall to a 'boy with teen appeal' playing 'raucous rock 'n' roll'. Interestingly, Burchill also commented on how uncomfortable some of the audience appeared during Robinson's set: 'One teenage girl near me was obviously somewhat alarmed at the fairly profuse references to homosexual love throughout the set ... whenever such a song seemed imminent she ran quickly off to the can, only to venture out when ... normality ruled OK once more. The boys she was with also seemed uncomfortable, and took great pains to show they weren't *together* by moving a seat apart from each other, which made it necessary for them to yell loudly when they wanted to communicate. As an exercise in human frailty, it was some gig' [and some review].[43]

Throughout 1977–78, Robinson became central to the debate as to punk's political potential and meaning. Not only was he a stalwart of Rock Against Racism (RAR), but the Tom Robinson Band's set-list covered the gamut of progressive causes. On 1978's *Rising Free* EP, 'Glad to Be Gay' (originally written for 1975's Campaign for Homosexuality Equality conference) was coupled with the self-explanatory 'Right On Sister' and 'Martin', a social-realist tale of juvenile delinquents with hearts of gold. As a result, Robinson was courted by the Socialist Workers Party (SWP) and the 'TRB' were lauded as 'the most important band in Britain' before accusations of earnestness and sloganeering took hold.[44] But it was Robinson's openness about his sexuality that broke new ground. 'Glad to Be Gay' and 'Long Hot Summer', referencing the 1969 Stonewall riots in New York that activated the more assertive gay rights movement of the 1970s, were particularly pertinent. As Phil McNeill noted, Robinson was 'the first major rock singer to simply *be* homosexual rather than pose about and use the "abnormality" of gayness as titillation ... he has a horror/fear of appearing camp, because for him it's not a flirtation, it's a hard fact'.[45]

There were few other bands that engaged with homosexuality in punk's early period. Wire's '12XU' made oblique reference to cottaging, a version of which appeared on the seminal *Live at the Roxy* (1977) album before inclusion on *Pink Flag*. Wire's set also featured 'Mary Is a Dyke', a rare (albeit crude) reference to lesbianism in the 1970s punk canon.[46] Although gay women were very much a part of punk's formative milieus, and non-gender specific lyrics performed by female singers allowed for inclusivity, it was not really until the 1980s that distinct scenes began to develop, as around Brixton's 'rebel dykes'.[47] Elsewhere, The Stranglers' 'Hangin' Around' name-checked The Coleherne in Earl's Court, absorbing the sweaty ambience of London's notorious leather bar, while Elton Motello's tale of a fifteen-year-old boy's being spurned by an older man, 'Jet Boy Jet Girl' (1977), soon became a punk staple covered by The Damned's Captain Sensible, Chron Gen and others. Raped, featuring the openly gay Faebhean Kwest, projected a wilfully sleazy image on stage and recorded songs of youthful fumbling ('Foreplay Playground'); Dead Fingers Talk, older counterculturalists from Hull, produced 'Nobody Loves You When You're Old and Gay' and 'Harry', a song deriding pejorative social attitudes to homosexuality.[48] By contrast, Gene October chose to keep his counsel, steering Chelsea towards anthemic social realism despite the music press sniggering at his gay porn past.[49] As for The Homosexuals, their name was chosen as a statement of anti-commerciality rather than sexual orientation.

Surprisingly, anarcho-punk appeared to harbour relatively conventional attitudes to sexuality beneath its radical veneer.[50] This, perhaps, was more to do with a suspicion of all things overtly fun than any intolerance to sexual preference. The focus on challenging and circumnavigating the forces of oppression took priority over declarations of desire, be they sexual or emotional.[51] Nevertheless, The Apostles, keen as ever to distinguish themselves from other anarchist bands, showed willing to explore themes of homosexuality, drawing on Andy Martin's experience as a gay man and volunteer at a gay youth club in London's King's Cross during the mid-1970s. Accordingly, songs such as 'Fucking Queer' tackled homophobia, telling of a 'queer-basher' who later realises his own repressed homosexuality. 'The Curse', written in 1982–83, relayed Martin's own sense of sexual alienation. 'Dave [Fanning] accepts his own bisexuality', Martin wrote of his band mate in the sleevenotes, '[but] to me it is The Curse, it is the blow nature struck me just when I'd got everything else in my life sorted out'.[52] More positively, 'Hello Mark' served as a personal paean to the 'love that dare not speak its name'.[53]

Martin was a complex character. His urge to challenge political preconceptions led him to write songs and essays – in his *Scum* fanzine – that proved contentious. Despites his own sexual orientation, 'Kill or Cure' was explicitly homophobic. Indeed, Martin harboured a fascination with the hyper-masculinity of skinhead culture, which in the early 1980s could lead to contact with the politics of the far right.[54] His solo cassette, *The Obscure Recluse* (1983), featured Nicky Crane on the cover, the gay British Movement skinhead who later died of AIDS and had previously graced the front of 1981's controversial *Strength Thru Oi!* album. As unusually, Martin also recorded songs with fascist lyrics ('Rock Against Communism'; 'Master Race') and advertised Skrewdriver's *White Power* EP in his fanzine as a protest against calls to ban it.[55]

Coil's relationship to homosexuality was more overt, though their interest in all things arcane ensured they imbued same-sex relations with transgressive intent. Centred on the partnership (professional and personal) of John Balance and Peter Christopherson, Coil's first release – 'How to Destroy Angels' (1984) – was described as 'ritual music for the accumulation of male sexual energy'. It came in a red sleeve that inferred Mars as the 'deification of the forces within man' and comprised seventeen minutes of drones and gong-tones designed to be listened to in 'exclusively male' circumstances.[56]

There was a darkness to Coil. They consciously sought out the marginal and embraced the deviant, incorporating samples and subjects that pushed to the extremes of sexuality. 'I think that gay people have the advantage in that when they realise they're gay it's tangible proof that the world is not the way it's represented', Christopherson later suggested.[57] In the early 1980s, moreover, the emergence of AIDS cast an ominous shadow. Coil's response was to record a version of 'Tainted Love', Gloria Jones' northern soul classic that in 1981 provided the breakthrough single for Marc Almond's Soft Cell. Where Almond's vocal delivery – and accompanying *Top of the Pops* performance – gave the song a sexual ambiguity that surreptitiously celebrated the sensual possibilities of homosexuality, Coil's 1985 version slowed the song down to become a lament for those who had died of AIDS (with proceeds donated to the Terrence Higgins Trust).[58] On the subsequent album, *Horse Rotorvator* (1986), themes of sex and death predominated, opening with a 'dizzying descent' down 'The Anal Staircase'. Meanwhile, in the charts, Frankie Goes To Hollywood – a band formed from within Liverpool's punk milieu – took the sexual practices venerated by Coil to number one in early 1984. With 'Relax', marketed by Paul Morley in a sadomasochistic sleeve and accompanied by an orgiastic video featuring moustachioed leathermen and simulated watersports, the fetishes that first informed punk's aesthetic were filtered through the 'pleasuredomes' of gay club land. At last, with Frankie Goes To Hollywood courting controversy as a kind of 'Disco Pistols', their confrontation sumptuously produced by Trevor Horn and directed towards the dancefloor, the homosexuality that had long simmered beneath the surface of pop music culture was finally and fully unleashed.[59]

Boys Don't Cry

Overt sexual reference was integral to providing punk and its related cultures with a sense of subversion, be it to reveal the messy truths of (male) sexuality, to make explicit what had long been implicit in pop music and rock 'n' roll, or to simply swear and say things deemed socially improper. Simultaneously, punk's tendency to critique ensured that constructed indications of masculinity – strength, pride, status, aggression, fortitude – were exposed and ridiculed. This often took the form of caricature: the drunken mug whose self-image was at odds with his actions (The Specials' 'Stereotype' or Seething Wells' 'Tetley Bitter Men'); the workplace drone (The Jam's 'Smithers-Jones'); the fascist thug (Garry Johnson's 'Boy About Town'); the army-type keen to prove his manhood (Gang of Four's 'I Love a Man in Uniform' or Cock Sparrer's 'Riot Squad').[60] But punk-informed critiques also set out to expose the foundations of contemporary maleness, be it in terms of childhood 'Games for Boys' that reinforced gender stereotypes or media images that buttressed hegemonic ideas of what a man *should be*.[61] So, for example, Jon Savage's contributions to *The Secret Public* (Figure 7.1) complemented Linder's decoding of 'woman', splicing together clichéd signifiers of masculinity with images from men's magazines: office blocks, technology, weapons, bodybuilding.[62]

Anarchist and socialist critiques developed these themes. The former tended to relate the constructs of masculinity to the oppressive impact of 'the system'. Where Crass' 'Big Man, Big M.A.N.' contrasted the 'myth of manhood' against a grim résumé of domestic abuse, porno-stimulated masturbation and war, so Flux of Pink Indians offered a double album that obsessed with gender conditioning. Titled *The Fucking Cunts Treat Us Like Pricks* (1984), its horror show of modern life presented a bleak portrait of masculinity shaped by a media barrage of advertising, pornography and violence.[63] On the

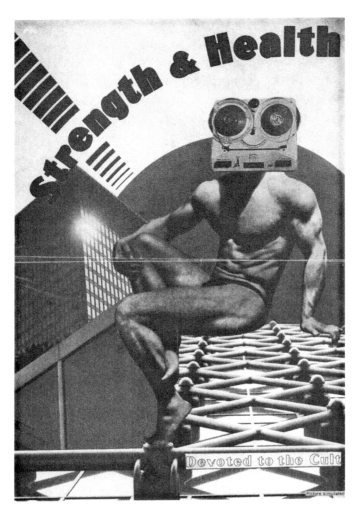

Figure 7.1 Jon Savage, *The Secret Public* (ORG 2, 1978).

left, meanwhile, a 'conscious' masculinity evolved to show awareness of socially conditioned gender traits while retaining a commitment to a politics of struggle that venerated the male working class. Hence the Newtown Neurotics followed their call to 'Get Up and Fight' with a dissection of sexual double standards ('No Respect') and a lament for repressed male emotion ('Agony').[64] Billy Bragg, too, combined a bloke-ish demeanour with crafted love songs that sought to personalise rather than objectify his female companions in the 'ideological cuddle'.[65]

Not surprisingly, such critiques brokered alternative responses. If punk never quite ventured into the exaggerated macho terrain of heavy metal, then The Clash's 'street-tough' stance drew from a recognisably rebel-male tradition that was repeated over and over on record sleeves and photos: young punks, leaning against a graffiti-covered wall, caught between the stoic and defiant.[66] Somewhat more elaborately, The Stranglers' Jean-Jacques Burnel developed his own masculine ideal derived from past and present warrior hordes: Vikings, Samurais, Hell's Angels. On record and in interviews he revered their outlaw codes of brotherhood, up to and including homosexual practice that drew men closer to their fellow warriors. Burnel even engaged in same-sex relations on occasion, as revealed in Steve Strange's autobiography.[67]

The Clash model of the rebel-male proved the more enduring. In particular, punk-informed social realism attracted masculine identities honed in the back streets and, in some cases, on the terraces. From The Clash themselves being presented as 'thinking men's yobs' through the Sham Army that followed Sham 69 to The Militia of New Model Army, punk harboured homosocial tendencies bound by a sense of style and commitment. This was rarely intellectualised, though Garry Bushell's conceptualisation of Oi! endeavoured to combine punk and skinhead into a predominantly masculine form of working-class protest. In other words, punk's rebellion was interpreted as a raucous response to a 'middle class and middle-aged controlled society which has guaranteed [young people] No Future and left them to fester in their frustrations'. In effect, Bushell sought to reclaim the idea of machismo, repudiating the negative connotations ascribed by 'wet/liberal/middle-class' critics in favour of a definition based on the core values of 'honour, loyalty, courage, strength and endurance'. And while the danger of such 'noble ideals' giving way to 'brutality, bullying and bigotry' was recognised, Bushell nevertheless argued they remained 'preferable to the introspective wimp advanced by the hipsters'.[68]

As should be clear, Oi! reflected a class-based masculinity perceived to be under threat from two intersecting sources: on the one hand deindustrialisation and the associated dissolution of communities built on collective class experience; on the other, the advance of cultural-political struggles that challenged the assumptions of standard male working-class identity.[69] For this reason, Oi! could appear defensive. Not unlike the skinhead culture it ascribed to, Oi! combined a fatalistic sense of a deteriorating present with a commitment to retaining those class-cultural signifiers deemed to give life a sense of purpose and excitement. In terms of masculinity, The Last Resort's 'King of the

Jungle' captured one such ideal: 'quiet and dignified', part of a 'pride', aware of threats all around but impassive, ready and able to fight when needs be.[70] Of course, such traits could indeed descend into 'brutality, bullying and bigotry', as played out too often via street-level style wars, football violence and, on the fringes, political combat.[71] Nevertheless, the way in which Oi! was caricatured and besmirched in the music press revealed the class prejudices that its aggressive demeanour steeled itself against to be very real.[72]

In a pop-cultural context, the Sex Pistols, The Clash and most other early punk bands conformed to the model of four-men-in-a-band. As punk evolved, however, so the associated trappings of rock masculinity were consciously rejected by the likes of Buzzcocks, Subway Sect and Scritti Politti, both in terms of music and performance. Not only were The Clash soon criticised for their apparent embrace of rock 'n' roll heroism (the last gang in town), but the likes of Devoto, Shelley, Godard and Gartside presented an erudite take on rock and pop that deliberately rubbed against any Bacchusian stereotype.[73] Thereafter, The Undertones, Orange Juice, The June Brides, The Pastels and The Smiths reaffirmed such an approach, providing a template – in terms of sound, style and lexicon – for a post-punk 'indie' culture that ran through the 1980s: literate but lovelorn, centred on a music shorn of rock's louche blues but in thrall to pop's adolescent thrill. Notably, too, such a culture consciously aspired to gender equality, a space for bands, fanzines and participants of either sex to coalesce on equivalent terms.[74]

Quite whether such ideals were realised is open to interpretation and personal experience. Beyond the vaguely androgynous sixties aesthetic that stylised eighties indie-pop (anoraks, t-shirts, flora, jeans and duffle coats), songs of unrequited love, blissful crushes and hazy existentialism tended to follow standard gender norms. There was, nevertheless, an evident attempt to soften the culture's masculine contours towards ideas of 'poetry, socialism, feminism, effeminism [sic]'.[75] For Orange Juice's Edwyn Collins, at least, it was important to take a stance against 'unrealistic' portrayals of masculine sexuality in popular music.[76] To this end, his lyrics were camp, witty and wordy: 'Ye gads, I'm simply thrilled honey'. The band appeared fey and unashamedly romantic, eschewing universal platitudes (be they emotional or political) in favour of personal songs of 'boys and girls being in love'.[77] 'It's not subversive to be aggressive anymore', Collins said in 1981, 'it's the sensual that matters now'.[78] As this suggests, Orange Juice ignored punk's early disavowal of love songs whilst retaining the more subtle intent of distorting the form. On 'Consolation Prize', as Collins muses over a girl whose love is bestowed to a bullying boyfriend, he concludes that 'I'll never be man enough for you'.[79]

The Smiths were more complex. The band's sound could be both delicate and muscular, a product of Johnny Marr's adept musicianship. Morrissey, meanwhile, brought literary and filmic influences to a pop music he believed should be 'straightforward, open and accessible'.[80] By so doing, he remained sure to keep his lyrics gender-neutral, an approach that fanned a protracted debate as to his sexuality. 'I'm very interested in gender', he told *Sounds* in an early interview, '[I'm] a prophet for the fourth sex. The third sex, that has been done and it's failed … I'm bored with men and I'm bored with women. All this sexual segregation that goes on, even in rock 'n' roll, I despise it.'[81] Instead, Morrissey was concerned with cultures, emotions and experiences that cut across the artificial divides of gender, talking of 'handsome women' and 'pretty men' towards new formulations of masculinity and femininity that transcended sexual preference ('gay' or 'straight').[82]

By 1983, as The Smiths emerged to become the defining group of the decade, they proved keen to move beyond the diffuse punk-informed cultures of the time. Nevertheless, Morrissey's approach was schooled in Manchester's punk milieu, born of discussions with Linder, Shelley, Devoto and Richard Boon. Indeed, Morrissey retained a recognisably punkish sense of provocation and directness, criticising post-punk tendencies to abstraction and reaffirming The Smiths' relevance to 'what's happening'. Place names, locales and cultural references gave social-realist shape to The Smiths' aesthetic, rooting the band in provincial back-street (bedroom) settings designed to resonate with their audience. Early interviews were also overtly political; railing against Thatcherism and the distorting effect of media spectacle. When the band signed to Rough Trade rather than a major, their rationale was explained in terms of retaining complete control over their artwork, music and style. And while Morrissey's lyrics often centred on the dynamics – and disappointments – of personal relationships, they also took in the Moors Murders, vegetarianism and alienation. A sense of conviction was essential to Morrissey, who spoke of communicating and urging people to think for themselves. 'You'll never catch me singing "oh baby, baby yeah"', he told Bill Black of *Sounds*. 'My only priority is to use lines and words in a way that [haven't] been heard before'.[83]

Looking back, Morrissey's vision of The Smiths owed much to Buzzcocks. Both bands sought to expand pop's lexicon by producing a run of innovative-but-unashamedly-accessible singles based on the complexities of personal relationships. Clichés were rejected or besmirched, while a mutual fascination with the tension between sex and love was cemented by Morrissey's later cover of Buzzcocks' 'You Say You Don't Love Me', one of Shelley's most prescient lyrics. Running over three verses, the song explored the varied scenarios of unrequited love in an ostensibly simple but poignant way. In all cases, the relationship – the friendship – trumped the emotional urge for something more. 'I try to relate to people as people', Shelley told Garry Bushell in 1978. 'I have boyfriends, I have girlfriends and if you can relate to people as people you realise that sex doesn't really matter'.[84]

With regard to questions of gender and male sexuality, Shelley presaged much of Morrissey's later rhetoric, albeit articulated in softer hue. Not only was he open about his sexuality, sporting a 'Campaign for Homosexual Equality' badge in an early interview (and an 'I Like Boys' badge on *Top of the Pops*), but his songs tended to be sung from an insider perspective as opposed to Morrissey's outsider-stance. Even so, Shelley's deliberately presenting his lyrics as 'ambisexual' was no doubt informative. 'If I was a great butch macho rock guitarist singing songs about laying all the groupies then it wouldn't mean anything to women or the people I work with', Shelley explained to *NME* in 1977. 'I don't like excluding people from ideas simply because of their gender'.[85] Instead, Buzzcocks' peerless run of singles – from 'Orgasm Addict' and 'What Do I Get' through 'Love You More', 'Ever Fallen in Love (With Someone You Shouldn't've)' and 'Everybody's Happy Nowadays' – was designed to serialise the complexities of modern romance.[86] Having helped pioneer punk's ethos of DIY, Buzzcocks also widened pop's vocabulary and challenged the hoary clichés of rock masculinity.

My Sex Is a Wanting Wardrobe ... My Sex Is Savage

By the mid-1970s and early 1980s, the letters' pages of the weekly music press had become a forum for a mix of petty musical gripes, subcultural squabbles and political comment. Alongside complaints of journalistic prejudice and undeserved media hype, readers' letters covered a range of subjects, from gig-related violence, nuclear disarmament and the validity of Marxism to sexism and the machinations of the music industry. Of course, the pitch was often queered by editorial policy, not to mention the journalists' habit of making up letters and, in the case of the *NME* especially, tail-ending correspondence with condescending comment. Nevertheless, the 'mailbags' and the 'gasbags' proved pop music to be more than mere entertainment. It provoked opinion, shaped identities and, despite those readers who complained that pop and politics should not mix, was recognised to have relevance beyond chart sales and personal taste.[87] Punk, not surprisingly, oft-featured in such conversation, informing questions of cultural meaning, political relevance and personal empowerment long into the 1980s.[88]

One particular strand of debate revolved around gender, relating both to subcultural and sexual identity. This was often trite. In *Sounds*, a discussion sparked by 'punkettes' from Tyne and Wear as to why punk boys dated non-punk girls ran for several issues over late 1979.[89] But it also fed into broader feminist concerns and, occasionally, questions of gender constructs. As always, opinion varied. Just as music press coverage of RAR and the Campaign for Nuclear Disarmament (CND) led to regular complaints of leftist or 'trendy' bias, so letters that touched on sexism or homosexuality received abusive replies. More generally, punk's stylistic evolution rekindled glam-era debates on masculinity, especially with the advent of 'Blitz Kids' and proto-gothic milieus channelling the spirit of Bowie.[90] By 1982, the 'punkette' debate in *Sounds* had moved onto 'men in frocks' following a letter from a self-professed Bauhaus fan ('Edna'). 'Speaking from the groin', she demanded more 'beautiful boys' in 'suspenders and stockings and stiletto heels' as a contrast to 'mindless' skinheads and headbangers.[91] Bauhaus' Peter Murphy and the Virgin Prunes' Gavin Friday were the new ideal: individuals transcending 'society's labels' to 'be themselves'.[92]

As this suggests, youth culture's blurring of gender boundaries continued through punk. Many a young punk had previously committed to Bowie, whose fusion of delinquent, bohemian and homosexual outsiderdom continued to appeal into the mid-1970s and after. Be they apprentice 'brickies in lippy' drawn to glam's stomp (à la Slaughter and The Dogs) or suburban would-be decadents searching for sleaze (the Bromley contingent), Bowie's disciples found portals to new worlds and influences: to the Velvet Underground, Warhol, Iggy Pop, Berlin, Burroughs, Genet, Crowley and Nietzsche.[93] New romanticism, obviously, extended the Bowie-punk continuum to its sartorial extreme, plundering and juxtaposing historical styles in ways that disguised gender beneath folds of cloth and layers of make-up. Perpetual self-reinvention enabled fluid sexualities that moved beyond mere androgyny; the guitar, which Daniel Miller of Mute Records described as an 'offensive male instrument', was replaced by synthesisers and the amatory pulse of disco.[94]

Goth also emerged in the early 1980s, a stylistic culture forged from a range of pre- and post-punk influences.[95] At its core lurked a dark aesthetic alluding to sexual transgression, including the vampiric and sadomasochistic. Over time, moreover, male goths came to be defined by their androgyny.[96] 'The sex thing, that's what's been missing from music for such a long time', Ollie Wisdom, the singer with Specimen and co-founder of London's Batcave club insisted, dressed in tights and a 'kiss kiss, bang bang' belt with lipstick bullets. 'Not as in obscenity but as in being sensuous with people'.[97]

In truth, goth's origins were diverse and androgyny but one component of its search for what Blood and Roses' Bob Short described as new feelings and emotions.[98] Writing in 1983, Richard Cabut (under the name Richard North) was the first to outline the basis of what eventually became codified as 'goth', pointing to the 'erotic politics' of The Doors and the 'tense dusky danger' of the Velvet Underground as early musical forebears. From punk, particularly the Sex Pistols, came the 'amalgam of style and direction'. Siouxsie and the Banshees provided the imagination (their 1981 album *JuJu* took the band's already morbid fascination into even darker recesses); Adam and the Ants, who in 1977–79 drew heavily from the sadomasochist accoutrements collated in SEX and Seditionaries, proffered the 'sensuous black style'. Both 'explored the edges of light and dark and some of the areas in between': fetishism, sex, magic, abjection and death.[99]

By 1980–81, these influences had begun to coalesce. Bauhaus, another band formed in the wake of seeing the Sex Pistols and whose cavernous 'Bela Lugosi's Dead' 12-inch was released in August 1979, revelled in a theatre of macabre imagery and linguistic signifiers: 'Dark Entries', 'St Vitus Dance', 'Hollow Hills', 'Lagartija Nick'. Though mocked in the music press, the band were popular (appearing on *Top of the Pops* to perform Bowie's 'Ziggy Stardust' in 1982), their vibrant live shows bathed in a blackness that was cut open by stark white light to suggest a mood of infernal communion.[100] Stage-front was Peter Murphy: lithe, accentuated cheek bones, dressed in black, imperious. Contemporaneously, UK Decay emerged from Luton with the self-proclaimed objective of evoking nightmares. Labelled as 'gothic punksters' by *Sounds*' Steve Keaton – performing a 'punk gothique' – their music and imagery drew from the 'darker side of life', a whirring mesh of taught guitar and tribal drums serving as a backdrop to tales of necrophilia, werewolves, possession and the occult.[101] In addition, the influence of Joy Division, whose gothic overtones were oft-noted, helped fuel the gloomy aesthetics of a post-punk culture showcased across the Futurama festivals organised by John Keenan from Leeds between 1979 and 1983. The Cure, along with Killing Joke and Theatre of Hate, provided further sources of dark inspiration.[102]

Come 1982 and proto-gothic bands were legion, dominating the line-ups of both Futurama and the end-of-year Last Christmas on Earth punk festival.[103] As it was, Blood and Roses, Brigandage, Sex Gang Children and Southern Death Cult formed the nucleus of what Cabut termed a 'positive punk', evolving from the post-punk diaspora to seek 'sensual revolution' beyond the 'macho mentality' of Oi! and the 'sexless' anarchism of Crass.[104] A few formative gigs took place at the Centro Iberico, revealing a crossover with punk's anarchist milieu. But goth's roots were also tendered at such venues as The Clarendon in Hammersmith, the Tribe Club in central London, The Cage in Manor House and, most redolently, the Batcave in Soho.[105] On the ground, *Artificial Life*, *Grim Humour*, *Kick*, *Kill Your Pet Puppy*, *Panache* and *Vague* documented the emergent scene, offering 'make-up tips for urban guerrillas' and distancing punk from the 'self-destructive' glue-sniffing image that was becoming 'some sort of punk common denominator' by 1981–82.[106] To the east, 13th Chime and Gothic Girls both ventured into bleak panoramas of fire, death and devils. In the north, proto-gothic tribes developed in and around Leeds, emerging from clubs such as the F-Club, The Warehouse and Le Phonographique to form-then-follow the likes of Danse Society (Barnsley), March Violets, 1919 (Bradford), Red Lorry Yellow Lorry, Sisters of Mercy and Skeletal Family (Keighley).[107] *Mass Murder* and *Whippings and Apologies* gave coverage. Back-combed hair, make up, skeletal jewellery and church-yard poses became the prerequisite signifiers of a culture that took up much of the alternative charts throughout the mid-1980s.

Goth evidently lent itself to androgyny. Just as Bauhaus' David Jay (David Haskins) talked of challenging 'traditional sexual attitudes and roles', so goth's stylistic reinventions defied gender norms.[108] On 'Mauritia Mayer', released as a single in 1983, Sex Gang Children told the tale of 'a man who can't handle having homosexual tendencies'. It was conceived as a 'sympathetic look into transvestism', Andi Sex Gang (Andrew Hayward) explained in an interview that pondered the fluidity of sexual identity. 'The name has two appeals: a feminine name that sounds very butch and masculine'.[109] Nevertheless, the culture's formative period also brokered alternative masculinities. For Adam Ant, a key influence on those who provided goth's early stirrings, his stated objective was 'the destruction of … social and sexual taboo'.[110] To this end, the Ants' early aesthetic drew from Westwood and McLaren's designs (rubber, leather, bondage), but also the fetishistic artworks of Allen Jones and films such as Liliana Cavani's *The Night Porter* (1974), which fused sadomasochism and Nazi chic. Posters and badges utilised drawings from John Willie's *The Adventures of Sweet Gwendolyn* (1974), featuring cartoon S&M imagery of leather-clad women, corseted and high-heeled. Live, Ant threw himself around the stage and into the crowd, taking the bruises with masochistic glee. His set-list doubled as a fetishist's inventory: 'Bathroom Function', 'Beat My Guest', 'Deutscher Girls', 'Fat Fun', 'Ligotage', 'Physical (You're So)', 'Rubber People', 'Whip in My Valise'.[111] Notably, however, Ant's 'sex people' both pushed at and replicated the boundaries of sexual norms; his was very much a male heterosexuality for which use of Nazi chic and images of women bound and gagged drew criticism even as he endeavoured to expand erotic horizons.[112]

Proto-gothic culture also retained links to punk's aggressive impulse, finding outlet in the hard-edged music of the Birthday Party, Killing Joke and others.[113] Both bands cultivated followings that related (in different ways) to a very physical male sexuality. Where Nick Cave's group specialised in brutal songs of sexual violence, literally collapsing their rockabilly-inflected rock 'n' roll into what Barney Hoskyns called the 'soul and dirt' of 'physical desire', Killing Joke presaged a new dark age driven by primal instinct.[114] The primitive feeling was getting closer Jaz Coleman prophesied amidst live 'gatherings' and war dances built on propulsive rhythms that sought to bind 'brain and body'.[115] He and others spoke of tribes, evoking images of wild youth (gangs, packs, cults, societies) creating new cultures amidst the rubble of Britain's

decaying inner cities.[116] By 1983's *Fire Dances*, this translated into orgiastic carnival, with conscience left behind to frenzy and 'Lust Almighty'.
Coleman even talked of becoming 'all man' on stage; a 'pure male spe-
cies' reaching for 'timelessness'.[117] On 'Tabazan' – from 1985's *Night
Time* – he sung of 'virile young men' running amok, breaking free from
the sexual repression that both shaped and stunted society. 'Semen and
blood is all I've got', Coleman gasped as the music throbbed towards
a point of climax: 'Push it between her legs and stretch the lips mother
relieve me … Shoot forth the new gold and at last reason makes perfect
sense'.[118]

There were pagan undercurrents to Killing Joke.[119] Members
of the band self-schooled across a range of arcane knowledge that fed
into and directed their music's form and practice.[120] Ritual and magick
coalesced to unleash a chaos of cathartic, sometimes transcendent dark
energy. Here was a masculinity bound to nature, through which male
strength and virility were venerated as visceral. Sex, in turn, became a
primal act, a physical conjunction captured also by New Model Army,
whose 'Sex (The Black Angel)' was a tense, contorted depiction of
carnality. As a result, proto-gothic gigs could be violent affairs.[121] For
Terry Macleay of Sex Gang Children, the dervish-like response of their
audience – lost amidst a churning noise overlaid with lyrics of death,
flesh, beasts and the abyss – related to repressed sexual desire. 'Go to
housing estates, a deprived area', he told *Sounds*, '[and] you see that the
kids there hang around in gangs and they're bounded by their desire to
cause trouble. It's a sexual urge. That's what a Sex Gang should be'.[122]
By contrast, goth's glam roots facilitated less aggressively physical male
identities, evolving towards an androgynous masculinity that complemented the distinctly feminine image of goth women.[123] Footage of the
Batcave shot in 1983 captures goth at its moment of crystallisation.
The interior is swathed in webbing and decorated with S&M-bound
mannequins. B-movie horror tat from the 1950s and black plastic
abound. The tropes of goth are clearly apparent, even as recognisably
punk signifiers remain in the boots, spikes, leather jackets and tattered
clothes of those Wisdom described as 'crawling' out from the 'dullness
of the cities' they live in.[124]

Punk's masculinities were complex and often contradictory. The
cultures that evolved from 1976 continued to push at gender boundaries and play with sexuality, just as their forebears had done. In Wayne
County, who moved to London in 1977 and became Jayne County from

1979, British punk adopted an important link back to the gay, drag and performance-art scenes of Warhol's New York.[125] Simultaneously, however, a tendency to associate sexuality with transgression served also to reaffirm socially conservative assumptions: punk's and goth's 'otherness' was dependent, in part, on aligning with the socially marginal. As intriguingly, punk's etymological fusion of juvenile and sexual 'delinquency' attracted conflicting bedfellows, hence its shared influence on new romanticism and Oi!

Taken generally, punk's critical impulse picked up on and fed into broader debates around the socioeconomic processes transforming notions of masculinity (and sexuality) over the late twentieth century.[126] More specifically, punk-informed youth cultures grappled intuitively with these processes, recognising signs of change while struggling to reconcile their significance. An example: references to soldiers and war were manifold across punk and post-punk, from The Clash through Stiff Little Fingers, Joy Division and Theatre of Hate onto The Exploited, Anti Pasti, Discharge and countless others. Second-hand army fatigues and wartime memorabilia became cultural-wear, part of the often indistinct styling of the punk diaspora. But the masculine ideal they evoked forever gave way to physical desolation and futility: dead heroes, tin soldiers, blown to bits, maimed and slaughtered.[127] While Ian Curtis' early lyrics contemplated the 'failures of the modern man', so Johnny Rotten used 'Belsen Was a Gas' to push twentieth-century masculinity into the void. Never released but played live as the Sex Pistols themselves hurtled towards their end, images of the Holocaust were saved from trivialisation by Rotten's concluding rant: 'Be a man, a real man, be someone, kill someone, kill yourself'.[128]

8 NO FUTURE: PUNK AS DYSTOPIA

> As long as the music's loud enough we won't hear the world
> falling apart...
>
> Borgia Ginz[1]

Between 23 August and 6 September 1980, the *NME* published a
three-part essay entitled '1984: Our Frightening Future'. Could it be,
the paper posited, that George Orwell's 'vision of a nightmare Britain –
overpopulated, overspent and overseen – ... is now an imminent
reality'? Written by Ian MacDonald, the series began with a history
of totalitarianism that located Orwell's novel in a political and cultural tradition encompassing Futurists, Bolsheviks, Fascists, National
Socialists and the dystopian science fiction of H. G. Wells and Aldous
Huxley. His thesis was that while *1984* offered a discerning critique
of Stalin's Soviet Union transferred to Britain, Orwell's concept of a
totalitarian system that utilised the structures of power and media
to maintain its authority and subjugate the individual could in fact
be applied to either side of the Iron Curtain, as well as to various
corporate interests beyond those of government. Looking forward,
MacDonald pointed to the arms industry, consumerism, population
growth, global economic crises and technological advances as conduits for a totalitarian future. The 'coming of machine science', he
argued with an eye on automation, alienation and the perennial threat
of nuclear annihilation, made the idea of total control 'perfectly and
permanently realisable'. In other words, competing economic systems
were transforming into competing control systems, just as Orwell
predicted.[2]

MacDonald's essay captured a sense – a feeling, a fear – that permeated the time. Throughout the 1970s, concerns relating to industrial conflicts and economic crises began to conflate with the ramifications of new technologies to presage either imagined clampdowns or socioeconomic collapse. From 1979, heightened Cold War tensions renewed the nuclear possibilities of a bleak near future. And where political and media rhetoric conjured up visions of socioeconomic disarray, so doomsday scenarios continued to be offered as cultural complements to the promised dark tomorrow.[3] Among the most popular were James Herbert's *The Rats* (1974), depicting a London plagued by urban decay; Terry Nation's television series *Survivors* (1975), imagining a civilization all but wiped out by a deadly virus; Richard Allen's youth cult novels for New English Library (*Skinhead*, *Suedehead*, *Boot Boys*, *Sorts*, etc.), revelling in teenage violence; *Threads* (1984) and *Edge of Darkness* (1985), two distinct but equally chilling responses to the nuclear threat. Even Peter Watkins' *The War Game* finally found airtime twenty years after being withdrawn by the BBC in 1965 for its predicting imminent nuclear war, while John Wyndham's *The Day of the Triffids* (1951) was adapted for television in 1981 to portray the results of bioengineering and social breakdown. In most cases, military solutions featured as barbarity and violence reigned.

Orwell, with his notions of 'newspeak', 'doublethink', total surveillance and perpetual war, remained among the most convincing. For MacDonald, the signs of a 'Big Brother' society were all but in place. Monetarism was leading towards entrenched unemployment and welfare cuts. Living standards for the majority were predicted to plateau (then fall) as the money supply tightened and the population increased. To maintain control, the state was becoming ever more centralised, with surveillance techniques extending through CCTV, phone tapping and the collation of databases. Simultaneously, the threat of nuclear war had paved the way for contingency plans that – following the severe industrial struggles of the early 1970s – could be applied in peacetime, particularly against trade unions or activist groups.[4] The militarisation of the police, meanwhile, was discernible in the actions of task forces such as the Special Patrol Group (SPG) and the provision of riot shields, helmets and weaponry to quell instances of social unrest. A 'secret hierarchy of power' was forming, MacDonald argued, purposely equipped to oversee a fearful, violent and mechanised society that harboured growing contempt for human frailty. 'Welcome', he wrote with a flourish, 'to [Orwell's] nightmare'.[5]

Orwell's spectre certainly haunted British punk. Reference to his novel recurred, from The Clash's countdown on '1977' to Crass' cataloguing their releases in similarly foreboding fashion, starting at '621984' in 1978 and numbering down (521984, 421984) each year until 1984, when the band resolved to split.[6] The Jam, on 'Standards' from their 1977 album *This Is the Modern World*, evoked 1984's principal character Winston Smith (a nom de plume, also, of *Sounds'* Richard Newson, who covered punk); The Unwanted's debut single from the same year came backed with a summation of 1984 that insisted 'newspeak don't keep the world free'.[7] '84' featured in the names of bands keen to intimidate (Combat 84, Condemned 84); it signified authoritarianism, as in Crisis' 'PC One Nine Eight Four'; it enveloped premonitions of national dissolution (Subhumans' *The Day the County Died* [1983]) and reflections on the miners' strike (New Model Army's '1984').[8] Often read in school over the 1970s and 1980s – not to mention being an influence on Bowie's *Diamond Dogs* (1974) – 1984 resonated in young minds coming of age as Orwell's portent beckoned.[9] 'Orwell said it all', the 4-Skins declared in their own tribute to the novel, 'he stared the future in the face'.[10]

In line with MacDonald's analysis of Britain's drift towards a militarised police state, the election of Margaret Thatcher's Conservative government was soon read by many as a validation of punk's grim foresight. Where Jon Savage's 1976 essay in *London's Outrage* had pre-cast Thatcher as the 'Mother Sadist' to British fascism, so the prime minister from 1979 was regularly portrayed as a 'Big Sister' figure: the wielder of law and order, the harbinger of war (The Falklands), the ally of American imperialism (allowing US cruise missiles to turn Britain into 'Airstrip One') and the public persona of a system willing to crush those seeking to exist outside or challenge the precepts of free market capitalism and the moral boundaries of a bygone Victorian age (see Figure 8.1).[11] '1984 has become a memory', Penny Rimbaud wrote in 1982, 'a clumsy hypothesis that fell hopelessly short in its failure to allow for the horrific escalation in technological "hardware"'.[12] The book itself, Rimbaud noted a year later, had forewarned the danger of totalitarianism. But 'under Thatcher's unfeeling guidance the scenario is one year early. With the cold mechanism of the pin-ball arcade, we're flicked around as numbers by the hidden computers: software in the

Figure 8.1 Cover of Russ Dunbar's *Acts of Defiance*, 6 (1983).

hardware; documented and filed.'[13] For Conflict, 'the village bobbies of yesteryear' had 'transformed into the riot squads of Maggie's '84', a scenario they substantiated with reference to the violence meted out by police on the miners striking to prevent pit closures and the associated break-up of their communities. The 'Battle of Orgreave', during which miners picketing a Yorkshire coking works were flanked and brutally battered by police, took place in June 1984.[14]

Like Orwell, punk dramatised the shifting dynamics of state power and social order. Just as the battle armour of Britain's police became a staple of Conflict's iconography, so visions of life caged and conditioned infused punk-informed records and imagery. As an example, Antisect's *In Darkness, There Is No Choice* (1984) portrayed a society of 'anonymous' lives imprisoned by institutions and indoctrination. In the self-flagellating essay that accompanied the record, the band expounded on people's willingness to repress their own free will to the needs of an 'authoritarian society'.[15]

Two other sources of fictional-dystopia proved especially influential among punk-related cultures. Anthony Burgess' *A Clockwork Orange* (1962), made into a film by Stanley Kubrick in 1971 but withdrawn following its being linked to real incidents of violence in the weeks after release, felt especially prescient in an age of football hooliganism and turf warfare dressed up in youth-cultural finery.[16] Revolving around Alex and his gang of 'droogs', the film's urban-concrete setting and stylised 'ultraviolence' proved to be as enticing as it was disturbing. Consequently, reference to the film's imagery and the book's argot fed into the youth cultures they commented on. In punk terms, the droog uniform was adopted by Cock Sparrer on their 1977 video for 'We Love You' and later by bands such as The Adicts, Major Accident and Violators (see Figure 8.2). Scars, from Edinburgh, utilised the book for 'Horrowshow' on their debut Fast Product release. In Sheffield, both Clock DVA and Heaven 17 chose names derived from the book/film, their penchant for electronic sounds drawn in part from Walter Carlos' innovative soundtrack. The motif of a clockwork orange was also used by the Angelic Upstarts ('Teenage Warning') and Sham 69 ('That's Life'), representing both an ominous commentary on a broken society where violence served as an outlet for youthful frustration and, to quote Major Accident's Con Larkin, 'the ultimate culmination of youth cults today, with its own language and way of life'.[17]

Not dissimilarly, J. G. Ballard's novels provided suitably bleak premonitions of the near future. Books such as *Crash* (1973), *Concrete Island* (1974) and *High Rise* (1975) were set in urban landscapes laid waste by town planners and reconstructed in the guise of concrete blocks, bland suburbs, intersecting roadways and shadowy underpasses. Therein, technology forged new realities and new pathologies, with human relations distorting against the topography of media simulacra. As a result, violence and sexuality were pushed to extremes, searching for a means to transcend the bland uniformity of what Ballard called the 'conforming suburb of the soul'.[18]

Figure 8.2 Major Accident, 'Mr Nobody' b/w 'That's You'. (Step Forward Records, 1983.)

Ballard's post-industrial visions found expression as punk's angry stare turned to alienation. Joy Division's Ian Curtis was a keen reader of Ballard, writing 'Atrocity Exhibition' in homage to the 1970 book of the same title; Comsat Angels, from Sheffield, named themselves after a Ballard short story, writing desolate songs of urban isolation. Daniel Miller's The Normal, too, launched Mute Records in 1978 with a single that included 'Warm Leatherette', a piston-churning mechanical interpretation of *Crash* that followed the book's fetishisation of car accidents towards a melange of twisted metal and punctured limbs. The b-side was entitled 'TV OD'. Indeed, those enamoured by the futuristic hum of early synthesisers often reproduced the detached anomie of Ballard's work. Ultravox's first records and John Foxx's *Metamatic* (1980) explored 'high rise overspills' and artificial lives, their faceless characters standing alone in the underpass or caught on celluloid as they moved in the flicker of artificial light.[19] By 1980–83, concurrent with the charts' embrace of synth-pop, punk's do-it-yourself (DIY) ethos had fused with industrial's tech-fascination to forge a network of cassette labels specialising in homemade electronica crafted on the ever more affordable synths becoming available from the late 1970s. Traced through Dave Henderson's seminal 'Wild Planet' supplement for *Sounds*, Ballard's – and William Burroughs' – influence was obvious.[20] SPK's Graeme Revell even wrote an essay on Ballard for *Sounds* in 1983, extolling the writer's ability to portray 'external reality transformed into media-scape', while such titles as *The Crystal World* (1966), *The Unlimited Dream Company* (1979) and *Myths of the Near Future* (1982) featured in the reading lists compiled by *RE/Search* for their *Industrial Culture Handbook* of 1983.[21]

Clearly, the punk-informed cultures evolving from 1976 bore dystopian sensibilities that found expression in the 1970s and 1980s.[22] Be it the void staring back from the Sex Pistols' 'No Future' or the perceived 'control' enacted on lives framed by media representation and the threat of nuclear devastation, punk conjured visions that were post-industrial, post-democratic and post-apocalyptic. Cult reading and viewing provided one source of inspiration; so too did events and perceptions from the time: deindustrialisation, unemployment, inner-city riots, the Falklands War, the Cold War, the neutering of trade unions, the closing down of the Greater London Council, the repositioning of Britain as an entrepreneurial economy driven by the needs of individual consumers. Such processes were hard fought. And as they unfolded, so punk mapped its own variations of a future that had yet to be written.

This Is the City of the Dead

Dystopian visions of post-industrialism were fuelled by long-running concerns as to the trajectory of Britain's economy. It was in the late 1970s that the term 'deindustrialisation' first began to find common usage, a less arresting – but perhaps more apposite – complement to the discourse of 'decline' that infused the period.[23] As Jim Tomlinson has argued, processes of deindustrialisation underpinned Britain's economic, social and political development over the late twentieth century.[24] For all the attention given to GDP figures as a measure of national virility and economic prowess, their ebbs and flows reveal little about broader structural and cultural change. By contrast, deindustrialisation pertains to the drawn-out transformation of Britain from an industrial to a primarily service economy.

The consequences of such a transition are complex and contested, be it with regard to class formation, social cohesion, income distribution, unemployment, consumption or the gendered distribution of labour. Across the 1970s and early 1980s, however, during which Britain's deindustrialisation reached 'a crescendo in 1979–82', the insecurities rendered by change prompted the imagining of post-industrial tomorrows.[25] In punk terms, reference to boredom and the dole queue provided one immediate association, as the promise of full employment was consigned to the past. The banality of a predetermined future in a monotonous job now competed with the banality of unemployment or piecemeal work, a conundrum caught perfectly by Mark Perry's Alternative TV: 'Life's about as wonderful as the record mart/ I don't like selling albums, but I don't want to go to work .../ Life's about a wonderful as the dole queue/ but I've got no choice, that's why I'm standing in the queue.'[26]

But more dramatic possibilities were also offered. The film *Jubilee* (1978), directed by Derek Jarman, was set in a desolate London of rubble and ruins. Young punks are seen killing time in the debris, among them Jordan, The Slits, Toyah, Adam Ant and Gene October, while a demented media mogul runs operations from a studio in Buckingham Palace, signing bands to exploit as cheap entertainment. England has all but collapsed into a morass of ennui and violence, wherein the police serve only as the most brutal and well-armed mob. 'When, on my fifteenth birthday', Jordan's character (Amyl Nitrate) narrates, 'law and order were finally abolished, all those statistics that were a substitute for reality disappeared, the crime-rate dropped to zero'.[27] Early reviews – and Jordan herself – suggested the film anticipated the England of 1984.[28] Certainly, it presented a prophecy of a country en route to oblivion, framed as it was by the device of John Dee conjuring up the spirit Ariel to show Queen Elizabeth I the future.[29]

In fact, Jarman was quite able to use contemporary settings to capture his vision. The crumbling docks of Butler's Wharf, where Jarman lived in a derelict warehouse that once worked as a grain store, provided a suitably post-industrial backdrop. All around, streets remained broken by the bomb-damage leftover from the war, with dented sheets of corrugated iron lined up to protect dilapidated buildings that nevertheless became playgrounds for local kids.[30] As recession

Figure 8.3 Cover and detail from Jon Savage, *London's Outrage*, 2 (1977).

began to bite, so areas raised for reconstruction were left to decay, overseen by cheaply built high rises and, along the Thames, signposts of Britain's declining manufacturing base.[31] In his second issue of *London's Outrage* (Figure 8.3), published in 1977, Jon Savage collated similar scenes to offer an effective snapshot of the topography that reflected punk's sensibility.[32]

Such imagery gave sense to the spatial dynamics that informed punk's cultural practice, by which the husk of British industry provided room for creativity and performance. In Manchester, T. J. Davidson's on Little Peter Street offered Joy Division and others opportunity to rehearse, a remnant of the city's industrial past described by Mick Middles as a complex of 'dusty rooms, all framed by fearsome junctions of industrial piping and all too soon filled with crisp packets, crushed beer cans and cigarette dimps'.[33] Not dissimilarly, Manchester's industrial remains soon fed into the city's punk and post-punk cultures. The Electric Circus stood in the wastelands of Collyhurst, a once heavily industrialised area that had fallen into disrepair by the 1970s. The very term Factory, first as the name for a club night at the Russell Club in Hulme and then as a record label, recalled Manchester's history, a fact emphasized by Peter Saville's in-house designs that initially drew from industrial iconography. Even more famously, the Hacienda nightclub was defined by Ben Kelly's use of industrial aesthetics to transform an old marina into an urbanised leisure space. In effect, Manchester's youth culture chartered the city's post-industrial transition, reclaiming and redefining the landscape in ways Tony Wilson could no doubt articulate in quasi-situationist terms.[34]

Similar observations have been made for Sheffield, a city with a contracting steel industry falling into disrepair by the onset of the 1980s. Although bands from the area were inspired by a range of cultural and aesthetic interests, their environment helped shape perceptions via reference to the city's 'grey air, thick with moisture, revealing vistas of factories, tower blocks, endless tightly-patterned semis'.[35] Sometime later, Simon Reynolds hypothesised that 'Sheffield's preference for electronic sounds' was connected to its 'role as one of the engines of the industrial revolution', with both Richard Kirk (Cabaret Voltaire) and Martyn Ware (The Future/Human League/Heaven 17) confirming their cultural practice was informed by an environment of blackened buildings and the crunching clangour of heavy industry.[36] Speaking in 1980, Cabaret Voltaire's Stephen Mallinder ruminated that his band's music was 'a reflection of a hell of a lot of your environment, social conditions, economic structures … a reflection of the times you live in'.[37] In 2012 he went further: '[Sheffield's] sounds during the 1980s were both a considered response and a practical resolution to the industrial atrophy that was well under way by this time. Against a backdrop of Thatcherite fiscal policy and regional confrontation, Sheffield's regeneration was in every sense post-industrial. Built upon the bones of its once-thriving steel and cutlery production, the abandoned offices and factories proved useful to would-be musicians, producers and artists who would come to occupy these lost properties. Cultural redemption came to those who were happy to exploit Youth Employment schemes and the cheap council housing of the time to provide their own solutions to southern capital abandonment'. Technology and creativity offered 'an escape route to an idealized future', albeit 'anchored in the more subversive dirt of reality'.[38] The band's first gig – in 1975 – was underpinned by a tape loop of drop-hammers; their classic single, 'Nag, Nag, Nag' (1978), was built on a percussion track of clanking metal keyboard legs.

Cabaret Voltaire's affinity to Throbbing Gristle and industrial culture was telling. Introducing their Institute of Contemporary Arts

(ICA) performance of October 1976, P-Orridge described Throbbing Gristle's music as a soundtrack to the breakdown of civilization. 'You know, you walk down the street and there's lots of ruined factories and bits of old newspapers with stories about pornography ... blowing down the street, and you turn the corner past the dead dog and you see old dustbins. And then over the ruined factory there's a funny noise'.[39] Speaking a few weeks later, he suggested Throbbing Gristle were 'writing about the future by looking at today. We look at this scabby, filthy, dirty, horrible society and transform it into this inhuman, emotionless parallel. That's the way it's going to be in 1984 for sure'.[40] The name Industrial Records was chosen to demystify cultural production, but it also signalled a music that offered 'vivid and accurate reportage, a precise description of the ailing industrial society in which [people] found themselves alienated and socially ill ... Industrial music was closest to journalism and to a documentary in black and white of the savage realities of fading capitalism'.[41]

Throbbing Gristle rehearsed and recorded in the basement of an old Hackney factory. This was the 'death factory', a name designed to reflect both its standing on the site of an old plague pit and the soul-destroying effects of automated labour. Now, in the 1970s, Throbbing Gristle manufactured culture, creating product to sell in multiples (albeit with subversive intent). South of the river, This Heat did similar, taking over an old meat-freezing warehouse in Brixton that they rechristened 'cold storage'. Therein, the band adopted an experimental 'all channels open' approach that fuelled confrontational live performances comprising harsh textures, improvisation, tape loops and proto-sampling.[42] Their second album, *Deceit* (1981), was a collage of dystopian possibilities that ranged from passive consumerism through social dislocation, overstretched welfarism, fascism and nuclear war. Test Dept, meanwhile, picked up, played and performed in the remnants of British industry.[43] Emerging from London's New Cross in 1981, they rehearsed in broken basements and gigged in railway arches, utilising discarded tools and industrial detritus to hammer percussive rhythms that clanked and ground in homage to the collective strength of the organised working class. 'There are two machines in operation', a group statement declared in November 1983. 'The machine which controls, dictates the rhythm of the modern state. This rhythm is impersonal. It has created a gradual furnace decline ... This force must be engaged with ... The human machine [must] cut back to basics ...

The past must be explored. Mistakes and propaganda exposed. Self-discipline, moving forward out of the chaotic present ... We will be fire and give strength to the new'.[44]

As this implies, the group's aesthetics drew from Soviet constructivism and John Heartfield's political montage, venerating industrial muscle in ways that soon correlated with the miners' strike of 1984–85. Accordingly, Test Dept were among those to the fore during the miners' struggle, performing a series of benefit gigs on their 'Fuel to Fight' tour and releasing an album, *Shoulder to Shoulder* (1985), in collaboration with the South Wales Miners' Choir. 'If the miners get fucked over this time then that's it!', one of the group predicted, having previously refused to declare their political leanings. 'Everyone is fucked – its downhill all the way ... this whole country is being deliberately run down. It's much more insidious than just a class struggle'.[45]

Much of this activity gestated in cheaply rented ramshackle houses, Victorian or Edwardian terraces transformed into transitory abodes for the poor and the marginal. As with the pre-punk counter-culture, some spaces proved more sustainable than others or continued in a tradition of radical squatting locales.[46] So, for example, London's early punk nexus was partly galvanised in squats that once housed hippie communes but later sheltered members of The Clash, The Slits, The Raincoats, pragVEC and others.[47] The area around 'Frestonia' (named after Freston Road, where squatters declared independence from the UK in 1977) also served as base for many connected to Rough Trade and for Tony Drayton on his relocation to London. As his *Ripped & Torn* fanzine transformed into the collectively produced *Kill Your Pet Puppy*, so Drayton moved from squat to squat across the city until a 'Puppy Mansions' was founded in West Hampstead and, later, Islington via the Black Sheep Housing Co-operative. Nettleton Road in New Cross, where Test Dept were based, offered another site of punk-related activity, with squats and housing co-ops providing space for creativity and recreational substance abuse. By this time, too, squats in and around Brougham Road (Hackney) served as headquarters for the capital's anarchist punk milieu, fusing politics and lifestyles in ways that found expression across an array of bands, fanzines and campaigns.[48] Nearby, Beck Road housed Throbbing Gristle/Psychic TV and various acolytes.

Squat scenes were less prevalent beyond London, though similar circumstances abounded in run-down, student or bohemian enclaves.

Bristol's early 1980s punk milieu formed around squats (including the 'Demolition Diner') located in the city's St Pauls, Montpelier, Cotham and Redland areas, from where the likes of Disorder, Chaos UK and others emerged in all their crusty, glue-inflected glory.[49] In Brighton, an entrenched squatting culture had taken an anarcho-punk 'turn' by the 1980s.[50] More typical, if not usually on so large a scale, were places such as Hulme in Manchester. Described by John Robb as a 'brave new world' of 'late sixties clearance and demolitions', the area saw students, squatters, bohemians and lost souls move into spaces deserted by families relocated by the council.[51]

Pocket-sized equivalents were evident elsewhere. The coalescing of students, fledgling creatives, the unemployed and the disaffected was important, sparking tensions but also fostering cross-class synergies that informed the youth cultures that flowered in the spaces between postwar redevelopment and urban regeneration. Accordingly, perhaps, accounts of punk as a lived experience – rather than a cultural process – combine resourcefulness with creativity; squalor with anxiety. The hardship of living in urban detritus was often compounded by fear of eviction, a visit from the police or, worse, bonehead gangs looking for easy targets. Drugs, and the sensual derangement engendered by a hand-to-mouth existence that deliberately rejected the time-line of an 'ordinary life', tended to reap grim consequences. Equally, camaraderie and the impetus to imagine new ways of living brought personal and creative reward.[52] Looking back on his time in Brougham Road, Zounds' Steve Lake remembered the dust and the corrugated iron, but also a community 'carrying on a radical, utopian tradition … we were building an alternative society'.[53]

Crucially, punk's tendency to engagement ensured that the cultures formed in the Sex Pistols' wake often reflected, documented and dramatised the environs in which they developed. Songs of urban decay and social dislocation were legion, foreseeing a future of dereliction and violence. These, in turn, were complemented by statements of self-sufficiency and self-interest, as if punk's anti-social impulse was as much a survival instinct as an adopted creed.[54] Given such a context, 'do-it-yourself' and 'I don't care' signified two related reactions to the breakdown of the postwar settlement and the perceived limitations of Labour social democracy. Come the 1980s, and the cultural effects of socioeconomic change were played out on records that sought to capture the changing mood. The Pack talked of being a generation 'forced to survive', their songs of 'death and damnation' signalling an impending cataclysm.[55] 'This civilization is dying', Kirk Brandon told *Sounds* after transforming The Pack into Theatre of Hate.[56] A new age was dawning, Brandon insisted, though he seemed hard pushed to explain exactly what this entailed.[57] Instead, portents of doom – Cold War animosities, Nazism, murderers, religious manias – ran through his lyrics: 'now something wicked this way comes'.[58] More specifically, Killing Joke sought to deliver the 'warning sounds for an age of self-destruction', their records rehearsing an array of doomsday scenarios through a noise that invoked tension and foreboding. In 1982, Jaz Coleman and guitarist Geordie (Kevin Walker) even fled to Iceland, searching for an island harnessed to nature and thereby equipped to survive the 'great upheaval'.[59] The band spoke of playing 'eighties music ... music that reflects pressure, because that's what [we] feel'.[60] To this end, one of their defining statements was named in honour of the decade, an inventory of the 1980s' prevailing values chanted over a pounding beat suffocated by the churn of Geordie's guitar as it hurtled towards chaos: 'I have to push, I have to struggle ... Get out my way ... I'll take all I can get'.[61]

By 1984, and despite signs of economic recovery, the onset of a year-long mining dispute and the continued problem of mass unemployment served only to reaffirm Britain's troubled transformation. Many of those drawn into punk's diaspora played or attended benefits for the miners, from Crass and Poison Girls to the Redskins, Billy Bragg and The Three Johns lining up with ranters, dub-poets and various left-leaning bands to lend support to those who embodied Britain's industrial base.[62] In punk terms, therefore, it was perhaps fitting that The Clash returned to update their vision of the UK. Where 1976–77 had seen the band present a Britain of simmering animosities, combustible, caught between disorder and clampdown, 1985's 'This is England' was more like a requiem. Slow paced with lyrics of 'cold voices' and 'hands freezing', the violence remained but was now wholly repressive. Nationalism fuelled by the Falklands War provided false comfort for a 'dying creed', inadequate cover for the closing industries. Sheffield steel no longer served as a site of class identity or collective pride, but only as a blunted knife to stab and attack. 'This is England', Joe Strummer mourned, looking out across Britain's post-industrial landscape, 'this is how we feel ...'[63]

State of Emergency

All but from the outset, dystopian punk visions intersected with prophesies of impending authoritarianism. 'Fascist' and 'fascism' were early punk trigger words, verbal accompaniments to the swastika's symbolic reminder of a previous descent into socioeconomic and political crisis.[64] The Nazi symbol captured the ugly 'vibe' of 1976, Hugh Cornwell suggested, as his Stranglers band mate Jean Jacques Burnel diagnosed a Britain 'due for tyranny' and the National Front marched in evermore confident fashion.[65] Certainly, the Sex Pistols' 'No Future' came with a nod to 'a fascist regime', as if slavish nationalism built on a hereditary monarchy presaged a peculiarly British despotism. Both The Clash and the Tom Robinson Band specialised in plotting scenarios of social unrest and government clampdowns, with 'heavy manners' leading to backs up against the wall. And while Penetration stood defiant ('don't dictate to me'), The Models' one and only 1977 single, 'Freeze', foretold an authoritarian solution to punk's youth 'revolution'.[66] Even songs unrelated to the politics of fascism used the term for provocative effect: The Cortinas' 'Fascist Dictator' was in fact a snotty paean to sexual self-interest that nevertheless attuned itself to Cornwell's vibe.

Not that far-right dictatorship was deemed the only possible outcome. The Jam's early hostility to a faltering Labour government led them regularly to accuse Jim Callaghan of 'trying for a police state', while Sham 69's 'Red London' appeared to suggest that the stifling uniformity of socialism paved the way for 'no democracy'.[67] 'People want to deviate, not join clubs', Mark Perry countered when quizzed as to his criticism of the Socialist Workers Party (SWP)'s role in Rock Against Racism (RAR). '[The red star] has caused as much trouble and animosity as the swastika', a thesis to which many in and around punk's anarchist and Oi! milieus would also later subscribe.[68] Though less common than portents of fascism, visions of communist tyranny occasionally found a punk outlet. The Stranglers' 'Curfew', for example, portrayed a Soviet invasion of Britain, cutting through a Europe softened by American cultural imperialism. Likewise, following the Russian intervention in Afghanistan in 1979, the Angelic Upstarts urged 'Guns for the Afghan Rebels' to prevent a Soviet advance. The Underdogs' 1983 single, 'East of Dachau', compared Soviet communism to the fascism it theoretically opposed.[69]

Quite how imminent was the post-democratic future remained a moot point. Many of the scenarios sketched in songs such as The Damned's 'I Just Can't Be Happy Today' – where evil reigned and books were burned under army command – were fantastical. Across the early 1980s, moreover, Anti Pasti, Chelsea, Conflict, Killing Joke, Mau Maus, The Skeptix and the UK Subs were among those to dramatise the onset of police states, curfews and clampdowns. The state was presented as omnipresent, signalling a brand new age of surveillance and repression. Violence and decay begat authoritarianism; the police acted with impunity; the military was poised to occupy the cities.[70] Though imagined, they pertained to an immediate future, tapping into Cold War paranoia and the perceived consequences of social dislocation.

Others, particularly among punk's social realists, focused on low-level state-sanctioned harassment to suggest encroaching authoritarianism. 'Freedom, there ain't no fucking freedom', Stinky Turner shouted to introduce the Cockney Rejects' 'Police Car', one of their many songs detailing scrapes, scraps and run-ins with the police.[71] Sham 69, Angelic Upstarts, Infa Riot and The Business also told tales of criminality that venerated villains as outsider-heroes or cast young delinquents as anti-social rebels. By so doing, they referred to a much longer historical struggle for the self-regulation of social space. Tensions between the forces of social control and working-class youth may be dated back to at least the nineteenth century, where police intervention into local street cultures brought resentment.[72] Be it hanging around on corners, coalescing in gangs, gambling or the football, urban space was contested; identities forged through locale, school, street, style and community were tendered and protected. If 'youth' – especially working-class youth and, in the post-1945 period, black youth – challenged a prescribed public order, then the police represented both a rival gang and a symbol of statist intervention; an irreconcilable 'other' to be opposed and never trusted. ACAB: All Coppers Are Bastards.[73]

Come the 1980s and many a young – and not so young – punk would claim to discern authoritarianism at the heart of Margaret Thatcher's mission. Disaffection with formal politics, including parliamentary politics, recurred across punk's cultures from 1976, be it for reasons of disinterest, distrust or preference for alternative political practice.[74] Simultaneously, a more overarching – and overtly anarchist – critique developed, positing democracy as a sham designed to mask broader systems of repression. 'Democracy is a lie', Penny Rimbaud wrote in the first issue of Crass' *International Anthem* (1977). 'Two party totalitarianism. The realities stay the same ... Democracy is a system and systems kill'.[75] Following Thatcher's election in 1979, such a perspective became entrenched. Predictions of legal crackdowns, detention centres and conscription began to fill fanzine columns; the 'clever con' of party politics was unpicked and revealed.[76]

Crass always pertained to offer hope. Their politics and practice demonstrated an alternative future. In the short term, however, they and others anticipated authoritarianism enforced by might, conformity and fear. 'The boundaries are becoming narrower as the state becomes more paranoid', Rimbaud contended as the Cold War's geo-politics cast an ever more ominous shadow.[77] Looking from the Falklands to the miners' strike to the war in Ireland to the deleterious economic situation, Crass predicted that 'the only way in which they [the government] are going to maintain their slavery of us is with the threat of a gun barrel'.[78] For this reason, the spectre of militarism became a common feature of the punk dystopia, the means by which control would be maintained once war was proclaimed or democracy untenable.

Punk's anarchist critiques were conceptual and theoretical. Nevertheless, they – and the impulses that informed punk's more general fascination with all things authoritarian – drew from real events and wider anxieties. Looking back, Nazism and the still-visible scars of World War II gave tangible sense to an averted post-democratic future that nevertheless continued to haunt the British psyche. The residues of the war – its horrors, symbols, rubble and losses – permeated the culture and politics of the postwar period, be it through film, literature, drama or the children's toys and comics that punk's participants grew up with.[79] In turn, images of Nazi brutality provided source material for many a punk song and record cover. From the Sex Pistols' 'Belsen Was a Gas' through Throbbing Gristle's death camp imagery onto lesser-known tracks such as The Prefects' 'Bristol Road Leads to Dachau', Crisis' 'Holocaust', Whitehouse's 'Buchenwald', Blitzkrieg's 'Lest We Forget' and Cult Maniax's 'Blitz', World War II provided a historical reminder of what could have been and what could still become. The cover of 1983's *Punk and Disorderly III* compilation even featured Adolf Hitler standing alongside Margaret Thatcher outside Downing Street. All around, punks lay dead on the roadside while others lined up for the firing squad or hung from a lamp post.[80]

As this suggests, the heightened political climate of the 1970s and early 1980s fuelled punk's post-democratic imaginings. The states of emergency called by Ted Heath throughout his bedevilled 1970–74 government had already served to implant the idea of democratic fragility. Ongoing economic and political upheavals only reaffirmed matters: power cuts and strikes; inflation and recession; IRA bombs and the Angry Brigade. As each new chronicler of the 1970s makes clear, fears of 'ungovernability' led to hushed talk of military coups finding outlet in private clubs, diaries and the more subterranean corridors of power.[81] Alongside doomsday dramas and novels depicting trade union takeovers or militarised responses to crisis, newspaper editorials predicted chaos and political commentators announced 'the death of British democracy'. 'Having been the most stable and prosperous industrial nation', Stephen Haseler wrote in a book that foresaw the 'social democratic age' give way to the 'ordered totalitarian control' of the far left, 'Britain has now become a potential arena for revolutionary political change. The centre of British politics may, at last, not hold'.[82]

Thatcherism, meanwhile, was positioned as a response to the fractures appearing in the British polity – either a necessary antidote to the nation's perceived ills or the realisation of 'popular authoritarianism'.[83] Consequently, political and economic solutions to problems both real and imagined fed into and informed British youth culture. In punk (and British reggae) terms, reference to the police tended to revolve around instances of harassment and the use of 'SUS', a section of the 1824 Vagrancy Act that allowed the arrest of someone on suspicion of loitering to commit a crime.[84] This, in turn, reflected the expansion of police numbers over the 1970–80s and the more assertive policing of inner-city areas sanctioned in response to rising crime rates and, by the 1970s, the terrorist threat posed by the IRA.[85] Engagement with the police became more common, bringing with it the tensions and confrontations that erupted in the riots of 1981. Not dissimilarly, emergent revelations of police corruption, brutality and racism served only to reinforce punk's critical position, with the deaths of Liddle Towers, Richard Campbell, James Kelly, Blair Peach – and the beating of Clarence Baker – inspiring a series of records.[86] More generally, 'SUS', 'SPG', 'police cars' and 'borstal' became embedded into punk's lexicon: symbols of repression utilised to signal subjugation and control.

And then there was Ireland. The Troubles of the 1960s–90s had a long history, pertaining to colonial and religious issues carved deep into the Anglo–Irish past.[87] By the late 1960s, with an Irish republic established in the Catholic south and a predominantly Protestant north bound within the UK, the question of civil rights for the Catholic population of Northern Ireland generated a challenge to the uneasy status quo that successive British governments had sought to maintain since the partition of 1921. Very quickly, demonstrations were met by counter demonstrations. Religious sectarianism, often concentrated in specific neighbourhoods, found renewed expression. The heavy-handed approach of the Protestant-dominated Royal Ulster Constabulary (RUC) served only to stoke – rather than quell – the mounting tension, leading to an upsurge in violence and the deployment of British troops in 1969.

At the dawn of the 1970s, the situation was acute. Paramilitary groups and patrolling British soldiers had transformed Ulster into a warzone, with bombs, beatings and barricades defining a new everyday reality. Most famously, the Provisional IRA was founded in 1969 to rekindle the armed struggle for a united Ireland, sniping at British soldiers and mounting a series of bomb attacks. Simultaneously, the British government's sanctioning of internment without trial and interrogation techniques later condemned by the European Commission of Human Rights as inhuman and degrading appeared to bolster the IRA's cause. In March 1972, just weeks after British soldiers killed thirteen unarmed civil rights protestors on the 'Bloody Sunday' of 30 January, direct rule was declared by the British government.[88]

The ramifications of all this were as brutal as they were complex. An erratic but determined mainland bombing campaign was launched by the IRA with bloody consequences. In Ulster itself, the influence of paramilitary groups in communities on either side of the religious divide brokered turf wars and no-go areas. Thousands were killed and injured, many of whom were civilians.[89] More generally, the presence of armed British troops suggested an occupation and contributed to a pervasive sense of threat and intimidation. Following the summer of 1972, Belfast city centre was surrounded by a 'ring of steel', the metal-gated fence preventing unchecked entry a response to the IRA's detonation of more than twenty incendiary devices in a single day, 21 July. Looking back, Terri Hooley – the founder of Good Vibrations, Belfast's premier record shop and punk label – recalled the late 1960s as 'the start of the dark ages': violence increased, clubs closed, cross-community contact diminished, anxious interaction with paramilitaries and British soldiers recurred.[90]

Given punk's dystopian tendencies, Ulster might have provided a suitably immediate example of the post-democratic future. The IRA and UDA (Ulster Defence Association) formed part of the acronym-shrapnel that splintered from the Sex Pistols' 'Anarchy in the UK'. Famously, too, The Clash visited Belfast in October 1977, lining up for photos at the barricades before insurance problems meant their gig was cancelled. True to form, the RUC moved in to disperse the disappointed young punks who had gathered early for the gig, provoking a minor riot and fuelling punk mythology.[91] Elsewhere, Sham 69 ('Ulster') and Theatre of Hate ('The Wake') evoked Ireland as a site of futile division, while Killing Joke released a debut album enveloped by Don McCullin's 1971 photograph of young Londonderry kids clambering over walls to escape clouds of CS gas fired by British soldiers. Even at a superficial level, Ulster offered visual signifiers to the UK's sociopolitical dislocation.

For groups of a more explicit political bent, Northern Ireland represented the most blatant example of British state oppression – a 'training ground for what the authorities believe is going to happen on the mainland', according to Rimbaud.[92] In fact, Gee Vaucher had intended the fourth issue of *International Anthem* to concentrate on Ireland, before deciding the subject was simply 'too much' to cover.[93] Nevertheless, anarchist bands offered intermittent statements on a conflict they defined as a contrivance of imperialism and proof of religious intolerance.[94] 'Crass would like to declare', the band commented on the back of Hit Parade's *Bad News* EP (1982), 'that we no more support the republican (generally Catholic) IRA ... than we do the unionist (generally Protestant) UDR (Ulster Defence Regiment) or RUC ... Nor do we support the presence in Northern Ireland of the British army'. The EP itself, put out on Crass Records but conceived by Dave Hyndman, included the song 'H Block' and a long essay on the use of rubber bullets. 'All of these organisations', Crass stated, 'are concerned with the seizure, or maintenance, of power and the control and manipulation of the unionist, republication and non-sectarian population ... As long as populations are unable to take a united stand against all forms of repression, they will remain subservient to it'.[95]

Bands coming from a leftist perspective covered similar terri-
tory. Gang of Four wrote of the damage done by 'Armalite Rifles' and
dropped reference to the H-blocks of Long Kesh prison that housed
Ireland's political prisoners and later staged the republican hunger
strikes of 1980–81. The Pop Group went further, setting Amnesty
International's 'report on British army torture of Irish prisoners' to a
dislocated funk rhythm, while Fallout's 'Tell Me About It' conflated
British intervention in Ireland with state terrorism: 'the Great British
nation, your creation, religious segregation … it's your finger on
the trigger'.[96] Others pointed to activism. The Passage, for example,
released 'Troops Out' in support of the UK-based movement of the
same name. In one Au Pairs interview (whose 'Armagh' again focused
on the torture of Irish prisoners), band members even debated the
extent to which they should give support to the IRA.[97] Alternatively,
the plight of British squaddies posted to Northern Ireland – among
them The Exploited's Wattie Buchan[98] – provided an effective example
of young working-class lives being sacrificed to the interests of power.
'Last Night, Another Soldier' by the Angelic Upstarts and Anti Pasti's
'Another Dead Soldier' provide just two examples.

Such 'outside' interventions came in for criticism. 'The kids are
sick of the violence here', Hooley insisted. '[They] are fed up too of
groups like The Clash coming over here and posing in front of soldiers'.[99]
In the *NME*, one Derry reader (and close friend of The Undertones)
complained: 'We've had bands like Killing Joke, Theatre of Hate and
other no-hopers writing songs about us, using us for covers, good copy;
when not one of them have the slightest clue what goes on here'.[100]
Protex – from Belfast – agreed, suggesting it was impossible to explain
what it was like to live in Ulster to someone from outside.[101] Or, as the
unfinished issue of *International Anthem* suggests, the complexities of
the Irish situation proved too difficult to distil into punk's essentially
pop format. When Poison Girls visited Belfast in 1981, their 'Take the
Toys from the Boys' badges were objected to by Irish anarchists who
felt they misunderstood how the gun-men were seen by communities in
Northern Ireland. That is, the paramilitaries were recognised by some
as protectors as well as oppressors.[102]

In Ulster itself, indigenous punk cultures mainly endeavoured
to transcend sectarian division, coming together in the Harp Bar where
a democratic committee ran a 'punk workshop' to sustain a local system of self-help. 'Politics, surprisingly, play no part in the songs [of Irish

punk bands]', Harry Doherty reported for *Melody Maker* in 1977, quoting The Undertones' pre-empting of Hooley's comment by saying they were 'sick of living with politics day after day'.[103] As a result, attempts to launch a Rock Against Sectarianism and Repression campaign akin to RAR soon stalled.[104] Instead, bands tended towards self-organisation with the assistance of people such as Hooley and Hyndman. The anarchist centre of late 1981 (revived briefly in 1982) took over where the Harp Bar left off, providing space for punks to meet and thereby pave the way for the on-going Warzone Collective to establish itself in 1984.[105] 'We always try to write positive songs – we don't believe in writing songs of gloom', Rudi's Ronnie Matthews explained. '[We're] trying to put over the fact that there is a way out and … the only way out of Belfast is to claw your way out'.[106]

There were exceptions. As well as Hit Parade and the gaggle of anarchist bands that formed in and around the Warzone Collective, Stiff Little Fingers' early records were specifically designed to bring attention to the situation in Northern Ireland (see Figure 8.4).[107] 'Suspect Device', the band's ferocious debut single released in 1978, both embodied the Troubles and rejected their logic: 'Inflammable material planted in my head, it's a suspect device that's left two thousand dead'. The b-side, 'Wasted Life', eschewed the call of the paramilitaries, paving the way for an 'Alternative Ulster' and the album, *Inflammable Material* (1979), to fully apply The Clash's punk template to Belfast's streets. Indeed, the band's lyrics were often co-written with Gordon Ogilvie, a journalist in his late twenties enthused by punk's reportage. It was he who encouraged Stiff Little Fingers to hone in on the day-to-day lives of Ulster's youth, to 'write about what you believe in'.[108] 'Punks in England moan about hassles on the street', Jake Burns noted, 'but they've never seen hooded men at a barricade. Their cops don't carry sub-machine guns'.[109] To prove the point, Burns claimed to have received letters from Belfast kids saying they had resisted joining a local paramilitary group after listening to his band's records.[110]

The Defects' debut EP from 1981 also touched on Irish politics, 'Brutality' culminating in the 'SS RUC' chant oft-heard at Belfast's punk gigs (and previously used by Rudi on 'Cops').[111] Nevertheless, both they and Stiff Little Fingers maintained either a critical attitude towards those who dabbled in a situation they did not fully understand or urged caution. 'You can't sit in London and sing about Northern Ireland if you haven't been here for three or four months', Burns

Figure 8.4 (a) Stiff Little Fingers, 'Suspect Device' (Rigid Digits, 1978) and (b) Hit Parade, *Bad News* EP (Crass Records, 1982).

argued, picking out Sham 69's 'Ulster' as a case in point.[112] 'Singing political songs gets you in trouble,' The Defects' Buck [Ian Murdock] admitted. 'Protestants and Catholics got together and mixed when punk came along … We want to keep playing to mixed audiences as long as we're in Belfast.'[113]

Buck's comments tally with the prevailing narrative of Northern Irish punk.[114] For Brian Young of Rudi, places like the Harp Bar and Good Vibrations provided neutral spaces. '[You] were a punk rocker first', he remembered: religious, class and political divisions were secondary.[115] The *Shellshock Rock* film, directed by John T. Davis and released in 1979, also emphasised punk's non-sectarianism, its rough and ready survey of Ulster's punk scene capturing what Martin MacLoone calls a 'new space – mental as well as physical, musical as well as social, economic as well as political – that has been opened up in an otherwise claustrophobic world'.[116] Hand-held cameras track Belfast's darkened streets, cutting to live footage of bands and interviews that articulate punk's non-sectarian identity. Of course, pressures were still felt.[117] Stiff Little Fingers and The Undertones had a running media debate as to whether they were respectively exploiting or ignoring the Troubles.[118] Contemporary and subsequent accounts recall the young Ulster punks' penchant for escaping the attention of paramilitaries and routine stop-and-searches via substance abuse, with one review of The Defects describing an audience with bags clamped to faces reeling from a double hit of glue and music.[119] As this suggests, travelling to and from punk's neutral spaces remained dangerous, while the release of the Sex Pistols' 'God Save the Queen' reputedly stoked a spate of punk beatings.[120] Nevertheless, punk's emergence was generally perceived as positive. 'Punk brought us together and we want to stay together', a friend of The Defects said in 1982.[121] In the face of Ulster's very real state of emergency, punk provided a cultural rather than political solution to a country in lockdown. Asked to define his idea for an 'Alternative Ulster', Jake Burns' reply was simple: 'playing a guitar'.[122]

The actions of the British state in Ulster and elsewhere did much to enflame punk's post-democratic imaginings. As politics flailed in Westminster and played out in the street through pickets, protests, demonstrations, delinquency, marches and bombs, so state-sanctioned responses served to both manage and provoke confrontation. Ulster, the riots of 1981 and the violence of the 1984–85 miners' strike would provide the most spectacular expressions of such antagonism. But images from Notting Hill, Lewisham, Grunwick, Southall, Brighton, Wapping and Wiltshire's Beanfield also informed the cultural memory, not to mention day-to-day experiences going on beneath the media radar.[123] Of course, freedom could also be lost through disinterest and malaise. A somnolent population too distracted or conditioned to recognise the connivance of power was another dystopian possibility played out through punk. Commodification, regeneration and the tightening strictures of state benefits and housing provision further contained the space for alternative cultures to form and function. Generally, however, punk – especially those who held fast to the term into the 1980s – appeared to exist under siege. Writing as 1984 turned to 1985, Conflict's Colin Jerwood surveyed a year of peace protests (Greenham Common), miners' struggles, Stop the City demonstrations, animal rights' actions and an IRA bomb that almost killed the prime minister as she prepared to speak at her party's annual conference on 12 October.[124] The government was becoming increasingly concerned with the 'scale of public awareness and the threat of mass civil unrest', Jerwood insisted. The police state was being 'brought to its peak'; the media and politicians had fallen into line. And as Conflict prepared to soundtrack and participate in the fight back, Jerwood reaffirmed his anarchist beliefs: 'Fuck authority … your oppression creates the hate'.[125]

Gimme World War Three, We Can Live Again

Part-way through the first side of Crass' *The Feeding of the Five Thousand*, a silence interrupts the noise. It lingers, disconcertingly longer than is normal for a typical segue, before a discordant guitar signals for Steve Ignorant to take up the lyric from where he left off: 'Twenty-odd years now, waiting for the flash ... all of the odd balls, thinking we'll be ash'.[126] The song's title, 'They've Got a Bomb', provided an obvious explanation. Live, however, the unexpected interlude made more sense, with lights simultaneously shutting down as film of an atomic bomb-blast projected into the sensorial vacuum. With the ultimate symbol of the Cold War lighting up the darkness, so the countdown began: four-three-two-one, fire.[127]

    Being Crass, this was no schlock-horror media affectation. It related to Rimbaud's long-standing support for the anti-war movement and sought deliberately to inform punk's countercultural position.[128] After all, the spectre of nuclear war – and the legacy of the atomic bombs dropped on Hiroshima and Nagasaki by the US military in August 1945 – had forever hung heavy over postwar youth and pop culture, fuelling what Jon Savage described as a kind of 'forced existentialism, of having to live for and in the moment'.[129] Jeff Nuttall even attributed 'the bomb' to the widening generation gap he perceived in the 1950s and 1960s, suggesting that 'the people who had not yet reached puberty at the time of the bomb were incapable of conceiving life with a future'.[130] Consciously or unconsciously, living in a world poised between the destructive might of two super-powers, each capable of unleashing wholesale devastation, had cultural ramifications that played out in myriad ways.

    Arguably, the 1970s saw some respite. Sino-American rapprochement and talk of 'peaceful coexistence' between the Soviet Union and US allowed for a period of détente to at least challenge the logic of Mutually Assured Destruction (MAD).[131] Enmities – and the perennial threat of nuclear conflict – remained, but discussion of arms limitation briefly replaced the brinksmanship that had peaked during the Cuban missile crisis of 1962.[132] As a result, Crass' raising the prospect of nuclear war and lending support to the Campaign for Nuclear Disarmament (CND) was relatively unusual in punk's early period. Although Rotten dropped reference to a 'potential H-bomb' in 'God Save the Queen', it was not until 1980, with the Cold War reigniting following the Soviet intervention in Afghanistan (1979) and the election of Ronald Reagan to the US presidency, that post-apocalyptic futures began to recur as punk dystopia. In particular, the confirmation in late 1979 that Britain would provide base for 160 American nuclear-armed cruise missiles rekindled both CND and latent fears.[133] In Margaret Thatcher, moreover, Britain had an 'iron lady' whose reputation was built on her irreconcilable opposition to Soviet communism.[134]

Political and cultural responses to what has been coined the 'second cold war' were soon apparent.[135] Publically, the women's peace camp at Greenham Common and the mass rallies organised by CND in the early 1980s offered the most overt displays of resistance. Labour also adopted unilateral disarmament and opposed accommodation of American missiles from 1980. Culturally, nuclear themes began to permeate everything from TV dramas, novels and documentaries to comics, comedies and the singles chart.[136] So, for example, Frankie Goes To Hollywood's 'Two Tribes' spent nine weeks at number one in June–August 1984, a pounding summation of the Cold War accompanied by a video that depicted Reagan and the Soviet leader Konstantin Chernenko wrestling in a bear-pit. Gruesome television also made an impact, with *Threads*' dramatisation of a nuclear strike on Sheffield being especially notorious among those of certain age. More generally, the Glastonbury music festival aligned with CND from 1981, raising money and the profile of the anti-war movement in the process.[137] In the *NME*, 'Plutonium Blondes' began as a regular column in the same year, featuring updates of nuclear-related developments and protests.[138]

Not surprisingly, punk-informed cultures proved quick to engage with the shifting geo-political climate. Crass' principal statement on the subject was 'Nagasaki Nightmare' (1980), a disturbing single that brought the horror of any future nuclear war into sharp focus. The song itself begins with Eve Libertine intoning the details of August 1945: the dates of the atomic explosions, the deaths, the radioactive consequences. Gong tones, bamboo flutes and a dislocated Japanese voice provide accompaniment, before the music builds up, disassembles and reforms over Rimbaud's shifting but incessant beat. Screeched vocals then bleed in and out, repeating the title around reference to man-made pain and deadly rain. Across the foldout sleeve, the minutiae of Nagasaki's nightmare – 'charred flesh, skin hanging in strips, maggots boiling out of wounds' – is related in words and pictures alongside essays on the power politics of nuclear proliferation. Opened-up, a Gee

Figure 8.5 (a) Discharge, *Why* (Clay, 1981) and (b) The Mob, 'No Doves Fly Here' (Crass Records, 1982).

Vaucher painting depicts cheerful world leaders set against an apocalyptic backdrop, while contact addresses for CND complement a map of the UK's nuclear sites and home defence structures. 'H-bombs are mind control. They kill people a little bit every day'.[139]

Crass were not alone in using the imagery of nuclear war to forewarn a post-apocalyptic future (see Figure 8.5). Discharge's relentless exploration of war's atrocities often drew on nuclear tropes filtered through brutal slabs of noise. 'It's the most important thing in our lives (threat of nuclear war) isn't it?', Bones (Tony Roberts) said when asked about his band's fixation.[140] Together with stark lyrics ('the final bloodbath's coming, it's just around the corner') and self-explanatory song-titles ('Two Monstrous Nuclear Stockpiles'), photographs of dead and radiated bodies covered their record sleeves. On 1982's *Hear Nothing See Nothing Say Nothing*, the songs 'Cries of Help' and 'The Possibility of Life's Destruction' were even conjoined by an excerpt from *The War Game*, the voice imparting data and survival advice over sounds of a bomb-blast and children in pain.[141] 'The message is peace', Cal (Kelvin Morris) told *Sounds* whilst touring under the banner of 'Apocalypse Now'. 'Our slogan says "I want to grow up, not blow up"'.[142]

Others made similar comment. From Killing Joke's 'Turn to Red' and the UK Subs' 'Warhead' through to Conflict's 'The Day Before' and Chaos UK's 'Four Minute Warning', the threat of nuclear war infused 1980s punk. Bands such as The Varukers, clearly inspired by Discharge, began to specialise in songs of nuclear holocaust, whilst the Subhumans tried to imagine the moment 'When the Bomb Drops'. Among the ever-growing number of anarchist bands emerging into the early 1980s, reflective accounts of the post-apocalyptic landscape sometimes offset the carnage. The Mob's 'No Doves Fly Here' presented a desolate portrait of the bomb's devastation, its celestial synths and choir suggesting a requiem for the empty cities and rural wastelands left in the aftermath.[143] Typically, however, the likes of Amebix, Anti-System, Flux of Pink Indians and The System preferred to depict broken bodies and war-torn cities amidst a barrage of angry noise, the death and destruction a by-product of power in the pursuit of profit.[144] And as the ramifications of 'Another Hiroshima' (to cite Dead Man's Shadow) were imagined, so lyrics and artworks oft-located punk in the fallout. Be it Vice Squad's 'Last Rockers' stumbling through the rubble of a blasted city or the sleeve to The Exploited's *Troops of Tomorrow* (1982) featuring the band caught in a bleak underpass surrounded by mutated skeletal creatures, punk appeared to embody the battered remnants of a society blown to bits. '[To] me', Wattie Buchan told *Sounds*, 'the punks now could be the troops of tomorrow, an' the cover jist shows like the skeletons an' that efter a nuclear attack, y'ken yer body wid jist be like waste [sic]'.[145] By 1984, peace symbols and images of mushroom clouds had become almost de rigueur across punk-informed artworks, serving both as sociopolitical commentary and, in some cases, a signal of committed activism.[146]

Less explicitly, perhaps, the overriding threat of the bomb may be read into the temper and tenor of punk and post-punk politics. It affirmed punk's oppositionism, appearing to represent the state's disdain for its citizens, replete with class connotations and a sense of 'us and them'. It was not just The Varukers who insisted 'They're the ones declare the war, you're the ones die for the cause'.[147] Similar sentiments were expressed in songs by 4-Skins, The Adicts, Chron Gen, GBH, The Samples and UK Decay – none of whom defined themselves as political in the commonly understood sense.[148] The bomb also reinforced punk's nihilist traits: the ultimate No Future. 'I might as well stay unemployed', Chron Gen reasoned as they viewed the mounting geo-political tensions surrounding Afghanistan and the US-led boycott of the Moscow Olympics, ''cos pretty soon, all life will be void'.[149] Even the dark ambience of much post-punk can be understood in relation to the bomb, tapping into a mood of disconcertion and unease.[150] According to Pete Wylie, whose various incarnations of Wah! emerged from Liverpool's punk milieu, 'apocalypse is in all the songs', lurking behind the paranoia of titles such as 'Seven Minutes to Midnight'.[151] We could go on: noting Young Marble Giants' 'The Final Day', The Sound's 'Missiles', the apocalyptic overtones of This Heat's *Deceit* (1981) and the obsessions of a (proto-) gothic culture that aestheticised death, ruin and decay. The point, of course, is that the threat of a post-nuclear future pervaded punk-related cultures (as it did culture and society more generally), finding creative expression in songs, artworks, writings and aesthetics.

It also crossed over into active political engagement. Alongside the collages of war and essays on militarism that filled many a fanzine over the 1980s, reports of anti-war groups and critical dissections of CND's effectiveness nestled between gig reviews and interviews.[152] Punk-informed bands held countless benefit gigs for anti-war causes and contributed to fund-raising records such as *Life in the European Theatre* (1982) and *Wargasm* (1982).[153] Young punks attended anti-war demonstrations. Where Crass distributed CND literature to those who wrote to them at Dial House, The Pop Group's Mark Stewart began working from CND's head office in 1980.[154] Paul Weller, whose lyric to 'Going Underground' sensed the darkening geo-political mood, even issued communiqués through the music press about the need to oppose nuclear weapons.[155]

Given such a context, the outbreak of the Falklands War fed into punk's bleak vision. The conflict began in earnest in April 1982, a British taskforce crossing the Atlantic to do combat with an Argentinian junta that had illegally occupied islands to which it staked a historic claim. It was also quickly won, with the British retaking control in June 1982 amidst much patriotic fervour.[156] Indeed, the war is generally recognised to have marked something of a turning point, both in terms of British self-perception and the status of Margaret Thatcher as a strong and decisive leader.[157] Popular and political support was forthcoming, despite the government being caught unawares and concern that expenditure cuts had undermined Britain's naval capabilities. The fact that Argentina, a dictatorship, had instigated the war also lent legitimacy to the government's actions. Nevertheless, the speed and the relish to which Britain went to war was alarming for some. Thatcher's bellicose rhetoric – conflating military combat abroad with industrial combat at home[158] – and the jingoism exemplified by *The Sun*'s 'Gotcha' headline following the sinking of the Argentinian *General Belgrano*, was both crude and disturbing.[159] To those of a critical disposition, the war appeared less a righteous cause than a politically-motivated distraction, an old-fashioned imperial power-play to rally the nation and bury domestic antagonisms beneath a patriotic veneer.

As may be expected, Crass immediately took up an anti-war position. The Falklands crisis had engendered an 'atmosphere of war', the band reasoned, thereby bringing the 'reality of nuclear' devastation ever closer.[160] First, therefore, a short statement condemning the war was hurriedly added to the booklet included with *Christ – The Album* (1982), before a rushed – and rather clumsy – dismissal of the conflict as an exercise in macho-posturing and imperial misadventure ('Sheep Farming in the Falklands') was issued anonymously as a flexi-disc.[161] Much sharper was 'How Does It Feel (To Be the Mother of a Thousand Dead)?', a splenetic anti-war statement that held Margaret Thatcher accountable for the misery, death and pain that 'you inflicted, you determined, you created, you ordered: it was your decision, to have those young boys slaughtered'. It was this that irked the moral scruples of Tim Eggar MP, who objected both to the record's anti-war sentiment and the b-side's rant against 'shit-head slimy got it all' politicians, grinding their 'bloodied teeth' in self-interest as they betrayed the dead from behind a Downing Street fortress.[162] Undeterred, Crass continued to agitate. Anti-war statements were printed and distributed at gigs, forewarning that 'the same squad of Falklands heroes will be smashing your head when you finally realise you've had enough of her [Thatcher's] madness'.[163] An 'open letter to rock 'n' rollers everywhere' was sent to the music press urging greater opposition to the Thatcher government. The 'Thatchergate' tape was also distributed, its spliced conversation between Reagan and Thatcher causing a brief media furore and hinting that the HMS *Sheffield* was deliberately sacrificed to Argentinian bombs in order to protect Prince Andrew on the *Ark Royal*.[164] Finally, on *Yes Sir, I Will*, recorded and released in 1983, Rimbaud endeavoured to distil the band's position over forty-four minutes of relentless noise broken only occasionally by moments of musical respite. An extended essay provided the lyric, locating the Falklands War as part of a more insidious political agenda: 'a callous and savage piece of electioneering to cover up horrific domestic problems'. Inside the album's sleeve, an image from *The Sun* was blown up to form a poster: Simon Weston, burnt horribly during the war, is photographed meeting Prince Charles. '"Get well soon", the Prince said. And the heroic soldier replied: "Yes, sir, I will."'[165]

Such a vehemently anti-war position was not universally accepted. In interviews and letters to the music press, varied responses to the conflict may be found among punk-informed milieus. So, for instance, Vice Squad's Beki Bondage initially supported Britain's going to war before reading up on the conflict and changing her mind. Nevertheless, at least one of her band mates felt the government had to respond.[166] Not dissimilarly, Mensi from the Angelic Upstarts worried that the crisis meant people 'forgetting there's three million, probably four million, on the dole'. But he recognised the war was fought against a 'fascist force' and insisted that 'if the call-up papers came [then] I'd fight'.[167] Cock Sparrer made similar comments, as did the 4-Skins, who saw the conflict as Britain 'fighting fascist aggression'.[168] Mark E. Smith also combined support for the war with 'Marquis Cha Cha', The Fall's tale of a 'loathsome traitor, victim of educated aimlessness', broadcasting pro-Argentinian propaganda from Buenos Aires.[169] Less assuredly, Mayhem claimed their song 'Patriots' was anti-fascist rather than nationalist (despite its 'what shall we do with the Argie bastards' intro), while to punk's right the likes of Combat 84 and The Ovalteenies revelled in Britain's military show of strength.[170] Generally, however, a sense that the war was exploited by Thatcher – either to distract from problems in Britain or as part of a broader geo-political power struggle – persevered, feeding into fanzine articles, interviews and songs such as 'Spirit of the Falklands' by New Model Army.[171] In effect, the specificities of the war became less important than the wider context. Not only had the conflict served to bolster the Conservatives' grip on government, but it turned an abstract fear of war into reality.

By 1984, military themes and visions of post-nuclear holocaust had become something of a punk cliché. Certainly, they informed one clearly visible strand of punk's aesthetic, taken to an extreme in the fledgling crust image of battered fatigues and almost wilful degradation. Notions of cider-punks and dogs-on-a-string were gestating, the oft-heard request from bedraggled punks loitering in city centres or outside gigs – 'have you got 10p' – was gently satirised by The Ejected.[172] And yet, for all the fatalism that imbued imaginations filled with apocalyptic doomsdays, punk still provided space to engage with and articulate the anxieties of what Extreme Noise Terror later called *A Holocaust in Your Head* (1989). More generally, any creative or political response to the threat of impending nuclear disaster cut to the nub of punk's dialectic: that its negation served as a stimulus. For this reason, punk and post-punk cultures may still be seen to offer what Raymond Williams described as a 'resource of hope'. In the politically informed DIY practice of Rough Trade or the sexual politics of The Raincoats lay alternate ways of thinking, living and doing. To be in a band was to work collectively; it was 'a strategy, a practice, a response to an incredibly barren and uncompromising landscape', Kevin Lycett of The Mekons remembered.[173] But we may also extend such reasoning to the anarchist praxis of Crass or the socialist sensibilities of the Newtown Neurotics and Redskins; to the boisterous defiance of Oi!; the esoteric explorations of industrial culture and the sensual transgressions of goth. Cast in the shadow of potential nuclear war, punk-informed responses were sometimes as ugly as the dystopias they envisaged. By engaging, however, they signalled both warnings and alternative possibilities. 'We're the future, your future' ....

ALTERNATIVES: CHAOS AND FINISH

We never sat down and wrote a thesis. There's no rules, and no order. We just do it, which is more to the point. Do it, and when you can't do it no more, then don't do it at all.[1]

Johnny Rotten (1977)

Having started *Sniffin' Glue* in 1976, Mark Perry soon formed one of punk's seminal bands, Alternative TV. Their first album was released in May 1978, opening with 'Alternatives' (originally titled 'Alternatives to NATO'), a slow-chugging freeform live staple of ATV's set that revolved around Perry reflecting on whatever came to mind (or hand).[2] That it musically referenced the experimental German band Faust confirmed Perry was keen to push beyond the limits of any pre-determined punk format.[3] As previously revealed on the single 'How Much Longer' (1977), Perry envisioned a punk of possibilities rather than clichés. Like Rotten, he urged invention rather than replication, confrontation rather than conformity.[4] Live, 'Alternatives' served as a provocation. Caught on record, it provided a freeze-frame of punk's fractious evolution.

The album version was recorded at London's 100 Club in February 1978. On this occasion, Perry offered the stage to the audience, reasserting punk's impetus to both do-it-yourself (DIY) and provide a platform for expression. The young crowd seem uncertain at first, as Perry invites people onto the 'soapbox'. Eventually, someone jumps up to berate the audience for being brainwashed by the media and politicians. He urges co-ordinated protest, for which he is shouted down, while Perry tells those dancing on the stage to get off ('we are spoilsports'). Another audience member takes the initiative, asking people to audition for his band (The Dead). Subcultural tensions then ensue as a skinhead calls out the punks and is met by a volley of derision. Perry steps in: 'Right, you stupid bastards, off the stage ... One of you people gets the chance to say something and what happens? There's a fight. That's all you can do ... I just wanted to make a point, right. I love all you people but I hate you when you act like stupid idiots, 'cos that's when they grind you down!' A disembodied documentary clip briefly cuts in, suggesting cultural spaces are where 'battles are fought, imaginations expressed, differences confronted and ... in which all kinds of movements can develop'.[5] The live recording then returns, with Perry insisting rock 'n' roll allows just such a space, but that it is not enough for punk bands simply to get on television. 'What you're getting is diluted, diluted shit ... No way have you won brother. Oh no, I talk like a communist. No way have you won sister. Someone said they know the problems, [but] what's the answer? This is really depressing 'cos there ain't no fucking answer'. A final audience member comes up to say that songs and words will never 'change the country', only actions can make a difference. Perry calls an end, telling the band: 'Let's have some chaos, chaos and finish'.[6]

Reviewing *The Image Has Cracked* (1978) for the *NME*, Paul Morley recognised how the album traced Perry's enthusiasms and frustrations across the punk culture he had helped disseminate. Perry was 'confused' and so 'confusing', Morley suggested, but the album's juxtaposition of experimentation and simplicity pointed towards the very answers Alternative TV were looking for. That is, to the 'problems of rock and its restrictions, fame and its dilutions'.[7] More than that, 'Alternatives' captured punk's combination of idealism, futility and violence. It set punk agency alongside idiocy, oppositionism against a disdain for all things political, collective endeavour against cultural animosity, purpose against fun, 'we' against 'them', an awareness of media distortion against suspicion of cultural impotency. Over its nine-or-so minutes, 'Alternatives' exposed the conflicting nature of punk's politics and tendered divisions that would fracture into the 1980s.

Vicarious Living Rids Your Boredom

As we know, Britain did not wholly succumb to the Orwellian future that The Clash and others envisaged for 1984 (though portents flicker brightly still). Nor did global nuclear war descend. But the sociopolitical *moment* from which punk emerged – as a faltering postwar 'consensus' gave way to the free-market doctrines of neoliberalism and the Cold War approached its endgame – did move beyond the contingent to the realised.[8] Aside from defeating the miners in 1984–85 and thereby breaking the back of a British labour movement already wracked by splits and division in the Labour Party, Margaret Thatcher's 1983 general election victory allowed for privatisation to push to the forefront of the government's agenda. Tax cuts and welfare restrictions followed, among them changes to unemployment benefit and, by the end of the 1980s, student grants. Local government powers were further curbed, including the abolition of the left-leaning Greater London Council (GLC); the sale of council houses was extended. In the City of London, financial services were deregulated in 1986 to precipitate a 'big bang' that fundamentally realigned the UK economy. Crucially, of course, such a transition was compounded by analogous policies in the United States and Mikhail Gorbachev's ascension to the Soviet leadership in 1985, setting in train a series of events that led to the collapse of European communism in 1989–91. Even the onset of recession in 1990 and violent protests against the Poll Tax failed to reset the economic agenda. Margaret Thatcher resigned in November 1990, but the socioeconomic changes she effected continued to form the basis of Conservative and (New) Labour policy thereafter.

Amidst all this, youth cultures evolved to find new forms that both complemented and countered the broader socioeconomic and political context of which they were part. Pop music did likewise, adopting and adapting to the technological innovations that charged the 'circuit of culture'.[9] Guitars began to give way to synths, sequencers and samplers; hip hop emerged from New York's South Bronx to further reimagine the possibilities of popular music; cheaper equipment paved the way for the same DIY impulse that fuelled punk to initiate new dance music and instigate the cultural sea change of rave.[10] By 1989, Tony Moon's famous directive – published originally in his 1977 *Sideburns* fanzine – that 'This is a chord, this is another, this is a third, now form a band', had been transformed.[11] Another fanzine, *Boy's Own*, passed on the new instructions: 'Here's a sampler, here's two decks, now go and form a band'.[12] On the streets (and soon-to-be outlawed terraces), sportswear and brand-affinity signalled status. More generally, the already nebulous boundaries of subcultural style became evermore fluid, sometimes circumventing media definition to distinguish class, cultural and emotional dispositions across different places and spaces, sometimes playing among an array of commercialised 'lifestyle choices'.[13]

Within the music and media industries, lessons were learnt and new challenges faced. Punk-related independent labels and bands were absorbed by the majors, with faux-independents set up to encroach on the 'alternative' market: 'indie' became a genre rather than a process or position.[14] The inkies' near monopoly of popular music coverage was also broken by greater tabloid interest in pop and the advent of style magazines that aestheticised the commodification of youth and music-based cultures. MTV and video transmitted through new mediums and revenue supplies. As for Band Aid, the 'super-group' brought together by Bob Geldof in 1984 to raise money for the Ethiopian famine, this soon benefited the pop establishment as much as those it strove to feed. In Dorian Lynskeys' words, the subsequent Live Aid concert of 1985 marked 'the end of strange, subversive statements such as [Frankie Goes To Hollywood's] "Two Tribes" and the beginning of phoney protest songs by artists with little grasp of politics who nonetheless felt obliged to make a Big Statement'.[15] And if Chumbawamba titling their first album *Pictures of Starving Children Sell Records* (1986) read a little harsh, then careers were certainly revitalised as one-time punks shared stages with a rock aristocracy they formerly decried and the grass-roots protests of the previous period segued into acts of paternalism: charity eclipsed commitment/intervention (see Figure C.1).[16] In the shops, meanwhile, compact discs helped shatter pop's sense of continual change, initiating the reissue of back catalogues to allow the past to exist in a perennial present. No longer were lost or marginal cultural resources recovered and reimagined; they existed concurrently to be collated, imitated, decontextualised and disarmed.[17]

As a result of such developments, the spaces opened up through punk began to contract. Equally, the differences that had always contested punk's point and purpose hardened as cultural forms evolved away from their initial stimulus. Bands ran out of ideas and energy; cultural changes and technology enabled competing sites of adolescent attention. Arguably, in terms of form and function, hip hop's emergence provided a more apposite cultural means of engaging with an age of postmodernism and neoliberalism; rave exposed the tensions existent between social control and the commodification of leisure/

Figure C.1 Label to Chumbawamba, *Pictures of Starving Children Sell Records* (Agit-Prop Records, 1986).

pleasure. Already, by the early 1980s, media interest in all things punk had begun to dim as its innovations became embedded in the cultural fabric and the music industry searched for new stars and styles. Sales of punk and punk-related records fell. According to Reynolds, 'average sales of an independent single in 1985 were half what they had been in 1980'.[18] For The Fits, at least, the reason was clear. It had 'nothing to do with George Orwell' and 'nothing to do with the bomb'. Rather, as Mick Crudge sung on 'Action', it was '1984 [and] we don't shock anymore'.[19]

As this suggests, new times begot new expressions. Across the independent chart of the mid-to-late 1980s, punk's diasporic subscenes evolved and dissolved, sometimes pushing to extremes (as with Napalm Death et al.'s grindcore), but more typically distilling aspects of pop's past in a variety of ways. Cultural obsessions – primarily referencing back to the 1950s–60s – and entrenched DIY strictures indicated conscious alternatives to chart-pop's technologically refined sheen, though these often appeared more retreat than critique. Soul-cialism infused leftist attempts to offer a positive riposte to Thatcherism, aspiring to *passion* amidst an uneasy mix of stylised appropriation and faux-sophistication. Goth recovered rock, all bluster and 4/4 beats, while industrial culture ventured further into the arcane or began journeys to the inner self that found synergy with the dance cultures flowering in the mid-to-late 1980s. Not dissimilarly, peace convoys provided a bucolic way out of the city for a section of punk's anarcho-milieu, looking back to connect with the hippie counterculture and, in some cases, forward to rave.[20] With the media focus elsewhere and the bill-board charts out of reach, avowedly punk-informed scenes dug-in to forge subterranean networks – both local and global – that maintain into the twenty-first century.[21] Existing beyond the spectacle and no longer pertaining to be a poison *inside* the machine, punk continued – and continues – to provide a means of agency and a platform, even as its cultural traces are archived, appropriated and, as here, historicised.

The years 1976–84 saw punk emerge and evolve as a musical form, a fashion, an attitude, an aesthetic and, significantly, a process of critical engagement. The Sex Pistols marked a moment of departure, facilitating a cultural critique that initiated a broader exposition of the faultlines that ran through a period of socioeconomic and political change.[22] By so doing, punk reasserted youth culture as both a site of refusal ('fuck off', two-fingers, 'up yours') and a means of expression: a space to forge individual identities; to have a voice; to explore a range of cultural and political possibilities.[23] Consequently, punk's politics – its *meanings* and *practice* – were disputed even as they revolved around a sense of disaffection, be it with the state of pop music or, to quote The Prefects, 'things in general'.

As importantly, Sex Pistols – and punk thereafter – served as stimulus. The impetus to form a band, write a fanzine, organise a gig or make a record was an immediate answer to Rotten's challenge ('get off your arse'/'no future'), not to mention punk's wider disdain for the choices provided through the culture industry. Accordingly, punk rejuvenated and re-energised popular music, inserting marginal voices, vocabularies and ideas into pop while endeavouring to (re)connect with the youth cultures that sustained and formed around it. This, in turn, affirmed punk claims to relevance.[24] But it also enabled Linder's conviction that punk took away the question '*Can* I do this?' If punk was a process, a way of doing, then it helped enable the experiments of post-punk and industrial just as much as the upsurge of activity that defined 1976–77. Or, to quote a member of Swell Maps, a band from Solihull who helped pioneer punk's DIY ethos, 'you can say anything you want, it's your attitude to what you are doing that counts'.[25]

Ultimately, punk's 'attitude' bore a critical impulse that both informed and corroded the related cultures that developed from 1976. Very quickly, 'punk' accrued a range of signifiers that defined a recognisable sound, image and approach – fast and furious rock 'n' roll, spitting, spikes, anti-social, rebellious. But there was also an awareness, oft-repeated in fanzines and interviews, that to label something was to disarm it. For this reason, punk was disavowed and reacted against just as much as it was adopted, instigating what Reynolds recognised as the creative 'spirit of adventure and idealism' that informed the 'long aftermath of punk'.[26] Among the handwritten notes for the second *Anarchy in the UK* fanzine compiled – but never issued – from within the Sex Pistols' inner circle was the statement 'punk is dead'.[27] This was early 1977, just as punk had been codified within the media. A year later, the same logic infused Crass' 'Punk is Dead', a song that critiqued punk's co-option by the music industry.[28] To be *that what is not* lay at the heart of the impulse to which punk gave (multiple) expression, a sensibility that could engender conscious sociopolitical engagement but more-often-than-not cut across or challenged the socioeconomic, cultural and ideological strictures of late twentieth-century polity in pursuit of individuality or new collectivities. Subsequently, the debate as to what punk *was* or *should be* rumbled on, even as those happy to leave the term behind continued to employ the processes that sparked the cultural ructions of 1976–77.[29]

Punk's politics were messy. They could be contradictory and formative; implicit and explicit; liberatory and reactionary. Meanings were projected onto punk, but also cultivated from within. Amidst the clashing political symbols that helped frame punk's emergence and the anti-political rhetoric that bore testament to youthful disdain, Rock Against Racism (RAR) and the practices associated with Rough Trade gave shape to punk's (future) purpose. The far right touted for young recruits, keen to channel punk's ire in an ultra-nationalist, often violent, direction. Anarchy, of a sort, found practical application in the cultures that coalesced around Crass; the influences of dada, situationist theory, Ballard, Burroughs and others were often evident. As importantly, questions of class, gender and sexuality fed into and informed punk's aesthetic, shaping the dialogues that ensued as cultural spaces opened up.

At root, punk signified a negation that enabled agency and empowerment, demystifying processes of cultural production in order to do-it-yourself. This could be fun and exciting, revelling in the temporal thrill of real or imagined transgressions. Not only did punk engender creativity, it also forged cultures that challenged prevailing social (and socioeconomic) norms in irreverent and provocative ways. Equally, punk's critical sensibility – and tendency to social commentary – allowed for deeper interpretation, filtering countercultural, artistic and ideological influences through a youth cultural lens at a time of broader socioeconomic and political change. Like pop more generally, punk both reflected lives being lived and uncovered portals to other worlds and ideas: to politics, history, cultural antecedents, provincial frustrations, adolescent insecurities and social antagonisms. This was always contentious. Attempts to apply formal politics or prescribed theories to youth culture and pop music were often seen to bind rather than enable. Nevertheless, themes ran through punk and its associated cultures that related to contemporaneous sociopolitical questions as well as the travails of youth. There was, moreover, an awareness as to the routines of media manipulation, commercial co-option and cultural appropriation that infused punk's practice and aesthetic. As a result, punk inspired both political engagement and cynicism. It also encouraged, alongside the industrial culture that emerged simultaneously, the exploration of sexual, psychological and delinquent extremes; anything to escape the banality of late twentieth-century living. To understand punk's politics, therefore, is not to find philosophical clarity or the basis of a *movement*. Rather, the politics of punk resided in its refusal and its practice: a recognition that 'blind acceptance is a sign of stupid fools who stand in line'.[30]

Notes

Teenage Warning: Punk, Politics and Youth Culture

1 John Peel speaking on BBC's *Brass Tacks* in August 1977.
2 Persons Unknown, *Persons Unknown* (London: Persons Unknown, 1979); *Persons Unknown*, directed by Gordon Carr (1980); David Clark, '18 Months in the Waiting', *The Leveller*, October 1979, pp. 7–8. The six arrested were Ronan Bennett, Stewart Carr, Trevor Dawton, Dafydd Ladd, Iris Mills and Vince Stevenson. Carr pleaded guilty and received nine years; Ladd jumped bail before the trial; the rest were acquitted. For an evocative glimpse of British anarchism in the 1970s, see Ian Walker, 'Anarchy in the UK', in Paul Barker (ed.), *The Other Britain: A New Society Collection* (London: Routledge, 1982), pp. 53–63.
3 Sleevenotes to Crass, 'Bloody Revolutions' b/w Poison Girls, 'Persons Unknown', Crass Records, 1980. Ronan Bennett contributed to the sleevenotes; the money made by the record was used to set up an anarchist centre in Wapping, London, which ran from August 1981 to March 1982.
4 For accounts of the Conway Hall incident, see 'Crass – "Heavy Mob" Invade', *The Leveller*, October 1979, p. 6; Crass and Poison Girls, Untitled Pamphlet, October 1979; Crass, 'Statement', *Kill Your Pet Puppy*, 1, 1980, pp. 13–15; Penny Rimbaud, *Shibboleth: My Revolting Life* (Edinburgh: AK Press, 1998), pp. 118–24; Martin Lux, *Anti-Fascist* (London: Phoenix Press, 2006), pp. 89–95; Sean Birchall, *Beating the Fascists: The Untold Story of Anti-Fascist Action* (London: Freedom Press, 2010), pp. 41–3.
5 See, for example, the accounts of Bernard Nossiter, *Britain: A Future that Works* (London: Houghton, 1978); Christopher Brooker, *The Seventies: Portrait of a Decade* (London: Allen Lane, 1980); Phillip Whitehead, *The Writing on the Wall: Britain in the Seventies* (London: Michael Joseph, 1985); Francis Wheen, *Strange Days Indeed: The Golden Age of Paranoia* (London: Fourth Estate, 2009). See the text that follows for more recent accounts of the 1970s that begin to question such interpretation.

6 This has not always been the case. For a few notable exceptions see Arthur Marwick, 'Youth in Britain, 1920–60', *Journal of Contemporary History*, 5:1 (1970), 37–51; Bill Osgerby, *Youth Culture in Britain Since 1945* (London: Routledge, 1998); David Fowler, *Youth Culture in Modern Britain, c. 1920–c.1970* (Basingstoke: Palgrave Macmillan, 2008); Adrian Horn, *Juke Box Britain: Americanisation and Youth Culture, 1945–1960* (Manchester: Manchester University Press, 2009); Subcultures Network, 'Youth Culture, Popular Music and the End of "Consensus" in Britain', *Contemporary British History*, 26:3 (2012 special issue); Keith Gildart, *Images of England through Popular Music: Class, Youth and Rock 'n' Roll, 1955–1976* (Basingstoke: Palgrave Macmillan, 2013). It was this observation that led me, Keith Gildart and Lucy Robinson to join with scholars from other academic disciplines to form the Interdisciplinary Network for the Study of Subcultures, Popular Music and Social Change (Subcultures Network).

7 Sex Pistols, 'Anarchy in the UK' b/w 'I Wanna Be Me', EMI Records, 1976; *Anarchy in the UK*, 1, 1976, p. 8.

8 Caroline Coon, 'Clash: Down and Out and Proud', *Melody Maker*, 13 November 1976, p. 33.

9 For an engaging account, see Steve Jones, *Lonely Boy: Tales from a Sex Pistol* (London: William Heinemann, 2016).

10 Len Richmond, 'Buy Sexual', *Forum*, June 1976, pp. 20–1; Paul Stolper and Andrew Wilson, *No Future: SEX, Seditionaries and the Sex Pistols* (London: The Hospital, 2004).

11 The definitive account of the Sex Pistols is Jon Savage, *England's Dreaming: Sex Pistols and Punk Rock* (London: Faber & Faber, 1991). But see also Fred and Judy Vermorel, *The Sex Pistols: The Inside Story* (London: Universal, 1978); Caroline Coon, *1988: The New Wave Punk Rock Explosion* (London, Omnibus, 1982); *Punk and the Pistols*, directed by Paul Tickell (1995); *The Filth and the Fury*, directed by Julien Temple (2000); Alan Parker with Mick O'Shea, *Young Flesh Required: Growing Up with the Sex Pistols* (London: Soundcheck Books, 2011); Clinton Heylin, *Anarchy in the UK: The Sex Pistols, The Clash and the Class of '76* (Pontefract: Route, 2016); John Scanlon, *Sex Pistols: Poison in the Machine* (London: Reaktion Books, 2016).

12 Savage, *England's Dreaming*, p. 478.

13 See, for example, 'Terrorise Your Fans the Sex Pistols Way', *NME*, 8 May 1976, p. 11.

14 Neil Spencer, 'Don't Look Over Your Shoulder, the Sex Pistols Are Coming', *NME*, 21 February 1976, p. 31; Jonh [sic] Ingham, 'The Sex Pistols ...', *Sounds*, 24 April 1976, pp. 10–11; Caroline Coon, 'Punk Rock: Rebels Against the System', *Melody Maker*, 7 August 1976, pp. 24–5; Jonh Ingham, 'Welcome

to the (?) Rock Special', *Sounds*, 9 October 1976, pp. 22–7; Caroline Coon, 'Rotten to the Core', *Melody Maker*, 27 November 1976, pp. 34–5.

15 Quoted in Vermorel and Vermorel, *The Sex Pistols*, p. 182.

16 Jonh Ingham, 'The Sex Pistols …', pp. 10–11.

17 Coon, 'Rotten to the Core', pp. 34–5.

18 Alongside Barker, Ballion and Bailey, the core Bromley contingent comprised Bertie Marshall (Berlin), Simone Thomas, Sharon Hayman and, on returning from the University of Sussex, Billy Broad (Billy Idol). Their wider circle included Linda Ashby, a dominatrix who worked out of London's St James' Hotel. Important, too, alongside Jordan, were Alan Jones, Helen Wallington-Lloyd, Marco Pirroni, Nils Stevenson, Debbie Wilson (Debbie Juvenile), Sue Lucas (Soo Catwoman), Tracie O'Keefe and Chrissie Hynde, all of whom worked in SEX or were close to McLaren and Westwood. John Lydon's friends, including John Beverley (Sid Vicious), John Gray and John Wardle (Jah Wobble), provided the menace.

19 Simon Barker, *Punk's Dead* (London: Divus, 2011); Bertie Marshall, *Berlin Bromley* (London: SAF Publishing), 2007; Billy Idol, *Dancing With Myself* (London: Simon & Schuster, 2014), pp. 39–59; Savage, *England's Dreaming*, pp. 181–2.

20 Nick Crossley, 'Pretty Connected: The Social Network of the Early UK Punk Movement', *Theory, Culture and Society*, 25:6 (2008), 89–116.

21 David Nolan, *I Swear I Was There: The Gig That Changed the World* (Shropshire: IMP, 2006).

22 Among these were *Alternative Ulster* (Belfast), *Bombsite* (Liverpool), *Bondage* (London), *Chainsaw* (London), *48 Thrills* (London), *Ghast Up* (Manchester), *Gun Rubber* (Sheffield), *Hanging Around* (Edinburgh), *In the City* (London), *Jamming* (London), *Jolt* (London), *Kid's Stuff* (Chesington), *Loaded* (Bristol), *London's Outrage* (London), *New Pose* (Leeds), *Panache* (Staines), *Ripped & Torn* (Glasgow) and *Shy Talk* (Manchester). See also Mark Perry, *Sniffin' Glue: The Essential Punk Accessory* (London: Sanctuary, 2000). For analysis, see Matthew Worley, 'Punk, Politics and British (fan)zines, 1976–84: "While the world was dying, did you wonder why?"', *History Workshop Journal*, 79 (2015), 76–106; Teal Triggs, *Fanzines* (London: Thames & Hudson, 2010); idem, 'Scissors and Glue: Punk Fanzines and the Creation of a DIY Aesthetic', *Journal of Design History*, 19: 1 (2006), 69–83; idem, 'Alphabet Soup: Reading British Fanzines', *Visible Language*, 29:1 (1995), 72–87.

23 Between September and November 1976, the band appeared on Granada's *So It Goes* (28 August), the BBC's *Nationwide* (12 November) and LWT's *London Weekend Show* (28 November). Some sources state that *So It Goes* was broadcast on 4 September, but the *TV Times* and Granada suggest otherwise.

24 Savage, *England's Dreaming*, p. 253.

25 'Anarchy in the Singles', *Sniffin Glue*, 5, 1976, p. 9.

26 Brian Southall, *Sex Pistols: 90 Days at EMI* (London: Bobcat Books, 2007). Stories differ: either the Queen video had not been cleared by the Musicians' Union or Queen's singer, Freddie Mercury, had failed to recover from a dental appointment.

27 Savage, *England's Dreaming*, pp. 263–75; Keith Gildart, '"The Antithesis of Humankind": Exploring Responses to the Sex Pistols' Anarchy Tour 1976', *Cultural and Social History*, 10:1 (2013), 129–49; Mick O'Shea, *The Anarchy Tour* (London: Omnibus Press, 2012).

28 'The Filth and Fury!' and 'Who Are These Punks?', *Daily Mirror*, 2 December 1976, pp. 1–2; 'Foul Mouthed Yobs', *Evening Standard*, 2 December 1976, p. 1; 'Revolting', *Evening Standard*, 4 January 1977, p. 1.

29 For examples, see 'Punk Rock Revolution', *Sunday People*, 12 June 1977, pp. 20–1; Brian Case, 'Punk People: Why They Go For Punk Rock', *The Observer Magazine*, 30 January 1977, pp. 18–21; Gordon Burn, 'Good Clean Punk', *Sunday Times Magazine*, 17 July 1977, pp. 28–33; Dave Marsh, 'Dole Queue Rock', *New Society*, 20 January 1977, pp. 112–14.

30 'Big Brother Declares War on the New Wave', *NME*, 4 June 1977, p. 3; 'New Wave Dossier', *Sounds*, 18 June 1977, p. 3. Alongside the Sex Pistols, The Stranglers were a particular target of the GLC and councils elsewhere. Material relating to the GLC's 'Code of Practice for Pop Concerts' (1976) and related newspaper reports are collected in the London Metropolitan Archive.

31 Colin Wills, 'Punk Rock Jubilee Shocker', *Sunday Mirror*, 12 June 1977, p. 1.

32 'Sex Pistols: Banned', *NME*, 25 June 1977, p. 52. Among those banning the single were BBC Radio One, Capital Radio, WH Smith, Boots and Woolworths. It was also reported that the nations' Brewers had refused to allow the Sex Pistols on their Juke Boxes.

33 Jon Savage, 'What Did You Do on the Jubilee?', *Sounds*, 18 June 1977, pp. 9–10; idem, *England's Dreaming*, pp. 358–67. Paul Cook was also attacked at this time, though this appears more related to punk-teddy boy antagonisms. See also, 'Messing About on the River', *Sounds*, 18 June 1977, p. 2.

34 Sex Pistols, 'Holidays in the Sun' b/w 'Satellite', Virgin 1977.

35 Savage, *England's Dreaming*, p. 424; James Johnson and Kevin Murphy, 'Police Move in on Punk Disc Shops', *Evening Standard*, 9 November 1977, p. 1; Brian Dixon, 'And the Same to You', *The Sun*, 25 November 1977, p. 1.

36 The messy aftermath of the Sex Pistols is covered extensively in Savage's *England's Dreaming*, pp. 474–541. See also *The Great Rock 'n' Roll Swindle*, directed by Julien Temple (1980).

37 'Terror in Southall', *Daily Mail*, 4 July 1981, p. 1; 'Race Riots', *Daily Mirror*, 4 July 1981, p. 1; 'Blood On Our Streets', *News of the World*, 5 July 1981, p. 1; Dorian Lynskey, *33 Revolutions per Minute: A History of Protest Songs* (London: Faber & Faber, 2010), pp. 433–50.

38 Andrew Czezowski and Susan Carrington, *The Roxy, London 1976–77: The Club That Forged Punk* (London: Carrczez, 2016).

39 Dick Hebdige, *Subculture: The Meaning of Style* (London: Routledge 2007 originally published 1979), p. 87.

40 The Perry quote is from 'The Sex Pistols for *Time Out*', *Sniffin' Glue*, 6, 1977, pp. 3–4.

41 Savage, *England's Dreaming*, pp. 277–9 and 396–9; Dave Laing, 'Interpreting Punk Rock', *Marxism Today*, April 1978, pp. 123–8; idem, *One Chord Wonders: Power and Meaning in Punk Rock* (Milton Keynes: Open University Press, 1985), pp. 104–5; Simon Frith, *Sound Effects: Youth, Leisure and the Politics of Rock 'n' Roll* (London: Pantheon, 1981), pp. 158–63.

42 Matthew Worley, 'Oi! Oi! Oi!: Class, Locality, and British Punk', *Twentieth Century British History*, 24:4 (2013), 606–36.

43 Matthew Worley, 'One Nation Under the Bomb: The Cold War and British Punk to 1984', *Journal for the Study of Radicalism* 5:2 (2011), 65–83.

44 Richard Cross, 'The Hippies Now Wear Black: Crass and the Anarcho-Punk Movement, 1977–84', *Socialist History*, 26 (2004), 25–44; George Berger, *The Story of Crass* (London: Omnibus, 2006). The term 'anarcho' floated around the early 1980s, being used in anarchist fanzines such as *Acts of Defiance*, *Fack* and *Kill Your Pet Puppy*, as well as cropping up in the journalism of Garry Bushell. Richard North (Richard Cabut) and Tony Drayton both used the term in their writing for the *NME* in 1982–83.

45 David Rimmer, *Like Punk Never Happened: Culture Club and the New Pop* (London: Faber & Faber, 2011 edition); Graham Smith and Chris Sullivan, *We Can Be Heroes* (London: Unbound, 2012); Mick Mercer, *Gothic Rock Black Book* (London: Lulu, 2009, originally published 1988).

46 Simon Ford, *Wreckers of Civilisation: The Story of COUM Transmissions and Throbbing Gristle* (London: Black Dog, 1995). For an excellent analysis of industrial music, see S. Alexander Reed, *Assimilate: A Critical History of Industrial Music* (Oxford: Oxford University Press, 2013).

47 Jon Savage, 'New Musick', *Sounds*, 26 November 1977, p. 23; Paul Morley, *Ask: The Chatter of Pop* (London: Faber & Faber, 1986); Simon Reynolds, *Rip It Up and Start Again: Post-Punk, 1978–84* (London: Faber & Faber, 2005).

48 Mick Middles, *From Joy Division to New Order: The True Story of Anthony H. Wilson and Factory Records* (London: Virgin, 2002); John Robb, *The North Will Rise Again: Manchester Music City, 1976–96* (London: Aurum, 2009); Tony Beesley, *Our Generation: The Punk and Mod Children of Sheffield, Rotherham and Doncaster* (Peterborough: Fastprint, 2009); Martin Lilleker, *Beats Working for a Living: Sheffield Popular Music, 1973–1984* (Sheffield: Juma, 2005); Sean O'Neill and Guy Trelford, *It Makes You Want to Spit: The Definitive Guide to Punk in Northern Ireland* (Belfast: Reekus, 2003); Jaki Florek and Paul Whelan, *Eric's: All the Best Clubs Are Downstairs, Everybody Knows That …* (Runcorn: Feedback, 2009).

49 Matthew Worley, 'Shot by Both Sides: Punk, Politics and the End of "Consensus"', *Contemporary British History*, 26:3 (2012), 333–54.

50 Barry Miles, 'Eighteen Flight Rock and the Sound of the Westway', *NME*, 11 December 1976, p. 14.

51 Garry Bushell, *Hoolies: True Stories of Britain's Biggest Street Battles* (London: John Blake, 2010).

52 *Nationwide*, broadcast 12 November 1976.

53 Joe Gibbs and The Professionals' *State of Emergency*, Record Globe, 1976.

54 The Clash, 'White Riot' b/w '1977', CBS Records, 1977; Charles Hamblett and Jane Deverson, *Generation X* (London: Tandem Books, 1965); Stanley Cohen, *Folk Devils and Moral Panics* (London: MacGibbon and Kee, 1972).

55 Richard Clutterbuck, *Britain in Agony: The Growth of Political Violence* (London: Penguin, 1978); Stephen Haseler, *The Death of British Democracy* (London, Elek Books, 1976); Isaac Kramnick, *Is Britain Dying? Perspectives on the Current Crisis* (New York: Ithaca, 1979). See also John Barr, *Derelict Britain* (London: Pelican, 1969); Tony Bunyan, *The History and Practice of the Political Police in Britain* (London: Quartet, 1977); Stuart Hall, *Policing the Crisis: Mugging, the State, and Law and Order* (Basingstoke: Macmillan, 1978); John Harrison and Andrew Glyn, *The British Economic Disaster* (London: Pluto, 1980); Anthony King, *Why Is Britain Becoming Harder to Govern?* (London: BBC, 1976).

56 Tom Nairn, *The Break-up of Britain: Crisis and Neo-Nationalism* (London: Verso, 1981 originally published 1977).

57 Andy Beckett, *When the Lights Went Out: Britain in the Seventies* (London: Faber & Faber, 2009), pp. 166–9 and 376–82. See also Alwyn W. Turner, *Crisis? What Crisis? Britain in the 1970s* (London: Aurum, 2008), pp. 128–9; Roger King and Neil Nugent (eds.), *Respectable Rebels: Middle Class Campaigns in Britain in the 1970s* (London: Hodder & Stoughton, 1979); Barrie Penrose and Roger Courtiour, *The Penrose File* (London: Secker & Warburg, 1978).

58 Beckett, *When the Lights Went Out*, p. 177.

59 See, for example, Colin Hay, 'Narrating the Crisis: The Discursive Construction of the "Winter of Discontent"', *Sociology*, 30:2 (1996), 253–77; idem, 'Chronicles of a Death Foretold: The Winter of Discontent and Construction of the Crisis of British Keynesian', *Parliamentary Affairs*, 63:3 (2010), 446–70; Nick Tiratsoo, '"You've Never Had It So Bad": Britain in the 1970s', in idem (ed.), *From Blitz to Blair: A New History of the Britain since the 1970s* (London: Weidenfield & Nicolson, 1997), 163–90; Mark Garnett, *From Anger to Apathy: The British Experience since 1975* (London: Jonathan Cape, 2007); Joe Moran, '"Stand Up and Be Counted": Hughie Green, the 1970s and Popular Memory', *History Workshop Journal*, 70:1 (2010), 173–98; Lawrence Black, Hugh Pemberton and Pat Thane (eds.), *Reassessing the Seventies* (Manchester: Manchester University Press, 2013). See also Dominic Sandbrook, *State of Emergency: The*

Way We Were: Britain, 1970–74 (London: Penguin, 2011); idem, *Seasons in the Sun: The Battle for Britain, 1974–79* (London: Allen Lane, 2012).

60 James Denman and Paul McDonald, 'Unemployment Statistics from 1881 to the Present Day', *Labour Market Trends*, January 1996, pp. 5–18; Sean Glynn and Alan Booth, *Modern Britain: An Economic and Social History* (London: Routledge, 1996); Richard Coopey and Nicholas Woodward (eds.), *Britain in the 1970s: The Troubled Economy* (London: UCL Press, 1995).

61 Denman and McDonald, 'Unemployment Statistics from 1881 to the Present Day', pp. 5–18. The percentage of those unemployed peaked in mid-1982 at 14 per cent. The highest yearly average of registered unemployment also occurred in 1982: 13 per cent.

62 Stuart Hall, 'The Great Moving Right Show', *Marxism Today*, January 1979, 14–20. For a historical account, see Andrew Gamble, *The Free Economy and the Strong State: The Politics of Thatcherism* (Basingstoke: Palgrave Macmillan, 1994 edition). For a comprehensive overview, see Brian Harrison, *Finding a Role? The United Kingdom, 1970–1990* (Oxford University Press, 2010).

63 See, for example, Bart Moore-Gilbert (ed.), *The Arts in the 1970s: Cultural Closure?* (London: Routledge, 1994); John A. Walker, *Left Shift: Radical Art in 1970s Britain* (London: I. B. Tauris, 2002).

64 Nik Cohn, *Awopbopaloobop Alopbamboom: Pop from the Beginning* (London: Pimlico, 2004 edition); Charlie Gillett, *The Sound of the City: The Rise of Rock & Roll* (London: Souvenir, 2004 edition).

65 For the emergence and development of pre–Second World War youth cultures, see Jon Savage, *Teenage: The Creation of Youth, 1875–1945* (London: Pimlico, 2008); David Fowler, *The First Teenagers: The Lifestyle of Young Wage-Earners in Interwar Britain* (London: Woburn Press, 1995); John Springhall, *Coming of Age: Adolescence in Britain, 1860–1960* (Gill & Macmillan, 1986).

66 Peter Doggett, *There's a Riot Goin' on: Revolutionaries, Rocks Stars, and the Rise and Fall of '60s Counter-Culture* (London: Canongate Books, 2008).

67 This was not just a UK phenomenon, of course. See the essays in Axel Schildt and Detlef Siegfried (eds.), *Between Marx and Coca-Cola: Youth Cultures in Changing European Societies, 1960–1980* (Oxford: Berghahn, 2006).

68 See, for example, Frederic Thrasher, *The Gang: A Study of 1,313 Gangs in Chicago* (Chicago: University of Chicago Press, 1927); Albert K. Cohen, *Delinquent Boys: The Culture of the Gang* (London: Taylor & Francis, 1956). The term 'youth culture' appears to have first been used by Talcott Parsons in a paper on age and sex in the United States (1942).

69 Radcliffe's articles appeared in *Anarchy*, *Rebel Worker* and his own *Heatwave* in 1965–66. See Jon Savage, *1966: The Year the Decade Exploded* (London: Faber & Faber, 2015), pp. 374–6.

70 Phil Cohen, 'Subcultural Conflict and Working Class Community', *Working Class Papers in Cultural Studies*, 2 (1972), pp. 4–51; John Clarke, Stuart Hall, Tony

Jefferson and Brian Roberts, 'Subcultures, Cultures and Class: A Theoretical Overview', in Stuart Hall and Tony Jefferson (eds.), *Resistance Through Rituals: Youth Subcultures in Post-War Britain* (London: Hutchinson & Co., 1976), pp. 9–74.

71 For a good overview of the debate see Paul Hodkinson, 'Youth Cultures: A Critical Outline of Key Debates', in Paul Hodkinson and Wolfgang Deicke (eds.), *Youth Cultures: Scenes, Subcultures and Tribes* (London: Routledge, 2007), pp. 1–22.

72 A point well made in Steve Redhead, *The End of the Century Party: Youth and Pop Towards 2000* (Manchester: Manchester University Press, 2000), p. 25.

73 In relation to punk, see David Muggleton, *Inside Subculture: The Postmodern Meaning of Style* (Oxford: Berg, 2000).

74 See, for example, Angela McRobbie and Jenny Garber, 'Girls and Subcultures: An Exploration', in Hall and Jefferson (eds.), *Resistance Through Rituals*, pp. 209–22; Angela McRobbie, 'Working Class Girls and the Culture of Femininity', in Women's Studies Group, *Women Take Issue* (London: Hutchinson, 1978), pp. 96–108.

75 See David Muggleton and Rupert Weinzierl (eds.), *Post-Subcultures Reader* (London: Berg, 2003); Andy Bennett and Keith Kahn-Harris (eds.), *After Subculture: Critical Studies in Contemporary Youth Culture* (Basingstoke: Palgrave Macmillan, 2004).

76 Hebdige, *Subcultures*, p. 105. The term is borrowed from Umberto Eco.

77 Cockney Rejects, 'Join the Rejects' on Cockney Rejects, *Greatest Hits Vol. 1*, EMI, 1980. *Leaving the 20th Century: The Incomplete Works of the Situationist International* (London: Free Fall, 1974) was compiled by Christopher Gray and designed by Jamie Reid.

78 This borrows from Jon Savage's rationale for his *1966*, pp. vii–xii.

79 Jamie Reid and Jon Savage, *Up They Rise: The Incomplete Works of Jamie Reid* (London: Faber & Faber, 1987); Ray Stevenson, *Sex Pistols File* (London: Omnibus, 1978); Dennis Morris, *Rebel Rock: A Photographic History of the Sex Pistols* (London: Omnibus Press, 1985). Early photos were also taken by Kate Simon and Peter Christopherson.

80 Mark Perry, 'The Last Page', *Sniffin' Glue*, 1, 1976, p. 8.

81 *Sex Pistols No. 1*, directed by Julien Temple (1977); *Punk in London*, directed by Wolfgang Büld (1977); *The Punk Rock Movie*, directed by Don Letts (1978). See also Büld's follow up film, *Punk in England* (1980), along with *Rough Cut and Ready Dubbed*, directed by Hasan Shah and Dom Shaw (1982); *UKDK: A Film about Punks and Skinheads*, directed by Christopher Collins and Ken Lawrence (1983).

82 Isabelle Anscombe and Dike Blair, *Punk: Rock/Style/Stance/People/Stars That Head the New Wave in England and America* (New York: Urizen Books, 1978); Virginia Boston, *Punk Rock* (London: Plexus, 1978); Julie Davis, *Punk* (London: Millington, 1977); Val Hennessy, *In the Gutter* (London: Quartet,

1978); Ray Stevenson, *Sex Pistols Scrap Book* (London: self-published, 1977 reissued as *Sex Pistols File* (London: Omnibus Press, 1978); John Tobler, *Punk Rock* (London: Phebus, 1977); Anon., *100 Nights at The Roxy* (London: Big O, 1978).

83 The exception, perhaps, is Caroline Coon's *1988: The New Wave Punk Rock Explosion* (1977), which compiles her 1976–77 *Melody Maker* articles.

84 Rotten, cited in Vermorel and Vermorel, *The Sex Pistols*, p. 130; Sex Pistols, 'No Fun', b-side of 'Pretty Vacant' (Virgin Records, 1977).

85 For oral histories see Legs McNeil and Gillian McCain, *Please Kill Me: The Uncensored Oral History of Punk* (London: Abacus, 1997); Nils & Ray Stevenson, *Vacant: A Diary of the Punk Years, 1976–79* (London: Thames & Hudson, 1999); Stephen Colegrave and Chris Sullivan, *Punk: A Life Apart* (London: Cassell & Co., 2001); John Robb, *Punk Rock: An Oral History* (London: Ebury Press, 2006); Nolan, *I Swear I Was There*; Paul Marko, *The Roxy London WC2: A Punk Rock History* (London, Punk77 Books, 2007); Simon Reynolds, *Totally Wired: Post-Punk Interviews and Overviews* (London Faber & Faber, 2009); Jon Savage, *The England's Dreaming Tapes* (London: Faber & Faber, 2009); Daniel Rachel, *Walls Come Tumbling Down: The Music and Politics of Rock Against Racism, 2-Tone and Red Wedge* (London: Picador, 2016). For collections, see Gavin Walsh, *Punk on 45: Revolution on Vinyl, 1976–79* (London: Plexus, 2006); Toby Mott, *Loud Flash: British Punk on Paper* (London: Haunch of Venison, 2010); Russ Bestley and Tony Brook, *Action Time Vision* (London: Unit Editions, 2016); The Mott Collection, *Oh So Pretty: Punk in Print, 1976–80* (London: Phaidon Press, 2016). For an important collection of photos, see Jonh Ingham, *Spirit of '76: London Punk Eyewitness* (Brooklyn: Anthology Editions, 2017).

86 Jon Savage, *Punk 45: Original Punk Rock Singles Cover Art* (London: Soul Jazz, 2013); Johan Kugelberg and Jon Savage (eds.), *Punk: An Aesthetic* (New York: Rizzoli, 2012); Johan Kugelberg with Jon Savage and Glenn Terry (eds.), *God Save Sex Pistols* (New Tork: Eizzoli, 2016). See also PunkPistol, *SEX and Seditionaries* (London: PunkPistol, 2007).

87 This was especially evident during the 2016 fortieth anniversary, where several books were republished and repackaged to fit in with various exhibitions and protracted media interest.

88 General histories would include Clinton Heylin, *Babylon's Burning: From Punk to Grunge* (London: Penguin, 2007); Phil Strongman, *Pretty Vacant: A History of Punk* (London: Orion Books, 2007); Alvin Gibbs, *Destroy: The Definitive History of Punk* (London: Britannia Press, 1996). See also Alex Ogg, *No More Heroes: A Complete History of UK Punk from 1976 to 1980* (London: Cherry Red, 2006). A list of (auto)biographies and band histories is provided in the bibliography, but see for some of the better examples: Berger, *The Story of*

Crass; David Buckley, *No Mercy: The Authorised and Uncensored Biography* (London: Hodder & Stoughton, 1997); Ford, *Wreckers of Civilization*; idem, *Hip Priest: The Story of Mark E Smith and The Fall* (London: Quartet Books, 2003); Pat Gilbert, *Passion is a Fashion: The Real Story of The Clash* (London: Auram Press, 2009 edition); Marcus Gray, *The Clash: Return of the Last Gang in Town* (London: Helter Skelter, 2001); Wilson Neate, *Read & Burn: A Book About Wire* (London: Jawbone Press, 2013); Viv Albertine, *Clothes, Clothes, Clothes, Music, Music, Music, Boys, Boys, Boys* (London: Faber & Faber, 2014); Marc Almond, *Tainted Life: The Autobiography* (London: Sidgwick & Jackson, 1999); Julian Cope, *Head On: Memories of the Liverpool Punk Scene and the Story of The Teardrop Explodes* (London: Thorsons, 1999 edition); Steve Ignorant with Steve Pottinger, *The Rest is Propaganda* (London: Southern, 2010); John Lydon with Keith & Kent Zimmerman, *Rotten: No Irish, No Blacks, No Dogs* (London: Plexus, 1994); John Lydon, *Anger Is an Energy: My Life Uncensored* (London: Simon & Schuster, 2014); Mick Middles and Lindsey Reade, *Torn Apart: The Life of Ian Curtis* (London: Omnibus Press, 2006); Penny Rimbaud, *Shibboleth: My Revolting Life* (Edinburgh: AK Press, 1998); Chris Salewicz, *Redemption Song: The Definitive Biography of Joe Strummer* (London: HarperCollins, 2006); Jah Wobble, *Memoirs of a Geezer* (London: Serpent's Tail, 2009).

89 Reynolds, *Rip It Up and Start Again*, pp. xvi–xxxi.

90 Greil Marcus, *Lipstick Traces: A Secret History of the Twentieth Century* (London: Faber & Faber, 1989); Stewart Home, *The Assault on Culture: Utopian Currents from Lettrisme to Class War* (Stirling: AK Press, 1991); Tom Vague, *King Mob Echo: From Gordon Riots to Situationists and Sex Pistols* (London: Dark Star, 2000); Paul Gorman, David Thorp and Fred Vermorel, *Joining the Dots: From the Situationist International to Malcolm McLaren* (Southampton: John Hansard, 2015). See also Vague's *Vague* fanzine, selections from which are published as *The Great British Mistake*, Vague 1977–92 (Edinburgh: AK Press, 1994). For the Gordon Riots, see Christopher Hibbert, *King Mob: The Story of Lord George Gordon and the Riots of 1780* (London: Longmans, 1958). King Mob also became the name of a pro-Situ grouping formed in London in the late 1960s, to which Malcolm McLaren, via Fred Vermorel, had links. See David Wise, *King Mob: A Critical Hidden History* (London: Bread and Circuses, 2014); Fred Vermorel, 'Growing Up as a Genius in the Sixties', in his *Fashion + Perversity: A Life of Vivienne Westwood and the Sixties Laid Bare* (London: Bloomsbury 1997), pp. 107–211.

91 Julie Burchill and Tony Parsons, *The Boy Looked at Johnny: The Obituary of Rock and Roll* (London: Pluto Press, 1978); David and Stuart Wise, 'The End of Music', in Stewart Home (ed.), *What Is Situationism? A Reader* (Edinburgh: AK Press, 1996), originally published as a pamphlet, 'Punk, Reggae: A Critique', in 1978. See also Garry Johnson, *The Story of Oi!: A View from the Dead End*

of the Street (Manchester: Babylon Books, 1982); Stewart Home, *Cranked Up Really High: Genre Theory and Punk Rock* (Hove: Codex, 1995).

92 As well as Berger's book-length history (2006), see Mike Dines and Matthew Worley (eds.), *The Aesthetic of Our Anger: Anarcho-Punk, Politics and Music* (Colchester: Minor Compositions, 2016); Brian Cogan, '"Do They Owe Us a Living? Of Course They Do!" Crass, Throbbing Gristle, and Anarchy and Radicalism in Early English Punk Rock', *Journal for the Study of Radicalism*, 1:2 (2007), 77–90; Cross, 'The Hippies Now Wear Black', 25–44; Ian Glasper, *The Day the Country Died: A History of Anarcho Punk, 1980–1984* (London: Cherry Red, 2006); George McKay, *Senseless Acts of Beauty: Currents of Resistance since the Sixties* (London: Verso, 1996); Alastair Gordon, *Throwing Out the Punk Rock Baby with the Dirty Bath Water: Crass and Punk Rock, A Critical Appraisal* (Nottingham: Do One Press, 1996, republished as *Crass Reflections*, Portsmouth: Itchy Monkey Press, 2016). For independent labels and DIY, see Alex Ogg, *Independence Days: The Story of UK Independent Record Labels* (London: Cherry Red, 2009); David Hesmondhalgh, 'Post-Punk's Attempt to Democratise the Music Industry: The Success and Failure of Rough Trade', *Popular Music*, 16:3 (1997), 25–74. For label histories, see Martin Aston, *Facing the Other Way: The Story of 4AD* (London; Friday Project, 2013); David Cavanagh, *The Creation Records Story: My Magpie Eyes Are Hungary for the Prize* (London: Virgin, 2001); Simon Goddard, *Simply Thrilled Honey: The Preposterous Story of Postcard Records* (London: Ebury Press, 2014); James Nice, *Shadowplayers: The Rise and Fall of Factory Records* (London: Aurum, 2010); Neil Taylor, *Document and Eyewitness: An Intimate History of Rough Trade* (London: Orion, 2010); Rob Young, *Rough Trade* (London: Black Dog, 2006).

93 A few exceptions would include Dave Thompson, *Wheels Out of Gear: 2 Tone, The Specials and a World on Fire* (London: Helter Skelter, 2004); idem, *The Dark Reign of Gothic Rock: In the Reptile House with The Sisters of Mercy, Bauhaus and The Cure* (London: Helter Skelter, 2002 and republished as *Twenty-Five Years in the Reptile House: British Gothic Rock, 1976–2001* in 2015). See also Ian Glasper, *Burning Britain: A History of UK Punk, 1980–84* (London: Cherry Red, 2004) and John Robb, *Death to Trad Rock* (London: Cherry Red, 2009).

94 Most, too, look at punk as part of a broader overview of youth culture or popular music. See, for example, Mike Brake, *The Sociology of Youth Culture and Youth Subculture* (London: Routledge & Kegan Paul, 1980); Ellis Cashmore, *No Future: Youth and Society* (London: Heinemann, 1984); Iain Chambers, *Urban Rhythms: Pop Music and Popular Culture* (New York: St Martin's Press, 1985). For the 'politics of pop', see John Street, *Rebel Rock: The Politics of Popular Music* (Oxford: Blackwell, 1986); idem, *Music and Politics* (Cambridge: Polity, 2012).

95 Hebdige, *Subculture*; Laing, One Chord Wonders; Simon Frith and Howard Horne, *Art into Pop* (London: Methuen & Co., 1987). See also Tricia Henry, *Break All Rules: Punk Rock and the Making of a Style* (Ann Arbor: University of Michigan Press, 1989); Neil Nehring, *Flowers in the Dustbin: Culture, Anarchy and Postwar England* (Ann Arbor: University of Michigan Press, 1993); R. H. Tillman, 'Punk Rock and the Construction of "Pseudo-Political" Movements', *Popular Music and Society*, 7:3 (1980), 165–75. For a more recent discussion of punk and postmodernism, see Ryan Moore, 'Postmodernism and Punk Subculture: Cultures of Authenticity and Deconstruction', *The Communication Review*, 7 (2004), 305–27.

96 Roger Sabin (ed.), *Punk Rock: So What? The Cultural Legacy of Punk* (London: Routledge, 1999). As well as Kugelberg and Savage's massive *Punk: An Aesthetic* (cited earlier), see Gee Vaucher, *Crass Art and Other Pre-postmodernist Monsters* (Edinburgh: AK Press, 1999); Philip Hoare et al., *Linder – Works, 1976–2006* (Zürich: JRP/Ringer, 2006); Gerald Matt (ed.), *Punk: No-One is Innocent* (Nuremberg: Kunsthalle Wien, 2008); Russ Bestley and Alex Ogg, *The Art of Punk: Posters + Flyers + Fanzines + Record Sleeves* (London: Omnibus Press, 2012).

97 Rachel, *Walls Come Tumbling Down*, pp. 1–227; Ian Goodyer, *Crisis Music: The Cultural Politics of Rock Against Racism* (Manchester Manchester University Press, 2009); Dave Renton, *When We Touched the Sky: The Anti-Nazi League, 1977–81* (Cheltenham: New Clarion Press, 2006); David Widgery, *Beating Time: Riot 'n' Race 'n' Rock 'n' Roll* (London, Chatto & Windus, 1986); Robert Forbes and Eddie Stampton, *The White Nationalist Skinhead Movement, UK & USA, 1979–1993* (London: Feral House, 2015); Nick Lowles, *White Riot: The Violent Story of Combat 18* (London: Milo 2001); Ryan Shaffer, 'The Soundtrack of Neo-Fascism: Youth and Music in the National Front', *Patterns of Prejudice*, 47:4–5 (2013), 458–82. See also, for a compendium of texts on punk and race, Stephen Duncombe and Maxwell Tremblay (eds.), *White Riot: Punk Rock and the Politics of Race* (London: Verso, 2011). For a rather different take on the question of identity, see Ruth Adams, 'The Englishness of English Punk: Sex Pistols, Subcultures, and Nostalgia', *Popular Music and Society*, 31:4 (2008), 468–88.

98 David Wilkinson, *Post-Punk, Politics and Pleasure in Britain* (Basingstoke: Palgrave Macmillan, 2016).

99 Subcultures Network, *Fight Back: Punk, Politics and Resistance* (Manchester: Manchester University Press, 2015).

100 Helen Reddington, *The Lost Women of Rock Music: Female Musicians of the Punk Era* (Aldershot: Ashgate, 2007); Sarah Whitely, *Too Much Too Young: Popular Music, Age and Gender* (London: Routledge, 2005); Maria Raha, *Cinderella's Big Score: Women of the Punk and Indie Underground* (Emeryville, CA: Seal Press, 2004); Caroline O'Meara, 'The Raincoats:

Breaking Down Punk Rock's Masculinities', *Popular Music*, 22:3 (2003), 299–313; Lauraine Leblanc, *Pretty in Punk: Girls' Gender Resistance in a Boys' Subculture* (New Brunswick, NJ: Rutgers University Press, 1999); Lucy O'Brien, *She Bop: The Definitive History of Women in Rock Pop and Soul* (London: Penguin, 1995), chapter five. See also *She's a Punk Rocker UK*, directed by Zillah Minx (2010).

101 Pete Dale, *Anyone Can Do It: Empowerment, Tradition and the Punk Underground* (Aldershot: Ashgate, 2012). For a now rare article on punk and class, see David Simonelli, 'Anarchy, Pop and Violence: Punk Rock Subculture and the Rhetoric of Class, 1976–78', *Contemporary British History*, 16:2 (2002), 121–44.

102 Nick Crossley, *Networks of Style, Sound and Subversion: The Punk and Post-Punk Worlds of Manchester, London, Liverpool and Sheffield, 1975–80* (Manchester: Manchester University Press, 2015).

103 *Punk and Post-Punk* is published by Intellect.

104 This is not to suggest punk ended in 1984; it did not and continues to evolve and develop today, both in Britain and across the world. The bulk of sociological studies now concerned with punk trace its continued relevance and expression.

105 See, for a sociological account of US punk that begins from a similar premise, Ryan Moore, *Sells Like Teen Spirit: Music, Youth Culture and Social Crisis* (New York: New York University Press, 2010).

1 What's This For? Punk's Contested Meanings

1 'The Punk Debate', *Sounds*, 25 December 1982, pp. 16–18.

2 Garry Bushell, 'Punk Is Dead!', *Sounds*, 4 December 1982, p. 11.

3 Taken from the *NME*, 25 December 1982, p. 2.

4 The fact that the Sex Pistols, Joy Division and certain other punk-informed bands dominated the 'All-Time Festive 50' from 1977 meant Peel ceased to collate it from 1982. 'Anarchy in the UK' was voted number one in 1978, 1979, 1980 and 1982; it came second to Joy Division's 'Atmosphere' in 1981. Already in 1982, Peel had decided to compile a chart based only on releases from the preceding twelve months. It was this format that he followed thereafter.

5 Hansard, House of Commons Debates, 26 October 1982, Vol. 29, c335W. For an overview, see Berger, *The Story of Crass*, pp. 212–28.

6 Bushell, 'Punk Is Dead!', p. 11.

7 Ibid; Bushell, 'The Punk Debate', pp. 16–18. For a 'musical' reply to Bushell's prognosis that 'punk is dead', see The Exploited, 'Singalongabushell', on the *Rival Leaders* EP, Pax Records, 1983.

8 Letters, *Sounds*, 25 December 1982, pp. 36–7.

9 For a twenty-first century pondering of this question, see Lisa Sofianos, Robin Ryde and Charlie Waterhouse (eds.), *The Truth of Revolution, Brother: An Exploration of Punk Philosophy* (London: Situation Press, 2014). Also Craig O'Hara, *The Philosophy of Punk: More Than Noise!* (Oakland, CA: AK Press, 2001).

10 'The Punk Debate', pp. 16–18.

11 Ibid, pp. 16–18.

12 Street, *Rebel Rock*, p. 210.

13 Ibid, p. 84. Street suggests that writers, rather than musicians, gave punk a social meaning.

14 See, for example, Charles Shaar Murray, 'Are You Alive to the Jive of ... The Sound of '75', *NME*, 8 November 1975, pp. 5–6. For an overview see Clinton Heylin, *From the Velvets to the Voidoids: The Birth of American Punk* (London: Penguin, 1993). It should also be noted that nascent punk scenes were forming elsewhere, such as in Cleveland, Ohio.

15 Lester Bangs, Dave Marsh and Mike Saunders had used the term 'punk' as a musical descriptor from 1969 to 1970, before Lenny Kaye's 1972 sleeve-notes to a *Nuggets* (Elektra, 1972) compilation of mid-1960s garage bands helped cement the term in relation to rock music stripped down to its bare essentials. Billy Altman and Joe Fernbacher also ran a *Punk* music magazine for two issues while at the University of Buffalo in 1973, featuring garage bands and The Stooges. But see also Nick Tosches' article, 'The Punk Muse', in *Fusion*, 10 July, 1970. In short, punk rock's template combined attitude with noise.

16 Savage, *England's Dreaming*, p. 134. We should note again that similar impulses were apparent beyond London and New York. Progenitors of punk's sound and aesthetic may also be found in Australia, Canada, France and Germany, not to mention other locales within the UK and US. Over time, bands such as Crushed Butler, Electric Eels, Figures of Light, Hollywood Brats, Pink Fairies, Radio Birdman, Rocket from the Tombs, The Saints and various others have been touted as prefacing punk's 'moment' in 1976–77.

17 Chris Salewicz, 'The Doomwatch Report', *NME*, 27 July 1974, pp. 32–3; Simon Reynolds, *Shock and Awe: Glam Rock and Its Legacy* (London: Faber & Faber, 2016), pp. 521–2.

18 Spencer, 'Don't Look Over Your Shoulder', p. 31.

19 Paul Gorman, *In Their Own Write: Adventures in the Music Press* (London: Sanctuary, 2001); Pat Long, *The History of the NME* (London: Portico, 2012).

20 Nick Kent, *Apathy for the Devil: A 1970s Memoir* (London: Faber & Faber, 2010); idem, *The Dark Stuff: Selected Writings on Rock Music, 1972–1993* (London: Penguin, 1994).

21 Figures are drawn from the Audit Bureau of Circulation and cited in Patrick Glen, '"Sometimes Good Guys Don't Wear White": Morality in the Music Press, 1967–1983' (University of Sheffield, PhD thesis, 2012), p. 22.

22 Reynolds, *Rip It Up and Start Again*, pp. xxvi–xxvii.

23 In his *Teenage Kicks: My Life as an Undertone* (London: Omnibus, 2016), Michael Bradbury describes how the *NME* was shared around his family and friends. The National Readership Survey for 1977 estimated that each copy of *Melody Maker* was read by 10.7 people, *NME* by 9.5 and *Sounds* by 6.1 (cited in Glen, '"Sometimes Good Guys Don't Wear White"', p. 23).

24 Glen, '"Sometimes Good Guys Don't Wear White"', pp. 22–3. There were, of course, other music magazines at this time, such as *Record Mirror*, *ZigZag* and various US titles.

25 Ingham, 'The Sex Pistols …', pp. 23–4.

26 Jonh Ingham, 'Anarchy in the UK', *Sounds*, 31 July 1976, p. 41; *Sounds*, 9 October 1976.

27 Ingham, 'Welcome to the (?) Rock Special', pp. 22–7.

28 Coon, 'Rotten to the Core', pp. 34–5.

29 Coon, 'Rebels Against the System', pp. 24–5.

30 Caroline Coon, 'The Violent World of The Damned' and 'Clash: Down and Out and Proud', *Melody Maker*, 13 November 1976, pp. 32–3.; idem, 'Rotten to the Core', pp. 34–5.

31 Caroline Coon, 'The Revolution Starts Here …', *Melody Maker*, 27 November 1976, p. 23.

32 Coon, 'Punk Rock', pp. 24–5; idem, 'Parade of the Punks', *Melody Maker*, 2 October 1976, pp. 26–7, 63; idem, 'Punk Power', *Melody Maker*, 27 November 1976, pp. 33–9; idem, 'London's Swinging Again – And the Whole World's Listening', *Melody Maker*, 21 May 1977, pp. 30–6; Ingham, 'Welcome to the (?) Rock Special', pp. 22–7.

33 Such a tendency was reinforced by the snobbish rejoinders to punk penned by writers tied to rock classicism. See, for example, Allan Jones, 'But Does Nihilism Constitute Revolt?', *Melody Maker*, 7 August 1976, pp. 24–5; Michael Watts, 'So Shock Me, Punks', *Melody Maker*, 11 September 1976, p. 37.

34 Julie Burchill, '1976', *NME*, 1 January 1977, pp. 17–20.

35 Tony Parsons, 'Go Johnny Go', *NME*, 2 October 1976, p. 29.

36 Julie Burchill, *I Knew I Was Right* (London: Arrow Books, 1998).

37 Long, *The History of the NME*, pp. 108–16.

38 See, for example, Tony Parsons, 'Clean Punk: The Menace to our Kids', *NME*, 29 January 1977, p. 11 (on Generation X); idem, 'Are These Men Prats?', *NME*, 25 June 1977, p. 14 (on The Cortinas); idem, 'Punk', *NME*, 29 October 1977, p. 23.

39 Julie Burchill and Tony Parsons, 'Fear and Loathing at The Roxy', *NME*, 19 March 1977, pp. 38–9, 52; Julie Burchill, 'The Jam Kick Out the Jams – Maggie

Thatcher Style', *NME*, 25 June 1977, p. 38; idem, Siouxsie and the Banshees live review, *NME*, 17 September 1977.

40 Julie Burchill and Tony Parsons, 'Dedicated Followers of Fascism', *NME*, 20 August 1977, p. 11.

41 Tony Parsons, 'Locker Room Sexuality and Six Figure Rebels', *NME*, 8 October 1977, pp. 7–8, 61. See also Burchill's' review of *Never Mind the Bollocks, Here's the Sex Pistols* (Virgin, 1977): 'I'm sick of unlimited tolerance and objectivity because it leads to annihilation' (*NME*, 5 November 1977, p. 31).

42 Burchill and Parsons, *The Boy Looked at Johnny*, pp. 85–95.

43 *London's Outrage*, 1, 1976; interview with Jon Savage in Vague, *The Great British Mistake*, pp. 93–100 (from *Vague*, 21 [1989]).

44 Savage, 'New Musick', p. 23.

45 For a collection of Savage's writings, see Jon Savage, *Time Travel: From the Sex Pistols to Nirvana: Pop, Media and Sexuality, 1977–96* (London: Chatto & Windus, 1996).

46 For a kind-of autobiography, see Paul Morley, *Nothing* (London: Faber & Faber, 2000).

47 Paul Morley, 'Manchester Madmen', *NME*, 27 November 1976, p. 50; idem, 'They Mean in M-a-a-a-nchester', *NME*, 30 July 1977, pp. 6–7. See also Nick Crossley, 'The Man Whose Web Expanded: Network Dynamics in Manchester's Post/Punk Music Scene, 1976–1980', *Poetics*, 37 (2009), 24–49.

48 Paul Morley, review of Sham 69, *That's Life* (Polydor, 1978), *NME*, 4 November 1978, p. 37; idem, live review of the Angelic Upstarts, *NME*, 27 January 1979, p. 40.

49 Paul Morley, 'New Stirrings on the North West Frontier', *NME*, 13 January 1979, pp. 7–8.

50 See, for example, his review of an RAR 'carnival' in Manchester, 'Chaos and Concern', *NME*, 22 July 1978, pp. 7–8; idem, 'In the Tradition that made Pinocchio Great', *NME*, 6 January 1979, p. 30.

51 Paul Morley, 'Breaking Down the Walls of Art-ache', *NME*, 20 March 1982, pp. 24–6.

52 Paul Morley, 'Lie Back and Think of England', *NME*, 22 May 1982, pp. 24–5, 51. Morley's theories would culminate in the label ZTT and his presentation of Frankie Goes To Hollywood.

53 Perry, 'The Sex Pistols for *Time Out*', pp. 3–4.

54 Garry Bushell, *Bushell on the Rampage: The Autobiography of Garry Bushell* (Clacton-on-Sea: Apex Publishing, 2010).

55 Garry Bushell, 'Sex Pistols: Whose Finger on the Trigger?', *Socialist Worker*, 18 December 1976, p. 11.

56 Garry Bushell, 'The New Breed', *Sounds*, 1 November 1980, pp. 32–3; idem, 'Oi! – The Column', *Sounds*, 17 January 1981, p. 11. See also Matthew Worley,

'Hey Little Rich Boy, Take a Good Look at Me: Punk, Class and British Oi', *Punk & Post-Punk*, 3:1 (2014), pp. 5–20.

57 Garry Bushell, 'Punk's Not Dead!', *Punk's Not Dead*, 1 (1981), p. 1.

58 For example, his review of Crass' *The Feeding of the Five Thousand* EP in *Sounds*, 24 March 1979, p. 35; idem, review of The Clash, *London's Calling*, *Sounds*, 15 December 1979, p. 28.

59 Bushell, 'Oi! – The Column', p. 11.

60 See comments in Rachel, *Walls Come Tumbling Down*, pp. 236–41, pp. 257–72 and pp. 293–5.

61 Richard North, 'Punk Warriors', *NME*, 19 February 1983, pp. 12–15; Steve Keaton, 'The Face of Punk Gothique', *Sounds*, 21 February 1981, pp. 16–17; Mercer, *Gothic Rock Black Book*, pp. 130–2.

62 V. Vale (ed.), *Industrial Culture Handbook* (San Francisco: RE Search, 1983); Christopher Neal (ed.), *Tape Delay* (Harrow: SAF Publishing, 1987).

63 For a general study see Martin Cloonan, 'Exclusive! The British Press and Popular Music: The Story So Far …' in Steve Jones (ed.), *Pop Music and the Press* (Philadelphia: Temple University Press, 2002). For a discussion of the relationship between media and youth culture, see Sarah Thornton, *Club Cultures: Music, Media and Subcultural Capital* (London: Polity Press, 1995).

64 Bill Osgerby, *Youth Media* (London: Routledge, 2004). For a pre-history, see John Springhall, *Youth, Popular Culture and Moral Panics: Penny Gaffs to Gangsta-Rap, 1830–1996* (Basingstoke: Macmillan, 1998).

65 A few examples: David Alford, Clive Entwistle and Steve Simpson, 'Punk Rock Revolution', *Sunday People*, 12 June 1977, pp. 20–1; Carolyn Martin, 'Here Come the Punkesses', *News of the World*, 16 January 1977, p. 3; 'Who Are These Punks?', *Daily Mirror*, 2 December 1976, p. 9.

66 Paul Rock and Stanley Cohen argue this in relation to teddy boys in their 'The Teddy Boy', in Vernon Bogdanor and Robert Skidelsky (eds.), *The Age of Affluence, 1951–64* (London: Macmillan, 1970), pp. 288–318.

67 Osgerby, *Youth Media*, pp. 83–4.

68 Judi Wade, 'Freakin' On', *The Sun*, 15 October 1976, pp. 16–17; Denis Cassidy, 'Look What Pop Kids Do Now', *Sunday People*, 3 October 1976, p. 1. Steve Strange and Chris Sullivan would both become integral to the new romantic scene that grew from one of punk's fragments. See Steve Strange, *Blitzed: The Autobiography of Steve Strange* (London: Orion, 2002).

69 BBC, *Nationwide*, broadcast 12 November 1976; LWT, *Weekend Show*, broadcast 28 November 1976; Case, 'Mad About Punk Rock', pp. 18–20; Burn, 'Good Clean Punk', pp. 28–33.

70 See Marsh, 'Dole Queue Rock', pp. 112–14; Steve Turner, 'The Anarchic Rock of the Young and Doleful', *The Guardian*, 2 December 1976, p. 13. The term was also used by Parsons in the *NME* in late 1976.

71 Throbbing Gristle were formed on 3 September 1975 and had played live before the *Prostitution* show. Nevertheless, the group recognised the ICA event as marking 'the end of COUM Transmissions as an active part within the Art Establishment and the emergence of Throbbing Gristle into the Music Establishment' (sleevenotes to reissued version of *The Second Annual Report of Throbbing Gristle*, originally released on Industrial Records, 1977). Throbbing Gristle's 'industrial music' always had a contentious relationship with punk, though there were clear overlaps in terms of personnel, audience, approach and subject matter.

72 Ford, *Wreckers of Civilization*, pp. 6.19–6.26. Ford quotes the *Daily Telegraph*, 19 October 1976, as saying the exhibition celebrated 'every social evil'.

73 *Daily Mail*, 19 October 1976, p. 1.

74 'These Revolting VIPs', *Evening News*, 4 January 1977, p. 1; Kenny Everett's 'Gizzard Puke' was perhaps the most renowned punk caricature, but *The Goodies*, *Terry & June*, *Metal Mickey* and *Keep It in the Family* all offer good examples.

75 Geoffrey Pearson, *Hooligan: A History of Respectable Fears* (London: Macmillan, 1983).

76 Alford, Entwistle and Simpson, 'Punk Rock Revolution', pp. 20–1; idem, 'The Punk Rock Exploiters', *Sunday People*, 19 June 1977, pp. 8–9; 'Editorial', *Daily Mirror*, 22 June 1977.

77 See, for example, the comments of Pastor John Cooper on BBC, *Brass* Tacks, broadcast in 1977: 'I feel this is the pay-off of a punk society ... We have punk parents, punk politicians, we have punk clergymen, and we have punk sportsmen.'

78 John Blake, 'Rock's Swastika Revolution', *Evening News*, 7 May 1977, p. 11.

79 'Danger on the Right', *TV Eye*, ITV Documentary, 1980; Peter Evans, 'When Being a Skinhead Becomes Part of Life', *The Times*, 16 February 1981, p. 6; Simon Kinnersley, 'The Skinhead Bible of Hate from an Establishment Stable', *Daily Mail*, 9 July 1981, pp. 18–19; Paul Donovan and Pat Evans, 'Exposed: The Racist Thug on the Cover of this Evil Record', *Daily Mail*, 10 July 1981, p. 3; Lucy Hodges, 'Racists Recruit Youth Through Rock Music', *The Times*, 3 August 1981, p. 3.

80 'Punish the Punks', *Sunday Mirror*, 12 June 1977, p. 15.

81 Worley, 'Shot By Both Sides', 333–54.

82 This began with Martin Jacques, 'Trends in Youth Culture: Some Aspects', *Marxism Today*, September 1973, pp. 268–80, and continued through until April 1975. For some discussion, see Evan Smith, 'When the Party Comes Down: The CPGB and Youth Culture, 1976–91', *Twentieth Century Communism*, 4 (2011), 38–75; Matthew Worley, 'Marx–Lenin–Rotten–Strummer: British Marxism and Youth Culture in the 1970s', *Contemporary British History*, 30:4 (2016), 505–21.

83 Paul Bradshaw, 'Trends in Youth Culture in the 1970s', *Cogito*, 3 (1976), 3–13.

84 'Open Letter to the Sex Pistols', *Challenge*, August–September 1977, p. 11.

85 Roger Huddle, 'Punk Rock Rules?', *Socialist Worker*, 11 December 1976, p. 5; Roger Huddle, 'Hard Rain', *Socialist Review*, July–August 1978, pp. 12–13.

86 Letters on punk appeared irregularly over the late 1970s into the 1980s. For articles on culture and politics, see John Hoyland, 'How Do Music and Socialism Connect?', *Comment*, 11 June 1977, pp. 200–2; Paul Thompson, 'Youth Politics and Youth Culture', *Revolutionary Socialism*, Spring 1978, pp. 11–15; Alex Callinicos, 'When the Music Stops' and John Hoyland and Mike Flood Page, 'You Can Lead a Horse to Water', *Socialist Review*, June 1978, pp. 15–18; Matthew Lynn, 'Music and Politics', *Challenge*, December 1979, p. 7; Vivien Goldman, 'Only Rock 'n' Roll?', *The Leveller*, December 1979, p. 27; Noel Halifax, 'The Sounds of Struggle', *Socialist Review*, March 1983, pp. 27–8.

87 For punk's supposed fascism, see 'Editorial', *News Line*, 2 December 1976, p. 2; Julian Leach's regular critiques in *Young Socialist* in 1976–78; the anonymous 'The Politics of Punk', *Young Socialist*, 7 January 1978, p. 5. For favourable coverage, see reports of WRP events in *Young Socialist*, 10, 24 June, 22 July, 12 and 19 August 1978.

88 For just a few examples, see *Challenge*, April–May 1978; *Red Rebel*, January–February, 1979; also the 'Notes' column in *Socialist Worker* from late 1978; *Big Flame*'s early 1980s music reviews; and *The Leveller* throughout the late 1970s and early 1980s.

89 See *Temporary Hoarding* for a record of RAR-related gigs.

90 *Temporary Hoarding*, 7, 1979, p. 22; Goodyer, *Crisis Music*, pp. 11–12. For an analysis of the relationship between RAR and ANL, see Paul Gilroy, *There Ain't No Black in the Union Jack* (London: Routledge, 2002 edition), pp. 151–77.

91 'Trafalgar Square, 26.10.80', *NME*, 1 November 1980, p. 11.

92 CP/YCL/21/1, Minutes of the [CPGB] Arts and Leisure Committee, 11 November 1976 (Labour History Archive and Study Centre [LHASC], Manchester); Laing, 'Interpreting Punk Rock', pp. 123–8.

93 Wise and Wise, 'The End of Music', pp. 63–102; Simon Frith, 'Post-Punk Blues', *Marxism Today*, March 1983, pp. 18–21.

94 The quote is from Colin Jordan's letter to the *British Patriot*, May–June 1977, p. 3; John Tyndall, 'The Kind of Britain I Want', *Spearhead*, March 1981; idem, 'Advice to a Young Nationalist', *Spearhead*, May 1981, pp. 10–11.

95 A. Critic, 'Rock and Reich', *British Patriot*, January–February 1977, pp. 3–4.

96 Garry Bushell, '(Sk)in the Beginning', *Sounds*, 2 August 1980, p. 27. See also 'Johnny Rotten: "I Despise the NF": We're Shattered', *NF News*, 10, 1977, p. 1; 'Sub-Cultures Imposed', *British Patriot*, March 1978, p. 4.

97 Derek Holland, 'The National Front – A Youth Wing?', *Spearhead*, June 1977, p. 9; Joe Pearce, 'The Importance of a Young National Front',

Spearhead, February 1978, p. 5; Ray Hill and Andrew Bell, *The Other Face of Terror: Inside Europe's Neo-Nazi Network* (Glasgow: Grafton, 1988).

98 Joe Pearce, *Race with the Devil: My Journey from Racial Hatred to Rational Love* (St Benedict Press: North Carolina, 2013).

99 *British News*, September 1978, p. 6–7; Eddy Morrison, *Memoirs of a Street Fighter: A Life in White Nationalism* (Leeds: Imperium Press, 2003).

100 Hill and Bell, *The Other Face of Terror*, pp. 134–9.

101 Eddy Morrison, 'Tomorrow Belongs To Those Who Can Hear It Coming', *British News*, August, 1978, p. 4; idem, 'Don't Condemn Pop!', *Spearhead*, April 1981. The article was prefaced by an editorial comment insisting that it did not reflect the opinions of the editor (Tyndall).

102 *Bulldog*, 18, 1980, p. 3. Some Bizarre was a label that specialised in signing electronic and industrial bands to major record companies. Stevo regularly denounced the politics of his brother.

103 See *Bulldog*, nos. 18–39, 1979–84 (esp, nos. 18, 20, 22, 25, 29).

104 'Oi! The New Wave of Skinhead Bands', *Bulldog*, 24, 1981, p. 3.

105 'White Riot at Bad Manners Gig', *Bulldog*, 27, 1982, p. 3.

106 Nick Lowles and Steve Silver (eds.), *White Noise: Inside the International Nazi Skinhead Scene* (London: Searchlight, 1998), pp. 9–47.

107 Forbes and Stampton, *The White Nationalist Skinhead Movement*, pp. 79–278.

108 For example, Neil Spencer's term as editor of *NME* (1978–85) imbued the paper with a consciously leftist perspective. For an excellent discussion see Street, *Rebel Rock*, pp. 83–7.

109 BBC, *Nationwide*, broadcast 12 November 1976. For similar comment on punk as a media term, see Paul Weller in the *NME*, 22 October 1977, p. 20.

110 Savage, *England's Dreaming*, p. 159; Jonh Ingham interviewed in Savage (ed.), *England's Dreaming Tapes*, p. 487.

111 Parsons, 'Go Johnny Go', p. 29; idem, 'Rats Out of Hell', *NME*, 13 November 1976, p. 17.

112 Paul Morley, *Out There*, summer 1976, quoted in Kugelberg and Savage (eds.), *Punk*, p. 351; Ingham, 'Welcome to the (?) Rock Special', p. 22.

113 Coon recognised differences between US and UK punk, primarily the latter's futurism compared to the former's nostalgia, but evidently felt their approach to rock 'n' roll was similar enough to warrant a shared name (Coon, 'Punk Rock', pp. 24–5). For examples of locating a punk lineage or defining punk via 1960s roots, see Giovanni Dadomo, 'The A to Z of Punk', *Sounds*, 17 July 1976, pp. 23–6; Charles Shaar Murray, untitled review of Sex Pistols, *NME*, 11 September 1976, p. 41; Mike Oldfield, 'Phase 3' [on 'punk pioneers'], *Melody Maker*, 27 November 1976, p. 40.

114 Tony D started his influential *Ripped & Torn* fanzine in Cumbernauld in late 1976 before moving to London and starting *Kill Your Pet Puppy*; Steve Burke

started Manchester's *Shy Talk* in early 1977; Paul Bowers wrote Sheffield's *Gun Rubber* with Adi Newton. The *Toxic Grafity* quote comes from the 'mental liberation issue' 5, 1980, p. 15.

115 The Ramones' first album was released in spring 1976; they played gigs in Britain over the summer.

116 This is evident in reminiscences of local scenes, such as Tony Beesley's *Our Generation* (about south Yorkshire) and the interviews with the bands listed by Ogg in *No More Heroes*, pp. 4–5. See also Paul Harvey, 'Doing the Right Things for the Right Reasons: Looking for Authenticity in Punk and Stuckist Practice', *Punk & Post-Punk*, 2:1 (2013), 43–71.

117 McLaren talks about this aspect of punk in Nick Kent, 'Meet the Col Tom Parker of the Blank Generation', *NME*, 27 November 1976, pp. 26–7.

118 The Damned, 'Politics', *Music for Pleasure*, Stiff Records, 1977; Andy Blade, *The Secret Life of a Teenage Punk Rocker* (London: Cherry Red, 2005).

119 Good early examples of this eclectic approach would be *Chainsaw*, *In the City*, *Jamming*, *Panache* and *Sniffin' Glue*.

120 *Jolt*, 1–3, 1977; 'When Did You Stop Wearing Nazi Paraphernalia?', *Ripped & Torn*, 7, 1977, p. 7; 'Perhaps You Think This Is a Bit Strong', *Ripped & Torn*, 14, 1978, p. 24. The first issue of *Kill Your Pet Puppy* was January 1980.

121 Tom Vague, 'Vague Post-Punk Memories', in Gavin Butt, Kwodo Eshun and Mark Fisher, *Post Punk Then and Now* (London: Repeater, 2016), pp. 250–82.

122 *Rapid Eye*, Vols. 1–2 (London: Annihilation Press, 1989–92). A third volume was published by Creation books in 1995. These include essays on, for example, Aleister Crowley, William Burroughs, Derek Jarman and Charles Manson.

123 The spelling of 'graffiti' changed with each issue – e.g. Graffitti, Grafitty, Grafity and Graffity.

124 Russ Bestley, '"I Tried to Make Him Laugh, He Didn't Get the Joke …": Taking Punk Humour Seriously', *Punk and Post-Punk*, 2:2 (2013), 119–45.

125 Vermorel, *Fashion + Perversity*, p. 81.

126 Quoted in Carline Coon, 'Public Image', *Sounds*, 22 July 1978, pp. 14–15.

127 Paul Morley, 'Don't Follow Leaders', *NME*, 12 November 1977, pp. 9–10.

128 Dave McCullough, 'The Nitty Gritty on Scritti Politti', *Sounds*, 13 January 1979, p. 11; Barney Hoskyns, 'Where Radical Meets Chic', *NME*, 31 October 1981, pp. 30–1; Vicki Bonnet, 'Scritticisms and Politticisms', *Let's Be Adult About This*, 1, 1979, pp. 18–21.

129 Penny Rimbaud, 'The Last of the Hippies – An Hysterical Romance', in Crass, *A Series of Shock Slogans and Mindless Token Tantrums* (London: Exitstencil Press, 1982), p. 3.

130 *Punk Lives*, issues 1–11, 1982–3. See also the exchange between Penny Rimbaud, Garry Bushell, the Special Duties and various readers in *Sounds*, May–August 1982.

131 Dale, *Anyone Can Do It*, pp. 90–1.

132 Sleevenotes to *The House That Man Built*, Crass Records, 1982.

2 Rock and Roll (Even): Punk as Cultural Critique

1 Chris Brazier, 'Subway Go Underground', *Melody Maker*, 18 March 1978, p. 35.

2 Coon, 'Rotten to the Core', p. 34.

3 The Clash, '1977' on the b-side of 'White Riot', CBS, 1977.

4 Robb, *Punk Rock*, pp. 39–97.

5 Quoted in Coon, 'Rotten to the Core', p. 34.

6 Hugh Felder, 'Crisis? Rock Crisis?', *Sounds*, 3 January 1976, p. 6; Neil Spencer, *NME*, 13 December 1975, in which Spencer claims that 'nothing happened this year'. Mick Farren, 'The Titanic Sails at Dawn', *NME* 19 June 1976, p. 5. For precursors to this, see Lester Bangs' 1971 essay 'James Taylor Marked for Death', in his *Psychotic Reactions and Carburettor Dung* (London: Heinemann, 1988), pp. 53–81 and the editorial to *The Hot Flash* fanzine (1975), cited in C. P. Lee, *Shake, Rattle and Rain: Popular Music Making in Manchester, 1955–95* (London: Hardinge Simpole, 2002), p. 111.

7 Quoted in Anthony O'Grady, 'Rock 'n' Roll Is Dead', *RAM*, 26 July 1975.

8 Laing, *One Chord Wonders*, pp. 1–40; Hesmondhalgh, 'Post-Punk's Attempt to Democratise the Music Industry', 255–74. The 'big six' were EMI, CBS, WEA, RCA, Polygram and Decca, all of which signed, manufactured and distributed the artists and records produced. Such concentration also had an impact on retail, as the majors reduced their services to small retailers in preference to larger retail outlets, including Boots, WH Smith and Woolworths.

9 See, for example, the letters pages of *Melody Maker*, *NME* and *Sounds* in 1976 as punk emerged and articles such as Morley, 'They Mean It M-a-a-a-nchester', pp. 5–7; Andy Gill and Adrian Thrills, 'This Week's Leeds: Sheffield, Yorks', *NME*, 9 September 1978, pp. 6–8; Tony D, 'Scottish Punk', *Ripped & Torn*, 2, January 1977, pp. 7–8; and early editions of fanzines such *Alternative Ulster*, *Ghast Up*, *Gun Rubber*, *Hangin' Around*, *Heat*, *Loaded*, *Private World* etc.

10 See *Melody Maker* mailbag, 3, 10 January 1976, 31 July, 16 October 1976; Chris Charlesworth, 'Plantations', *Melody Maker*, 14 February 1976, p. 8; Farren, 'The Titanic Sails at Dawn', p. 5.

11 Dale, *Anyone Can Do It*, pp. 90–1.

12 The T-shirt's lists of 'Hates' and 'Loves' are listed in Savage, *England's Dreaming*, pp. 84–5.

13 Tony Parsons, 'Eye Witness Pistols Whipping', *NME*, 18 June 1977, pp. 10–11; Danny Baker, 'You Don't Have to Read This of Course', *Sniffin' Glue*, 12, 1977, p. 26. See, too, Allan Jones, 'Rotten', *Melody Maker*, 4 June 1977, pp. 8–9, 52.

14 Savage, 'A Punk Aesthetic', p. 146.

15 Mark Perry, 'The Last Page', p. 8.

16 Tony D, 'Can Rich "Stars" Rock?', *Ripped & Torn*, 1, 1976, pp. 5–6.

17 The quote here is from *Chainsaw*, 1, 1977, p. 2. See also *Fair Dukes!*, 2, 1977, p. 4, which insisted the Sex Pistols had 'the essential ingredient to any punk music, energy'.

18 Criticism of 'rock star trips' was evident in early Sex Pistols interviews, as in Coon, 'Rotten to the Core', pp. 34–35. Bands also denied their objective was fame or stardom: see Lester Bangs' *NME* interview with The Clash, 10 December 1977, pp. 31–34; Brian Case, 'Angels With Dirty Faces', NME, 11 March 1978, pp. 32–33; Harry Doherty, 'Pete Shelley ...', *Melody Maker*, 30 September 1978, p. 11; Ian Pye, 'Postcards from Scotland', *Melody Maker*, 22 August 1981, p. 20. Within punk, The Clash and Siouxsie and the Banshees often got the most criticism – the former because of their strict ideals and subsequent focus on the US, the latter for their rejection of punk's egalitarian principles and stated desire to enjoy the trappings of stardom on their own terms.

19 Mark Perry, 'Damned Interview', *Sniffin' Glue*, 3, 1976, pp. 3–6.

20 Rick O'Shea, 'Punk Rock Rules ...', *Heat*, 2, 1977, p. 13.

21 Rotten's quote is from Coon, 'Rotten to the Core', pp. 34–5. See Laing, *One Chord Wonders*, pp. 27–32 for an analysis of early subject matter.

22 Quoted in *Ghast Up*, 1, 1977, pp. 6–7.

23 This was captured most explicitly in The Clash's early interviews, which helped cultivate punk's concept of year zero. Also heard, however, were comments such as Mick Jones': 'Call it what you want – all the terms just stink. Call it rock 'n' roll' (Tony Parsons, 'Sten Guns in Knightsbridge', *NME*, 2 April 1977, p. 22).

24 Craig Bromberg, *The Wicked Ways of Malcolm McLaren* (New York: Harper & Row, 1988); Scanlon, *Sex Pistols*, pp. 31–4; Ingham, 'The Sex Pistols', pp. 10–11. The designs for Let It Rock, Too Fast to Live and SEX included homages to teddy boys and early rock 'n' rollers. Similarly, the jukebox in SEX was filled with 1960s garage singles and 1950s rockers, as compiled on *SEX: Too Fast To Live Too Young To Die*, OLLA Records, 2003.

25 Kent, 'Meet the Col Tom Parker of the Punk Generation', pp. 26–7.

26 See the Generation X singles 'Your Generation' b/w 'Day By Day', Chrysalis, 1977 and 'Ready Steady Go' b/w 'No No No', Chrysalis, 1978. In his interview for Fred and Judy Vermorels' *The Sex Pistols* (p. 137), Johnny Rotten said: 'It's only one generation have become stars and that's the 60s bands. Before them like rock 'n' rollers, I mean they weren't out of touch, were they? They kept their roots. Cos they had it in them. It's all the 60s bands have just got bullshitty.'

27 The list is endless, but three random examples could be The Boys' 'I Don't Care', The Cortinas' 'Fascist Dictator' and Menace's 'GLC'.

28 Monica Sklar, *Punk Style* (London: Bloomsbury, 2013).

29 See, for example, *Heat, Negative Reaction, Ripped & Torn, Rotten to the Core, Sniffin' Glue* and *White Stuff*. These refer mostly to Lou Reed, John Cale, Iggy Pop and Patti Smith, but also to glam and Bowie.

30 For Mark E. Smith on punk and rock 'n' roll, see the interview in *Jamming*, 9, 1979, pp. 24–7. Smith described rock 'n' roll as a 'spirit' that was not about technique or effects, or bringing out a single and going on tour.

31 Steve Clarke, 'Union Jacks? ...' *NME*, 7 May 1977, p. 28; Chas de Whalley, 'Boy Wonders Make the Big Step', *Sounds*, 25 June 1977, pp. 26–8; Steve Mick, 'The Jam', *Sniffin' Glue*, 8, 1977, pp. 3–5.

32 'Thrills', *NME*, 15 September 1979, p. 11.

33 See, for example, the comments by Secret Affair in Garry Bushell, 'Mods Without Parkas', *Sounds*, 9 June 1979, p. 16.

34 George Marshall, *Spirit of '69: A Skinhead Bible* (Dunoon: ST Publishing, 1991).

35 Chris Bohn makes this case with regard to new mod in 'Ready Steady Go Live', *Melody Maker*, 24 August 1979, pp. 17–18.

36 For a round-up of the scene's background, see the *NME* rockabilly special on 16 February 1980.

37 It was from the upsurge in DIY labels that compilations of UK garage tracks from the 1960s – such as *The Rubble Collection* – were issued by the Bam Caruso label in the mid-1980s.

38 'A New Direction ...', *Hungry Beat*, 1, 1984, pp. 3–6.

39 For a good overview, see Dale, *Anyone Can Do It*, pp. 149–64.

40 The Clash singled out The George Hatcher Band in their *Sniffin' Glue* interview (issue 4, 1976, p. 4), focusing on the stage poses, long hair, cowboy shirts and trousers: 'This is what rock 'n' roll's supposed to look like'.

41 Steve Mick, 'The Subway Sect', *Sniffin' Glue*, 5, 1976, pp. 5–6; Paul Morley, 'Down in the Subway Where the Sect Hang Out', *NME*, 4 March 1978, pp. 18–19; Dave McCullough, 'The Northern Soul of Vic Godard', *Sounds*, 2 December 1978, pp. 16–17; Paul Morley, 'War Poet of the Modern World', *NME*, 9 December 1978, pp. 9–10.

42 Subway Sect, 'Rock and Roll Even', also titled 'Different Story' b/w 'Ambition' Rough Trade, 1978.

43 McNeill, 'We Are Not Showroom Dummies', pp. 7–8; Andy Gill, 'Wire', *NME*, 16 September 1978, pp. 27–8; Harry Doherty, 'Barbed Wire', *Melody Maker*, 9 December 1978, pp. 26–8. For a history of Wire in the punk period, see Neate, *Read & Burn*, pp. 38–69.

44 Morley, 'They Mean It M-a-a-a-nchester', pp. 6–7; Jon Savage, 'The Worst', *Sounds*, 11 February 1978, p. 22.

45 Footage of the early Slits is included in Don Letts' *The Punk Rock Movie* (1977).

46 See, for example, Greil Marcus, 'It's Fab, It's Passionate, It's Wild, It's Intelligent! It's the Hot New Sound of England Today', *Rolling Stone*, 24 July 1980, reprinted in Greil Marcus, *In the Fascist Bathroom: Writings on Punk, 1977–82* (London: Viking, 1993), pp. 109–30.

47 Paul Rambali, 'The Group Who Fell to Earth', *NME*, 3 March 1979, pp. 7–8.

48 Adrian Thrills, 'The Year of the Great Leap Four-Wards', *NME*, 20 January 1979, pp. 7–8; Frank Worrall, 'The Seduction Line', *Melody Maker*, 6 February 1982, p. 10. See also *Brass Lip*, *City Fun* and *Jolt* for analysis of pop music and gender.

49 *After Hours*, 1, 1979, p. 7. Aspinall was a trained violinist.

50 Neil Spencer, 'Johnny Doesn't Live Here Anymore', *NME*, 27 May 1978, pp. 7–8.

51 'A Punk and His Music – Capital Radio', *Sounds*, 23 July 1977, p. 9 and p. 30. Among the records played were those by Tim Buckley, Can, Captain Beefheart, Kevin Coyne and Peter Hammill.

52 Danny Baker, 'The Odd Combo', *NME*, 16 June 1979, pp. 24–6.

53 Bonnet, 'Scritticisms and Politticisms', pp. 18–23.

54 Paul Morley, 'The Heart and Soul of Cabaret Voltaire', *NME*, 29 November 1980, pp. 16–17.

55 *New Gold Dream: The Sound of Young Scotland*, directed Grant McPhee, 2016.

56 See, for example, Steve Walsh, 'Pop Group Mania', *NME*, 18 February 1978, p. 19; Paul Morley, 'Rental & Leer and the Secret of Synthesis', *NME*, 4 November 1978, p. 11; Ian Cranna, 'Product, Packaging and Rebel Music', *NME*, 13 January 1979, pp. 22–4; Thrills, 'The Year of the Great Leap Four-Wards', pp. 7–8.

57 Oliver Lowenstein, 'Prima Donnas Have More Fun', *Melody Maker*, 10 February 1979, p. 25; Ian Pye, 'The Punks Who Don't Die', *Melody Maker*, 14 November 1981, p. 21.

58 Laing, *One Chord Wonders*, p. 1.

59 The quotes are from Patti Smith at the end of her cover version of The Who's 'My Generation' and Johnny Rotten talking on LWT, *Weekend Show*, 28 November 1976.

60 Writers assigned to the music papers from beyond London included Ian Cranna, Paul Du Noyer, Andy Gill, Gavin Martin, Paul Morley and Emma Ruth. Writers such as Burchill, Bushell, Parsons and Savage also entered the music press through punk's opening up the requisite space. Among the other 'stars' born through punk, we could point to Bob Geldof, Mick Hucknall and Sting.

61 See John Orme, 'What Next After Punk?', *Melody Maker*, 29 April 1978, p. 20, which quotes Maurice Oberstein predicting that 'every star of the eighties is

in a punk band today'. See also Peter Ross, 'An Organizational Analysis of the Emergence, Development and Mainstreaming of British Punk Rock Music', *Popular Music and Society*, 20:1 (1996), 155–73.

62 David George, 'The End', *Dirt*, 1, 1978, p. 3.

63 Mark P, "Ope I Die Before I Get Old', *Sniffin' Glue*, 3 ½, 1976, p. 4.

64 Tony Medlycott, 'The Opposition (New Underground)', *Aftermath*, 3, 1980, p. 13.

65 Lucy Toothpaste, 'Marxism and the Media', *Jolt*, 2, 1977, p. 5.

66 Minutes of the [CPGB] Arts and Leisure Committee, 11 November 1976.

67 Mary Harron, 'Dialectics Meet Disco', *Melody Maker*, 26 May, 1979, pp. 17–18 and 52; Graham Lock, 'Gabba Gabba Hegel', *NME*, 13 October 1979, pp. 6–8. King's comments may have been influenced by the ideas of Walter Benjamin, as explored in Laing, 'Interpreting Punk Rock', pp. 123–8. See also Michael Hoover and Lisa Stokes, 'Pop Music and the Limits of Cultural Critique: Gang of Four Shrinkwraps Entertainment', *Popular Music and Society*, 22:3 (1998), 21–38.

68 For examples, see Chris Salewicz, 'On Tour with The Clash', *NME*, 15 July 1978, pp. 27–30; Chris Burkham, 'Prepare to Meet Your Mecca', *Sounds*, 25 July 1981, p. 18; Barney Hoskyns, 'This is the Hoax that Joke Built', *NME*, 27 February 1982, pp. 11–12; Garry Bushell, 'War of Independents', *Sounds*, 7 August 1982, pp. 10–11.

69 Ian Pye, 'Aural Postcards from Scotland', *Melody Maker*, 22 August 1981, p. 20. See Tony Mitchell, 'Mr Bizarro', *Sounds*, 25 December 1982, pp. 8–9 (on Some Bizarre), and Edwyn Collins of Orange Juice in Steve Sutherland, 'And the Souls Were Sold', *Melody Maker*, 14 November 1981, p. 13. 'Our ultimate goal has always been to get a record in the charts, not just for ego-gratification but to reach the maximum number of people … Pop music is useless unless it's truly populist'.

70 Introduction to 'Hold on', *Redskins Live*, Dojo, 1994.

71 Letter from Martin Hewes to *Socialist Review*, June 1983, p. 32.

72 Lynden Barber, 'Red on Arrival', *Melody Maker*, 8 December 1984, pp. 12–13; 'Redskins', *Artificial Life*, 9, 1984, pp. 9–10.

73 The Redskins' appearance on Channel 4's *The Tube* in 1984 featured a Durham miner taking the stage to speak in support of his striking fellow-workers, only for his microphone to mysteriously cut out.

74 See the special issue of the *NME*, 22 July 1978.

75 For details see Bromberg, *The Wicked Ways of Malcolm McLaren*, pp. 235–7.

76 Parsons, 'Locker Room Sexuality and Six Figure Rebels', pp. 7–8; Danny Baker, 'Dies Ist der Modernische Welt', *NME*, 17 March 1979, pp. 20–1; Adrian Thrills, 'Overtones Undertones Sideways Down', *NME*, 15 September 1979, pp. 32–3; Dave McCullough, 'Off the Beaten Track', *Sounds*, 7 June 1980, pp. 32–3.

77 *NME*, 17 September 1977, p. 4.

78 Chris Bohn, 'The Clash: One Step Beyond', *Melody Maker*, 29 December 1979, p. 20; Charles Shaar Murray, 'Up the Hill Backwards', *NME*, 29 May 1982, pp. 30–1.

79 Garrett, who – along with Linder and Peter Saville, the designer for Factory Records – attended Manchester Poly, continued to worked closely with Buzzcocks thereafter.

80 Bestley and Ogg, *The Art of Punk*, pp. 38–41.

81 See, for example, Tony Parsons, 'Around the World in Eighty Daze', *NME*, 30 July 1977, pp. 18–19; Adrian Thrills, 'Complete Control: Siouxsie in Wonderland', *NME*, 24 June 1978, pp. 18–19; Chris Burkham, 'Alphabet Spaghetti', *Sounds*, 5 September 1981, p. 23. Jill Mumford, who art-directed some of the early Siouxsie and the Banshees releases, remembered the band maintaining 'strict control'. See Bestley and Ogg, *The Art of Punk*, pp. 98–9.

82 John Orme, 'Muzak and Movement', *Melody Maker*, 27 September 1980, p. 21.

83 Chris Bohn, 'Sir Keith Talks Bluntly to EEC Management Consultants', *NME*, 5 July 1980, pp. 36–7. See also Heaven 17, whose idea was to frame their British Electric Foundation as an ironic play on the entrepreneurial aesthetics of early Thatcherism. Lynden Barber, 'Into the Heavenly Music Corporation', *Melody Maker*, 3 October 1981, p. 17. Heaven 17 were a classic example of a band that eschewed 'punk rock' but recognised punk's importance in creating a space or opportunity within pop.

84 See Secret Affair's complaints about Arista and the band's i-Spy imprint in Sandy Robertson, 'The End of the Affair', *Sounds*, 26 April 1980, pp. 18–20.

85 A well-known early example was The Jam changing the word 'fuck' to 'damn' for the single release of 'This Is the Modern World' in 1977.

86 See, for example, Ian Pye, 'Green's Peace', *Melody Maker*, 10 March 1984, pp. 10–11.

87 The Clash formally opened The Roxy on 1 January 1977, but 'trial' punk gigs were held during December 1976. See Marko, *The Roxy London*, pp. 60–5.

88 The criteria for inclusion in the independent chart was that a 'record had to be independently manufactured, distributed and marketed without recourse to the machinery of the majors' (Ogg, *Independence Days*, p. 369).

89 John Orme, 'Crisis? *This* Crisis!', *Melody Maker*, 30 June 1979, p. 21; Andrew Tyler, 'Cold Wind Hits Record Industry', *NME*, 22 May 1982, p. 3; Ogg, *Independence Days*, p. 164.

90 John Orme, 'Riding the New Wave', *Melody Maker*, 9 July 1977, pp. 26–7 and 38; Paul Rambali, 'Independents Day Revisited', *NME*, 5 August 1978, pp. 14–16.

91 Both Robinson and Riviera had been active in London's music scene for some time prior to 1976, primarily as mangers. See Bert Muirhead, *Stiff: The Story*

of a Record Label (Poole: Blandford Press, 1983); Richard Balls, *Be Stiff: The Stiff Records Story* (London: Soundcheck Books, 2014). Other early labels of a similar ilk included Do It, The Label, Lightning and Safari, along with Copeland's Deptford City Fun and Illegal.

92 Taylor, *Document and Eyewitness*, pp. 206–20.

93 For an introduction, hear the *Messthetics* cd compilations released on Hyped2Death. See Mick Sinclair's DIY 'Cassette Pets' column in *Sounds* and 'Garageland' in *NME*.

94 'Six Minute War Interview', *Intensive Care*, 1, 1980, p. 10.

95 Sleevenotes to 'The Medium Is Tedium' b/w 'Don't Back the Front', Refill Records, 1977.

96 Interview with Desperate Bicycles by Graham Kennedy, *Challenge*, April–May 1978, p. 5.

97 Notable examples include The Door and Window, The Drive, The Outsiders, Reptile Ranch, Six Minute War, Spherical Objects, Swell Maps, Television Personalities. For an overview, see Paul Morley and Adrian Thrills, 'Independent Discs', *NME*, 1 September 1979, p. 23.

98 This became common, as with The Door and Window's first EP, which came with a 'How We Did It' pamphlet.

99 'Scritlock's Door', on *2nd Peel Session* EP, Rough Trade/St Pancras, 1979.

100 Scritti produced a guide to 'making your own record' with Rough Trade. See Taylor, *Document and Eyewitness*, p. 19.

101 'From the Pressing Plants to the Concert Halls, We Want Control', *After Hours*, 1, 1979, pp. 15–20.

102 Taylor, *Document and Eyewitness*, pp. 44–64. Its early founders and staff included Travis, John Kemp, Jo Slee, Ken Davison and Steve Montgomery, all of whom brought with them a countercultural heritage of varied hue.

103 See Essential Logic and Raincoats interviews in *Mental Children*, 1, 1980.

104 Quoted in Marcus, 'It's Fab …', pp. 120–1. This was echoed by The Slits in an interview with *Grinding Halt*, 5, 1980. The band left Island to work with Y and Rough Trade, complaining that Island was only interested in money.

105 Tony Wilson, *24 Hour Party People: What The Sleeve Notes Never Tell You* (London: Channel 4 Books, 2002), pp. 66–8; Nice, *Shadowplayers*, p. 62 (a more conventional 50/50 deal was then arranged prior to the release of 1979's *Unknown Pleasures*); Harry Doherty, 'Packing Up Good Vibrations', *Melody Maker*, 3 November 1979, p. 9.

106 'bIG fLAME – Statement of Intent', undated [originally drafted c. 1983], in the booklet to *Rigour, 1983–86*, Drag City, 1995.

107 For an interesting discussion, see Pete Dale, 'It Was Easy, It Was Cheap, So What?' Reconsidering the DIY Principle of Punk and Indie Music', *Popular Music History*, 3:2 (2008), pp. 171–93.

108 See, for example, 'Thorn–EMI', anarchist leaflet, 1983, printed in *Paid in Full*, 1, 1985, p. 15; 'Notes' in Conflict, 'This Is Not Enough' b/w 'Neither Is This', Mortarhate Records, 1985.

109 Penny Rimbaud, 'Crass at the Roxy', *International Anthem*, 1, 1977, pp. 5–10; Crass 'Punk is Dead', on *The Feeding of the Five Thousand*, Small Wonder, 1978.

110 See also Wise and Wise, 'The End of Music', pp. 63–102.

111 Poison Girls', 'State Control', on *Total Exposure*, Xntrix, 1981; *The Impossible Dream*, 2, 1980.

112 Graham Lock, 'Crass By Name, Cross By Nature', *NME*, 20 January 1979, p. 16. Recorded and dated 1978, the record's release was delayed into the new year because of the situation at the Irish pressing plant. English plants then refused the record for being 'obscene'. In the event, the Irish plant pressed the record once 'Asylum' was removed (and replaced with two minutes of silence titled 'The Sound of Free Speech').

113 For an insight into Crass' approach to their label, see their interview in *Artificial Life*, 2, 1982, pp. 6–8.

114 Cranna, 'Product', pp. 22–4; Nice, *Shadowplayers*, pp. 25–50; *Industrial News*, Nos. 1–4, 1978–80.

115 Hesmondhalgh, 'Post-Punk's Attempts to Democratise the Music Industry', pp. 263–7.

116 Cranna, 'Product', pp. 22–4; Charles Shaar Murray, 'Gang Floored', *NME*, 15 May 1982, pp. 14–15; Frith, 'Post-Punk Blues', pp. 18–21.

117 See, for example, Johnny Rotten's comments on Stiff Records in Brian Harrigan, 'Punk Comes of Age', *Melody Maker*, 19 March 1977, pp. 38–9; Bushell, 'War of Independents', *Sounds*, pp. 10–11. For a dismissive overview of punk's independents by 1984, see Lynden Barber, 'Electric Dreams', *Melody Maker*, 1 December 1984, p. 11.

118 The reasons for Rough Trade refusing to handle a record/band/fanzine were varied. Nurse With Wound's debut album, *Chance Meeting on a Dissecting Table of a Sewing Machine and an Umbrella* (1979) was initially rejected because of its sado-masochist cover image. Raped, whose name and *Pretty Paedophiles* EP (1977) were obviously designed to offend, were similarly chastised. See also Paul Morley's coverage of Postcard in *NME*, 4 October 1980, pp. 24–5; Colin Irwin, 'The Decline and Fall in Iceland', *Melody Maker*, 26 September 1981, p. 24.

119 Quoted in Paul Rambali, 'Malcolm and Bernard: Rock 'n' Roll Scoundrels', *NME*, 9 August 1980, pp. 25–9 and p. 49.

120 Quoted in Lock, 'Gabba Gabba Hegel', pp. 6–8.

121 The EP was originally released in late 1979 (under the name The Licks) by Stortbeat Records, a deal that soon led to difficulties. 'We've found that a lot of people who claim to be punks are no better than the businessmen who exploit us'. By 1981, the band was known as Flux of Pink Indians.

122 Jon Savage, 'Consuming Passion: Cash from Chaos Becomes Profits', *Melody Maker*, 22 September 1979, p. 12.

123 Harrison, *Finding A Role?*, p. 408.

124 John Cunningham, 'National Daily Newspapers and Their Circulations in the UK, 1908–78', *Journal of Advertising History*, 4 (1981), p. 17.

125 Marshall McLuhan, *Understanding Media: The Extensions of Man* (London: Routledge & Paul, 1964); Marshall McLuhan and Quentin Fiore, *The Medium Is the Massage* (London: Penguin, 1967); Stanley Cohen and Jock Young (eds.), *The Manufacturing of News: Social Problems, Deviance and the Mass Media* (London: Constable, 1973); Glasgow University Media Group, *Bad News* (London: Routledge and Kegan Paul, 1976); Stuart Hall, Chas Critcher, Tony Jefferson, John Clarke, Brian Roberts, *Policing the Crisis: Mugging, the State, and Law and Order* (Basingstoke: Palgrave Macmillan 2002, originally published 1978).

126 Examples taken from The Pop Group, *For How Much Longer Do We Tolerate Mass Murder?*, Y Records, 1979; Sham 69, *That's Life*, Polydor Records, 1978; The Exploited, *Dead Cities* EP, Secret Records, 1981.

127 *The Secret Public*, 1, 1978.

128 Sex Pistols, 'I Wanna Be Me', b-side of 'Anarchy in the UK', EMI 1976.

129 The Clash, 'London's Burning', on *The Clash*, CBS 1977.

130 Subway Sect, 'Nobody's Scared' b/w 'Dontsplitit', Braik Records, 1978.

131 McNeill, 'We Are Not Showroom Dummies', pp. 7–8.

132 The Members, 'Phone-In Show', on *At The Chelsea Nightclub*, Virgin, 1979.

133 See, for example, *Breakdown*, 1, 1977 and Pete Nasty, 'Punk Hits the Glossies', *Heat*, 2, 1977, p. 3.

134 Quoted in *Negative Reaction*, 5, 1977, p. 5.

135 Mark Perry, 'The Last Page', p. 8; 'We've Had Enough!', *City Fun*, 17, 1980, p. 6; *Cobalt Hate*, 3, 1980, p. 2.

136 Guy Debord, *Society of the Spectacle* (Michigan: Black & Red, 1983 edition, originally published 1967), p. 2.

137 Ibid., p. 1.

138 Ibid., pp. 56–7.

139 As in Marcus, *Lipstick Traces*, pp. 19–21; David Thorp, 'Joining the Dots', in Gorman, Thorp, Vermorel, *Joining the Dots*, pp. 8–16; Vermorel, 'Growing Up as a Genius in the Sixties', pp. 107–211.

140 Dick Witts interviewing Tony Wilson in *Temporary Hoarding*, 5, Spring 1978.

141 The French comic-strip was titled *Le Retour De La Colonne Durutti* (1966). The album was released in January 1980, but pressed and manufactured in 1979.

142 Ivan Chtcheglov, 'Formulary for a New City', in Ken Knabb (ed.), *Situationist International Anthology* (Berkeley: Bureau of Public Secrets, 1981), pp. 1–4.

143 See various articles in *A System Partly Revealed*, 2, 1982; *And Don't Run Away You Punk*, 1, 1984; *Vague*, 16/17, 1985. *Kill Your Pet Puppy* was also informed by situationist ideas and approaches.

144 Rimbaud, 'The Last of the Hippies', p. 4.

145 See Duffield's *Christ the Movie* (1990) and the three editions of *International Anthem*. Numerous pamphlets were printed and distributed by the band through until the mid-1980s.

146 Crass, *Yes Sir, I Will*, Crass Records, 1983. For all Crass' lyrics, see Crass, *Love Songs* (Hebden Bridge: Pomona Books, 2003).

147 Song titles relate to Conflict, Rubella Ballet, Rudimentary Peni, Flux of Pink Indians and Antisect.

148 The quote is from a 1979 letter from Genesis P. Orridge, in Ford, *Wreckers of Civilisation*, p. 9.27.

149 Quoted in Ian Pye, 'Genesis: the Movie', *Melody Maker*, 6 November 1982, p. 19.

150 'Throbbing Gristle', *Industrial Culture Handbook*, pp. 6–19.

151 *Industrial News*, 1–4, 1978–80.

152 See Richard Kirk, in Paul Morley, 'The Heart and Soul of Cabaret Voltaire', *NME*, 29 November 1980, pp. 16–17, stating: 'In a way we're like journalists, we're taking things in and reporting'. P-Orridge also described industrial music being 'closest to journalism', documenting 'the savage realities of capitalism'. See 'Terry Gold' [Genesis P-Orridge], Sleevenotes to *The Industrial Records Story*, Industrial Records, 1984; Sandy Robertson, 'Art Throbs', *Sounds*, 6 January 1979, p. 9.

153 Neal, *Tape Delay*, p. 153.

154 Adam Sweeting, 'Cabs x 45', *Melody Maker*, 26 June 1982, p. 10.

155 The reference is to 'I Wanna Be Me', the b-side of 'Anarchy in the UK' (1976).

3 Tell Us the Truth: Reportage, Realism and Abjection

1 Quoted in Pete Silverton, 'Sham 1969/1977', *Sounds*, 29 October 1977, pp. 14–15.

2 Steve Walsh, 'The Very Angry Clash', *Sniffin' Glue*, 4, 1976, p. 3.

3 LWT, *London Weekend Show*, 28 November 1976.

4 Harrison, *Finding A Role?*, p. 200.

5 LWT, *London Weekend Show*, 28 November 1976.

6 For an interesting account by Strummer, see Max Farrar, 'Is It More Than Rock 'n' Roll?', *The Leveller*, July/August 1977, p. 17.

7 Tony Parsons, review of *The Clash*, *NME*, 16 April 1977, p. 33.

8 Reportage is recognised to mean the recording or depiction of actual events or the dramatised survey of a contemporary socioeconomic and political landscape.

9 Coon, 'Clash: Down and Out and Proud', p. 33; Walsh, 'The Very Angry Clash', p. 3–6.

10 Billy Bragg, the Redskins' Chris Dean and Attila the Stockbroker are three examples of those inspired by The Clash; the Angelic Upstarts' Mensi is another. See also articles and letters in *Challenge*, the newspaper of the YCL, and *Socialist Worker* throughout 1977–79. For The Clash and the left more generally, see Matthew Worley, 'Revolution Rock? The Clash, Joe Strummer and the British Left in the Early Days of Punk', in Barry Faulk and Brady Harrison (eds.), *Punk Rock Warlord: Critical Perspectives on the Life and Work of Joe Strummer* (Farnham: Ashgate, 2014), pp. 81–92.

11 Caroline Coon, 'Clash Personality', *Melody Maker*, 23 April 1977, p. 29.

12 Social realism is understood to mean the dramatisation of everyday life. In the context of punk, it refers to attempts to capture the young lives lived by those who identified with punk or took up early punk claims that popular music should reflect the experiences of those who made and listened to it. As this suggests, such a definition recognises that punk's social realism also informed musical forms and bands who did not necessarily sound or dress as 'punk', but who related to punk's tendency to social commentary.

13 Laing, *One Chord Wonders*, p. 29.

14 Michael Bracewell, *England Is Mine: Pop Life in Albion, From Wilde to Goldie* (London: Flamingo, 1998), pp. 76–108. Weller also made the connection in conversation with Paul Morley, 'The Revolution Will Start When Paul Weller Has Supped His Pint', *NME*, 3 November 1979, pp. 37–9.

15 The Jam. 'Saturday's Kids', on *Setting Sons*, Polydor Records, 1979.

16 See, for example, Garry Bushell's interview with The Ruts in *Sounds*, 16 June 1979, pp. 16–18 and the 4-Skins in 'The New Breed', pp. 32–3. Or, for The Clash, see Strummer in Mikal Gilmore, 'The Clash: Anger on the Left', *Rolling Stone*, 8 March 1979, p. 22.

17 Such a critique is most articulately argued in Simon Frith's 'Post-Punk Blues', pp. 18–21. But see also, for example, Paul Morley's review of The Jam at the Music Machine, *NME*, 6 January 1979, p. 30.

18 Mick Duffy, 'Playing with Fire – And Other Skin Problems' and Neil Spencer, 'Oi! – The Disgrace', *NME*, 11 July 1981, pp. 4–5; Joanna Rollo, 'Sounds Familiar', *Socialist Worker*, 18 July 1981, p. 4.

19 Quoted in Beckett, *When the Lights Went Out*, p. 335.

20 Whitbread, *The Writing on the Wall*, pp. 184–201; Beckett, *When the Lights Went Out*, pp. 317–57.

21 Glynn and Booth, *Modern Britain*, pp. 188–276.

22 Jim Tomlinson, 'Thrice Denied: "Declinism" as a Recurrent Theme in British History in the Long Twentieth Century', *Twentieth Century British History*, 20:2 (2009), 227–51.

23 Turner, *Crisis? What Crisis?*, pp. 181–204.

24 Moran, '"Stand Up and Be Counted"', 173–98.

25 Robert Saunders, 'Thatcherism and the Seventies', in Ben Jackson and Robert Saunders (eds.), *Making Thatcher's Britain* (Cambridge University Press, 2012), p. 30. The paper was titled 'Themes' and produced in February 1978. See also John Shepherd, *Crisis? What Crisis? The Callaghan Government and the British 'Winter of Discontent'* (Manchester University Press, 2013).

26 See, for example, Keith Waterhouse, 'The Punk of Politics', *Daily Mirror*, 11 August 1977, p. 11. Similarly, of course, Coon, Ingham and Parsons' reading of punk made just such a connection.

27 *London's Outrage*, p. 5.

28 Quoted in Phil McNeill, 'Watch Out It's the Angry "Young" Men', *NME*, 4 December 1976, p. 5. The Stranglers' summed up this mood on their single 'Something Better Change' b/w 'Straighten Out', United Artists, 1977.

29 Mark Perry, 'The Truth', *Sniffin' Glue*, 9, 1977, p. 9.

30 The Jam, 'Time for Truth', on *In The City*, Polydor, 1977.

31 Quoted in Paul Morley, 'Belfast's Ripped Backsides', *NME*, 17 February 1979, pp. 7–8.

32 Renton, *When We Touched the Sky*, pp. 136–55; Roland Link, *Love in Vain: The Story of The Ruts* (London: Cadiz Music, 2015), pp. 124–8. Hear also, and see the sleeve for, Alien Kulture, 'Asian Youth' b/w 'Cultural Crossover', RARecords, 1980.

33 Garry Bushell, 'The Ruts Bleed for You', *Sounds*, 16 June 1979, p. 18.

34 For an overview, see Worley, 'Punk, Politics and British (fan)zines, 1976–84', 76–106.

35 Subhumans, 'Black and White', *The Day the Country Died*, Spider Leg Records, 1983.

36 Vinen, *Thatcher's Britain*, pp. 101–33.

37 Jon Lawrence and Florence Sutcliffe-Braithwaite, 'Margaret Thatcher and the Decline of Class Politics', in Jackson and Saunders (eds.), *Making Thatcher's Britain*, pp. 132–47. Lilley's list, read out at the 1992 Tory conference and based on the executioner's song from Gilbert and Sullivan's 'The Mikado', went thus: 'I've got a little list/Of benefit offenders who I'll soon be rooting out/And who never would be missed/They never would be missed/There's those who make up bogus claims/In half a dozen names/And councillors who draw the dole/To run left-wing campaigns/... Young ladies who get pregnant just to jump the housing list/And dads who won't support the kids of ladies they've just kissed/And I haven't even mentioned all those sponging socialists/They'd none of them be missed'.

38 The Anti-Nowhere League also guested on the tour.

39 Chris Bohn, 'Premature Burial', *NME*, 18 July 1981, pp. 32–3.

40 Ibid, pp. 32, 61.

41 Lord Scarman, *The Scarman Report: The Brixton Disorders, 10–12 April 1981* (London, Pelican, 1982).

42 Matthew Worley, 'Riotous Assembly: British Punk's Diaspora in the Summer of '81', in Knud Andresen and Bart van der Steen (eds.), *A European Youth Revolt: European Perspectives on Youth Protest and Social Movements in the 1980s* (Basingstoke: Palgrave Macmillan, 2016), pp. 217–27.

43 Quoted in Neil Rowland, 'Anti-Christ Crusade', *The Other Side*, 1, 1981, pp. 5–9.

44 Strummer made this observation in 'Garageland' on *The Clash* (1977).

45 Parsons, 'Go Johnny Go', p. 29; idem, interview with The Damned, *NME*, 13 November 1976, p. 16. Coon's and Ingham's pieces also made regular reference to the dole queue and the backgrounds of the early punk bands.

46 Marsh, 'Dole Queue Rock', pp. 112–14. Denman and McDonald, 'Unemployment Statistics from 1881 to the Present Day', p. 112.

47 Frith, 'Beyond the Dole Queue', pp. 77–9; idem, 'The Punk Bohemians', *New Society*, 9 March 1978, pp. 535–6.

48 A band called Social Security also formed in Bristol.

49 'SS Snoopers' was a song by Poison Girls featured on *Total Exposure*, Xntrix, 1981. Hear also 'Working' by Cock Sparrer on *Shock Troops*, Razor, 1983.

50 'Vicious Circle' on Abrasive Wheels, *Vicious Circle* EP, Riot City, 1981.

51 YOP was a reference to the Youth Opportunities scheme introduced by Labour in 1978 and extended by the Conservatives in 1980. For songs predicting conscription, see – for but a few examples – Abrasive Wheels, 'Army Song', Chron Gen, 'Puppets of War', The Clash, 'The Call Up', Dead Man's Shadow, 'When Our Blood is Spilled', Killing Joke, 'Tomorrow's World', Subhumans, 'Who's Gonna Fight in the Third World War'.

52 Harrison, *Finding a Role?*, p. 248.

53 For a discussion, see Alwyn W. Turner, *Rejoice! Rejoice! Britain in the Eighties* (London: Aurum, 2010), pp. 86–9.

54 'DHSS Do Discharge', *NME*, 20 June 1981, p. 11.

55 Action Pact, 'Suicide Bag', on *Suicide Bag* EP, Fallout Records, 1982; A-Heads, *Dying Man* EP, TW Records, 1982.

56 Quoted in Garry Bushell, 'Anti People Are the Warriors', *Sounds*, 5 September 1981, pp. 18–19.

57 Quoted in Harry Doherty, 'A Mod at 20', *Melody Maker*, 20 January 1979, p. 13. See also Steve Clarke's interview with Paul Weller in *NME*, 7 May 1977, p. 28, wherein Weller says he formed The Jam because 'I didn't want to work, I didn't want to become Mr Normal'.

58 Quoted in Paul Morley, 'Hey Mac...', *NME*, 6 October 1979, pp. 6–8.

59 Quoted in Parsons, 'Sten Guns in Knightsbridge', p. 6.

60 The Fall, 'Industrial Estate', on *Live at the Witch Trials*, Step Forward, 1979; Sham 69 'I Don't Wanna', on *I Don't Wanna* EP released by Step Forward, 1977.

61 A version can be heard on the film *Punk Kebab*, directed by Pedro Rojas, 1977.

62 See, for example, poems collected in *Another Day Another World*, 1, 1982.

63 The documentary was filmed in 1983 but broadcast in 1984.

64 Six Minute War, 'Strike', on *Six Minute War* EP, Six Minute War, 1980.

65 The Members, 'Solitary Confinement' b/w 'Rat Up a Drainpipe', Stiff Records, 1978; Newtown Neurotics, 'Living with Unemployment' on *Beggars Can Be Choosers*, Razor Records, 1983.

66 Paul Rambali, 'Rock 'n' Roll Scoundrels', *NME*, 9 August 1980, pp. 25–9. McLaren's ideas gave a degree of substance to the fledgling new romantic scene gathered around clubs such as Billy's in Covent Garden. That most of the club's early entourage – including Steve Strange and Boy George (George O'Dowd) – were squatting in the late 1970s, allowed their flamboyance to be read as a counter to both unemployment and the greyness of work. The end-game came with Wham's 'Wham Rap! (Enjoy What You Do)', released in 1982 and again in 1983.

67 Pete Scott, 'W.O.R.K.N.O', *Vague*, 14, 1983, pp. 10–11.

68 Mike Diboll, 'The Admition', *Toxic Grafity*, 5, 1980, p. 18. Also, for just a few examples, 'Work Slavery', *Acts of Defiance*, 4, 1982, p. 13; 'Owe Us A Living', *Fack*, 6, 1981, p. 23; 'Work', *Knee Deep in Shit*, 1, 1981, p. 3.

69 See reports in *NME*, 10 September 1977, p. 5; *Young Socialist*, 10 June 1978, p. 5; *Sounds*, 5 August 1978, p. 10.

70 See the comments of Gene October, 'fuck the unions', in 'Chelsea', *Sniffin' Glue*, 10, 1977, pp. 4–5.

71 Wise, *King Mob*, p. 59; Savage, *London's Outrage*, 2, 1977, pp. 3–8.

72 Quoted in Rina Vergano, 'Poly Styrene', *The Leveller*, March 1978, pp. 118–19.

73 Garry Bushell, 'We Have a Right to Work', *Sounds*, 16 September 1978, pp. 14–15 and 22; Ray Lowry, 'The Walker Brothers', *NME*, 23 May, 1981, p. 29 and p. 55; X. Moore, 'The Road to Blackpool Pier', *NME*, 24 October 1981, pp. 31–5. See also fanzines pieces such as 'Unemployed? So Are They', *Guttersnipe*, 7, 1979, pp. 8–9.

74 Paul Morley review of *That's Life*, NME, 4 November 1978, p. 37.

75 The BBC *Arena* documentary was called 'Tell Us the Truth', broadcast in 1979 and directed by Jeff Perks.

76 The quotes come from 'Who Gives a Damn' and 'That's Life' from *That's Life*, Polydor, 1978.

77 The description of Pursey is from Paul Morley, 'Don't Follow Leaders', *NME*, 12 November 1977, pp. 9–10.

78 Danny Baker, 'Sham 69', *Sniffin' Glue*, 12, 1977, pp. 19–23.

79 Tony Parsons, 'Next Week's Big Thing', *NME*, 29 August 1977, p. 31.

80 Quoted in Bushell, '(Sk)in the Beginning', p. 27.

81 See, for example, the interview with Pursey by Brian Case in *NME*, 11 March 1978, pp. 32–3.

82 'Song of the Street', free single with Sham 69, *Tell Us the Truth*, Polydor, 1978.

83 The quotes refer to Slaughter and the Dogs' 'Where Have All the Boot Boys Gone?' and Menace's 'Insane Society'.

84 Quoted in Garry Bushell, 'Harder than the Rest', *Sounds*, 8 March 1980, pp. 32–4.

85 Advert for a Cock Sparrer gig at the London Greyhound, *NME*, 26 November 1977, p. 46.

86 Cock Sparrer, 'Runnin' Riot' b/w 'Sister Suzie', Decca, 1977 and 'Chip on My Shoulder' b/w 'We Love You', Decca, 1977.

87 Garry Bushell, 'Minding Our Own Business', *Sounds*, 27 February 1982, pp. 18–19.

88 Infa Riot, 'Feel the Rage' on Various Artists, *Britannia Waives the Rules* EP, Secret, 1982.

89 For overlaps see Garry Bushell, *Dance Craze* (London: Spotlight, 1981); Marshall, *Spirit of '69*, pp. 82–97; idem, *The Two Tone Story* (Lockerbie: ST Publishing, 1997 version).

90 Garry Bushell, 'Rude Boys Can't Fail', *Sounds*, 15 March 1980, pp. 31–3; Chris Salewicz, 'The Specials: Stop The Tour, I Want To Get Off', *NME*, 27 September 1980, pp. 30–3; Paul Wellings, 'The Greatest Show on Earth', *The Other Half*, 1, 1981, pp. 15–18.

91 Russ Bestley, 'From "London's Burning" to "Sten Guns in Sunderland"', *Punk and Post-Punk*, 1:1 (2012), 41–71.

92 Simon Reynolds, 'Younger Than Yesterday: Indie-Pop's Cult of Innocence', in his *Bring the Noise: Twenty Years of Writing About Hip Rock and Hip Hop* (London: Faber & Faber, 2007), pp. 13–19. The essay was originally published in *Melody Maker* in 1986.

93 Simon Frith, 'Youth in the Eighties: A Dispossessed Generation', *Marxism Today*, November 1981, pp. 12–15.

94 Quoted in Miles, 'Eighteen Flight Rock', p. 14. For similar sentiments by Johnny Rotten, see interview in *Temporary Hoarding*, 2, 1977.

95 Words are from 'Make Me Mad', on The Selecter, *Too Much Pressure*, Chrysalis, 1980.

96 The Jam, 'Town Called Malice' b/w 'Precious', Polydor, 1982.

97 Scanlon, *Sex Pistols*, pp. 92–9; Charles M. Young, 'Rock Is Sick and Living in London: A Report of the Sex Pistols', *Rolling Stone*, 20 October 1977, p. 72.

98 Rick Szymanski, 'Would You Buy A Rubber T-Shirt From This Man?', *Street Life*, 1–14 May 1976, p. 11; Jon Savage, '430 King's Road', in PunkPistol, *SEX and Seditionaries*, n.p.

99 Reed, *Assimilate*, pp. 3–25.

100 Rotten, *No Irish*, p. 235. 'Annalisa' and 'Poptones' are the songs referred to here.

101 Vivien Goldman, 'Siouxsie Sioux who R U?', *Sounds*, 3 December 1977, pp. 26–7; Chris Brazier, 'Siouxsie: Cold and Confrontational', *Melody Maker*, 17 June 1978, pp. 8–9.

102 Paul Morley, 'A World Domination by 1984 Special', *NME*, 14 January 1978, pp. 7–8.

103 The quote comes from a 'Statement on COUM' (1975), cited in Ford, *Wreckers of Civilization*, p. 5:10.

104 'Terry Gold' [Genesis P-Orridge], sleevenotes to *The Industrial Records Story*, Illuminated Records, 1984.

105 'The Sewage Worker's Birthday Party', on Coil, *Scatology*, Force & Form, 1984 (though the album did not come out until February 1985); 'Coil', in Neal, *Tape Delay*, pp. 115–25. The story was taken from a Swedish magazine, *Mr SM*.

106 For an interesting discussion, see Alex Ogg, 'For You Tommy, The War is Never Over', *Punk & Post-Punk*, 2:3 (2013), 282–304.

107 Discharge, 'Maimed and Slaughtered', on *Why*, Clay Records, 1981.

108 A 'Cambridge Rapist' T-shirt and reference to Myra Hindley formed part of the SEX and Seditionaries collection. Hear also Throbbing Gristle, 'Very Friendly', a version of which is on *The First Annual Report of Throbbing Gristle*, Yeaah, 2001. The Moors Murderers were formed by Steve Strange, Chrissie Hynde and others for shock effect in 1977: see Bruce Elder, 'The Moors Murderers', *Sounds*, 7 January 1978, pp. 7–8. For references to the Yorkshire Ripper, hear Siouxsie and the Banshees, 'Nightshift', *JuJu*, Polydor, 1981; The Exploited, 'Ripper', on *Punk's Not Dead*, Secret Records, 1981; The New Order, *Bradford Red Light District*, Come Organisation, 1981. Sutcliffe Jugend took part of their name from the Yorkshire Ripper and released a ten cassette pack, *We Spit On Their Graves*, Come Organisation, 1982, with each tape named after one of the female victims.

109 Gang of Four, 'Ether', on *Entertainment*, EMI, 1979.

110 Richard Osborne, 'A Great Friggin' Swindle? Sex Pistols, School Kids and 1979', *Popular Music and Society*, 38:4 (2015), 432–49.

111 This did not spare the Banshees and SEX's early coterie from criticism, see Burchill and Parsons, 'Fear and Loathing at the Roxy', p. 38; Julie Burchill, 'The Kid Who Wouldn't Wear Clarke's Sandals', *NME*, 15 April 1978, pp. 7–8.

112 Ka-Tzetnik 135633, *House of Dolls* (London: Panther, 1965 version); Dave McCullough, 'Pseud Yourself', *Sounds*, 11 August 1979, pp. 16–17.

113 Peter Webb, *Exploring the Networked Worlds of Popular Music: Milieu Cultures* (London: Routledge, 2007), pp. 65–86. Douglas Pearce continues to record as Death in June; the third original member was Patrick Leagas, later of Sixth Comm.

114 Sleevenotes to Whitehouse, *Birthdeath Experience*, Come Organisation, 1980; Sleevenotes to Whitehouse, *Psychopathia Sexualis*, Come Organisation, 1982. See also the Come Organisation's *Kata*, nos. 1–20 (1980–84) and *Intolerance*, nos. 1–5 (1982), produced by Philip Best just prior to his joining Whitehouse.

115 Related records were dedicated to Albert DeSalvo, Peter Kürten, Dennis Nilsen and Peter Sutcliffe. *Buchenwald* (1981) and *New Britain* (1982) were both Whitehouse albums, *Für Ilse Koch* (1982) was a compilation. In the same spirit, a *White Power* cassette compilation was released on the Iphar label in 1983. For background, see David Keenan, *England's Hidden Reverse: A Secret History of the Esoteric Underground* (London: Strange Attractor, 2016, originally published 2003) pp. 96–111.

116 Mark Crumby (ed.), *Whitehouse: Still Going Strong* (Amersham: Impulse Publications, 1994 edition). For an overview of the power electronics scene that evolved from Whitehouse via industrial culture, see Jennifer Wallis (ed.), *Fight Your Own War: Power Electronics and Noise Culture* (London: Headpress, 2016).

117 Quoted in Graham Lock, 'Stopping, Starting and Falling All Over Again', *NME*, 7 April, 1979, p. 7.

118 Michael Goddard and Benjamin Halligan, 'Introduction', in Michael Goddard and Benjamin Halligan (eds.), *Mark E. Smith and The Fall: Art, Music and Politics* (Farnham: Ashgate, 2010), pp. 1–15.

119 Quoted in Dave McCullough, 'The Famous Five Fight On', *Sounds*, 21 April, 1979, pp. 20–1.

120 The Fall, 'Fiery Jack' b/w '2nd Dark Age' and 'Psykick Dancehall', Step Forward, 1980.

121 Mark Fisher, '"Memorex for the Krakens": The Fall's Pulp Modernism', in Goddard and Halligan (eds.), *Mark E. Smith and The Fall*, pp. 95–110.

122 For an insightful overview of The Fall, see David Wilkinson, 'Prole Art Threat: The Fall, the Blue Orchids and the Politics of the Post-Punk Working Class Autodidact', *Punk & Post-Punk*, 3:1 (2014), 67–82.

123 Steve Clarke, 'Cooper Clarke's in the Kitchen, Mixin' up the Medicine', *NME*, 28 January 1978, pp. 7–8.

124 John Parham, '"Flowers of Evil": Ecosystem Health and the Punk Poetry of John Cooper-Clarke', in Subcultures Network (ed.), *Fight Back*, pp. 119–38.

125 John Cooper Clarke, *Ten Years in an Open Necked Shirt* (London: Arena, 1983).

4 Suburban Relapse: The Politics of Boredom

1 *The Great Rock 'n' Roll Swindle*, directed by Julien Temple, 1980.

2 Raoul Vaneigem, *The Revolution of Everyday Life* (London: Rebel Press, 1994, originally published 1967), p. 178.

3 Buzzcocks, *Spiral Scratch*, New Hormones, 1977.

4 'Howard Devoto interviewed by Johnny Rachy, 1977', in sleevenotes to *Time's Up*, Mute Records, 2000. *Time's Up* was originally released as a bootleg in 1977 and comprised Buzzcocks' early demo recordings from 1976.

5 Reynolds, *Rip It Up and Start Again*, p. 92. The reference is to 'orgone', Reich's notion of a life force. Devoto also cited Dostoyevsky and Camus as influences on the record's prevailing themes.

6 Nick Kent, 'Meet the Col Tom Parker of the Blank Generation', p. 26.

7 Sex Pistols, 'Pretty Vacant' b/w 'No Fun', Virgin Records, 1977. The sleeve was designed by Jamie Reid, drawing on an idea developed in his pre-Pistol Suburban Press days. According to Reid in his *Up They Rise*, the image was printed as a poster in 1973 and 'sent to Point Blank! [a pro-situ group] in San Francisco, who used them in a pamphlet about city transit policy' (Reid and Savage, *Up They Rise*, pp. 68–9). Alternately, a pamphlet featuring the 'Nowhere' bus – 'Space Travel: an official guide for San Francisco commuters' (1973) – was produced by David Jacobs in Berkeley and sent to Reid, who then used it for a poster and, later, the Sex Pistols. The Berkeley pamphlet image is reproduced in Kugelberg with Savage and Terry, *God Save Sex Pistols*, p. 177.

8 Vaneigem, *The Revolution of Everyday Life*, p. 35; quoted in the transcript to Rotten's radio interview with Tommy Vance, *Sounds*, 16 July 1977, pp. 9, 30. See also The Clash's Joe Strummer speaking to Caroline Coon ('Clash: Down and Out and Proud', p. 33), saying London had 'nowhere to go, [nothing] to do'.

9 See the first issue of *Breakdown* fanzine (1977) from Southampton, which included a satirical list of 'good words to use in conversation'. 'Boredom' was one such, along with 'repression', 'cliché', 'plastic death' and 'revolt'. The strapline to *Nihilist Vices*, 1, 1979, was 'Stop Terminal Boredom Now'.

10 The nods here are to The Clash's 'London's Burning' and 'I'm So Bored with the USA', The Adverts' 'Bored Teenagers', The Damned's 'Politics' and 'I'm Bored', Slaughter and the Dogs' 'You're a Bore', The Slits' 'A Boring Life', Crass' 'Chairman of the Bored', Honey Bane's 'Boring Conversations' and The Prats' 'Nothing'. There are countless others, including many from the USA (Ramones' 'Now I Wanna Sniff Some Glue', Iggy Pop's 'I'm Bored' etc.). The Stooges' 'No Fun', covered by the Sex Pistols, is arguably the punk urtext.

11 Coon, 'Punk Rock', p. 24.

12 Some references here could include The Damned, 'So Messed Up', Menace 'Screwed Up', The Clash, 'Cheat', The Users, 'Sick of You', Hollywood Brats and subsequently The Boys, 'Sick on You', The Damned, 'Sick of Being Sick', Skrewdriver, *All Skrewed Up* (1977).

13 Nick Kent, 'Howard Devoto: The Compete Fatalist', *NME*, 28 April 1979, pp. 28–9.

14 Notes for the unrealised Sex Pistols book 'When Tutor Takes Over from Practice', in Kugelberg with Savage and Terry, *God Save Sex Pistols*, p. 306.

15 Two versions of the song were recorded. The single version, which reached number twelve in the UK charts in 1979, is shorter and contains fewer verses than the album version on *At The Chelsea Nightclub*, Virgin, 1979.

16 Rupa Huq, *Making Sense of Suburbia Through Popular Culture* (London: Bloomsbury, 2013); Roger Silverstone (ed.), *Visions of Suburbia* (London: Routledge, 1997).

17 The 'reality' of suburbia was obviously more complex. See Mark Clapson, *Invincible Green Suburbs, Brave New Towns: Social Change and Urban Dispersal in Post-War England* (Manchester: Manchester University Press, 1998).

18 Bracewell, *England Is Mine*, esp. chapter five; Simon Frith, *Music for Pleasure: Essays in the Sociology of Pop* (London: Polity, 1988), pp. 44–63.

19 Bracewell, *England Is Mine*, p. 25.

20 Quoted in Savage, *England's Dreaming Tapes*, p. 336.

21 *Dressing For Pleasure*, directed by John Samson, 1977; Burchill, 'The Kid Who Wouldn't Wear Clarkes Sandals', pp. 7–8; Savage, *The England's Dreaming Tapes*, pp. 33–52. See also the emergent new romantics and the fledgling goth style that evolved from punk through the 1980s.

22 Andy Medhurst, 'Negotiating the Gnome Zone: Versions of Suburbia in British Popular Culture', in Silverstone (ed.), *Visions of Suburbia*, pp. 240–68.

23 From *The Fall and Rise of Reginald Perrin* (1976–9), *Abigail's Party* (1977), *George & Mildred* (1976–9) and *The Good Life* (1975–8) respectively.

24 For an interesting discussion, see John Parham, 'A Concrete Sense of Place: Alienation and the City in British Punk and New Wave', *Green Letters: Studies in Ecocriticism*, 15:1 (2011), 76–88.

25 Pete Silverton, 'The Most Elitist Band in the World', *Sounds*, 25 November 1978, pp. 30–34. It also denies the aspirations of many working-class couples and families keen to buy into the suburban ideal.

26 Nick Kent, 'The Cure: A Demonstration of Household Appliances', *NME*, 19 May 1979, pp. 7–8; Barbarian, Steve Sutherland and Robert Smith, *The Cure: Ten Imaginary Years* (London: Zomba Books, 1988); Lol Tolhurst, *Cured: The Tale of Two Imaginary Boys* (London: Quercus, 2016).

27 John Reed, *Paul Weller: My Ever Changing Moods* (London: Omnibus, 1997 edition); Morrissey, *Autobiography* (London: Penguin, 2013).

28 For an excellent discussion, see Vicky Labeau, 'The Worst of All Possible Worlds', in Silverstone (ed.), *Visions of Suburbia*, pp. 280–97.

29 Bruce Wood, 'Urbanisation and Local Government', in Albert Henry Halsey (ed.), *British Social Trends since 1900* (Basingstoke: Palgrave Macmillan, 1988), pp. 325–6. For sociological accounts, see Michael Young and Peter Willmott, *Family and Class in a London Suburb* (London: Routledge & Kegan Paul, 1960); Phil Cohen, 'Subcultural Conflict and Working Class Community', in Stuart Hall, Dorothy Hobson, Andrew Lane and Paul Willis (eds.), *Culture, Media, Language* (London: Unwin Hyman, 1980).

30 Wood, 'Urbanisation and Local Government', pp. 325–30; Harrison, *Finding a Role?*, pp. 77–92; Sandbrook, *State of Emergency*, p. 360.

31 Brian Harrison, *Seeking a Role: The United Kingdom, 1951–1970* (Oxford: Oxford University Press, 2009), pp. 146–56; Peter Scott, *The Making of the Modern British Home: The Suburban Semi and Family Life between the Wars* (Oxford: Oxford University Press, 2013); Robert Fishman, *Bourgeois Utopias: The Rise and Fall of Suburbia* (New York: Basic Books, 1987). See also Julian Barnes' novel, *Metroland* (London: Jonathan Cape, 1980).

32 For an excellent case study, see Ben Jones, *The Working Class in Mid-Twentieth-Century England: Community, Identity and Social Memory* (Manchester: Manchester University Press, 2012). See also John Grindrod, *Concretopia: A Journey Around the Rebuilding of Postwar Britain* (London: Old Street, 2014); Lynsey Hanley, *Estates: An Intimate History* (London: Granta, 2007).

33 Ignorant, *The Rest is Propaganda*, pp. 31–3.

34 Harrison, *Seeking a Role*, pp. 158–64.

35 Colin Amery and Dan Cruickshank, *The Rape of Britain* (London: Harper Collins, 1975); Jeremy Seabrook, *City Close-Up* (London: Penguin, 1973 edition). Listen also to The Jam, 'The Planner's Dream Goes Wrong', on *The Gift*, Polydor, 1982.

36 From the cover of *Suburban Press*, 3 (undated), included in Reid and Savage, *Up They Rise*, p. 37.

37 PiL, 'No Birds', *Metal Box*, Virgin, 1979. 'Satellite', a scathing attack on suburban youth, was reputedly inspired by Shanne Hasler (Shanne Bradley), a St Albans art student from Ware in Hertfordshire and later member of the Nipple Erectors (along with Shane MacGowan).

38 The Skids, 'Sweet Suburbia' b/w 'Open Sound', Virgin, 1978; Action Pact, 'Stanwell' on *Suicide Bag* EP, Fallout, 1982.

39 Mark Clapson, *A Social History of Milton Keynes: Middle England/Edge City* (London: Fran Cass, 2004).

40 'Change Your Life – Move to one of Britain's New Towns', in Reid and Savage, *Up They Rise*, p. 43. Listen also to 'Come to Milton Keynes' by The Style Council, Paul Weller's post-Jam group, and to Eddie Stanton's 'Milton Keynes We Love You', released in 1980 on Black Eye Records.

41 Skroteez, *Overspill* EP, Square Anarchy Music, 1982.

42 Quoted in Carol Clerk, 'A Town Called Malady', *Melody Maker*, 29 January 1983, p. 29. See also Attila the Stockbroker, 'News from Nowhere', *NME*, 13 March 1982, pp. 26–7; Paul Castles, 'Band of Hope and Glory', *Punk Lives*, 11, 1983, p. 6. The Gangsters also came from Harlow, producing an album that featured them standing beneath a modernist concrete block and including 'Harlow Town', an ode to new town boredom and dulled aspiration.

43 For just a few examples, see the covers to Alternative TV, 'How Much Longer' b/w 'You Bastard', Deptford Fun City Records, 1977; The Cortinas, 'Defiant

Pose' b/w 'Independence', Step Forward, 1977; The Cure *Three Imaginary Boys*, Fiction 1979; Punishment of Luxury, 'Puppet Life' b/w 'The Demon', Small Wonder, 1978.

44 *International Anthem*, 2, 1979.

45 Poison Girls, *Hex*, Small Wonder, 1979.

46 Adam and the Ants, 'Cartrouble' on *Dirk Wears White Sox*, Do It, 1979.

47 Quoted in Neville Wiggins, 'On the Anti-Pop Road to Somewhere', *Punk Lives*, 1, 1982, pp. 22–3.

48 Soft Cell, *Mutant Moments* EP, A Big Frock Rekord, 1980.

49 As sung by Rotten in 'Anarchy in the UK'.

50 Simon Frith makes the point that English cities are themselves effectively 'suburban', given that cultural and political power is concentrated in London. See Simon Frith, 'The Suburban Sensibility in British Rock and Pop', in Silverstone (ed.), *Visions of Suburbia*, p. 270. For an expression of this, see the interview with Pauline Murray from Penetration in *Bored Stiff*, 1, 1977.

51 The Mob, 'Witch Hunt' b/w 'Shuffling Souls', All the Madmen, 1980.

52 The Head, 'Nothing to do in a Town like Leatherhead' b/w 'University '79', Ellie Jay Records, 1980; Nuclear Socketts, 'Play Loud' b/w 'Shadow on the Map', Subversive Records, 1981; 'O' Level, 'East Sheen' b/w 'Pseudo Punk', Psycho, 1978. There are others, such as O21's 'Solihull Revisited' *ad infinitum*.

53 New Model Army, 'Smalltown England', on *Vengeance*, Abstract, 1984. Hear also 'Ambition' and 'Better Than Them' on *No Rest for the Wicked*, EMI, 1985.

54 'There's An Army Coming', *Rigor Mortis*, 1 (1984), pp. 8–13.

55 Jack Barron, 'Re-Make Re-Model', *Sounds*, 16 June 1984, p. 16. Sullivan actually came from Buckinghamshire, but moved to Bradford to attend college. The rest were Yorkshire natives, as was Joolz.

56 New Model Army, 'Green and Grey', on *Thunder and Consolation*, EMI, 1989.

57 Gildart, *Images of England*, p. 198.

58 This point is well made by John Robb in his *Death to Trad Rock*, p. 10.

59 Debbie Wilson interviewed in Savage, *The England's Dreaming Tapes*, pp. 381–94; Ant, *Stand & Deliver*, p. 5. See also Boy George, who grew up on an Eltham council estate. Boy George with Spencer Bright, *Take It Like a Man* (London: Sidgwick & Jackson, 1995).

60 Bernard Sumner, *Chapter and Verse: New Order, Joy Division and Me* (London: Bantam Press, 2014), pp. 26–45.

61 See, for example, Mark Abrams, *The Teenage Consumer* (London: Press Exchange, 1959); John Clarke, 'Style', in Hall and Jefferson (eds.), *Resistance Through Rituals*, pp. 175–91: Paul Willis, *Profane Culture* (London: Routledge and Kegan Paul, 1978); Simon Frith, *The Sociology of Rock* (London: Constable, 1978), pp. 19–74; Hebdige, *Subculture*, pp. 100–27; Street, *Rebel Rock*, p. 112; Paul Willis, *Common Culture: Symbolic Work at Play in the Everyday Cultures of the Young* (Milton Keynes: Open University, 1990); Steven Miles, Cliff Dallas and Vivien Burr, ' "Fitting In and

Sticking Out": Consumption, Consumer Meanings and the Construction of Young People's Identities', *Journal of Youth Studies*, 1:1 (1998), pp. 81–96; Steven Miles, *Youth Lifestyles in a Changing World* (Buckingham: Open University Press, 2000); David Buckingham, 'Selling Youth: The Paradoxical Empowerment of the Young Consumer', in David Buckingham, Sara Bragg and Mary Kehily (eds.), *Youth Cultures in the Age of Global Media* (Basingstoke: Palgrave Macmillan, 2014).

62 Osgerby, *Youth in Britain*, pp. 30–49; Peter Wicke, 'Music, Dissidence, Revolution and Commerce: Youth Culture between Mainstream and Subculture', in Schildt and Siegfried (eds.), *Between Marx and Coca-Cola*, pp. 109–26.

63 Two classic examples would be Richard Hoggart, *The Uses of Literacy* (Harmondsworth: Penguin, 1958); L. T. Wilkins, *Delinquent Generation* (London: HMSO, 1960).

64 Robert Hewison, *Too Much: Art and Society in the Sixties, 1960–75* (London: Methuen, 1986), p. 149.

65 Herbert Marcuse, *One-Dimensional Man: Studies in the Ideology of Advanced Industrial Society* (London: Routledge, 1991 edition, originally published in 1964).

66 Hebdige, *Subculture*, p. 103.

67 Ibid., pp. 92–106; Willis, *Common Culture*, p. 21.

68 Osgerby, *Youth Media*, pp. 135–41.

69 Willis, *Profane Culture*, pp. 177–222; Hebdige, *Subculture*, pp. 103–17. Willis and Hebdige took up these terms from Claude Lévi-Strauss to explain how the meaning of objects and texts could be transformed when applied in a different context (bricolage) and how a relatively coherent subcultural form could be constructed from seemingly disparate elements (homology).

70 Rimbaud, *Shibboleth*, pp. 24–8.

71 Quoted in Savage (ed.), *The England's Dreaming Tapes*, pp. 597–608.

72 Ian Birch, 'Poly Rhythms', *Melody Maker*, 22 April 1978, p. 8.

73 X-Ray Spex, *Germfree Adolescents*, EMI, 1978.

74 BBC, 'Who Is Poly Styrene', *Arena*, directed by Ted Clisby, broadcast January 1979; Julie Burchill, 'You Don't Need X-Ray Spex to See Flying Saucers', *NME*, 21 October 1978, pp. 7–8.

75 *Temporary Hoarding*, 4, 1977, pp. 11–12. See Styrene's comments in Tony Parsons, 'Oh Philistines! Up Yours!, *NME*, 5 November 1977, pp. 28–9.

76 Bestley and Ogg, *The Art of Punk*, pp. 104–5.

77 Quoted in Oliver Lowenstein, 'The Case for the Buzzcocks', *Dangerous Logic*, 3, 1978, pp. 12–16. The press release was for 'Orgasm Addict' b/w 'Whatever Happened To ...?', United Artists, 1977.

78 Hipgnosis was a design group that had long produced record covers for major labels. From 1974, they included Peter Christopherson, later to become a member of Throbbing Gristle.

79 Bob Last quoted in Cranna, 'Product, Packaging and Rebel Music', pp. 22–4.

80 John Willett (ed.), *Brecht on Theatre: The Development of an Aesthetic* (London: Methuen, 1964); Reynolds, *Rip It Up and Start Again*, p. 117.

81 Reynolds, *Rip it Up and Start Again*, pp. 117–18; Bestley and Ogg, *The Art of Punk*, pp. 114–15.

82 Extract from *The Quality of Life*, 2, in sleevenotes to *Fast Product: Rigour and Discipline*, EMI, 1993.

83 Fraser Sutherland, 'Permission to Disobey: The Emergence of DIY Culture in the Post-Punk Era, 1978–82' (University of Birmingham, MA thesis, 2016).

84 The Mekons, 'Trevira Trousers', on *The Quality of Mercy Is Not Strnen*, Virgin, 1979.

85 Garry Bushell, 'The Gang's All Here', *Sounds*, 2 June 1979, pp. 29–31; Jon Savage, review of *Entertainment!*, *Melody Maker*, 6 October 1979, p. 32.

86 Reynolds, *Rip It Up and Start Again*, p. 121.

87 Hear also 'Dream Time' and 'In the Crowd' by The Jam. The Clash's *Cost of Living* EP (1979) came in a sleeve that parodied soap powder packaging.

88 Crass, 'Buy Now, Pay As You Go', on *Christ – The Album*, Crass Records, 1982; Annie Anxiety, *You Can't Sing The Blues While Drinking Milk* (Coventry: Tin Angel, 2012).

89 For a few examples: The Business, 'Product', Crass, 'End Result', The Epileptics, 'The 1970s Have Been Made in Hong Kong', Fatal Microbes, 'Beautiful Pictures', Patrick Fitzgerald, 'Buy Me Sell Me', The Normal, 'Warm Leatherette', Public Image Ltd, 'Public Image', Zounds, 'Knife'.

90 Vital Disorders, 'Prams' on *EP*, Lowther International, 1981.

91 Wilkinson, *Post-Punk, Politics and Pleasure in Britain*, chapter six; Simon Reynolds and Joy Press, *The Sex Revolts: Gender, Rebellion and Rock 'n' Roll* (London: Serpent's Tail, 1995), pp. 352–3.

92 Hence, 'alienation' became a staple of the music press discourse. See, for just a few examples, Morley, 'They Mean It M-a-a-a-nchester', pp. 6–7; Phil McNeill, 'Sing if You're Glad to be Grey', *NME*, 12 November 1977, p. 48; Jon Savage 'Throbbing Gristle: All the Fun of the Holocaust', *Melody Maker*, 23 December 1978, p. 27; Ian Penman review of Scritti Politti and pragVEC, *NME*, 18 November 1978, p. 31; Charles Shaar Murray, 'Coping with the 80s', *NME*, 31 March 1979, p. 35; Dave McCullough live review of Siouxsie and the Banshees, *Sounds*, 21 April 1979, p. 54; Mick Sinclair, 'Demystification', *Sounds*, 19 September 1981, p. 22.

93 Johnny Rotten to BBC Radio 1's *Rock On* programme, November 1977 (private tape). See also the interview with The Pop Group in *Dangerous Logic*, 1, 1978.

94 Interview with Poison Girls in *Anathema*, 1, 1982, pp. 31–2.

95 In the UK, punk-informed criticism of 'disco' related more to the disco-thèque as a space than disco as a musical form. The high-street disco was oft-seen to represent commercialised leisure (and punk a self-determined alternative). Where discos provided an escape from 'reality', punk-related events were deemed to engage or better reflect the indigenous culture of those attending. Where punks could find themselves under attack from 'baggy-trousered disco boys', 'straights', 'trendies' and 'normals', punk gigs offered space for the disaffected outsider or self-proclaimed rebel. Of course, the music was sometimes criticised, often in quasi-Adorno terms of functionality or inauthenticity. See, for example, the letter to *Sounds*, about being picked on by 'disco boys', 27 May 1978, p. 63; Gang of Four, 'At Home He Feels Like a Tourist'; The Molesters, 'Disco Love'; Specials, 'Night Klub' and 'Friday Night, Saturday Morning'; interview with The Raincoats in *Mental Children*, 1, 1980, pp. 14–18; Chron Gen, 'Discotheque'; Crass, 'Deadhead'; Attila the Stockbroker's 'Pap Music for Wrecks'; Garry Bushell, 'Minding Their Own', *Sounds*, 27 February 1982, pp. 18–20 and interview with The Business on *UK/DK* (1983). Typical was The Business' 'Smash the Discos', described by the band's Kev Boyce as a rejection of the disco 'dream world where everything is fine and you can forget about Thatcher'.

96 Rimmer, *Like Punk Never Happened*, pp. 7–23; Reynolds, *Rip it Up and Start Again*, pp. 361–82.

97 The quotes here come from Paul Morley, 'Pink Military: Post-modernist Pop Music', *NME*, 12 January 1980, pp. 6–7.

98 The term new romanticism eventually won-out over various other descriptors bandied around at the time: The Movement, Futurists, Blitz Kids.

99 Beyond London, equivalent scenes developed in places such as Birmingham's Rum Runner (which spawned Duran Duran) and Leeds' Adelphi Club and Warehouse (where Marc Almond and Kris Neate hosted and DJ'd). Elsewhere, Bowie/Roxy nights and gay clubs provided home for the flam-boyant, among them Pip's in Manchester and Cagney's in Liverpool. See Dave Haslam, *Life After Dark: A History of British Nightclubs and Music Venues* (London: Simon & Schuster, 2015), pp. 258–77.

100 Dave Rimmer, *The Look: New Romantics* (London: Omnibus, 2003); Andy Bennett, '"Fade to Grey": The Forgotten History of the British New Romantic Movement', in Christine Feldman-Barrett (ed.), *Lost Histories of Youth Culture* (New York: Peter Lang, 2015), pp. 51–64.

101 Robert Hewison, *Future Tense: A New Art for the Nineties* (London: Methuen, 1990).

102 Savage, 'An Enclosed World: The New Romantics', in his *Time Travel*, pp. 121–2 (originally published in *Time Out*, January–February 1981).

103 Quoted in Paul Tickell 'Top of the Fops', *NME*, 13 December 1980, pp. 11–12; Rimmer, *The Look*, p. 10.

104 Jon Savage, 'The Toytown Nihilists', in his *Time Travel*, pp. 181–3 (originally published in *The Face*, December 1985).

105 Rimmer, *The Look*, p. 10. Arguably, Duran Duran's video for 'Rio' (1983) was the apotheosis of this.

106 See Harrold Schellinck, 'Scritti Politti: "We're Gonna Be Big!"', *Vinyl*, November 1981; Reynolds, *Rip It Up and Start Again*, pp. 366–70. The sleeve designs for 'The Sweetest Girl', 'Faithless' and 'Asylums in Jerusalem' were based on the packaging for Dunhill cigarettes, Dior Eau Sauvage perfume and Courvoisier brandy.

107 Barney Hoskyns, 'Where Radical Meets Chic', *NME*, 31 October 1981, pp. 30–31. See also Kwodo Eshun, '"The Weakest Link in Every Chain, I Always Want to Find it": Green Gartside in Conversation', in Butt, Eshun and Fisher (eds.), *Post Punk Then and Now*, pp. 166–96.

108 For the dissemination of these ideas, see Ben Jackson, 'The Think-Tank Archipelago: Thatcherism and Neo-Liberalism', in Jackson and Saunders (eds.), in *Making Thatcher's Britain*, pp. 43–61.

109 Joseph Schumpeter, *The Theory of Economic Development* (Oxford: Oxford University Press, 1961).

110 Among the designers associated with the new romantic club scene were Melissa Caplan, John Galliano and Darla Jane Gilroy.

111 Paul Morley, 'It's as Easy as ABC', *NME*, 20 December 1980, p. 28.

112 Quoted in Andy Beckett, *Promised You a Miracle: UK 80–82* (London: Allen Lane, 2015), p. 192.

113 Quoted in Adrian Thrills, 'Spandau Ballet: A Solar Eclipse on the Social Calendar', *NME*, 1 August 1981, pp. 25–7.

114 The Ruts, 'In a Rut' b/w 'H-Eyes', People Unite, 1979.

115 See also 'H-Eyes' and 'Love in Vain'.

116 'Savage Circle' was a rumination on life's brutality included on The Ruts, *The Crack*, Virgin, 1979.

117 Link, *Love in Vain*, 261–81.

118 See Savage, *1966*, pp. 39–67. For a classic exploration of such themes in literature, and a book well-known within many a punk milieu, see Colin Wilson, *The Outsider* (London: Gollancz, 1956).

119 Robert C. Solomon, *Existentialism* (Oxford: Oxford University Press, 2004 edition).

120 Quoted in Barry Cain, 'Johnny knows he's not mad', *Record Mirror*, 11 December 1976, p. 6.

121 See Coon, 'Rotten to the Core', pp. 34–5; Tommy Vance Capital Radio interview with Rotten, 'A Punk and His Music', *Melody Maker*, 16 July 1977, pp. 9,30.

122 See, for example, Alternative's *In Nomine Patri* EP, Crass Records, 1982; Rudimentary Peni, 'Religion' booklet with *Rudimentary Peni* EP, Outer Himalayan Records, 1981. For fanzine examples, see 'This Is Religion', *Acts of Defiance*, 3, 1982, pp. 11–16; 'Church Control', *Anathema*, 1, 1982, p. 19; untitled rant, *Concrete Beaches*, 6, 1981, p. 6; 'Religious Carnage', *Toxic Grafity*, 5, 1980, p. 17. For a critique of Crass' take on religion, see *Aftermath*, 5, 1980, p. 8.

123 See, for example, 'David Tibet' in Neal (ed.), *Tape Delay*, pp. 209–11; Current 93, 'The Mystical Body of Christ in Chorazaim', *Nature Unveiled*, L.A.Y.L.A.H., 1984.

124 The Damned, 'Anti-Pope', on *Machine Gun Etiquette*, Chiswick, 1979; The Blood, *Megalomania* EP, No Future, 1983.

125 Coon, 'Public Image', *Sounds*, 22 July 1978, pp. 14–15.

126 Alternative TV, 'Life' b/w 'Love Lies Limp', Deptford Fun City Records, 1978. Similar reflections repeated across ATV's early works, as in 'Another Coke', 'Good Times', 'Lost in a Room' and 'Splitting in Two'. Hear also The Pigs, 'Youthanasia', released on their debut EP (New Bristol, 1977). Buzzcocks also played with existential themes, as exemplified on 'I Believe' from *A Different Kind of Tension*, United Artists, 1979.

127 Pete Haynes, *God's Lonely Men: The Lurkers* (London: Headhunter Books, 2007). See also Haynes' *Malayan Swing* (London: London Books, 2009), a fine 'outsider' novel. For Robertson, see his *White Stuff* fanzine and Genesis P-Orridge's 1977 essay reproduced in the sleevenotes to Alternative TV with Genesis P-Orridge, *The Industrial Sessions*, Overground Records, 1996.

128 See also Vi Subversa talking about existential pain in Graham Lock, 'Poison Girls Come Out to Play', *NME*, 24 November 1979, p. 60 and Colin Latter from Flux of Pink Indians suggesting 'I believe more in a simple kind of existentialism' to Barney Hoskyns in 'A Constant State of Punk', *NME*, 26 September 1981, p. 51.

129 Jon Savage, 'Introduction', in Deborah Curtis and Jon Savage (eds.), *So This Is Permanence: Ian Curtis Joy Division Lyrics and Notebooks* (London: Faber & Faber, 2014), p. xxvii.

130 Ian Curtis, Handwritten Note, in Curtis and Savage (eds.), *So This Is Permanence*, p. 216.

131 Paul Morley and Adrian Thrills, 'Don't Walk Away in Silence', *NME*, 14 June 1980, pp. 38–40; Jon Savage, Review of *Unknown Pleasures*, *Melody Maker*, 21 July 1979, p. 27.

132 Quoted in Savage, 'Joy Division: Someone Takes These Dreams Away', in his *Time Travel*, p. 366.

133 'Editorial', *Dangerous Logic*, 1, 1978, p. 2; Worley, 'One Nation Under the Bomb', pp. 65–83.

134 David Stubbs, *Future Days: Krautrock and the Building of Modern Germany* (London: Faber & Faber, 2014), p. 435

135 See Paul Morley's feature on Postcard Records, *NME*, 4 October 1980, pp. 24–5.

136 Robert Smith was a keen reader of modern literature. The run of albums, from *Three Imaginary Boys* (1979) through *Seventeen Seconds* (1980), *Faith* (1981) and *Pornography* (1982), mined a deep trough of existential angst.

137 The Pop Group, 'Trap' on *We Are Time*, Rough Trade, 1980; Paul Rambali, 'The Pop Group', *NME*, 30 September 1978, pp. 7–8.

138 GBH, *No Survivors* EP, Clay, 1982; The Exploited, 'Attack' b/w 'Alternatives', Secret Records, 1982.

139 The Partisans, 'Blind Ambition', on *Blind Ambition* EP, Cloak & Dagger Records, 1983.

140 For a fictional account, see Nick Blinko, *Primal Screamer* (Oakland: PM Press, 2012). For an overview of Rudimentary Peni, see Glasper, *The Day the Country Died*, pp. 81–8.

141 Quoted in Allan Jones, 'Rotten', p. 52. See also Ingham, 'Welcome to the (?) Rock Special', pp. 22–7; Nick Kent, 'Never Mind the Sex Pistols, Here Comes the Wrath of Sid', *NME*, 17 December 1977, pp. 22–3, 50; Vermorel (eds.), *The Sex Pistols*, pp. 153–8. For a biography of Vicious, see Alan Parker, *Sid Vicious: No-one is Innocent* (London: Orion, 2007).

142 The The emerged from the more experimental side of the punk diaspora. Prior to *Soul Mining* (1983), an unreleased album was provisionally titled 'The Pornography of Despair'. Hear also Matt Johnson's solo LP, *Burning Blue Soul* (1981) on 4AD.

143 Giovanni Dadomo, 'The Rotten Interview', *Sounds*, 27 August 1977, pp. 16–18.

144 Jah Wobble, interviewed on *Punk in '76: From SEX to the Sex Pistols*, directed by Mark Sloper and Alan Byron (2013).

145 Sex Pistols, 'Anarchy in the UK', on Granada TV's *So It Goes* (1976).

5 Who Needs a Parliament? Punk and Politics

1 Sleevenotes to Poison Girls/Crass, 'Persons Unknown' b/w 'Bloody Revolutions', Crass Records, 1980 (spelling as in the original). Bennett was one of those arrested in the persons unknown case.

2 Worley, 'Shot by Both Sides', 333–54.

3 Allan Jones, 'Rotten!', *Melody Maker*, 4 June 1977, pp. 8–9, 52.

4 Parsons, 'Sten Guns in Knightsbridge', p. 22; Vivien Goldman, 'Siouxsie Sioux who R U?', *Sounds*, 3 December 1977, pp. 26–7; Clarke, 'Union Jacks? ...', p. 28.

5 Paul Morley, 'Tartan Terror for the 90s', *NME*, 14 April 1979, p. 48; Lynn Hanna, 'Into the Valley of the Voodoo Doll', *NME*, 15 August 1981, p. 44.

6 Tony Parsons, 'Around the World in Eighty Daze', *NME*, 30 July 1977, pp. 18–19.

7 Red Wedge was a campaign to engage young people with politics and mobilise support for the Labour Party in opposition to Margaret Thatcher. See Rachel, *Walls Come Tumbling Down*, pp. 383–446.

8 For Rotten, listen to the recording of Sex Pistols live at Chelmsford prison, 17 September 1976. For Strummer, see Coon, *1988: Punk Rock Explosion*, pp. 73–4.

9 There were limits to this. A rather unscientific but entertaining *Sounds* poll of musicians (5 May 1979) found most 'rock 'n' rollers' and nearly all 'punk rockers' intended to vote Labour in 1979. Among others, the article quoted Joe Strummer, Jimmy Pursey, Mensi and The Ruts, Generation X, Gang of Four, The Mekons, UK Subs and The Members in support of Labour. Of those asked, only Dave Greenfield of The Stranglers committed to the Conservatives.

10 Evan Smith and Matthew Worley (eds.), *Against the Grain: The British Far Left from 1956* (Manchester: Manchester University Press, 2014).

11 Rich Cross, 'British Anarchism and the End of Thatcherism', in Smith and Worley (eds.), *Against the Grain*, pp. 133–52.

12 Crossley, *Networks of Sounds*, pp. 163–90.

13 Walker, *Left Shift: Radical Art in the 1970s Britain*, pp. 1–20.

14 Walsh, 'The Very Angry Clash', p. 6.

15 'Politics', on The Damned, *Music For Pleasure*, Stiff Records, 1977.

16 The following two paragraphs draw from John Hoyland, 'How Do Music and Socialism Connect?', *Comment*, 11 June 1977, pp. 200–2; Ian Walker, 'Whole Lotta Shakin' Goin' On', *The Leveller*, July–August 1977, pp. 18–20; Simon Frith, 'Beyond the Dole Queue: The Politics of Punk', *Village Voice*, 24 October 1977, pp. 77–9.

17 It is not clear what film this was. Julien Temple's sister, Nina Temple, was in the CPGB (and later become its general secretary), so it may have been *Sex Pistols No. 1* (1977), a 25-minute short comprised of TV and live footage from 1976–77.

18 Phil McNeill, 'Who Is Cornelius Cardew?', *NME*, 10 September 1977, pp. 11–12. Cardew also wrote an article on punk for *Cogs and Wheels*, the Maoist journal of the Progressive Cultural Association.

19 'The Politics of Punk', *Young Socialist*, 7 January 1978, p. 5; Letter from T. Broadbent, *Challenge*, June–July 1977, p. 2.

20 Letter from Paul Wilson, *Challenge*, July 1977, p. 2.

21 *Challenge*, August–September 1977, p. 11 and November–December, 1977, p. 3.

22 Dennis Dworkin, *Cultural Marxism in Post War Britain: History, the New Left and the Origins of Cultural Studies* (Durham, NC: Duke University Press, 1997); John Callaghan, *The Far Left in British Politics* (Oxford: Blackwell, 1987).

23 Letters, *NME*, 11 September 1976, p. 50. Saunders' co-authors were Peter Bruno, Dave Courts, Angela Follett, Roger Huddle, Mike Stradler and Jo Wreford.

24 *Socialist Worker*, 2 October 1976, p. 11.

25 See *Temporary Hoarding*, 8, 1979; Steve Clarke, 'Master-minding the Militant Roadshow', *NME*, 31 March 1979, pp. 18, 46.

26 Carnivals were also held in Manchester, Edinburgh, Cardiff and Harwich. A second London event, at Brockwell Park, took place in September 1978. A final carnival took place in Leeds in 1981.

27 Angus Mackinnon and Charles Shaar Murray, 'RAR: It's Number One, It's Top of the Agit Props', *NME*, 24 March 1979, pp. 24–5, 52. We should note that Ian Goodyer estimates that RAR constituted between sixty and seventy branches by 1979 (Goodyer, *Crisis Music*, p. 12).

28 Widgery, *Beating Time*, p. 62; Goodyer, *Crisis Music*, p. 12.

29 Rachel, *Walls Come Tumbling Down*, pp. 215–26.

30 *Sounds*, 12 January 1980, p. 3, reporting on RAR organising Rock Against Thatcher events.

31 Renton, *When We Touched the Sky*, p. 11.

32 ibid, pp. 74–95. Beyond Clapton's prejudice, RAR also responded to David Bowie's controversial allusions to fascism and the ugly spectacle of reggae bands being jeered at the annual Reading festival. See John Street, *Music & Politics*, pp. 80–1.

33 *Socialist Worker*, 2 October 1976, p. 11

34 Walsh, 'The Very Angry Clash', p. 5. Simonon and Rotten, not to mention Paul Cook, ATV's Mark Perry, Crass' Steve Ignorant and many others, boasted of skinhead pasts to explain the reggae connections.

35 Miles, 'Eighteen Flight Rock', p. 14; Parsons, 'Sten Guns in Knightsbridge', p. 22'; Charles Shaar Murray, 'The Social Rehabilitation of the Sex Pistols', *NME*, 6 August 1977, pp. 23–6; Vivien Goldman, 'Jah Punk: New Wave Digs Reggae OK?', *Sounds*, 3 September 1977, pp. 23–7.

36 Quoted in Miles, 'Eighteen Flight Rock', p. 14; Don Letts, *Culture Clash: Dread Meets Punk Rockers* (London: SAF Publishing, 2007); Mark Perry interview with Letts, 'Black–White', *Sniffin' Glue*, 7, 1977, pp. 8–10.

37 The Members and The Ruts proved particularly adept; the less said about Generation X's 'Wild Dub' the better. For other examples, covering or incorporating dub, reggae or ska, hear Alternative TV ('Love Lies Limp'), Angelic Upstarts ('I Understand'), Blitz ('Nation on Fire'), Case ('Oh'), Dead Man's Shadow ('Greed'), The Fits ('Peace and Quiet'), 4-Skins ('Plastic Gangster', 'Seems To Me'), Newtown Neurotics ('Newtown People'), Peter and the Test Tube Babies ('Trapper Ain't Got A Bird'), Stiff Little Fingers ('Johnny Was', 'Bloody Dub' and 'Roots, Radicals, Rockers and Reggae'), Subhumans ('Human

Error'). We could also include Bauhaus' 'Bela Lugosi's Dead' b/w 'Boys', Small Wonder Records, 1979, for proto-gothic dub.

38 Dick Hebdige, 'Aftershock: From Punk to Pornification to "Let's Be Facebook Frendz!!"', in Subcultures Network (ed.), *Subcultures, Popular Music and Social Change* (Newcastle: Cambridge Scholars, 2014), pp. 271–3.

39 Several punk, post-punk and, of course, 2-Tone bands comprised multiracial or non-white line-ups – among them Alien Kulture, Anti-Nowhere League, Basement 5, Bow Wow Wow, Demob, Hagar the Womb, Killing Joke, Magazine, Rip Rig and Panic, Southern Death Cult, UK Decay and X-Ray Spex. See also Bradford's Apathy Collective and Jayna Brown, '"Brown Girl in the Ring": Poly Styrene, Annabella Lwin and the Politics of Anger', *Journal of Popular Music Studies*, 23:4 (2011), 455–78.

40 Stephen Duncombe and Maxwell Tremblay, 'White Riot?', in idem (eds.), *White Riot*, pp. 1–17. The Clash's 'White Riot' and '(White Man) in Hammersmith Palais' are two good examples; The Stranglers' 'I Feel Like a Wog' a more cumbersome one.

41 Roger Sabin, '"I Won't Let That Dago By": Rethinking Punk and Racism", in Sabin (ed.), *Punk Rock: So What?*, pp. 199–218. Sabin's article is named after a line from Adam and the Ants' 'Puerto Rican'.

42 See Thrills' review of The Clash live at Guildford Civic Hall, 48 *Thrills*, 4, 1977.

43 Goldman, 'Siouxsie Sioux, Who RU?', pp. 26–7.

44 RAR letter to *Socialist Worker*, 9 April 1977, p. 12. For the breadth of RAR activity, see *Temporary Hoarding*. We should note, too, that punk and reggae acts played together outside of RAR as well as within.

45 As Roger Sabin has revealed, there were examples of bands claiming to only play RAR gigs because they were paid or because they were asked. See Sabin, '"I Won't Let That Dago By"', p. 206.

46 Savage, *England's Dreaming*, p. 483.

47 Parsons and Burchill, 'Dedicated Followers of Fascism', p. 11.

48 Explicitly anti-NF songs included 'Don't Back the Front' by The Desperate Bicycles; 'National Front' by The Pigs; 'Fuck the Front' by 2.3. The two singles with the RAR/ANL slogan were Crisis, 'White Youth' b/w 'UK '79', Ardkor Records, 1979; Angelic Upstarts, 'Kids on the Street' b/w 'The Sun Never Shines', EMI, 1979. For fanzines, see *Flicks*, 4, with its 'Smash Fascism' cover and *Guttersnipe* (1978–80), a Telford fanzine with links to the local RAR club. The band China Street also released the single 'Rock Against Racism', EMI, 1978, while Virgin issued a 1980 compilation album called *RAR's Greatest Hits* featuring Stiff Little Fingers, The Members, X-Ray Spex and, of course, the Tom Robinson Band.

49 Quoted in Mackinnon and Murray, 'RAR', pp. 24–5, 52.

50 Douglas Pearce, 'Crisis', *Temporary Hoarding*, 8, 1979, p. 6.

51 *Dry Rot*, 1, 1979, pp. 5–7.

52 'Militant' was an early, unreleased song; 'White Youth' b/w 'UK78', Ardkor Records, 1979; 'Red Brigades', *Hymns of Faith*, Ardkor Records, 1980.

53 See, for example, *Sounds*, 25 March 1978, for an anti-racism special issue.

54 See, for example, Helen Reddington's discussion of Brighton punk in *The Lost Women of Rock Music*, pp. 84–8.

55 Chris Brazier, 'One Love, One Aim, One Destiny', *Melody Maker*, 30 September 1978, pp. 37–9.

56 See, for example, *Guttersnipe* fanzine, the Rock Against Sexism campaign (see Chapter 6) or The Passage, 'Troops Out' b/w 'Hip Rebels', Night & Day, 1981.

57 *Socialist Worker*, 16 December 1978, p. 10; *Red Rebel*, January–February, 1979, pp. 4–5.

58 Gavin Butt, 'Being in a Band: Art School Experiment and the Post-Punk Commons', in Butt, Eshun and Fisher, *Post Punk Then and Now*, pp. 57–83.

59 Brian Case, 'Angels with Dirty Faces', *NME*, 11 March 1978, pp. 32–3. Despite playing for RAR and touring with The Cimarons, Sham 69 still came in for criticism: *Temporary Hoarding*, 5, 1978; Terry Allcock, 'The Sham in Sham 69', *Socialist Worker*, 25 November 1978, p. 10.

60 David Brazil, 'Spittin' Hate at the Future of Rock 'n' Roll', *The Leveller*, October 1979, pp. 18–19; interview with Mark Perry, *Temporary Hoarding*, 5, 1978; Lucy Toothpaste, 'Wouldn't You Like to Rip Him to Shreds?' [Adam and the Ants] and interview with Jimmy Pursey, *Temporary Hoarding*, 6, 1978. On 2-Tone, see *Temporary Hoarding*, 12, 1980, pp. 8–9.

61 Quoted in Ian Penman, 'Between Innocence and Forbidden Knowledge', *NME*, 19 August 1978, pp. 7–8.

62 Savage makes this point well in *England's Dreaming*, p. 484. See also *Temporary Hoarding*, 4, 1977, pp. 2–3; Mackinnon and Murray, 'RAR', pp. 24–5, 52; Brazil, 'Spittin' Hate', pp. 18–19; idem, 'Gatecrashers', *The Leveller*, November 1979, pp. 26–7. For an example of someone complaining about RAR defining punk's politics, see letter from Mark Adams (Swansea), *NME*, 2 December 1978, p. 66.

63 'Jaws', *Sounds*, 22 July 1978, p. 10; 'Nazis Firebomb London Rock Venues', *NME*, 22 July 1978, p. 3; Renton, *When We Touched the Sky*, pp. 131–5; Rachel, *Walls Come Tumbling Down*, pp. 112–13.

64 'Jaws', *Sounds*, 3 November 1979, p. 10; 'Cut Out the Aggro', *Melody Maker*, 3 November 1979, p. 3.

65 *Big Flame*, June 1977, p. 10 (Strummer); *Temporary Hoarding*, 5, 1978 (Pursey); Steve Clarke, 'The Rise of the Ruts', *NME*, 14 July 1979, pp. 7–8 (Owen).

66 This was also the case in *Temporary Hoarding*, where letter writers asked about RAR's politics and links to the SWP. For one example, see letter from

Chesham City Rocker in No. 5, 1978. 'We know you're socialist. But how far do you go? How tied up in the SWP are you?'

67 Paul Morley, 'Chaos and Confusion', *NME*, 22 July 1978, pp. 7–8. Similar criticism – balanced by recognition of the carnival and the importance of the preceding march – was made by Simon Frith and Chris Brazier in 'Play Power '78', *Melody Maker*, 30 September 1978, pp. 37–9.

68 Rick Joseph, 'Nazi Hordes Foiled', *NME*, 28 April 1979, p. 59.

69 *Temporary Hoarding*, 2, 1977.

70 *Temporary Hoarding*, 5, 1978. For this Perry was rebuked by Tony Parsons: 'Listen, mate, the Left didn't start these altercations. The Airfix-inhaling one seems totally oblivious as to what would be the fate of Black people in this country ... if the National Front ever got to power. Perry should get down on his knees in gratitude to the Left. All we are doing is defending. What are YOU doing, Mark?' (*NME*, 25 March, 1978, pp. 25–6).

71 Lindsey Boyd, 'Alternativevision', *Sounds*, 24 December 1977, p. 12.

72 Crass, 'White Punks on Hope', *Stations of the Crass*, Crass Records, 1979. See also, for the adoption of Crass' argument, *Cobalt Hate*, 3, p. 11; *New Crimes*, 4, 1981, pp. 10–11; *Toxic Grafitty*, 4, 1979, p. 6.

73 See, for example, Frank Worrall, 'Anarchy Lives on Radio Crass', *Melody Maker*, 20 November 1982, p. 5.

74 *Kill Your Pet Puppy*, 1, 1980, pp. 13–15. For Poison Girls, see interview in *New Crimes*, 5, 1982, pp. 6–9.

75 Crass, 'Bloody Revolutions' b/w Poison Girls, 'Persons Unknown', Crass Records, 1980.

76 *Big Flame*, August 1979, p. 11. The conference resolved that regional repre-sentation was essential. Quarterly policy-making conferences were to be held henceforth, at which delegates from all over the country would make decisions to direct the RAR national organisation without curbing local autonomy.

77 *Big Flame*, November 1977, p. 10. A similar issue was raised in Brighton, where feminists intervened against the sexism of the Fabulous Poodles. See Lyndsey Cooper, 'Rock Around the Cock', *The Leveller*, October 1979, pp. 10–12.

78 Graham Lock, 'Rock Against Conferences', *NME*, 16 December 1978, p. 11; Rachel, *Walls Come Tumbling Down*, pp. 81–4.

79 For example, see letters in *Sounds*, 5 May 1979, p. 48. Also Renton, *When We Touched the Sky*, p. 135. For young NF kids going to the carnival to watch the bands, see Ian Walker, 'A Quiet Day at the Match', in Barker (ed.), *The Other Britain*, p. 231.

80 Quoted in Reddington, *The Lost Women of Rock Music*, p. 85. See also the interview with Redskins in *Artificial Life*, 9, 1984, pp. 9–10.

81 Red Saunders in *The Leveller*, January 1977, pp. 12–13, cited in Street, *Music & Politics*, p. 93.

82 Robb, *Death to Trad Rock*, pp. 8–14. We could also point to bands such as the Anti-Social Workers and Burial, who had ties to Red Action, and to Easterhouse and McCarthy, who included Revolutionary Communist Party members.

83 This took place in the music press, between bands and in political journals. See, for example, Noel Halifax, 'The Sound of Struggle, *Socialist Review*, March 1983, pp. 27–8. For Rough Trade, see Taylor, *Document and Eyewitness*, pp. 126–7.

84 For a semi-official history of RAC, see Robert Forbes and Eddie Stampton, *When the Storm Breaks: Rock Against Communism, 1979–93* (London: Forbes/Stampton, 2014).

85 Shaffer, 'The Soundtrack of Neo-Fascism', 458–82; Matthew Worley and Nigel Copsey, 'White Youth: The Far Right, Punk and British Youth Culture, 1977–87', *Journalism, Media and Cultural Studies*, 9 (2016), 27–47.

86 Eddy Morrison, 'Don't Condemn Pop!', *Spearhead*, April, 1981, p. 20.

87 Reynolds, *Shock and Awe*, pp. 547–53.

88 Letter from Eddy Morrison to *Sounds*, 1 April 1977. My thanks go to Jon Savage for providing a copy of the letter. At the time, Morrison was national organiser of a small right-wing faction called the British National Party. This had fused into the NF by 1978.

89 'Gang of Three/Quarters', *Temporary Hoarding*, 9, 1977, pp. 11–14.

90 Interview with Alan Peace of The Ventz, *British News*, September 1978, pp. 6–7.

91 According to one report, Joe Pearce claimed ten bands had affiliated to RAC by 1979, though some of those listed later denied the association. See Garry Bushell, 'Rock Against Cretinism', *Sounds*, 10 March 1979, p. 10; Brazil 'Spittin' Hate', pp. 18–19.

92 Vivien Goldman, 'Seeing Red at RAC', *Melody Maker*, 25 August 1979, p. 9; Mark Ellen, 'No Fun with the Front', *NME*, 25 August 1979, p. 17.

93 Colin Ward and Chris Henderson, *Who Wants It?* (Mainstream: Edinburgh, 2002 edition), pp. 60–2.

94 A few examples were listed in Brazil, 'Spittin' Hate', pp. 18–19: A Crass benefit for the Southall Defence Fund in June 1979; Scritti Politti at a Stevenage RAR gig; a Crisis gig at the Albany in Deptford; the Angelic Upstarts in Wolverhampton; Sham 69 at the Rainbow Theatre.

95 Quoted in Bushell, '(Sk)In the Beginning', p. 27.

96 The mood of The Vortex was captured by The Jam on '"A" Bomb in Wardour Street', a joint A-side with 'David Watts', Polydor, 1978.

97 See Stuart's letter to *NME*, 18 March 1978, p. 62. For a run through of Skrewdriver's various line-up changes, see Joe Pearce, *Skrewdriver: The First Ten Years* (London: Skrewdriver Services, 1987).

98 For the story of Blood & Honour, the splits, murder and recriminations, see Lowles, *White Noise*, pp. 100–9. Stuart died in a car accident in 1993, by which time he had become a fêted figure in the global neo-Nazi underground.

99 *Bulldog*, 16, 1979, p. 3; *Rocking the Reds*, no number, 1982. The Skids' song 'Blood and Soil' also made it into the RAC chart (*Bulldog*, 26, 1982, p. 3).

100 Quoted in Vivien Goldman, 'Only Rock 'n' Roll?', *The Leveller*, December 1979, p. 27.

101 *Bulldog*, Nos. 21 and 27, 1981 and 1982, both p. 3.

102 Morrison, 'Don't Condemn Pop', p. 20.

103 *Bulldog*, 29, 1982, p. 3. Death in June's first single, 'Heaven Street', New European Recordings, 1981, journeyed into the gas chamber. Also featured was 'We Drive East', an account of the Third Reich's march into Russia.

104 *Bulldog*, 33, 1983, p. 3. The gig was held in Stratford.

105 See, for example, 'Silly Boys Lose Prestige Gig', *NME*, 5 May 1979, p. 5. For Red Action, see *We Are … Red Action* (London: Red Action, undated).

106 For an early expression of skinhead anti-fascism, see Garry Bushell, 'Putting the Boot on the Left Foot', *Sounds*, 9 September 1978, p. 11. For the 1980s, see fanzines such as *Hard as Nails*, *Boots & Braces*, *Bovver Boot*, *Skinhead Havoc*, *Stand Up and Spit*, *Street Feeling* and *Tell Us the Truth*.

107 See, for example, *Spy Kids* from Glasgow.

108 Turner, *Cockney Reject*, pp. 58–62.

109 As well as *Blood & Honour*, see *British Oi!*, *Last Chance*, *White Noise*.

110 Martin Langebach and John Raabe, 'Inside the Extreme Right: The "White Power" Music Scene', in Andrea Mammone, Emmanuel Godin, Brian Jenkins (eds.), *Varieties of Right-Wing Extremism in Europe* (Abingdon: Routledge, 2013), pp. 249–64; Timothy S. Brown, 'Subcultures, Pop Music and Politics: Skinheads and "Nazi Rock" in England and Germany', *Journal of Social History*, 38:1 (2004), 157–78; John Cotter, 'Sounds of Hate: White Power Rock and Roll and the Neo-Nazi Skinhead Subculture', *Terrorism and Political Violence*, 11:2 (1999), 111–40; Ana Raposo, '30 Years of Agitprop: The Representation of "Extreme" Politics in Punk and Post-Punk Music Graphics in the United Kingdom from 1978 to 2008' (London University of the Arts, PhD thesis, 2012).

111 Lowles, *White Riot*, pp. 220–33.

112 Diary entry for 29 November 1976, in Vermorel and Vermorel, *The Sex Pistols*, p. 28. See also the interview with Richmond in Savage, *The England's Dreaming Tapes*, pp. 426–40.

113 Savage, *London's Outrage*, 1, 1976, p. 8–12.

114 Stéphanie François, 'The Euro-Pagan Scene: Between Paganism and Radical Right', *Journal for the Study of Radicalism*, 1:2 (2007), 35–54; Alexander

Reed, *Assimilate*, pp. 185–205. Above the Ruins' name evoked Julius Evola's *Men Among the Ruins* (1953). Evola's ideas began to exert a notable influence among certain far-right circles in the early1980s.

115 As Sandbrook has noted, quoting *The Times'* fear that the 'vanguard of anarchy is loose in the world', the term 'anarchy' formed part of the media's crisis-ridden lexicon during the mid-1970s. Sandbrook, *Seasons in the Sun*, p. 125.

116 Fred Vermorel, 'Blowing Up The Bridges So There Is No Way Back', in Gorman, Thorp and Vermorel, *Joining the Dots*, pp. 18–27.

117 Kent, 'Meet the Col Tom Parker of the Blank Generation', pp. 26–7.

118 Jones, 'Rotten!', p. 52.

119 Russ Bestley, 'Big A Little A: The Graphic Language of Anarchy', in Dines and Worley (eds.), *The Aesthetic of Our Anger*, pp. 43–66.

120 Mick Farren, 'Fascism in the UK '77', *NME*, 22 January 1977, pp. 20–1. See also the questions put to McLaren and Rotten on *Nationwide* (12 November 1976) and the criticism of punk in *News Line*, 3 December 1976, p. 2.

121 Sex Pistols press handout, April 1976, cited in Savage, *England's Dreaming*, p. 162.

122 Ingham, 'The Sex Pistols', pp. 10–11.

123 Quoted in Chris Salewicz, 'Really Nice Guys', *NME*, 9 September 1978, pp. 23–5, 57.

124 For an enlightening discussion of anarchy's different meanings in a punk context, see Jim Donaghey, 'Bakunin Brand Vodka: An Exploration into Anarchist-Punk and Punk-Anarchism', *Anarchist Developments in Cultural Studies*, 1 (2013), 138–70.

125 Rimbaud, 'The Last of the Hippies', pp. 3–13; Cross, 'The Hippies Now Wear Black', 25–44; Rich Cross, '"There Is No Authority But Yourself": The Individual and the Collective in British Anarcho-Punk', *Music and Politics*, 4:2 (2010), 1–20; Berger, *The Story of Crass*, pp. 75–95.

126 Russell Southwood and Tony Nicholls, 'Crass', *The Leveller*, April 1979, pp. 24–5. The band's emblem was designed by Dave King to represent various forms of repression. The symbol is enveloped by snakes eating their own tails.

127 Sleevenotes to the first pressing of *The Feeding of the Five Thousand*, Small Wonder Records, 1978. Crass later issued the song as a single – 'Reality Asylum' b/w 'Shaved Women' – on their own Crass Records imprint in 1979.

128 We should note that Dial House had existed as a collective and creative space long before 1977.

129 Vi Subversa speaks of selling *Freedom* in an interview with *Anarchy*, 34, 1981, pp. 5–11.

130 Rimbaud, 'The Last of the Hippies', p. 11.

131 This was the term used in the 1979 Conservative Party manifesto.

132 Rimbaud, 'The Last of the Hippies', pp. 10–11.

133 Mick Duffield, 'A Nightmare Ends …', in Crass, *A Series of Shock Slogans and Mindless Token Tantrums*, p. 20–3.

134 Crass, *Yes Sir, I Will*, Crass Records, 1983; Crass, *You're Already Dead* (Epping: Dial House, 1984) and the EP of the same name on Crass Records; Crass essay in *Fight Back*, 1, 1984, pp. 6–9; Rimbaud, *Shibboleth*, pp. 262–9.

135 McKay, *Senseless Acts of Beauty*, pp. 73–101.

136 Winston Smith, 'This Is Squat We Want', *Sounds*, 1 January 1983, p. 13. The initial plan was to squat the Rainbow Theatre, but the venue was switched at the last minute.

137 National Archives, PREM 19/1380, 'Forged Recording …' (1983–84); Rimbaud, *Shibboleth*, pp. 250–5; Martin Cloonan, '"I Fought the Law": Popular Music and British Obscenity Law', *Popular Music*, 14:3 (1995), 349–63.

138 Cross, 'British Anarchism and the End of Thatcherism', p. 136.

139 Rich Cross, '"Take the Toys from the Boys": Gender, Generation and the Anarchist Intent in the Work of Poison Girls', *Punk & Post-Punk*, 3:2 (2015), 117–45.

140 The Mob emerged from Somerset in the late 1970s, playing free festivals and relocating to London in 1981.

141 Anxiety, *You Can't Sing the Blues*, pp. 95–129.

142 Steve Lake, *Zounds Demystified* (London: Active/Bev, 2013).

143 See, for a few fanzine examples, 'Slaughter of the Innocent', *Fack*, 6, 1981, pp. 25–7; 'Blood Sports', *Guilty of What*, 3, 1982, p. 32; 'Animal Liberation', *New Crimes*, 5, 1981, p. 22; Steve Hansell, 'The Animal's Film', *Tender Mercy*, 1, 1982, p. 7.

144 Alistair Livingstone, 'With a Little Help From My Friends', *Punk Lives*, 6, 1983, p. 16.

145 See *Pigs for Slaughter*, issues 1–3, 1981–82. For a semi-fictional but evocative description of the Autonomy Centre, see Blinko, *The Primal Screamer*, pp. 82–5. Fanzines associated with the centre included *Book of Revelations*, *Enigma*, *Paroxysm Fear*, *Pigs for Slaughter* and *Precautions Essentielles Pour La Bonne*. Numerous bands formed – or were dreamt up – at the centre, with Hagar the Womb among the most notable.

146 Al A [Alistair Livingstone], 'Punk Lives in the Strangest Places', *Punk Lives*, 4, 1983, pp. 28–9; Chris Low, 'The Centro Iberico August 1982: A Spectator's Point of View', in Gregory Bull and Mickey 'Penguin' (eds.), *Not Just Bits of Paper* (Charleston: Perdam Babylonis Nomen, 2015), pp. 166–71.

147 Gary Cavanagh, *Bradford's Noise of the Valleys* (New Romney: Bank House Book, 2009); *Knee Deep in Shit* fanzine, first published 1981 and linked to the 1in12 Club.

148 *Acts of Defiance*, 4, 1982, pp. 13–14.

149 Francis Stewart, 'The Outcasts: Punk in Northern Ireland during the Troubles', in Gregory Bull and Mike Dines (eds.), *Tales from the Punkside* (Portsmouth: Itchy Monkey, 2014), pp. 47–64.

150 Tony Puppy, 'Apocalypse Now, Part 1', *Kill Your Pet Puppy*, 2, 1980, pp. 4–6.

151 Mike Diboll, 'Exit-Stance', *Toxic Grafity*, 5, 1980, p. 31 (spelling as in the original). Issue number '5' was actually the third issue of the fanzine. It had previously been titled *No Real Reason*.

152 'Life Today ... Is It Really Life?', *Anathema*, 1, 1982, pp. 17–18. 'Anarchy in the UK Again', *Acts of Defiance*, 3 (1982), p. 5; 'Anarchy: A Way of Life Not Death', *FACK*, 5, 1980, p. 19.

153 Quotes taken from *Kick*, Nos. 3 and 4, 1980–82. For 'ranters', see Jerome Friedman, *Blasphemy, Immorality and Anarchy: Ranters and the English Revolution* (Athens: Ohio University Press, 1987); Christopher Hill, *The World Turned Upside Down: Radical Ideas during the English Revolution* (London: Penguin, 1991, originally published 1972).

154 Conflict, *To a Nation of Animal Lovers* EP, Corpus Christi, 1983.

155 Robert Dellar, *Splitting in Two: Mad Pride and Punk Rock Oblivion* (London: Unkant Press, 2014); Gibson, *A Punk Rock Flashback*, pp. 130–88; Joseph Porter, *Genesis to Revelation: The Curse of Zounds Demystified* (Downwarde Spiral/Bedsit Press, 2012), pp. 99–115; Bob Short, *Trash Can: Tales of Lowlife Losers and Rock & Roll Sleaze* (London: Lulu, 2007). See also Gregory Bull, *Perdam Babylonis Nomen* (Charleston: Gregory Bull, 2012).

156 For an excellent overview, see Rich Cross, '"Stop the City Showed Another Possibility": Mobilisation and Movement in Anarcho-Punk', in Dines and Worley (eds.), *The Aesthetic of Our Anger*, pp. 117–56.

157 Radicals in the London Greenpeace group issued the leaflet calling for a Stop the City protest in the summer of 1983, as detailed in Cross, '"Stop the City Showed Another Possibility"', pp. 122–4.

158 'Stop the City?', *Peace News*, 22 July 1983, p. 18 and 16 September 1983, p. 9; 'Stop the City', *Freedom*, 16 July 1983, p. 7 and 27 August 1983, p. 7; 'Together we can Stop "The City" Sept 29th', London: London Greenpeace, 1983.

159 Cross, '"Stop the City Showed Another Possibility"', pp. 117–56; 'Mob Goes on Rampage in City Centre', *Eastern Daily Press*, undated clipping (Norwich); *Paid in Full*, 1, 1984 (report of Birmingham 'Reclaim the City' protest), p. 8.

160 Penny Rimbaud, 'Stop the City!', *Punk Lives*, 10, 1983, pp. 19–22.

161 'Stop the Cities', *Peace News*, 13 April 1984, p. 3; *Stop the City, London 29.3.1984*, directed by Mick Duffield and Andy Palmer (1984).

162 See discussion in Cross, '"Stop the City Showed Another Possibility"', pp. 117–56.

163 Conflict, 'Stop the City', on *Increase the Pressure*, Mortarhate, 1984. See also 'Rats' by Subhumans, which analysed the impact of the Stop the City campaign.

164 Wise and Wise, 'The End of Music', pp. 70–4.

165 'Crass', *Anarchy*, 34, 1982, pp. 4–5.

166 'Strength Through @!', *Anarchy*, 34, 1982, pp. 10–11.

167 Porter, *Genesis to Revelation*, pp. 130–1.

168 Tom Vague, 'Crass', *ZigZag*, February 1982, pp. 38–9; idem, 'Those Not So Loveable Spikey Tops', *Vague*, 14, 1983.

169 North, 'Punk Warriors', pp. 12–15; Marek Kohn, 'Punk's New Clothes', *The Face*, April 1983, pp. 16–21. See also *Kill Your Pet Puppy*, Nos. 4–6, 1981–83; *Kick*, 4, 1982; *Vague*, Nos. 12–15, 1982–84; copies of Mick Mercer's *Panache* fanzine from 1980 and the relaunched *ZigZag* in 1983, which was built around the ideas of a positive punk and the emergence of goth.

170 See, for example, Buenaventura Makhno, 'Peaceful Pro-Crass-tination', *Kill Your Pet Puppy*, 1, 1980, p. 16; 'Crass', *Pigs for Slaughter*, Pilot Issue, 1981.

171 Class War, *This Is Class War* (Stirling: AK Distribution, 1991 edition), p. 3.

172 Quoted in Bone, *Bash the Rich*, p. 119.

173 See Ian Bone's letter to *Sounds*, 26 June 1982, p. 46.

174 Bone had helped put on Crass gigs in Swansea from 1979; he also performed in bands and released records, including an EP on Conflict's Mortarhate label.

175 Sleevenotes to Conflict, *Increase the Pressure*, Mortarhate, 1984.

176 For expressions of this, see *Class War* and Bone's pre-Class War publication *Fuck Off*, pilot issue, 1982; *London CND Rally: An Anarchist Viewpoint*, pamphlet, 1983; *Like a Summer with a Thousand July's* (London: BM Blob, 1982); Riot Not to Work Collective, *We Want to Riot Not to Work: The 1981 Brixton Uprisings* (London: Riot Not to Work), 1982.

177 One Andy Martin communiqué on anti-fascism – 'There Can Be No Spectators', circa 1982 – ended with the sign off: 'Stuff Pacifism and Existential Bollocks – Put the Fucking Boot In: Hard!'

178 Parson's review is in *NME*, 24 March 1979, p. 34. See also Paul Tickell, 'The Revolution Will Not Be Hippified', *Melody Maker*, 19 January 1980, p. 13.

179 Garry Bushell, 'Obscene Oaths Do Not the Revolution Make', *Sounds*, 24 March 1979, p. 34; idem, 'The Mystic Revelations of Crasstafari', *Sounds*, 30 August 1980, pp. 18–19; idem, 'Bushell Bites Back', *Sounds*, 12 June 1982, pp. 38–9.

180 'Camera' on *Six Minute War* EP, Six Minute War, 1980; *Intensive Care*, Nos. 1 and 2, 1980; *No More Than That*, 1, 1981, pp. 2–3.

181 See X Moore's live review of Crass in Halifax, *NME*, 7 November 1981, pp. 48–9.

182 See The Exploited's 'I Believe in Anarchy', *Punk's Not Dead*, Secret Records, 1981. The title of the album was itself a riposte to Crass' 'Punk Is Dead' on *The Feeding of the Five Thousand*.

183 Special Duties, 'Bullshit Crass' b/w 'You're Doing Yourself No Good', Rondelet 1982.

184 Rimbaud, 'Last of the Hippies', pp. 4–6. See also Rimbaud's letter to *NME*, 20 February 1982, p. 50, telling X Moore [Chris Dean] to 'piss off' for suggesting Crass hid away in their 'safe' home. Moore replied, essentially calling Rimbaud a hippie in a critique along the same lines as Bushell's.

185 Sleevenotes to Conflict, 'Only Stupid Bastards Help EMI', Mortarhate, 1985.

186 Crass, *Life Amongst the Little People* (Epping: Dial House, 1978). See also *Antigen*, 1, 1982 and *Incendiary*, 1, 1984. We should note that other strands of punk culture could display similar tendencies.

187 Dale, *Anyone Can Do It*, pp. 93–108.

188 Zounds, 'Demystification' b/w 'Great White Hunter', Rough Trade, 1981.

6 Anatomy Is Not Destiny: Punk as Personal Politics I

1 Quoted in Chris Brazier, 'United They Fall', *Melody Maker*, 31 December 1977, p. 9.

2 Quoted in Parsons and Hamblett, 'Leeds: Mill City UK', *NME*, 5 August 1978, pp. 7–8.

3 Paul Tickell, 'Gang of Four', *The Leveller*, December 1979, pp. 26–7.

4 For background, see Stephen Brooke, *Sexual Politics: Sexuality, Family Planning and the British Left from the 1880s to the Present Day* (Oxford: Oxford University Press, 2011); Jodi Burkett, *Constructing Post-Imperial Britain: Britishness, 'Race' and the Radical Left in the 1960s* (Basingstoke: Palgrave Macmillan, 2013); Celia Hughes, *Young Lives on the Left: Sixties Activism and the Liberation of the Self* (Manchester: Manchester University Press, 2016); Lucy Robinson, *Gay Men and the Left in Post-War Britain: How the Personal Got Political* (Manchester: Manchester University Press, 2007); Natalie Thomlinson, *Race and Ethnicity in the Women's Movement in England, 1968–93* (Basingstoke: Palgrave Macmillan, 2016).

5 Arthur Marwick, *The Sixties: Cultural Revolution in Britain, France, Italy and the United States, c. 1958–c. 1974* (Oxford: Oxford University Press, 1998).

6 Geoff Andrews, Richard Cockett, Alan Hooper and Michael Williams (eds.), *New Left, New Right and Beyond: Taking the Sixties Seriously* (Basingstoke: Palgrave Macmillan, 1999).

7 Quoted in Morley, 'Don't Follow Leaders', pp. 9–10.

8 Quoted in Chris Salewicz, 'God What a Bummer! Stuck Here with Joe Strummer', *NME*, 3 September 1977, pp. 7–8. See also Paul Simonon's comments in Chris Salewicz, 'Clash on Tour', *NME*, 15 July 1978, pp. 27–30. Simonon claimed not to understand politics, just 'what's right and wrong'.

9 Quoted in Chris Bohn, 'Sir Keith Talks Bluntly to EEC Management Consultants', *NME*, 5 July 1980, pp. 26–7.

10 Quoted in Bushell, 'Minding Their Own', pp. 18–20.

11 The Business, 'Suburban Rebels', on *Carry on Oi!*, Secret Records, 1981. See also comments from Jam fans in Kris Needs, 'Modern Meets Real World – Hundreds Hurt', *NME*, 26 November 1977, p. 14 and such letters as to *Melody Maker*, 18 June 1978, p. 13; *NME*, 5 May 1979, p. 55; *Sounds*, 13 February 1982, pp. 62–3.

12 *Plaything*, No. 2, 1978, p. 1.

13 David Wilkinson, 'Ever Fallen in Love (With Someone You Shouldn't Have): Punk, Politics and Same-Sex Passion', *Key Words*, 13 (2015), pp. 57–76.

14 See Ingham, 'The Sex Pistols', pp. 10–11; Ingham, 'Welcome to the (?), Rock Special', pp. 22–7; Paul Simonon made the dope quote on LWT's *London Weekend Show*, 28 November 1976.

15 Quoted in Charles Shaar Murray, 'John, Paul, Steve and Sidney: The Social Rehabilitation of the Sex Pistols', *NME*, 6 August 1977, pp. 23–6

16 Emily Robinson, Camilla Schofield, Florence Sutcliffe-Braithwaite and Natalie Thomlinson, 'Telling Stories about Post-war Britain: Popular Individualism and the "Crisis" of the 1970s', *Twentieth Century British History*, 28:2 (2017), 268–304.

17 Frank Cartledge, 'Distress to Impress? Local Punk Fashion and Commodity Exchange', in Sabin (ed.), *Punk Rock: So What?*, pp. 143–53.

18 Quoted in Allan Jones, 'Scotland the Grave', *Melody Maker*, 24 September 1977, p. 17. 'Individuals rule' was the rallying cry of Sham 69's 'Red London'. For later reassertions of punk meaning to 'be an individual', see Johnny Waller, 'Join the Exploited Army', *Sounds*, 3 January 1981, pp. 11–12; Beki Bondage's letter to *Sounds*, 11 July 1981, p. 51, stating that punk had two rules: 1) no rules; 2) be individual; Paul Du Noyer, 'Rebel With a Brain' [Theatre of Hate], *NME*, 6 February 1982, pp. 22–6.

19 Malcolm McLaren, 'The Haberdasher', in PunkPistol, *SEX and Seditionaries*, pp. 4–9. See also Szymanski, 'Would You Buy a Rubber T-Shirt from This Man?', p. 11.

20 See Phil McNeill's interview with the Sex Pistols, 'Spitting into the Eye of the Hurricane', *NME*, 15 January 1977, pp. 16–17.

21 Crass, 'Big A Little A' b/w 'Nagasaki Nightmare', Crass Records, 1980; P-Orridge quoted in Chris Bohn, 'A Leak into the Future', *NME*, 25 September 1982, pp. 6–7.

22 'First Transmission' [1981], quoted in Keenan, *England's Hidden Reverse*, pp. 55–6.

23 North, 'Punk Warriors', pp. 12–15.

24 Ted Polhemus, *Streetstyle: From Sidewalk to Catwalk* (London: Thames & Hudson, 1994).

25 See the short essay in *Acts of Defiance*, 7, 1983, p. 20. 'If power cannot be exercised anywhere else, it can be exercised here, the body …'

26 Lesley Woods, 'roxex', *Brass Lip*, 1, 1979, pp. 16–17. The term 'cock rock' was reputedly first used in the US countercultural paper *Rat* in 1970.

27 See, for example, Margaret Geddes, 'Roll Over and Rock Me Baby', *Spare Rib*, May 1973, pp. 6–8; Liz Waugh and Terri Goddard, 'Love 'em and Leave 'em', *Spare Rib*, August 1975, pp. 37–9; Northern Women's Liberation Rock Band, *Manifesto* (Manchester: NWLRB, 1974). Debate was also creeping into the music press before punk broke. See 'Woman: No Longer Nigger of the World', *Melody Maker*, 3 January, 1976, p. 13. For background, see Anna Coote and Beatrix Campbell, *Sweet Freedom: The Struggle for Women's Liberation* (Oxford: Blackwell, 1982).

28 Mavis Bayton, *Frock Rock: Women Performing Popular Music* (Oxford: Oxford University Press, 1998); Marion Fulger, 'The Stepney Sisters', *Spare Rib*, May 1979, pp. 6–8. As well as countless locally organised workshops, a 'Women and Music Conference' was held in Liverpool in 1976. Leftist groups also hosted regular discussions. See, for examples, John Hoyland, 'How Do Music and Socialism Connect?', *Challenge*, 11 June 1977, pp. 200–2.

29 Women's Liberation Music Projects Group, *Sisters in Song* (WLMPG, undated), pp. 4–7.

30 Woods, 'roxex', pp. 16–17; *Jolt*, Nos. 1–3, 1977. For related arguments within the feminist press, see Sue Denim, 'Women 'n' Punk', *Spare Rib*, July 1977, pp. 48–53.

31 Lynn Hutchinson, 'Women and Punk', *Challenge*, April 1978, p. 5; Lindsey Cooper, 'Rock Around the Cock', *The Leveller*, October 1978, pp. 10–12; Simon Frith and Angela McRobbie, 'Rock and Sexuality', *Screen Education*, 29 (1978–79), pp. 3–19; Lucy Whitman, 'Women and Popular Music', *Spare Rib*, June 1981, pp. 6–8 and pp. 20–1; Sue Steward, 'Sound Barriers', *Marxism Today*, May 1982, pp. 36–7.

32 Caroline Coon, 'Punk Alphabet', *Melody Maker*, 27 November 1976, p. 33. See also Burchill and Parsons, *The Boy Looked at Johnny*, p. 74: 'Punk rock in 1976 was the first rock and roll phase *ever* not to insist that women should be picturesque topics and targets of songs; punks were too hung up on tower blocks to be power-driven cock-of-the-walk'.

33 O'Brien, *She-Bop*, pp. 131–74; Cazz Blasé, 'Writing Women Back into Punk', *The f-word* (2010).

34 One of these was Chrissie Hynde, whose memoirs recall her time in the shop. See Chrissie Hynde, *Reckless: My Life* (London: Ebury Press, 2015).

35 This was also the case at a local level, where young women created their own punk styles. So, for example, Linder took photos of Manchester punk women such as Jodi and Denise (see *Linder: Works*, pp. 17, 25).

36 Ian Cranna, 'Macho Boys Murder Their Repertoire', *NME*, 18 February 1978, p. 43; Buckley, *No Mercy*, pp. 80–100.

37 The Stranglers, 'Bring on the Nubiles', on *No More Heroes*, United Artists, 1977.

38 Phil McNeill, 'Women are Strange when You're a Strangler', *NME*, 30 April 1977, p. 35; Caroline Coon, 'Stranglers: It's Good Noose', *Melody Maker*, 14 May 1977, p. 38; Parsons, 'Locker Room Sexuality and Six Figure Rebels', pp. 7–8, 61; Chris Brazier, 'Black Side of the Stranglers', *Melody Maker*, 3 June 1978, p. 8; Salewicz, 'Really Nice Guys', pp. 23–5. For a defence, see Phil Knight, *Strangled: Identity, Status, Structure and The Stranglers* (London: Zero Books, 2015).

39 Quoted in Lucy O'Brien, 'The Woman Punk Made Me', in Sabin (ed.), *Punk Rock? So What*, pp. 194–5. For a recent critique of punk misogyny, see Maria Kouvarou, 'Deconstructing the "Bodies": Reading the Feminine Approach to the Sex Pistols', *Popular Music and Society*, 38:4 (2015), 450–65. See also, Reddington, *The Lost Women of Rock Music*, pp. 59–65.

40 For just four examples, Chris Salewicz, live review of The Adverts, *NME*, 11 June 1977, p. 44; Dave McCullough, 'Shrieks from the Groove' [review of The Raincoats], *Sounds*, 8 December 1979, p. 35; live review of The Slits by Ian Penman, *NME*, 13 January 1979, p. 35; Giovanni Dadomo, review of The Slits' *Cut*, *Sounds*, 1 September 1979, p. 33. The letter pages of *Melody Maker*, *NME* and *Sounds* regularly contained pro- and anti-feminist correspondence.

41 Caroline Coon, 'White Riot on the Road', *Melody Maker*, 25 June 1977, p. 39. See also Zoe Street Howe, *Typical Girls? The Story of The Slits* (London: Omnibus, 2009).

42 Quoted in Deanne Pearson, 'Cute, Cute, Cutesy, Goodbye', *NME*, 29 March 1980, pp. 27–30.

43 Quoted in Pearson, 'Cute, Cute', p. 29. See also, for Siouxsie Sioux, Lynn Hanna, 'Into the Valley of the Voodoo Doll', *NME*, 15 August 1981, p. 44.

44 Woods, 'roxex', p. 17. See also comments by Mary Jenner from The Mekons in the same issue of *Brass Lip* (pp. 18–21) and by The Raincoats' Vicky Aspinall in *NME*, 9 June 1979, p. 23.

45 For discussion on this, see Wilkinson, *Post-Punk, Politics and Pleasure in Britain*, chapter six; Reddington, *The Lost Women of Rock Music*, pp. 175–83; Amanda M., 'A Woman's Place Is in the Movement', *Anathema*, 1, 1982, p. 4. For a broader debate on strands within feminist politics, see Lynne Segal, *Is the Future Female? Troubled Thoughts on Contemporary Feminism* (London: Virago, 1994).

46 See Gina Birch speaking in *Brass Lip*, 1, 1979, pp. 4–7.

47 See The Slits interviewed in *Jolt*, 2, 1977, pp. 2–4; Poly Styrene interview in *Jolt*, 3 (1977), pp. 2–6; Pearson, 'Cute, Cute', pp. 27–30.

48 O'Brien, *She Bop*, pp. 131–7.

49 Brian Cogan, 'Typical Girls? Fuck Off, You Wanker! Re-evaluating The Slits and Gender Relations in Early British Punk and Post-Punk', *Women's Studies*, 4 (2012), 121–35; Helen Reddington, 'The Political Pioneers of Punk (Just

Don't mention the F-Word)', in Dines and Worley (eds.), *The Aesthetic of Our Anger*, pp. 91–116.

50 Of those listed, only Pauline Black has so far written a memoir: *Black By Design: A 2-Tone Memoir* (London: Serpent's Tail, 2011); but see also Shane Baldwin, *Last Rockers: The Vice Squad Story* (Bristol: ACM Retro, 2016).

51 Hélène Cixous, 'The Laugh of the Medusa', *Signs*, 1:4 (1976), pp. 875–93; Amy Britton, 'Harmony in Differentiation: Post Punk and *écriture féminine*', *Louder Than War*, 28 January 2015.

52 Brown, '"Brown Girl in the Ring"', 455–78.

53 For the Mo-Dettes and Gymslips' differing ideas on feminism, see Paulo Hewitt, 'Mo-Dettes Out For Fun', *Melody Maker*, 26 July 1980, p. 9 and Robbi Millar, '(Not) the Sweetest Girls', *Sounds*, 23 January 1982, p. 22, 38.

54 Reddington, *The Lost Women of Rock Music*, pp. 67–98; Robb, *The North Will Rise Again*, pp. 92–4; O'Brien, 'The Woman Punk Made Me', pp. 186–98. Women such as Karen Ablaze, Cath Carroll, Liz Naylor and Clare Wadd are among those who carried on the fanzine tradition.

55 Veit Görner and Heinrich Dietz (eds.), *Linder: Woman/Object* (Paris: Musée d'Art Moderne, 2013).

56 Paul Du Noyer, 'Militant Words in a Rock 'n' Roll Vacuum', *NME*, 5 September 1981, pp. 12–13; Frank Worrall, 'The Seduction Line', *Melody Maker*, 6 February 1982, p. 10.

57 See Linder talking to Paul Morley, 'Ludus: Strange Band. And Getting Stranger', *NME*, 17 February 1979, p. 14.

58 Linder quoted in Nice, *Shadowplayers*, p. 199.

59 O'Brien, 'The Woman Punk Made Me', p. 197. Linder's performance was also a response to the recent success of Bucks Fizz in winning the Eurovision song contest. As part of their performance, the two men in Bucks Fizz whipped off the long skirts of their two female partners, an act coinciding with the line 'If you want to see some more'.

60 Linder, 'Northern Soul', in Hoare et al., *Linder: Works*, pp. 16–47. 'Anatomy Is Not Destiny' was the b-side to 'My Cherry is in Sherry', New Hormones, 1980. A 1997 show was entitled: 'What did you do in the punk war, mummy?'

61 Cosey Fanni Tutti, *Art, Sex, Music* (London: Faber & Faber, 2017).

62 Ford, *Wreckers of Civilisation*, pp. 5.10–5.11 and, for later performances pushing to further extremes, pp. 6.30–6.33.

63 Cosey Fanni Tutti, Sleevenotes to *Time to Tell*, CTI, 2000 (written 25 May 1988), pp. 1–2. As an aside, a few other women involved in punk also featured in pornographic magazines, though none stated the same objectives as Cosey.

64 Ibid.

65 *Industrial News*, 3, 1979, p. 22: Cosey lists 'Women's Lib' as one of her dislikes.

66 Cosey Fanni Tutti, lecture at Leeds polytechnic, 19 May 1982, reprinted in *Time to Tell* sleevenotes, pp. 3–10; Steve Sutherland, 'The Creative Technology Institute', *Melody Maker*, 19 June 1982, p. 16.

67 Maria Fusco and Richard Birkett (eds.), *Cosey Complex* (London, Koenig Books, 2012); 'Girlie Magazines Featuring Cosey Fanni Tutti', *Industrial News*, 4, 1980, p. 8.

68 *Compulsion* Online interview with Cosey Fanni Tutti, www.compulsiononline. com/falbum2.htm (Accessed 29 January 2016).

69 COUM statement, c. 1975, quoted in Ford, *Wreckers of Civilisation*, p. 5.10.

70 Kathy Acker, Diamanda Galas, Lydia Lunch and Johanna Went were non-UK artists who crossed over, worked with or associated with industrial groups. See Neal (ed.), *Tape Delay*, pp. 41–9, 197–201; Re/Search, *Industrial Culture Handbook*, pp. 118–27.

71 Keenan, *England's Hidden Reverse*, pp. 121–2, and 145–9. Rogerson worked closely with Steven Stapleton of Nurse With Wound. Hear also *The Inevitable Chrystal Belle Scrodd Record*, United Dairies, 1985.

72 Reed, *Assimilate*, p. 175; Paul Hegarty, *Noise/Music* (London: Bloomsbury, 2013 edition), pp. 119–25.

73 Ian Penman, review of Rainbow in *NME*, 29 April 1978, pp. 40–1; Paul Morley's review of Judas Priest in *NME*, 18 February 1978, p. 46.

74 Martha Zenfell, 'Love Sex, Hate Sexism?', *NME*, 7 April 1979, p. 15.

75 *Big Flame*, August 1979, p. 11.

76 'Grass Roots and Brass Tacks', *Drastic Measures*, 1, 1979, p. 2.

77 RAS formed just as the 'Corrie Bill' (named after John Corrie MP) was introduced to amend the 1967 Abortion Act. The Bill was unsuccessful.

78 Angele Veltmeijer, 'Sexuality on Stage', *Drastic Measures*, 1, 1979, p. 6; Lucy Toothpaste, 'Sex & Violence & Rock & Roll', *Drastic Measures*, 3, 1980, pp. 6–7; 'Sexism in the Rock Media', *Drastic Measures*, 5, 1981, pp. 4–5; *Big Flame*, March 1981, p. 13.

79 'Grass Roots and Brass Tacks', p. 2.

80 The Raincoats discuss the problems of RAS bureaucracy in *Brass Lip*, 1, 1979, pp. 4–7.

81 'Gig Guide', *Drastic Measures*, 1, 1979, p. 8. For criticism, see Zenfell, 'Love Sex, Hate Sexism?', p. 15.

82 *Drastic Measures*, 1, 1979, p. 3.

83 Lock, 'Gabba Gabba Hegel', pp. 6–8; O'Brien, 'Can I Have a Taste of Your Ice-Cream', *Punk and Post-Punk*, 1:1 (2012), 27–40.

84 For the Gang of Four discussing gender politics, see Adrian Thrills, 'The Year of the Great Leap Four-Wards', *NME*, 20 January 1979, pp. 7–8.

85 The lyric is from 'You', the b-side to 'Anticipation', Rough Trade, 1980; O'Brien, 'Can I Have a Taste of Your Ice-Cream?', 31–3.

86 Greil Marcus, 'Suspicious Minds', in his *In the Fascist Bathroom*, pp. 151–8.

87 See the interview Lynden Barber, 'Sex Without Stress', *Melody Maker*, 12 June 1982, p. 8. See also, Graham Lock, 'Come On Out and Do the Sexual Dance', *NME*, 10 November 1979, p. 19.

88 *The Leveller*, 7–20 August 1981, pp. 12–13.

89 Au Pairs, 'Come Again', on *Playing With a Different Sex*, Human Records, 1981.

90 Quoted in Reynolds, *Rip It Up and Start Again*, p. 214.

91 Lynden Barber, 'Odymusic and Body Shapes', *Melody Maker*, 26 September 1981, p. 26.

92 Quoted in Graham Lock, 'Raincoats Keep Falling on Their Feet', *NME*, 22 December 1979, pp. 34–5.

93 Lynn Hanna, 'Shape Some Action', *NME*, 22 August 1981, p. 22.

94 Quoted in Lock, 'Raincoats Keep Falling on Their Feet', pp. 34–5. See also, Vivien Goldman, 'New Raincoats Don't Let You Down', *Melody Maker*, 1 December 1979, p. 24. For an interesting discussion, see O'Meara, 'The Raincoats', 299–313.

95 Wilkinson, Post-*Punk, Politics and Pleasure in Britain*, p. 6.

96 Cross, '"Take the Toys from the Boys"', pp. 117–45; Reddington, *The Lost Women of Rock Music*, pp. 67–97.

97 Lock, 'Poison Girls Come Out to Play', p. 25 and p. 60; 'Poison Girls', *Anarchy*, 34, 1981, pp. 5–11.

98 *Chappaquiddick Bridge*, Crass Records, 1981.

99 Poison Girls, 'Offending Article', on *7-Year Scratch*, Xntrix, 1984.

100 Jerry Harris, 'The Final Cut', *Sounds*, 24 September 1983, pp. 35–6; Cross, '"Take the Toys from the Boys"', pp. 137–8.

101 Quoted in Mike Parker, Making Connections, *The Leveller*, 2–15 October, 1981, p. 18.

102 Quoted in Helen Fitzgerald, 'One Girl's Poison', *Melody Maker*, 27 August 1983, p. 25.

103 Poison Girls, 'Statement', flexi-disc with *Chappaquiddick Bridge*, Crass Records, 1980; Pete Silverton, 'Old People Can Be Rebels Too', *Sounds*, 24 November 1979, p. 23; *In the City*, 13, 1980, pp. 24–8.

104 A few examples include 'A Women's Place Is in the Movement", *Anathema*, 1, 1982, p. 4; 'Consumer Guide to Feminism', *Antigen*, 1, 1982; 'Their Morality is Our Fatality', *Coming Attack*, 2, 1981, p. 19; 'Underneath They're All Angry', *Fack*, 6, 1981, p. 6; 'The Female Role in Society', *Protesting Children Minus the Bondage*, No. 1, 1981, p. 6.

105 *Toxic Grafity*, 5, 1980, p. 23. See also, *The Impossible Dream*, 2, 1981, p. 15; *Anathema*, 1, 1982, p. 5.

106 For example, Conflict's 'I've Had Enough', Flux of Pink Indians' 'Background of Malfunction', Omega Tribe's 'Man Made'.

107 'Toxic Shock', *Paid in Full*, 1, 1984, pp. 2–3; Lost Cherrees, *A Man's Duty ... A Woman's Place* EP, Mortarhate Records, 1984. Fender also played in Omega Tribe.

108 Crass, 'Reality Asylum' b/w 'Shaved Women', Crass Records, 1979. Lyrics also reproduced in Crass, *Love Songs*, pp. 51–3.

109 *International Anthem*, 2, 1979.

110 Crass, *Penis Envy*, Crass Records, 1981.

111 Berger, *The Story of Crass*, pp. 258–61; Cloonan, '"I Fought the Law"', 349–63.

112 Goldman, 'Only Rock 'n' Roll?', p. 27.

113 For a good example, see Greil Marcus, 'It's Fab, It's Passionate, It's Wild', pp. 112–13.

114 Jon Savage, 'The Secret Public', in Hoare et al., *Linder: Works*, p. 13; Ian Birch, 'Looking Behind the Buzzcocks Myth', *Melody Maker*, 18 March 1978, p. 8; Taylor, *Document and Eyewitness*, p. 124; Lake, *Zounds Demystified*, pp. 40–1.

115 Anna Gough-Yates, '"A Shock to the System": Feminist Interventions in Youth Culture – The Adventures of Shocking Pink', *Contemporary British History*, 26: 3 (2012), 375–403.

116 Lisa Darms (ed.), *The Riot Grrrl Collection* (New York: The Feminist Press 2013).

7 Big Man, Big M.A.N.: Punk as Personal Politics II

1 P. Oetloreate [sic], 'Poem', *Black Dwarf*, 2, 1979, p. 16.

2 Lydon, *Anger Is an Energy*, pp. 20–4.

3 Coon, 'Rotten to the Core', p. 35.

4 LWT's *London Weekend Show*, 28 November 1976. See also Rotten being 'told off' by Bill Grundy on the infamous *Today* programme interview.

5 Jordan interviewed in Savage, *The England's Dreaming Tapes*, p. 47; Albertine, *Clothes, Music, Boys*, pp. 113–15.

6 George McKay, '"Crippled with Nerves": Popular Music and Polio, with Particular Reference to Ian Dury', *Popular Music*, 28:3 (2009), 341–66. See also George McKay, *Shakin' All Over: Popular Music and Disability* (Ann Arbor: University of Michigan Press, 2013).

7 Timothy Heron, '"We're Only Monsters": Punk Bodies and the Grotesque in 1970s Northern Ireland', *Études Irlandaises*, 42:1 (2017), 139–54.

8 Rotten quoted in Coon, 'Rotten to the Core', p. 35.

9 Vicious in Ingham, 'Welcome to the (?) Rock Special', p. 26.

10 Rotten quoted in Coon, 'Rotten to the Core', p. 35. For a book rejecting heteronormative conventions with direct reference to the Sex Pistols, see Lee Edelman, *No Future: Queer Theory and the Death Drive* (Durham, NC: Duke University Press, 2004).

11 Savage, *England's Dreaming*, p. 151; Kugelberg with Savage and Terry (eds.), *God Save Sex Pistols*, pp. 23–4 and 41. For 'A Punk Etymology', see Kugelberg and Savage (eds.), *Punk*, pp. 348–51.

12 Robert Price and George Sayers Bain, 'The Labour Force', in Halsey (ed.), *British Trends since 1900*, pp. 162–201.

13 Harrison, *Seeking a Role*, pp. 234–55; idem, *Finding a Role?*, pp. 220–40; Pat Thane, 'Women and the 1970s', in Black, Pemberton and Thane (eds.), *Reassessing 1970s Britain*, pp. 167–86.

14 Bracewell, *England Is Mine*, p. 78.

15 Pete Townsend, *Who I Am* (London: HarperCollins, 2012), p. 65. See also Gildart, *Images of England*, p. 97; Sarah Whiteley (ed.), *Sexing the Groove: Popular Music and Gender* (London: Routledge, 1997).

16 Savage, *1966*, pp. 281–334.

17 For an excellent discussion of music and masculinity, see Sam de Boise, *Men, Masculinity, Music and Emotion* (Basingstoke: Palgrave Macmillan, 2015).

18 Hugh Cornwell, *A Multitude of Sins* (London: HarperCollins, 2004), p. 100.

19 Sleevenotes to Whitehouse, *Birthdeath Experience*, Come Organisation, 1980. The song titles come from the LPs *Total Sex* (1980), *Peter Kürten: Sadist and Mass Slayer* (1981) and *Right to Kill, Dedicated to Dennis Andrew Nilsen* (1983), all released by the Come Organisation.

20 The Passage, *No Love Songs*, Object Music, 1978. See also Paul Morley, 'New Stirrings on the North West Frontier', *NME*, 13 January 1979, pp. 7–8. Later, on *Pindrop*, Object Records, 1980, 'Carnal' mused on male and female attitudes to sex and the relationship between the emotional and physical.

21 The Damned, 'New Rose' b/w 'Help', Stiff Records, 1976.

22 John Peel and Sheila Ravenscroft, *Margrave of the Marshes* (London: Bantam Press, 2005), pp. 312–14.

23 Alternative TV, 'Love Lies Limp', S.G. Records, 1977 (a one-sided flexi-disc given away with *Sniffin' Glue*). The Snivelling Shits, a joke band formed by *Sounds* journalist Giovanni Dadomo, also offered 'I Can't Come', a crude depiction of an amphetamine side effect.

24 For example, The Boy's 'I Don't Care', The Cortinas' 'Fascist Dictator' or The Users' 'Sick of You'.

25 The Slits, 'Love and Romance', on *Cut*, Island Records, 1979.

26 Hear the album version on *Entertainment!*, EMI, 1979.

27 Kris Needs, 'Psychic TV', *ZigZag*, February 1983, pp. 22–3.

28 Psychic TV, *First Transmission*, TOPY, 1982; Keenan, *England's Hidden Reverse*, pp. 315–25.

29 Jon Savage, 'The Conflicted History of Queer Punks', *Attitude*, April 2016, pp. 100–3.

30 Wilkinson, 'Ever Fallen in Love', pp. 61–6.

31 Savage, *England's Dreaming*, pp. 102–3.

32 Quoted in Burchill, 'The Kid Who Wouldn't Wear Clarke's Sandals', pp. 7–8.

33 Barker, *Punk's Dead*, pp. 3–10; Marshall, *Berlin Bromley*, pp. 43–50. See also Billy Idol's comments in Chris Welch, 'Road Test', *Melody Maker*, 18 March 1978, p. 36.

34 Marko, *The Roxy*, pp. 39–43.

35 Paul Du Noyer, *Liverpool Wondrous Place: Music from the Cavern to the Coral* (London: Virgin Books, 2004), p. 117; Cope, *Head On*, pp. 14–42; Holly Johnson, *A Bone in My Flute*, London: Century, 1994; Savage, *England's Dreaming*, pp. 298–9. See also Peter Alan Lloyd, *Bombed Out! Tales of 70s–80s: Music, Punk, Eric's and Beyond* (Liverpool: PAL Publishing, 2014).

36 Quoted in Gavin Martin, 'Pink and Perky', *NME*, 5 November 1983, pp. 32–3.

37 Matthew Worley, *Young Offenders: Punk in Norwich* (Norwich: Bestley Press, 2016). Jon Fry was Norwich's resident punk DJ, playing at The Woolpack from 1978 and organising nights at The Jacquard from 1979.

38 For just a few examples, Infa Riot's 'Friday Oh Friday', on *Still Out of Order*, Secret, 1982; Dave Hepworth, 'Could It Happen Here? My Night of Disco Horror', *Sounds*, 14 April, 1979, pp. 30–1; Dave McCullough, 'No Poofters', *Sounds*, 13 October 1979, pp. 28–30; Richard Grabel, 'Spandaus Invade America!', *NME*, 16 May 1981, pp. 8 and 13; Biba Kopf's review of Bronski Beat's *Age of Consent*, *NME*, 24 October 1984, p. 33; Garry Bushell, singles review, *Sounds*, 24 October 1984, p. 27.

39 Lesley Hall, *Sex, Gender and Social Change in Britain since 1800* (Basingstoke: Palgrave Macmillan, 2000).

40 For complaints about homophobia, see 'Gay Punx', *Kill Your Pet Puppy*, 4, 1981, p. 17.

41 See, for example, *City Fun*, 2, 1978.

42 Ian Birch 'Here's to You, Mr Robinson', *Melody Maker*, 13 August 1977, p. 10; Steve Clarke, '3-5-7-9 (Laying It on) the Little White Line', *NME*, 22 October 1977, pp. 7–8.

43 Julie Burchill review of the Tom Robinson Band at London's Golden Lion, *NME*, 29 January 1977, p. 31.

44 See Kim Davis' live review in *NME*, 17 September 1977, p. 48 and Tony Parson's review in *NME*, 8 April 1978, p. 50. For the SWP, see *Socialist Worker*, 6 May 1978 (Robinson on the front cover) and *Temporary Hoarding*, 4, 1977. For criticism, see Nick Kent's review of *Power in the Darkness*, *NME*, 20 May 1978, p. 37.

45 Phil McNeill, 'Tom Robinson', *NME*, 11 February 1978, pp. 25–30. See also Ray Coleman, 'Power in the Darkness', *Melody Maker*, 22 October 1977, pp. 30–2.

46 Punk-related fanzines such as *City Fun*, *Drastic Measures*, *Guttersnipe* and *Scum* included articles relating to female same-sex relationships.

47 For an international overview, see Maria Katharina Wiedlack, *Queer-Feminist Punk: An Anti-Social History* (Veinna: Zaglossus, 2015). See also Reddington, *The Lost Women of Rock*, pp. 89–93, for the Brighton scene and Devil's Dykes.

48 'Raped', *Ripped & Torn*, 11, 1978, pp. 12–13; 'Dead Fingers Talked', *Ripped & Torn*, 9, 1978, p. 6. Hear also The Drug Addix's 'Gay Boys in Bondage' (featuring Kirsty MacColl on backing vocals), a Chiswick single released from punk's r'n'b fringe.

49 'Blackmail Corner', *NME*, 16 September 1978, p. 3.

50 For an exception, see Andy Palmer's artworks, poems and writing in his *The Eklektik* fanzine.

51 Hear, for example, Conflict's 'The Serenade Is Dead' on their EP of the same name released on Mortarhate Records in 1983.

52 'The Apostles, 'Fucking Queer', on *Blow It Up, Burn It Down, Kick It Til It Breaks* EP, No Label, 1982; idem, 'The Curse' on *The Curse of the Creature* EP, Scum Records, 1984.

53 'Hello Mark', on *2nd Dark Age*, BBP Records, 1982. In *Twisted Nerve*, 3, 1982, Martin claimed that his singing the song 'nearly got me gay-bashed at the Autonomy Centre'. Then again, the anarcho-scene continued to provide space for its own dissidents, even those – such as Martin – keen to attempt acts of 'heresy'.

54 For analysis, see Murray Healy, *Gay Skins: Class, Masculinity and Queer Appropriation* (London: Continuum, 1996). See also 'Skin Complex', *Out*, Channel 4, broadcast 29 July 1992, which featured Crane. In *Scum*, 3, 1980, p. 19, Martin claimed to have been 'active member' of the NF until he 'realised what a lot of shit politics all was, left or right …' See also, in the same issue (p. 28), 'Gay Skinheads OK'.

55 *Scum*, 6, 1983, p. 10; The Apostles, *The Giving of Life Costs Nothing* EP, Scum Records, 1984, and *The Lives and Times of The Apostles*, Children of the Revolution Records, 1986.

56 Sleevenotes to Coil, 'How to Destroy Angels', L.A.Y.L.A.H. Antirecords, 1984.

57 Quoted in Keenan, *England's Hidden Reverse*, p. 180.

58 Almond, a perennial Coil collaborator, appeared in the accompanying video as an angel of death.

59 Reynolds, *Rip It Up and Start Again*, p. 503. Less blatant – but still subversive – was Boy George's late 1982 appearance on *Top of the Tops* with his band Culture Club. The music, 'Do You Really Want to Hurt Me?', was rendered irrelevant next to the ensuing debate as to George's sex and gender. Like Marc Almond, however, George was initially unforthcoming about his sexuality. Bronksi Beat, a group that aligned gay and leftist politics, also broke through in 1984.

60 Ranter poets proved particularly adept at this. See also Nick Toczek's 'Stiff with a Quiff', in *Wake Up*, 7, 1986, p. 36 and performed with The Burial on *The Oi! of Sex*, Syndicate Records, 1984.

61 Television Personalities, 'Games for Boys', on *They Could Have Been Bigger Than the Beatles*, Whaam Records, 1982.

62 *The Secret Public*, pp. 4–5 and 8–9.

63 Flux of Pink Indians, *The Fucking Cunts Treat Us Like Pricks*, Spider Leg, 1984.

64 Newtown Neurotics, *Beggars Can Be Choosers*, Razor Records, 1983.

65 Billy Bragg, 'Greetings to the New Brunette', on *Talking to the Taxman About Poetry*, Go Discs, 1986.

66 By the 1980s, a few punk bands – Discharge, GBH, English Dogs, Broken Bones, The Blood – had begun to bolster their sound and style with aspects of heavy metal, while others – including the Cockney Rejects – deliberately moved in a more obviously rock direction. A punk-metal crossover would eventually find fruition among the grindcore and hardcore scenes of the mid-to-late 1980s.

67 Strange, *Blitzed*, pp. 28–9; Parsons, 'Locker Room Sexuality and Six Figure Rebels', pp. 7–8 and 61; Knight, *Strangled*, pp. 140–50. For a related discussion, see Eve Sedgwick, *Between Men: English Literature and Male Homosocial Desire* (New York: Columbia University Press, 1985).

68 Bushell, 'The New Breed', pp. 32–3.

69 Worley, 'Oi!, Oi!, Oi!', pp. 606–36.

70 Last Resort, 'King of the Jungle', on Various Artists, *Carry On Oi!*, Secret Records, 1981.

71 See, for a snapshot, Tony Fletcher, 'Tribalism Rules OK', *Jamming*, 9, 1979, p. 28.

72 Duffy, 'Playing with Fire', pp. 4–5.

73 Chris Brazier, 'Subway Go Overground', *Melody Maker*, 18 March 1978, p. 35; Ian Penman, 'Black 'n' White Drop Outasite', *NME*, 4 November 1978, p. 47. For a discussion, see Reynolds and Press, *The Sex Revolts*, pp. 66–74.

74 Key fanzines covering the evolution of this culture were *Adventure in Bereznik!*, *Are You Scared to Get Happy?*, *Baby Honey*, *Communication Blur*, *Hungry Beat*, *Kvatch*, *Simply Thrilled*, *Trout Fishing in Leytonstone!* and *Turn!* For background, see Michael White, *Popkisss: The Life and Afterlife of Sarah Records* (New York: Bloomsbury, 2016), pp. 1–23.

75 The quote is from an advert for Sarah Records, November 1992.

76 Dave McCullough, 'OJ and OK', *Sounds*, 24 October 1981, pp. 26–7.

77 Collins quoted in Gavin Martin, 'Fresh Juice Sweet Dreams', *NME*, 26 September 1981, pp. 29–30.

78 Quoted in McCullough, 'OJ and OK', pp. 26–7.

79 'Consolation Prize', on Orange Juice, *You Can't Hide Your Love Forever*, Polydor Records, 1982.

80 Ian Pye, 'Magnificent Obsessions', *Melody Maker*, 26 September 1983, pp. 24–5.

81 Quoted in Dave McCullough, 'Handsome Devils', *Sounds*, 4 June 1983, p. 13. See also, Frank Worrall, 'The Cradle Snatchers', *Melody Maker*, 3 September 1983, p. 7.

82 Cath Carroll, 'Prune Features', *NME*, 14 May 1983, p. 11.

83 Frank Worrall, 'The Cradle Snatchers', *Melody Maker*, 3 September 1983, pp. 26–7; Pye, 'Magnificent Obsessions', pp. 24–5; Bill Black, 'Keep Young and Beautiful', *Sounds*, 19 November 1983, pp. 8–9; Barney Hoskyns, 'These Disarming Men', *NME*, 4 February 1984, pp. 12–13; Ian Pye, 'A Hard Day's Misery', *Melody Maker*, 3 November 1984, p. 24.

84 Quoted in Garry Bushell, 'The Art of Love', *Sounds*, 23 September 1978, pp. 13–14.

85 Quoted in Caroline Coon, 'Whatever Happened to the Buzzcocks?', *Sounds*, 17 September 1977, pp. 20–1; Tony Parsons, 'Electronically Tested', *NME*, 3 December 1977, p. 37.

86 See Shelly's comments in Paul Rambali, 'The Lust Train Stops Here', *NME*, 14 October 1978, pp. 7–8.

87 For an explicit example, see Steve Tope's letter to *NME*, 1 May 1982, pp. 59–9, insisting the paper should not restrict itself to 'just music' when music is 'becoming increasingly bound up with everything else that's going on'.

88 See, for example, *Sounds*, 10 December 1984, p. 28, for two letters musing on punk's problems and how to move forward again.

89 The debate begins in *Sounds*, 1 September 1979.

90 For a discussions of glam and gender, see Gildart, *Images of England*, pp. 168–73; Andrew Branch, 'All the Young Dudes: Educational Capital, Masculinity and the Uses of Popular Music', *Popular Music*, 31:1 (2012), 25–44.

91 *Sounds*, 6 March 1982, p. 46.

92 Edna's follow-up letter in *Sounds*, 10 April 1982, p. 63.

93 Gildart, in *Images of England*, p. 165, quotes Steve Fitzgerald, a fourteen-year old working class boy from Essex: 'Bowie was a bolt out of the blue to me ... I wanted to be just like him. His lyrics took me to a different, exciting almost alien world'.

94 Quoted in Vivien Goldman, 'Mute Speak', *NME*, 2 May 1981, pp. 25–6.

95 Joshua Gunn, 'Gothic Music and the Inevitability of Genre', *Popular Music and Society*, 23:1 (1999), 31–50; Alexander Carpenter, 'The "Ground Zero" of Goth: Bauhaus, "Bela Lugosi's Dead" and the Origins of Gothic Rock', *Popular Music and Society*, 35:1 (2012), 25–52; Mercer, *Gothic Rock Black Book*, pp. 130–3; Chris Roberts, Hywel Livingstone and Emma Baxter-Wright, *Gothic: The Evolution of a Dark Subculture* (London: Goodman, 2014), pp. 128–73; Thompson, *Twenty-Five Years in the Reptile House*, pp. 9–27. See also the essays collected in Lauren Goodlad and Michael Bibby (eds.), *Goth: Undead Subculture* (Durham, NC: Duke University Press, 2007).

96 Paul Hodkinson, *Goth: Identity, Style and Subculture* (Oxford: Berg, 2002), pp. 48–56; Carol Siegel, *Goth's Dark Empire* (Bloomington: Indiana University Press, 2005); Dunja Brill, *Goth Culture: Gender, Sexuality and Style* (Oxford: Berg, 2008).

97 Quoted in Richard North, 'Making a Specimen of Themselves', *NME*, 12 February 1983, p. 13. Wisdom had previously been in The Unwanted, one of the most ramshackle bands to feature on the seminal *Live at The Roxy* album (1977).

98 LWT, 'Positive Punk', *Watford Gap*, broadcast 18 March 1983.

99 North, 'Punk Warriors', pp. 12–15. See also the interview with Brigandage in *Incendiary*, 1, 1984, pp. 11–13.

100 Barney Hoskyns, live review, 13 March 1982, p. 51.

101 'Tips for '81', *Sounds*, January 1981, p. 17; Keaton, 'The Face of Punk Gothique', pp. 16–17; idem, 'The Rot Sets In', *Sounds*, 3 April 1982, p. 20.

102 For example see Martin Hannett's comment in *Melody Maker*, 29 September 1979, p. 19.

103 A shift was clear in that the 1981 Christmas on Earth festival in Leeds was headlined by The Exploited and The Damned and featured such bands as GBH, Vice Squad and the Anti-Nowhere League. The 1982 festival (at London's Lyceum) was initially conceived to follow in similar fashion – with Discharge, GBH and Chelsea touted – but was eventually headlined by Sex Gang Children alongside Alien Sex Fiend, The Sisters of Mercy and Ritual. See *Sounds*, 25 December 1982, p. 3.

104 *Kick*, 4, 1982, p. 3. See also the report in *Sounds*, 3 July 1982, p. 12.

105 The Batcave opened in July 1982 at the Gargoyle Club in London's Soho. It later moved through various other venues in central London. See Thompson, *Twenty-Five Years in the Reptile House*, pp. 219–43; Haslam, *Life After Dark*, pp. 273–4.

106 'Make Up Tips for Urban Guerrillas', *Kill Your Pet Puppy*, 5, 1982, pp. 11–13; *Kick*, No, 4, pp. 2–4.

107 Captain Swing, *The Black Book: The Life and Crimes of Richard Rouska* (Leeds: 1977cc, 2014). We should note that Southern Death Cult also formed in Bradford.

108 Quoted in *Kick*, 3, 1980, p. 11.

109 Tony Puppy, 'Sex in Your Own Home', *Punk Lives*, 10, 1983, p. 32

110 Andy Courtney, 'The Great Smell of Brutality', *Sounds*, 11 November 1978, pp. 14–15.

111 'The Ants', *Ripped & Torn*, 8, 1977, pp. 5–6; Vivien Goldman, 'Whip in My Valise', *Sounds*, 10 November 1977, p. 14; 'Adam and the Ants', *Ripped & Torn*, 14, 1978, pp. 11–13. Later, of course, Ant took on the masculine identity of Red Indian warrior, pirate, highwayman and decadent prince.

328 / Notes to pages 212–214

112 Nick Kent 'Termites Devour Part of New Wave', *NME*, 11 February 1978, p. 46.
113 Kimberly Jackson, 'Gothic Music and the Decadent Individual', in Ian Peddie (ed.), *The Resisting Muse: Popular Music and Social Protest* (Aldershot: Ashgate, 2006), pp. 177–88.
114 Barney Hoskyns, 'Pleasure Heads Must Burn', *NME*, 17 October 1981, pp. 29–30.
115 Quoted in Valac Van Der Veene, 'Live from the Theatre of Destruction', *Sounds*, 31 January 1981, pp. 26–8.
116 For tribes, see interviews with The Pack, *Panache*, 9, 1979, pp. 36–7; Adam Ant in *Sounds*, 5 January 1980, pp. 14–15; Killing Joke in *Sounds*, 31 January 1981, pp. 26–8, *Anti-Climax*, 8, 1981, pp. 8–10 and *NME*, 27 February 1982, pp. 11–12; Sex Gang Children, in *Artificial Life*, 2, 1982, pp. 6–7; Southern Death Cult, *NME*, 2 October 1982, pp. 16–17.
117 See comments in Mat Snow, 'He Man and All That Jazz', *NME*, 20 August 1983, pp. 24–5.
118 'Tabazan', on *Night Time*, EG Records, 1985.
119 Jason Pitzel-Waters, 'The Darker Shade of Pagan: The Emergence of Goth', in Donna Weston and Andy Bennett (eds.), *Pop Pagans: Paganism and Popular Music* (Durham: Acumen, 2013), pp. 76–90.
120 Jaz Coleman, *Letters from Cythera* (London: KJ Books, 2014).
121 This was also true for Bauhaus. Peter Murphy would sometimes assault the audience, as in Glasgow and Nottingham on the 'Mask' tour of 1981. See David J. Haskins, *Who Killed Mister Moonlight: Bauhaus, Black Magick and Benediction* (London: Jawbone Press, 2014), p. 83); 'Murphy's War – Bauhaus Style', [Norwich] *Evening News*, cutting, 18 October 1982.
122 Quoted in Thompson, *Twenty-Five Years in the Reptiles House*, p. 228.
123 Brill, *Goth Culture*, pp. 75–98; Claire Nally, 'Goth Beauty, Style and Sexuality: Neo-Traditional Femininity in Twenty-First Century Subcultural Magazines', *Gothic Studies* (forthcoming).
124 BBC, *Riverside*, broadcast 31 October 1983. See *Time Out*, 8–14 December 1983, for its 'Gothic Punk' cover featuring Specimen's Jonny Slut (Jonny Melton) on the cover.
125 Reynolds, *Shock and Awe*, pp. 373–88.
126 1976 was also the year that Michel Foucault's *Histoire de la sexualité*, Vol. I: *La Volonté de savoir* was published by Gallimard.
127 There are nods here to songs by The Samples, Stiff Little Fingers, The Exploited and Discharge.
128 Sex Pistols, 'Belsen Was a Gas', appears on various live recordings, including the band's final gig: *Live at Winterland*, Sanctuary Records, 2001. A demo version was also included on Sex Pistols, *Never Mind the Bollocks, Here's The Sex Pistols*, Virgin, 2012.

329 / Notes to pages 215–218

8 No Future: Punk as Dystopia

1 Taken from the film *Jubilee*, directed by Derek Jarman, 1978. Also quoted by Adam Ant in Goldman, 'Whip in My Valise', p. 14. Adam played a lead part in *Jubilee*.

2 Ian MacDonald, 'The NME Consumers' Guides to 1984', *NME*, 23 August 1980, pp. 29–32.

3 Beckett, *When the Lights Went Out*, pp. 157–82; Turner, *Crisis? What Crisis?*, pp. 59–76; idem, *Rejoice! Rejoice!*, pp. 96–122; Bart Moore-Gilbert, 'Apocalypse Now? The Novel in the 1970s', in Moore-Gilbert (ed.), *The Arts in the 1970s*, pp. 152–75.

4 MacDonald pointed here to the Emergency Powers Act (1964), used in 1977–78 in response to the firemen's strike.

5 Ian MacDonald, 'The NME Consumers' Guides to 1984', parts 2 and 3, *NME*, 30 August 1980, pp. 25–32 and 6 September 1980, pp. 31–4.

6 Explicit reference to Orwell is made by Crass' Andy Palmer in 'Crass Interview', *Anathema*, 1, 1982, pp. 12–15.

7 The Unwanted, 'Withdrawal' b/w '1984' and 'Bleak Outlook', Raw Records, 1977. Orwellian references were also made in relation to the banning of punk bands following the Sex Pistols' 'Anarchy' tour. See 'Big Brother Declares War on New Wave', *NME*, 4 June 1977, p. 3; *Heat*, 2, 1977, p. 2.

8 Imagery relating to 1984 was also sometimes used, as on Poison Girls' 'Are You Happy Now?', Illuminated Records, 1983, with its cover adapted from the 1956 film of Orwell's book. Here, however, 'Big Brother' becomes an object of ridicule, a figure inviting defiance; his image recast as satire. My thanks to Rich Cross for this observation.

9 For Paul Weller's reading the book at school, see Hewitt, *Paul Weller*, pp. 72–3. See also 'Deterrence is a theory based on possibilities, not certainties', *Bits*, 1, 1981. For the US, see James Morey's designs for the Dead Kennedys under the name 'Winston Smith'.

10 4-Skins, '1984', on *Strength Thru Oi!*, Decca, 1981.

11 Savage, *London's Outrage*, p. 11. See also the essay in *Nihilistic Vices*, 1, 1979: 'we're near enough to 1984 … with Maggie, we'll get even closer' (p. 4).

12 Rimbaud, 'Last of the Hippies', p. 12.

13 Crass, *Yes Sir, I Will*, Crass Records, 1983.

14 Conflict, sleevenotes to 'This Is Not Enough' b/w 'And Neither Is This', Mortarhate Records, 1985. The 'Battle of Orgreave' took place on 18 June 1984. See *Still the Enemy Within*, Dartmouth Films, 2014, directed by Owen Gower; Penny Green, *The Enemy Without: Policing and Class Consciousness in the Miners' Strike* (Buckingham: Open University Press, 1990); Seamus Milne, *The Enemy Within: The Secret War Against the Miners* (London: Verso, 1991). For a literary take that captures a mood, see David Peace, *GB84* (London: Faber & Faber, 2005).

15 Antisect, *In Darkness, There Is No Choice*, Spider Leg Records, 1984.

16 Stuart McDougal, *Stanley Kubrick's A Clockwork Orange* (Cambridge: Cambridge University Press, 2010).

17 Quoted in Ben Fleet, 'Major Accident', *Sounds*, 29 January 1983, p. 10. Hear also New Order's 'Ultraviolence', on *Power, Corruption and Lies*, Factory Records, 1983; and, for visuals, see the covers of *Aftermath*, 5, 1980 and *Strangled*, 7, 1978.

18 Quoted in 'Interview', *RE/Search*, Nos. 8–9, San Francisco: Re/Search, 1984, p. 8.

19 Ultravox, *Ultravox!* (1977), *Ha!-Ha!-Ha!* (1977) and *Systems of Romance* (1978), all on Island Records; John Foxx, *Metamatic*, Virgin, 1980. We could also point to Tubeway Army's *Replicas*, Beggars Banquet, 1979 and Gary Numan's *The Pleasure Principle*, Beggars Banquet, 1979 – especially 'Cars'.

20 Dave Henderson, 'Wild Planet', parts 1 and 2, *Sounds*, 7 and 14 May, 1983, pp. 23–6 and 27–8. Among such labels were Broken Flag, Cause For Concern, Color, Flowmotion, Snatch and Third Mind.

21 *Sounds*, 24 December 1983, p. 12; RE/Search, *Industrial Culture Handbook*, pp. 49, 67, 91 and 105.

22 Herbert Pimlott, '"Militant Entertainment"?: "Crisis Music" and Political Ephemera in the Emergent "Structure of Feeling"', in Subcultures Network (ed.), *Fight Back*, pp. 268–86.

23 Frank Thomas Blackaby (ed.), *De-industrialisation* (London: Heinemann, 1978); Tom Sheriff, *A De-industrialised Britain* (London: Fabian Society, 1979).

24 Jim Tomlinson, 'De-industrialisation Not Decline: A New Meta-narrative for Post-war British History', *Twentieth Century British History*, 77:1 (2016), 76–99. See also Jim Tomlinson, *The Politics of Declinism: Understanding Post-War Britain* (Oxford: Longman, 2000).

25 Tomlinson, 'De-industrialisation Not Decline', 87; Stephen Brooke, 'Living in "New Times": Historicizing 1980s Britain', *History Compass*, 12:1 (2014), 20–32.

26 Alternative TV, 'Life' b/w 'Love Lies Limp', Deptford Fun City, 1978.

27 *Jubilee*, directed by Derek Jarman, 1978.

28 Nick Kent, 'On the Town: The Unpleasant Vision of "Punk 1984"', *NME*, 18 February 1978, pp. 41–3; Jordan, cited in Burchill, 'The Kid Who Wouldn't Wear Clarke's Sandals', pp. 7–8.

29 Derek Jarman, *Dancing Ledge* (London: Quartet Books, 1991 edition), pp. 168–81.

30 The Adverts' 'Bombsite Boy' captures this very well, as confirmed by its author, TV Smith, in an interview with Alex Ogg: 'For You, Tommy, the War Is Never Over', p. 282.

31 Jon Savage, 'The World's End: London Punk, 1976–77', in Matt (ed.), *Punk*, pp. 40–6; *London's Outrage*, 2, 1977.

32 *London's Outrage*, 2, 1977. For similar images in relation to Liverpool, see Dave Sinclair, *Liverpool in the 1980s* (Stroud: Amberley, 2014).

33 Middles, *From Joy Division to New Order*, p. 85.

34 Haslam, *Life After Dark*, pp. 303–5.

35 Jon Savage, 'Cabaret Voltaire', *Sounds*, 15 April 1978, pp. 16–17.

36 Reynolds, *Rip It Up and Start Again*, pp. 150–1. See also Lilleker, *Beats Working for a Living*, p. 5.

37 Quoted in Paul Morley, 'The Heart and Soul of Cabaret Voltaire', *NME*, 29 November 1980, pp. 16–17.

38 Stephen Mallinder, 'Foreword', in Reed, *Assimilate*, p. xiii.

39 Quoted in Ford, *Wreckers of Civilisation*, p 6.28.

40 Quoted in Harrigan, 'From Genesis – Revelations', pp. 50 and 55.

41 Sleevenotes to *The Industrial Records Story*, Industrial Records, 1984. See also Gregory Steirer, 'The Art of Everyday Life and Death: Throbbing Gristle and the Aesthetics of Neoliberalism', *Postmodern Culture*, 22:2 (2012), 1–16.

42 Oliver Lowenstein, 'A Question of Identity', *Sounds*, 19 August 1978, p. 21.

43 Rose Rouse, 'Electronically Tested for Your Protection', *Sounds*, 13 August 1983, pp. 19–20; Don Watson, 'One-Two One-Two Testing!', *NME*, 13 August 1983, pp. 6–7.

44 Test Dept, 'November Reprisal' (1983), in Graham Cunnington, Angus Farquhar and Paul Jamrozy, *Test Dept: Total State Machine* (Bristol: PC Press, 2015), p. 40.

45 Susan Williams [Steven Wells], 'A Working Class Hero Is Nothing to Be', *NME*, 15 December 1984, pp. 25 and 35.

46 For background, see Ron Bailey, *The Squatters* (London: Penguin, 1973); Nick Wates and Christian Wolmar (eds.), *Squatting: The Real Story* (London: Bay Leafy Books, 1980); Nicholas Saunders, *Alternative London* (London: Saunders, 1978); Lucy Finchett-Maddock, 'Squatting in London: Squatters' Rights and Legal Movement(s)', in Bart Van Der Steen, Ask Katzeff and Leendert Van Hoogenhuijze (eds.), *The City Is Ours: Squatting and Autonomous Movements from the 1970s to the Present* (Oakland: PM Press, 2014), pp. 207–31. See also Matt Cook, '"Gay Times": Identity, Locality, Memory, and the Brixton Squats in 1970s London', *Twentieth Century British History*, 24:1 (2013), 84–109.

47 Richard Dudanski, *Squat City Rockers: Proto-Punk and Beyond* (London: Dudanski/Romero, 2013); Crossley, *Networks of Sound*, p. 129. Other early punk squats included New Court, Lutton Terrace (Hampstead), that briefly housed Johnny Rotten, and Carol Street (Camden), where Scritti Politti were based. Steve Strange writes of living in a squat in Alperton with Jamie Reid (*Blitzed*, pp. 36–7), while many connected to the new romantic scene squatted on Warren Street in central London. Boy George squatted in nearby Great Titchfield Street, Carburton Street and Goodge Street.

48 The Apostles, '62 Brougham Road', on *Punk Obituary*, Mortarhate Records, 1986; Porter, *Genesis to Revelations*, pp. 176–77; Gibson, *A Punk Rock Flashback*, pp. 139–44; Mickey 'Penguin', 'My Journey to All the Madmen Records and Back Again', in Bull and 'Penguin' (eds.), *Not Just Bits of Paper*, pp. 124–55.

49 Peter Webb, 'Dirty Squatters, Anarchy, Politics and Smack: A Journey through Bristol's Squat Punk Milieu', in Dines and Worley (eds.), *The Aesthetic of Our Anger*, pp. 179–98; Justine Butler, 'Disgustin' Justin', in Bull and Dines (eds.), *Tales From the Punkside*, pp. 85–94.

50 Bash Street Kids, 'Ebb and Flow: Autonomy and Squatting in Brighton, 1973–2012', in Van Der Steen, Katzeff and Van Hoogenhuijze (eds.), *The City Is Ours*, pp. 159–60.

51 Robb, *The North Will Rise Again*, pp. 216–19.

52 For varied accounts, see Alistair Livingston, 'Diary of an Anarcho-Goth-Punk Fiend', unpublished, 1983 (my thanks to Al for sending me a copy of this); Porter, *Genesis to Revelations*, pp. 104–113 and 184–90; Short, *Trash Can*, pp. 78–95; Gibson, *A Punk Rock Flashback*, pp. 145–72; Rebecca Binns, 'They May Have Beds, But They Don't Use Sheets', in Bull and Dines (eds.), *Tales From the Punkside*, pp. 119–35; Rebecca Binns et al., *They've Taken Our Ghettos: A Punk History of Woodberry Down Estate* (London: Active, 2015).

53 Lake, *Zounds Demystified*, p. 71. Hear also Zounds, 'Dirty Squatters', on *The Curse of Zounds*, Rough Trade, 1981.

54 Just a few examples from 1977–79: The Adverts, 'Bombsite Boy'; The Art Attacks, 'Rat City'; The Boys, 'Turning Grey'; Chelsea, 'High Rise Living'; The Clash, 'Hate and War'; The Jam, 'Down in the Tube Station at Midnight'; Menace, 'Insane Society'; The Members, 'Fear on the Streets'; 999, 'No Pity'; The Panik, 'Urban Damnation'; The Ruts, 'Babylon's Burning'; Sham 69, 'Song of the Streets'; The Stranglers, 'Down in the Sewer'; UK Subs, 'World War'. And, from 1980–84: Blitz, 'Your Revolution'; Chaotic Youth, 'No Future UK'; The Defects, 'Survival'; Disorder, 'Today's World'; 4-Skins, 'Wonderful World'; One Way System, 'Ain't No Answers'; Partisans, '17 Years of Hell'; Red Alert, 'Crisis'; Special Duties, 'Violent Society'; Ultra-Violent, 'Dead Generation'.

55 'The Pack', *Jamming*, 9, 1979, pp. 36–7.

56 Quoted in Johnny Waller, 'You Are What You Hate', *Sounds*, 15 August 1981, pp. 22–3.

57 See Paul Du Noyer, 'Rebel with a Brain', *NME*, 6 February 1982, pp. 22–6; Neville Wiggins, 'Theatre of Hate and the Spirit of '76', *Punk Lives*, 1, 1982, pp. 28–9.

58 The quote is from Theatre of Hate, 'Rebel Without a Brain' b/w 'My Own Invention', Burning Rome, 1981.

59 Coleman quoted in Van Der Veene, '"Live" from the Theatre of Destruction', pp. 26–8.

60 Quoted in *Anti-Climax*, 8, 1981, pp. 8–10.

61 Killing Joke, 'Eighties' b/w 'Eighties (The Coming Mix)', EG Records, 1984.

62 The list of bands playing benefits for the miners in *Sounds*, 7 July 1984 (p. 3) included the Style Council, UB40, Spear of Destiny, Madness, Crass and Flux of Pink Indians. See also the list of miners' benefit gigs in *Sounds*, 8 December 1984 (p. 3), comprising Redskins, Poison Girls, Omega Tribe, The Three Johns, The Creepers, Pink Industry and bIG fLAME. Over the course of the strike, there were hundreds of gigs featuring numerous bands.

63 The Clash, 'This Is England' b/w 'Do It Now', CBS, 1985.

64 For contemporary comments along the same lines, see Turner, *Crisis? What Crisis?*, p. 24.

65 Quoted in McNeil, 'Watch Out It's the Angry "Young" Men', p. 5.

66 The Models, 'Freeze' b/w 'Man of the Year', Step-Forward Records, 1977.

67 For Weller's fears of a police state, see the interview in *48 Thrills*, 2, 1977; hear 'In the City' and 'Time for Truth' on *In the City*, Polydor (1977); and see comments in Clarke, 'Union Jacks?', pp. 28–9. Pursey claimed 'Red London' was not meant to be seen as anti-socialist, though the lyric is ambiguous. The 'red' could be understood to mean blood. See Penny Valentine, 'Jimmy Pursey, Mirror Man', *Melody Maker*, 4 February 1978, p. 14.

68 Quoted in Lindsey Boyd, 'Alternativevision', *Sounds*, 24 December 1977, p. 12. For an anarchist comment along similar lines, see Colin Jerwood in Garry Bushell, 'It's Time to Hear What's What', *Sounds*, 30 April 1983, pp. 15–17; and for an Oi! quote, see the 4-Skins in Paul Castles, '4 Play', *Punk Lives*, 8 (1983), pp. 6–7.

69 The Stranglers, 'Curfew', on *Black and White*, United Artists, 1978; Angelic Upstarts, 'Guns for the Afghan Rebels', on *2,000,000 Voices*, Zonophone, 1981; The Underdogs, 'East of Dachau' b/w 'Johnny Go Home' and 'Dead Soldier', Riot City, 1983.

70 Anti Pasti, 'Freedom Row'; Chelsea, *Evacuate*, IRS, 1982; Conflict, 'The Serenade Is Dead'; Killing Joke, 'Wardance'; Mau Maus, 'Clampdown', The Skeptix, 'Curfew' and UK Subs, 'Police State' are just a handful of examples.

71 Cockney Rejects, 'Police Car' on *Flares 'N' Slippers* EP, Small Wonder, 1979.

72 Stephen Humphries, *Hooligans or Rebels? An Oral History of Working Class Childhood and Youth, 1889–1939* (Oxford: Blackwell, 1981); Phil Cohen, 'Policing the Working-Class City', in Mike Fitzgerald, Gregor McLennan and Jennie Pawson (eds.), *Crime and Society: History and Theory* (London: Routledge and Kegan Paul, 1981), pp. 118–36; Osgerby, *Youth in Britain*, pp. 68–9.

73 The origins of 'ACAB' pre-date punk by several decades, though the 4-Skins wrote a typically direct song of the same title. For a pre-punk reference, see 'Class Divisions in Attitudes to Crime', *The Times*, 22 May 1959, p. 4.

74 Pete Shelley, when asked if he had political views, replied: 'Lots … I don't vote 'cos I don't believe in organised political parties … I've got this idea of personal

politics – which is how people relate to each other'. Quoted in Davies, *Punk*, p. 22, taken from an interview in *The New Wave* fanzine (1977). Billy Idol, meanwhile, said: 'We haven't a set political stance. We're not communists or fascists. Something new must be sorted out. Like communism is great, but British communism stinks' (*More On*, 3, 1977).

75 *International Anthem*, 1, 1977, pp. 5–10.

76 See, for example, *Toxic Grafitty*, 4, 1979, p. 3; 'The Art of Politics/A Clever Con', *Anathema*, 1, 1982, p. 28; 'Democracy?', *Incendiary*, 1, 1984, p. 20.

77 Crass, *Yes Sir, I Will*; Crass, *Love Songs*, pp. 63–91.

78 Crass, *You're Already Dead*, p. 5.

79 Ogg, 'For You, Tommy, the War Is Never Over', 281–304.

80 Various, *Punk and Disorderly III: The Final Solution*, Anagram, 1983.

81 Beckett, *When the Lights Went Out*, pp. 166–82 and 376–82; Garnett, *From Anger to Apathy*, pp. 18–26 and 72–78; Sandbrook, *Seasons in the Sun*, pp. 66–72 and 124–49; Wheen, *Strange Days Indeed*, pp. 201–25; Turner, *Crisis? What Crisis?*, pp. 108–9.

82 Haseler, *The Death of British Democracy*, pp. 7–16.

83 Ben Jackson and Robert Saunders, 'Varieties of Thatcherism', in Jackson and Saunders (eds.), *Making Thatcher's Britain*, pp. 1–21; Hall, 'The Great Moving Right Show', pp. 14–20.

84 The most obvious example is 'SUS' by The Ruts, on *The Crack*, Virgin, 1979.

85 Robert Reiner, *The Politics of the Police* (Hemel Hempstead: Harvester Wheatsheaf, 1992); Harrison, *Finding a Role?*, pp. 475–8.

86 Angelic Upstarts, 'The Murder of Liddle Towers' (1978) and 'I Understand' (1981); Dave Goodman and Friends, 'Justifiable Homicide' (1978); The Ruts, 'Jah War' (1979); Tom Robinson Band, 'Blue Murder' (1979); The Pop Group, 'Justice' (1980); The Partisans, 'Police Story' (1981); Crux, 'Liddle Towers' (1982).

87 For an overview, see Tim Pat Coogan, *The Troubles: Ireland's Ordeal and the Search for Peace* (Basingstoke: Palgrave Macmillan, 2002 edition).

88 Beckett, *When the Lights Went Out*, pp. 101–13.

89 Harrison, *Finding a Role?*, p. 104.

90 Terri Hooley and Richard Sullivan, *Hooligan: Music, Mayhem, Good Vibrations* (Belfast: Blackstaff Press, 2010), pp. 38–46.

91 O'Neill and Trelford, *It Makes You Want to Spit*, pp. 46–51; Gray, *The Clash: Return of the Last Gang in Town*, p. 256; Gilbert, *Passion Is a Fashion*, p. 161. For an eye-witness account of the RUC 'lashing out' at the young punks, see *NME* letters page, 5 November 1977, p. 42. Rudi's song 'Cops' was written in response to these events. The Clash returned to play Belfast in December 1977.

92 Rimbaud, 'Last of the Hippies', p. 11.

93 Vaucher, *Crass Art*, pp. 52–7.

94 See Rimbaud, 'Last of the Hippies', pp. 10–11; Conflict, 'Northern Ireland', in sleevenotes to *The House That Man Built* EP, Crass 1982; Liberty, 'We Have the

Real Power ...', sleevenotes to *The People Who Care Are Angry*, Mortarhate, 1986. For related songs, hear Alternative's 'Ireland', Assassins of Hope's 'Battle of the Boyne', Dirt's 'Belfast', Exit-stance's 'Ballykelly Disco', Liberty's 'As Fools Rush in' and Rubella Ballet's 'Belfast'.

95 Hit Parade, *Bad News* EP, Crass Records, 1982.

96 Fallout, 'Tell Me About It', on *Butchery*, Fallout Records, 1985.

97 Graham Lock, 'Creature from the Noordzee', *NME*, 11 July 1981, pp. 12–13. For a strong rebuke of the Au Pairs' position, see Gavin Martin's review of the Northern Carnival Against Racism, *NME*, 11 July 1981, pp. 38–9. Martin was an *NME* writer from Bangor and co-founder of *Alternative Ulster* fanzine. He was unimpressed by the Au Pairs' 'homage to an organisation which has admitted to putting bombs in places where innocent people have been blown to bits'.

98 Garry Bushell, 'Exploited Exported', *Sounds*, 21 November 1981, pp. 18–21. 'Army Life' on the band's debut EP of the same name (1980), and the b-side of 'Dogs of War' b/w 'Blown to Bits' (1981), both allude to Buchan's experience in the army.

99 Quoted in Ian Birch, 'Ulster on a Thin Wire', *Melody Maker*, 14 October 1978, pp. 32–4. Joe Strummer would also be criticised for stating his belief that the British should leave Ireland in a feature on the 1979 general election in *NME*.

100 Letter from Domnhall McDermott, *NME*, 6 June 1981, p. 58. For McDermott, see Bradley, *Teenage Kicks*, p. 34.

101 Dave McCullough, 'Heard the one about the Irish prophylactic?', *Sounds*, 6 January 1979, pp. 10–11. McCullough, who had previously contributed to *Alternative Ulster* fanzine, was also critical of Theatre of Hate's attempts to sing about the Irish situation. See his review of Theatre of Hate's, *Who Dares Wins*, *Sounds*, 28 March 1981, p. 36. Bands like Gang of Four denied such accusations, stating that it was a 'terrible myth that you can only sing about your direct experience'. See Thrills, 'The Year of the Great Leap Four-Wards', pp. 7–8.

102 Johnny Waller, 'The Poison in the Machine', *Sounds*, 16 January 1982, pp. 22–3.

103 Harry Doherty, 'Land of Ire', *Melody Maker*, 12 November 1977, p. 53.

104 'Thrills', *NME*, 11 November 1978, p. 11; Gavin Martin, 'Rock Against Sectarianism – New Angles', *NME*, 18 November 1978, p. 15; Letters to *NME*, 2 and 9 December 1978, p. 66 and p. 58 respectively.

105 O'Neill and Trelford, *It Makes You Want to Spit*, pp. 2–12.

106 Quoted in Colin Irwin, 'Clawing Out of Toytown', *Melody Maker*, 27 March 1982, p. 6.

107 Roland Link, *Kicking Up a Racket: The Story of Stiff Little Fingers* (Belfast: Appletree Press, 2009), pp. 68–113. Hear also early 1980s records by Alienated, Asylum, Catch 22, Self Defence, Stalag 17 and Toxic Waste.

108 Link, *Kicking Up a Racket*, pp. 57–67.

109 Quoted in Tony Stewart, 'It's A Dog's Life in Today's Belfast', *NME*, 25 March 1978, p. 11.

110 Harry Doherty, 'Heroes for Credibility', *Melody Maker*, 29 March 1980, p. 16.

111 The Defects, *Dance (Until You Drop)* EP, Casualty Records, 1981. See also Tina Calder, *Survival: The Story of The Defects* (Belfast: Ravage Publishing, 2011).

112 Quoted in Birch, 'Ulster on a Thin Wire', p. 34. See also comments on Sham 69's 'Ulster Boy' in Doherty, 'Heroes for Credibility', p. 16. For a defence of Sham 69, see the live review in *Alternative Ulster*, 1 (1978), p. 3.

113 Quoted in Carol Clerk, 'Metal Walls and Dead Cities', *Melody Maker*, 6 February 1982, p. 8.

114 O'Neill and Trelford, *It Makes You Want to Spit*, p. v; Francis Stewart, '"Alternative Ulster": Punk Rock as a Means of Overcoming the Religious Divide in Northern Ireland', in John Wolffe (ed.), *Irish Religious Conflict in Comparative Perspective* (Basingstoke: Palgrave Macmillan, 2014), pp. 76–90; Stewart, 'The Outcasts', pp. 47–63; Timothy Heron, 'Alternative Ulster: Punk and the Construction of Everyday life in 1970s Northern Ireland', *Popular Culture Today: Imaginaries*, 9 (2015), 1–17.

115 Quoted in Hooley, *Hooleygan*, pp. 138–43.

116 *Shellshock Rock*, directed by John T. Davis, 1979; Martin McLoone, 'Punk Music in Northern Ireland: The Political Power of "What Might Have Been"', *Irish Studies Review*, 12:1 (2004), 29–38.

117 Gavin Martin, 'Northern Ireland: The Fantasy and the Reality', *NME*, 11 October 1980, pp. 31–4 and 61.

118 Birch, 'Ulster on a Thin Wire', p. 34.

119 Johnny Waller, live review of Poison Girls and The Defects in Belfast, *Sounds*, 16 January 1982, p. 29. See also Steve Ignorant's comments in Berger, *The Story of Crass*, p. 225.

120 Link, *Kicking Up a Racket*, p. 52. Link writes of 'anti-punk gangs' (p. 325), often with connections to Loyalist organisations, targeting punks from 1977.

121 Quoted in Clerk, 'Metal Walls and Dead Cities', p. 8.

122 Quoted in Paul Morley, 'Belfast's Ripped Back Sides', *NME*, 17 February 1979, pp. 7–8.

123 Andy Worthington, *Stonehenge: Celebration and Subversion* (Loughborough: Alternative Albion, 2014).

124 The bomb exploded at the Grand Hotel, Brighton. Five people were killed; many more were seriously injured.

125 Conflict, sleevenotes and lyrics to 'This Is Not Enough' b/w 'Neither Is This', Mortarhate, 1985.

126 Crass, 'They've Got a Bomb', on *The Feeding of the Five Thousand*, Small Wonder, 1978.

127 For a gig review describing Mike Duffield's use of nuclear imagery for films projected at Crass gigs, see Edwin Pouncey, 'Tea and Anarchy', *Sounds*, 20 June 1981, pp. 24–5.

128 Rimbaud, *Shibboleth*, pp. 109–10.

129 Savage, 1966, p. 32.

130 Jeff Nuttall, *Bomb Culture* (London: Paladin, 1970, originally published 1968), p. 20.

131 MAD referred to the doctrine – most clearly defined by US Secretary of Defence Robert McNamara in the 1960s – that assumed either side of the Cold War had the nuclear capability to destroy the other, be it initially or in retaliation.

132 For an overview, see John Lewis Gaddis, *The Cold War: A New History* (New York: Penguin Press, 2005); Sean Greenwood, *Britain and the Cold War, 1945–91* (Basingstoke: Palgrave Macmillan, 1999).

133 Paul Byrne, *The Campaign for Nuclear Disarmament* (Croom Helm: London, 1988); Kate Hudson, *CND – Now More Than Ever: The Story of a Peace Movement* (London: Vision, 2005 edition).

134 The moniker of 'Iron Lady' was given to Thatcher by the Soviets following her 'Britain Awake' speech of January 1976.

135 See, for example, Fred Halliday, *The Making of the Second Cold War* (London: Verso, 1983).

136 Turner, *Rejoice! Rejoice!*, pp. 96–105; Worley, 'One Nation Under the Bomb', 65–83.

137 *Threads*, directed by Mick Jackson, 1984; George McKay, *Glastonbury: A Very English Fair* (London: Verso, 2000).

138 All three of the main music papers gave extensive coverage to CND events, including interviews with Bruce Kent (*Sounds*, 31 December 1983, pp. 12–13). The *NME* letters' page regular featured discussion of CND and the paper's anti-nuclear position.

139 Crass, 'Nagasaki Nightmare' b/w 'Big A Little A', Crass Records, 1980.

140 Quoted in Winston Smith, 'Hear Nothing, See Nothing, Say Nothing', *Punk Lives*, 3, 1983, pp. 12–13.

141 Discharge, *Hear Nothing See Nothing Say Nothing*, Clay Records, 1982. Discharge would also show *The War Game* at concerts. My thanks go to Nic Bullen for passing this information to me.

142 Quoted in Garry Bushell, 'Night of the Punk Undead', *Sounds*, 11 July 1981, pp. 26–7.

143 The Mob, 'No Doves Fly Here' b/w 'I Hear You Laughing', Crass Records, 1981. The record was pressed in 1981 but came out in 1982.

144 Amebix, *Who's The Enemy* EP, Spider Leg Records, 1982, 'Winter' b/w 'Beginning of the End', Spider Leg Records, 1983 and *No Sanctuary*, Spider Leg Records, 1984; Anti-System, *Defence of the Realm* EP, Pax, 1983; Flux of Pink Indians, *Strive to Survive Causing Least Suffering Possible*, Spider Leg Records, 1982 (released 1983); The System, *The Warfare* EP, Spider Leg Records, 1982.

145 Quoted in Sandy Robertson, 'Fighting Talk ...', *Sounds*, 10 July 1982, p. 23; hear also, The Exploited, 'Computers Don't Blunder' b/w 'Addiction', Secret Records, 1982 and *Rival Leaders* EP, Pax Records, 1983.

146 For an insightful essay on the *sound* of punk's anti-nuclear protest, see George McKay, '"They've Got a Bomb": Anti-Nuclearism in the Anarcho-Punk Movement, 1978–84', draft article. My thanks to George for letting me see a copy.

147 The Varukers, 'Die for Your Government' b/w 'All Systems Fail', Riot City, 1983.

148 Hear also The Clash, 'The Call Up' b/w 'Stop the World', CBS, 1980.

149 Chron Gen, 'Puppets of War', on *Puppets of War* EP, Gargoyle Records, 1981. Hear also The Insane, 'Nuclear War', on *El Salvador* EP, No Future, 1982: 'Why bother anyway, 'there's gonna be a nuclear war'.

150 See, for example, comments in Paul Du Noyer's interview with Theatre of Hate, *NME*, 6 February 1982, pp. 22–6. Brandon felt the threat of nuclear war would give youth a common purpose for change.

151 Sleevenotes to Wah!, *Nah=POO: The Art of Bluff*, Sanctuary 2001 (original LP released on Eternal, 1981).

152 For just a few examples, see *Acts of Defiance*, 3, 1982 and 7, 1983; *Apathy* ('CND Issue'), 3, 1981; *Bring Into Being*, 1, 1983, pp. 7–9; *Fack*, 5, 1980, p. 14; *FM–LB* [named after the bombs dropped in August 1945], 4, 1982; *Mental Block*, 1, 1982; *New Crimes*, 6, 1982; *Toxic Graffity*, 6, 1982.

153 Various Artists, *Life in the European Theatre*, WEA, 1982; Various Artists, *Wargasm*, Pax Records, 1982. The former record included The Clash, The Jam, The Stranglers, The Beat and The Specials; the latter featured Poison Girls, Flux of Pink Indians, Infa Riot, Angelic Upstarts, Mau Maus and Danse Society.

154 *Melody Maker*, 18 October 1980, p. 3.

155 Paul Weller, 'The Eve of Destruction?', *Melody Maker*, 28 November 1981, p. 20.

156 David George Boyce, *The Falklands War* (Basingstoke: Palgrave Macmillan, 2001); Helen Parr, 'National Interest and the Falklands War', in Timothy Edmunds, Jamie Gaskarth and Robin Porter (eds.), *British Foreign Policy and the National Interest: Identity, Strategy and Security* (Basingstoke: Palgrave Macmillan, 2014), pp. 62–82.

157 Beckett, *Promised You a Miracle*, pp. 255–87; Andy McSmith, *No Such Thing As Society: A History of Britain in the 1980s* (London: Constable, 2011), pp. 111–35; Graham Stewart, *Bang! A History of Britain in the 1980s* (London: Atlantic Books, 2013), pp. 130–68; Turner, *Rejoice! Rejoice*, pp. 105–22; Richard Vinen, *Thatcher's Britain: The Politics and Social Upheaval of the 1980s* (London: Simon & Schuster, 2009), pp. 134–53.

158 See, for example, Thatcher's speech at a Conservative rally in Cheltenham on 3 July 1982, quoted in Stewart, *Bang!*, p. 168.

159 Robert Harris, *Gotcha: The Media, The Government and the Falklands Crisis* (London: Faber and Faber, 1983).

160 Crass, *The Party's Over* (Epping: Dial House, 1982); *Artificial Life*, 2, 1982, pp. 9–11.

161 Crass, *A Series of Shock Slogans*, p. 21.

162 Crass, 'How Does It Feel (To Be the Mother of a Thousand Dead)' b/w 'The Immortal Death' and 'Don't Tell Me You Care', Crass Records, 1982; *Hansard*, 26 October 1982, Vol. 29 c335W; Paul Du Noyer, 'Official – Crass "Not Obscene"', *NME*, 6 November 1982, p. 5.

163 Crass, *The Party's Over*, p. 2.

164 Berger, *The Story of Crass*, pp. 229–48.

165 Crass, *Yes Sir, I Will*, Crass Records, 1983.

166 Betty Page, 'The Sanity Squad', *Sounds*, 22 May 1982, pp. 22–5.

167 Quoted in Garry Bushell, 'Upstate with the Upstarts', *Sounds*, 26 June 1982, pp. 116–17.

168 Garry Bushell, 'Strictly for the Birds', *Sounds*, 20 November 1982, p. 14; idem, 'Four Go Mad in Shoreditch', *Sounds*, 4 June 1983, p. 22.

169 Ford, *Hip Priest*, p. 108. The song was intended to be a single, but was never properly released as such. It appeared on *Room to Live*, Kamera, 1982, and a limited number of 7-inch copies came out in 1983.

170 For Mayhem, see *IQ32*, 2, 1983, pp. 16–17; Combat 84, 'Right to Choose', on *Rapist* EP, Victory, 1983 (and the album *Send in the Marines*, Rock-O-Rama, 1984); The Ovalteenies, 'Argentina', on *British Justice* EP, BAA, 1983. The Crack also issued 'The Troops Have Landed' in support of those who fought on the b-side of 'Going Out', RCA, 1982, while Special Duties' Steve Arrogant insisted 'we did a great job in the Falklands' (Letter to *Sounds*, 14 August 1982, p. 42). The Ejected's 'England Ain't Dead' was another celebratory account of the Falklands war.

171 'Conflict in the Falklands', *Anathema*, 2, 1982, p. 22; 'Glorious Victory of Falklands Farce', *Bring Into Being*, 1, 1983, p. 12; Paul Wellings, 'Scalp Hunters' [Redskins], *Sounds*, 14 August 1982, p. 23; Garry Bushell, 'It's Time to See What's What' [Conflict], 30 *Sounds*, 1983, pp. 15–17; New Model Army 'Spirit of the Falklands', on *Vengeance*, Abstract 1984. Hear also Elvis Costello's 'Shipbuilding', released as a single by Robert Wyatt on Rough Trade in 1982 and Billy Bragg's 'Island of No Return', on *Brewing Up With Billy Bragg*, Go Discs!, 1984. Non-punk responses to the war included Pink Floyd's *The Final Cut*, Columbia, 1983.

172 The Ejected, *Have You Got 10p* EP, Riot City, 1982.

173 This is a point well made in Wilkinson, *Post-Punk, Politics and Pleasure in Britain*, p. 5; Butt, 'Being in a Band', in Butt, Eshun and Fisher (eds.), *Post Punk Then and Now*, pp. 61–7. See also Raymond Williams, 'Culture Is Ordinary', in Robin Gable (ed.), *Resources of Hope: Culture, Democracy, Socialism* (London: Verso, 1989).

Alternatives: Chaos and Finish

1 Quoted in Murray, 'John, Paul, Steve and Sidney', pp. 23–6.

2 For an early version, hear Alternative TV, *Live at the Rat Club*, Crystal Records, 1979. Recorded on 14 September 1977, Perry reads from an anarchist magazine article that imagines how the media would respond to a Soviet invasion.

3 The opening of 'Alternatives' recalls Faust's 'Why Don't You Eat Carrots' (*Faust*, Polydor, 1971).

4 Alternative TV, 'How Much Longer' b/w 'You Bastard', Deptford City Fun Records, 1977.

5 According to Perry, the clip came from a BBC documentary about the Other Cinema (which became the Scala Cinema soon after). Alternative TV played a gig there in late 1977, supporting a showing of the film *Blank Generation*. Correspondence with the author, 15 September 2016.

6 Alternative TV, 'Alternatives', on *The Image Has Cracked*, Deptford City Fun Records, 1978.

7 Paul Morley, 'Let's Crack Again Like We Did Last Summer, *NME*, 24 June 1978, p. 37.

8 Moore, *Sells Like Teen Spirit*, pp. 5–12; David Harvey, *A Brief History of Neoliberalism* (Oxford: Oxford University Press, 2005).

9 Richard Johnson, 'What Is Cultural Studies?', *Social Text*, 16 (1986), 38–80; Paul Du Gay and Stuart Hall, *Doing Cultural Studies: The Story of the Sony Walkman* (London: SAGE, 1997).

10 Drugs helped too, of course.

11 *Sideburns*, 1 (1977), p. 2.

12 *Boy's Own*, 8 (1989), p. 23.

13 Steve Redhead, *Subcultures to Clubcultures: An Introduction to Popular Cultural Studies* (Oxford: Blackwell, 1997); Muggleton and Weinzierl (eds.), *The Post-Subcultures Reader*; Andy Bennett and Keith Kahn-Harris, *After Subculture*.

14 David Hesmondhalgh, 'Flexibility, Post-Fordism and the Music Industries', *Media, Culture and Society*, 18 (1996), 461–79; idem, 'Indie: The Institutional Politics and Aesthetics of a Popular Music Genre', *Cultural Studies*, 13:1 (1999), 34–61.

15 Lynskey, *33 Revolutions per Minute*, p. 486.

16 For more sophisticated analysis, see Lucy Robinson, 'Putting the Charity Back into Charity Singles: Charity Singles in Britain, 1984–95', *Contemporary British History*, 26:3 (2012), 405–25. We should also note that Red Wedge attempted another approach, linking with the Labour Party to encourage political participation at the 1987 general election via gigs, day events and publications. See Rachel, *Walls Come Tumbling Down*, pp. 407–46; Simon Frith and John Street, 'Rock Against Racism and Red Wedge: From Music to Politics, from Politics to Music', in Reebee Garofalo (ed.), *Rockin' the Boat:*

Mass Music and Mass Movements (London: South End Press, 1992), pp. 67–80.

17 They could also be mixed imaginatively and admirably, of course. See David Toop, *The Rap Attack: African Jive to New York Hip Hop* (London: Pluto, 1994); Paul D. Miller, *Sound Unbound: Sampling Digital Music and Culture* (London: MIT Press, 2008).

18 Reynolds, *Rip It Up and Start Again*, p. 518.

19 The Fits, 'Action' b/w 'Achilles Heel', Trapper Records, 1984.

20 McKay, *Senseless Acts of Beauty*, pp. 45–72 and 103–26.

21 Ian Glasper, *Trapped in a Scene: UK Hardcore, 1985–89* (London: Cherry Red, 2010); Kevin Dunn, 'Never Mind the Bollocks: The Punk Rock Politics of Global Communication', *Review of International Studies*, 34 (2008), 193–210; Kevin Dunn and May Summer Farnsworth, '"We ARE the Revolution": Riot Grrrl Press, Girl Empowerment and DIY Self-Publishing', *Women's Studies*, 41:2 (2012), 136–57.

22 Robinson, Schofield, Sutcliffe-Braithwaite and Thomlinson, 'Telling Stories about Post-war Britain', 268–304.

23 Such a suggestion chimes with Black and Pemberton's reading of the 1970s as a period of possibility as well as 'decline'. See their 'The Benighted Decade?' Reassessing the 1970s', in Black, Pemberton and Thane (eds.), *Reassessing 1970s Britain*, pp. 1–24. See also Wilkinson, *Post-Punk, Politics and Pleasure in Britain*, pp. 195–7.

24 For an amusing take on this, see Billy Idol in Chris Welch, 'Road Test', *Melody Maker*, 18 March 1978, p. 36. 'I never liked songs about wizards', Idol says just before the allure of pop stardom transformed him into a willing rock 'n' roll cliché. 'Does a wizard drive a bus, or work in Woolworth's? I've never seen a wizard in my life.'

25 *Peroxide*, 1, 1980, p. 5. Swell Maps started their own Rather Records in 1977, having experimented in bedrooms for some time before being inspired to greater action by the Sex Pistols.

26 Reynolds, *Rip It Up and Start Again*, pp. xiv–xv.

27 The notes are located in the Jon Savage Archive at John Moores University, Liverpool, and quoted in Kugelberg and Savage (eds.), *Punk*, p. 351.

28 Crass, 'Punk Is Dead', on *The Feeding of the Five Thousand*, Small Wonder, 1978. See also 'Punk Is Dead', *International Times*, February 1977.

29 See, for example, the bIG fLAME statement cited in Chapter 2 or John Hyatt of The Three Johns' discussion of live performances deconstructing the image of a band on stage in echo of his fellow John's (Jon Langford's) time in The Mekons (Bill Black, 'Ello John', *Sounds*, 10 December 1984, p. 14).

30 Sex Pistols, 'EMI', *Never Mind the Bollocks, Here's the Sex Pistols*, Virgin, 1977.

Bibliography

Archives

The bulk of the material used for this book comes from records, interviews, fanzines and artworks (including posters and flyers) produced in the period under review. These are scattered across a range of public and private collections and number too many to list in a manageable bibliography. As such, the archives in the following list were drawn upon for fanzine material, the music press, political periodicals, ephemera and other documentation.

Bodleian Library, Oxford: political periodicals
British Library, London: fanzine collection and music papers
Caversham Archive, Reading: BBC documents
Chris Low Collection: fanzines, periodicals and ephemera
Feminist Archive, Leeds: fanzines, papers, documents
Hansard: parliamentary debates
Jon Savage Archive, Liverpool John Moores University: fanzines and ephemera
Labour History Archive and Study Centre, Manchester: political papers and documents
London College of Communications: fanzines
London Metropolitan Archive, London: Greater London Council material
Marx Memorial Library, London: political periodicals and papers
Mott Collection: fanzines and ephemera
National Archive: government papers
Victoria and Albert Museum: fanzines
Women's Liberation Music Archive: fanzines, pamphlets and political periodicals
Working Class Movement Library, Salford: political periodicals and papers

Fanzines, Music Press and Political Periodicals

Fanzines

48 Thrills
Ability Stinks
A Boring Fanzine
Acts of Defiance
Adventures in Reality
Adventuring into Basketry
After Hours
Ain't Been to No Art School
Allied Propaganda
All the Poets
Alternative Sounds
Alternative Ulster
Anarchy in the UK
Anathema
And Don't Run Away You Punk
Another Day Another Word
Anti-Climax
Antigen
Apathy
Artificial Life
A System Partly Revealed
A Trip into Realism
Attack on Bzag
Back Issue
Barbecued Iguana
Barricade
Between the Lines
Bigger Problem Now
Bits
Black Dwarf
Blackpool Rox
Blades 'n' Shades
Blam!
Blast
Blaze

Blown to Bits
Blue Blanket
Bombsite
Bondage
Book of Revelations
Bored Stiff
Brains Thinking
Brass Lip
Breakdown
Bring into Being
Cardboard Theatre
Cells
Censored
Chainsaw
Chargesheet
City Chains
City Fun
Cliché
Cobalt Hate
Codeye
Coming Attack
Concrete Beaches
Confidential
Cool Notes
Crash Bang
Dangerous Logic
Dayglow
Defused
Dirt
Do You Know Vanessa Redgrave?
Dry Rot
Eklektik. The
Encyclopaedia of Ecstasy
Enigma
Fack

Fair Dukes

Fight Back

Final Curtain

Flicks

FM-LB

For Adolpfs Only

Gabba Gabba Hey

Ghast Up

God on the Screen

Grim Humour

Grinding Halt

Guilty of What

Guilty Without Trial

Gun Rubber

Guttersnipe

Hanging Around

Hard as Nails

Harsh Reality

Hate and War

Have a Good Laugh

Heat

Here's the Sex Pistols

Hit Ranking

Hungry Beat

Impossible Dream. The

Incendiary

Industrial News

Inside Out

Intensive Care

International Anthem

In the City

Intolerance

IQ32

Jamming

Jolt

Jungleland

Kata

Kick

Kid's Stuff

Kill Your Pet Puppy

Kingdom Come

Knee Deep in Shit

Let's Be Adult About This

Live Wire

Loaded

London's Burning

London's Outrage

Mental Block

Mental Children

Monkey Talk

More On

Mucilage

Murder by Fanzine

Music Works

Negative Reaction

New Crimes

New Mania

New Pose

New Systems

New Wave. The

Next Big Thing. The

Nihilist Vices

NN4 9PZ

No Comment

No More of That

Non-LP B-Side

Northern Spikes

Paid in Full

Panache

Peroxide

Phaze One

Pigs for Slaughter

Pink Flag

Pistol Whipped

Plaything

Précautions Essentielles Pour
   la Bonne

Pretty Vacant

Printed Noises
Private World
Problem Child
Protesting Children Minus the
  Bondage
Other Side. The
Rabid
Raising Hell
Ranting on the Barricades
Rapid Eye Movement
Ready to Ruck
Red Tape
Rigor Mortis
Ripped & Torn
Rising Free
Rotten to the Core
Rough Justice
Sanity is Boring
Scrobe
Scum
Secret Public. The
Shelters for the Rich
Shews
Shocking Pink
Sideburns
Situation 3
Situation Vacant
Skinhead Havoc
Skins
Skum
Sniffin' Glue
So What
Spuno
Stabmental
Stand Up and Spit
Stay Free
Still Dying
Stranded
Strangled

Stringent Measures
Suburban Revolt
Subvert
Summer Salt
Sunday Mirra
Sunday the 7th
Surrey's Burning
Surrey Vomet
Suspect Device
Tell Us the Truth
Tender Mercy
Terminal Boredom
Testament of Reality
Tidal Wave
Tirane Thrash
To Hell With Poverty
Totally Wired
Toxic Grafity
Trees and Flowers
Twisted Nerve
Urban Royalty
Vague
Vibes
Voice of Buddha
V-Sign
Wake Up
What Culture
White Stuff
Wool City Rocker
Young Offenders
Zip Vinyls

Music Papers

Dance Craze
Face. The
Melody Maker
New Musical Express

Punk Lives
Punk's Not Dead
Record Mirror
Rolling Stone
Smash Hits
Sounds
Street Life
Village Voice
ZigZag

Political Periodicals and Papers

Anarchy
Angry
Big Flame
Britain First
British News
British Patriot
Bulldog
Challenge
Class War
Cogito
Comment

Drastic Measures
Forum
Fuck Off
International Discussion Bulletin
Leveller. The
Marxism Today
Militant
Morning Star
News Line
New Society
NF News
Red Action
Red Rebel
Revolution
Revolutionary Socialism
Rocking the Reds
Searchlight
Socialist Challenge
Socialist Review
Socialist Worker
Spare Rib
Spearhead
Temporary Hoarding
Young Socialist

Books

Punk-Related

Albertine, Viv. *Clothes, Clothes, Clothes, Music, Music, Music, Boys, Boys, Boys*. London: Faber & Faber, 2014.
Almond, Marc. *Tainted Life: The Autobiography*. London: Sidgwick & Jackson, 1999.
Anon. *100 Nights at The Roxy*. London: Big O, 1978.
Anscombe, Isabelle and Dike Blair. *Punk: Rock/Style/Stance/People/Stars That Head the New Wave in England and America*. New York: Urizen Books, 1978
Ant, Adam. *Stand & Deliver: The Autobiography*. London: Sidgwick & Jackson, 2006.

Anxiety, Annie. *You Can't Sing The Blues While Drinking Milk*. Coventry: Tin Angel, 2012.

Aston, Martin. *Facing the Other Way: The Story of 4AD*. London; Friday Project, 2013.

Baldwin, Shane. *Last Rockers: The Vice Squad Story*. Bristol: ACM Retro, 2016.

Balls, Richard. *Be Stiff: The Stiff Records Story*. London: Soundcheck Books, 2014.

Barbarian, Steve Sutherland and Robert Smith. *The Cure: Ten Imaginary Years*. London: Zomba Books, 1988.

Barker, Simon. *Punk's Dead*. London: Divus, 2011.

Beesley, Tony. *Our Generation: The Punk and Mod Children of Sheffield, Rotherham and Doncaster*. Peterborough: Fastprint, 2009.

Berger, George. *The Story of Crass*. London: Omnibus, 2006.

Bestley, Russ and Tony Brook. *Action Time Vision*. London: Unit Editions, 2016.

Bestley, Russ and Alex Ogg. *The Art of Punk: Posters + Flyers + Fanzines + Record Sleeves*. London: Omnibus, 2012.

Binns, Rebecca et al. *They've Taken Our Ghettos: A Punk History of Woodberry Down Estate*. London: Active, 2015.

Black, Pauline. *Black By Design: A 2-Tone Memoir*. London: Serpent's Tail, 2011.

Blade, Andy. *The Secret Life of a Teenage Punk Rocker*. London: Cherry Red, 2005.

Blinko, Nick. *Primal Screamer*. Oakland: PM Press, 2012.

Boston, Virginia. *Punk Rock*. London: Plexus, 1978.

Bradley, Michael. *Teenage Kicks: My Life as an Undertone*. London: Omnibus, 2016.

Bromberg, Craig. *The Wicked Ways of Malcolm McLaren*. New York: Harper & Row, 1988.

Bruce, Steve. *The Best Seat in the House: A Cock Sparrer Story*. London: Cherry Red, 2010.

Buckley, David. *No Mercy: The Authorised and Uncensored Biography*. London: Hodder & Stoughton, 1997.

Bull, Gregory. *Perdam Babylonis Nomen*. Charleston: Gregory Bull, 2012.

Bull, Gregory and Mike Dines (eds.). *Tales From the Punkside*. Portsmouth: Itchy Monkey, 2014.

Bull, Gregory and Mike Dines (eds.). *Some of Us Scream, Some of Us Shout*. Portsmouth: Itchy Monkey, 2016.

Bull, Gregory and Mickey 'Penguin' (eds.). *Not Just Bits of Paper*. Charleston: Perdam Babylonis Nomen, 2015.

Burchill, Julie and Tony Parsons. *The Boy Looked at Johnny: The Obituary of Rock and Roll*. London: Pluto Press, 1978.

Butt, Gavin, Kwodo Eshun and Mark Fisher. *Post Punk Then and Now*. London: Repeater, 2016.

Cain, Barry. *'77 Sulphate Strip*. London: Ovolo, 2007.

Calder, Tina. *Survival: The Story of The Defects*. Belfast: Ravage Publishing, 2011.

Captain Swing. *The Black Book: The Life and Crimes of Richard Rouska*. Leeds: 1977cc, 2014.

Cavanagh, David. *The Creation Records Story: My Magpie Eyes Are Hungry for the Prize*. London: Virgin, 2001.

Clarke, Victoria Mary and Shane MacGowan. *A Drink with Shane MacGowan*. London: Pan Books, 2002.

Colegrave Stephen and Chris Sullivan. *Punk: A Life Apart*. London: Cassell & Co., 2001.

Coleman, Jaz. *Letters from Cythera*. London: KJ Books, 2014.

Collins, Bob and Ian Snowball. *The Kids Are All Square: Medway Punk and Beyond, 1977–85*. Hitchin: Countdown, 2014.

Coon, Caroline. *1988: The New Wave Punk Rock Explosion*. London: Orbach & Chambers, 1977; London, Omnibus, 1982.

Cooper Clarke, John. *Ten Years in an Open Necked Shirt*. London: Arena, 1983.

Cope, Julian. *Head On: Memories of the Liverpool Punk Scene and the Story of The Teardrop Explodes. 1976–82*. London: Thorsons, 1999 edition.

Cornwell, Hugh. *A Multitude of Sins*. London: Harper Collins, 2004.

Crass. *A Series of Shock Slogans and Mindless Token Tantrums*. London: Exitstencil Press, 1982.

Crass. *You're Already Dead*. Epping: Dial House, 1984.

Crass. *Love Songs*. Hebden Bridge: Pomona Books, 2003.

Crossley, Nick. *Networks of Style, Sound and Subversion: The Punk and Post-Punk Worlds of Manchester, London, Liverpool and Sheffield, 1975–80*. Manchester: Manchester University Press, 2015.

Crumby, Mark (ed.). *Whitehouse: Still Going Strong*. Amersham: Impulse Publications, 1994 edition.

Cunnington, Graham, Angus Farquhar and Paul Jamrozy. *Test Dept: Total State Machine*. Bristol: PC Press, 2015.

Curtis, Deborah. *Touching from a Distance: Ian Curtis and Joy Division*. London: Faber & Faber, 1995.

Curtis, Deborah and Jon Savage (eds.). *So This Is Permanence: Ian Curtis Joy Division Lyrics and Notebooks*. London: Faber & Faber, 2014.

Czezowski, Andrew and Susan Carrington, *The Roxy, London 1976–77: The Club That Forged Punk* (London: Carrczez, 2016).

Dale, Pete. *Anyone Can Do It: Empowerment, Tradition and the Punk Underground*. Aldershot: Ashgate, 2012.

D'Ambrosio, Antonio (ed.). *Let Fury Have the Hour: The Punk Rock Politics of Joe Strummer*. New York: Nation, 2004

Darms, Lisa (ed.). *The Riot Grrrl Collection*. New York: The Feminist Press, 2013.

Davis, Julie. *Punk*. London: Millington, 1977.

Dellar, Robert. *Splitting in Two: Mad Pride and Punk Rock Oblivion*. London: Unkant Press, 2014.

Dines, Mike and Matthew Worley (eds.). *The Aesthetic of Our Anger: Anarcho-Punk, Politics and Music*. Colchester: Minor Compositions, 2016.

Drummond, Bill. *45*. London: Abacus, 2001.

Dudanski, Richard. *Squat City Rockers: Proto-Punk and Beyond*. London: Dudanski/Romero, 2013.

Duncombe, Stephen and Maxwell Tremblay (eds.). *White Riot: Punk Rock and the Politics of Race*. London: Verso, 2011.

Dwyer, Simon. *Rapid Eye*, Vols. 1–2. London: Annihilation Press, 1989–92.

Eddington, Richard. *Sent From Coventry: The Chequered Past of Two Tone*. London: Independent Music Press, 2004.

Fanni Tutti, Cosey, *Art, Sex, Music*. London: Faber & Faber, 2017.

Faulk, Barry and Brady Harrison (eds.). *Punk Rock Warlord: Critical Perspectives on the Life and Work of Joe Strummer*. Farnham: Ashgate, 2014.

Fielding, Garry. *The Business: Loud, Proud 'n' Punk*. Dunoon, ST Publishing, 1996.

Fish, Mick. *Industrial Evolution: Through the Eighties with Cabaret Voltaire*. London: SAF Publishing, 2002.

Fish, Mick and Dave Hallbery. *Cabaret Voltaire: The Art of the Sixth Sense*. London: SAF, 1989.

Fitzsimons, Ronan. *I'm An Upstart: The Decca Wade Story*. Cottingham: Ardra, 2013.

Fletcher, Tony. *Boy About Town: A Memoir*. London: William Heinemann, 2013.

Florek, Jaki and Paul Whelan. *Eric's: All the Best Clubs are Downstairs, Everybody Knows That ....* Runcorn: Feedback, 2009.

Forbes, Robert and Eddie Stampton. *When the Storm Breaks: Rock Against Communism, 1979–93*. London: Forbes/Stampton, 2014.

Forbes, Robert and Eddie Stampton. *The White Nationalist Skinhead Movement, UK & USA, 1979–1993*. London: Feral House, 2015

Ford, Simon. *Wreckers of Civilization: The Story of COUM Transmissions and Throbbing Gristle*. London: Black Dog, 1999.

Ford, Simon. *Hip Priest: The Story of Mark E Smith and The Fall*. London: Quartet Books, 2003.

Fusco, Maria and Richard Birkett (eds.). *Cosey Complex*. London, Koenig Books, 2012.

Furness, Zack (ed.). *Punkademics: The Basement Show in the Ivory Tower*. Wivenhoe: Minor Composition, 2012.

George, Boy with Spencer Bright. *Take It Like a Man*. London, Sidgwick & Jackson, 1995.

Gibbs, Alvin. *Destroy: The Definitive History of Punk*. London: Britannia Press, 1996.

Gibson, Lee. *A Punk Rock Flashback*. London: Lulu Press, 2013.

Gilbert, Pat. *Passion Is a Fashion: The Real Story of The Clash*. London: Auram Press, 2009 edition.

Glasper, Ian. *Burning Britain: A History of UK Punk, 1980–84*. London: Cherry Red, 2004.

Glasper, Ian. *The Day the Country Died: A History of Anarcho Punk, 1980–1984*. London: Cherry Red, 2006.

Glasper, Ian. *Trapped in a Scene: UK Hardcore, 1985–89*. London: Cherry Red, 2010.

Goddard, Michael and Benjamin Halligan (eds.). *Mark E. Smith and The Fall: Art, Music and Politics*. Farnham: Ashgate, 2010.

Goddard, Simon. *Simply Thrilled Honey: The Preposterous Story of Postcard Records*. London: Ebury Press, 2014.

Goodman, Dave. *My Amazing Adventures with the Sex Pistols*. London: Bluecoat Press, 2006.

Goodyer, Ian. *Crisis Music: The Cultural Politics of Rock Against Racism*.Manchester: Manchester University Press, 2009.

Gordon, Alastair. *Throwing Out the Punk Rock Baby With the Dirty Bath Water: Crass and Punk Rock, A Critical Appraisal*. Nottingham: Do One Press, 1996.

Görner, Veit and Heinrich Dietz (eds.). *Linder: Woman/Object*. Paris: Musée d'Art Moderne, 2013.

Gray, Marcus. *The Clash: Return of the Last Gang in Town*. London: Helter Skelter, 2001.

Hanley, Steve and Olivia Pickarski. *The Big Midweek: Life Inside The Fall*. Pontefract: Route, 2014.

Haskins, David J. *Who Killed Mister Moonlight: Bauhaus, Black Magick and Benediction*. London: Jawbone Press, 2014.

Haynes, Pete. *God's Lonely Men: The Lurkers*. London: Headhunter Books, 2007.

Hegarty, Paul. *Noise/Music*. London: Bloomsbury, 2013 edition

Hennessy, Val. *In the Gutter*. London: Quartet, 1978.

Henry, Tricia. *Break All Rules: Punk Rock and the Making of a Style*. Ann Arbor: University of Michigan Press, 1989.

Hewitt, Paolo. *The Jam: A Beat Concerto*. London: Omnibus Press, 1983.

Hewitt, Paolo. *Paul Weller: The Changing Man*. London: Corgi, 2007.

Heylin, Clinton. *From the Velvets to the Voidoids: The Birth of American Punk*. London: Penguin, 1993.

Heylin, Clinton. *Babylon's Burning: From Punk to Grunge*. London: Penguin, 2007.

Heylin, Clinton. *Anarchy in the UK: The Sex Pistols, The Clash and the Class of '76*. Pontefract: Route, 2016.

Hoare, Philip et al. *Linder – Works, 1976–2006*. Zürich: JRP/Ringer, 2006.

Home, Stewart. *Cranked Up Really High: Genre Theory and Punk Rock*. Hove: Codex, 1995.

Hook, Peter. *Unknown Pleasures: Inside Joy Division*. London: Simon & Schuster, 2012.

Hooley, Terri and Richard Sullivan. *Hoolygan: Music, Mayhem, Good Vibrations*. Belfast: Blackstaff Press, 2010.

Hynde, Chrissie. *Reckless: My Life*. London: Ebury Press, 2015.

Idol, Billy. *Dancing With Myself*. London: Simon & Schuster, 2014.

Ignorant, Steve with Steve Pottinger. *The Rest Is Propaganda*. London: Southern, 2010.

Ingham, Jonh, *Spirit of '76: London Punk Eyewitness* (Brooklyn: Anthology Editions, 2017).

Johnson, Garry. *The Story of Oi!: A View from the Dead End of the Street*. Manchester: Babylon Books, 1982.

Johnson, Mark. *An Ideal for Living: A History of Joy Division*. London: Bobcat Books, 1986.

Johnstone, Rob (ed.). *John Lydon: Stories of Johnny*. New Malden: Chrome Dreams, 2006.

Jones, Steve. *Lonely Boy: Tales From a Sex Pistol*. London: William Heinemann, 2016.

Keenan, David. *England's Hidden Reverse: A Secret History of the Esoteric Underground*. London: Strange Attractor, 2016.

Knight, Phil. *Strangled: Identity, Status, Structure and The Stranglers*. London: Zero Books, 2015.

Kugelberg, Johan and Jon Savage (eds.). *Punk: An Aesthetic*. New York: Rizzoli, 2012.

Kugelberg, Johan with Jon Savage and Glenn Terry (eds.). *God Save Sex Pistols*. New York: Eizzoli, 2016.

Laing, Dave. *One Chord Wonders: Power and Meaning in Punk Rock*. Milton Keynes: Open University Press, 1985.

Lake, Steve. *Zounds Demystified*. London: Active/Bev, 2013.

Langebach, Martin and John Raabe. 'Inside the Extreme Right: The "White Power" Music Scene', in Andrea Mammone, Emmanuel Godin, Brian Jenkins (eds.). *Varieties of Right-Wing Extremism in Europe*. Abingdon: Routledge, 2013.

Leblanc, Lauraine. *Pretty in Punk: Girls' Gender Resistance in a Boys' Subculture*. New Brunswick: Rutgers University Press, 1999.

Letts, Don. *Culture Clash: Dread Meets Punk Rockers*. London: SAF Publishing, 2007.

Lilleker, Martin. *Beats Working for a Living: Sheffield Popular Music, 1973–1984*. Sheffield: Juma, 2005.

Link, Roland. *Kicking Up a Racket: The Story of Stiff Little Fingers*. Belfast: Appletree Press, 2009.

Link, Roland. *Love in Vain: The Story of The Ruts*. London: Cadiz Music, 2015.

Lloyd, Peter Alan. *Bombed Out! Tales of 70s–80s: Music, Punk, Eric's and Beyond*. Liverpool: PAL Publishing, 2014.

Lohmas, Ross with Steve Pottinger. *City Baby: From Highgate to Hawaii … Life and GBH*. London: Ignite Books, 2013.

Lowles, Nick and Steve Silver (eds.). *White Noise: Inside the International Nazi Skinhead Scene*. London: Searchlight, 1998.

Lydon, John with Keith and Kent Zimmerman. *Rotten: No Irish, No Blacks, No Dogs*. London: Plexus, 1994.

Lydon, John. *Anger Is an Energy: My Life Uncensored*. London: Simon & Schuster, 2014.

Marcus, Greil. *Lipstick Traces: A Secret History of the Twentieth Century*. London: Faber & Faber, 1989.

Marcus, Greil. *In the Fascist Bathroom: Writings on Punk, 1977–82*. London: Viking, 1993.

Marko, Paul. *The Roxy London WC2: A Punk Rock History*. London, Punk77 Books, 2007.

Marshall, Bertie. *Berlin Bromley*. London: SAF Publishing, 2007.

Marshall, George. *The Two Tone Story*. Lockerbie: ST Publishing, 1997 version.

Matlock, Glen. *I Was a Teenage Sex Pistol*. London: Reynolds & Hearn, 2006 edition.

Matt, Gerald (ed.). *Punk: No-One Is Innocent*. Nuremberg: Kunsthalle Wien, 2008.

McNeil, Legs and Gillian McCain. *Please Kill Me: The Uncensored Oral History of Punk*. London: Abacus, 1997.

Mercer, Mick. *Gothic Rock Black Book*. London: Lulu, 2009 edition.

Middles, Mick. *From Joy Division to New Order: The True Story of Anthony H. Wilson and Factory Records*. London: Virgin, 2002.

Middles, Mick and Lindsey Reade. *Torn Apart: The Life of Ian Curtis*. London: Omnibus Press, 2006.

Middles, Mick and Mark E. Smith. *The Fall*. London: Omnibus Press, 2008 edition.

Monk, Noel and Jimmy Guterman. *12 Days on the Road: The Sex Pistols and America*. New York: William Morrow & Co., 1990.

Moore, Ryan. *Sells Like Teen Spirit: Music, Youth Culture and Social Crisis*. New York University Press, 2010.

Morley, Paul. *Ask: The Chatter of Pop*. London: Faber & Faber, 1986.

Morley, Paul. *Nothing*. London: Faber & Faber, 2000.

Morley, Paul. *Joy Division Piece By Piece: Writings About Joy Division, 1977–2007*. London: Plexus, 2008.

Morris, Dennis. *Rebel Rock: A Photographic History of the Sex Pistols*. London: Omnibus Press, 1985.

Morrissey. *Autobiography*. London: Penguin, 2013.

Mott, Toby. *100 Fanzines: 10 Years of British Punk*. New York: PPP Editions, 2010.

Mott, Toby. *Loud Flash: British Punk on Paper*. London: Haunch of Venison, 2010.

Mott, Toby. *Oh So Pretty: Punk in Print, 1976–80*. London: Phaidon Press, 2016.

Muirhead, Bert. *Stiff: The Story of a Record Label*. Poole: Blandford Press, 1983.

Myers, Ben. *John Lydon: The Sex Pistols, PiL and Anti-Celebrity*. London: Independent Music Press, 2004.

Neal, Christopher (ed.). *Tape Delay*. Harrow: SAF Publishing, 1987.

Neate, Wilson. *Read & Burn: A Book About Wire*. London: Jawbone Press, 2013.

Needs, Kris. *Joe Strummer and the Legend of The Clash*. London: Plexus, 2005.

Nehring, Neil. *Flowers in the Dustbin: Culture, Anarchy and Postwar England*. Ann Arbor: University of Michigan Press, 1993.

Nice, James. *Shadowplayers: The Rise and Fall of Factory Records*. London: Aurum, 2010.

Nolan, David. *I Swear I Was There: The Gig That Changed the World*. Shropshire: IMP, 2006.

Ogg, Alex. *No More Heroes: A Complete History of UK Punk from 1976 to 1980*. London: Cherry Red, 2006.

O'Hara, Craig. *The Philosophy of Punk: More Than Noise!*. Oakland: AK Press, 2001.

O'Neill, Sean and Guy Trelford. *It Makes You Want to Spit: The Definitive Guide to Punk in Northern Ireland*. Belfast: Reekus, 2003.

O'Shea, Mick. *The Anarchy Tour*. London: Omnibus Press, 2012.

Panter, Horace. *Ska'd For Life: A Personal Journey with The Specials*. London: Pan 2008.

Parker, Alan. *Sid Vicious: No-one Is Innocent*. London: Orion, 2007.

Parker, Alan with Mick O'Shea. *Young Flesh Required: Growing Up with the Sex Pistols*. London: Soundcheck Books, 2011.

Paytress, Mark. *Siouxsie and the Banshees: The Authorised Biography*. London: Sanctuary, 2003.

Pearce, Joe. *Skrewdriver: The First Ten Years*. London: Skrewdriver Services, 1987.

Perry, Mark. *Sniffin' Glue: The Essential Punk Accessory*. London: Sanctuary, 2000.

Porter, Joseph. *Genesis to Revelation: The Curse of Zounds Demystified*. Downwarde Spiral/Bedsit Press, 2012.

PunkPistol. *SEX and Seditionaries*. London: PunkPistol, 2007.

Rachel, Daniel. *Walls Come Tumbling Down: The Music and Politics of Rock Against Racism, 2-Tone and Red Wedge*. London: Picador, 2016.

Rawlings, Terry. *Steve Diggle's Harmony in My Head*. London: Helter Skelter, 2003.

Reddington, Helen. *The Lost Women of Rock Music: Female Musicians of the Punk Era*. Aldershot: Ashgate, 2007.

Reed, John. *Paul Weller: My Ever Changing Moods*. London: Omnibus, 1997 edition.

Reed, S. Alexander. *Assimilate: A Critical History of Industrial Music*. Oxford: Oxford University Press, 2013.

Reid, Jamie and Jon Savage. *Up They Rise: The Incomplete Works of Jamie Reid*. London: Faber & Faber, 1987.

Reynolds, Simon. *Rip It Up and Start Again: Post-Punk, 1978–84*. London: Faber & Faber, 2005.

Reynolds, Simon. *Totally Wired: Post-Punk Interviews and Overviews*. London Faber & Faber, 2009.

Rimbaud, Penny. *Shibboleth: My Revolting Life*. Edinburgh: AK Press, 1998.

Rimmer, Dave. *The Look: New Romantics*. London: Omnibus, 2003.

Rimmer, David. *Like Punk Never Happened: Culture Club and the New Pop*. London: Faber & Faber, 2011 edition.

Robb, John. *Punk Rock: An Oral History*. London: Ebury Press, 2006.

Robb, John. *The North Will Rise Again: Manchester Music City, 1976–96*. London: Aurum, 2009.

Robb, John. *Death to Trad Rock*. London: Cherry Red, 2009.

Sabin, Roger (ed.). *Punk Rock: So What? The Cultural Legacy of Punk*. London: Routledge, 1999.

Salewicz, Chris. *Redemption Song: The Definitive Biography of Joe Strummer*. London: Harper Collins, 2006.

Savage, Jon. *England's Dreaming: Sex Pistols and Punk Rock*. London: Faber & Faber, 1991.

Savage, Jon. *Time Travel: From the Sex Pistols to Nirvana: Pop, Media and Sexuality, 1977– 96*. London: Chatto & Windus, 1996.

Savage, Jon. *The England's Dreaming Tapes*. London: Faber & Faber, 2009.

Savage, Jon. *Punk 45: Original Punk Rock Singles Cover Art*. London: Soul Jazz, 2013.

Scanlon, John. *Sex Pistols: Poison in the Machine*. London: Reaktion Books, 2016.

Short, Bob. *Trash Can: Tales of Lowlife Losers and Rock & Roll Sleaze*. London: Lulu, 2007.

Simpson, Dave. *The Fallen: Life In and Out of Britain's Most Insane Group*. Edinburgh: Canongate, 2008.

Sklar, Monica. *Punk Style*. London: Bloomsbury, 2013.

Smith, Graham and Chris Sullivan. *We Can Be Heroes*. London: Unbound, 2012.

Smith, Mark E. *Renegade: The Lives and Tales of Mark E. Smith*. London: Viking, 2008.

Sofianos, Lisa, Robin Ryde and Charlie Waterhouse (eds.). *The Truth of Revolution, Brother: An Exploration of Punk Philosophy*. London: Situation Press, 2014.

Southall, Brian. *Sex Pistols: 90 Days at EMI*. London: Bobcat Books, 2007.

Staple, Neville with Tony McMahon. *Original Rude Boy: From Borstal to The Specials*. London: Aurum, 2009.

Stevenson, Nils and Ray. *Vacant: A Diary of the Punk Years, 1976–79*. London: Thames & Hudson, 1999.

Stevenson, Ray. *Sex Pistols File*. London: Omnibus, 1978.

Stevenson, Ray. *Siouxsie and the Banshees: Photo Book*. London: Symbiosis, 1983.

Stolper Paul and Andrew Wilson. *No Future: SEX, Seditionaries and the Sex Pistols*. London: The Hospital, 2004.

Strange, Steve. *Blitzed: The Autobiography of Steve Strange*. London: Orion, 2002.

Street Howe, Zoe. *Typical Girls? The Story of The Slits*. London: Omnibus, 2009.

Strongman, Phil. *Pretty Vacant: A History of Punk*. London: Orion Books, 2007.

Subcultures Network (ed.). *Subcultures, Popular Music and Social Change*. Newcastle: Cambridge Scholars, 2014.

Subcultures Network. *Fight Back: Punk, Politics and Resistance*. Manchester: Manchester University Press, 2015.

Sumner, Bernard. *Chapter and Verse: New Order, Joy Division and Me*. London: Bantam Press, 2014.

Taylor, Neil. *Document and Eyewitness: An Intimate History of Rough Trade*. London: Orion, 2010.

Thompson, Dave. *The Dark Reign of Gothic Rock: In the Reptile House with The Sisters of Mercy, Bauhaus and The Cure*. London: Helter Skelter, 2002.

Thompson, Dave. *Wheels Out of Gear: 2 Tone, The Specials and a World on Fire*. London: Helter Skelter, 2004.

Tobler, John. *Punk Rock*. London: Phebus, 1977.

Tolhurst, Lol. *Cured: The Tale of Two Imaginary Boys*. London: Quercus, 2016.

Triggs, Teal. *Fanzines*. London: Thames & Hudson, 2010.

Turner, Jeff with Garry Bushell. *Cockney Reject*. London: John Blake, 2010.

Vague, Tom. *The Great British Mistake*, Vague 1977–92. Edinburgh: AK Press, 1994.

Vale, V. (ed.). *Industrial Culture Handbook*. San Francisco: RE Search, 1983.

Valls, Jordi. *The London Punk Tapes*. Barcelona: Actar, 2016.

Vaucher, Gee. *Crass Art and Other Pre-Postmodernist Monsters*. Edinburgh: AK Press, 1999.

Vaucher, Gee. *Introspective*. Colchester: Firstsite, 2016.

Vermorel, Fred. *Fashion + Perversity: A Life of Vivienne Westwood and the Sixties Laid Bare*. London: Bloomsbury, 1997.

Vermorel, Fred and Judy. *The Sex Pistols: The Inside Story*. London: Universal, 1978.

Wallis, Jennifer (ed.). *Fight Your Own War: Power Electronics and Noise Culture*. London: Headpress, 2016.

Walsh, Gavin. *Punk on 45: Revolution on Vinyl, 1976–79*. London: Plexus, 2006.

Westwood, Vivienne and Ian Kelly. *Vivienne Westwood*. London: Picador, 2014.

Whalley, Boff. *Footnote**. Hebden Bridge: Pomona, 2003.

White, Michael. *Popkisss: The Life and Afterlife of Sarah Records*. New York: Bloomsbury, 2016.

Widgery, David. *Beating Time: Riot 'n' Race 'n' Rock 'n' Roll*. London, Chatto & Windus, 1986.

Wiedlack, Maria Katharina. *Queer-Feminist Punk: An Anti-Social History*. Vienna: Zaglossus, 2015.

Wilkinson, David. *Post-Punk, Politics and Pleasure in Britain*. Basingstoke: Palgrave Macmillan, 2016.

Williams, Paul. *You're Wondering Now: The Specials from Conception to Reunion*. London: Cherry Red, 2009.

Wilson, Tony. *24 Hour Party People: What The Sleeve Notes Never Tell You*. London: Channel 4 Books, 2002.

Wobble, Jah. *Memoirs of a Geezer*. London: Serpent's Tail, 2009.

Wood, Lee. *Sex Pistols: Day by Day*. London: Omnibus Press, 1988.

Young, Rob. *Rough Trade*. London: Black Dog, 2006.

Historical Context and Theory

Abrams, Mark. *The Teenage Consumer*. London: Press Exchange, 1959.

Adlington, Robert (ed.). *Red Strains: Music and Communism Outside the Communist Bloc*. Oxford: British Academy, 2013.

Amery, Colin and Dan Cruickshank. *The Rape of Britain*. London: Harper Collins, 1975.

Andresen, Knud and Bart van der Steen (eds.). *A European Youth Revolt: European Perspectives on Youth Protest and Social Movements in the 1980s*. Basingstoke: Palgrave Macmillan, 2016.

Andrews, Geoff, Richard Cockett, Alan Hooper and Michael Williams (eds.). *New Left, New Right and Beyond: Taking the Sixties Seriously*. Basingstoke: Palgrave Macmillan, 1999.

Bailey, Ron. *The Squatters*. London: Penguin, 1973.

Bangs, Lester. *Psychotic Reactions and Carburetor Dung*. London: Heinemann, 1988.

Barker, Paul (ed.). *The Other Britain: A New Society Collection*. London: Routledge, 1982.

Barnes, Julian. *Metroland*. London: Jonathan Cape, 1980.

Barr, John. *Derelict Britain*. London: Pelican, 1969.

Bayton, Mavis. *Frock Rock: Women Performing Popular Music*. Oxford University Press, 1998.

Beckett, Andy. *When the Lights Went Out: Britain in the Seventies*. London: Faber & Faber, 2009.

Beckett, Andy. *Promised You a Miracle: UK 80–82.* London: Allen Lane, 2015.

Bennett, Andy and Keith Kahn-Harris (eds.). *After Subculture: Critical Studies in Contemporary Youth Culture.* Basingstoke: Palgrave Macmillan, 2004.

Birchall, Sean. *Beating the Fascists: The Untold Story of Anti-Fascist Action.* London: Freedom Press, 2010.

Black, Lawrence, Hugh Pemberton and Pat Thane (eds.). *Reassessing the Seventies.* Manchester: Manchester University Press, 2013.

Blackaby, Frank Thomas (ed.). *De-industrialisation.* London: Heinemann, 1978.

Boyce, David George. *The Falklands War.* Basingstoke: Palgrave Macmillan, 2001.

Bracewell, Michael. *England Is Mine: Pop Life in Albion, From Wilde to Goldie.* London: Flamingo, 1998.

Brake, Mike. *The Sociology of Youth Culture and Youth Subculture.* London: Routledge & Kegan Paul, 1980.

Brill, Dunja. *Goth Culture: Gender, Sexuality and Style.* Oxford: Berg, 2008.

Brooke, Stephen. *Sexual Politics: Sexuality, Family Planning and the British Left from the 1880s to the Present Day.* Oxford University Press, 2011.

Brooker, Christopher. *The Seventies: Portrait of a Decade.* London: Allen Lane, 1980.

Buckingham, David, Sara Bragg and Mary Kehily (eds.). *Youth Cultures in the Age of Global Media.* Basingstoke: Palgrave Macmillan, 2014.

Bunyan, Tony. *The History and Practice of the Political Police in Britain.* London: Quartet, 1977.

Burchill, Julie. *I Knew I Was Right.* London: Arrow Books, 1998.

Burkett, Jodi. *Constructing Post-Imperial Britain: Britishness, 'Race' and the Radical Left in the 1960s.* Basingstoke: Palgrave Macmillan, 2013.

Bushell, Garry. *Hoolies: True Stories of Britain's Biggest Street Battles.* London: John Blake, 2010.

Bushell, Garry. *Bushell on the Rampage: The Autobiography of Garry Bushell.* Clacton-on- Sea: Apex Publishing, 2010.

Byrne, Paul. *The Campaign for Nuclear Disarmament.* Croom Helm: London, 1988.

Callaghan, John. *The Far Left in British Politics.* Oxford: Blackwells, 1987.

Cashmore, Ellis. *No Future: Youth and Society.* London: Heinemann, 1984.

Cavanagh, Gary. *Bradford's Noise of the Valleys.* New Romney: Bank House Book, 2009.

Chambers, Iain. *Urban Rhythms: Pop Music and Popular Culture.* New York: St Martin's Press, 1985.

Clapson, Mark. *Invincible Green Suburbs, Brave New Towns: Social Change and Urban Dispersal in Post-War England.* Manchester: Manchester University Press, 1998.

Clapson, Mark. *A Social History of Milton Keynes: Middle England/Edge City.* London: Fran Cass, 2004.

Clarke, John, Chas Critcher and Richard Johnson (eds.). *Working Class Culture: Studies in History and Theory.* London: Hutchinson, 1979.

Class War. *This Is Class War.* Stirling: AK Distribution, 1991 edition.

Clutterbuck, Richard. *Britain in Agony: The Growth of Political Violence.* London: Penguin, 1978.

Cohen, Albert K. *Delinquent Boys: The Culture of the Gang.* London: Taylor & Francis, 1956.

Cohen, Stanley. *Folk Devils and Moral Panics.* London: MacGibbon and Kee, 1972.

Cohen, Stanley and Jock Young (eds.). *The Manufacturing of News: Social Problems, Deviance and the Mass Media.* London: Constable, 1973.

Cohn, Nik. *Awopbopaloobop Alopbamboom: Pop from the Beginning.* London: Pimlico, 2004 edition.

Coogan, Tim Pat. *The Troubles: Ireland's Ordeal and the Search for Peace.* Basingstoke, Palgrave Macmillan, 2002.

Coopey, Richard and Nicholas Woodward (eds.), *Britain in the 1970s: The Troubled Economy.* London: UCL Press, 1995.

Coote, Anna and Beatrix Campbell. *Sweet Freedom: The Struggle for Women's Liberation.* Oxford: Blackwell, 1982.

Cutler, Chris. *File Under Popular: Theoretical and Critical Writings on Music.* London: November, 1985.

Davis, John. *Youth and the Condition of Britain: Images of Adolescent Conflict.* London: Athlone Press, 1990.

de Boise, Sam. *Men, Masculinity, Music and Emotion.* Basingstoke: Palgrave Macmillan, 2015.

Debord, Guy. *Society of the Spectacle.* Michigan: Black & Red, 1983 edition.

Denslow, Robin. *When the Music's Over: The Story of Political Pop.* London: Faber & Faber, 1989.

Doggett, Peter. *There's a Riot Goin' on: Revolutionaries, Rocks Stars, and the Rise and Fall of '60s Counter-Culture.* London: Canongate Books, 2008.

Du Gay, Paul and Stuart Hall. *Doing Cultural Studies: The Story of the Sony Walkman.* London: SAGE, 1997.

Duncombe, Stephen. *Notes From the Underground: Zines and the Politics of Alternative Culture.* London: Verso, 1997.

Du Noyer, Paul. *Liverpool Wondrous Place: Music from the Cavern to the Coral.* London: Virgin Books, 2004.

Dworkin, Dennis. *Cultural Marxism in Postwar Britain: History, the New Left and the Origins of Cultural Studies.* Durham, NC: Duke University Press, 1997.

Edelman, Lee. *No Future: Queer Theory and the Death Drive.* Durham, NC: Duke University Press, 2004.

Edmunds, Timothy, Jamie Gaskarth and Robin Porter (eds.). *British Foreign Policy and the National Interest: Identity, Strategy and Security.* Basingstoke: Palgrave Macmillan, 2014.

Feldman-Barrett, Christine (ed.). *Lost Histories of Youth Culture.* New York: Peter Lang, 2015.

Fishman, Robert. *Bourgeois Utopias: The Rise and Fall of Suburbia.* New York: Basic Books, 1987.

Fitzgerald, Mike, Gregor McLennan and Jennie Pawson (eds.). *Crime and Society: History and Theory.* London: Routledge and Kegan Paul, 1981.

Fowler, David. *The First Teenagers: The Lifestyle of Young Wage-Earners in Interwar Britain.* London: Woburn Press, 1995.

Fowler, David. *Youth Culture in Modern Britain, c. 1920–c.1970.* Basingstoke: Palgrave Macmillan, 2008.

Friedman, Jerome. *Blasphemy, Immorality and Anarchy: Ranters and the English Revolution.* Athens, OH: Ohio University Press, 1987;

Frith, Simon. *The Sociology of Rock.* London: Constable, 1978.

Frith, Simon. *Sound Effects: Youth, Leisure and the Politics of Rock 'n' Roll.* London: Pantheon, 1981.

Frith, Simon. *Music for Pleasure: Essays in the Sociology of Pop.* London: Polity, 1988.

Frith, Simon and Howard Horne. *Art into Pop.* London: Methuen & Co., 1987.

Fry, Jamie. *A Licence to Rock and Pop.* London: JWF, 2014.

Gable, Robin (ed.). *Resources of Hope: Culture, Democracy, Socialism.* London: Verso, 1989.

Gaddis, John Lewis. *The Cold War: A New History.* New York: Penguin Press, 2005.

Gamble, Andrew. *The Free Economy and the Strong State: The Politics of Thatcherism.* Basingstoke: Palgrave Macmillan, 1994 edition.

Garnett, Mark. *From Anger to Apathy: The British Experience since 1975.* London: Jonathan Cape, 2007.

Garofalo, Reebee (ed.). *Rockin' the Boat: Mass Music and Mass Movements.* London: South End Press, 1992.

Gildart, Keith. *Images of England Through Popular Music: Class, Youth and Rock 'n' Roll, 1955–1976*. Basingstoke: Palgrave Macmillan, 2013.

Gillett, Charlie. *The Sound of the City: The Rise of Rock & Roll*. London: Souvenir, 2004 edition.

Gilroy, Paul. *There Ain't No Black in the Union Jack*. London: Routledge, 2002 edition.

Glasgow University Media Group. *Bad News*. London: Routledge and Kegan Paul, 1976.

Glynn, Sean and Alan Booth. *Modern Britain: An Economic and Social History*. London: Routledge, 1996.

Goodlad, Lauren, Michael Bibby (eds.). *Goth: Undead Subculture*. Durham, NC: Duke University Press, 2007.

Gorman, Paul. *In Their Own Write: Adventures in the Music Press*. London: Sanctuary, 2001.

Gorman, Paul, David Thorp and Fred Vermorel. *Joining the Dots: From the Situationist International to Malcolm McLaren*. Southampton: John Hansard, 2015.

Gray, Christopher. *Leaving the 20th Century: The Incomplete Works of the Situationist International*. London: Free Fall, 1974.

Green, Penny. *The Enemy Without: Policing and Class Consciousness in the Miners' Strike*. Buckingham: Open University Press, 1990.

Greenwood, Sean. *Britain and the Cold War, 1945–91*. Basingstoke: Palgrave Macmillan, 1999.

Grindrod, John. *Concretopia: A Journey Around the Rebuilding of Postwar Britain*. London: Old Street, 2014.

Hall, Lesley. *Sex, Gender and Social Change in Britain since 1800*. Basingstoke: Palgrave Macmillan, 2000.

Hall, Stuart, Chas Critcher, Tony Jefferson, John Clarke and Brian Roberts. *Policing the Crisis: Mugging, the State, and Law and Order*. Basingstoke: Macmillan, 1978.

Hall, Stuart and Tony Jefferson (eds.). *Resistance Through Rituals: Youth Subcultures in Post- War Britain*. London: Hutchinson & Co., 1976.

Hall, Stuart, Dorothy Hobson, Andrew Lane and Paul Willis (eds.). *Culture, Media, Language*. London: Unwin Hyman, 1980.

Halliday, Fred. *The Making of the Second Cold War*. Verso: London, 1983.

Halsey, Albert Henry (ed.). *British Social Trends since 1900*. Basingstoke: Palgrave Macmillan, 1988.

Hamblett, Charles and Jane Deverson. *Generation X*. London: Tandem Books, 1965.

Hanley, Lynsey. *Estates: An Intimate History*. London: Granta, 2007.

Harris, Robert. *Gotcha: The Media, The Government and the Falklands Crisis*. London: Faber and Faber, 1983.

Harrison, Brian. *Seeking a Role: The United Kingdom, 1951–1970.* Oxford: Oxford University Press, 2009.

Harrison, Brian. *Finding a Role? The United Kingdom, 1970–1990.* Oxford University Press, 2010.

Harrison, John and Andrew Glyn. *The British Economic Disaster.* London: Pluto, 1980.

Harvey, David. *A Brief History of Neoliberalism.* Oxford University Press, 2005.

Haseler, Stephen. *The Death of British Democracy.* London, Elek Books, 1976.

Haslam, Dave. *Young Hearts Run Free: The Real Story of the 1970s.* London: Harper Perennial, 2007.

Haslam, Dave. *Life After Dark: A History of British Nightclubs and Music Venues.* London: Simon & Schuster, 2015.

Haynes, Pete. *Malayan Swing.* London: London Books, 2009.

Healy, Murray. *Gay Skins: Class, Masculinity and Queer Appropriation.* London: Continuum, 1996.

Hebdige, Dick. *Subculture: The Meaning of Style.* London: Routledge 2007 edition.

Hewison, Robert. *Too Much: Art and Society in the Sixties, 1960–75.* London: Methuen, 1986.

Hewison, Robert. *Future Tense: A New Art for the Nineties.* London: Methuen, 1990.

Hibbert, Christopher. *King Mob: The Story of Lord George Gordon and the Riots of 1780.* London: Longmans, 1958.

Hill, Christopher. *The World Turned Upside Down: Radical Ideas during the English Revolution.* London: Penguin, 1991.

Hill, Ray and Andrew Bell. *The Other Face of Terror: Inside Europe's Neo-Nazi Network.* Glasgow: Grafton, 1988.

Hodkinson, Paul. *Goth: Identity, Style and Subculture.* Oxford: Berg, 2002.

Hodkinson, Paul and Wolfgang Deicke (eds.). *Youth Cultures: Scenes, Subcultures and Tribes.* London: Routledge, 2007.

Hoggart, Richard. *The Uses of Literacy.* Harmondsworth: Penguin, 1958.

Home, Stewart. *The Assault on Culture: Utopian Currents from Lettrisme to Class War.* Stirling: AK Press, 1991.

Home Stewart (ed.). *What Is Situationism? A Reader.* Edinburgh: AK Press, 1996.

Horn, Adrian. *Juke Box Britain: Americanisation and Youth Culture, 1945–1960.* Manchester: Manchester University Press, 2009.

Hudson, Kate. *CND – Now More Than Ever: The Story of a Peace Movement.* London: Vision, 2005.

Hughes, Celia. *Young Lives on the Left: Sixties Activism and the Liberation of the Self*. Manchester: Manchester University Press, 2016.

Humphries, Stephen. *Hooligans or Rebels? An Oral History of Working Class Childhood and Youth, 1889–1939*. Oxford: Blackwell, 1981.

Huq, Rupa. *Making Sense of Suburbia Through Popular Culture*. London: Bloomsbury, 2013.

Jackson, Ben and Robert Saunders (eds.). *Making Thatcher's Britain*. Cambridge: Cambridge University Press, 2012.

Jarman, Derek. *Dancing Ledge*. London: Quartet Books, 1991 edition.

Jones, Ben. *The Working Class in Mid Twentieth-Century England: Community, Identity and Social Memory*. Manchester: Manchester University Press, 2012.

Ka-Tzetnik 135633. *House of Dolls*. London: Panther, 1965 version.

Kent, Nick. *The Dark Stuff: Selected Writings on Rock Music, 1972–1993*. London: Penguin, 1994.

Kent, Nick. *Apathy for the Devil: A 1970s Memoir*. London: Faber & Faber, 2010.

King, Anthony. *Why Is Britain Becoming Harder to Govern?*. London: BBC, 1976.

King, Roger and Neil Nugent (eds.). *Respectable Rebels: Middle Class Campaigns in Britain in the 1970s*. London: Hodder & Stoughton, 1979.

Knabb, Ken (ed.). *Situationist International Anthology*. Berkeley: Bureau of Public Secrets, 1981.

Kramnick, Isaac. *Is Britain Dying? Perspectives on the Current Crisis*. New York: Ithaca, 1979.

Lee, C. P. *Shake, Rattle and Rain: Popular Music Making in Manchester, 1955–95*. London: Hardinge Simpole, 2002.

Long, Pat. *The History of the NME*. London: Portico, 2012.

Lowles, Nick. *White Riot: The Violent Story of Combat 18*. London: Milo 2001.

Lux, Marin. *Anti-Fascist*. London: Phoenix Press, 2006.

Lynskey, Dorian. *33 Revolutions per Minute: A History of Protest Songs*. London: Faber & Faber, 2010.

Mammone, Andrea, Emmanuel Godin, Brian Jenkins (eds.). *Varieties of Right-Wing Extremism in Europe*. Abingdon: Routledge, 2013.

Marcuse, Herbert. *One-Dimensional Man: Studies in the Ideology of Advanced Industrial Society*. London: Routledge, 1991 *edition originally published in* 1964.

Marshall, George. *Spirit of '69: A Skinhead Bible*. Dunoon: ST Publishing, 1991.

Marwick, Arthur. *The Sixties: Cultural Revolution in Britain, France, Italy and the United States, c. 1958–c.1974*. Oxford University Press, 1998.

McDougal, Stuart. *Stanley Kubrick's A Clockwork Orange*. Cambridge University Press, 2010.

McKay, George. *Senseless Acts of Beauty: Currents of Resistance since the Sixties*. London: Verso, 1996.

McKay, George. *Glastonbury: A Very English Fair*. London: Verso, 2000.

McKay, George. *Shakin' All Over: Popular Music and Disability*. Ann Arbor: University of Michigan Press, 2013.

McLuhan, Marshall. *Understanding Media: The Extensions of Man*. London: Routledge & Paul, 1964.

McLuhan, Marshall and Quentin Fiore. *The Medium Is the Massage*. London: Penguin, 1967.

McSmith, Andy. *No Such Thing as Society: A History of Britain in the 1980s*. London: Constable, 2011.

Melly, George. *Revolt into Style: The Pop Arts*. London: Faber & Faber, 2008.

Miles, Barry. *London Calling: A Countercultural History of London since 1945*. London: Atlantic, 2010.

Miles, Steven. *Youth Lifestyles in a Changing World*. Buckingham: Open University Press, 2000.

Miller, Paul D. *Sound Unbound: Sampling Digital Music and Culture*. London: MIT Press, 2008.

Milne, Seamus. *The Enemy Within: The Secret War Against the Miners*. London: Verso, 1991.

Moore-Gilbert, Bart (ed.). *The Arts in the 1970s: Cultural Closure?*. London: Routledge, 1994.

Morrison, Eddy. *Memoirs of a Street Fighter: A Life in White Nationalism*. Leeds: Imperium Press, 2003.

Muggleton, David. *Inside Subculture: The Postmodern Meaning of Style*. Oxford: Berg, 2000.

Muggleton, David and Rupert Weinzierl (eds.). *Post-Subcultures Reader*. London: Berg, 2003.

Mungham, Geoff and Geoff Pearson (eds.). *Working Class Youth Cultures*. London: Routledge & Kegan Paul, 1976.

Nairn, Tom. *The Break-up of Britain: Crisis and Neo-Nationalism*. London: Verso, 1981 edition.

Northern Women's Liberation Rock Band. *Manifesto*. Manchester: NWLRB, 1974.

Nossiter, Bernard. *Britain: A Future That Works*. London: Houghton, 1978.

Nuttall, Jeff. *Bomb Culture*. London: Paladin, 1970.

O'Brien, Lucy. *She Bop: The Definitive History of Women in Rock, Pop and Soul*. London: Penguin, 1995.

Ogg, Alex. *Independence Days: The Story of UK Independent Record Labels*. London: Cherry Red, 2009.

Osgerby, Bill. *Youth Culture in Britain since 1945*. London: Routledge, 1998.

Osgerby, Bill. *Youth Media*. London: Routledge, 2004.

Peace, David. *GB84*. London: Faber & Faber, 2005.

Pearce, Joe. *Race with the Devil: My Journey from Racial Hatred to Rational Love*. St Benedict Press: North Carolina, 2013.

Pearson, Geoffrey. *Hooligan: A History of Respectable Fears*. London: Macmillan, 1983.

Peddie, Ian (ed.). *The Resisting Muse: Popular Music and Social Protest*. Aldershot: Ashgate, 2006.

Peel, John and Sheila Ravenscroft. *Margrave of the Marshes*. London: Bantam Press, 2005.

Penrose, Barrie and Roger Courtiour. *The Penrose File*. London: Secker & Warburg, 1978.

Persons Unknown. *Persons Unknown*. London: Persons Unknown, 1979.

Polhemus, Ted. *Streetstyle: From Sidewalk to Catwalk*. London: Thames & Hudson, 1994.

Raha, Maria. *Cinderella's Big Score: Women of the Punk and Indie Underground*. Emeryville, CA: Seal Press, 2004.

Red Action. *We Are … Red Action*. London: Red Action, undated.

Redhead, Steve. *Subcultures to Clubcultures: An Introduction to Popular Cultural Studies*. Oxford: Blackwell, 1997.

Redhead, Steve. *The End of the Century Party: Youth and Pop Towards 2000*. Manchester: Manchester University Press, 2000.

Reiner, Robert. *The Politics of the Police*. Hemel Hempstead: Harvester Wheatsheaf, 1992.

Renton, Dave. *When We Touched the Sky: The Anti-Nazi League, 1977– 81*. Cheltenham: New Clarion Press, 2006.

Reynolds, Simon. *Blissed Out: The Raptures of Rock*. London: Serpent's Tail, 1990.

Reynolds, Simon. *Bring the Noise: Twenty Years of Writing About Hip Rock and Hip Hop*. London: Faber & Faber, 2007.

Reynolds, Simon. *Shock and Awe: Glam Rock and Its Legacy*. London: Faber & Faber, 2016.

Reynolds, Simon and Joy Press. *The Sex Revolts: Gender, Rebellion and Rock 'n' Roll*. London: Serpent's Tail, 1995.

Roberts, Chris, Hywel Livingstone and Emma Baxter-Wright. *Gothic: The Evolution of a Dark Subculture*. London: Goodman, 2014.

Robinson, Lucy. *Gay Men and the Left in Post-War Britain: How the Personal Got Political*. Manchester: Manchester University Press, 2007.

Sandbrook, Dominic. *State of Emergency: The Way We Were: Britain, 1970–74*. London: Penguin, 2011.

Sandrook, Dominic. *Seasons in the Sun: The Battle for Britain, 1974–79*. London: Allen Lane, 2012.

Saunders, Nicholas. *Alternative London*. London: Saunders, 1978.

Savage, Jon. *Teenage: The Creation of Youth, 1875–1945*. London: Pimlico, 2008.

Savage, Jon. *1966: The Year the Decade Exploded*. London: Faber & Faber, 2015.

Scarman, Lord. *The Scarman Report: The Brixton Disorders, 10–12 April 1981*. London, Pelican, 1982.

Schildt, Axel and Detlef Siegfried (eds.). *Between Marx and Coca-Cola: Youth Cultures in Changing European Societies, 1960–1980*. Oxford: Berghahn, 2006.

Schumpeter, Joseph. *The Theory of Economic Development*. Oxford University Press, 1961.

Scott, Peter. *The Making of the Modern British Home: The Suburban Semi and Family Life between the Wars*. Oxford: Oxford University Press, 2013.

Seabrook, Jeremy. *City Close-Up*. London: Penguin, 1973 edition.

Sedgwick, Eve. *Between Men: English Literature and Male Homosocial Desire*. New York: Columbia University Press, 1985.

Segal, Lynne. *Is the Future Female? Troubled Thoughts on Contemporary Feminism*. London: Virago, 1994.

Shepherd, John. *Crisis? What Crisis? The Callaghan Government and the British 'Winter of Discontent'*. Manchester: Manchester University Press, 2013.

Sheriff, Tom. *A De-industrialised Britain*. London: Fabian Society, 1979.

Siegel, Carol. *Goth's Dark Empire*. Bloomington: Indiana University Press, 2005.

Silverstone, Roger (ed.). *Visions of Suburbia*. London: Routledge, 1997.

Sinclair, Dave. *Liverpool in the 1980s*. Stroud: Amberley, 2014.

Smith, Evan and Matthew Worley (eds.). *Against the Grain: The British Far Left from 1956*. Manchester: Manchester University Press, 2014

Solomon, Robert C. *Existentialism*. Oxford: Oxford University Press, 2004 *edition*.

Springhall, John. *Coming of Age: Adolescence in Britain, 1860–1960*. Dublin: Gill & Macmillan, 1986.

Springhall, John. *Youth, Popular Culture and Moral Panics: Penny Gaffs to Gangsta-Rap, 1830–1996*. Basingstoke: Macmillan, 1998.

Stewart, Graham. *Bang! A History of Britain in the 1980s*. London: Atlantic Books, 2013.

Street, John. *Rebel Rock: The Politics of Popular Music*. Oxford: Blackwell, 1986.

Street, John. *Music and Politics*. Cambridge: Polity, 2012.

Stubbs, David. *Future Days: Krautrock and the Building of Modern Germany*. London: Faber & Faber, 2014.

Subcultures Network (ed.). *Subcultures, Popular Music and Social Change*. Newcastle: Cambridge Scholars, 2014.

Subcultures Network (ed.). *Youth Culture, Popular Music and the End of 'Consensus'*. London: Routledge, 2015.

Thomlinson, Natalie. *Race and Ethnicity in the Women's Movement in England, 1968–93*. Basingstoke: Palgrave Macmillan, 2016.

Thornton, Sarah. *Club Cultures: Music, Media and Subcultural Capital*. London: Polity Press, 1995.

Thrasher, Frederic. *The Gang: A Study of 1,313 Gangs in Chicago*. Chicago: University of Chicago Press, 1927.

Tiratsoo, Nick (ed.). *From Blitz to Blair: A New History of the Britain since the 1970s*. London: Weidenfield & Nicolson, 1997.

Tomlinson, Jim. *The Politics of Declinism: Understanding Post-War Britain*. Oxford: Longman, 2000.

Toop, David. *The Rap Attack: African Jive to New York Hip Hop*. London: Pluto, 1994.

Townsend, Pete. *Who I Am*. London: Harper Collins, 2012.

Turner, Alwyn W. *Crisis? What Crisis? Britain in the 1970s*. London: Aurum, 2008.

Turner, Alwyn W. *Rejoice! Rejoice! Britain in the Eighties*. London: Aurum, 2010.

Vague, Tom. *King Mob Echo: From Gordon Riots to Situationists and Sex Pistols*. London: Dark Star, 2000.

Van Der Steen, Bart, Ask Katzeff and Leendert Van Hoogenhuijze (eds.). *The City Is Ours: Squatting and Autonomous Movements from the 1970s to the Present*. Oakland: PM Press, 2014.

Vaneigem, Raoul. *The Revolution of Everyday Life*. London: Rebel Press, 1994.

Vinen, Richard. *Thatcher's Britain: The Politics and Social Upheaval of the 1980s*. London: Simon & Schuster, 2009.

Walker, John A. *Left Shift: Radical Art in 1970s Britain*. London: I.B.Tauris, 2002.

Ward, Colin and Chris Henderson. *Who Wants It?* Mainstream: Edinburgh, 2002 edition.

Wates, Nick and Christian Wolmar (eds.). *Squatting: The Real Story*. London: Bay Leafy Books, 1980.

Webb, Peter. *Exploring the Networked Worlds of Popular Music: Milieu Cultures*. London: Routledge, 2007.

Weston, Donna and Andy Bennett (eds.). *Pop Pagans: Paganism and Popular Music*. Durham, UK: Acumen, 2013.

Wheen, Francis. *Strange Days Indeed: The Golden Age of Paranoia*. London: Fourth Estate, 2009.

Whitehead, Phillip. *The Writing on the Wall: Britain in the Seventies*. London: Michael Joseph, 1985.

Whiteley, Sarah (ed.). *Sexing the Groove: Popular Music and Gender*. London: Routledge, 1997.

Whitely, Sarah. *Too Much Too Young: Popular Music, Age and Gender*. London: Routledge, 2005.

Wilkins, L. T. *Delinquent Generation*. London: HMSO, 1960.

Willett, John (ed.). *Brecht on Theatre: The Development of an Aesthetic*. London: Methuen, 1964.

Willis, Paul. *Profane Culture*. London: Routledge & Kegan Paul, 1978.

Willis, Paul. *Common Culture: Symbolic Work at Play in the Everyday Cultures of the Young*. Milton Keynes: Open University, 1990.

Wilson, Colin. *The Outsider*. London: Gollancz, 1956.

Wise, David. *King Mob: A Critical Hidden History*. London: Bread and Circuses, 2014.

Wolffe, John (ed.). *Irish Religious Conflict in Comparative Perspective*. Basingstoke: Palgrave Macmillan, 2014.

Women's Liberation Music Projects Group. *Sisters in Song*. WLMPG, undated.

Women's Studies Group. *Women Take Issue*. London: Hutchinson, 1978.

Worthington, Andy. *Stonehenge: Celebration and Subversion*. Loughborough: Alternative Albion, 2014.

York, Peter. *Style Wars*. London: Sedgwick & Jackson, 1983.

Young, Michael and Peter Willmott. *Family and Class in a London Suburb*. London: Routledge & Kegan Paul, 1960.

Articles

Punk Related

Adams, Ruth. 'The Englishness of English Punk: Sex Pistols, Subcultures, and Nostalgia'. *Popular Music and Society*, 31:4 (2008).

Albiez, Sean. 'Know History! John Lydon, Cultural Capital and the Prog/Punk Dialectic'. *Popular Music*, 22:3 (2003).

Bestley, Russ. 'From "London's Burning" to "Sten Guns in Sunderland"'. *Punk and Post-Punk*, 1:1 (2012).

Bestley, Russ. '"I Tried to Make Him Laugh, He Didn't Get the Joke …": Taking Punk Humour Seriously'. *Punk and Post-Punk*, 2:2 (2013).

Blasé, Cazz. 'Writing Women Back into Punk'. *The f-word* (March 14, 2010).

Brown, Jayna. '"Brown Girl in the Ring": Poly Styrene, Annabella Lwin and the Politics of Anger'. *Journal of Popular Music Studies*, 23:4 (2011).

Brown, Timothy S. 'Subcultures, Pop Music and Politics: Skinheads and "Nazi Rock" in England and Germany'. *Journal of Social History*, 38:1 (2004).

Carpenter, Alexander. 'The "Ground Zero" of Goth: Bauhaus, "Bela Lugosi's Dead" and the Origins of Gothic Rock'. *Popular Music and Society*, 35:1 (2012).

Cogan, Brian. '"Do They Owe Us a Living? Of Course They Do!" Crass, Throbbing Gristle, and Anarchy and Radicalism in Early English Punk Rock'. *Journal for the Study of Radicalism*, 1:2 (2007).

Cogan, Brian. 'Typical Girls? Fuck Off, You Wanker! Re-evaluating The Slits and Gender Relations in Early British Punk and Post-Punk'. *Women's Studies*, 4 (2012).

Cotter, John. 'Sounds of Hate: White Power Rock and Roll and the Neo-Nazi Skinhead Subculture'. *Terrorism and Political Violence*, 11:2 (1999).

Cross, Richard. 'The Hippies Now Wear Black: Crass and the Anarcho-Punk Movement, 1977–84'. *Socialist History*, 26 (2004).

Cross, Rich. '"There Is No Authority But Yourself": The Individual and the Collective in British Anarcho-Punk'. *Music and Politics*, 4:2 (2010).

Cross, Rich. '"Take the Toys from the Boys": Gender, Generation and the Anarchist Intent in the Work of Poison Girls'. *Punk & Post-Punk*, 3:2 (2015).

Crossley, Nick. 'Pretty Connected: The Social Network of the Early UK Punk Movement'. *Theory, Culture and Society*, 25:6 (2008).

Crossley, Nick. 'The Man Whose Web Expanded: Network Dynamics in Manchester's Post/Punk Music Scene, 1976–1980'. *Poetics*, 37 (2009).

Dale, Pete. 'It Was Easy, It Was Cheap, So What?' Reconsidering the DIY Principle of Punk and Indie Music'. *Popular Music History*, 3:2 (2008).

Donaghey, Jim. 'Bakunin Brand Vodka: An Exploration into Anarchist-Punk and Punk- Anarchism'. *Anarchist Developments in Cultural Studies*, 1 (2013).

Dunn, Kevin. 'Never Mind the Bollocks: The Punk Rock Politics of Global Communication'. *Review of International Studies*, 34 (2008).

Dunn, Kevin and May Summer Farnsworth. '"We ARE the Revolution": Riot Grrrl Press, Girl Empowerment and DIY Self-Publishing'. *Women's Studies*, 41:2 (2012).

Gildart, Keith. '"The Antithesis of Humankind": Exploring Responses to the Sex Pistols' Anarchy Tour 1976'. *Cultural and Social History*, 10:1 (2013).

Gunn, Joshua. 'Gothic Music and the Inevitability of Genre'. *Popular Music and Society*, 23:1 (1999).

Harvey, Paul. 'Doing the Right Things for the Right Reasons: Looking for Authenticity in Punk and Stuckist Practice'. *Punk & Post-Punk*, 2:1 (2013).

Heron, Timothy. 'Alternative Ulster: Punk and the Construction of Everyday life in 1970s Northern Ireland'. *Popular Culture Today: Imaginaries*, 9 (2015).

Heron, Timothy. '"We're Only Monsters": Punk Bodies and the Grotesque in 1970s Northern Ireland'. *Études Irlandaises*, 42:1 (2017).

Hesmondhalgh, David. 'Post-Punk's Attempt to Democratise the Music Industry: The Success and Failure of Rough Trade'. *Popular Music*, 16:3 (1997).

Hesmondhalgh, David. 'Indie: The Institutional Politics and Aesthetics of a Popular Music Genre'. *Cultural Studies*, 13:1 (1999).

Hoover, Michael and Lisa Stokes. 'Pop Music and the Limits of Cultural Critique: Gang of Four Shrinkwraps Entertainment'. *Popular Music and Society*, 22:3 (1998).

Kouvarou, Maria. 'Deconstructing the "Bodies": Reading the Feminine Approach to the Sex Pistols'. *Popular Music and Society*, 38:4 (2015).

McKay, George. '"Crippled With Nerves": Popular Music and Polio, with Particular Reference to Ian Dury'. *Popular Music*, 28:3 (2009).

McLoone, Martin. 'Punk Music in Northern Ireland: The Political Power of "What Might Have Been"'. *Irish Studies Review*, 12:1 (2004).

Moore, Ryan. 'Postmodernism and Punk Subculture: Cultures of Authenticity and Deconstruction'. *The Communication Review*, 7 (2004).

Nally, Claire. 'Goth Beauty, Style and Sexuality: Neo-Traditional Femininity in Twenty-First Century Subcultural Magazines'. *Gothic Studies* (forthcoming).

O'Brien, Lucy. 'Can I Have a Taste of Your Ice-Cream'. *Punk and Post-Punk*, 1:1 (2012).

Ogg, Alex 'For You, Tommy, the War Is Never Over'. *Punk & Post-Punk*, 2:3 (2013).

O'Meara, Caroline. 'The Raincoats: Breaking Down Punk Rock's Masculinities'. *Popular Music*, 22:3 (2003).

Osborne, Richard. 'A Great Friggin' Swindle? Sex Pistols, School Kids and 1979'. *Popular Music and Society*, 38:4 (2015).

Parham, John. 'A Concrete Sense of Place: Alienation and the City in British Punk and New Wave'. *Green Letters: Studies in Ecocriticism*, 15:1 (2011).

Ross, Peter. 'An Organizational Analysis of the Emergence, Development and Mainstreaming of British Punk Rock Music'. *Popular Music and Society*, 20:1 (1996).

Shaffer, Ryan. 'The Soundtrack of Neo-Fascism: Youth and Music in the National Front'. *Patterns of Prejudice*, 47:4–5 (2013).

Simonelli, David. 'Anarchy, Pop and Violence: Punk Rock Subculture and the Rhetoric of Class, 1976–78'. *Contemporary British History*, 16:2 (2002).

Steirer, Gregory. 'The Art of Everyday Life and Death: Throbbing Gristle and the Aesthetics of Neoliberalism'. *Postmodern Culture*, 22:2 (2012).

Tillman, R. H. 'Punk Rock and the Construction of "Pseudo-Political" Movements'. *Popular Music and Society*, 7:3 (1980).

Triggs, Teal. 'Alphabet Soup: Reading British Fanzines'. *Visible Language*, 29:1 (1995).

Triggs, Teal. 'Scissors and Glue: Punk Fanzines and the Creation of a DIY Aesthetic'. *Journal of Design History*, 19: 1 (2006).

Wilkinson, David. 'Prole Art Threat: The Fall, the Blue Orchids and the Politics of the Post-Punk Working Class Autodidact'. *Punk & Post-Punk*, 3:1 (2014).

Wilkinson, David. 'Ever Fallen in Love (With Someone You Shouldn't Have): Punk, Politics and Same-Sex Passion'. *Key Words*, 13 (2015).

Worley, Matthew. 'One Nation Under the Bomb: The Cold War and British Punk to 1984'. *Journal for the Study of Radicalism*, 5:2 (2011).

Worley, Matthew. 'Shot By Both Sides: Punk, Politics and the End of "Consensus"'. *Contemporary British History*, 26:3 (2012).

Worley, Matthew. 'Oi! Oi! Oi!: Class, Locality, and British Punk'. *Twentieth Century British History*, 24:4 (2013).

Worley, Matthew. 'Hey Little Rich Boy, Take a Good Look at Me: Punk, Class and British Oi'. *Punk & Post-Punk*, 3:1 (2014).

Worley, Matthew. 'Punk, Politics and British (fan)zines, 1976–84: "While the World Was Dying, Did You Wonder Why?"'. *History Workshop Journal*, 79 (2015).

Worley, Matthew and Nigel Copsey. 'White Youth: The Far Right, Punk and British Youth Culture, 1977–87'. *Journalism, Media and Cultural Studies*, 9 (2016).

Historical Context and Theory

Branch, Andrew. 'All the Young Dudes: Educational Capital, Masculinity and the Uses of Popular Music'. *Popular Music*, 31:1 (2012).

Brooke, Stephen. 'Living in "New Times": Historicizing 1980s Britain'. *History Compass*, 12:1 (2014).

Cixous, Hélène. 'The Laugh of the Medusa'. *Signs*, 1:4 (1976).

Cloonan, Martin. '"I Fought the Law": Popular Music and British Obscenity Law'. *Popular Music*, 14:3 (1995).

Cohen, Phil. 'Subcultural Conflict and Working Class Community'. *Working Class Papers in Cultural Studies*, 2 (1972).

Cook, Matt. '"Gay Times": Identity, Locality, Memory, and the Brixton Squats in 1970s London'. *Twentieth Century British History*, 24: 1 (2013).

Cunningham, John. 'National Daily Newspapers and their Circulations in the UK, 1908–78'. *Journal of Advertising History*, 4 (1981).

Denman, James and Paul McDonald. 'Unemployment Statistics from 1881 to the Present Day'. *Labour Market Trends* (January 1996).

François, Stéphanie. 'The Euro-Pagan Scene: Between Paganism and Radical Right'. *Journal for the Study of Radicalism*, 1:2 (2007).

Frith, Simon and Angela McRobbie. 'Rock and Sexuality'. *Screen Education*, 29 (1978–79).

Gough-Yates, Anna. '"A Shock to the System": Feminist Interventions in Youth Culture – The Adventures of *Shocking Pink*'. *Contemporary British History*, 26: 3 (2012).

Hay, Colin. 'Narrating the Crisis: The Discursive Construction of the "Winter of Discontent"'. *Sociology*, 30:2 (1996).

Hay, Colin. 'Chronicles of a Death Foretold: The Winter of Discontent and Construction of the Crisis of British Keynesian'. *Parliamentary Affairs*, 63:3 (2010).

Hesmondhalgh, David. 'Flexibility, Post-Fordism and the Music Industries'. *Media, Culture and Society*, 18 (1996).

Johnson, Richard. 'What Is Cultural Studies?'. *Social Text*, 16 (1986)

Marwick, Arthur. 'Youth in Britain, 1920–60'. *Journal of Contemporary History*, 5:1 (1970).

Miles, Steven, Cliff Dallas and Vivien Burr. '"Fitting In and Sticking Out": Consumption, Consumer Meanings and the Construction of Young People's Identities'. *Journal of Youth Studies*, 1:1 (1998).

Moran, Joe. '"Stand Up and Be Counted": Hughie Green, the 1970s and Popular Memory'. *History Workshop Journal*, 70:1 (2010).

Robinson, Emily, Camilla Schofield, Florence Sutcliffe-Braithwaite and Natalie Thomlinson. 'Telling Stories about Post-war Britain: Popular Individualism and the "Crisis" of the 1970s'. *Twentieth Century British History*, 28:2 (2017).

Robinson, Lucy. 'Putting the Charity Back into Charity Singles: Charity Singles in Britain, 1984–95'. *Contemporary British History*, 26:3 (2012).

Smith, Evan. 'When the Party Comes Down: The CPGB and Youth Culture, 1976–91'. *Twentieth Century Communism*, 4 (2011).

Subcultures Network. 'Youth Culture, Popular Music and the End of "Consensus" in Britain'. *Contemporary British History*, 26:3 (2012 special issue).

Tomlinson, Jim. 'Thrice Denied: "Declinism" as a Recurrent Theme in British History in the Long Twentieth Century'. *Twentieth Century British History*, 20:2 (2009).

Tomlinson, Jim. 'De-industrialisation Not Decline: A New Meta-narrative for Post-war British History'. *Twentieth Century British History*, 77:1 (2016).

Worley, Matthew. 'Marx–Lenin–Rotten–Strummer: British Marxism and Youth Culture in the 1970s'. *Contemporary British History*, 30:4 (2016).

Chapters in Edited Collection

Punk Related

Bennett, Andy. '"Fade to Grey": The Forgotten History of the British New Romantic Movement'. In Christine Feldman-Barrett (ed.), *Lost Histories of Youth Culture*. New York: Peter Lang, 2015.

Bestley, Russ. 'Big A Little A: The Graphic Language of Anarchy'. In Mike Dines and Matthew Worley (eds.), *The Aesthetic of Our Anger: Anarcho-Punk, Politics and Music*. Colchester: Minor Compositions, 2016.

Binns, Rebecca. 'They May Have Beds, But They Don't Use Sheets'. In Gregory Bull and Mike Dines (eds.), *Tales From the Punkside*. Portsmouth: Itchy Monkey, 2014.

Butler, Justine. 'Disgustin' Justin'. In Gregory Bull and Mike Dines (eds.), *Tales From the Punkside*. Portsmouth: Itchy Monkey, 2014.

Butt, Gavin. 'Being in a Band: Art School Experiment and the Post-Punk Commons'. In Gavin Butt, Kodwo Eshun and Mark Fisher (eds.), *Post Punk Then and Now*. London: Repeater Books, 2016.

Cartledge, Frank. 'Distress to Impress? Local Punk Fashion and commodity Exchange'. In Roger Sabin (ed.), *Punk Rock: So What? The Cultural Legacy of Punk*. London: Routledge, 1999.

Cross, Rich. 'British Anarchism and the End of Thatcherism'. In Evan Smith and Matthew Worley (eds.), *Against the Grain: The British Far Left from 1956*. Manchester: Manchester University Press, 2014.

Cross, Rich. '"Stop the City Showed Another Possibility": Mobilisation and Movement in Anarcho-Punk'. In Mike Dines and Matthew Worley (eds.), *The Aesthetic of Our Anger: Anarcho-Punk, Politics and Music*. Colchester: Minor Compositions, 2016.

Eshun, Kwodo. '"The Weakest Link in Every Chain, I Always Want to Find it": Green Gartside in Conversation'. In Gavin Butt, Kodwo Eshun and Mark Fisher (eds.), *Post Punk Then and Now*. London: Repeater Books, 2016.

Fisher, Mark. '"Memorex for the Krakens": The Fall's Pulp Modernism'. In Michael Goddard and Benjamin Halligan (eds.), *Mark E. Smith and The Fall: Art, Music and Politics*. Farnham: Ashgate, 2010.

Jackson, Kimberly, 'Gothic Music and the Decadent Individual'. In Ian Peddie (ed.), *The Resisting Muse: Popular Music and Social Protest*. Aldershot: Ashgate, 2006.

Low, Chris. 'The Centro Iberico August 1982: A Spectator's Point of View'. In Gregory Bull and Mickey 'Penguin' (eds.), *Not Just Bits of Paper*. Charleston: Perdam Babylonis Nomen, 2015.

O'Brien, Lucy. 'The Woman Punk Made Me'. In Roger Sabin (ed.), *Punk Rock: So What? The Cultural Legacy of Punk*. London: Routledge, 1999.

Parham, John. '"Flowers of Evil": Ecosystem Health and the Punk Poetry of John Cooper- Clarke'. In Subcultures Network (ed.), *Fight Back: Punk, Politics and Resistance*. Manchester: Manchester University Press, 2015.

'Penguin', Mickey. 'My Journey to All the Madmen Records and Back Again'. In Gregory Bull and Mickey 'Penguin' (eds.), *Not Just Bits of Paper*. Charleston: Perdam Babylonis Nomen, 2015.

Pimlott, Herbert. '"Militant Entertainment"?: "Crisis Music" and Political Ephemera in the Emergent "Structure of Feeling"'. In Subcultures Network (ed.), *Fight Back: Punk, Politics and Resistance*. Manchester: Manchester University Press, 2015.

Pitzel-Waters, Jason. 'The Darker Shade of Pagan: The Emergence of Goth'. In Donna Weston and Andy Bennett (eds.), *Pop Pagans: Paganism and Popular Music*. Durham: Acumen, 2013.

Reddington, Helen. 'The Political Pioneers of Punk (Just Don't Mention the F-Word'). In Mike Dines and Matthew Worley (eds.), *The Aesthetic of Our Anger: Anarcho-Punk, Politics and Music*. Colchester: Minor Compositions, 2016.

Reynolds, Simon. 'Younger Than Yesterday: Indie-Pop's Cult of Innocence'. In Simon Reynolds, *Bring the Noise: Twenty Years of Writing About Hip Rock and Hip Hop*. London: Faber & Faber, 2007.

Sabin, Roger. '"I Won't Let That Dago By": Rethinking Punk and Racism". In Roger Sabin (ed.), *Punk Rock: So What? The Cultural Legacy of Punk*. London: Routledge, 1999.

Savage, Jon. 'The World's End: London Punk, 1976–77'. In Gerald Matt (ed.), *Punk: No-One Is Innocent*. Nuremberg: Kunsthalle Wien, 2008.

Stewart, Francis. '"Alternative Ulster": Punk Rock as a Means of Overcoming the Religious Divide in Northern Ireland'. In John Wolffe (ed.), *Irish Religious Conflict in Comparative Perspective*. Basingstoke: Palgrave Macmillan, 2014.

Stewart, Francis. 'The Outcasts: Punk In Northern Ireland During the Troubles'. In Gregory Bull and Mike Dines (eds.), *Tales From the Punkside*. Portsmouth: Itchy Monkey, 2014.

Tramner, Jeremy. 'Rocking Against Racism: Trotskyism, Communism and Punk in Britain'. In Robert Adlington (ed.), *Red Strains: Music and Communism Outside the Communist Bloc*. Oxford: British Academy, 2013.

Vague, Tom. 'Vague Post-Punk Memories'. In Gavin Butt, Kwodo Eshun and Mark Fisher, *Post Punk Then and Now*. London: Repeater, 2016.

Webb, Peter. 'Dirty Squatters, Anarchy, Politics and Smack: A Journey through Bristol's Squat Punk Milieu'. In Mike Dines and Matthew Worley (eds.), *The Aesthetic of Our Anger: Anarcho-Punk, Politics and Music*. Colchester: Minor Compositions, 2016.

Wise, David and Stuart 'The End of Music' [1978]. In Stewart Home. ed., *What Is Situationism? A Reader*. Edinburgh: AK Press, 1996.

Worley, Matthew. 'Revolution Rock? The Clash, Joe Strummer and the British Left in the Early Days of Punk'. In Barry Faulk and Brady Harrison (eds.), *Punk Rock Warlord: Critical Perspectives on the Life and Work of Joe Strummer*. Farnham: Ashgate, 2014.

Worley, Matthew. 'Riotous Assembly: British Punk's Diaspora in the Summer of '81'. In Knud Andresen and Bart van der Steen (eds.), *A European Youth Revolt: European Perspectives on Youth Protest and Social Movements in the 1980s*. Basingstoke: Palgrave Macmillan, 2016.

Historical Context and Theory

Buckingham, David. 'Selling Youth: The Paradoxical Empowerment of the Young Consumer'. In David Buckingham, Sara Bragg and Mary Kehily (eds.), *Youth Cultures in the Age of Global Media*. Basingstoke: Palgrave Macmillan, 2014.

Clarke, John, 'Style'. In Stuart Hall and Tony Jefferson (eds.), *Resistance Through Rituals: Youth Subcultures in Post-War Britain*. London: Hutchinson & Co., 1976.

Clarke, John, Stuart Hall, Tony Jefferson and Brian Roberts. 'Subcultures, Cultures and Class: A Theoretical Overview'. In Stuart Hall and Tony Jefferson (eds.), *Resistance through Rituals: Youth Subcultures in Post-War Britain*. London: Hutchinson & Co., 1976.

Cloonan, Martin. 'Exclusive! The British Press and Popular Music: The Story So Far ...' In Steve Jones (ed.), *Pop Music and the Press*. Philadelphia: Temple University Press, 2002.

Cohen, Phil. 'Subcultural Conflict and Working Class Community'. In Stuart Hall, Dorothy Hobson, Andrew Lane and Paul Willis (eds.), *Culture, Media, Language*. London: Unwin Hyman, 1980.

Cohen, Phil. 'Policing the Working-Class City'. In Mike Fitzgerald, Gregor McLennan and Jennie Pawson (eds.), *Crime and Society: History and Theory*. London: Routledge and Kegan Paul, 1981.

Finchett-Maddock, Lucy. 'Squatting in London: Squatters' Rights and Legal Movement(s'. In Bart Van Der Steen, Ask Katzeff and Leendert Van Hoogenhuijze (eds.), *The City Is Ours: Squatting and Autonomous Movements from the 1970s to the Present*. Oakland: PM Press, 2014.

Frith, Simon. 'The Suburban Sensibility in British Rock and Pop'. In Roger Silverstone (ed.), *Visions of Suburbia*. London: Routledge, 1997.

Frith, Simon and John Street. 'Rock Against Racism and Red Wedge: From Music to Politics, from Politics to Music'. In Reebee Garofalo (ed.), *Rockin' the Boat: Mass Music and Mass Movements*. London: South End Press, 1992.

Hebdige, Dick. 'Aftershock: From Punk to Pornification to "Let's Be Facebook Frendz!!"'. In Subcultures Network (ed.), *Subcultures, Popular Music and Social Change*. Newcastle: Cambridge Scholars, 2014.

Hodkinson, Paul. 'Youth Cultures: A Critical Outline of Key Debates'. In Paul Hodkinson and Wolfgang Deicke (eds.), *Youth Cultures: Scenes, Subcultures and Tribes*. London: Routledge, 2007.

Jackson, Ben. 'The Think-Tank Archipelago: Thatcherism and Neo-Liberalism'. In Ben Jackson and Robert Saunders (eds.), *Making Thatcher's Britain*. Cambridge: Cambridge University Press, 2012.

Jackson, Ben and Robert Saunders. 'Varieties of Thatcherism'. In Ben Jackson and Robert Saunders (eds.), *Making Thatcher's Britain*. Cambridge: Cambridge University Press, 2012.

Labeau, Vicky. 'The Worst of All Possible Worlds'. In Roger Silverstone (ed.), *Visions of Suburbia*. London: Routledge, 1997.

Lawrence, Jon and Florence Sutcliffe-Braithwaite. 'Margaret Thatcher and the Decline of Class Politics'. In Ben Jackson and Robert Saunders (eds.), *Making Thatcher's Britain*. Cambridge: Cambridge University Press, 2012.

McRobbie, Angela. 'Working Class Girls and the Culture of Femininity'. In Women's Studies Group, *Women Take Issue*. London: Hutchinson, 1978.

McRobbie, Angela and Jenny Garber. 'Girls and Subcultures: An Exploration'. In Stuart Hall and Tony Jefferson (eds.), *Resistance Through Rituals: Youth Subcultures in Post-War Britain*. London: Hutchinson & Co., 1976.

Medhurst, Andy. 'Negotiating the Gnome Zone: Versions of Suburbia in British Popular Culture'. In Roger Silverstone (ed.), *Visions of Suburbia*. London: Routledge, 1997.

Moore-Gilbert, Bart. 'Apocalypse Now? The Novel in the 1970s'. In Bart Moore-Gilbert (ed.), *The Arts in the 1970s: Cultural Closure?* London: Routledge, 1994.

Parr, Helen. 'National Interest and the Falklands War'. In Timothy Edmunds, Jamie Gaskarth and Robin Porter (eds.), *British Foreign Policy and the National Interest: Identity, Strategy and Security*. Basingstoke: Palgrave Macmillan, 2014.

Price, Robert and George Sayers Bain. 'The Labour Force'. In Albert Henry Halsey (ed.), *British Social Trends since 1900*. Basingstoke: Palgrave Macmillan, 1988.

Rock, Paul and Stanley Cohen. 'The Teddy Boy'. In Vernon Bogdanor and Robert Skidelsky (eds.), *The Age of Affluence, 1951–64*. London: Macmillan, 1970.

Saunders, Robert. 'Thatcherism and the Seventies'. In Ben Jackson and Robert Saunders (eds.), *Making Thatcher's Britain*. Cambridge University Press, 2012.

Tiratsoo, Nick. '"You've Never Had It So Bad": Britain in the 1970s'. In idem (ed.), *From Blitz to Blair: A New History of the Britain since the 1970s*. London: Weidenfield & Nicolson, 1997.

Walker, Ian. 'Anarchy in the UK'. In Paul Barker (ed.), *The Other Britain: A New Society Collection*. London: Routledge, 1982.

Wicke, Peter. 'Music, Dissidence, Revolution and Commerce: Youth Culture between Mainstream and Subculture'. In Axel Schildt and Detlef Siegfried(eds.), *Between Marx and Coca-Cola: Youth Cultures in Changing European Societies, 1960–1980*. Oxford: Berghahn, 2006.

Williams, Raymond, 'Culture Is Ordinary'. In Robin Gable (ed.), *Resources of Hope: Culture, Democracy, Socialism*. London: Verso, 1989.

Wood, Bruce. 'Urbanisation and Local Government'. In Albert Henry Halsey(ed.), *British Social Trends since 1900*. Basingstoke: Palgrave Macmillan, 1988.

Films and Documentaries

Punk Related

Angelic Upstarts (dir.), *Play at Home* (1984)

Büld, Wolfgang (dir.), *Punk in London* (1977).

Büld, Wolfgang (dir.), *Punk in England* (1980).

Clisby, Ted (dir.), 'Who Is Poly Styrene', *Arena* (1979).

Collins, Christopher and Ken Lawrence (dir.), *UK/DK: A Film about Punks and Skinheads* (1983).
Duffield, Mick (dir.), *Christ The Movie* (1990).
Hazen, Jack and David Mingay (dir.), *Rude Boy* (1980).
Jarman, Derek (dir.), *Jubilee* (1978).
Letts, Don (dir.), *The Punk Rock Movie* (1978).
Letts, Don (dir.), *Westway to the World* (2000).
McPhee, Grant, *New Gold Dream: The Sound of Young Scotland* (2016).
Minx, Zillah (dir.), *She's a Punk Rocker UK* (2010).
Oey, Alexander (dir.), *The Sound of Progress* (1988).
Perks, Jeff (dir.), 'Tell Us the Truth', *Arena* (1979).
Psychic TV, *First Transmission* (1982).
Rojas, Pedro (dir.), *Punk Kebab* (1977).
Samson, John (dir.), *Dressing For Pleasure* (1977).
Shah, Hasan and Dom Shaw (dir.), *Rough Cut and Ready Dubbed* (1982).
Sloper, Mark and Alan Byron (dir.), *Punk in '76: From SEX to the Sex Pistols* (2013).
Temple, Julien (dir.), *Sex Pistols No. 1* (1977).
Temple, Julien (dir.), *Punk Can Take It* (1979).
Temple, Julien (dir.), *The Great Rock 'n' Roll Swindle* (1980).
Temple, Julien (dir.), *The Filth and the Fury* (2000).
Tickell, Paul (dir.), *Punk and the Pistols* (1995).

Historical Context and Theory

Carr, Gordon (dir.), *Persons Unknown* (1980).
Gower, Owen (dir.), *Still the Enemy Within* (2014).
Jackson, Mick (dir.), *Threads* (1984).

Theses

Glen, Patrick. '"Sometimes Good Guys Don't Wear White": Morality in the Music Press, 1967–1983'. University of Sheffield, PhD thesis, 2012.
Raposo, Ana. '30 Years of Agitprop: The Representation of "Extreme" Politics in Punk and Post-Punk Music Graphics in the United Kingdom from 1978 to 2008'. London University of the Arts, PhD thesis, 2012.
Sutherland, Fraser. 'Permission To Disobey: The Emergence of DIY Culture in the Post-Punk Era, 1978–82'. University of Birmingham, MA thesis, 2016.

Index

Printed in Great Britain
by Amazon

24628476R00235